TESTIMONIES OF RESISTANCE

TESTIMONIES OF RESISTANCE

Representations of the Auschwitz-Birkenau Sonderkommando

Edited by Nicholas Chare and Dominic Williams

berghahn
NEW YORK • OXFORD
www.berghahnbooks.com

First published in 2019 by
Berghahn Books
www.berghahnbooks.com

© 2019, 2023 Nicholas Chare and Dominic Williams
First paperback edition published in 2023

All rights reserved. Except for the quotation of short passages for the purposes of criticism and review, no part of this book may be reproduced in any form or by any means, electronic or mechanical, including photocopying, recording, or any information storage and retrieval system now known or to be invented, without written permission of the publisher.

Library of Congress Cataloging-in-Publication Data
Names: Chare, Nicholas, editor. | Williams, Dominic, editor.
Title: Testimonies of resistance : representations of the Auschwitz-Birkenau Sonderkommando / edited by Nicholas Chare and Dominic Williams.
Description: New York ; Oxford : Berghahn Books, [2019] | Includes bibliographical references and index. |
Identifiers: LCCN 2019015105 (print) | LCCN 2019016147 (ebook) | ISBN 9781789203424 (ebook) | ISBN 9781789203417 (hardback : alk. paper)
Subjects: LCSH: Auschwitz (Concentration camp)--Biography. | Birkenau (Concentration camp)--Biography. | Sonderkommandos--Poland--Biography. | Holocaust, Jewish (1939-1945)--Poland--Personal narratives. | Holocaust, Jewish (1939-1945)--Poland--Influence.
Classification: LCC D805.5.A96 (ebook) | LCC D805.5.A96 T444 2019 (print) | DDC 940.53/1853862--dc23
LC record available at https://lccn.loc.gov/2019015105

British Library Cataloguing in Publication Data
A catalogue record for this book is available from the British Library

ISBN 978-1-78920-341-7 hardback
ISBN 978-1-80073-915-4 paperback
ISBN 978-1-78920-342-4 ebook

https://doi.org/10.3167/9781789203417

Contents

List of Figures and Tables	viii
Foreword	ix
Anne Karpf	
Acknowledgements	xiv
Note on Transliteration	xv
Introduction. Testimonies of Resistance	1
Nicholas Chare and Dominic Williams	

Part I. Historical and Ethical Questions of Representation

Chapter 1. Knowing Cruelty: The Negation of Death and Burial in SS Violence — 33
Griselda Pollock

Chapter 2. What Makes the Grey Zone Grey? Blurring Factual and Ethical Judgements of the Sonderkommando — 69
Dominic Williams

Part II. Witnessing from the Heart of Hell

Chapter 3. Farewell Letter from the Crematorium: On the Authorship of the First Recorded 'Sonderkommando-Manuscript' and the Discovery of the Original Letter — 91
Andreas Kilian

Chapter 4. To Read the Illegible: Techniques of Multispectral Imaging and the Manuscripts of the Jewish Sonderkommando of Auschwitz-Birkenau — 102
Pavel Polian and Aleksandr Nikityaev

Chapter 5. 'Like a True Greek': The Last Will and Testimony of Marcel Natzari   106
   K.E. Fleming

Chapter 6. Disinterred Words: The Letters of Herman Strasfogel and Marcel Nadjary   111
   Nicholas Chare, Ersy Contogouris and Dominic Williams

Chapter 7. The Letter of Herman Strasfogel   131
   Translated by Ersy Contogouris

Chapter 8. The Letter of Marcel Nadjary   138
   Translated by Ersy Contogouris

Chapter 9. The Religious Life of Sonderkommando Members inside the Killing Installations in Auschwitz-Birkenau   143
   Gideon Greif

Part III. Retrospective Representations

Chapter 10. Doubly Cursed: The Sonderkommando in the Documents of the International Tracing Service   159
   Dan Stone

Chapter 11. Enduring Witness: David Olère's Visual Testimony   182
   Carol Zemel

Chapter 12. The Sonderkommando and the Auschwitz-Birkenau Memorial Museum   193
   Dominic Williams and Isabel Wollaston

Chapter 13. Early and Late Testimonies of the Sonderkommando Survivors   215
   Gideon Greif

Chapter 14. From Special Operations Executive to Sonderkommando: Sebastian Faulks and the Anxiety of Invention   230
   Sue Vice

Chapter 15. Out of the Plan, Out of the Plane 2: Stripping, Fourth Letter to Gerhard Richter   247
   Georges Didi-Huberman

Chapter 16. Greeks in the Birkenau Sonderkommando: Representation and Reality   265
   Steven Bowman

Part IV. Cinema and the Sonderkommando

Chapter 17. 'We Did Something': Framing Resistance in
Cinematic Depictions of the Sonderkommando   287
  Barry Langford

Chapter 18. 'We Can't Know What We're Capable Of':
Approaching the 'Grey Zone' in Holocaust Film   307
  Adam Brown

Chapter 19. The Sonderkommando on Screen   332
  Philippe Mesnard

Afterword. Tracing Topographies of Memory and Mourning   346
  Victor Jeleniewski Seidler

Index   369

Figures and Tables

Figures
Figure 10.1 CNI card for Jakow (Yaakov) Gabai.   163
Figure 10.2 Death certificate for Chaim Herman, 1996.   164
Figure 10.3 CNI card for Hersz Strasfogel.   165
Figure 10.4 IRO DP identity card for Szloma Dragon, 1948.   167
Figure 10.5 First page of Abraham Dragon's IRO application, 13 January 1948.   168
Figure 10.6 Fourth page of Abraham Dragon's IRO application.   169
Figure 10.7 Abraham Dragon's IRO certificate of eligibility, December 1948.   170
Figure 10.8 Daniel Bennahmias' certificate of incarceration, 1968.   172
Figure 10.9 T/D inquiry card for Filip Müller.   173
Figure 12.1 Birkenau. Memorial boards, near the site of Crematorium 4 (V).   197
Figure 12.2 Auschwitz I, Block 4. Model of Crematorium 1 (II) and one of the Sonderkommando photographs.   199

Tables
Table 4.1 Gain of read text (in pages) of Marcel Nadjary's manuscript.   104
Table 12.1 Online lessons, Google exhibitions and *Episodes from Auschwitz* graphic novels.   203
Table 12.2 Breakdown of tweets mentioning 'sonderkommando' from @AuschwitzMuseum.   207

Foreword

Anne Karpf

It is hardly surprising that it has taken so long for representations of the Sonderkommando (SK), the 'special squads' of Jewish prisoners grotesquely tasked with the running of the crematoria in the extermination camps, to be accorded sustained, scholarly examination of the kind offered here. Even as more testimony left by these toilers at the epicentre of terror was unearthed (at times literally), so too did the analytic tools available seem inadequate to the task. Primo Levi's 'grey zone' – 'the space that separates . . . the victims from the persecutors'[1] in which the 'hybrid class of the prisoner-functionary'[2] SK had to operate – appears with the passage of time to have got greyer and darker still. So fraught with ethical complexity is the subject of the SK that, for a long time, it was cordoned off from what one contributor to this volume calls *le champ du visible*, its exclusion from the scrutiny afforded other aspects of the Holocaust horribly confirming its 'specialness'.

The editors of this volume, however, make the persuasive claim that the SK is central to our understanding of the Holocaust. (As Levi insisted, it is 'indispensable to know [the occupants of the grey zone] if we want to know the human species'.)[3] They also, correctly, see it as a form of resistance, a way of foiling attempts to 'conceal the crime'. Yet this is a book about how the unimaginable has been imagined. The unimaginability of the SK experience is compounded by the undesirability of imagining it – a reluctance to enter inside the abject, the innermost circle of hell, a place of negation of life. So, a book like this must break a taboo: it involves the transgressive act of imaginatively entering, if not the gas chamber itself, then its environs – and to do so not as a potential victim and without lapsing into voyeurism. As Levi also said, 'one is tempted to turn away with a grimace and close one's mind: this is a temptation one must resist'.[4]

If one does indeed resist, one enters a world so unmoored from normal structures of meaning and feeling that it risks the dissolution of language itself. It is shocking to read, for example, in Herman Strasfogel's letter to his wife and daughter that, when he arrives in Birkenau, he is sent to work in the SK supposedly as a member of the Chevra Kadischa. This most honourable of voluntary roles involves preparing the body of a deceased Jew for burial with respect and reverence: the members of Chevra Kadischa ritually clean and then dress the body. Although the letter does not make clear whether 'Chevra Kadischa' was a term employed by the Nazis or (more probably) Strasfogel himself, its use in this context to denote a process in which the body is treated with the utmost contemptuous savagery illuminates in a flash the inversion and perversion of the *univers concentrationnaire*.

For such material, a new kind of transdisciplinary approach is therefore needed, one that can synthesize the critical tools provided not only by history but also by literary and film criticism, cultural studies, linguistics, semiotics, translation studies – indeed, archaeology itself. This volume makes rich use of such a transdisciplinary approach to explore written and visual testimony and representation in the form of texts, photographs, painting, drawing, film and fiction. To an extent, the lapse of time since the end of the Second World War facilitates such an approach: with the death of the surviving members of the SK, scholarly scrutiny seems in some sense – even if this is irrational – less 'personal'. At the same time, however, even more detective work is now required to explore and analyse traces of traces, inevitably sometimes leading to conjecture and speculation. This in no sense diminishes the careful scholarship of the book. On the contrary, this is history and historiography of the finest order, simultaneously analysing representations of the SK and the difficulties of such analysis, a treatise on the limits of representation and interpretation, but also the necessity of doing so. In its refusal of claims to absolute knowledge, its deployment of diverse and sometimes divergent perspectives, and by drawing attention to missing fragments of evidence, this volume (like its two predecessors)[5] honours the ultimate ineffability of its subject.

There can be no disagreement about the enormity of the challenge of representing the SK, especially in film. This has been reflected in the heated and sometimes hostile reactions to scenes in the most feted filmic depictions, *Shoah* and *Son of Saul*. When Claude Lanzmann in *Shoah* (1985) ruthlessly goaded the barber Abraham Bomba, a member of the Treblinka SK, to retell his testimony while cutting hair in a barbershop that Lanzmann re-created in Tel Aviv, Bomba became, as one of the contributors to this volume puts it, 'an actor of his own testimony' in an iconic but controversial sequence that made terribly visible the return of the repressed and that has been accused of retraumatizing the survivor.[6]

Son of Saul, on the other hand, has been mostly lauded for its eschewal of a survivor-centred story, its refusal to provide redemptive narrative relief and its acoustically dense soundtrack. László Nemes' 2015 film, which has played an important role in foregrounding the SK in recent cultural memory, is nevertheless critiqued in this volume in a number of sympathetic ways. The film and the debate surrounding it raise questions arising from one of the major challenges faced by filmmakers and writers in representing the SK: the need to find a cultural form that cannot easily be assimilated into the surrounding cultural products but remains distinctive, without at the same time falling back on self-regarding aesthetic devices.

What liberties can be legitimately taken to make a cultural product readable or watchable – indeed, bearable? In attempting to make it possible to even think about the most grotesque aspects of the Holocaust, the chapters gathered here raise a host of other, often unanswerable, questions too. What, apart from the attempted SK rebellion, can meaningfully be classed as resistance? How can a scholarly engagement with the subject of the SK avoid becoming occluded by a visceral reaction of revulsion or, at the other extreme, the objectification and dehumanization experienced by SK members themselves? How can both scholars and creative artists engage with the subject without sacralizing, banalizing or decomplexifying it? (Levi's own thinking about the subject was anything but schematically reductive: as a chapter here points out, it was sometimes inconsistent and contradictory.) And, finally, what lies between the heroization and the stigmatisation of the members of the SK – and beyond the dispensing of moral judgements?

The contributors work hard to avoid such polarizations and, in their examination of both the testimony of the SK and their representation, exhibit a sensitive reckoning of fact, after-effect and after-affect. The tender care with which evidence and its provenance are treated is itself moving – in its keen sense of the different nationalities and cultural identities from which the SK were drawn, for instance. (Particularly valuable is the material on the Greek members, curiously marginalized in mainstream Holocaust narratives for so long.) For this volume not only reclaims the SK's legitimate and important place in Holocaust research but also re-endows its members as far as is possible with the humanity that the Nazis so violently despoiled, along with the scraps of physical and moral agency remaining to them. (The traces of vanity that are visible in some of the SK testimony, for instance, while shocking, at the same time show that, even in extreme circumstances, such forms of human preoccupation remain.) As such, this collection has a strong moral as well as historical dimension, serving not just as scholarship but also as an example of the mourning to which scholarship can contribute – research as a form of Shiva.

Mourning, in the case of the Holocaust in general and specifically the SK, can never be completed; in Freud's terms, we can never overcome the loss of the object.[7] This book nevertheless is an important and timely contribution to a vital aspect of the Holocaust that will itself seed further research and debate, and will significantly enlarge our understanding of forced labour in the Auschwitz crematoria and its representation.

Anne Karpf is a writer, journalist and sociologist. She is a regular broadcaster for BBC Radio and contributor to *The Guardian*; her books include a family memoir, *The War After: Living with the Holocaust* and *The Human Voice*. Co-editor of *A Time to Speak Out: Independent Jewish Voices on Israel, Zionism and Jewish Identity*, she has written and spoken widely on the Holocaust and is a past recipient of a British Academy Thank-Offering to Britain Fellowship for her research. She is Professor of Life Writing and Culture at London Metropolitan University.

Notes

1. Primo Levi, 'The Grey Zone' (1986), in *The Drowned and the Saved*, trans. Raymond Rosenthal (London: Abacus, 1989), 25.
2. Ibid., 27.
3. Ibid., 25–26.
4. Ibid., 37.
5. Nicholas Chare and Dominic Williams (eds), *Representing Auschwitz: At the Margins of Testimony* (Basingstoke: Palgrave Macmillan, 2013); Nicholas Chare and Dominic Williams, *Matters of Testimony: Interpreting the Scrolls of Auschwitz* (Oxford: Berghahn Books, 2016).
6. Dominick LaCapra, *History and Memory after Auschwitz* (Ithaca, NY: Cornell University Press, 1998).
7. Sigmund Freud, 'Mourning and Melancholia' (1914), in *The Standard Edition of the Complete Works of Sigmund Freud*, vol. 14, trans. James Strachey (London: Hogarth Press, 1957), 237–58.

Bibliography

Chare, Nicholas, and Dominic Williams. *Matters of Testimony: Interpreting the Scrolls of Auschwitz*. Oxford: Berghahn Books, 2016.

———. (eds). *Representing Auschwitz: At the Margins of Testimony*. Basingstoke: Palgrave Macmillan, 2013.

Freud, Sigmund. 'Mourning and Melancholia' (1914), in *The Standard Edition of the Complete Works of Sigmund Freud*, vol. 14, trans. James Strachey. London: Hogarth Press, 1957, 237–58.

LaCapra, Dominick. *History and Memory after Auschwitz*. Ithaca, NY: Cornell University Press, 1998.

Levi, Primo. *The Drowned and the Saved*, trans. Raymond Rosenthal. London: Abacus, 1989.

Acknowledgements

We wish to thank Doris Bergen, Aurélia Kalisky, Silvestra Mariniello, Suzanne Paquet, Nikos Papastergiadis, Wolfgang Schneider, Milena Marinkova and Angela Mortimer for their intellectual and, sometimes, practical support during the preparation of this volume.

While we were editing the book, Nicholas Chare was the Diane and Howard Wohl Fellow in the Jack, Joseph and Morton Mandel Center for Advanced Holocaust Studies at the United States Holocaust Memorial Museum, and thanks are therefore due to the excellent staff at the Library and Archives Reference Desk there for their help in locating relevant references and sources. We are therefore particularly beholden to Liviu Carare, Megan Lewis, Larissa Reed, Vincent Slatt and Elliott Wrenn. We are also thankful to Wojciech Płosa at the Auschwitz Museum. We are grateful to the Fortunoff Video Archive for Holocaust Testimonies as well, for granting access to view pertinent video testimonies.

Additionally, we are indebted to the three anonymous reviewers of the manuscript for their thoughtful and constructive advice, and to the commissioning and production team at Berghahn Books, including Chris Chappell, Mykelin Higham, Jon Lloyd, Caroline Kuhtz and Soyolmaa Lkhagvadorj, who were a pleasure to work with throughout.

Note on Transliteration

The editors have endeavoured to make the spelling of transliterated names consistent across the volume but inevitably with different scholars working from different sources this has not always been possible. Quotations and citations retain the original spelling. The index entry for a name also indicates variant spellings that occur in the text because of this (or in other common references to the person in question).

Introduction

Testimonies of Resistance

Nicholas Chare and Dominic Williams

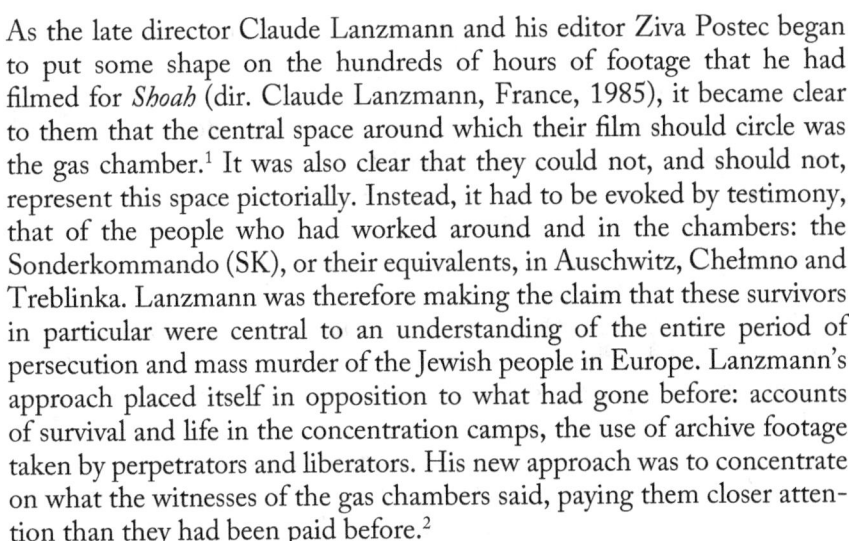

As the late director Claude Lanzmann and his editor Ziva Postec began to put some shape on the hundreds of hours of footage that he had filmed for *Shoah* (dir. Claude Lanzmann, France, 1985), it became clear to them that the central space around which their film should circle was the gas chamber.[1] It was also clear that they could not, and should not, represent this space pictorially. Instead, it had to be evoked by testimony, that of the people who had worked around and in the chambers: the Sonderkommando (SK), or their equivalents, in Auschwitz, Chełmno and Treblinka. Lanzmann was therefore making the claim that these survivors in particular were central to an understanding of the entire period of persecution and mass murder of the Jewish people in Europe. Lanzmann's approach placed itself in opposition to what had gone before: accounts of survival and life in the concentration camps, the use of archive footage taken by perpetrators and liberators. His new approach was to concentrate on what the witnesses of the gas chambers said, paying them closer attention than they had been paid before.[2]

The SK had indeed been a group that had been given less consideration than might be expected. They were forced to labour at the heart of one of the killing centres of the Holocaust. At Auschwitz in particular, they witnessed, as they worked, hundreds of thousands of fellow Jews from all over Europe being brought into the crematorium buildings of Birkenau, tricked or forced into undressing and entering the gas chambers. The SK then had to handle their bodies once they had been murdered, clearing them from the gas chambers and burning them in specially installed ovens or, when the ovens were not enough, in pits. They were thus eyewitnesses to genocide. They managed to record some of what they saw, and what they felt, in photographs smuggled outside the camp and writings that they buried in the grounds of the crematoria. But these vital, contemporaneous efforts to document the Final Solution long met with a puzzling degree of neglect. Their witness was often seen as compromised by the role that they had been forced to fulfil, and from those who survived, many were reluctant to talk of their experiences because of their supposed 'collaboration'. The main way that they were remembered was for their act of rising up in October 1944, attacking guards and burning a crematorium, before most of them were killed.[3]

In turning to their testimony, therefore, Lanzmann acknowledges their importance as eyewitnesses of a key aspect of the Holocaust: industrialized extermination by gassing. But even he chooses to use them in a particular manner, not acknowledging all the ways that they bore witness or other important parts of their history. Lanzmann ignores both their writings and their photographs in order to focus solely on the SK's retrospective words and the re-enactments that bring moments of incarnation, the past coming into the present. Adam Brown suggests that asking survivors to undergo this painful process might indicate Lanzmann's own sense that they bear some guilt for being compelled to work servicing the machinery of extermination.[4] And although *Shoah* does show how forced labourers in the gas chambers came to the conclusion that violent resistance was the only possible response to the universe of extermination, nothing of any of their uprisings is detailed in the film.

These aspects were at least touched upon by a number of texts that were almost exactly contemporaneous with *Shoah*. Raul Hilberg revised his 1963 account of the *Destruction of the European Jews* (1985) to include Filip Müller and Zalman Lewental's descriptions of the Auschwitz SK uprising of 7 October 1944, although with little effect on his account and none on his interpretive framework.[5] Martin Gilbert's chronicle of the Holocaust of 1986, an attempt to stitch together the testimony of the victims into a coherent, chronological whole, made extensive use of documents probably written by Leyb Langfus.[6] Đorđe Lebović's radio play *Traganje po pepelu* (*Searching the Ashes*) (1985) based on the Scrolls of Auschwitz was translated and broadcast by many European radio stations.[7] And, of course, Primo Levi's essay 'La zona grigia' also appeared in 1986, placing the SK at the heart of his troubled enquiry into the damage inflicted on the moral integrity of victims and survivors of the Shoah. Hilberg aside, all of these texts could be said to make the SK more central to ideas of the Holocaust than they had been before, although what that centrality consisted of took different forms in each of the texts.

More than thirty years later, we can see that the mid 1980s did not mark a definitive point at which discussion of the SK entered the mainstream of Holocaust consciousness. The changes in study of the Holocaust during the 1990s wrought by the collapse of East European communism and the reunification of Germany, the accelerating surge in public and state interest in the Holocaust, and perhaps even the academic theories of testimony prompted in part by Lanzmann's film did not produce a version of the Holocaust in which the SK would play a central part. Newly accessible archives shifted attention more to the east of Europe, while public debates and controversies focused more on German responsibility for the crime.[8] Influential theories of testimony saw it as inherently retrospective.[9] And although the public was prepared to view, and the Academy of Motion Picture Arts was eager to reward, stories of rescue and maintaining hope such as *Schindler's List* and *Life is Beautiful*, predictions of success for an American film on the SK fell flat.[10]

The mid 1980s can nonetheless be seen as one moment at which it became possible to consider the SK's significance. It might be said that now is another such moment. Once more, thinking about and finding ways to represent the SK have come to be central to the ways in which the Holocaust is currently figured. Most notable perhaps is the Academy Award given to *Son of Saul* (2015), but we can add to that the set of paintings by Gerhard Richter made in response to their photographs (*Birkenau*, 2014), and the new editions of and interpretations of their writings that have recently been published.[11]

At this point, then, addressing the question of how at some points the SK have been central to understanding the Holocaust and at others have been excluded from that understanding is one of the major motivations for putting together this collection. The volume explores the kinds of insights a focus on the SK, on their personal testimonies and on testimonies inspired by them can provide for histories of the Holocaust. Although Lanzmann rightly treats the death camps as operating on a continuum in terms of embodying Nazi genocidal policies, each of the death camps also possessed unique characteristics and this extended to their use of slave labour. In this volume we have restricted ourselves to a consideration of the Auschwitz-Birkenau SK. There is often crossover between the SK at Auschwitz and those working at camps such as Treblinka and Sobibór in terms of their duties and outlook, but there are also important differences. A major feature of the Auschwitz SK, for instance, was the sheer quantity of testimony they produced from within the extermination camp. Another distinction is the quantity of retrospective testimonies and portrayals of the Auschwitz SK. These factors have informed our decision to build the volume around this group in particular. Lanzmann's reliance on incarnation to bypass the vagaries of memory bespeaks a distrust of mediation. Similarly the cover image for this volume, in which someone has crossed out the man filming the crematorium, indexes a desire to redact content that draws attention to the visual testimony's mediatedness. We, however, are interested in the ways that the SK and their forced labour in the crematoria have been mediated and represented in works of cultural memory. Such representations raise crucial questions about the ethics of representation and the responsibility of the present to past victims.

Different definitions and interpretations of the Holocaust as a whole necessarily give the SK different places within their arguments. An Auschwitz- and gas chamber-centric approach will see them as absolutely central, whereas other interpretations will place less importance on them. Accounts that rely mainly on perpetrator documents will pay them less attention than those which insist that the victims' voices are heard. Different approaches to how victims can bear witness will also frame the SK's position differently. Ones that conceptualize testimony as retrospective will give the SK's contemporary accounts less weight or will struggle to accommodate them. A narrative of the Holocaust explaining how it was administered or improvised by the perpetrators will be less focused on the SK than one that takes an interest in what happened to the victims. Questions of how victims reacted, what level of agency they had, under what circumstances they were able to resist and when they could be made to comply, or what meaning they gave to the events, are all ones that the SK can speak to, but to what extent they can be included depends on how the relationship between them and the rest of the victims is conceptualized. Were they part of an exterminatory universe cut off completely from the worlds of the concentration camp and ghettos? Or are there commonalities between these different spaces that can be explored? Can the concentration camp system of Kapos and prisoner-administered hierarchies help to make sense of the way the SK were co-opted into the exterminatory process or of the privilege from which they (in some sense) benefited? Does the grey zone in which they are often placed have clear boundaries or does it blur into the lives of all victims? Looking at the place of the SK within different conceptions of the Holocaust therefore helps to illuminate how these conceptions operate.

Matters of Resistance

The SK of Auschwitz-Birkenau are well known for the uprising they planned and in which many of them participated on 7 October 1944. This event is the focus of much retrospective testimony and also of one major document produced from within the Birkenau death factory. The preparations for armed resistance are discussed at length by the SK member Zalman Lewental in a manuscript he composed in the immediate aftermath of the revolt. Many postliberation representations of the SK discussed in the chapters in this volume also make reference to the uprising. The film *Son of Saul*, for example, culminates with the revolt and the efforts of some members of the SK to flee Birkenau.[12] The history and identity of the SK is now bound up with an act of violent resistance that occurred towards the end of their existence. The revolt, however, was not the only form of resistance engaged in by members of the SK. Many of their activities can be conceived of as kinds of rebellion against Nazi oppression.

Resistance as it manifested in the SK and by Jewish communities and individuals in the Shoah more broadly is complex, taking multiple guises through the history of persecution. The revolt for which the SK has become celebrated, for example, has been viewed by some as inspired by the Warsaw ghetto uprising of 1943. For Ber Mark, the Warsaw ghetto uprising reverberated through all the places in which Jews were being oppressed and murdered. He writes that subsequently in Auschwitz, as well as other camps, 'the heroic fight of the Warsaw ghetto resounded in a powerful echo'.[13] In his Foreword to *Armed Resistance of the Jews in Poland*, Joseph Tenenbaum also suggests that 'the revolt of the ghetto was to be the beginning of a general resurrection in Poland – or so some believed it to be'.[14] Yet, Melech Neustadt suggests that prior to, and at the same time as, the uprising in Warsaw, there were other efforts at self-defence in Poland (he lists Kraków, Mińsk Mazowiecki, Lwów, Będzin, Białystok and Częstochowa).[15] These efforts never attained the symbolic status of the Warsaw uprising, yet they should not be overlooked.

Warsaw came to embody proof of a capacity for Jewish resistance and was particularly rousing. Yisrael Gutman writes: 'I can remember how the eyes of the Jews flamed with pride and fervour when I arrived in Auschwitz, and told them the story of the revolt and the fight against the enemy in the Warsaw ghetto'.[16] Lewental also refers to the heroism of the defenders of the ghetto in his addendum to a diary written in the Łódź ghetto.[17] Gutman goes on to relate that the SK uprising at Auschwitz had a similarly inspirational effect on other prisoners at the camp complex: 'the day of the revolt was a symbol of vengeance and encouragement for the prisoners'.[18] It is clear that the day was memorable, although some prisoners in video-testimony have also denied that the uprising greatly changed their feelings of desperation and hopelessness.[19]

Aside from armed struggle, many other forms of resistance were enacted by Jews across Europe. Neustadt also recognizes the existence of what he refers to as 'passive heroism' which manifested itself through clandestine schools, illegal workshops and soup kitchens.[20] Neustadt admits of this 'passive heroism' that: 'We did not appreciate it as it was deserved. We did not regard it as the miracle it was'.[21] As Yehuda Bauer observes in his Foreword to Shmuel Krakowski's exploration of Jewish resistance in Poland, *The War of the Doomed*, 'examples of active resistance, although without arms, are many and their importance is vast'.[22] Unarmed resistance is explored by Bauer in *Rethinking the Holocaust* where he considers *amidah*, which he describes as encompassing activities such as organizing education, engaging in clandestine political life and embarking on social welfare efforts.[23]

The term *amidah*, which means steadfastness or standing firm, was employed very early on in the history of Holocaust historiography by Meir Dworzecki to describe acts of resistance without arms.[24] Many of the forms of resistance Dworzecki discusses in his book *Histoire de la resistance anti-nazie juive, 1933–45*, which offers an extended and nuanced consideration of resistance, can be understood as forms of *amidah*. He refers, for example, to spiritual resistance, youth activism, illegal border crossings, sabotage, testimonies of Nazi crimes and clandestine assertions of Jewish culture (such as ghetto schools). In relation to youth activism, Dworzecki provides his own eyewitness testimony of nonconformity in the Vilna ghetto that included children putting up signs with slogans and, on one occasion, dressing in rags of diverse colours and smearing their faces in an effort to embody different 'races' while singing these (misremembered or improvised) words of I.L. Peretz: 'Alle mentschen zenen brider / Weiss, gelbe, schwarze / Rasen – an eusgetracht majsse' (All men are brothers, white, yellow, or black, race is just a simple invention).[25] Dworzecki was himself part of the Jewish resistance movement in the ghetto.[26] He knew of resistance in practical terms before he came to study it historically.

Dworzecki's conception of *amidah* is contentious in its seeking to extend the idea of revolt beyond violent uprising. As Or Rogovin recounts, there was criticism of a 1968 Yad Vashem Conference on Manifestations of Jewish Resistance during the Holocaust at which Dworzecki outlined his idea of *amidah* in a paper entitled 'The Day to Day Stand of the Jews'.[27] Some, such as Lucy Dawidowicz, felt that the term 'resistance' was becoming too broad to be useful. Dworzecki, however, was motivated by a desire to ensure that inconspicuous acts of rebellion, less spectacular modes of resistance, were accorded their due. For him, any effort to resist

Nazi efforts at dehumanization should be recognized and affirmed. Irene Weiss observes of her time at Auschwitz: 'If you could maintain your sense of humanity – it was a sense of defiance'.[28] In this context, small gestures, gestures that are now mostly unknown or remain overlooked, were of immense importance. If Dworzecki's perspective is embraced, such small gestures, when recorded, can be recognized for their oppositional character. It then becomes possible to detect resistance manifesting in unlikely situations in the concentration camp experience. Defiance, for instance, was already apparent at the moment of tattooing, a key event in the process of dehumanization in many survivor testimonies.

Henryk Mandelbaum, a survivor of the SK, recounts in oral testimony that sometimes during tattooing, people asked for small numbers – although he did not and clearly feels that he missed a trick – explaining of his arrival at Auschwitz in relation to the tattooist that some said: '"Make small numbers for me!" And he made the small numbers. He was French the man who made the number'.[29] Shlomo Venezia also notes, while showing his 'fairly big' (*abbastanza grande*) tattoo to the cameraperson during video-testimony, that such requests were possible and successful.[30] Women would similarly sometimes resist during this assault upon identity. Erna Low writes:

> 'Make mine small!' I implored the woman who was working on my arm, 'So that I can get rid of it some day'. In the light of what was to come, how ridiculous was my attitude! She gave me a look that puzzled me and obliged.[31]

Lucia Franco recalls women rubbing their tattoos immediately after receiving them in an effort to remove as much ink as possible.[32] An account of resistance that only accords significance to armed struggle or its preparation will neglect instances such as these that might be referred to as quotidian, yet far from insignificant rebellion. There are numerous examples of such acts among inmates in the concentration camps.

For a period of time, workers in Kanada (known by the Nazis as the *Effektenlager*), the part of the camp where the possessions of prisoners and of those murdered in the gas chambers were sorted, were barracked in the main camp of Birkenau at night, travelling to and from the warehouses each day. This gave them considerable opportunity for smuggling clothing and other items back to their barracks. In her memoir, Erika Myriam Kounio Amariglio recounts:

> I remember that one of the 'Canada' girls brought me a pink blouse to wear under my striped dress. It was such a luxury! I even let a bit of pink show above the neckline of my uniform. Naturally I considered myself very elegant. I wore the blouse constantly until we left Auschwitz.[33]

Here the girl flouts the rule against taking items from among the possessions deposited in Kanada and Amariglio, in her turn, rebels against the uniform dress code of the inmates. She sticks her neck out through permitting the (likely thin) patch of pink to be visible above the neckline. This scrap of pink as symbolic resistance both individualizes her and affirms her femininity, two qualities the Nazis had sought to deprive her of.[34]

One of the most celebrated examples of armed resistance at Birkenau prior to the SK revolt was carried out by a woman, possibly the professional ballerina Franceska Mann, who shot and killed the SS officer Josef Schillinger (and injured another member of the SS) in the undressing room of Crematorium 1 (II).[35] Hermann Langbein, favouring Rudolf Höss' (the Commandant of Auschwitz at the time) account of the event, in which the role of a woman in this act of resistance is suppressed, dismisses Mann's purported actions as legendary.[36] Zalman Lewental, however, makes reference to the woman's rebelliousness in his 'Addendum to the Łódź Manuscript'.[37] It is clear the attack on the SS, an attack that fits easily into definitions of active resistance, was performed by a woman. Efforts to downplay this reality reflect fears of emasculation among perpetrators and some male resistance members.

For Roger Gottlieb, resistance is bound up with contesting oppression. He states that 'to seek to resist oppression means to seek to thwart, limit, or end the actions of the oppressor'.[38] Henryk Tauber recalls resistance that could be categorized as of this kind occurring on occasion inside the gas chamber itself. The metallic grille that protected the peephole in the interior of Crematorium 1 (II) was installed in response to those being gassed repeatedly breaking the small window the Nazis used to observe the progress of a gassing.[39] Even the addition of the grille did not prevent this from happening, so the window had to be recessed through the addition of planks or metal plates. Those being murdered also sometimes damaged the ventilation system and electrical cables.[40] These efforts were, of course, borne of desperation, yet they attest to people fighting by whatever means available to them to prevent the gassing being successful. That their efforts failed does not negate their intent. The damage they caused likely also led to delays in the killing process as repairs had to be carried out. When the crematoria were being dismantled, Morris K. also recounts that the SK found valuables concealed in the ventilation ducts of the gas chambers: 'jewellery hidden away in the openings'.[41] These acts of concealment carried out in the most appalling circumstances also index a defiance that should not pass unremarked.

The activities of the SK themselves fit into many of the categories identified by Dworzecki, including spiritual resistance, attestation to Nazi crimes, and the use of humour and satire (which Dworzecki acknowledges requires further research). The letter signed 'Herman', composed in November 1944, which was discovered shortly after the liberation of Auschwitz and is published in a new translation in this volume, alludes to ongoing religious life in the SK. Its author writes in French, but was originally from Poland. For Dworzecki, there was a particular propensity toward spiritual resistance in Eastern European Jewish communities. Heroism had become interlocked (*enchevêtrée*) with spiritual heroism and martyrdom.[42]

In a recent important book, Amos Goldberg criticizes the concepts of resistance and *amidah* for presenting the Shoah as a crisis instead of a trauma. Such thinking, he claims, misrepresents the Shoah as a difficult process with the possibility of redemption at the end, rather than the destructive and incapacitating event that it really was. Placing emphasis on the ways victims resisted, or interpreting all of their actions as resistance, fails to acknowledge that destruction, which can be identified in the writings he considers. As an 'extreme case', Goldberg cites Zalman Lewental, one of the chroniclers of the SK, who describes his 'very own death': 'We were like dead men, like robots'.[43] Here, Goldberg simply ignores the word 'like' (*vi*), a small but significant indication that Lewental is *figuring* what happened to him when he was first recruited into the SK: he is using a simile, comparing their state to things that they are not, and thus allowing him to make more than one comparison, to robots as well as dead men. This doubling fits into Lewental's use of repetitive parallel structures, which run throughout the passage Goldberg cites.[44] Such repetitions serve to figure the state of being an automaton, but also to manage feelings arising from contemplating it and even to communicate them to a reader. They do not (at least not straightforwardly) index it in the way that Goldberg seems to believe. While Goldberg may be right to say that the experience of psychic damage and collapse of meaning is scanted by some accounts of resistance, his sense of trauma (heavily reliant on the classic definitions provided by Dori Laub, Shoshana Felman and Cathy Caruth) places far too simple a boundary between it and accounts of agency, self-understanding and, indeed, resistance.[45] It is quite clear that one of Lewental's chief motivations in writing was to document the resistance attempts and plans by the SK that led up to the revolt of 7 October 1944.

Writing as a mode of resistance arises in many contexts in the Shoah. In Chełmno, for instance, notes were written and concealed by Jewish prisoners. A sheet of squared paper annotated with the names of twelve Jewish male prisoners and inscribed with a short message is now held in the archives of Yad Vashem.[46] It was discovered in the ruins of the extermination camp. The current condition of the sheet, its multiple creases, attests to the need to hide it. Judging from the creases and staining, it was seemingly repeatedly folded in half (five times in total), with the paper becoming more resistant each time, to produce a small, squat rectangle that was easily concealable. The names are on the inner face of the folded paper. They have been documented in a conscious effort to accord the men, who knew they were going to die, a nominal afterlife. Through the list, they managed to leave a record of their fate. The short message explains that the roll has been prepared in the hope that friends or relatives of the men will one day be able to read it and learn of their fate. It concludes: 'if you survive you must take revenge'.[47] This command, for that is what it is, manifests something important about how the anonymous author (perhaps Josef Herskowicz, the first name on the list) conceived of their writing. They expected the message to function as a prompt to action, to exercise a kind of agency.

Here, Alfred Gell's conception of agency as he develops it in the context of art is enlightening. For Gell, agents (of which works of art form an example) are things which intend events to happen and perform social actions. In Gell's terms, the author who penned the demand for vengeance was the 'primary' intentional agent and the note as artefact functions as a 'secondary' intentional agent, an agent that indexes but acts independently of the primary agent.[48] Gell provides a framework for conceptualizing how documents such as the one from Chełmno and also the Scrolls of Auschwitz (the manuscripts written and then concealed by members of the SK) function not simply to register acts of resistance but also potentially to engender such acts. Taking one of the Scrolls as an example, Zalman Gradowski's account of a transport from the Kiełbasin camp to Auschwitz, the reader is invited by the narrator to bear witness. The narrator, who leads the reader on a journey through the destruction wrought on Europe's Jews, can be read as incarnating the text's own 'secondary' agency. Documents such as Gradowski's should be understood as active rather than passive artefacts.[49] One of the issues with understandings of textuality such as Goldberg's is that this agential capacity is downplayed. For him, writing either serves its author, enabling them to work through their (traumatic) experiences, or provides a means by which those experiences are imprinted. It is afforded no will of its own. Many of the authors writing during the Shoah, however, display an open or implicit belief in writing's inherent agency.

The Scrolls usually involve a conscious effort to bear witness to Nazi atrocity so that the Nazis can subsequently be held to account for their actions. They were conceived as agents to bear witness against the Nazis. Marcel Nadjary's letter, again likely written in November 1944 and also published in a new translation for this volume, provides one such agential example. There are clear efforts to specify numbers of those murdered and detail the method of killing in the letter. These sit uneasily beside heartfelt messages from Nadjary to those closest to him who he believes are still alive. The four photographs taken by a member of the SK to record the extermination process which were smuggled out of Birkenau in August 1944 would also comprise artefacts embodying resistance of this kind.[50] The Scrolls of Auschwitz as examples of resistance, particularly those written in Yiddish, can also be understood to thwart Nazi efforts at cultural genocide.

The Grey Zone

Dworzecki's efforts to advance a broader definition of *amidah* are motivated by an ethical concern that anonymous efforts to preserve humanity are not forgotten. Acts of the kind Dworzecki has in mind, minimal yet momentous actions such as the sharing of a piece of bread, often feature in retrospective testimonies provided by members of the SK. In the context of these men, however, slave-labourers in an extermination camp rather than inmates in a concentration camp, such stories might be interpreted as efforts to expiate because of their crucial, if unwilling, role in the perpetration of mass murder. The SK as a group have prompted intense ethical debate from the beginning, even as the special squad was still in operation in Birkenau. Among the writings of SK members buried in the grounds of the crematoria, Zalman Lewental provided both an analysis of how the SS forced men to perform this role and a lacerating self-examination of the will to live that kept them at it. In his letter, which was written to friends in Greece, Marcel Nadjary imagined them wondering how he could have carried out his tasks. Both Lewental and 'Herman' believed that something would be known of the SK and in different ways wanted to put some of that record straight. Indeed, knowledge of this group was passed on in moments where they did manage to breach the barrier kept between them and other prisoners, but it also circulated the camp in the form of rumour, by prisoners shocked and horrified by what the SK were forced, or were allowing themselves, to do. In conversation with Claude Lanzmann, Filip Müller described these rumours as 'myths' and 'figments of the imagination'.[51]

Müller also acknowledged that some of the crematoria were very close to the women's camp, and early testimony from women survivors of Auschwitz, such as that of Seweryna Szmaglewska (*Smoke over Birkenau*, 1945, English trans. 1947) and Krystyna Żywulska (*I Survived Auschwitz* 1946, English trans. 1951) found the position of the SK hard to accept and described them in harsh terms, although they acknowledged some complexity in what they had witnessed in the words and deeds of the men themselves. Not everyone brought moral questions to the fore, however.

In David Boder's interviews with survivors in 1946, a number mentioned the Sonderkommando, including one who stated that her brother was in the SK.[52] They cited them usually to help explain what they knew of the mass murder, as informed or shown by members of the SK. People who had managed to escape the camps could also be fascinated by this group from early on. Günther Anders wrote a poem inspired by newspaper reports of prisoners forced to burn bodies, asking simply 'What would you have done?' (1948).[53] The speaker and their addressee are haunted by the image of a member of the SK, unable to imagine what he was thinking, but compelled to try to place themselves in his position.

Early discussions of what was seen as the morally compromised position of the SK need to be seen in a wider context of suspicion of survivors. Initial attempts to consider the wrongs inflicted upon the victims and survivors of the Shoah often focused on the logic of forcing people to participate in their own victimization. In many cases, this took the form of asking at what cost to their own moral integrity people had survived. The SK provided a ready example – indeed, in some of the earliest novels in English that touch on the Holocaust, principal characters are survivors of the SK.[54]

By the early 1960s, criticisms of Jewish victims had shifted to focus on their passivity. The SK were often (albeit not in depth) referenced in such texts, not as a unique group, but simply as an extreme case of what was true in general. Bruno Bettelheim applied his characterization of prisoners straightforwardly to the behaviour of the SK. In his preface to Miklós Nyiszli's testimony, alongside the harsh criticisms of Nyiszli himself, the SK played a dual role. Thirteen of the supposed fourteen squads of SK simply accepted their lot, and so, for Bettelheim, took up the same position as all other Jews who marched unresisting to their deaths. The so-called twelfth SK who resisted served as a rebuke to the others. Bettelheim fitted them into his general schema of those who wished to 'protect the body' and those who wished to 'survive as men'.[55] In this the differences within the SK were the same as those within the Jewish people in Europe: the majority accepted their fate and did not resist; a small minority did not. Raul Hilberg used the uprisings of the SK and their equivalent in Treblinka to show that the only point at which Jews were prepared to fight back was when they 'were aware of everything'. It was only at this point, Hilberg argued, that 'long-forgotten and long-repressed powers of combat may be recalled'; the slightest degree of ignorance or uncertainty allowed 'Jewish submissiveness' to prevail.[56]

For Hannah Arendt, however, the extremity of the situation of the SK seems to have led her simply to refuse to consider whether ordinary men might have been forced to do this work. While she wanted to consider the difficult moral question of how much one should acknowledge complicity by Jewish elites, for her, the 'death commandos' must have been drawn from 'criminal elements' and 'the worst'. Their existence for her, therefore, 'was only horrible, it was no moral problem'.[57] While this position seems to show little interest in the SK, it does actually share commonalities with Arendt's description in *The Origins of Totalitarianism* (1951) of 'the murder of the moral person in man' in the camps. Arendt places this particular 'murder' into a system of destroying the humanity of human beings (as Griselda Pollock discusses in her chapter in this book). One of the steps in this process is making prisoners complicit in the crime against them, with the result that 'the distinguishing line between the persecutor and persecuted, the murderer and his victim is constantly blurred'. But for Arendt, while it is important to document this process, there is no moral insight to be gained from the experience of being in the camps, which 'can communicate no more than nihilistic banalities'. Arendt's point is that the experience of the concentration camp (and here she means extermination as well as concentration camps) was morally meaningless, precisely because the camps expunged people's moral being as part of a scheme of nullifying their lives.[58]

In a number of these cases, therefore, the extremity of the position of the SK does provoke some consideration, but it is mostly to confirm the writer's overall thesis. For Bettelheim, it simply demonstrates how his argument applies to everyone. For Hilberg, the SK confirm the extremes to which Jews had to be pushed to change their passive behaviour. In Arendt's case, they are unworthy of consideration, but do seem to fit into a general sense that there are no moral lessons to learn from the camps.

Compared to these cases, Primo Levi's consideration of the SK shows itself to be far more open to the possibility of different experiences of prisoners. He might also be said to return to an early form of response, by people such as Żywulska and Anders, who were puzzled and unable (or unwilling) to answer the questions 'what would you have done?' and 'why don't you resist?' As Dominic Williams' chapter in this volume notes, Levi's idea of the grey zone has prompted much consideration of ethical questions and the Shoah, but not everyone has engaged with the SK as one of the zone's key groups. Tzvetan Todorov's insistence that there was such a thing as moral life in the camps, criticized so virulently by Lawrence Langer, does draw upon their testimony, particularly that of Zalman Gradowski and Filip Müller. But while some of his concepts, such as 'fragmentation', might seem particularly useful for considering the grey zone, he gives little space to addressing their specific situation. In Judith Butler's recent essay on ethics of fiction and testimony, the 'grey zone' once more becomes a concept applicable to all survivors. In this essay, she suggests that the zone 'offers a way of thinking about witnessing as something other than expiating guilt' – a position that she sees as applying to Levi just as much as any of the figures that he discusses (the specifics of which she does not engage with).[59]

Langer's term 'choiceless choices' might seem to apply most aptly to the SK. However, his only direct reference to the SK in *Holocaust Testimony* is to Filip Müller's book *Sonderbehandlung* and its translation into English. He dismisses this written text as 'drawing on the temptations of teleology or the appeal of representative patterns'. Langer's point seems to be that if even someone who worked in the SK succumbs to the temptation of morally framing his written testimony, then writing in general might be unworthy of trust.[60] Langer's famous characterization of the Holocaust victims as living in a world without morality incorporates Levi's idea of the grey zone quite unproblematically. He writes that the zone 'represents those moments when staying alive could not be practiced as a common pursuit'.[61] For Langer, actions to save oneself made at someone else's expense have little difference from the questions of collaboration and privilege that Levi considers himself to be examining. While acknowledging the extreme position of the SK to a degree, Langer essentially sees them as of a piece with the rest of the victims and survivors.

Other discussions of the 'grey zone' sometimes do recognize the particular position of the SK, but find it hard to work out their place within it. For Claudia Card, the SK might be called the most extreme example of the grey zone. She cites Primo Levi's descriptions of them at a number of points when she wishes to emphasize the evil (what she calls diabolical evil) of the zone, which forces others to corrupt themselves and lose their potential for goodness.[62] This is, as she puts it, 'as diabolical an evil as I can imagine', which she matches to Primo Levi's description of the creation of the SK as 'National Socialism's most demonic crime'.[63] However, she also acknowledges that the SK are not typical of the zone, not clearly bearers of any guilt and having minimal choice in comparison with others.[64] If the ultimate evil of the grey zone is that it corrupts others, then the SK may not be the best example to choose. And yet its ultimate evil seems to be summed up in their figures, as its limit case, perhaps.

Giorgio Agamben's thinking about ethics is one of the best known responses to Levi, although he focuses on a different figure discussed by Levi: the Muselmann, an inmate who has reached an extreme state of emaciation and fatigue, who is barely alive.[65] He describes the Muselmann as 'the guard on the threshold of a new ethics'.[66] For Agamben, ethics needs to be rethought without the irredeemably legal terms of judgement and responsibility. This argument, however, also makes reference to the SK. They are important because Agamben perceives the grey zone to be a space before law and the SK are the extreme figure of this zone.⁶⁷ Agamben's engagement with the grey zone and with the SK more broadly has been severely critiqued by Philippe Mesnard and Claudine Kahan. For them, Agamben divides the grey zone too neatly in dualisms and therefore obscures the shades of grey that characterize Levi's essay.⁶⁸ They suggest that Agamben skirts the nuances that Levi emphasizes.⁶⁹ Mesnard and Kahan explore Agamben's interpretation of Levi's analysis of the football match between the SK and the SS, which he extracts from the testimony of Miklós Nyiszli and cites during his discussion of the grey zone. For Levi, this match represents a clear expression of the blurring of bounds between victim and persecutor. Mesnard and Kahan question whether Levi fully appreciated the intense pressure that members of the SK would be under to participate in such a match. If they refused to join in, they would be signing their death warrants. They also foreground Nyiszli's status difference from the SK, a difference that Agamben, in contrast to Levi, fails to recognize.⁷⁰

For Agamben, the football match is 'never over; it continues as if uninterrupted'.⁷¹ As Debarati Sanyal explains as part of her reading of *Remnants of Auschwitz*: 'Agamben's claim for the continuing relevance of Levi's gray zone transforms the aberrant event of a soccer match played in Auschwitz – and the complex web of complicity between victims and executioners that such a game reveals – into an emblem for a recurrent, unlocatable, and transhistorical violence, one contaminating the civilian world of even a liberal democracy and its daily rituals and spectacles'.⁷² Sanyal is troubled by Agamben's turning of the football match into 'the figure for a historical violence that is completely unleashed from its spatiotemporal moorings'.⁷³ His rhetorical manoeuvres, Sanyal observes, also render us 'analogous to the SS and the SK'.⁷⁴ For her, this convertibility that informs Agamben's understanding of the football match as it features in his project to reconceptualize ethics is viewable as ethically suspect. Both Sanyal, and Mesnard and Kahan foreground Agamben's failure to attend to the historical specificities of the grey zone.

This difficulty of assigning a place to be given to the SK is not surprising. Any attempt to conceptualize one group of prisoners will find it difficult to acknowledge both their particularity and their place in the wider 'society' of prisoners in the camp. But some of these difficulties seem to be particularly brought to the fore by the SK: their (seeming) centrality to the killing process (central both to the camp regime, who thought them particularly useful, and to the prisoners. who found them particularly guilty of collaboration, although members of the SK themselves disputed it); their centrality therefore to witnessing extermination; the extreme psychological suffering that this caused them and thus the extreme reactions that it might have provoked, at the same time as the fairly high level of privilege that they were granted. The chapters collected in this volume are not assembled to answer this problem, but to think through its implications.

From Within to Without

The first part of this volume includes chapters by Griselda Pollock and Dominic Williams that explore historical and ethical questions regarding representation through the prism of a consideration of the SK. Pollock considers the particular assault on the moral integrity that the Nazis had devised. Through her use of Arendt's theorization of the destruction of prisoners' moral worlds (based in large part on ideas from David Rousset) to think through the specific way in which members of the SK were morally assaulted, she demonstrates that (with care and a clear sense of the differences) some conceptual links can be drawn between concentration camps and extermination sites. Williams argues that the difficult ethical status of the grey zone is bound up with anxieties over cognizing this space. Taking off from a reading of Primo Levi's essay, he shows how ascertaining facts about the SK and their environment is always bound up with ethical questions. Indeed, even the way in which the SK gained knowledge of the machinery of destruction, by working within it, is often seen to contaminate them in a way that obscures the possibility for moral action against it that this knowledge sometimes gave them.

The volume then moves on to consider representations of the SK produced from within Birkenau. Two letters by members of the SK that were discovered buried in the grounds of the crematoria are published (in new translations) together here for the first time. The letters, written by a Polish Jewish émigré who was deported from France, and a Greek Jew, were found in 1945 and 1980 respectively. The majority of manuscripts discovered in the grounds of the crematoria were composed in Yiddish, while these two letters were written in French and Greek. This section is able to draw on new discoveries for both of them. The original of the letter in French, attributed to Chaim Herman, was considered lost. New research into its authorship has established that the actual author was Herman Strasfogel. His family held the original manuscript, which they then donated to the archives of the *Mémorial de la Shoah* in Paris. Andreas Kilian's chapter explains how this discovery was made. We have been able to incorporate corrections to the transcription of the letter into the new translation. For a long time, Marcel Nadjary's letter in Greek was largely unreadable, but in 2017, Pavel Polian and Aleksandr Nikityaev revealed that through multispectral analysis of a scan of the letter, they had been able to render visible much of the hitherto illegible text. The technique they used is detailed in a short initial chapter.

In Chapter 5, K.E. Fleming provides a sensitive analysis of the emotional tenor of Nadjary's letter and also what it reveals about his relationship to his Greek heritage. As Fleming foregrounds, Nadjary formed part of the first generation of truly 'Greek Jews', navigating his identity through both his religion and a fierce sense of nationalism. The next chapter, by Nicholas Chare, Ersy Contogouris and Dominic Williams, provides context and some interpretation of the two letters, tracing similarities and differences between them. The letters themselves then follow. The new translations both seek to replicate something of the original, at times confused, syntax of the letters. This syntax registers the horrific conditions under which the missives were both composed. The fact that so much more of Nadjary's text has recently been deciphered causes us to accord it considerable importance in this part. Doing so also serves to foreground the presence of Greek prisoners in the SK at Birkenau. The role of Greek SK members in acts of resistance has been somewhat overlooked, a theme also taken up by Steven Bowman in the third part. The part ends with a thoughtful meditation by Gideon Greif on the religious life of the SK in the crematoria.

The third part of the book considers various forms of retrospective representations of the SK. Chapter 10 by Dan Stone explores what material relating to the SK exists in the archives of the International Tracing Service (ITS). Drawing on his extensive work on this archive and previous theorizations of its nature, Stone shows how even the most minimal registration of SK experience can provide telling insights into the ways the SK have been remembered, and the ways archives operate to make certain memories possible. In the next chapter, Carol Zemel provides a sensitive and sophisticated engagement with the difficult corpus of works that were produced by the artist David Olère, a survivor of the Sonderkommando, to record what he had witnessed in the camps (he was liberated from Ebensee like many other former members of the SK). Prior to his deportation, Olère worked as a film poster designer in Paris. His works relating to his Holocaust experiences take varied forms. In the immediate postwar years, for instance, he produced a series of drawings in pen and ink, sometimes supplemented with wash, which detailed his experiences in the SK and in Auschwitz more generally. Later he would incorporate elements from these drawings into a number of paintings. Zemel traces how the effects of trauma are registered across his different practices and approaches. Her reading also examines gender issues in relation to Olère's corpus, particularly the voyeurism that manifests in some of his compositions. There has been a reluctance to engage in depth with Olère's works, but Zemel demonstrates that they form important testimony and offer valuable historical insights.

Dominic Williams and Isabel Wollaston consider the part played by the SK in the range of exhibitions and sites curated by the Auschwitz-Birkenau State Museum, both in the physical locations of Auschwitz-Birkenau and in a broader network of publications and online and social media activity. The inconsistent picture that emerges of the SK both speaks to the complexities and inconsistencies of the museum's organization and appears as a solution to the problems that the SK present for an institution. In Chapter 13, Gideon Greif then discusses reports and oral testimonies provided by survivors who were members of the SK. Through examining both early postwar testimonies and more recent accounts, he is able to foreground how our understanding of the SK and their experiences has shifted over time. In the next chapter, Sue Vice considers what might be called a doubly fictional version of the SK – that presented by Sebastian Faulks in his novel *A Possible Life*, drawing on the fake elements of Donald Watt's memoir *Stoker*. Vice shows how an Anglocentric version of the Second World War, adhered to by Faulks in his choice of intertexts and his English protagonist, produces an impossible version of the SK, one that subordinates the specific history of this group to the experience of British prisoners of war (POWs).

This part also includes a letter by Georges Didi-Huberman that is published here for the first time in English translation. It is the final one of four letters addressed to the German artist Gerhard Richter by Didi-Huberman. The communications began following a visit to Richter's studio at the artist's invitation in December 2013. It is necessary to give some sense of the letters as a whole in order to fully appreciate the fourth letter. The first letter in the quartet is dated 19 February 2014 and the last 8 July 2016. Each of Didi-Huberman's letters had to be translated into German for Richter before he was able to fully read them. The four letters were published as two pairs under the title 'Sortir du plan' in issues 135 and 137 of *Les Cahiers du Musée national de l'art modern*, one of France's most prestigious art history journals. 'Sortir du plan' is a title with multiple connotations in French.[75] As well as meaning blueprint or outline, 'plan' can also refers to the picture plane and to a cinematic shot (*gros plan*, for example, translates as close-up). Throughout the letters, Didi-Huberman particularly exploits the first two meanings of the word. The second pairing of letters also received a subtitle, *L'écorcement*, a term that translates as peeling, stripping or debarking. All these connotations are important to Didi-Huberman at different times. The four letters, written over two years, span the preparation, creation and subsequent exhibition of what came to be known as the *Birkenau* series of artworks.

The *Birkenau* series was inspired by Richter's encounters at various times and in differing contexts with the four photographs taken by a member of the SK at Birkenau to bear witness to mass murder.[76] Richter initially copied the photographs in outline onto four canvases. He then overpainted these figurative works to produce four abstract paintings. The *Birkenau* series also features four photographic works of the paintings. The four photographs upon which Richter's series is based form the subject of Didi-Huberman's 2003 work *Images malgré tout* (translated into German in 2006).[77] Richter was familiar with Didi-Huberman's analyses of the images when he invited the art historian to visit his studio. For both the artist and the art historian, the photographs hold a longstanding interest. Richter explains to Didi-Huberman at one point after 'finishing' the series that he is still engaged (*impliqué*) with their subject. Didi-Huberman, similarly, has continued to think about these photographs subsequent to the publication of *Images malgré tout*. They form part of the discussion of his 2011 book *Écorces* and, as these letters attest, continue to inspire reflection in him.[78] The correspondence between Didi-Huberman and Richter seems to provide a medium for both men to work towards an understanding of how to approach and think through these troubling images, two of which depict the burning of corpses and two of which seek to record a group of naked women in woodland near to Crematorium 4 (V) who will shortly be gassed.[79]

Each of Didi-Huberman's letters can be read as a particular foray in understanding, offering distinct ways to find words to illuminate the seen in the face of the initial quietude of the images. There are, however, continuities across the quartet. A major aim, for instance, appears to be to offer a corrective to the interpretive template Benjamin Buchloh, perhaps Richter's most significant interlocutor, has provided for the works.[80] Didi-Huberman perceives Buchloh as striving to situate Richter's works either in relation to Clement Greenberg's formalist criticism or Theodor Adorno's ideas about the value of autonomous art. In his second letter to Richter, he pointedly describes the painter not as someone who moves from the culture industry to the avant-garde, but rather as being far more subtle and dialectical, working across such divides rather than occupying a polarising position with regard to them.

In the letter we have translated here, Didi-Huberman moves on to a consideration of Richter's works in relation to Aristotelean ideas about subject and form and then in terms of their archaeological qualities. As a means to make sense of this aspect, Didi-Huberman turns to the psychoanalytic thinking of Nicolas Abraham and Maria Torok, specifically to their idea of the shell (*l'écorce*) and the kernel (*le noyau*).[81] Abraham and Torok were primarily interested in speech (such as that of the analysand), but Didi-Huberman wants to tease out the implications of their thinking for the visual. He describes painting as becoming the shell of the subject. The abstract overlays of the paintings, their shells, covering the kernels of the four photographs. These kernels *survive* their overpainting, continuing to resonate from within their abstract shells. This description of Richter's practice through the tropes of the shell and the kernel builds on ideas advanced in *Écorces* in particular. The choice of the trope of the kernel as survivor also unwittingly echoes language used by Zvi Radlitzky (also Radlitzki) in a diary of his experiences in the Lwów ghetto. Radlitzky describes those in the ghetto as being like kernels of grain (גרעיני התבואה), some of which briefly escape the action of the millstone.[82] For Radlitzky, any survival is only temporary; yet, in spite of this, his prose provides the ghetto inhabitants with a posthumous phantom presence. The writer's imagery also induces a kind of survival in the face of annihilation, his text avoiding the millstone.

In the last chapter of this part, Steven Bowman offers a valuable overview of extant sources relating to the experiences of Greek members of the SK. He draws on both testimony produced from within Birkenau and postwar accounts to assemble a compelling picture of the sometimes singularity of experience of Greek members of the SK in contrast with their Eastern European counterparts.

The next part engages with depictions of the SK in film. The first chapter in this part is by Barry Langford. Langford considers the two best-known filmic portrayals of the SK: *The Grey Zone* (dir. Tim Blake-Nelson, United States, 2001) and *Son of Saul* (dir. László Nemes, Hungary, 2015). Exploring the ways in which resistance is seen primarily in cinematic terms as violence, Langford argues that this fails to acknowledge the fact that the SK had a life and that their attempts to preserve it also need to be seen as a form of resistance. This argument speaks to some of what Williams argues in Chapter 2 about the need to credit the SK with a daily life that enabled as well as stymieing action on their part.

Adam Brown also surveys a range of films and television representations of the SK, situating a discussion of *The Grey Zone* and *Son of Saul* within this context. Unlike the other attempts to figure the SK, which Brown characterizes as appropriating them for other political purposes, these two films show the potential of fiction to prompt engagement with the ethical issues that Levi outlined in his essay on the grey zone.

In Chapter 19, Philippe Mesnard provides a detailed overview of varied approaches to the portrayal of the SK across narrative cinema and documentary. Mesnard argues persuasively that sometimes fictional devices – such as the crafted *mise-en-scène* in *Shoah* of a barber shop in which Abraham Bomba, a former slave labourer from Treblinka, gives his testimony – provide invaluable truths about Holocaust experiences. Films such as *Shoah*, involving stagings, fictional elements conceived to enhance the emotional impact of the testimony, form hinge cases existing somewhere between narrative cinema and straightforward documentary. Finally, in a coda to the volume, Victor Seidler offers a personal reflection on the insufficiency of paradigms of silence and postmemory, weaving it together with his response to the reading we provide of Zalman Gradowski in *Matters of Testimony*, and the possible intertwinings of Gradowski's and his family histories.

All the chapters in this volume seek in some way to broaden or develop thinking regarding how representations of the SK as forms of testimony intersect with ethical questions and/or address issues concerning resistance. They speak to the need to engage thoughtfully with some of the difficult questions posed by the actions of SK and how they have been portrayed retrospectively, if we are to continue to enhance our understanding of the Holocaust. Too often, the SK have been viewed as peripheral or as a taboo topic. This is a tendency that *Testimonies of Resistance* seeks to stand against. The SK need to be accorded due importance in histories of the Holocaust more broadly. The chapters here form a small contribution to the ongoing, immense, and immensely important research, which seeks to deepen our knowledge of the Holocaust. In this, they contribute to a vital kind of struggle. For Dworzecki, as Boaz Cohen implies, scholarship itself comprises a form of resistance, albeit a belated one. Among other things, documentation of the Holocaust provides a means to 'foil the murderers' attempts to conceal the crime'.[83]

Nicholas Chare is Associate Professor in the Department of History of Art and Film Studies at the Université de Montréal. In 2018 he was Diane and Howard Wohl Fellow at the Jack, Joseph and Morton Mandel Center for Advanced Holocaust Studies at the United States Holocaust Memorial Museum, Washington DC. He is the author of *Auschwitz and Afterimages: Abjection, Witnessing and Representation* (2011) and the co-author (with Dominic Williams) of *Matters of Testimony: Interpreting the Scrolls of Auschwitz* (2016) and *The Auschwitz Sonderkommando: Testimonies, Histories, Representations* (2019).

Dominic Williams is Senior Lecturer in Holocaust and Genocide Studies at Northumbria University. He has published articles on modernist writing and antisemitism, contemporary Jewish poetry, and Holocaust memory and testimony. He and Nicholas Chare have coedited *Representing Auschwitz: At the Margins of Testimony* (2013), and co-authored *Matters of Testimony:*

Interpreting the Scrolls of Auschwitz (Berghahn Books, 2016) and *The Auschwitz Sonderkommando: Testimonies, Histories, Representations* (2019).

Notes

1. For a recent filmic exploration of Postec's role in the creation of *Shoah* see *Ziva Postec: La monteuse derrière le film Shoah* (dir. Catherine Hébert, Canada, 2018). For an extended examination of how the Sonderkommando are represented in *Shoah*, see Nicholas Chare and Dominic Williams, *The Auschwitz Sonderkommando: Testimonies, Histories, Representations* (Basingstoke: Palgrave Macmillan, 2019), Chapter 7.
2. Rémy Besson, *Shoah: Une double référence? Des faits au film, du film aux faits* (Paris: MkF, 2017); Ziva Postec, 'As Editor: *Shoah* Paris 1979–1985', http://www.postec-ziva.com/Shoah.php (retrieved 28 March 2019).
3. Nicholas Chare and Dominic Williams, *Matters of Testimony: Interpreting the Scrolls of Auschwitz* (New York: Berghahn Books, 2016).
4. Adam Brown, *Judging 'Privileged' Jews: Holocaust Ethics, Representation, and the 'Grey Zone'* (New York: Berghahn Books, 2013), 124–30.
5. Compare the accounts of the SK revolt and sources used in Raul Hilberg, *The Destruction of the European Jews* (Chicago: Quadrangle, 1961), 624–25 and Raul Hilberg, *The Destruction of the European Jews* (New York: Holmes & Meier, 1985), revised edn, vol 3, 1047–48.
6. Martin Gilbert, *The Holocaust: The Jewish Tragedy* (London: HarperCollins, 1986), esp. 649–53, but also 518, 633, 636–37, 667–68 and 749–50. Following the Auschwitz Museum, Gilbert attributes these passages to an anonymous author or Zalman Lewental. Far less extensive references are made to Lewental's account of the SK resistance (515–16, 744–46, 820), and one reference to Zalman Gradowski occurs (730).
7. Val Arnold-Forster, 'Weekend Arts: Taste of Ashes/Radio Review', *The Guardian*, 20 December 1986, p. 12.
8. Hannes Heer, 'The Difficulty of Ending a War: Reactions to the Exhibition "War of Extermination: Crimes of the Wehrmacht 1941 to 1944"', trans. Jane Caplan, *History Workshop Journal* 46 (Autumn 1998), 187–203; Andrew I. Port, 'Holocaust Scholarship and Politics in the Public Sphere: Reexamining the Causes, Consequences, and Controversy of the Historikerstreit and the Goldhagen Debate: A Forum with Gerrit Dworok, Richard J. Evans, Mary Fulbrook, Wendy Lower, A. Dirk Moses, Jeffrey K. Olick, and Timothy D. Snyder', *Central European History* 50(3) (2017), 375–403.
9. Most notably Shoshana Felman and Dori Laub, *Testimony: Crises of Witnessing in Literature, Psychoanalysis, and History* (New York: Routledge, 1992).
10. *Schindler's List* (dir. Steven Spielberg, 1993) and *Life is Beautiful* (dir. Roberto Benigni, 1997) won seven and three Oscars respectively. *The Guardian* predicted that with *The Grey Zone* (2001), its director Tim Blake Nelson was 'set to flower' and would 'show himself a heavyweight'. Andrew Pulver et al., 'New Year Special: Just Watch Us Go', *The Guardian*, 29 December 2000, p. 10. The film received a limited release in the United States and went straight to DVD in most countries, including

the United Kingdom. See https://www.imdb.com/title/tt0252480/?ref_=ttrel_rel_tt (retrieved 28 March 2019).
11. The chapters in this collection by Griselda Pollock, Barry Langford, Adam Brown and Philippe Mesnard include at least some discussion of *Son of Saul*. We also include a translation of one open letter from Georges Didi-Huberman to Richter about his *Birkenau* series. On the Scrolls of Auschwitz, see Chare and Williams, *Matters of Testimony* and Nicholas Chare and Dominic Williams, *The Auschwitz Sonderkommando*, Chapter 2. New translations include Zalmen Gradowski, *From the Heart of Hell: Manuscripts of a Sonderkommando Member in Auschwitz*, trans. Barry Smerin and Janina Wurbs (Oświęcim: Auschwitz-Birkenau State Museum, 2017); and Salmen Gradowski, *Die Zertrennung*, ed. Aurélia Kalisky, trans. Almut Seiffert and Miriam Trinh (Frankfurt: Suhrkamp, forthcoming).
12. For a discussion of *Son of Saul* in relation to writings by members of the SK, see our article 'Questions of Filiation: From the Scrolls of Auschwitz to *Son of Saul*', *Mémoires en jeu* 2 (2016), 63–72. For a recent, powerful reading of *Son of Saul*, one which draws on the writings of Zalman Gradowski for context, see Isabel Wollaston, '(Re-)Visualizing the "Heart of Hell"? Representations of the Auschwitz Sonderkommando in the Art of David Olère and Son of Saul (László Nemes, 2015),' *Holocaust Studies* (2019), https://doi.org/10.1080/17504902.2019.1625119.
13. Ber Mark, *The Extermination and the Resistance of the Polish Jews during the Period 1939–1945*, trans. Adam Rutkowski (Warsaw: Jewish Historical Institute, 1955), 15.
14. Joseph Tenenbaum, 'Foreword', in Jacob Apenszlak and Moshe Polakiewicz, *Armed Resistance of the Jews in Poland* (New York: American Federation for Polish Jews, 1944), 7.
15. Melech Neustadt, 'The Year of Extermination', in *The Last Stand: Jewish Resistance in Nazi Europe and the Role of the Labour Zionist Movement* (New York: Poale Zion Organization of America, 1944), 7.
16. Israel Gutman, 'The Jewish Underground in Auschwitz', trans. Israel Meir Lask, in Zvi Szner (ed.), *Extermination and Resistance: Historical Records and Source Material, Volume I* (Lohamei Haghettaot: Ghetto Fighters House, 1958), 157.
17. Lewental probably found this diary in the effects of a person murdered in the gas chambers of Auschwitz-Birkenau. Ber Mark, *The Scrolls of Auschwitz* (Tel Aviv: Am Oved Press, 1985), 237.
18. Gutman, 'The Jewish Underground in Auschwitz', 160.
19. See, for instance, the testimony of Murray Kenig. When questioned about the revolt, Kenig states that: 'It had no significance'. When pressed, he says: 'Let me explain the hopelessness of the situation to you in real terms, not imaginatively or otherwise. Auschwitz was impregnable both ways. You couldn't get in and you couldn't get out'. He then observes that if there were any feelings following the revolt, they were not of hope, but of fear of retaliation. Murray Kenig interviewed by Josh Freed, 13 January 1982. USC Shoah Foundation. Interview Code 53607.
20. Neustadt is keen to link resistance activities with the Labor Zionist Movement and, without underplaying the role of the Movement, his approach demonstrates how efforts at rebellion can be retrospectively co-opted to serve political and other agendas.
21. Neustadt, 'The Year of Extermination', 9.
22. Yehuda Bauer, 'Foreword', in Shmuel Krakowski, *The War of the Doomed: Jewish Armed Resistance in Poland, 1942–1944*, trans. Orah Blaustein (New York: Holmes & Meier, 1984), vii.

23. Yehuda Bauer, *Rethinking the Holocaust* (New Haven: Yale University Press, 2001), 163.
24. Boaz Cohen, 'Dr Meir (Mark) Dworzecki: The Historical Mission of a Survivor Historian', *Holocaust Studies* 21(1–2) (2015), 24–37, at 28.
25. The original is: 'All men are brothers / Brown, yellow, black, white / Peoples lands and climates / Are a made up tale'. Dworzecki, *Histoire de la résistance anti-nazie juive (1933–1945) : Problèmes et méthodologie* (Tel Aviv: n.p., 1965), 27.
26. For a short biography of Dworzecki, see Cohen, 'Dr Meir (Mark) Dworzecki', 24–25.
27. See Or Rogovin, 'Between Meir Dworzecki and Yehiel Dimur: *Amidah* in the Writing of Ka-Tzetnik 135633', *Holocaust Studies* 24(2) (2018), 203–17, at 203–4.
28. Irene Weiss interviewed by Ileane Kenney, 26 July 1996. Shoah Foundation Number 17212.
29. Henryk Mandelbaum interviewed by Elliot Perlman in the spring of 2006. USHMM Accession Number: 2006.201. RG Number: RG-50.634.0001.
30. Shlomo Venezia interviewed by Manuela Consonni on 13 December 1997. USC Shoah Foundation Interview Code 36179.
31. Erna Low, 'I was in Oswiecim'. Unpublished memoir, 2. USHMM Accession Number: 2017.466.1.
32. Lucia Franco, *Et un jour, la joie de vivre s'arreta à . . . Auschwitz* (Owings Mills: Marla Stein Associates, 1994), 62.
33. Erika Myriam Kounio Amariglio, *From Thessaloniki to Auschwitz and Back: Memories of a Survivor from Thessaloniki*, trans. Theresa Sundt (London: Valentine Mitchell, 2000), 90.
34. For a discussion of symbolic resistance, see Michael R. Marrus, 'Jewish Resistance in the Holocaust', *Journal of Contemporary History* 30 (1995), 83–110, at 94–95.
35. For further discussion of this event, see Chare and Williams, *The Auschwitz Sonderkommando*, Chapter 2. Our numbering of the crematoria in this chapter, like some of the other chapters in the volume, follows that used by the majority of survivors of the SK in their retrospective testimonies and also by the authors of the Scrolls of Auschwitz (see, for example, the anonymous list of transports written in Polish discovered buried alongside manuscripts by Leyb Langfus and Zalman Lewental). In their lived experience, for the SK at Birkenau there were only four crematoria (although a very few had also worked at the crematorium at Auschwitz I). We have provided the Nazi numbering of the crematoria (which included the crematoria at both Auschwitz I and II) as roman numerals in parentheses. In this volume, some chapters follow the numbering system used by the camp regime and subsequently by many historians (who mostly relied on perpetrator documents). This system counts the crematorium at Auschwitz I as Crematorium I and the four at Birkenau as Crematoria II–V. In all cases, the numbers in Roman numerals are consistent, so Crematorium 1 (II) is the same as Crematorium II.
36. Hermann Langbein, *Against All Hope: Resistance in the Nazi Concentration Camps 1938–1945*, trans. Harry Zohn (New York: Paragon, 1994), 280.
37. Zalman Lewental, 'Addendum to the Łódź Manuscript', in Ber Mark, *The Scrolls of Auschwitz*, trans. Sharon Neemani (Tel Aviv: Am Oved, 1985), 236–40, at 238.
38. Roger S. Gottlieb, 'The Concept of Resistance: Jewish Resistance during the Holocaust', *Social Theory and Practice* 9(1), 31–49, at 41.
39. 'Protokół [Official Record] – Henryk Tauber', Proces Rudolfa Hoessa, Sygn. GK 196/93, NTN 93, Volume 11, 1946–47. USHMM Accession Number: 1998.A.0243 RG Number: RG-15.167M, 122–49; 129 (1-28; 8).

40. Ibid.
41. Morris K. interviewed by Lawrence Langer on 29 June 1989 (currently mistakenly listed in the Yale catalogue as 28 June). Fortunoff Collection HVT-1431.
42. Meir Dworzecki, *Histoire de la résistance anti-nazie juive (1933–1945) : Problèmes et méthodologie* (Tel Aviv: n.p., 1965), 26.
43. Amos Goldberg, *Trauma in First Person: Diary Writing during the Holocaust* (Indianapolis: Indiana University Press, 2017), 56–57, 40–41.
44. E.g. 'vos er tut, ven er tut, vos mit im tut zikh bikhlal'; 'kh'veys genoy, az keyner hot demolt fun undz nisht gelebt, nisht gedenkt, nisht getrakht'. Goldberg also ceases his quotation immediately before the words: 'That's how they treated us until we [*1 word illegible*] we began to regain our senses'. And a few lines later: 'Afterwards, coming to oneself in the block, when each man lay down to rest, then the tragedy began'.
45. Indeed, these theorizations of trauma as inherently retrospective fit uneasily with discussing diarists writing during the event. In fact, attempts to theorize an 'everyday' as opposed to a 'catastrophic' trauma might speak better to some of the aspects of what diarists and contemporaneous writers were doing. See especially Ann Cvetkovich, *An Archive of Feelings: Trauma, Sexuality, and Lesbian Public Cultures* (Durham, NC: Duke University Press, 2003).
46. 'Will written by 12 Jewish inmates who were labourers in Chełmno camp before they were murdered (undated)', Letters and Postcards Collection, Yad Vashem, Item ID 3539746.
47. 'Will written by 12 Jewish inmates who were labourers in Chełmno camp before they were murdered (undated)', Reuven Dafni and Yehudit Kleiman (eds), *Final Letters from Victims of the Holocaust* (New York: Paragon House, 1991), 120.
48. Alfred Gell, *Art and Agency: An Anthropological Theory* (Oxford: Clarendon Press, 1998), 21.
49. For a discussion of Gradowski's own notion of agency in relation to artefacts, see Nicholas Chare, 'Material Witness: Conservation Ethics and the Scrolls of Auschwitz', *symplokē* 24(1–2) (2016), 81–97.
50. For a recent analysis of these photographs see Chare and Williams, *The Auschwitz Sonderkommando*, Chapter 3.
51. Claude Lanzmann Shoah Collection, Interview with Filip Müller, Accession Number 1996:166; RG-60.5012. English translation of transcript of interview with Lanzmann, trans. Uta Allers, 89–90.
52. Jola Gross, 3 August 1946, Paris; Helen Tichauer, 23 September 1946, Feldafing, Germany. Retrieved 28 March 2019 from http://voices.iit.edu/david_boder.
53. Gideon Greif and Adam Brown have both cited this poem, but dated it by its appearance in the German-Jewish New York newspaper *Aufbau* in 1961. Brown, *Judging 'Privileged' Jews*, 202; Gideon Greif, *We Wept without Tears: Testimonies of the Jewish Sonderkommando from Auschwitz*, trans. Naftali Greenwood (New Haven: Yale University Press, 2005), 1–2. See Günther Anders, *Tagebücher und Gedichte* (Munich: Beck, 1985), 331–32.
54. E.g. Mordecai Richler, *A Choice of Enemies* (1957), Leon Uris, *Exodus* (1958), Edward Lewis Wallant, *The Pawnbroker* (1961) and Daniel Stern, *Who Shall Live, Who Shall Die* (1963).
55. Bruno Bettelheim, 'Afterword', in Miklós Nyiszli, *Auschwitz: A Doctor's Eyewitness Report* (London: Penguin, 2013) 173. Bettelheim's criticism of Nyiszli also appeared in *The Informed Heart* (Harmondsworth: Penguin, 1991), 261–62.

56. Hilberg, *The Destruction of the European Jews* (1st ed., 1961), 625n23; see also 624–25 and 631.
57. Hannah Arendt, *Eichmann in Jerusalem: A Report on the Banality of Evil* (New York: Penguin, 1994), 123–25.
58. Hannah Arendt, *The Origins of Totalitarianism* (London: Penguin, 2017), 451, 591. For the earliest version of this argument, see Hannah Arendt, 'The Concentration Camps (Review)', *Partisan Review* 15(7) (July 1948). Retrieved 28 March 2019 from http://www.bu.edu/partisanreview/books/PR1948V15N7/HTML/files/assets/basic-html/index.html#743.
59. Judith Butler, 'Fiction and Solicitude: Ethics and the Conditions for Survival', in Claudio Fogu, Wulf Kansteiner and Todd Presner (eds), *Probing the Ethics of Holocaust Culture* (Cambridge, MA: Harvard University Press, 2016), 335–36.
60. Lawrence Langer, *Holocaust Testimony: The Ruins of Memory* (New Haven: Yale University Press, 1991), 57–58. Langer's position is that the authenticity of Müller's written text is more questionable than that of the testimony provided for Claude Lanzmann in *Shoah*, on the basis that written testimony can be 'openly or silently edited', whereas in oral testimony 'every word spoken falls directly from the survivor's lips' (at 210n18). However, Müller's words are in fact heavily edited in *Shoah*. See Chare and Williams, *The Auschwitz Sonderkommando*, Chapter 7. For a general discussion of the complex role of editing in *Shoah*, see Rémy Besson, *Shoah une double référence: Des faits au film, du film aux faits* (Paris: MkF éditions, 2017). Recent work on Müller's book indicates that Helmut Freitag played a rather more complicated role than Langer believes him to have done and that Müller was responsible for some of the writing in German. See Peter Davies, *Witness between Languages: The Translation of Holocaust Testimonies in Context* (Rochester, NY: Camden House, 2018), 191–192.
61. Langer, *Holocaust Testimony*, 139.
62. Claudia Card, *The Atrocity Paradigm: A Theory of Evil* (New York: Oxford University Press, 2002), 212, 234.
63. Ibid., 217, 234.
64. Ibid., 222, 230.
65. For a recent discussion of the figure of the Muselmann, see Paul Bernard-Nourad, *Figurer l'autre: Essai sur la figure du 'musulman' dans les camps de concentration nazis* (Paris: Éditions Kimé, 2013).
66. Giorgio Agamben, *Remnants of Auschwitz: The Witness and the Archive*, trans. Daniel Heller-Roazen (New York: Zone Books, 1999), 69. For further discussion of Agamben's ethical framework in relation to the Sonderkommando, see Nicholas Chare, 'The Gap in Context: Giorgio Agamben's *Remnants of Auschwitz*', *Cultural Critique* 64 (Fall 2006), 40–68. We are grateful to Justin Clemens for sharing his insights about Agamben's philosophy.
67. Ibid., 24.
68. Philippe Mesnard and Claudine Kahan, *Giorgio Agamben à l'épreuve d'Auschwitz* (Paris: Éditions Kimé, 2001) 33.
69. Ibid., 36.
70. Ibid., 39.
71. Agamben, *Remnants of Auschwitz*, 26.
72. Debarati Sanyal, *Memory and Complicity: Migrations of Holocaust Remembrance* (New York: Fordham University Press, 2015), 32.
73. Ibid.
74. Ibid., 33.

75. We are grateful to Georges Didi-Huberman for his suggestion as to how best to translate the title.
76. These photographs are additionally discussed by Steven Bowman in his chapter in this volume.
77. Georges Didi-Huberman, *Images malgré tout* (Paris: Les Éditions de Minuit, 2004).
78. Georges Didi-Huberman, *Écorces* (Paris: Les Éditions de Minuit, 2011).
79. For further discussion of Didi-Huberman's engagement with these images, see Chare & Williams, *Matters of Testimony*, Chapter 6.
80. For Buchloh's own reading of Richter's *Birkenau* series, see Benjamin Buchloh, *Gerhard Richter's* Birkenau *Paintings* (Cologne: Verlag der Buchhandlung Walther König, 2016).
81. Nicolas Abraham and Maria Torok, *The Shell and the Kernel: Renewals of Psychoanalysis, Volume 1*, trans. Nicholas T. Rand (Chicago: University of Chicago Press, 1994).
82. Zvi Radlitzky, 'Reshimot miyemei hakibush haGermani BeLvov', *Yalqut moreshet* 21 (1976), 7–34, at 7.
83. Cohen, 'Dr Meir (Mark) Dworzecki', 26.

Bibliography

Abraham, Nicolas, and Maria Torok. *The Shell and the Kernel: Renewals of Psychoanalysis, Volume 1*, trans. Nicholas T. Rand. Chicago: University of Chicago Press, 1994.
Agamben, Giorgio. *Remnants of Auschwitz: The Witness and the Archive*, trans. Daniel Heller-Roazen. New York: Zone Books, 1999.
Amariglio, Erika Myriam Kounio. *From Thessaloniki to Auschwitz and Back: Memories of a Survivor from Thessaloniki*, trans. Theresa Sundt. London: Valentine Mitchell, 2000.
Anders, Günther. *Tagebücher und Gedichte*. Munich: Beck, 1985.
Arendt, Hannah. 'The Concentration Camps (Review)', *Partisan Review* 15(7) (July 1948), 743–63.
——. *Eichmann in Jerusalem: A Report on the Banality of Evil*. New York: Penguin, 1994.
——. *The Origins of Totalitarianism*. London: Penguin, 2017.
Bauer, Yehuda. 'Foreword', in Shmuel Krakowski, *The War of the Doomed: Jewish Armed Resistance in Poland, 1942–1944*, trans. Orah Blaustein. New York: Holmes & Meier, 1984, vii–viii.
——. *Rethinking the Holocaust*. New Haven: Yale University Press, 2001.
Bernard-Nourad, Paul. *Figurer l'autre: Essai sur la figure du 'musulman' dans les camps de concentration nazis*. Paris: Éditions Kimé, 2013.
Bettelheim, Bruno. *The Informed Heart*. Harmondsworth: Penguin, 1991.
Besson, Rémy. *Shoah une double référence: Des faits au film, du film aux faits*. Paris: MkF éditions, 2017.
Brown, Adam. *Judging 'Privileged' Jews: Holocaust Ethics, Representation, and the 'Grey Zone'*. New York: Berghahn Books, 2013.
Buchloh, Benjamin. *Gerhard Richter's* Birkenau *Paintings*. Cologne: Verlag der Buchhandlung Walther König, 2016.
Butler, Judith. 'Fiction and Solicitude: Ethics and the Conditions for Survival', in Claudio Fogu, Wulf Kansteiner and Todd Presner (eds), *Probing the Ethics of Holocaust Culture*. Cambridge, MA: Harvard University Press, 2016, 373–88.

Card, Claudia. *The Atrocity Paradigm: A Theory of Evil*. New York: Oxford University Press, 2002.
Chare, Nicholas. 'The Gap in Context: Giorgio Agamben's *Remnants of Auschwitz*', *Cultural Critique* 64 (Fall 2006): 40–68.
———. 'Material Witness: Conservation Ethics and the Scrolls of Auschwitz', *symplokē* 24(1/2) (2016): 81–97.
Chare, Nicholas, and Dominic Williams. *Matters of Testimony: Interpreting the Scrolls of Auschwitz*. New York: Berghahn Books, 2016.
———. 'Questions of Filiation: From the Scrolls of Auschwitz to *Son of Saul*', *Mémoires en jeu* 2 (2016): 63–72.
———. *The Auschwitz Sonderkommando: Testimonies, Histories, Representations*. Basingstoke: Palgrave Macmillan, 2019.
Cohen, Boaz. 'Dr Meir (Mark) Dworzecki: The Historical Mission of a Survivor Historian', *Holocaust Studies* 21(1/2) (2015), 24–37.
Cvetkovich, Ann. *An Archive of Feelings: Trauma, Sexuality, and Lesbian Public Cultures*. Durham, NC: Duke University Press, 2003.
Davies, Peter. *Witness between Languages: The Translation of Holocaust Testimonies in Context*. Rochester, NY: Camden House, 2018.
Didi-Huberman, Georges. *Images malgré tout*. Paris: Les Éditions de Minuit, 2004.
———. *Écorces*. Paris: Les Éditions de Minuit, 2011.
Dworzecki, Meir. *Histoire de la résistance anti-nazie juive (1933–1945): Problèmes et méthodologie*. Tel Aviv: n.p., 1965.
Franco, Lucia. *Et un jour, la joie de vivre s'arreta à . . . Auschwitz*. Owings Mills: Marla Stein Associates, 1994.
Gell, Alfred. *Art and Agency: An Anthropological Theory*. Oxford: Clarendon Press, 1998,
Gilbert, Martin. *The Holocaust: The Jewish Tragedy*. London: HarperCollins, 1986.
Goldberg, Amos. *Trauma in First Person: Diary Writing During the Holocaust*, trans. Shmuel Sermoneta-Gertel and Avner Greenberg. Indianapolis: Indiana University Press, 2017.
Gottlieb, Roger S. 'The Concept of Resistance: Jewish Resistance During the Holocaust', *Social Theory and Practice* 9(1), 31–49.
Greif, Gideon. *We Wept without Tears: Testimonies of the Jewish Sonderkommando from Auschwitz*, trans. Naftali Greenwood. New Haven: Yale University Press, 2005.
Gutman, Israel. 'The Jewish Underground in Auschwitz', trans. Israel Meir Lask, in Zvi Szner (ed.), *Extermination and Resistance: Historical Records and Source Material, Volume I*. Lohamei Haghettaot: Ghetto Fighters House, 1958, 153–61.
Hilberg, Raul. *The Destruction of the European Jews*. Chicago: Quadrangle, 1961.
———. *The Destruction of the European Jews*, revised edn. New York: Holmes & Meier, 1985.
Langbein, Hermann. *Against All Hope: Resistance in the Nazi Concentration Camps 1938–1945*, trans. Harry Zohn. New York: Paragon, 1994.
Langer, Lawrence. *Holocaust Testimony: The Ruins of Memory*. New Haven: Yale University Press, 1991.
Lewental, Zalman. 'Addendum to the Łódź Manuscript', in Ber Mark, *The Scrolls of Auschwitz*, trans. Sharon Neemani. Tel Aviv: Am Oved, 1985, 236–40.
Mark, Ber. *The Extermination and the Resistance of the Polish Jews during the Period 1939–1945*, trans. Adam Rutkowski. Warsaw: Jewish Historical Institute, 1955.
———. *The Scrolls of Auschwitz*, trans. Sharon Neemani. Tel Aviv: Am Oved Press, 1985.

Marrus, Michael R. 'Jewish Resistance in the Holocaust', *Journal of Contemporary History* 30 (1995), 83–110.

Mesnard, Philippe, and Claudine Kahan. *Giorgio Agamben à l'épreuve d'Auschwitz*. Paris: Éditions Kimé, 2001.

Neustadt, Melech. 'The Year of Extermination', in *The Last Stand: Jewish Resistance in Nazi Europe and the Role of the Labour Zionist Movement*, New York: The Poale Zion Organization of America, 1944, 5–34.

Nyiszli, Miklós. *Auschwitz: A Doctor's Eyewitness Report*, trans. Tibère Kremer and Richard Seaver. London: Penguin, 2013.

Radlitzky, Zvi. 'Reshimot miyemei hakibush haGermani BeLvov', *Yalqut moreshet* 21 (1976), 7–34.

Rogovin, Or. 'Between Meir Dworzecki and Yehiel Dimur: *Amidah* in the Writing of Ka-Tzetnik 135633', *Holocaust Studies* 24(2), 203–17.

Sanyal, Debarati. *Memory and Complicity: Migrations of Holocaust Remembrance*. New York: Fordham University Press, 2015.

Tenenbaum, Joseph. 'Foreword', in Jacob Apenszlak and Moshe Polakiewicz, *Armed Resistance of the Jews in Poland*. New York: American Federation for Polish Jews, 1944.

Wollaston, Isabel. '(Re-)Visualizing the "Heart of Hell"? Representations of the Auschwitz Sonderkommando in the Art of David Olère and *Son of Saul* (László Nemes, 2015),' *Holocaust Studies* (2019), https://doi.org/10.1080/17504902.2019.1625119.

Part I

Historical and Ethical Questions of Representation

Chapter 1

Knowing Cruelty

The Negation of Death and Burial in SS Violence

Griselda Pollock

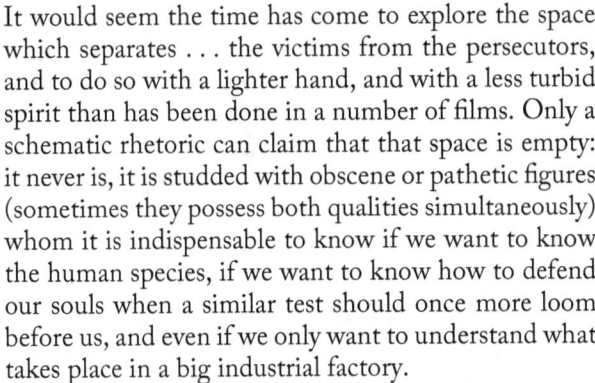

It would seem the time has come to explore the space which separates ... the victims from the persecutors, and to do so with a lighter hand, and with a less turbid spirit than has been done in a number of films. Only a schematic rhetoric can claim that that space is empty: it never is, it is studded with obscene or pathetic figures (sometimes they possess both qualities simultaneously) whom it is indispensable to know if we want to know the human species, if we want to know how to defend our souls when a similar test should once more loom before us, and even if we only want to understand what takes place in a big industrial factory.
—Primo Levi, 'The Gray Zone', 1986[1]

... you know – nay, you knew – and so I have to remind you of this now, that the Death Fugue is also this to me: an epitaph and a grave ... My mother, too, has only *this* grave.
—Paul Celan, letter to Ingeborg Bachmann, 12 November 1959[2]

Paul Celan's most famous poem *Todesfuge* (*Death Fugue*) shares two key ideas – *black milk* and *a grave in the air* – with fellow Romanian Jewish poets Rose Ausländer (1901–88) and Immanuel Weissglas (1920–79), all of them seeking an image in language for extreme suffering and impossible mourning. Celan's poem joins the two horrors. Black milk negates life as surely as maternal milk once enabled its daily increase. To prohibit burial enacts a moral violence on both the dead and those who, witnessing death, initiate mourning and preserve memory. It is the denial of a singular, personal death and an effacement of that person having been here, in life, by dissipating their remains into the no-place of air. Theodor Adorno wrote of both the crime and its legacy for all coming thereafter:

> The administrative murder of millions made of death a thing one had never yet to fear in just this fashion. There is no chance any more for death to come into the individual's empirical life as somehow conformable with the course of that life. The last, the poorest possession left to the individual is expropriated. That in the concentration camps it was no longer an individual who died, but a specimen – this is a fact bound to affect the dying of those who escaped the administrative measure.[3]

The sparse, sarcastic and repetitious incantation that is Celan's *Todesfugue* produces a cry of agony as it identifies a calculatedly *psychological* crime perpetrated through *physical* forms: malnutrition and defilement of the dead human body. It is unequivocal as to its origin: 'Death is a master from Germany'.[4]

From historical records and survivor testimonies from the various Sonderkommando (SK), we know that mass burial of gassed corpses was the initial practice in the death camps of Operation Reinhard on Polish soil.[5] Exhumation and open-pit burning and then industrial cremation was undertaken in response to the defeat of the German forces at Stalingrad in February 1943 when the possibility of losing the war as the victorious Red Army began to the Germans back into Poland and Germany made it imperative to remove traces of the mass killings. Side by side with such political exigencies, the processes officially decreed were elaborated in each location by the heads of the SS units placed in charge of each camp who thereby inducted, by daily enactment, the SS themselves into a universe of calculated, systematic cruelty that was, I shall argue, as psychologically destructive as it was physically brutal for their prisoners.

In the historical evolution of the camps, Hannah Arendt argues that the real horror began when the SS took over the running of camps from the SA – defined as 'beasts in human form, that is, men who really belonged in mental institutions and prisons' – and 'the old spontaneous bestiality gave way to an absolutely cold and systematic destruction of human bodies, calculated to destroy human dignity'. The camps then became 'drill grounds on which perfectly normal men were trained to be full-fledged members of the SS'.[6]

The use of radically *othered* prisoners – those selected from the Jewish concentration camp internees to form the SK – within this process of mass murder can also be considered, according to Hannah Arendt, ideological. She defines a dialectic in the camp between the perpetrator elite, SS and the terrorized victims, the SK, in order for a hierarchy, the essence of the totalitarian system, to come into being so as to justify its own extremity:

> Totalitarian domination attempts to achieve this goal both through logical indoctrination of the elite formations and through absolute terror in the camps; and the atrocities for which the elite formations are ruthlessly used becoming, as it were, the practical application of the ideological indoctrination – the testing ground in which the latter must prove itself – while the appalling spectacle of the camps themselves is supposed to furnish the 'theoretical' verification of the ideology.[7]

The SS were trained in the cultivation of cruelty by the complementary creation of a category of prisoners who were radically *differentiated* from the SS by the work they were made to perform, but were placed *in proximity* to the SS. The SK were thus not only general prisoners under a regime of intensifying dehumanization typical of the camp as instrument. As special – *sonder* – they were forced into this ghastly labour facilitating the killing process in a condition *when they were still known to be human*: conscious, morally sensitive and thinking beings. Their work traumatically breached their deepest morality and, in many cases, as religious Jewish men from the heartlands of Jewish life in Eastern Europe, the very definition of their identities. The physical violence of enforced starvation of the general population in the camp was mitigated for the SK by extra rations not only to enable them to work at the pace required, but also to make more acute the psychological agony that was inflicted as the price of remaining alive a little longer.

The cultivation of unimaginable cruelty created a regime for the SS that sustained them in a logic of utter atrocity because of their apparent superiority to the species into which they made the members of the SK. This is not, in any way, an argument for understanding the perpetrator as also a victim of this system. I am shifting the debate, cited as an epigraph, about Primo Levi's concept of a grey zone of Jewish prisoners compromised by complicity in genocide, however forced, to focus on the *systemic creation of a cruelty* that was not only produced by the SS. It functioned structurally as the ideological realization and iterative, performative enactment of what constituted the SS.

The selection of *Jewish* prisoners to be SK – the physical instruments of the mass murder kept at work by ruthless SS overseers – was part of this deep logic. Knowingly, this logic had to appal those powerlessly selected to perform it, soiling them by the intimacy with the SS universe. My argument is that the nature of this cruelty was pointed. SS actions demonstrated awareness of, and exploited a violation of, deep-rooted Jewish sensibilities and obligatory rituals of care for the dead. If we do not acknowledge this, we will never register the depth of the moral perversion imposed upon the SK as a knowing cruelty.

To explore this conjunction – defilement of the human dead and enforced participation in dehumanization – at the point of the power of the SS over their victims, I offer a reading the film *Son of Saul* (*Saul fia*) directed by László Nemes in 2015, which was hailed as a landmark in cinema's exploration of the core of the Shoah. I focus on the desecration of the dead in my reading. Coding the terms of generally enthusiastic critical responses to the film, I draw attention to what they do not discuss: the significance of burial and mourning as well as references for the central character as a figure already dead while still living, in Hungarian Jewish writing by survivors Elie Wiesel (1928–2016) and Imre Kertész (1929–2016).

Son of Saul tells the story of one attempt by a member of the SK to secure a ritual burial for one victim of the gas chambers at Auschwitz-Birkenau, one of the sites of the exterminatory factory system of genocidal destruction of Jewish and Roma Europeans in the years 1940–45. It has been hailed as a breakthrough film for daring to explore the most compromised of prisoners – the SK – by means of a powerfully immersive cinematic re-creation of the death factory across whose horrific landscape and soundscape we follow the aberrant and obsessed prisoner, Saul, in his quest. Despite the positive critical response to the film's faithfulness and its creation of immersive reality effects, I propose that *Son of Saul* is not a work of cinematic verism. I investigate it as cinematic allegory, obliquely invoking biblical and classical myth as much as the myth of cinema. The core narrative action of one man seeking a ritual burial for one corpse invokes two figures: Lazarus and Antigone. Antigone represents a moral action in defiance of the law. Lazarus prefigures a Christian promise of resurrection, while suggesting a state of being permanently touched by the tomb.[8] My purpose is, therefore, to examine the film's allegorical and mythic quality, its debts to tropes from classical and biblical literature, and its relation to other cinemas within the changing terms of the debate about the representability and representation of the Shoah.

In its form, *Son of Saul* is deeply reverential, referencing canonical cinematic engagements with the Shoah and the Parisian debates about representation and representability surrounding them. Thus, I will situate its intervention in that dense field to assess how *Son of Saul*, so clearly breaching the injunction not to show the process of mass murder, still accumulated acclaim, even from Claude Lanzmann himself. My own reading furthermore recasts the film's engagement with the SK by approaching its core themes, inhuman killing versus humanizing burial, through a political analysis of the SS system offered by Hannah Arendt and her definition of the concentrationary universe as a systematic destruction of the human condition that tortured its inmates not only physically but also psychologically.[9] This will enable me to argue ultimately that although the apparent project of *Son of Saul* is allegorical and although the film is deeply self-conscious aesthetically as a work of cinema, it effectively exposes the logic of atrocity that Arendt insisted constituted the SS. This means seeing the systematic enactment on its Jewish SK of a knowing cruelty by means of psychological torture involving the specific defilement of a Jewish concept of life, death and the body signified by the rituals of burial.

I am suggesting that the SS (ab)use of the SK produced a culturally specific anguish for a Jewish imaginary and subjectivity by the denial of the rites of burial and memorialization of the dead. This forms a critical dimension of the film's work that is neither identified nor acknowledged in the journalistic and the more critical commentary on *Son of Saul*. The undertone of a culturally specific psychological assault, involved in the very processes the SK were forced to undertake – not the killing, but the preceding (forced and mixed nakedness) and subsequent violations (mass non-burial) of the human beings whom the SS murdered – was not consciously introduced by the filmmaker. Rather, I propose that the narrative trope of a man seeking to say *Kaddish* for a dead child becomes an allegory of the film itself, with both man and child being the projections of the director working through the unprocessed traumatic legacies of the condition of being a member of the second and third generation, the condition theorized by literary theorist Marianne Hirsch as postmemory.[10] The film's affectivity, cinematic aesthetic and character-centred narrative then become a symptomatic inscription of trauma seeking to find a form that takes the film into a different space from what was hailed in its critical reception.[11]

At the heart of my argument is Hannah Arendt's political theory of the concentrationary society as a systematic assault on what she came to recognize, as a result of her analysis, as 'the human condition'. This concept is central, so let me define it right away. The human condition is neither a human essence nor a human nature. For Arendt, the human condition is the *unnatural* creation of political association between plural yet singular beings in a space of spontaneous action by subjects capable of moral choice. She came to define this condition through her analysis of the camps as the core instrument of totalitarian domination and therefore the site of its ideological realization that systematically destroyed person by person, individual psyche by individual psyche, such a human condition. Arendt defined the camp's assault on the human condition in three stages. The loss of civic identity, becoming a number, following arbitrary arrest is the first assault that is compounded by the third level: prolonged physical torture by cold, overwork and starvation that reduces the person ultimately to an organism desperate just to stay alive, a living corpse. The intermediate stage is also a systematic torture by rendering any action and any gesture of moral purpose meaningless.[12]

This, I am suggesting, is the condition of the SK and one that, significantly but incompletely, *Son of Saul* placed in the cinema. I conclude with my reappraisal, therefore, of the allegorical gesture of a ritual of *mourning* that is attempted by a character in the film while also being, in effect, performed as cultural memory by this still-problematic film *qua* cinematic (figurative, narrative, audio-visually immersive) representation of the life of the SK of Auschwitz-Birkenau. In the light of these levels of analysis – theoretical, critical, cinematic and allegorical – I argue that for the spectator, the film's troubling ending becomes paradoxically more Lazarean than Antigonian. This, perhaps, accounts unconsciously for the adoring reception of a problematic but daring cinematic exploration of the jeopardy of the SK.

My Problem and the Not-So-Tired Question of Representation

It has been some days since I inserted into my computer the DVD of *Son of Saul* (2015) in order to rewatch the film as part of my preparation for writing this chapter, focusing on the juxtaposition in the film of inhuman and dehumanizing killing with its mass effacement of the existences of millions of people and the narrative of one man seeking one religiously sanctioned burial of one victim. I have been unable to do so. This might well stymy the promised writing were it not for the fact that this very difficulty, reticence or even phobic paralysis, is itself indicative of the power of this topic, the SK, to disturb, even through remote or virtual cinematic encounter. My problem, however, is not with the subject matter, challenging as it is. It is the film *qua* film itself that detains me as it negotiates, *cinematically*, that weight of its subject matter and the theoretical debates surrounding our attempts to know, to remember and to represent the event, variously named – itself a fascinating issue – Holocaust and Shoah.[13]

Engaging with the discussions generated by the film as a 'representation' of the dark core of Auschwitz II-Birkenau itself, we are first of all weighed down by both cinematic and theoretical memory. For the last twenty years, I have been teaching and writing in Holocaust studies under the rubric of tracking the complex, belated and varied process of transformation of trauma into cultural memory. I have witnessed significant shifts in the representation and debates about representation of the Shoah.

The paradox is this. The initially traumatic nature of an unassimilable but also not fully grasped event would become (but only in retrospect) the focus of a belated return to it, when it was represented as a major theoretical, political and cultural issue for humanity itself. Thus, by the 1990s, the Holocaust/Shoah was elevated from a specific historical event these names arrived to designate to become *the* case of exception with implications at every level of human thought. The long process follows the classic structure of trauma: repression, latency and belated arrival. At the same time, as an issue of representation, this newly defined and named event, the Holocaust/Shoah, fell under the sign of unrepresentability.

When the historian Saul Friedländer convened a conference under the title *Nazism and the Final Solution: Probing the Limits of Representation* in April 1990, only two papers named the Holocaust. Friedländer admitted he had not assembled any of the usual suspects in Holocaust studies. The speakers were to address 'an event which demands a global approach and a general reflection on the difficulties that are raised by its representation'. He then stated:

> The extermination of the Jews of Europe is as accessible to both representation and interpretation as any other historical event. But we are dealing with an event which tests our traditional conceptual and representational categories, an 'event at the limits'.[14]

The Holocaust is not at all unrepresentable *per se*. As an unprecedented event, however, it falls at the very limits of existing schemes of representation. Representation, of which history as a discourse might be considered the paradigm, interprets events with reference to precedents. Comparative measurement enables the historians to determine the contours of an occurrence, its difference or similarity. Without comparison, the event that exceeds the limits of existing representation poses entirely new questions of historical understanding, pushing into related areas that might offer terms and tools to grapple with the excessive novelty of an event outstripping all known, recorded and represented human experience. Friedländer argues that because this event exceeded all known events and we have none comparable to it, we have no terms, no narratives, no codes, no phrasing. Thus, he invokes the philosopher Jean-François Lyotard, who defined 'Auschwitz' as *le différend*, the as-yet unphrased, that which, in effect, can only remain uncharacterized since language, based on the formula of signifier/signified = sign, fails before this novelty:

> Signs are not referents to be validated under the cognitive regimen, they indicate that something that should be able to be put into phrases cannot be phrased in the accepted idioms . . . The silence that surrounds the phrase 'Auschwitz was the extermination camp' is not a state of mind, it is a sign that something remains to be phrased which is not, something which is not determined.[15]

Yet Lyotard argued that we must work towards knowledge while accepting the deficiency of language and, behind its symbolic codes, the incapacity of the imagination to handle the shock of encounter out of which new concepts are formed.

Cinema and the Question of Representation

Paralleling these intellectual endeavours in forging cultural memory is the major cultural apparatus of the twentieth century: cinema. Both a historical object in its own right, having its own history of technical formation and stylistic/iconographic/generic development, and a site of historical representation or rather the machine for creating the present's representation of the historical, cinema adds to the debate cinematic idioms: image, sequence, montage, narrative, speech, music, the gaze and the politics of viewing. These are the terms of a technological-aesthetic representation that produces cultural memory through the trio of audiovisual image, story (duration) and spectatorship. Spectatorship and cinema have their own history of debates. Here I want to add to the general theories a specification of a difference produced by the aesthetic politics of different cinemas that produced the 'spectator as interpellated consumer' (Hollywood fiction) and the 'spectator as alienated, agitated observer' (critical cinema). The latter generates a politics of aesthetics opposing pleasured engagement by incited resistance.[16]

Two further positions now enter the debate. One involves Theodor Adorno and the other Jean-Luc Godard. In his eight-part video *Histoire(s) du cinema* (1988–98), Godard condemned twentieth-century cinema for its failure as a cultural form to address 'the camps'.[17] Whatever he meant by the phrase 'the camps' remains sufficiently vague yet evocative to serve as an observation and an indictment without assisting us at all in knowing what would be cinema *qua* cinema's engagement with 'the camps'.[18] At the other end of this string is Adorno's usually misrepresented comments on the paradox of the impossibility and the compelling necessity for art to address the era in which we now live, termed 'after Auschwitz' (hence after one iconic death camp) while acknowledging that art cannot adequately encompass 'Auschwitz' and, even in trying to do so, might transgress into obscenity. I make this distinction between era and name because, as with *the Holocaust*, we are already in the field of *phrasing* and the *differend*. Names are being used to stand for and allude to, while unable to signify what in effect we accept defies the relation between signifier and signified, but also, in historical terms, confuses specific and different systems with the Third Reich's political and killing machinery.

'Auschwitz' is, as Michael Rothberg argues, a chronotope.[19] This means a place (in fact historically a complex of over forty-eight camps with different purposes and degrees of terror and horror) and a time period from 1940 to 1945. These dates already indicate historical uncertainty as to what dimension of what activity took place in the barracks outside Oświęcim after April 1940, then in the new camp at Birkenau begun in the summer of 1941, on the industrial site at Monowitz from April 1941, when its construction began, or in the other satellite slave labour camps. Uncertainty rules as to what elements of this complex site we are imagining and using to stand in for much more than a process. For Adorno, the name of this time-space distils the rupture of a novel event. Yet for Adorno, and many people I suspect, 'Auschwitz' – its realities never witnessed by any Western European armies or observers and only liberated by the Red Army, and then claimed as a site of national suffering under fascism by the Communist regime in Poland following the war – *phrases* the industrial extermination process directed at the Jewish and Roma communities of Poland and Western Europe. Yet we should remember that the mass killing grounds of 1.5 million people in the Jewish communities in Ukraine, Lithuania, Belarus and Latvia by the Einsatzgruppen murder squads after the German invasion of the Soviet Union in the summer of 1941 are not part of the cultural memory evoked by 'Auschwitz', the factory of death. It also effaces the names of Treblinka, Sobibór, Bełżec and Chełmno, the dedicated Operation Reinhard camps in which over two million Jewish and Roma people, mostly from Poland, were murdered between 1942 and 1943.[20] Finally, the word 'camps' evokes for Western Europeans images of corpses and skeletal survivors of *concentration* camps such as Dachau, Buchenwald and Bergen Belsen, which the Allied troops liberated, Allied journalists reported and film crews recorded. Death camps leave no corpses. The Operation Reinhard camps were destroyed and effaced in 1943 once the war in the Soviet Union turned against Germany. What is the visual signifier for an image if it is to convey whatever it is 'Auschwitz' stands for in Adorno's vocabulary?

Writing on representation 'after Auschwitz', Adorno was not a theorist of the visual image. His cultural case studies were literature (Kafka and Beckett) and music (Schoenberg). Adorno asserted that the only art practice that could address 'Auschwitz' *without immediately betraying it* had to be what he defined as 'autonomous art', that is, self-consciously and formally aesthetic modernist contravention of consumable cultural forms. Adorno called for art to risk addressing 'Auschwitz' because art alone might address the extremity of suffering. Yet only autonomous, avant-garde formal practice can – and only for a moment – touch the event and agitate the reader or auditor without release. Even the most radical art, Adorno knew, will inevitably fall prey sooner or later to capture by the culture industry, for the latter forms the conditions of cultural production and consumption in the capitalist system that has totally disfigured art. Adorno allowed Samuel Beckett's work alone to pass this test because, in effect, Beckett theatrically created an endurance test the audience is forced to witness, never being allowed to spectate or to discern a coherent meaning from what had been endured in the physical present of being there in the antitheatrical theatre.[21]

Unphrased, at the limits of representation because it is unprecedented, an event which nonetheless has names that explain little and distort much encounters the difficulty of representation, both because it knows not what is to be represented – except through already prefigured representation (testimony or archive documentation) – and because even the most affectively disturbing and politically agitating work of art succumbs *in the end* to the terms of its own compromised existence as cultural commodity in capitalist society. Impatience at the powerfully modernist terms of such debates has led to experimental breaches, notably in the cultural industries and above all in cinema. In the 1990s, no longer awed by Adorno's worries or Lanzmann's negative injunction against any use of images of the Shoah, fiction cinema took up Jean-Luc Godard's challenge to cinema for its failure, but not in Godard's use of montage or Adorno's stark, Beckettian terms. Directors seemed to be asking themselves more freely: could not cinema's most compelling abilities in storytelling bring this event into wider view?

Indeed, the model that was already there is Steven Spielberg's wager in 1993 to make Hollywood look again at the Holocaust in terms of his grand scale of filmmaking.[22] *Schindler's List* exemplified the ways in which the Hollywood culture industry deals with history through its favoured strategies: historical reconstruction on an epic scale focalizing the viewer's engagement with the big picture by means of an individual's story set against the panorama of the massed historical. There has to be a hero, with other subsidiary characters to whom viewers can relate or against whom they will revolt. Above all, the film must tell a story that provides a point of bearable exit for the spectator, whatever has been experienced during the course of the narrative. To remain thus intact on leaving the cinema, the viewer may be moved by suffering, but he or she must also be protected from attachment to those who, for the sake of the narrative, must necessarily be sacrificed: collateral damage as it were. We, viewer-consumers, cannot, and do not, grieve for everyone, even in fictional space and time. Hollywood narratives engineer precise hierarchies of narrative agency and affective significance, which are shaped by and reshape the hierarchies in the social world they address and, in effect, constantly iterate. The Christological and the Lazarean figure strongly in Spielberg's Schindler and 'his' survivor families located in the State of Israel in the present.

Thus, by the beginning of the twenty-first century, the questions we faced as scholars of cultural memory of the Holocaust/Shoah had expanded to include the increasing number of fictional and narrative cinematic representations. Far from being neglected or rare, and 'silenced' by majestic monuments such as Lanzmann's *Shoah*, cinema now regularly takes us to the camps, the ghettoes, the rescuers, the partisans and the perpetrators, the harrowed or sympathetic bystanders and the warm-hearted rescuers. So far, it has, however, largely avoided, or not learnt from, Adorno's sense of 'Auschwitz'.

Let me be clear. Fiction does not imply falsification. Indeed, in Aristotelian terms, the poetic is what provides a form of intelligibility for the formless contingency of the mere succession of historical events. French philosopher Jacques Rancière glosses Aristotle when he argues 'to pretend is not to put forth illusions but to elaborate intelligible structures'. He suggests that poetry offers 'arrangements between actions' that the process of history leaves in 'empirical disorder'.[23] In considering the issue of poetics and intelligibility, Rancière identified three regimes of art. The one that matters here is named the aesthetic, which frames the Romantic and modern periods. In the aesthetic regime, the self-consciousness of both the classical (Plato) and Classical (seventeenth-century) poetic *ordering* is effaced to be replaced by forms of art that, in effect, replicate the terms in which we might describe the 'phenomena of the social and historical world'. This produces two poles: 'the potential meaning inherent in everything silent' (there is no hierarchy of what we can make art about) and 'the proliferation of modes of speech and levels of meaning' (again there is no hierarchy, as we find in the Classical representative regime, of the proper or the improper).[24] Everything becomes a possible meaning in forms that blur representation (self-consciously other) and fictional replication.

In literature and cinema, this produces not a structural, critical realism, but rather a confusion between the fictional form and that which it represents. In that light, I argue that the film *Son of Saul*, for instance, creates a reality effect that is not productive of structural knowledge of past or present, however much it immerses us in, and impresses upon us an intense virtual experience of and in its fictive time and space. If cinema has a history as well as being an instrument for purveying representations of historical events, and if its own history has moved out of avoidance into still stuttering or relatively rare engagements with the material of the Holocaust/Shoah, and if the forms of cinema engagement remain largely fictional but also still based on the primary principles of narrative, illusion-sustaining editing and so forth, what are the stakes of critical engagement with such a film as *Son of Saul*?

Reviewing *Son of Saul*

The critical reception in 2015–16 of *Son of Saul* was, with few exceptions, positive, if not adulatory, often accompanied by images of a smiling or bemused director clutching his Oscar for Best Foreign Language Film, a sign that the English-language American film community acclaimed it. I carried out a narrative analysis of the newspaper reviews. This revealed the pattern of language across the wealth of writing on the film. *Immersive* is the most widely used adjective to describe the effect of the film, a quality confirmed by statements from the director, who indeed aimed to 'immerse' the audience in the world his film was to evoke. In interviews, Nemes used the concept of immersion as a means both of produce knowledge of 'what the Holocaust was like' and to pierce the generalizing mythic quality of this named event:

> From my point of view, the film immerses the viewer and communicates in a very *visceral way* the *experience* of the individual in the concentration camp and it gives an *intuitive sense* of what limitations the individual had to face in the extermination process and what the Holocaust was like. That is important because the Holocaust became, in our common knowledge, a sort of *abstract thing* devoid of all meaning; it just became like the Titanic, a *sort of myth*.
>
> But understanding the individual and *how really to feel something* in the position of the individual is something that we never understood, *never felt* and that's why I made this film. I didn't want to make an intellectual film; I didn't want to make a film based on the distance and the sense of escape

that all films of fiction established with all their strategies aimed at reassuring the audience.²⁵

Nemes explains his demythicizing strategy: a focus on an individual in the specific condition of working around the gas chambers and crematoria. Yet does this idea of cinema taking us to this place and time conflict with the subject matter? In *The Times*, Kevin Maher wrote:

> 'Immersive' is not the word you want to use to describe a Holocaust drama. It seems too flippant and is too often applied to the whizzbangery of Hollywood 3D blockbusters that sell you fantastical dreams of utopian otherworlds. Yet it is the most fitting description of László Nemes' harrowing and hugely upsetting Oscar winner, *Son of Saul*, a film *that plunges you, shoulder height, into the horrors of Auschwitz-Birkenau* during the final days of the war.²⁶

Nemes suggests that immersion and individuation in cinematic recreation serve to bridge the gap between past and present to remind us that our present is contaminated by this inadequately remembered event, not as a political danger, but as a threat within human nature:

> I wanted to, on the contrary, to say something about the core of the nature of this human hell that is not that remote from us in time and in civilization or perspective, it is not that remote. We are living in a world of dreams and we might wake up in the nightmare if we don't fathom or try to understand the *potential evil lying within human nature*.²⁷

The immersive effect and its larger ambitions were achieved, and this is the second key trope in reviews: *technically*. The key was the tight framing of the central character, Saul Ausländer, which, in Mark Kermode's words: 'pushes the horrors that surround Saul to and beyond the edges of the film's 4x3 frame, the narrowness of the image somehow broadening the scope of its impact'. He also notes the relation of face to background: 'In several sequences set within the gas chambers and furnaces of Saul's netherworld existence, only Röhrig's face is in focus, the Boschian landscape of suffering and death in which he dwells remaining expressionistic rather than explicit', concluding:

> Focusing its tightly held, shallow-focus gaze on a single prisoner in whose face we see reflections of atrocities too hellish to depict, *Son of Saul* is indeed a *stylistic masterpiece*, a film of precise visual and aural design, executed with fearsome skill, precision and commitment. Yet far from being a 'technical' triumph, the claustrophobic aesthetic that Nemes employs has a powerful moral *raison d'etre*, seemingly born out of a desire to address a subject that arguably has no place in dramatic cinema.²⁸

In the *Financial Times*, Danny Leigh devoted a long review to the film underlying this third trope, the use of the main character's face:

> Then we see his face. From here, that is our default: the gaunt, stunned features of actor Géza Röhrig (more commonly a poet, here transcendent). Tightly framed, they are often the only thing in focus. Most of the film's horrors take place out-of-shot, or in the background, heard more than seen.[29]

Colin McCabe offered this summation of the 'triumph' of the film as a work of cinema:

> There is to my mind almost no doubt that Nemes is a great director. It is a long time, if ever, since I have seen a first-time film crackling with such cinematic intelligence. Nor have I any doubts about recommending that anyone who wants to see a great example of the seventh art get to a good cinema to see *Son of Saul* as soon as it is released.[30]

The only major dissenting voice was *New York Times* critic Manohla Dargis, who wrote on 20 May 2016:

> Directed by Laszlo Nemes, making his feature directing debut, this *radically dehistoricized, intellectually repellent* movie tracks the title *Sonderkommando*, one of the Jewish prisoners whom the Nazis forced to help run their death machines . . . Mr. Nemes' *technical virtuosity* is evident in every meticulously lighted, composed and shot step of the way, which means that your attention is continually *being guided as much to his cinematic abilities as to the misery on screen.*[31]

In these largely positive responses amongst newspaper reviewers as much as in this final devastating, but just, critique, the central question of the relationship between aesthetic process, the technicality of representation and the ethics or politics of the resulting representation as a work of cinematic art is being rehearsed. Yet from all the multitude of critics' writing I reviewed symptomatically, I conclude that the awesome aesthetics of the film dominated the impressions the critics took away from the film. Many refer not only to the cinematic language, but also to its many sources in the history of cinema avowed by Nemes himself: Robert Bresson, Jean-Pierre and Luc Dardenne, and, above all, the great Hungarian film director Béla Tarr, to whom Nemes was 'apprenticed'. Furthermore, because of the topic of the film *Shoah* by Claude Lanzmann is the monumental work of cinema clearly the haunting the film. It is the other with which the film is in dialogue, borrowing the trope of focusing on the face, aspiring to its grandeur and differing from it by committing the major transgression denounced by Lanzmann: depiction and fictionalization. One critic notes the paradox of this relationship:

> *Son of Saul* is most valuable for its attention to the themes and ideas in Lanzmann's work. Nemes admirably re-instigates discussion of the awe-inspiring, complex, and yet unassimilated experience of Lanzmann's films – and does so perhaps even more discerningly than much written criticism does. Yet without *Shoah*, *Son of Saul* would be meaningless; in the light of *Shoah*, *Son of Saul* though useful and provocative – is, nonetheless, nearly superfluous.[32]

Surprising many, Claude Lanzmann endorsed Nemes' film, as indeed has the other figure haunting the film's intellectual and politico-aesthetic imagination, Georges Didi-Huberman. The latter devoted a small book, written in the form of a personal letter addressed to the director to the film, *Sortir du noir*, which might translate as 'Emerging from the Darkness', to *Son of Saul*.[33] Confirming Lanzmann's influence, Nemes points us to what, in fact, Jacques Rancière had argued formed the core of what *Shoah*, purportedly a film refusing representation, actually represented – absence:[34]

> We became friends through the film. And I know he is very hard with fiction films ... We watched *Shoah* (1985) a lot before making this film. It inspired us. I think *Shoah* has a tremendous outer frame off stage. It's the vanished world of the Jews of Europe. The idea of an off-screen that is always there that fuelled our approach.[35]

'What is unrepresentable?', asks Rancière. Lanzmann, he argues, merely denies that equivalence can be created by the fictional embodiment of executioners and victims:

> For what is represented is not executioners and victims, but the process of a double elimination: the elimination of the Jews and the elimination of the traces of their elimination. Only it is not representable in the form of fiction or testimony, which by bringing the past 'back to life' renounces representing the second elimination.[36]

There can be no resurrection in cinema, no Lazarus.

I am arguing here that Nemes' evocation of 'the lost world of the Jews of Europe', clearly acknowledging the doubled elimination, tips these discussions of his film's project into the frame of mourning and commemoration. Thus, in the light of *Son of Saul*, one might retrospectively argue that the film *Shoah* was itself the performance of a cinematic *Kaddish* for the erasure of a whole civilization *embodied* in the now invisible people who were mercilessly destroyed, with their destroyers seeking to leave no trace of their physical existences, and notably the point at which they passed out of life.[37] Nemes shares this sense of a disappeared civilization of which he is an orphaned remnant:

> I'm not a religious person but I have a very deep connection to Judaism and I see how much destruction the European Jews have suffered. And I made this film to talk about this lost civilization and this lost world, and also because I'm angry that this happened, and Europe never really understood that.[38]

My review of reviews reveals that neither was mourning coupled with anger recognized in the critical responses, nor was the specific weight of the history of what happened to the Hungarian Jewry in 1944. Historically, the massacre of the substantial Jewish communities of Hungary (one million in 1939) was one of the most horrific elements of the genocidal crimes committed by the Third Reich. Despite the fact that it was increasingly clear that Germany was losing the war, in March 1944, the German army occupied Hungary in order to destroy its Jewish population. Eichmann was despatched to Hungary to force the already virulently antisemitic and fascist regime in Hungary to go beyond persecution and deliver up its Jewish population. Antisemitic laws had come into force in the late 1930s. Deportations to Ukraine and to labour camps had already begun in 1941. In a move that was unprecedented, however, even in the history of the Nazi assault on the Jewish world, in the spring of 1944, most of the 861,000 Jewish Hungarians were forced in to ghettos, and between 29 April and 9 July over 437,000 people were transported to Auschwitz-Birkenau. Figures vary as to how many were murdered on arrival: only between 28,000 and 100,000 may have been selected for slave labour. The destruction of Hungarian Jewry is therefore the most telling instance of the dedication of the Third Reich to the mass extinction of the European Jewry at whatever cost irrespective of the 'war'.

Significantly, the raising of the fate of the Jewish world of Hungary by László Nemes geopolitically and culturally extends the cinematic memorial to the Polish Jewry created by Claude Lanzmann in *Shoah*. It also speaks to the writings of Hungarian Jewish novelist and survivor Imre Kertész (1929–2016), whose novel *Fatelessness* (*Sorstalanság*, 1975), published in English as *Fateless* in 1995, was made into a highly regarded film *Fateless* by Lajos Koltai in 2005. This film follows the autobiographical story of a Hungarian Jewish teenager, rounded and deported first to Auschwitz and then to Buchenwald, where he almost dies from infected wounds, overwork and malnutrition. It also evokes the other major text of the Hungarian Jewish Holocaust, *Night*, written by Elie Wiesel in 1954 and published in French in 1958, since in both books, the authors convey the powerful and permanent estrangement experienced by the survivors from the world to which they are returned.[39] Kertész demanded, however, that works about the events of the Holocaust cannot be distanced from the continuing political realities of fascism in the present:

> I regard as kitsch any representation of the Holocaust that is incapable of understanding or unwilling to understand the organic connection between our own deformed mode of life (whether in the private sphere or on the level of 'civilization' as such) and the very possibility of the Holocaust. Here I have in mind those representations that seek to establish the Holocaust once and for all as something foreign to human nature; that seek to drive the Holocaust out of the realm of human experience. I would also use the term kitsch to describe those works where Auschwitz is regarded as simply a matter concerning Germans and Jews, and thereby reduced to something like the fatal incompatibility of two groups; when the political and psychological anatomy of modern totalitarianism more generally is disregarded; when Auschwitz is not seen as a universal experience, but reduced to whatever immediately 'hits the eye'.[40]

Neither of these two key and necessary reference points – Kertész and Wiesel – are mentioned by reviewers to situate Nemes' work in an enlarged Hungarian-Jewish context, nor is Koltai's cinematography and use of silence.

It is clear, however, that *Son of Saul* emerged not only from a Hungarian cinematic idiom identified with Béla Tarr, but above all from close engagement with a Parisian intellectual community that has acquired a specific centrality to discussions of representation and the Shoah/Holocaust. This circle does not indicate a community of colleagues, but of contesting intellectual positions.[41] This triangulation – Tarr, Lanzmann and Didi-Huberman – not only situates the film aesthetically and critically, it also encloses the film in a local debate, associated with particular individuals within a small world of both art and scholarship that has a number of centres focalized by key authors and film directors. This fact demands our attention because the intellectual politics of international academic or, shall we say, intellectual culture is itself a player, a factor, shaping the reception of this film in narrowed ways that trouble me profoundly.

We all know, from our own watching of *Shoah* and as underlined by scholars such as Shoshana Felman and Margaret Olin, that *faces* and *places* form the basic grammar of Claude Lanzmann's cinematic language.[42] Lanzmann often opens his films with a scene, an establishing shot in which the camera begins in wide shot and pans to the right, mostly to reveal the extended space of the place that is being used as an anchor, in the present, for the section about to begin. This space-become-place is, therefore, also located in the time of filming. The counterpoint to this element of Lanzmannian cinematic grammar is the tight shot held, often relentlessly, on the faces of the witnesses, on the faces of men (in general since there are so few women in the film) whose eyes have seen what their coaxed-out words often seek not to say. They carry that past behind their eyes so he has to film face to face. The rhythm of the close attention to the single speaker in the now and the broad encompassing of the space where the event had taken place is then punctuated by speech. Words pass between interviewer and interviewee, mediated at times by the translator and for many mediated further by subtitles that confer meaning on heard but not understood speech.

The Last of the Unjust (2013) is a film by Lanzmann set in Rome, where a highly educated and voluble scholar and former Jewish community leader provides extraordinarily precise accounts of day-to-day negotiation and actions relevant for this discussion of *Son of Saul* and the equivocal status of those Jewish people trapped in a role in the machinery of elimination. It serves as a contrast with *Son of Saul* insofar as both films share the project of investigating those Jewish men (and women) forced into this dreadful proximity to the SS executioners, for which fate they have been named collaborators or termed complicit. Lanzmann edited the many hours of interviews undertaken in 1975 in Rome with Rabbi Benjamin Murmelstein (1905–89), the last leader of the Jewish community in Terezin. These were placed into sequences of newly filmed locations that placed Lanzmann himself at the sites, reading to the camera passages he had composed or passages from other testimony. The mesmerizing effect of the director's French words spoken 'in place' of a past no longer visible or even imaginable in these sites produces a singular affect. The linearity of spoken language marks the time that we, the viewer, are invited to spend looking at cinematically created images that show nothing of the now-traceless historical event the words are describing. The mismatch specifically destroys the coincidence that Jacques Rancière defined as characterizing 'the aesthetic regime' where literary description swims as close as can be to factual description, while investing the banality of the normal with implied meaning.[43] The autonomy of spoken words from visual images keeps both apart enough to posit a viewer as the receiver of the impossibility of conferring sense on what is being heard, even while taking in information that has to be processed as making grammatical sense by the listening viewer. We ask ourselves: could this have been real? What will I do now knowing this?

Over three hours of edited film, Murmelstein describes in detail what he did when he and those like him were forced to work with Eichmann and the Nazis, if only to mitigate slightly the policies that were relentlessly and violently carried out. He defines his position as being a marionette, but a puppet who also pulled his own strings in the endless struggle to mediate the threat to his Jewish compatriots. He is seeking to explain the conditions in which he worked in Vienna after the Anschluss and in Terezín as one of the leaders of the Jewish community. In effect, this figure, denounced as a collaborator and disowned by the Jewish world, reveals above all the consistent and demonic cruelty, the deceit and the always-deadly intent of Eichmann and the system he created.[44] No banal or thoughtless bureaucratic efficiency is exposed. Instead, Eichmann is shown to have been a knowing, dedicated agent of the intended destruction of Jewish Europeans, against whom someone like Murmelstein acts in ever more limited measure to mitigate a little the demonic forces that have control over Jewish life and death.[45]

Son of Saul lies at the opposite pole to Lanzmann's incitement of all whom he interviews to speak, even when they cannot bear to form the words for what they have endured or seen. In *Son of Saul*, the grammar, deeply Tarr-ian in my sense of that director's searing cinema, is speechlessness. Nemes' film, like Tarr's cinema, creates a *mise-en-scène* for actions carried out by those whose abjected life has put them beyond speech even as speech, let alone writing, was specifically denied as part of the torture.[46] Words are exchanged, barked, heard, uttered on a soundtrack of cacophonous chaos, but the central character Saul does not inhabit speech.

This feature is in marked contrast to the volubility of Filip Müller (1922–2013), the Slovak Jewish survivor of the SK at Auschwitz-Birkenau, in his own memoir and as he was filmed in Lanzmann's *Shoah* (1985).[47] His extraordinary fluency and urgency in speaking was apparently slowed down in the editing, interrupted and paced by Lanzmann. Punctuated by the traumatic repeat of the word *plötzlich*, suddenly, there is only one section where words fail the ever-eloquent Müller. It is not silence but tears that halt his flow as a particular memory pierces the carapace of his rehearsed storytelling, so evidently a necessary, even a compulsive shield against the affects that break through on this one occasion as he tells of recognizing Slovak Jewish men and women from his own town being pushed into the gas chamber. He wants to join them and die alongside them. They reject his suicidal gesture. Live and tell our story, they say.

This story echoes the scene with Abraham Bomba also filmed by Lanzmann, which shows a man broken in the course of forced speech, and reveals how a moment of recognition deprives the hardened slave workers of their defences. Abraham Bomba was forced to cut the hair of the women before they were horribly and agonizingly gassed to death in Treblinka. Only in recounting a specific story of the encounter between a husband and wife in the gas chamber does Bomba stumble and refuse to speak anymore as he also breaks into tears, against which he bravely struggles on camera for long minutes. While the first viewing of these scenes has often raised ethical questions for student viewers, it is possible to read Lanzmann's insistence that Bomba tell this story or Muller shed his defence, as a necessity to move beyond the 'use' of the SK men as witnesses for historical documentation and to make us feel the human agony from which they seek perpetually to shield themselves.

This trope of recognition of a family member is taken up as the key narrative device for László Nemes to set the narrative of the film in motion, even if it is a mistaken identification of his son that enlivens the automaton-like SK worker, Saul Ausländer, into his dedicated purpose, to bury one body with some ritual that acknowledges a *Jewish* death. The main character thus becomes fixated on the corpse of a boy who survived the gassing only to be put immediately to death by an SS officer. This body is about to be autopsied to study why he did not succumb. To protect the child from being cut open and mutilated, a horror in Jewish tradition where one must return to the earth as whole as one entered life, Saul Ausländer conceives a compulsion to give him a Jewish burial. This is not a religious gesture, but an act of residual fidelity that performatively reclaims a Jewish identity of traditional dignity in contrast to the daily animalistic and eschatological insults from the SS.

This plot device is distilled from reading the *Scrolls of Auschwitz* as well as from watching other films. In finding a narrative form for elements culled from witness sources, however, *Son of Saul* is precipitated from the testimonial into the mythic and the allegorical. The SK worker is named *Saul Ausländer*. The surname translates as *Stranger*, the German word originating in middle German for a newcomer to a district or a farmer who cultivates land outside the district. Of course, in literary terms, the figure of the stranger originates in the historical narratives and ethical codes of the Jewish Bible as much as classical legend, for instance, the wandering Odysseus calling himself *No-name*. The biblical 'You were a stranger in a strange land' determines the mythic base of what becomes Jewish memory and it frames the Judaic ethical code. In modern times, from sociologists Georg Simmel to Zygmunt Bauman, the stranger has been theorized as a sociological character distinct from the outsider or the foreigner.[48] The stranger is not a visitor but a resident alien, an other who remains close but different. The stranger has thus become the allegorical figure for representing and understanding the place of 'the Jew' in modernity, a member of a permanent and longstanding community within European civilization, yet as 'the Jew', perceived by Christianist thought as a threatening presence for refusing to accept their Messiah and, under Nazism's fictional racist schema, ultimately delivered to a policy of extermination as the archetypal racialized contestant for universality. The openly Biblical name *Saul* derives from the Hebrew root שאל (*sha'al*), meaning to ask, inquire, borrow or beg. In its variations, it can mean a petition or a desire, while it is also linked to the sombre term שאול (*she-ol*), meaning grave or pit, and, in later Jewish mysticism, it is the equivalent of hell. These layers of meaning perfectly encode the figure of Saul in the film and the function of his desire in a place of hellish pits made all too real.

Holding on to the mythic dimension embedded in the name and narrative, which I am setting up in opposition to the immersion in the cinematic effect so enthralling to the critics, and anticipating a deeper exploration of the allegorical and mythic dimensions of the film, we need first to go deeper into the director's ambition, partially recognized in the responses of the critics, to deliver a historically based exploration of the human condition of a specific subject, the member of the SK in Auschwitz-Birkenau. For this I turn to the political analysis offered by Hannah Arendt.

The Political Analysis of the Concentrationary

Determining, in 1945, that the novel forms of evil enacted by Nazism and Stalinism would demand henceforth the ceaseless critical attention of all, Hannah Arendt composed her major study, *The Origins of Totalitarianism* (1951), through a close reading of all available documents, but notably the astute interpretations of 'the concentrationary universe' by its politically aware survivors largely of the concentration camps in Germany.[49] The study of what Arendt herself termed 'the concentrationary society' requires us to distinguish the vast network of concentration camps, largely in Germany and its occupied territories (over 10,000) from the dedicated death camps, of which there were four on Polish soil created as Operation Reinhard: Sobibór, Bełżec, and Treblinka (1942–43), and at Chełmno (1941–42 and in 1944). Only sixty-seven prisoners survived Treblinka, which was destroyed following an uprising of the SK in August 1943. Fifty-eight men and women survived the SK revolt of 300 prisoners in Sobibór on 14 October 1943. Of the fifty SK Jewish prisoners who escaped Bełżec, seven survived. Seven men are known to have survived the execution of the remaining SK at Chełmno on 18 January 1945, a day after the Russians took the neighbouring town. Unlike the Auschwitz complex, composed of three major and forty-eight minor camps, with Auschwitz II-Birkenau being the centre of mass killing for two years

(1942–44), these major sites of killing of the Jewish population of Poland, and to a lesser extent Western Europe, have not become widely known or commemorated. None has given their name to the memory of the entire horror for which the Germanized name of the complex near Oświęcim, *Auschwitz*, now serves because it was a major killing centre and was liberated by the Red Army.

One of the earliest articles written on Treblinka in November 1944 was by the Russian journalist and writer Vasily Grossman (1905–64) when he arrived at the site in September with the victorious Red Army. He collected testimonies from surviving Treblinka SK who escaped in the uprising. Treblinka operated as a death factory between 23 July 1942 and 19 October 1943. During these seventeen months of operation, between 700,000 and 900,000 Jewish Europeans and 2,000 Romani people were killed by carbon monoxide gas. It is the second-largest site of industrial mass murder after Auschwitz-Birkenau. Grossman writes of walking through the space of the camp whose effaced remains have been overplanted with lupins. He finds women's hair on the ground:

> Evidently these are the contents of a sack, just a single sack that somehow got left behind. Yes, it is all true. The last hope, the last wild hope that it was all just a terrible dream, has gone. And the lupine pods keep popping open, and the tiny peas keep pattering down – and this really does all sound like a funeral knell rung by countless little bells from under the earth. And it feels as if your heart must come to a stop now, gripped by more sorrow, more grief, more anguish than any human being can endure...[50]

Thus concludes the first published and still-devastating account – too gruesome to repeat but worth everyone reading – of unspeakable, hideous cruelty by the SS as they harried, beat, whipped, mutilated and violated the terrified people being driven to immediate death. As a little-known text, it records a different SK group, but what it reports could never be put on screen, fashioned into a story that might be told to commemorate the victims or to discern any kind of consolation, except that of the SK's concerted action, collective strategy and unbelievable courage in a doomed but ultimately effective revolt against the monstrous perpetrators.[51]

Arendt's analysis of the larger scheme of what was defined by political survivors as 'the concentrationary universe' helps us to grasp the issues of any representation of the *exterminatory* process that was effected within, and as the extreme element of, what Arendt and other political theorists argued was the object of the totalitarian experiment: the destruction, or the rendering superfluous of the human *qua* human person. Arendt states:

> Total domination, which strives to organize the infinite plurality and differentiation of human beings as if all humanity were just one individual, is possible only if each and every person can be reduced to a never changing identity of reactions, so that each of these bundles of reactions can be exchanged at random for any other.[52]

Arendt's postwar determination that plurality was a key element of 'the human condition', the title of the book, necessarily continued her thinking about the nature of the crime and the significance of the event in *The Origins of Totalitarianism*.[53] Plurality is not diversity, but the product of a human characteristic assaulted by the camp – spontaneity:

> The camps are not only meant to exterminate people and degrade human beings, but also serve the ghastly experiment of eliminating, under scientifically controlled conditions, spontaneity itself as an expression of human behaviour and of transforming the human personality into a mere thing, into something that even animals are not.[54]

Spontaneity is the capacity for action, for initiating the unforeseen that stands in radical contrast to regimentation and the systematic destruction of the conditions for human, and hence political, action, by total social isolation 'where terror enforces oblivion'.[55] This next step in preparing 'living corpses' is 'the murder of the moral person in the man' by making moral choices of any kind meaningless in a situation in which whatever action taken, such as suicide or escape, would lead to dreadful retributive harm to others.

The concentration camps are thus the extreme laboratory for the production of total domination that functions only insofar as the human condition of those incarcerated is compromised and effectively negated while some are kept just alive within it. The instrument of the most extreme form of this domination is the extermination camp. The SS cadres operating the system are trained precisely by what they do there to others who have to be so degradingly and atrociously treated – dehumanized – so that, in this dehumanization of the victims – both the prisoners being killed and the prisoners forced to operate the killing – the politically necessary creation of monstrosity in the perpetrators is consistently effected.

The logic of atrocity functioning as education of the SS constantly infested some prisoners with the horror of the SS's criminality by being degraded in work so that their degradation in servicing the machine seemingly justified the action of the SS to clear the earth of such depraved beings. Arendt is stressing the necessity of the political level of analysis of this circular, self-reinforcing process in order to penetrate its darkness by going beyond the residual sentiment that attaches to our feelings about the specific ethnic groups, Jewish and Romani, who were the victims targeted for immediate extinction or about the social, political and sexual groups targeted for concentrationary existence. Of course, mourning such deaths is a permanent imperative. Without a political analysis of its place in the totalitarian system, we have no defence against the recurrence of this now-ever present antipolitical possibility.

The SK form a unique element of this hideous performance of the racialized totalitarian experiment insofar as the majority who were ethnically selected, not merely for slave labour as opposed to immediate gassing on arrival, but to be the physical adjuncts to the SS's most secret and most fundamental, symbolic-practical project – the dedicated extinction of 11 million citizens of Europe – were those racially designated as the deepest threat to the SS's own order. That *Jewish* workers were forced to service the killing process should not lead us to debates about *Jewish* complicity and collaboration. The process itself was part of the theatrical elaboration of a mythic concept that had to produce a never-before-imagined radical division and hierarchy within humankind: SS versus Jews. In Nazism, the stake of their action exceeded existing discourses on racism and preceding, if also egregious, affronts to humanity.

Plurality, spontaneity and individuality – for Arendt, the indicators of the human condition as a speaking, acting, moral and political subject – were the symbolic and real enemies of that SS universe. For those selected to work in conditions without the extremity of regular concentrationary torture, cold, foodlessness, and ceaseless and often useless labour – I am thinking of the SK members – there was still a shared horror they feared and witnessed daily:

> The concentration camps, by making death itself anonymous (making it impossible to find out whether a prisoner is dead or alive), robbed death of its meaning as the end *of a fulfilled life*. In a sense they took away the individual's own death, proving that henceforth nothing belonged to him and he belonged to no one. *His death merely set a seal on the fact that he had never existed.* (Emphasis added)[56]

Arendt borrows a biblical figure for this state of living in a tomb-world:

> We attempt to understand the behaviour of the concentration camps inmates and SS-men psychologically, when the very thing that must be realized is that the psyche *can* be destroyed even without the destruction of the physical man; that, indeed, psyche, character, and individuality seem under certain circumstances to express themselves only through the rapidity or slowness with which they disintegrate. The end result in any case is inanimate men, i.e., men who can longer be psychologically understood,

whose return to the psychologically or otherwise intelligibly human world closely resembles the resurrection of Lazarus.[57]

The Catholic writer Jean Cayrol, surrealist poet and inmate of Mauthausen, also invoked the Lazarean as the state for those who survived to be 'liberated' and returned to a world who could never know what they had seen, been and were forever.[58] This political analysis of the camp system and Arendt's final turn to a biblical image opens on to my final section on another figure of the unburied from classical myth that haunts this film.

Burial, Myth and *Son of Saul*

Son of Saul also evokes the classical figure Antigone, the tragic daughter of an incestuous marriage who, after her father/brother's death (Oedipus), defied the law of Thebes to bury, at risk of capital punishment, her criminally treasonous brother, Polyneices, who had been condemned by her uncle, the ruler of Thebes, to an inhuman fate – to lie unburied as carrion for the birds of prey – as his punishment for his civil war against his own brother. Antigone risked her own life to fulfil an ethical law she espoused because of her sibling relation to the dead, which overrode her obedience to the state and political law. Through the trope of dedication to a doomed act of burial defying the law of the SS regime, *Son of Saul* inhabits Antigone's territory, but only in the vaguest way that offers to a film about an historical horror the potential to understand its story as myth in the terms of Greek tragedy. The tragic is, as we know, focused on the compromised hero acting and failing as a moral subject in a world predetermined and without escape. Is Saul raised to the level of a tragic hero?

The mythically named character *Saul* (distinctively Jewish) *the Foreigner* (*Ausländer*) feels compelled, at the risk of derailing an uprising of the Birkenau SK, to seek burial for a boy who has survived the gas chamber only to be immediately suffocated by the SS officer. Stealing and concealing the body while seeking a rabbi to say the words of the *Kaddish* at his burial, constitutes, however, a very different proposition from the Greek myth of Antigone. True, Saul breaks the SS law of Auschwitz-Birkenau by acting on his own and performing a spontaneous and moral act of seeking individual burial in stark contrast to the hideous act of mass cremation and dispersal of mingled ashes in the river, effacing every trace of human existence. Yet can we really draw on Hegel's timeless opposition between natural and political law in the case of the most lawless, modern apolitical experiment in total domination, which not only represents the Third

Reich as a fascist society, but also as a world apart ruled absolutely by that Reich's special creation, its death's head forces, the SS?

The ancient Greek imaginary, distilled into its classical dramaturgy of Sophocles' recasting in his play of 441 BCE of the ancient legend of the House of Thebes serves me, however, to distinguish that tradition of tragedy from the Jewish religious legend transformed into Rabbinic theological interpretations and liturgical formulations of obligations to the dead as figurations of concepts of time, not law. [59]

In this universe, in which all law has been suspended by the claim for absolute and arbitrary SS power over life and death, what is the meaning of the gesture of seeking burial as opposed to revolt and dying by an act of collective and hence political resistance that might save others? What is the significance of not merely seeking just burial as opposed to disposal by burning, grinding and dispersing of ash, but wanting to perform a formal, liturgical funeral involving a designated but not sacral voice to intone an ancient set of words, the *Kaddish*, in Aramaic, that represent a punctuation point of human life by defiantly magnifying the deity? At the end of parts of traditional Jewish services, but also to make and remember the end of a life, *Kaddish* is recited first to mark a mortal time and place and second to displace it with the eternal temporality of the divine. The recitation thus endows the mortal human with the meaning of a lived life that has followed the cycle of birth and death in relation to nonhuman or divine time imagined as the basis of many religions by people seeking to evade the fact of organic mortality by hoping for an afterlife. Philosophically and anthropologically, the invention of death, its humanization as mortality, ritually marked by care of the body and processes of burial or cremation or being delivered to the sea, indexes a historic emergence of human self-consciousness as a kind of being different from related animal peers (although we know now that certain animals also 'bury' their dead kin). The invention of death by the treatment of the dead person through burial or other rituals reflects back to define human life as human.

My reading of the SK thus derives from a specifically informed analysis of the ways in which the torture inflicted on the SK was calculated to maximize the offence against the meaning of burial and its associated rituals *in Jewish culture*, for which saying *Kaddish* is the incantatory core. Denying burial was thus an assault on a Jewish imaginary and the subjectivity it sustains. Irrespective of issues of religion and belief, those born into Jewish cultures and communities, whether religious or secular, enter the world through a different imaginary from the hegemonic Christian imaginary that triangulates death, burial and resurrection. I am proposing a specific understanding of the cultural violence that was inflicted on the

Jewish prisoners selected and forced on pain of horrible death to work in a SK, whose job was to 'assist' in the process of bringing Jewish people to the gas chambers, removing and burning their bodies.

The SK did not kill. Only the SS killed. The SK were made instruments of making death not only inhuman in the most general sense. This killing machine inflicted both a non-Jewish death and an un-Jewish no-death because it became nonhuman within the framework of the Jewish imaginary, whether the individual was religious or not. The SK both witnessed this intended inhumanity and were daily psychologically destroyed by the impossible choice they were given by being its instrument. To make this case more forcefully, I draw support from the profoundly insightful reading by Nicholas Chare and Dominic Williams of the Scrolls of Auschwitz as acts of aesthetic resistance.[60] Chare and Williams not only recognize the literary consciousness evident in the most agonizing texts by SK members Leyb Langfus, Zalman Gradowski and Zalman Lewental, they also recast the meaning of what is shown in three of the four photographs taken by an SK member by linking its imagery with what the Scrolls' authors also identify as core horrors for them: the forced nakedness of Jewish women and the burning of the corpses. Countering the use of these images as evidence of the gas chambers, Chare and Williams argue that the 'nucleus of the horrible' lay here:

> The burning of the bodies was, of course, the last indignity inflicted on the victims. Nonetheless, as the scrap of address book tests, Langfus appears to exhibit particular concern over this passage. On the draft composition, it is the *Sonderkommando* who must destroy the evidence, enabling the murderer to 'wash his bloody hands' by removing all traces of the crime. This clean-up operation *causes the Sonderkommando to become tainted by the crime* . . . It was they who formed, who worked, and who lived within this odious environment. This, for them, was the heart of Hell.[61]

Thus, an additional level of culturally specific sensibility is layered into these photographs by bringing back into view Jewish codes of bodily purity and modesty and around sensitivities to gendered dimensions of this hell and the erosion of gendered norms as an additional violence forced on the witnessing bearers of the secrets of this place – the SK. The aesthetic resistance enacted in and through the writing of the Scrolls and the photographic 'scrolls' exceeds testimony. They also indict when read with this cultural-analytically Jewish understanding of the role of the rituals for dying and being buried in Jewish culture.

My final question then is: do they cast light on Nemes' film as aesthetic resistance or as the symptom of an incomplete but intimated desire to inscribe a different moral sensibility into a film by setting in tension the one character who acts like a tragic hero against a background of the horror created by the SS?

This is not a question of conscious intent. We know Nemes read and studied the SK writings as diligently as he watched Lanzmann's and Tarr's films. László Nemes was raised outside Jewish religious practice, but he admits to being pierced, as so many of the second and third-generation Jewish survivor families are, by what he named a 'black hole' that inhabited him as soon as he learnt, aged five, what had happened to his family in the Shoah. I suggest that the film becomes a symptomatic site of that transmitted trauma seeking to create a form in the relation to cinematic language.[62] In doing this, however, it also iterates *affectively* a cultural anguish that Arendt's political analysis of the psychological assault on the human condition by dehumanization in the camps draws to our attention.

Conclusion

I still cannot bear to see *Son of Saul* again, mostly for trite reasons. I hate the tight framing that places the dead and dying as staffage for a portrait of *Saul*, as the blurred background that foregrounds the central character. I hate the fact that they have tried to imagine and re-create the sound and process, at once so precisely and yet so inadequately. No heat, no smell, no terror loosing the body. They cannot show us the twenty or more minutes it took to die of suffocation and terror in a gas chamber. There is no cinema on earth even in horror and torture genres to re-enact what actually happened when bodies are burnt in the open. I hate the fact that being a film historian, I researched the conditions of production and discovered the giveaway detail that extras were hired to play the dead, lying naked and getting cold during long hours of filming, and that some of these extras were hired from amongst the homeless. I found photographs of the filming revealing that the apparatus used to film Géza Röhrig in tight frame was a moving camera strapped to the body of the cameraman walking backwards with his guide through the carefully re-created set.

Yet, as work of art, however compromised, by a serious director engaging in an act of personal mourning and communal commemoration, the film exceeds its compromised conditions of cinematic production. Its narrative imagines a spontaneous act and individuates its agent as a moral subject by his seeking to oppose the fundamental horror of unburied no-death: Celan's 'grave in the air'. As such, it merits Arendtian acknowledgement. Yet it fails the Adornian test because, in the end, it offers consolation to the cinematic spectator.

In its final frames, it gives us Saul/Röhrig's ashen face yielding to a smile of deluded, visionary joy while the camera follows a living boy, from the world outside Auschwitz, whom Saul has glimpsed framed in the doorway of the escapees' temporary hiding place, running through the rich greenery, a reverse rhyme and echo of the opening device of filming Saul from the back as he goes to work. With this ending, the film is allowing the spectator to escape with the free child back into nature, even as the soundtrack registers the machine guns and grenades of the German soldiers who cross the boy's path before they wipe out the other ragged escapees hiding in a hut. Saul, the film seems to say, dies happy. A child lives. Samuel Beckett would never leave us so.

Mainstream film, it seems, cannot but betray. It has to give the audience hope, even if, in this film, this is being balanced in the credit sequence running against a black screen between the mournful voice of a plaintive Klezmer violin playing the film's theme tune and the eerie sound of flames. Having battled seriously and profoundly with the place of cinema in the challenge of knowing and mourning, *Son of Saul* ultimately abandons its allegorical and mythic work. One dead, one live child, blank screen. We go home.

Yet the film has, I acknowledge, made me work at it, working through its troubling attempt to touch the dark centre of the Shoah. In making so patently visible and so viscerally felt the knowing cruelty of the SS perpetrators who inflicted a Jewish agony on the SK, I find myself here, unable to watch it again.

Griselda Pollock is Professor of Social and Critical Histories of Art and Director of the Centre for Cultural Analysis, Theory and History (CENTRECATH) at the University of Leeds. Committed to creating and extending an international, postcolonial, queer feminist analysis of the visual arts, visual culture and cultural theory, she researches issues of trauma and the aesthetic in contemporary art expanding her concept of *the virtual feminist museum* through *After-Affects/After-Images: Trauma and Aesthetic Transformation in the Virtual Museum* (2013) and *Art in the Time-Space of Memory and Migration* (2013), which both offer a feminist rereading of Aby Warburg's concept of the *pathos formula* at the intersection with psychoanalytical aesthetics. Since 2007, in addition to writing on Holocaust memory, she has elaborated the concept of *concentrationary memory* in relation to the Arendtian critique of totalitarianism in four publications with Max Silverman: *Concentrationary Cinema* (Berghahn Books, 2011); *Concentrationary Memories: Totalitarian Terror and Cultural Resistance* (2013), *Concentrationary Imaginaries: Tracing*

Totalitarian Violence in Popular Culture (2015); and *Concentrationary Art* (Berghahn Books, 2019). Just published is her monograph: *Charlotte Salomon and the Theatre of Memory* (2018) and forthcoming are *Is Feminism a Bad Memory?* (2019); *The Case against 'Van Gogh': Memory, Place and Modernist Disillusionment* (2019); and *Monroe's Mov(i)es: Class, Gender and Nation in the Work, Image-Making and Agency of Marilyn Monroe* (2020).

Notes

1. Primo Levi, 'The Gray Zone', in *The Drowned and the Saved*, trans. Raymond Rosenthal (New York: Vintage, 1989 [1986]), 40.
2. Mads Rosenthal Thompson et al., *Literature: An Introduction to Theory and Analysis* (London: Bloomsbury, 2017), 140.
3. Theodor W. Adorno, 'Meditations on Metaphysics: After Auschwitz', in *Negative Dialectics*, trans. E.B. Ashton (New York: Routledge, 1973), 362.
4. 'Death Fugue', in *Poems of Paul Celan*, trans. Michael Hamburger (New York: Persea Books, 2001).
5. Yitzhak Arad, *Belzec, Sobibor, Treblinka: The Operation Reinhard Death Camps* (Bloomington: University of Indiana Press, 1987).
6. Hannah Arendt, 'The Concentration Camps', *Partisan Review* XV (1948), 758.
7. Ibid.
8. On the theme of Lazarus in literature emerging from the concentration camps, notably in the work of Jean Cayrol and taken up by Alain Resnais, see Griselda Pollock and Max Silverman (eds), *Concentrationary Art: Jean Cayrol, the Lazarean and the Everyday in Post-war Film, Literature, Music and the Visual Arts* (New York: Berghahn Books, 2019).
9. This term originates in the political writings of David Rousset, *L'Univers concentrationnaire* (Paris: Editions de Pavois, 1946); translated as *The Other Kingdom*, trans. Ramon Guthrie (New York: Reynal and Hitchcock, 1947) and reissued in 1951 as *A World Apart*. Rousset produced a political anatomy of the camp as system from his place as a political deportee to Buchenwald, one of the 10,000 concentration camps in Germany. These are distinct from the four to six dedicated sites of mass extermination of Jewish and Romani peoples that were sited in Poland, never seen by Allied troops and were largely destroyed by 1943. Auschwitz-Birkenau remained in action as a killing camp until October 1944. See Griselda Pollock and Max Silverman (eds), *Concentrationary Memories: Totalitarian Terror and Cultural Resistance* (London: I.B. Tauris, 2013).
10. Marianne Hirsch, *The Generation of Postmemory: Writing and Visual Culture after the Holocaust* (New York: Columbia University Press, 2012); Helen Epstein *Children of the Holocaust* (New York: Putnam, 1979); Dina Wardi, *Memorial Candles: Children of the Holocaust* (London: Routledge, 1992); Anne Karpf, *The War After: Living with the Holocaust* (London: William Heinemann Ltd., 1996).

11. For a detailed argument about the process in art of formulation, finding forms to hold the traces of traumatic affects, see Griselda Pollock, *After-Affects/After-Images: Trauma and Aesthetic Transformation in the Virtual Feminist Museum* (Manchester: Manchester University Press, 2013).
12. Hannah Arendt, 'Social Science Techniques and the Study of Concentration Camps', in Jerome Kohn (ed.), *Essays in Understanding 1930–1945* (New York: Schocken Books, 1994), 232–248, at 240.
13. How many major historical events have names, as opposed to descriptive titles associated with places or people? The word *holocaust* derives from the Greek *holokauston*: *holos*/whole *kaustos*/burnt, which is the translation of the Hebrew *ola*, which was the most significant sacrifice because it entailed an animal being entirely consumed by fire. It was already in general usage as a term for a catastrophic event, but was often associated with fire, such as the notion of a nuclear holocaust, although Churchill had used it of the genocide of Armenians during the First World War. As a term evoking the mass murder of millions of Jewish and Roma-Sinti people by the Third Reich between 1941 and 1945, Holocaust only came into general usage, replacing generalizing terms such as Nazi atrocities or the war, during the 1960s, although there a scattered precedents. The American TV series *Holocaust* gave the term widespread popular currency after 1978 in the United States and also Europe, where it was also broadcast in 1978–79. *Shoah* is a Hebrew word meaning calamity and in the Middle Ages was associated with destruction. It is mostly used in the Jewish world given the horrific implications of the notion of a sacrifice and the fact that the association with fire is horrifying as a memory, although that element does not reference the millions killed by direct shooting by *Einsatzgruppen* during the German invasion of the Soviet Union or the deaths by attrition and arbitrary killing in ghettoes, on transports and as slave labourers.
14. Saul Friedländer, *Probing the Limits of Representation: Nazism and the 'Final Solution'* (Cambridge, MA: Harvard University Press, 1992), 1–2.
15. Jean-François Lyotard, *The Differend: Phrases in Dispute*, trans. George van den Abeele (Minnesota: University of Minneapolis Press, 1988 [1983]), 56–57.
16. On the idea of creating an agitating, reflexive mode of memory in self-consciously aesthetic art working, see Griselda Pollock and Max Silverman, *Concentrationary Cinema: The Politics of Resistance in Alain Resnais' Night and Fog (1955)* (New York: Berghahn Books, 2011).
17. Jean Luc Godard, *Histoire(s) du Cinéma* (eight-part video, 1988–99), Part 1 (Episode 1A).
18. The images Godard uses are Allied photographs and films of the piled corpses of those who died in the concentration camps of Germany, such as Bergen-Belsen, diseased and left for weeks to starve when the SS abandoned their prisoners as the Allied forces approached. The confusion widespread in cultural memory and general parlance between the vast concentrationary camp system and the few death camps, mostly erased by 1943 and only visited by the Soviet forces, remains a major obstacle in understanding. On this issue see Pollock and Silverman, *Concentrationary Memories* and *Concentrationary Imaginaries: Tracing Totalitarian Terror in Popular Culture* (London: I.B. Tauris, 2015).
19. Michael Rothberg, 'After Adorno: Culture in the Wake of Catastrophe', in *Traumatic Realism: The Demands of Holocaust Representation* (Minneapolis: University of Minnesota Press, 2000), 25–58.
20. Yitzhak Arad, *Belzec, Sobibor, Treblinka: The Operation of the Reinhard Death Camps* (Bloomington: University of Indiana Press, 1987).

21. Theodor W. Adorno, 'The Problem of Suffering', section of 'Commitment' (1962), in Andrew Arato and Eike Gebhardt (eds), *The Essential Frankfurt School Reader* (Oxford: Basil Blackwell, 1978), 312. On Beckett, see 313–15.
22. There is a long history of cinema and the Holocaust plotted out by Judith Doneson, *The Holocaust in American Film* (Philadelphia: Jewish Publication Society, 1987; 2nd revised edn Syracuse, NY: University of Syracuse Press, 2002).
23. Jacques Rancière, 'Is History a Form of Fiction?', in *The Politics of Aesthetics*, trans. Gabriel Rockhill (London: Continuum, 2004), 37.
24. Ibid.
25. Emphases added.
26. Kevin Maher, *Son of Saul*, 29 April 2016, https://www.thetimes.co.uk/article/film-son-of-saul-vt65nqlg3 (retrieved 30 March 2019). Emphasis added. The historical confusion as to when the scenes depicted could have taken place is part of the problem of a film about an event for which precision is fundamental, while the generalization under the term 'Holocaust' allows for projection and inaccuracy at the same time. The uprising took place on 7 October 1944. The transports from Hungary arrived between 29 April and 7 July 1944. Gassing at Auschwitz ceased soon after the uprising as the advance of the Soviet Army led the Himmler to order the destruction of the gas chambers and crematoria on 25 November 1944 to destroy the evidence. The Soviet troops arrived on 27 January 1945.
27. Interviews with László Nemes on *Son of Saul*, https://m.imdb.com/name/nm1841577 (retrieved 30 March 2019).
28. Mark Kermode, *The Guardian*, 27 April 2016; republished 1 May 2016, https://www.theguardian.com/film/2016/apr/27/son-of-saul-review-profoundly-distressing (retrieved 30 March 2019). Emphasis added.
29. Danny Leigh, 'Son of Saul; Film Review – a Triumph', *FT*, 28 April 2016, https://www.ft.com/content/ca3be218-0d55-11e6-b41f-0beb7e589515 (retrieved 30 March 2019).
30. Colin McCabe, *Criterion*, 22 May 2016, https://criticsroundup.com/film/son-of-saul (retrieved 30 March 2019).
31. https://www.nytimes.com/2015/05/21/movies/at-the-cannes-film-festival-some-gems-midway-through.html?partner=rss&emc=rss (retrieved 30 March 2019). Emphasis added.
32. Richard Brody, *New Yorker*, https://www.newyorker.com/culture/richard-brody/son-of-saul-and-the-ungraspable-horrors-of-auschwitz?mbid=rss (retrieved 30 March 2019).
33. Georges Didi-Huberman, *Sortir du noir* (Paris: Editions de Minuit, 2015). See also Georges Didi-Huberman, *Écorces* (Paris: Editions de Minuit, 2011) for the author's photo-essay on his own journey around Auschwitz I and II.
34. Jacques Rancière, 'Are Some Things Unrepresentable?', first published under the title 'L'art et la mémoire des camps' in *Genre Humain* 36 (2001), reprinted in *Le Destin des images* (Paris: Editions La Frabrique, 2003) and translated in revised form in *The Future of the Image* (London: Verso, 2007), 109–38.
35. Interviews with László Nemes on *Son of Saul*, https://m.imdb.com/name/nm1841577/quotes (retrieved 30 March 2019).
36. Rancière, 'Are Some Things Unrepresentable?', 127.
37. *Kaddish*, relating to the Hebrew word *Kadosh*, meaning holy, refers to a 2,000-year-old Judaic hymn of praise, written in Aramaic. It does not refer to death or the dead, but is a blessing of an eternal God. It is used in all Jewish services, often several times

to punctuate or close each section. But it is also said as a mourner's prayer, at burials, and in weekly and annual remembrance of the names of the deceased, and is said on the anniversary of a death when lighting a candle of remembrance in the home. Kaddish cannot be recited alone. It does not require a rabbi, as rabbis are not in any way sacerdotal. The word rabbi does not refer to a priest but means my teacher.

38. Interviews with László Nemes on *Son of Saul*, https://m.imdb.com/name/nm1841577/quotes (retrieved 30 March 2019).
39. On the theme of Lazarus as a figure for the returnee in Wiesel, see Griselda Pollock, 'The Perpetual Anxiety of Lazarus', in Griselda Pollock and Max Silverman (eds) *Concentrationary Art: Jean Cayrol, the Lazarean and the Everyday in Post-war Film, Literature, Music and the Visual Arts* (New York; Berghahn Books, 2018).
40. Imre Kertész, 'Who Owns Auschwitz?', *Yale Journal of Criticism* 14(1) (2001), 267–72, at 270.
41. For major readings of these four photographs, see Dan Stone, 'The Sonderkommando Photographs', *Jewish Social Studies* 7(3) (Spring/Summer 2001), 132–48; Nicholas Chare, 'Afterimages', in *Auschwitz and Afterimages: Abjection, Witnessing and Representation* (London: I.B. Tauris, 2011), 125–50; and especially Nicholas Chare and Dominic Williams, 'The Camera Eye: Four Photographs from Birkenau', in *Matters of Testimony: Interpreting the Scrolls of Auschwitz* (New York: Berghahn Books, 2016), 182–213.
42. Shoshana Felman, 'In an Era of Testimony: Claude Lanzmann's *Shoah*', *Yale French Studies* 79 (1991), 39–81; Margaret Olin, 'Lanzmann's *Shoah* and the Topography of the Holocaust Film', *Representations* 57 (Winter 1997), 1–23.
43. Jacques Rancière, *The Politics of Aesthetics*, trans. Gabriel Rockhill (London: Continuum, 2004), 20–34.
44. He lived in Rome after being tried and released by the Czech communist regime, but on his death, the Roman Jewish community would not allow his burial with his wife, and his son was prevented from saying Kaddish for him by the same community. Anna Hájková, 'The Last of the Self-Righteous: Claude Lanzmann's version of Benjamin Murmelstein', http://www.histoire-politique.fr/index.php?numero=23&rub=comptes-rendus&item=499 (retrieved 28 March 2019).
45. For a soundly critical reading of Lanzmann's seduction by Murmelstein and other interpretations of his character and role, see Anna Hájková 'The Last of the Self-Righteous: Claude Lanzmann's version of Benjamin Murmelstein', http://www.histoire-politique.fr/index.php?numero=1&rub=comptes-rendus&item=499 (retrieved 28 March 2019). On studies of the complexities and ambiguity of Jewish experience under ruthless Nazi power that dispel myths of both collaboration and heroic resistance, Hájková references the following scholarly texts: Dan Diner, 'Historisches Verstehen und Gegenrationalität: Der Judenrat als erkenntnistheoretische Warte', in Frank Bajohr, Werner Johe and Uwe Lohalm (eds), *Zivilisation und Barbarei: Die widersprüchlichen Potentiale der Moderne. Detlev Peukert zum Gedenken* (Hamburg: Christians 1991), 307–21; Beate Meyer, *Tödliche Gratwanderung: Die Reichsvereinigung der Juden in Deutschland zwischen Hoffnung, Zwang, Selbstbehauptung und Verstrickung (1939–1945)* (Göttingen: Wallstein, 2011).
46. On the issue of being deprived of speech and writing, of language, in the concentrationary universe see Jean Améry's chapter, 'The Intellectual in Auschwitz', in *At the Mind's Limits* (Bloomington: Indiana University Press, 1980).
47. Filip Müller, *Eyewitness Auschwitz: Three Years in the Gas Chamber*, trans. Suzanne Flatauer (Chicago: Ivan R. Dee, 1979).

48. Georg Simmel, 'The Sociological Significance of the Stranger', in Donald Levine (ed.), *Georg Simmel: On Individuality and Social Forms* (Chicago: University of Chicago Press, 1971 [1908]), 143–50; Zygmunt Bauman, *Modernity and Ambivalence* (Cambridge: Polity Press, 1993).
49. Hannah Arendt, *The Origins of Totalitarianism* (New York; Shocken Books, 1951); Rousset, *L'Univers concentrationnaire*.
50. Vassily Grosman, 'The Hell of Treblinka', in Robert Chandler (ed.), *The Road*, trans. Robert and Elizabeth Chandler with Olga Mukovnikova (New York: New York Review Books, 2010), 160.
51. Claude Lanzmann released as a single film his long interview with Yehuda Lerner, member of the SK team that led the revolt in Sobibór: *Sobibor, October 14, 1943, 4pm* (2001).
52. Hannah Arendt, *The Origins of Totalitarianism* (New York: Harvest at Harcourt, Inc., 1968 [1951]), 438.
53. Hannah Arendt, *The Human Condition* (Chicago: University of Chicago Press, 1958).
54. Arendt, *The Origins of Totalitarianism*, 438.
55. Ibid., 443.
56. Arendt, 'The Concentration Camps', 756.
57. Ibid., 746.
58. See Pollock and Silverman, *Concentrationary Art*.
59. Respectful treatment of the dead is a fundamental obligation in Jewish societies. The first element of a new community is arrangements for secure burial. It is an obligation on all members of the society to accompany and indeed physically assist in the burial of the dead person. Each person has a unique grave that cannot be used again.
60. Chare and Williams, *Matters of Testimony*, 185.
61. Ibid., 199. Emphasis added.
62. For a detailed argument about the process in art of formulation, finding forms to hold the traces of traumatic affects, see Pollock, *After-Affects/After-Images*.

Bibliography

Adorno, Theodor W. *Negative Dialectics*, trans. E.B. Ashton. London and New York: Routledge, 1973.
——. 'The Problem of Suffering', section of 'Commitment' (1962), in Andrew Arato and Eike Gebhardt, eds, *The Essential Frankfurt School Reader*, Oxford: Basil Blackwell, 1978.
Améry, Jean. *At the Mind's Limits*. Bloomington: Indiana University Press, 1980.
Arad, Yitzhak. *Belzec, Sobibor, Treblinka: The Operation of the Reinhard Death Camps*. Bloomington: University of Indiana, 1987.
Arendt, Hannah. 'The Concentration Camps', *Partisan Review* XV (1948), 743–63.
——. *The Origins of Totalitarianism*. New York: Schocken Books, 1951.
Celan, Paul. *Poems of Paul Celan*, trans. Michael Hamburger. New York: Persea Books, 2001.
Cesarani, David, and Eric J. Sundquist. *After the Holocaust: Challenging the Myth of Silence*. London: Routledge, 2011.
Chare, Nicholas. *Auschwitz and Afterimages: Abjection, Witnessing and Representation*. London: I.B. Tauris, 2011.

Chare, Nicholas, and Dominic Williams, *Matters of Testimony: Interpreting the Scrolls of Auschwitz*. New York: Berghahn Books, 2016.
Didi-Huberman, Georges. *Écorces*. Paris: Editions de Minuit, 2011
———. *Sortir du Noir*. Paris: Editions de Minuit, 2015.
Diner, Dan. 'Historisches Verstehen und Gegenrationalität: Der Judenrat als erkenntnistheoretische Warte', in Frank Bajohr, Werner Johe and Uwe Lohalm (eds), *Zivilisation und Barbarei: Die widersprüchlichen Potentiale der Moderne. Detlev Peukert zum Gedenken*. Hamburg: Christians 1991, 307–321.
Doneson, Judith. *The Holocaust in American Film*. Philadelphia: Jewish Publication Society, 1987.
———. *The Holocaust in American Film*. 2nd revised edn. Syracuse NY: University of Syracuse Press, 2002.
Epstein, Helen. *Children of the Holocaust*. New York: Putnam, 1979.
Felman, Shoshana. 'In an Era of Testimony: Claude Lanzmann's *Shoah*', *Yale French Studies* 79 (1991), 39–81.
Friedländer, Saul. *Probing the Limits of Representation: Nazism and the 'Final Solution'*. Cambridge, MA: Harvard University Press, 1992.
Grossman, Vassily. 'The Hell of Treblinka', in Robert Chandler (ed.), *The Road*, trans. Robert and Elizabeth Chandler with Olga Mukovnikova, New York: New York Review Books, 2010, 116–62.
Hirsch, Marianne. *The Generation of Postmemory: Writing and Visual Culture after the Holocaust*. New York: Columbia University Press, 2012.
Karpf, Anne. *The War After: Living with the Holocaust*. London, William Heinemann Ltd., 1996.
Kertész, Imre. 'Who Owns Auschwitz?', *Yale Journal of Criticism* 14(1) (2001), 267–72.
Levi, Primo. *The Drowned and the Saved*, trans. Raymond Rosenthal. New York: Vintage, 1989 [1986].
Lyotard, Jean-François. *The Differend: Phrases in Dispute*, trans. George van den Abeele. Minnesota: University of Minneapolis Press, 1988 [1983].
Meyer, Beate. *Tödliche Gratwanderung: Die Reichsvereinigung der Juden in Deutschland zwischen Hoffnung, Zwang, Selbstbehauptung und Verstrickung (1939–1945)*. Göttingen: Wallstein, 2011.
Müller, Filip. *Eyewitness Auschwitz: Three Years in the Gas Chamber*, trans. Suzanne Flatauer. Chicago: Ivan R. Dee, 1979.
Olin, Margaret. 'Lanzmann's *Shoah* and the Topography of the Holocaust Film', *Representations* 57 (Winter 1997), 1–23.
Pollock, Griselda. *After-Affects/After-Images: Trauma and Aesthetic Transformation in the Virtual Feminist Museum*. Manchester: Manchester University Press, 2013.
———. 'The Perpetual Anxiety of Lazarus: The Gaze, the Tomb and the Body in the Shroud', in Griselda Pollock and Max Silverman (eds), *Concentrationary Art: Jean Cayrol, the Lazarean and the Everyday in Post-war Film, Literature, Music and the Visual Arts*. New York: Berghahn Books, 2019.
Pollock, Griselda, and Max Silverman (eds). *Concentrationary Cinema: The Politics of Resistance in Alain Resnais'* Night and Fog *(1955)*. New York: Berghahn Books, 2011.
———. *Concentrationary Memories: Totalitarian Terror and Cultural Resistance*. London: I.B. Tauris, 2013.
———. *Concentrationary Imaginaries: Tracing Totalitarian Terror in Popular Culture*. London: I.B. Tauris, 2015.

———. *Concentrationary Art: Jean Cayrol, the Lazarean and the Everyday in Post-war Film, Literature, Music and the Visual Arts* (New York and London: Berghahn Books, 2019).
Rancière, Jacques. 'S'il y a de l'irreprésentable', *Le Genre Humain* 36 (2001), 81–102.
———. *The Politics of Aesthetics*, trans. Gabriel Rockhill. London: Continuum, 2004.
———. *The Future of the Image*, trans. Gregory Elliott. London: Verso, 2007.
Rothberg, Michael. *Traumatic Realism: The Demands of Holocaust Representation*. Minneapolis: University of Minnesota Press, 2000.
Rousset, David. *L'Univers concentrationnaire*. Paris: Editions de Pavois, 1946.
———. *The Other Kingdom*, trans. Ramon Guthrie. New York: Reynal and Hitchcock, 1947.
———. *A World Apart*. New York: Secker & Warburg, 1951.
Stone, Dan. 'The Sonderkommando Photographs', *Jewish Social Studies* 7(3) (Spring/Summer 2001), 132–48.
Thompson, Mads Rosenthal et al. *Literature: An Introduction to Theory and Analysis*. London: Bloomsbury, 2017.
Wardi, Dina. *Memorial Candles: Children of the Holocaust*. London: Routledge, 1992.

Chapter 2

What Makes the Grey Zone Grey?
Blurring Moral and Factual Judgements of the Sonderkommando

Dominic Williams

―⦅⦆―

Describing the Auschwitz Sonderkommando (SK) as denizens of the grey zone is perhaps the most obvious way to characterize them. Their position within it is so important that mention of the grey zone often conjures the SK up as its ideal type. For many people, the first piece of writing in which they encounter the SK is Levi's essay of that title. And Levi's anguished meditation on the SK, their moral position and the possibility of judging, or even understanding, them is a major attempt to assess what their significance is. In this chapter I shall consider not only how Levi's essay regards the SK morally, but also how he ascertains what he knows about them: how he treats his sources and how he conceives of the facts. In examining the way he treats factual and moral judgements, sometimes blurring them, sometimes distinguishing them too rigidly, I will suggest that the grey zone is characterized by the uncertainty of both kinds of judgement. I will go on to argue that the knowledge that members of the SK gained by 'adapting', or 'getting used', to their situation was experienced as moral contamination, but also gave some possibility of moral action, as their own words testify.

The Blurred Boundaries of the Grey Zone

The idea of the grey zone has at least a ten-year history to it, although some aspects of it can be traced back to Levi's earliest postwar writing.[1]

Passages that touch on and work through the concept can be found from 1975 onwards. The first of these is in Levi's foreword to his own translation of Jacques Presser's *The Night of the Girondins* (1951, Levi's translation 1976), in which he suggests that 'the time has come to explore the space that separates the victims from the executioners'.[2] Levi also acknowledges the difficulty of judging Presser's character Cohn, while pronouncing him 'guilty'. A year later, a story on Chaim Rumkowski, Jewish head of the Łódź ghetto ('Il re dei Giudei'), appeared in *La Stampa*. This piece was included with only slight changes in the final essay. In 1984, the Italian translation of Hermann Langbein's *People in Auschwitz* was published, with Levi's introduction, which talked of the 'gray zone of the Kapos and the prisoners who were given a rank and authority', warned against generalizations 'which are so loved by totalitarian regimes', but still argued that 'to judge is necessary but difficult'.[3] Many of these ideas were the same as in 'The Grey Zone', including the term itself, even though only two years prior to it Levi was still asserting the importance of judging. When the final essay was published in 1986, it was divided into three parts: a general discussion (based around the seeds of what he had written in his introductions to Presser and Langbein about privilege and collaboration), a meditation on the SK (which had not appeared in any form before) and the story of Rumkowski.[4]

Based on texts written at different points when Levi had different ideas of the function of judgement, 'The Grey Zone' is, not surprisingly, a text that does not take an easily defined position on judging. The question of judgement is clearly central to Levi's essay, but it is actually very hard to extract what he says to provide guidance on how, or whether, one should judge people in the zone. Judgement is almost never straightforwardly described; it is always surrounded with hedging, counterfactuals and qualifications.[5] Levi says that he would 'light-heartedly absolve' minor functionaries 'if I were forced to judge' (29). Kapos 'bear their own share of the guilt', but 'are the vectors and instruments of the system's guilt', and require 'more delicate and varied' judgement (29). Chaim Rumkowski cannot be 'absolve[d] ... on the moral plane', but there are 'extenuating circumstances' (49) and we still stand paralysed in our *'impotentia judicandi'* before his case. Even the most forthright assertion – that 'no one is authorised to judge' the SK (42) – is qualified by the statement that those who did not go through the Lagers have less authority than those who did, and in asking that 'judgement of [the SK] be suspended' (43), Levi still treats all of his readers as judges.

The grey zone might therefore be best seen as a set of cases that Levi has assembled together to puzzle over, not some general principle that he applies to a defined category of prisoner.[6] But even his reasons for selecting these particular cases are not always easy to discern. The difficulty of making moral judgements is what Levi's essay is famous for, but it is also noticeable how much disagreement there is about even what might be called the factual elements of the zone: where it is located and who is part of it. The zone itself is extremely nebulous: applicable to the camps, to totalitarian societies and to situations of imbalance of power.[7] It seems mainly to encompass victims, but it might even expand to include a mass murderer such as Erich Muhsfeldt. Some writers have taken this nebulousness as a prompt to think about where it might be expanded further. Christopher Browning sees it as speaking to the situation of his 'ordinary men'; Tzvetan Todorov applies it to all people in a totalitarian society; Claudia Card uses it to conceptualize the position of many women within patriarchal structures.[8] Others have policed its boundaries more strictly than Levi himself. Berel Lang not only provides a straightforward definition of the zone, but lists many groups and situations to which he claims it is inapplicable, including perpetrators. Sander H. Lee has followed him in this rather reductive characterization.[9] Some of the difficulty seems to stem from decisions about the genre of this essay: philosophers read it as a work of moral philosophy (or at least transform it into that) and attribute to it (or supply it with) a rigorous precision. Others dwell more on its literary qualities, focusing on its ambiguities and paradoxes. Adam Brown, for example, argues that even when trying not to judge some people, Levi cannot avoid doing so.[10]

Such difficulties seem inherent to this particular essay, as they are not characteristic even of other essays in *The Drowned and the Saved*. Usually, Levi exhibits some precision, being able to make nuanced distinctions that give a sense of a pattern that might be discerned, even when they discuss difficult material. In 'Shame', the essay following 'The Grey Zone', for example, which touches on many of the same themes (privilege, camp 'morality' and guilt as well as shame itself), the discussion is far more balanced and patterned: lists and explanations are not asserted as exhaustive, and are self-consciously described as limited or simplified, but are not put forward simply to be taken back.

In 'The Grey Zone', however, Levi's consideration of the difficulty of ethical questions (of judging) shows how it also creates problems for cognitive ones (of understanding). Indeed, the blurring of the two is present from the very beginning of the essay, in which he traces how any attempts at understanding might turn into a simplification and thus a judgement. He then places the person trying to make sense of the life of the camps in the same position as the *Zugang*, the newly arrived prisoner, whose previous categories of judgement and understanding are of little use in their changed environment (22–24). Amos Goldberg describes this as the 'epistemological grey zone': a state in which the prisoner has difficulties simply cognizing the extreme situation, let alone judging it.[11] This difficulty seems to affect not simply those within the camp, such as the *Zugang*, and those who survived it, such as Levi, but anyone trying to conceptualize the grey zone itself: its borders are necessarily troubled ones.

Imagining the Sonderkommando

By introducing the SK, the only completely new part, to his essay, Levi troubled the grey zone even further. Although they are placed at its heart, their connections to what is written before and after are problematic. The first part of the essay elaborates the concept of the grey zone through the terms of privilege and collaboration. The SK, however, are introduced as follows:

> An extreme case [*un caso-limite*] of collaboration is represented by the Sonderkommandos of Auschwitz and the other extermination camps. Here one hesitates to speak of privilege. (34)

While the English translations of Raymond Rosenthal and Michael F. Moore (both of whom use the term 'an extreme case') suggest that Levi means to accuse the SK of the maximum degree of collaboration, in fact *caso-limite* might be better translated as 'borderline case' – a case that might be collaboration or might not.[12] Neither collaboration nor privilege, therefore, apply straightforwardly to the SK. Equally, Rumkowski and the SK are linked together with the idea that they both provoke the same '*impotentia judicandi*', but the 'morals' that the two sections draw are utterly opposed to each other. At the end of the SK section, Levi writes about the impossibility of putting oneself in their, or indeed anyone's, place, including that of one's future self. Rumkowski, however, is us. We see in Rumkowski 'a reflection of ourselves', his 'ambiguity' and 'fever' are 'ours': the section (and the essay) ends with a meditation on 'us', not Rumkowski (54).

In the SK section itself, Levi relied on three main sources: Miklós Nyiszli, Hermann Langbein and Filip Müller. Langbein's collection of testimony in *Menschen in Auschwitz*, important to Levi in formulating his thinking about the grey zone, provides the bulk of his material, with only a brief mention of Müller, who is only referenced once (41).[13] Miklós Nyiszli is the source most extensively discussed, even though he is used for only a small number of facts. Levi draws upon Nyiszli in particular to offer stories that are worth 'meditat[ing] upon' (38).

Levi is disturbed by the account of a football match between representatives of the SK and the SS.[14] For him, this is not some suspension of hostilities between the two groups, but rather a grotesque charade of normality, the ultimate sign that the SS feel that they have degraded the SK to their level of killers. Indeed, as at a few other points in the essay, Levi ventriloquizes the perpetrators here, rendering his version of their thoughts in direct speech (37–38). The meaning of this incident is given it by the SS, not the SK.

Another story is that of a teenage girl who was pulled alive and unconscious out of the gas chamber (38–41). As Nyiszli tells it, he was urgently summoned by the SK to resuscitate her and to ask Erich Muhsfeldt, an SS guard, to save the girl's life. Muhsfeldt considered Nyiszli's request, but decided it was impracticable and had the girl shot.[15] Levi sees this incident as significant because it is a point at which the SK see not a mass of victims, but one individual, who they then feel obliged to try to save. This story ends with a discussion of Muhsfeldt's actions, concluding that his hesitation, and his unwillingness to shoot the girl himself, might allow us not to redeem him, but to place him at the 'extreme boundary' of the grey zone.

Although the girl's individuality is important for Levi (a point to which this chapter will return), the question that has to be asked of the SK is not about individual behaviour, but about their situation – the 'convulsed questions' that they prompt are entirely general: 'why did they accept that task? why didn't they rebel? why didn't they prefer death?' (41). This whole section could be said to be groping towards answers to those questions and then rejecting them, or seeing that they do not actually apply to the SK. Catherine Mooney observes that Levi is not interested in the daily life of the SK and does not think it possible to imagine how they lived.[16] The only points that he is able to come towards anything like imagining them are boundary situations, at the moment of entry into the ranks of the Special Squad, and times when they stop being, or fulfilling their roles as, SK: they revolt or try to save a young girl's life. Mostly, however, Levi seems to find it easier to see what these incidents mean for the SS. Both of the two incidents taken from Nyiszli end up as a discussion of the perpetrators rather than the SK themselves: the football match becomes what the SS make it mean, while the rescue of the girl becomes a discussion of Muhsfeldt's responsibility rather than that of the SK. Indeed, the football match ends with him speaking in the voice of the Nazis, a turn that he takes at three points in the essay (35, 37 and 38).

By comparison, the SK's own words are treated with much greater suspicion:

It is evident that these things that were said, and the innumerable others which were probably said by them and among them but did not reach us, cannot be taken literally. From men who have known such extreme destitution one cannot expect a deposition in the juridical sense of the term, but something that is at once a lament, a curse, an expiation, and an attempt to justify and rehabilitate themselves. One should expect a liberating outburst instead of a Medusa-faced truth. (36)

This comment can be compared to that in the essay about the drowned and the saved in which Levi mentions the Gorgon's face (Medusa was, of course, a Gorgon): 'We who survived the camps are not true witnesses. We are those who, through prevarication, skill or luck, never touched bottom. Those who have, and who have seen the face of the Gorgon, did not return, or returned wordless' (63). Did the SK see the face of the Gorgon/Medusa in Levi's characterization? This is difficult to tell. Perhaps they did, and like all others who saw the Gorgon they are not able to put it into words. Or perhaps they did not, because they were among those who benefited from privilege, in some sense, and are therefore unable to tell of what they have not seen. This status of being possibly drowned, possibly saved, is another difficulty for Levi to make sense of them.

Establishing Facts

Although Levi does not place much store in the SK's own words, he (necessarily) draws on a set of facts to demonstrate the difficulty of imagining the SK's lives. A similar process happens at two points in the essay. Levi acknowledges the imperfection of the sources of information before going on simply to assert that they match each other and therefore provide the facts of the case. After a list that highlights the difficulty of finding information about the SK ('meagre depositions', 'admissions' from perpetrators, 'hints' from bystanders and 'feverishly written' diaries), Levi proclaims: 'All these sources are in agreement' (34–35). Later he describes the 'vague and mangled rumours [*voci vaghe e monche*] [about the SK that] circulated among us' before simply stating that they 'were confirmed afterwards' (36). This is at odds with much of what Levi says in other parts of the essay indicating that knowledge of the SK is by no means secure.[17] But at these two junctures, Levi treats the facts as unquestionable. On both occasions, he then moves on to say that even with these facts established, it is difficult to form or conjure up (at both points he uses the verb *costruirsi*) an image of the men's daily lives (35, 36).

At one level, the reason for doing this is quite straightforward and understandable: Levi wants the discussion to be about the morals of it and not to enter into discussions of what did or did not happen. His point might be something like that there is no set of facts that we could uncover that would give us insight into the SK, or even if we knew everything about them, we still would not understand them. But this is still a puzzling use of the idea of facts about the SK: that we have the pieces, but we cannot build out of them an image of who they were. It simply accepts the stories that have been handed down about the SK as true, even though they have been described in ways that Levi himself says makes them problematic. Actually, this approach can be seen as a consequence of the conclusion that it is impossible to imagine the SK. Precisely because the situation is deemed to be unimaginable, any 'fact' about it is equally thinkable (since all of them are unthinkable). This way of thinking about the facts simply leaves the grounds of any moral judgements, such as they are, unexamined. And further scrutiny of these facts shows, firstly, that they are not at all as well established as Levi presents them as being and, secondly, that they are not separate from the moral questions that Levi goes on to ask, but rather are inextricably bound together with them.

One of the cornerstones of Levi's thinking about the SK (and the final key detail taken from Nyiszli) is the idea that they were all killed every three or four months.[18] We know that this is not true because there were people who survived for much longer than that.[19] Here what purports to simply be a statement of fact actually allows us to build a particular moral picture of the SK. This supposed fact asserts that they were assured of death and so makes their 'choice' to be in the SK one of eking out a few more weeks of life with a definite end rather than to continue in an open-ended and uncertain existence. This story simplifies the facts, and knowledge of the facts, both for those thinking about the SK and for the members of the SK themselves. In this version, the SK *know* that they will die. Here what was really (at least in part) a judgement of fact – not knowing whether they would live or not – is neatened out into a judgement of value – what three months of life are worth. It turns the SK into a moral thought experiment.[20]

Equally, scholars make judgements of value in deciding what is taken to be valid evidence, including ethical judgements about what can be said about the SK. Hayden White has argued repeatedly that the choice of facts and their ordering (their emplotment or narrativity) involve an 'impulse to moralize reality'.[21] Even before this stage, deciding which facts to investigate, how to do so and what might be appropriate methods to establish them involves ethical decisions. As Hilary Putnam has argued, 'theory selection' of how to determine what is factually true also presupposes values, such as preferences for simplicity, coherence and plausibility.[22] Edith Wyschogrod's sense of the historian's primary calling as founded in 'an eros for the past and an ardor for those other in whose name there is a felt urgency to speak' contains the sense that the search for the truth of the past is a primarily ethical relationship.[23]

Levi chose what facts were appropriate for him to take from Hermann Langbein, for example. Langbein's account of the SK includes stories both of their actions to help others and of ways in which they abused their privilege.[24] Leaving these stories out means that Levi provides no variegated sense of how the SK acted. Langbein too must have made choices about which stories to accept and what was sufficient evidence for him to do so. Most of his stories are not based on the SK's own testimony, but on accounts of conversations with them by survivors or rumours that circulated in the camp. One example of these rumours is a claim that some members of the SK sexually interfered with the bodies of dead women in the gas chamber. Langbein does not seem to have considered the plausibility of this act; he gives an account of it happening immediately after their death that would have been physically impossible. But simply accepting this story as factual evidence on the SK had moral consequences, including facing a potential lawsuit for defaming the dead. Langbein agreed to leave the story out of other editions of his book.[25]

The testimony that Langbein used to make this claim (not from a member of the SK, but someone who, as a teenage boy, spoke to a member of the SK) might appear to give some insight into the sexuality of the SK or at least the ways in which stories of the SK were infused with sexual imaginings. It may simply be that this temptation to find meaning in it should be resisted.[26] Even considering the possibility, or making anything of this testimony, might be a betrayal of the SK's memory. But what is clear is that simply accepting the testimony and then trying to make moral sense of it is itself a moral abdication, one that stems from a sense that the lives of the SK are outside our imagining.

'Getting Used to It'

Another possibility is that we do not place the SK so absolutely beyond the bounds of imagination. We might, for a start, want to listen to their words rather more carefully than Levi himself does. The only time that Levi quotes words supposedly spoken by members of the SK, these are also taken from Langbein:

One of them declared: 'Doing this work, one either goes crazy the first day or gets accustomed to it [*si abitua*]'. Another, though [*un altro, invece*]: 'Certainly, I could have killed myself or got myself killed; but I wanted to survive, to avenge myself and bear witness. You mustn't think that we are monsters; we are the same as you, only much more unhappy'. (36)

An examination of Langbein reveals, however, that Levi has taken both of these statements from the same person:

'Do you people think that I volunteered for this work? What was I to do? Sure, I could have gone into the wire, like so many comrades. But I want to survive. Maybe a miracle will happen! We could be liberated today or tomorrow. And then I want to take revenge as a direct witness of their crimes'.

And he continued 'If this work doesn't make you crazy on the first day, you get used to it [*gewöhnt man sich daran*]. Do you think that those who work in a munitions factory have a much nobler occupation? Or the girls who sort the things in Canada so they can be taken to Germany? We're all working for them on their orders. Believe me, I don't want to survive for the sake of living. I don't have anyone anymore because they have gassed my whole family. But I want to live so I can report about it and take revenge'. This man's spontaneous outburst ended with the words: 'Do you think the members of the Sonderkommando are monsters? I tell you, they are like the others, only much more unhappy'.[27]

Instead of one man who provides a complex range of feelings and justifications, Levi splits him into two: a man who is accustomed to the work and the man who wants to bear witness and take revenge. In Levi's moral imagination, the states of being used to this work and of having the desire to resist it would seem to be incompatible. Being used to something has a wide range of meanings and implications: it means that something has been experienced many times and so is familiar. It is known (and thus knowable) and normal. The implication in many cases is that the situation is accepted as normal too.[28] Here, Levi's warning against seeing the SK as having an 'everyday' would seem to have most bite: if the life amidst death of the SK is simply normal to them, then they no longer see the utter abnormality of their situation, do not know it for what it truly is and are therefore not able to bear witness to it.[29] Amos Goldberg and Alexandra Garbarini have both noted points where Holocaust diarists feel they are no longer able to describe the events around them because they are used to them.[30] Goldberg goes further, reading this state as a kind of symbolic death, an acceptance of the Nazi signifier that turns the diarist into an automaton working towards its own destruction.[31]

Catherine Mooney adds to this a specific moral problem faced by the SK. Making powerful use of Martha Nussbaum's thinking on Greek tragedy (as interpreted by Ariel Meirav), Mooney finds the danger of 'getting used' to the morally repugnant tasks that one is forced to carry out.[32] Nussbaum does not blame Agamemnon, for example, for killing his daughter Iphigenia, but she points out that he 'put up with it; he did not struggle against it'.[33] To get used to their environment, as a number of SK cited by Mooney say they did, is a dangerous position to be in. It morally contaminates them because as they dull their senses in order to survive, they begin to be associated with the function that they carry out and become indifferent to victims' suffering.[34]

Indeed, Levi returns to the idea of 'being used to' the work in his discussion of the girl who survived the gas chamber, one of the incidents that he takes from Miklós Nyiszli:

> The men are perplexed [*perplessi*]; death is their trade at all hours, death is a habit [*consuetudine*] because, precisely, 'one either goes crazy the first day or gets accustomed to it', but this woman is alive. (39)

The quotation is from the SK's words that he provides earlier in the text. Here it is put into a contradictory relationship with the fact of the girl being alive. Only an exceptional event jolts the men out of their normal patterns of behaviour. Death is their job, their habit or custom. They have become part of the kingdom of death, and only by exiting this realm, by being confounded or perplexed, can they recognize someone as a human being.[35]

But all of this characterization is based on the idea that the man who has grown accustomed and the man who resists are not the same person – that one can only turn into the other in this most exceptional of circumstances. If we take these two states as less radically separate, the situation might be interpreted in a different way. Instead of thinking of 'being used' with reference to such extreme psychic states as automatism and dissociation,[36] the more everyday concept employed by Levi himself – habit – suggests other possibilities. Habit too is often seen as simply conforming to one's environment, but as Maurice Merleau-Ponty suggested, it also makes actions within that environment possible:

> To get used to [*s'habituer*] a hat, car or stick is to be transplanted into them, or conversely, to incorporate them into the bulk of our own body. Habit expresses our power of dilating our being-in-the-world, or changing our existence by appropriating fresh instruments.[37]

The instruments are no longer noticed in themselves, but allow other kinds of perceptions, and actions that respond to the environment. In a context in which the tools used and the environment inhabited are all designed to produce mass murder, this idea is disturbing. But this two-way movement, as Merleau-Ponty describes it, holds out the possibility that as well as, or instead of, simply reproducing that environment, a member of the SK might also inhabit it in order to achieve his own purposes. This more complex sense of what might have happened to the SK is also expressed in Filip Müller's rejection of the idea that members of the SK got used ('haben sich . . . gewöhnt') to the work, only to suggest that they had to adapt to the conditions ('mußten sich den Verhältnissen anpassen').[38]

Following this line, we might say that precisely because the SK are used to their circumstances, they understand how they normally operate and are therefore able to judge, more precisely, what the results of their actions might be. Seeing the girl survive does not transform unfeeling automata into humans, but rather presents them with an opportunity, one that they sense because they are accustomed to the workings of the death factory. And, as Levi and Nyiszli tell it, their judgement that it might be possible to save a life seems to be justified.[39] They know enough about Erich Muhsfeldt to see that he might be persuaded to let her live; Muhsfeldt does hesitate, ponders the possibility of not killing her and is not able to carry out the murder himself. For Levi, this ends in a consideration of Muhsfeldt's place in the grey zone, but it might equally be read as showing that the life of the SK alongside the SS allowed them not (or not simply) to be contaminated by them, but to provide them with knowledge that could be used, at times, to attempt to make a difference.

Granted, this particular attempt failed. The SK's knowledge was not in the vein of a thought experiment, in which one is always certain what will happen, but rather a calculation of risk or a feel for what might be possible. Granted too, these judgements were also made more uncertain by the extreme psychological stress, distress, shame and fear that they suffered. Some of the interpretations of the SK as having an everyday life do not take this sufficiently into account. Inga Clendinnen's suggestion that the adaptability demonstrated by the SK was part of a set of conventional moral virtues (such as inventiveness and perseverance) has the merit of trying to treat them as human. As Catherine Mooney points out, however, Clendinnen gives too little consideration to the damage that might have been done to them.[40] Clendinnen's interpretation of the football match in particular is troubling – accepting the normalcy that is imposed upon the situation, and that Levi finds so obscene.[41] Claudia Card's more rigorous examination does acknowledge that the evil of grey zones is that they sap people of the ability to behave morally, and she still decides in the end that we should respect the ways in which some of its denizens still want to think in moral categories.[42] Michael Rothberg argues that the everyday of the outside is not simply separated from the extremity of the inside by the barbed wire of the camp.[43] Equally, in their even more extreme circumstances, the SK's everyday is part of what characterizes their place in the grey zone. Attending to this everyday allows us to recognize the smaller, successful acts of aid provided by the SK, such as those recorded by Langbein, as part of their moral landscape.

Making Judgements within the Grey Zone

Let us take the man quoted by Primo Levi at his word. The SK asked to be seen as the same as us, not monsters. Indeed, allowing these victims to speak – with all the difficulties that this includes – is one of the ethical decisions that needs to be made. Listening to them, and treating what they have to say as having value, might risk underestimating what the grey zone did to them. It might be that it robbed them of an ability to give an account of themselves, as Levi argues. But even this extreme judgement can only be made by assessing the plausibility of the SK's testimony. As the examples above show, simply refusing to judge what is plausible and what is not leaves the SK open to any accusation. There is therefore no possibility of not judging, because as soon as we begin to give any account of the SK, we make morally significant judgements about what is acceptable as evidence and what is not. Deciding that their accounts cannot be believed is a moral judgement (even if it is one that tries to explain why that might be so). Accepting stories from other people is also a moral judgement. And they result in moral judgements too.

In the letters that they wrote to relatives and friends, Marcel Nadjary and Herman Strasfogel did think about the moral judgements that might be made of them.[44] Nadjary wrote:

> My dear friends when you read this you will wonder about the work I did, how was I Manolis or anyone else able to do this work burning my fellow believers I was also thinking that at the beginning many times I thought of going in with them as well so as to finish but what always kept me was the revenge I wanted and want to live in order to avenge the deaths of Dad of Mum and of my beloved darling sister Nelli.

Nadjary too indicates that in some sense, he has got used to the work: he only asked himself how he could do this work at the beginning, so presumably he does not ask that question anymore. He is prepared to continue with the work insofar as he can take revenge: presumably by resisting or perhaps even by bearing witness. Being used to the work (in some sense) is a requirement of being able to do so.

Strasfogel wrote in similar terms to his wife and daughter in France:

> if you live you will certainly read quite a few works written about the 'Sonder-Komando' but I ask you to never judge me badly as if among us there were good and bad I was certainly not among the latter. During this period I did everything I was able to, never thinking about the danger or risk to ease the fate of the wretched for reasons of discretion [*politiquement*] I cannot write to you about their fate, that my conscience is clear and on the eve of my death I can be proud.

Here Strasfogel is less interested in the idea of collaborating than in the idea that he has some power to do some good. He is probably sparing his family the details of what he does and he may be trying to make his condition more bearable to them by claiming that he is still some kind of moral being (as with his statements that he is fit and well, and that he looks good), but even the awareness that he needs to give this account of himself suggests something more than the utter moral abjection presented by Hannah Arendt. Strasfogel also makes it clear that members of the SK felt capable of judging each other and themselves. Acknowledging differences within the group (that some deserve judgement more than others) might even be a way of acknowledging differences within oneself, between the part of the person that is used to the work and the part that resists.

Nadjary and Strasfogel, both writing letters, put themselves into dialogue with someone from outside. They use that interlocutor as a way of imagining the moral judgement that they may have to face, or the judgement that they articulate about themselves. They both acknowledge that their situation itself may raise questions of their moral standing. But in both cases, they find an answer to it in their ability to act: to take revenge or to ease others' suffering. This is not, it seems to me, just an excuse, although many moral compromises are made in this form.[45] It demonstrates that the SK's moral thinking considered both their situation and their ability to act within its bounds. What both of these letters also show is that they *want* to think in moral terms, engaging in a dialogue that is – in part – that dialogue with the self that Hannah Arendt saw as crucial for taking a moral position.[46]

Levi's essay on the grey zone, therefore, not only meditates on but also enacts the difficulties of understanding and judging the SK. In the grey zone, a realm marked by shifting boundaries and uncertainty over who qualifies for membership, the SK hold a particularly troubled place for him. This status is certainly in part due to the difficulty of judging them morally, but bound up with this are questions of how knowledge of them is to be gained: what judgements are involved in establishing facts about them, what weight should be given to their own words and whether the knowledge that they themselves gained by being in their situation morally contaminated them. These are difficulties that anyone working on the Sonderkommando must face. They are also ones that members of the SK themselves wrestled with, as Nadjary and Strasfogel's letters demonstrate.

Dominic Williams is Senior Lecturer in Holocaust and Genocide Studies at Northumbria University. He has published articles on modernist writing and antisemitism, contemporary Jewish poetry, and Holocaust memory and testimony. He and Nicholas Chare have coedited *Representing Auschwitz: At the Margins of Testimony* (2013), and coauthored *Matters of Testimony: Interpreting the Scrolls of Auschwitz* (Berghahn Books, 2016) and *The Auschwitz Sonderkommando: Testimonies, Histories, Representations* (2019).

Notes

Thanks to Nicholas Chare and Milena Marinkova who read and commented on earlier drafts of this chapter.

1. The genesis of Levi's essay has been covered in some depth. See Philippe Mesnard, 'Primo Levi, cheminement vers la zone grise', in *La Zone grise: Entre accommodement et collaboration* (Paris: Kimé, 2010), 21–48; Martina Mengoni, 'The Rumkowski Variations: Up and Down the Trails of the Gray Zone', http://www.primolevi.it/@api/deki/files/1202/=MAUSC_E00003.pdf (retrieved 2 April 2019); Lina N. Insana, *Arduous Tasks: Primo Levi, Translation and the Transmission of Holocaust Testimony* (Toronto: University of Toronto Press, 2009), 56-92, 125–176.
2. Primo Levi, Foreword to *The Night of the Girondists* by Jacques Presser, *The Complete Works of Primo Levi*, ed. Ann Goldstein (New York: Liveright, 2015), 1220–23. The term is usually dated to 1975, in a letter Levi wrote to Gabriella Poli, although he refers in it to his translation of Presser. In a conversation with Giuseppe Grassano, he called it the 'fascia grigia' ('grey band'). Mesnard, 'Primo Levi', 23–24; Grassano, 'A Conversation with Primo Levi (1979)', in Marco Belpoliti and Robert Gordon (eds), *The Voice of Memory: Primo Levi*, trans. Gordon (Cambridge: Polity Press, 2001), 131.
3. Primo Levi, Foreword to *People in Auschwitz* by Hermann Langbein, *The Complete Works of Primo Levi*, ed. Ann Goldstein (New York: Liveright, 2015), 2671–74. Levi referred to this book in a paragraph of the Foreword to Presser that he incorporated into 'The Grey Zone' (Foreword to Presser, 1222; 'Grey Zone', 25–26). The conclusion to *People in Auschwitz* was included in Levi's own translation in *La ricerca delle radici: Antologia personale* (Turin: Einaudi, 1981), 221–27. Levi corresponded with

Langbein and had read the book in draft form in 1972. See Ian Thomson, *Primo Levi* (London: Hutchinson, 2002), 356.
4. My main references to this essay will be to the translation by Raymond Rosenthal, published in Primo Levi, *The Drowned and the Saved* (London: Michael Joseph, 1988), 22–51. Page references in brackets in the main body of the chapter are to this translation. I have also consulted the translation by Michael F. Moore in Primo Levi, *The Complete Works of Primo Levi*, ed. Ann Goldstein (New York: Liveright, 2015), 2430–56. References to the original Italian are to Primo Levi, 'La zona grigia', *I sommersi e i salvati* (Turin: Einaudi, 1986), 24–52.
5. Hence Stef Craps can say that Rumkowski escapes judgement and Adam Brown can say that the SK do not. For Craps see https://www.academia.edu/27978486/The_Grey_Zone_extended_version_. Brown, *Judging 'Privileged' Jews: Holocaust Ethics, Representation and the 'Grey Zone'* (New York: Berghahn, 2013), 42–75.
6. Cf. Robert Gordon's claim that: 'The individuals in Levi's world almost always have metonymic potential, but are not reduced to metonyms; they are partly representative, but representative precisely because each is unique'. '"Per mia fortuna . . .": Irony and Ethics in Primo Levi's Writing', *Modern Language Review* 92(2) (1997), 343.
7. See Yannis Thanassekos. 'La zone grise, un concept problématique?', in Philippe Mesnard and Yannis Thanassekos (eds), *La Zone grise: Entre accommodement et collaboration* (Paris: Kimé, 2010), 15–20.
8. Christopher Browning, *Ordinary Men: Reserve Police Battalion 101 and the Final Solution in Poland* (London: Penguin, 2001), 186–88; Tzvetan Todorov, *Facing the Extreme: Moral Life in the Concentration Camps*, trans. Arthur Denner and Abigail Pollack (London: Weidenfeld & Nicolson, 1999), 182; Claudia Card, *The Atrocity Paradigm: A Theory of Evil* (New York: Oxford University Press, 2002), 219–21, 228–33.
9. Berel Lang, *Primo Levi: The Matter of a Life* (New Haven: Yale University Press, 2013), 127; Sander H. Lee, 'Primo Levi's *Gray Zone*: Implications for Post-Holocaust Ethics', *Holocaust and Genocide Studies* 30(2) (Fall 2016), 276–97.
10. See the Introduction to this volume for a discussion of Giorgio Agamben's reading of 'The Grey Zone' and criticisms made of it.
11. Amos Goldberg, *Trauma in First Person: Diary Writing during the Holocaust* (Bloomington: Indiana University Press, 2017), 217–18.
12. Levi, 'The Gray Zone', trans. Moore, 2441; Levi, 'La zona grigia', 36. Thanks to Martine Grange and Agnieszka Smigiel for pointing this out to me.
13. Nyiszli and Müller are explicitly mentioned as his sources, but Langbein is not. However, Myriam Anissimov identifies Langbein as Levi's 'main source' on the SK: *Primo Levi: Tragedy of an Optimist*, trans. Steve Cox (London: Aurum, 1998), 146. The information about the SK provided by Levi matches that given by Langbein on the following points: the care with which the SK's writings were buried (Levi 35, Langbein 192); selection on the basis of physiognomy, strength and as a punishment (Levi 35, Langbein 192); the SK's habitual drunkenness (Levi 36, Langbein 193–94); the words spoken by a member of the SK (Levi 36, Langbein 194); the refusal of about 400 Jews from Corfu to work and their being gassed (Levi 41, Langbein 196); details of the 7 October 1944 uprising, including the numbers of SK dead and SS dead and wounded (Levi 41–42, Langbein 201). Page references are to Levi, 'The Grey Zone' and Hermann Langbein, *People in Auschwitz*, trans. Harry Zohn (Chapel Hill, NC: University of North Carolina Press, 2004). The fact that Langbein also quotes Zalman Lewental describing the SK as a 'small group of grey people' (*kleine*

Gruppe grauer Leute) (Langbein 192) is also highly noteworthy. The adjective 'grey' is not in the Yiddish original and appears to have been added in the Auschwitz Museum's Polish translation, the basis for the German translation that Langbein used. See Danuta Czech and Jadwiga Bezwińska (eds), *Inmitten des grauenvollen Verbrechens: Handschriften von Mitgliedern des Sonderkommandos* (Oświęcim: Verlag staatliches Auschwitz-Museum, 1972).

14. Miklós Nyiszli, *Auschwitz: A Doctor's Eyewitness Account*, trans. Tibère Kremer and Richard Seaver. (London: Penguin, 2013), 42–43. See also Langbein, *People in Auschwitz*, 130. Myriam Anissimov seems to take Levi's references to Nyiszli as indirect, via Langbein (Anissimov, *Primo Levi*, 147), but some details come directly from Nyiszli's memoir. Friedrich Herber and Andreas Kilian are sceptical about an actual match taking place between members of the SK and the SS: 'The two- or four-man squad of SS-men was without exception involved as spectators' (Miklós Nyiszli, *Im Jenseits der Menschlichkeit: Ein Gerichtsmediziner in Auschwitz*, trans. Angelika Bihari, ed. Andreas Kilian and Friedrich Herber (Berlin: Karl Dietz, 2005), 171n60). However, Kevin E. Simpson found other examples in testimony of football matches at Auschwitz between prisoners and SS that served 'as sacraments of degradation and domination for the SS'. See *Soccer under the Swastika: Stories of Resistance and Survival* (Lanham, MD: Rowman and Littlefield, 2016), 143–45.
15. Nyiszli, *Auschwitz*, 80–84. See also Langbein, *People in Auschwitz*, 415. Herber and Kilian note that some other SK survivors talked of people who survived the gassing, only to be shot afterwards. Nyiszli, *Im Jenseits*, 175–76n84.
16. Catherine Mooney, 'The Ethics of the Gray Zone', in Arthur Chapman and Minna Vuohelainen (eds), *Interpreting Primo Levi: Interdisciplinary Perspectives* (London: Palgrave Macmillan, 2016), 31.
17. E.g. the information about the uprising is 'neither complete nor without contradictions' (41).
18. The way in which this story of the SK is fundamental to much imagining of them can be seen in its inclusion as one of the key facts about them at the beginning of both of the films *Son of Saul* and *The Grey Zone*.
19. See Friedrich and Kilian's remarks in Nyiszli, *Im Jenseits*, 167n39. See also Nicholas Chare and Dominic Williams, *Matters of Testimony: Interpreting the Scrolls of Auschwitz* (New York: Berghahn Books, 2016), 5–7; and Nicholas Chare and Dominic Williams, *The Auschwitz Sonderkommando: Testimonies, Histories, Representations* (Basingstoke: Palgrave Macmillan, 2019), 20n8.
20. The most famous moral thought experiment is probably the so-called 'trolley problem', introduced by Philippa Foot in 'The Problem of Abortion and the Doctrine of the Double Effect', in *Virtues and Vices and Other Essays in Moral Philosophy* (Oxford: Oxford University Press, 2002 [1967]), 19–32. Here the decisions of a tram driver on where to steer to minimize loss of life are, characteristically, expressed in certainties ('anyone on the track he enters is bound to be killed'). But even in its very first discussion, the simplified terms of this thought experiment are contrasted with 'real life', in which results 'would hardly ever be certain' (23).
21. Hayden White, *The Content of the Form: Narrative Discourse and Historical Representation* (Baltimore: Johns Hopkins University Press, 1987), 14.
22. Hilary Putnam, *The Collapse of the Fact/Value Dichotomy and Other Essays* (Cambridge, MA: Harvard University Press), 30–31.
23. Edith Wyschogrod, 'Representation, Narrative, and the Historian's Promise', in David Carr, Thomas R. Flynn and Rudolf A. Makkreel (eds), *The Ethics of History*

(Evanston, IL: Northwestern University Press, 2004), 28–44, at 28. For a more traditional idea of the historian's obligation to truth, see Allan Megill, 'Some Aspects of the Ethics of History Writing: Reflections on Edith Wyschogrod's *An Ethics of Remembering*', in Carr, Flynn and Makkreel (eds), *The Ethics of History*, 45–75.

24. Langbein, *People in Auschwitz*, 191–202.
25. Hermann Langbein, *Menschen in Auschwitz* (Vienna: Europaverlag, 1972), 227 (this passage was not included in any English translation); Katharina Stengel, *Hermann Langbein: Ein Auschwitz-Überlebender in den erinnerungspolitischen Konflikten der Nachkriegszeit* (Frankfurt: Campus Verlag, 2012), 558n254.
26. Although that was not the approach taken in *Matters of Testimony*, where we used video testimony from the same survivor, Yehuda Bacon, to provide some context for the sexual imagery in Zalman Gradowski's writing. Chare and Williams, *Matters of Testimony*, 80.
27. Langbein, *People in Auschwitz*, 194, translation amended (see *Menschen in Auschwitz*, 224–225). The original source is Krystyna Żywulska, *Przeżyłam Oświęcim* (Warsaw: tCHu, 2004 [1946]), 221. Langbein used the French translation, which edits out small parts of the original: *J'ai survécu à Auschwitz* (Warsaw: Editions Polonia, 1957), 233. Whittled away in the process of transmission was Żywulska's own response to the SK member's words: 'I was shocked. So those guys over there in the crematorium – they feel, they reflect, they are emotional?' (*także czują, rozmyślają, przeżywają?* – lit. 'they too feel, reflect, experience?'); *I Survived Auschwitz* (Warsaw: tCHu, 2004), 253. For a brief discussion of this moment, see Chapter 1 of Chare and Williams, *The Auschwitz Sonderkommando*.
28. In addition to English meanings of 'being/getting used to', I have in mind its equivalents in the range of languages passed through by Krystyna Żywulska's testimony to reach Levi's essay: Polish (*przyzwyczaić się*), French (*s'habituer*), German (*sich gewöhnen*) and Italian (*abituarsi*). The words are often linked to words that mean 'habit' (*zwyczaj, habitude, Gewohnheit, abitudine*) and sometimes with words that mean 'ordinary' (*zwyczajny, gewöhnlich*).
29. In a recent conversation about *Son of Saul*, Clara Royer said that Saul 'doesn't see, because he's used to it'. Royer, in conversation with Ludger Schwarte, *Telling, Describing, Extermination: The Sonderkommando and their Legacy*, Zentrum für Literatur- und Kulturforschung, Berlin, 13 April 2018, https://www.dailymotion.com/video/x6nnvgs (retrieved 13 January 2019).
30. '[S]lowly one becomes accustomed to phenomena that are out of this world, and there is nothing to write in the diary', Fela Szeps, quoted in Goldberg, *Trauma*, 14; 'one quickly grew accustomed [*gewöhnte man sich*] to all these strange images, which lose their horror through habit [*Gewohnheit*]'. Richard Ehrlich, quoted in Garbarini, *Numbered Days: Diaries in the Holocaust* (New Haven: Yale University Press, 2006), 117.
31. Goldberg, *Trauma*, 90.
32. Catherine Mooney, 'Reading "The Grey Zone" in the Testimonial Literature of the Holocaust', *Holocaust. Studii și cercetări* 1(10) (2017), 227–45, at 236.
33. Martha Nussbaum, *The Fragility of Goodness: Luck and Ethics in Greek Tragedy and Philosophy* updated edn (Cambridge: Cambridge University Press, 2001), 36; Ariel Meirav, 'Tragic Conflict and Greatness of Character', *Philosophy and Literature* 26(2) (2002), 260–72.
34. Mooney, 'Reading "The Grey Zone"', 237–40.
35. This is one register in which SK themselves wrote about themselves, for example Leyb Langfus in his account 'The 3000 Naked Women'. See Chare and Williams, *Matters of*

Testimony, 110–11; and Dominic Williams, 'The Dead are My Teachers: The Scrolls of Auschwitz in Jerome Rothenberg's *Khurbn*', in Nicholas Chare and Dominic Williams (eds), *Representing Auschwitz: At the Margins of Testimony* (Basingstoke: Palgrave Macmillian, 2013), 72–73. However, as the passages quoted at the end of this chapter show, it was by no means the only one.

36. Some of the testimonies of the SK can be read this way. Zalman Lewental in one passage describes the SK being like robots (*oytomatn*). Dario Gabbai in interview said: 'I said to myself I am a robot, and I [he touches his temples with his index fingers and twists his hands] I did just this [he repeats the gesture] to my mind'. See https://www.youtube.com/watch?v=ysz4zzGhMhE (retrieved 2 April 2019). In both cases, however, that is a description of the initial reaction to the shock of the work, before they might be said to have 'got used' to it.
37. Maurice Merleau-Ponty, *Phenomenology of Perception*, trans. Colin Smith (London: Routledge, 2002), 166.
38. One of Müller's examples of adaptation was that 'even when we were unhappy, we played football'. Transcript of *Shoah*, 96–97, modified from listening to the recording, https://collections.ushmm.org/film_findingaids/RG-60.5012_01_trs_de.pdf (retrieved 2 April 2019). Recording available at: https://collections.ushmm.org/search/catalog/irn1003921, 06:30:15–06:30:45 and 06:59:54–07:01:41
39. This possibility is completely foreclosed in Richard Seaver's English translation of Tibère Kremer's French translation, where Nyiszli says that he was 'going to attempt something that I knew without saying was doomed to failure' (Nyiszli, *Auschwitz*, 82). The Hungarian original simply makes use of a standard phrase for 'attempt the impossible', which, as in English, denotes extreme difficulty, not the total absence of any chance of success: 'Magam próbálom a lehetetlent is megkisérelni' (Miklós Nyiszli, *Dr Mengele boncolóorvosa voltam az auschwitzi krematóriumban* (Budapest: Magvető, 2016 [1947]), 199). This might be better translated as 'I myself was prepared to attempt even the impossible'. Thanks to András Lenart and Zsombor Hunyadi for translating and explaining the connotations of this sentence.
40. Inga Clendinnen, *Reading the Holocaust* (Cambridge: Cambridge University Press, 1999), 78. Mooney, 'Reading "The Grey Zone"', 240, 242.
41. Clendinnen, *Reading the Holocaust*, 73.
42. Card, *The Atrocity Paradigm*, 227.
43. Michael Rothberg, *Traumatic Realism: The Demands of Holocaust Representation* (Minneapolis: University of Minneapolis Press, 2000), 118–29.
44. See Andreas Kilian's chapter in this volume for an explanation of why the letter that had been attributed to Chaim Herman now needs to be attributed to Herman Strasfogel.
45. As Hannah Arendt put it, 'those who choose the lesser evil forget very quickly that they chose evil'. See Hannah Arendt, 'Personal Responsibility under Dictatorship', in *Responsibility and Judgement* (New York: Random House, 2003), 36. Compare Card, *The Atrocity Paradigm*, 223. See the Introduction to this volume for a discussion of how Arendt saw the moral status of the SK.
46. Arendt, *Responsibility and Judgement*, 44–45.

Bibliography

Anissimov, Myriam. *Primo Levi: Tragedy of an Optimist*, trans. Steve Cox. London: Aurum, 1998.
Arendt, Hannah. *Responsibility and Judgement*. New York: Random House, 2003.
Belpoliti, Marco, and Robert Gordon (eds). *The Voice of Memory: Primo Levi*, trans. Robert Gordon. Cambridge: Polity Press, 2001.
Brown, Adam. *Judging 'Privileged' Jews: Holocaust Ethics, Representation and the 'Grey Zone'*. New York: Berghahn Books, 2013.
Browning, Christopher. *Ordinary Men: Reserve Police Battalion 101 and the Final Solution in Poland*. London: Penguin, 2001.
Card, Claudia. *The Atrocity Paradigm: A Theory of Evil*. New York: Oxford University Press, 2002.
Chare, Nicholas, and Dominic Williams. *Matters of Testimony: Interpreting the Scrolls of Auschwitz*. New York: Berghahn Books, 2016.
———. *The Auschwitz Sonderkommando: Testimonies, Histories, Representations*. Basingstoke: Palgrave Macmillan, 2019.
Clendinnen, Inga. *Reading the Holocaust*. Cambridge: Cambridge University Press, 1999.
Craps, Stef. 'The Grey Zone – Extended Version'. Retrieved 1 April 2019 from https://www.academia.edu/27978486/The_Grey_Zone_extended_version_.
Foot, Philippa. 'The Problem of Abortion and the Doctrine of the Double Effect' (1967), in *Virtues and Vices and Other Essays in Moral Philosophy* (Oxford: Oxford University Press, 2002), 19–32.
Garbarini, Alexandra. *Numbered Days: Diaries in the Holocaust*. New Haven: Yale University Press, 2006.
Goldberg, Amos. *Trauma in First Person: Diary Writing during the Holocaust*, trans. Shmuel Sermoneta-Gertel and Avner Greenberg. Bloomington: Indiana University Press, 2017.
Gordon, Robert. '"Per mia fortuna . . .": Irony and Ethics in Primo Levi's Writing', *Modern Language Review*, 92(2) (1997), 337–47.
Insana, Lina N. *Arduous Tasks: Primo Levi, Translation and the Transmission of Holocaust Testimony*. Toronto: University of Toronto Press, 2009.
Lang, Berel. *Primo Levi: The Matter of a Life*. New Haven: Yale University Press, 2013.
Langbein, Hermann. *Menschen in Auschwitz*. Vienna: Europaverlag, 1972.
———. *People in Auschwitz*, trans. Harry Zohn. Chapel Hill, NC: University of North Carolina Press, 2004.
Lee, Sander H. 'Primo Levi's *Gray Zone*: Implications for Post-Holocaust Ethics', *Holocaust and Genocide Studies* 30(2) (Fall 2016), 276–97.
Levi, Primo. *I sommersi e i salvati*. Turin: Einaudi, 1986.
———. *The Drowned and the Saved*, trans. Raymond Rosenthal. London: Michael Joseph, 1988.
———. *The Complete Works of Primo Levi*, ed. Ann Goldstein. New York: Liveright, 2015.
Megill, Allan. 'Some Aspects of the Ethics of History Writing: Reflections on Edith Wyschogrod's *An Ethics of Remembering*', in David Carr, Thomas R. Flynn and Rudolf A. Makkreel (eds), *The Ethics of History*. Evanston, IL: Northwestern University Press, 2004, 45–75.
Meirav, Ariel. 'Tragic Conflict and Greatness of Character', *Philosophy and Literature* 26(2) (2002), 260–72.

Mengoni, Martina. 'The Rumkowski Variations: Up and Down the Trails of the Gray Zone'. Retrieved 1 April 2019 from http://www.primolevi.it/@api/deki/files/1202/=MAUSC_E00003.pdf.

Merleau-Ponty, Maurice. *Phenomenology of Perception*, trans. Colin Smith. London: Routledge, 2002.

Mesnard, Philippe (ed.). *La Zone grise: Entre accommodement et collaboration*. Paris: Kimé, 2010.

Mooney, Catherine. 'The Ethics of the Gray Zone', in Arthur Chapman and Minna Vuohelainen (eds), *Interpreting Primo Levi: Interdisciplinary Perspectives* (London: Palgrave Macmillan, 2016), 21–35.

——. 'Reading "The Grey Zone" in the Testimonial Literature of the Holocaust', *Holocaust. Studii și cercetări* 1(10) (2017), 227–45.

Nussbaum, Martha. *The Fragility of Goodness: Luck and Ethics in Greek Tragedy and Philosophy*, updated edn. Cambridge: Cambridge University Press, 2001.

Nyiszli, Miklós. *Im Jenseits der Menschlichkeit: Ein Gerichtsmediziner in Auschwitz*, trans. Angelika Bihari, ed. Andreas Kilian and Friedrich Herber. Berlin: Karl Dietz, 2005.

——. *Auschwitz: A Doctor's Eyewitness Account*, trans. Tibère Kremer and Richard Seaver. London: Penguin, 2013.

——. *Dr Mengele boncolóorvosa voltam az auschwitzi krematóriumban*. Budapest: Magvető, 2016 [1947].

Putnam, Hilary. *The Collapse of the Fact/Value Dichotomy and Other Essays*. Cambridge, MA: Harvard University Press.

Rothberg, Michael. *Traumatic Realism: The Demands of Holocaust Representation*. Minneapolis: University of Minneapolis Press, 2000.

Simpson, Kevin E. *Soccer under the Swastika: Stories of Resistance and Survival*. Lanham, MD: Rowman & Littlefield, 2016.

Stengel, Katharina. *Hermann Langbein: Ein Auschwitz-Überlebender in den erinnerungspolitischen Konflikten der Nachkriegszeit*. Frankfurt: Campus Verlag, 2012.

Thanassekos, Yannis. 'La zone grise, un concept problématique?', in Mesnard (ed.), *La Zone grise*, 15–20.

Thomson, Ian. *Primo Levi*. London: Hutchinson, 2002.

Todorov, Tzvetan. *Facing the Extreme: Moral Life in the Concentration Camps*, trans. Arthur Denner and Abigail Pollack. London: Weidenfeld & Nicolson, 1999.

White, Hayden. *The Content of the Form: Narrative Discourse and Historical Representation*. Baltimore: Johns Hopkins University Press, 1987.

Williams, Dominic. 'The Dead are My Teachers: The Scrolls of Auschwitz in Jerome Rothenberg's *Khurbn*', in Nicholas Chare and Dominic Williams (eds), *Representing Auschwitz: At the Margins of Testimony* (Basingstoke: Palgrave Macmillian, 2013), 58–84.

Wyschogrod, Edith. 'Representation, Narrative, and the Historian's Promise', in David Carr, Thomas R. Flynn and Rudolf A. Makkreel (eds), *The Ethics of History*. Evanston, IL: Northwestern University Press, 2004, 28–44.

Żywulska, Krystyna. *J'ai survécu à Auschwitz*. Warsaw, translator uncredited. Editions Polonia, 1957.

——. *I Survived Auschwitz*, trans. Krystyna Cenkalska, Lech Czerski and Sheila Callahan Warsaw: tCHu, 2004.

——. *Przeżyłam Oświęcim*. Warsaw: tCHu, 2004 [1946].

Part II

Witnessing from the Heart of Hell

Chapter 3

Farewell Letter from the Crematorium
On the Authorship of the First Recorded 'Sonderkommando-Manuscript' and the Discovery of the Original Letter

Andreas Kilian

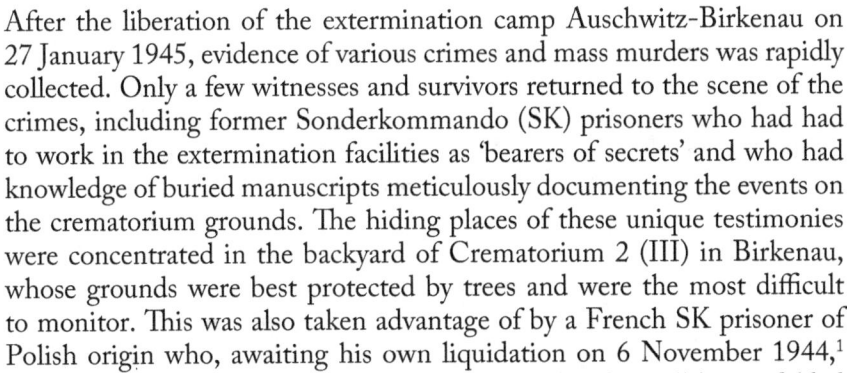

After the liberation of the extermination camp Auschwitz-Birkenau on 27 January 1945, evidence of various crimes and mass murders was rapidly collected. Only a few witnesses and survivors returned to the scene of the crimes, including former Sonderkommando (SK) prisoners who had had to work in the extermination facilities as 'bearers of secrets' and who had knowledge of buried manuscripts meticulously documenting the events on the crematorium grounds. The hiding places of these unique testimonies were concentrated in the backyard of Crematorium 2 (III) in Birkenau, whose grounds were best protected by trees and were the most difficult to monitor. This was also taken advantage of by a French SK prisoner of Polish origin who, awaiting his own liquidation on 6 November 1944,[1] wrote and left a moving eight-paged, double-sided farewell letter, folded in the middle, with his final greeting to his wife and daughter.

The writer of this letter, who signed it with his first name 'Herman', will in the following be consistently referred to as the 'author'. About two weeks after the liberation of the camp, a volunteer from Poland's Red Cross, Andrzej Zaorski, found the letter, which eventually made its way to Paris and led to a search of the recipient.[2] The efforts were not successful however, and the author could not be identified unambiguously. Authorship was attributed to a certain 'Mr. Herrmann', subsequently 'Chaim Herman' and to a 'Georges Bermann' at one point.[3]

The attribution to Chaim Herman was made between 1968 and 1970 by Jadwiga Bezwińska and Danuta Czech, two historians of the Auschwitz museum.⁴ They merely relied on the personal data in the deportation list of the 49th transport from Drancy, with which, according to his own information, the author arrived at Auschwitz. In the following, the reasons that speak against the authorship of Chaim Herman are examined and the essential arguments for the redetermination are named, which have finally been confirmed by information from family members and by the discovery of the original letter.

Correspondence from Birkenau

The author states at the beginning of his conspiratorial letter that he received a letter from his wife and daughter four months earlier, namely at the beginning of July, but had not had a chance to reply because of the high risk and danger. Writing home was forbidden for SK members as 'bearers of secrets' in principle and they were generally excluded from a postcard initiative commanded by the SS.⁵ A recent find, however, proves that in exceptional cases SK prisoners from France took part in the prescribed official correspondence and were able to send at least one sign of life back home.

Chaim Herman did send a postcard to his prior address in Paris, which arrived on 12 October 1943.⁶ Postcards were knowingly gathered by the administration of the camp and sent out collectively, which means the actual date could be earlier.⁷ Many senders were no longer alive at the time of arrival. The sender's address was 'House 17a' in 'Birkenau', which was obviously misleading information as the number indicated that Chaim Herman was living in the main camp in Auschwitz (an 'a' was added to the number for the first floor of its two-storeyed buildings). In Chaim Herman's case, it can be assumed that he was not a member of the SK when he wrote his postcard. This assumption may be supported by two cases of SK inmates, whose postcards, presumably from a time before being transferred to the SK, are preserved: Filip Müller used the address 'House 11' in Birkenau and was housed in the main camp, and David Olère, who had sent two postcards that arrived on 12 October and 29 November 1943.⁸ It can be presumed that Olère was housed and working in a satellite camp in Neu-Dachs in Jaworzno at least until 20 August 1943.⁹ While it is unknown when exactly he was transferred to the SK in Birkenau, he might have written his cards during the postcard campaign in July 1943, when he was deployed in the satellite camp. However, two postcards from Hersz Strasfogel, written while he was in the SK, arrived in Paris on 18 October 1943 and 27 March 1944. They were answered by four letters in the period from 18 January to 20 May 1944.¹⁰

Transfer to the Sonderkommando

In contrast to Müller and Olère, there is neither evidence nor testimony for Chaim Herman's forced labour in the SK. The author's statement that one hundred men on his transport (i.e. apparently all the men taken into the camp) had been transferred into the SK the next morning is not borne out by other evidence. At least eight men that survived transport no. 49 from Drancy were not members of the SK.[11] Moreover, records of the camp administration, preserved at the Auschwitz-Birkenau state museum, show that not every man could have been sent immediately or even at all to the SK. Some men were deployed in other work detachments or were delivered to the mortuary of the main camp.[12]

State of Health

Chaim Herman's postcard reached Paris in the middle of October 1943 – seven months after his deportation to Auschwitz. It is unknown whether he was still alive at the time of its arrival; his chance of survival was low, however, because of his poor state of health. This is proven by a document kept in Drancy that listed all interned Jews that suffered from oedema and were suggested to be released. This document shows that Chaim Herman was indeed released 11 weeks after internment in Drancy on 4 November 1941, before being imprisoned again on 21 February 1943 and being deported to Auschwitz on 2 March 1943.[13] The only sign of life of Chaim Herman in Auschwitz is one entry in the record book of the X-ray station four months after his arrival, on 3 July 1943.[14] It supplies his prisoner number and the diagnosis of an incurable respiratory disease, scarred respiratory tracts, that can lead to death if not treated. The diagnosis did not permit a long life expectancy under inhuman camp conditions, nor is it consistent with the contents of the crematorium letter: 'My physical suffering ended in September 1943 . . . I am in perfect health'.[15]

Family Status and Employment

The letter from the crematorium is addressed to the author's wife and daughter. While the name of the wife is not stated, his beloved daughter Simone is named many times. At the beginning of the letter, he suggests getting together with a producer of knitted goods to safeguard their future. He regrets that he has not left much to them materially. This statement seems to indicate the author's own occupation. According to his Internment card of the camp at Drancy, Chaim Herman was not married and had no children. Moreover, he was employed as a dental technician.[16]

Verified Names and Witnesses from the Sonderkommando

The only five known, verified names from the reports of (former) SK prisoners that were also listed on the deportation list from Drancy are: Josef Dorembus, Jankiel Handelsman, David Lahana, David Olère and Hersz Strasfogel, with the last being named by the Greek SK survivors Leon Cohen and Marcel Nadjary, who were friends with Strasfogel.[17] In Leon Cohen's book, Strasfogel is described as the 'Parisian industrialist'.[18] The author of the letter writes that he was friends with David Lahana, a manufacturer and merchant of fur goods, and sharing the fate of Leon Cohen, whom he therefore also knew well.

The author's family details cannot be reconciled with the history of Dorembus and Handelsman, who died during the uprising of the SK before the letter was written. Both were deported with their wives, who were killed in Auschwitz-Birkenau. Furthermore, Josef and Pola (Pesa) Dorembus only had one son, Marcel, who was born in Paris on 20 April 1938, survived the German occupation and later committed suicide in the 1960s.[19] Hersz Strasfogel was deported to Auschwitz together with his older cousin Izak Strasfogel. Olère was deported alone, but did not have a daughter. He had a son, Alexandre, born in 1930, whom he left together with his wife.[20] Lahana's death is recorded in the letter; his sons, Marcel and Albert, born in 1938, survived in Toulouse.[21]

The author states that he was 'one of the oldest' inmates in the SK. Amongst the known deportees of transport no. 49, Hersz Strasfogel, almost forty-nine years old (born in 1895), was the oldest; Chaim Herman was five-and-a-half years younger.

Crucial Indications in the Letter

The author mentions that among the SK comrades was a cousin of the father 'of our Figlarz'. In 2011, the Memorial de la Shoah in Paris received a collection of family photos from Charles Figlarz, amongst them a portrait of Hersz Strasfogel.[22] According to Figlarz, Strasfogel, who was born on 16 December 1895, was his uncle. When asked about the name of Strasfogel's daughter, Figlarz promptly replied 'Simone', the same name mentioned six times in the letter from the crematorium.[23] Simone (Sima) was born on 21 January 1927 in Vilna. Her mother was Chiona Strasfogel (née Winicka in Grodno, 1898).[24] Chiona and Hersz were married in Warsaw on 10 July 1920 and took up permanent residence in Paris on 5 March 1930. Simone's daughter later confirmed that her brother Laurent possessed a letter from Birkenau.[25] Her grandfather and his wife produced knitted goods, which may explain some hints in the letter and which explains calling Strasfogel the 'industrialist' by Cohen.[26] Monsieur Vanhems, also mentioned in the letter as taking care of Simone, was the addressee of Hersz Strasfogel's postcards from Birkenau. His apartment was in the neighbouring street only three minutes away from Strasfogel's apartment and atelier.

Signature and Name Specification

The author signed his farewell letter to his wife and daughter twice with 'Herman', once at the end of the letter and once in the postscript at the left and lower margin. Everything indicates that the author had signed with his first name, but not with his last name. Historians of the Auschwitz museum checked in the late 1960s every name on the deportation list and found four men with the name 'Herman(n)': two Germans and one Ukrainian, aged sixty-three to seventy-four, and one of unknown nationality, aged forty-three.[27] They chose the youngest one, despite it being unlikely to sign a letter to your loved ones with your last name. Moreover, they neglected the possibility of naturalized names. Some of the deported Jews from Drancy had naturalized first names, which were not always included in the administrative files or had been concealed by the Jews themselves when they were registered.

Strasfogel provides a perfect example of this: there is a grave at Bagneux cemetery in Paris commemorating the 'family members who perished during deportation in 1942–1945', with 'Herman Strasfogel' being one of them. Next to the name is a photograph of a slender man that resembles Hersz Strasfogel's portrait in Figlarz's collection. The age of the person at the time of death '49', which matches that of Hersz Strasfogel. The granddaughter finally confirmed that Hersz was using the naturalized name 'Herman', who was falsely recorded as 'Heinz' in a list of names from Drancy,[28] and that his memorial place is indeed in Bagneaux. Consequently, Strasfogel was the one signing the farewell letter from the crematorium with the name 'Herman'.

The Address and the Search for Family Members

How and when the letter signed with 'Herman' came into the possession of the family was made known for the first time at the official presentation of the original letter to the Mémorial de la Shoah in Paris. A memorandum states that the letter was handed over to Strasfogel's daughter on 2 March 1948.[29] According to the grandchildren, however, the author's daughter found the letter within the estate of her late mother.[30] Zaorski's statement that the family's address inside the letter was 'in France' does not fit with the surviving manuscript.[31] On the current outermost page is actually written in French as well in Russian (with the same handwriting):

> Prayer of a dying person to deliver this letter to the Consulate of France or to the International Red Cross to forward it to the address given. Thank you.

However, according to a letter from the Ministry of Former Veterans and War Victims, dated 5 February 1948, the following note was also written on another sheet of paper (now apparently lost): 'To Mister VANHEMS, 16 rue du Grand Prieuré, PARIS XIe, to deliver to Madam or Miss Simone'. For security reasons, the author only gave the address of his friend Vanhems.[32]

The addressee then appears to have informed the wife or daughter of Strasfogel. The memories of the visit of former comrade Leon Cohen with the Strasfogels during his stay in Paris in 1946 prove that the letter had not reached the addressee at this point in time.[33] Cohen does not mention the letter in connection with Hersz Strasfogel.[34] Moreover, the transcript of the letter was printed as a shortened, one-paged version in February 1948 in the bulletin 'Après Auschwitz' of 'L'amicale des anciens déportés d'Auschwitz' in order to find relatives. In the introduction of the published version, it says:

> In the following we are publishing a copy of a letter that was just sent to us by the Department of Veterans Affairs ... The investigation conducted by the Department to find Family Hermann and the named persons has been unsuccessful to date. We are thankful for everyone helping with the investigation and inform us as soon as possible.[35]

Just after his return from the United States in 1953, Cohen learned by June 1955 in Saloniki about the printed version of a letter written in the crematorium in the bulletin 'Après Auschwitz' and only via third parties about his own name in the hidden letter. He did, however, write about it as 'my farewell letter' apparently without knowing that the letter was written by his friend Strasfogel.[36]

The Discovery of the Original Letter

In parallel to the discovery of the true author on the basis of thorough analyses of all available sources, the original letter, which had been lost until then, was found in Paris and finally handed over by the author's grandchildren to the archives of the Museum Mémorial de la Shoah on 7 October 2018.[37] The original letter featured in a four-minute television report on France 2 on 27 January 2019 and presented to the public for the first time in excerpts at the Mémorial de la Shoah on 10 March 2019 at an event attended by numerous members of Hersz Strasfogel's family.[38]

The main contents of the letter are now understood for the first time thanks to new biographical background information. Understanding errors in the transcription can be proven by the original. The original can be used to refute misinterpretations of the document and complete missing parts, such as the missing cover text and the dual signature.[39] Ultimately, the mystery about the author and several people mentioned in the letter can be solved. The farewell letter was confirmed as an authentic testimony and document that proves the mass murders in Auschwitz-Birkenau and the humanity of the author, which is also expressed in the indestructible love for his family.

Andreas Kilian is a historian and former staff member at the International Youth Meeting House Auschwitz and the Claims Conference Forced Laborer Fund. He has been researching the history of the Jewish Sonderkommandos in Auschwitz since 1992 and is a board member of the German 'Lagergemeinschaft Auschwitz' (Auschwitz Camp Community). He is the author and editor of numerous publications on the Sonderkommando Auschwitz, including the first SK monograph *Zeugen aus der Todeszone* (*Witnesses from the Death Zone*, with Eric Friedler and Barbara Siebert, 2002) and the newly edited memoir from Miklós Nyiszli entitled *Im Jenseits der Menschlichkeit* (*Beyond Humanity*, edited by Friedrich Herber, 2005). He is scientific advisor of the first TV documentary on the history of the SK, *Sklaven der Gaskammer* (*Slaves of the Gas Chamber*, dir. Eric Friedler, 2000), founder of the internet portal www.sonderkommando-studien.de (2003), and also wrote essays for the latest editions of Marcel Nadjari's and Filip Müller's memoirs (in Greek and Czech respectively, 2018).

Notes

1. In fact, on that day, the work detachment from Crematorium 2 (III) was transferred to the men's camp in Birkenau. The liquidation took place about three weeks later.
2. APMA-B, statement A. Zaorski from 11 March 1971, statements collection, ed. 70, 212–13. Certificate of service in Auschwitz of Andrzej Zaorski, APMAB Bd. XXIV, micro film no. 1358/114.
3. For the edition history and development of the name attribution, see Andreas Kilian, 'Abschiedsbrief aus dem Krematorium: das verschollene Original und sein anonymer Verfasser. Zur Autorschaft des ersten überlieferten Sonderkommando-Manuskripts', *Mitteilungsblatt der Lagergemeinschaft Auschwitz, Freundeskreis der Auschwitzer* 38(1) (2018), 5–21. In November 2015, the intensive search for the original letter began, during which the authorship of Chaim Herman became questionable.
4. Transcript of the 'Herman'-letter, APMAB Bd. XXIV, Bl. 91, D-RO/147 sent from Paris on 6 December 1967 by the 'Amicale des déportés d'Auschwitz et des camps de Haute-Silésie' to the Auschwitz Museum. Correspondence with the Deputy Head of Archive of the Auschwitz-Birkenau State Museum, Szymon Kowalski, from 18 December 2018. The first publication of 'Chaim Herman's' letter in Poland was prepared for print in October 1970: *Wśród koszmarnej zbrodni: Rękopisy członków Sonderkommando, Zeszyty Oświęcimskie* 2 (1971), 175–84.
5. Several similar initiatives were forced on Jewish prisoners from 1942 to 1944. The content has been specified and was used to calm the public. See also the secret message by Stanisław Kłodziński from 20 June 1943 in Andrea Rudorff (ed.), *Das KZ Auschwitz 1942–1945 und die Zeit der Todesmärsche 1944/45* (Berlin: de Gruyter, 2018), 266 and 279.
6. Mailing list card of Chaim Herman, correspondence no. 1154 to his neighbour, Service historique de la defense, DAVCC, Caen.
7. Secret message by Kłodziński from 14 July 1943 in Rudorff, *Auschwitz*, 279: 'On July 13 all Jews were ordered to write home, with the exception of the Greek and the Polish. They were ordered to ask for food and to write that they were healthy and well. They wrote and gave as their address the labour camp Birkenau, Post Neu Berun'.
8. The postcard (12.IX.1942) was purposely not sent to relatives but to neighbours in Sered; Müller estate. Witness report Filip Müller (n.d, n.p.), Austrian state archive, Vienna, estate Hermann Langbein, E/1797, folder 49, 1 and 13. Mailing list card David Olère, correspondence no. 1218 and 3143, Service historique de la defense, DAVCC, Caen. However, a recent archive find suggests that during the letter campaign in July 1943, French prisoners in the SK also received permission to write postcards as an exception. Hersz Strasfogel demonstrably sent two postcards from Birkenau – one of them self-dated July 1943 – which arrived in Paris in October 1943 and March 1944. He sent his first postcard to a man named Goldberg in Paris. The receipt of apparently the reply to his postcard from March – presumably from his wife – was confirmed in July 1944 by him. Mailing list card Hersz Strasfogel, Service historique de la defense, DAVCC, Caen.
9. Record of work shifts of inmates in Neu Dachs, August 1943, APMAB, folder Jaworzno, Bd. I, Bl. 189–90. The satellite camp was opened in mid June 1943. Olère is listed by his camp number, not by his name. It must be stated that the documented

number 106144 had been corrected by the writer: the number '5' was changed into a '6' or written so misleadingly that it looked like a '6' and was clarified again to a '5'.
10. Mailing list card of Hersz Strasfogel, correspondence no. 1771 and 3886 to M. Vanhems, 16 rue du Grand Prieuré in Paris, Service historique de la defense, DAVCC, Caen.
11. In the late 1970s, four names were known. See Serge Klarsfeld (ed.), *Le Memorial de la déportation des Juifs de France* (Paris: Éditions Klarsfeld, 1978), n.p. By 2018, it was nine (including Olere): Pejsach Bajnwelzweig, Rubin Bruder, Chaim Hausman, Mazal Leonoff, Bernard Melman, Simon Neumann, Noé Nysenbaum and Rachmil Szulklaper. Correspondence with S. Klarsfeld from 20 October 2018.
12. APMAB, 'Drancy-49-m-1943-03-04 106088 – 106187', list of Krystyna Lesniak, Biuro ds. Byłych Więźniów, from 1 June 2018. In addition to the eight known survivors, there were at least twenty-four other men.
13. List from 2 November 1941, SHD/Caen AC 27P 93, LA 15518 (at 672). Chaim Herman's name was marked 'released on 4/11/1941' and crossed out (Rudorff, *Auschwitz*, 505n2).
14. APMAB, record books of the camp hospital X-ray station (VII. Röntgen-Station 22.VI.-19.VII.43), Bd. 14, Bl. 39.
15. Doc. 152, letter by Chaim Herman, in: Rudorff, *Auschwitz*, 507. By 'physical pain' the author refers to hunger; diseases are not mentioned.
16. Record of internment in camp Drancy of Chaim Herman, Fichiers de la Préfecture de police de la Seine et des camps de Drancy, Pithiviers et Beaune-la-Rolande (1940–45), Archives Nationales, MIC/F/9/5700/3. Rudorff, *Auschwitz*, 505n2.
17. Marcel Nadjary, *Manuscripts 1944–1947: From Thessaloniki to the Sonderkommando of Auschwitz* (Athens: Alexandria, 2018) (in Greek), 77.
18. Leon Cohen, *From Greece to Birkenau: The Crematoria Workers Uprising* (Athens: Kyanavgi, 2017), 124.
19. Email from M. Dorembus, 2 September 2018.
20. Email from A. Oler, 20 October 2004
21. Email from M. Lahana, 24 August 2018. M. Lahana clarified misconceptions concerning statements of the author about Family Lahana and Babani.
22. C.D.J.C., Coll. Charles Figlarz, MXII_10219, portrait from the 1930s, http://bdi.memorialdelashoah.org/internet/jsp/media/MmsMediaDetailPopup.jsp?mediaid=1161360 (retrieved 2 April 2019). Charles Figlarz was born in 1933 to Hersz's sister Chaja (1907–1991) in Paris.
23. Phone conversation with Charles Figlarz on 19 August 2018.
24. Email from C. Figlarz, 26 August 2018 and 4 September 2018. Simone got married in 1949, bore three children in 1951 and 1955, and died on 25 January 2017.
25. Phone conversation with Beatrice Muntlak (granddaughter of Hersz Strasfogel), on 4 September 2018. However, she did not remember the exact content and date of the letter.
26. Phone conversation with B. Muntlak on 8 October 2018.
27. List of deportation no. 49, B.d.S. France, 2 March 1943, 1.1.9.1 / 11182649/ ITS Digital Archive, Bad Arolsen.
28. List of names in Drancy, departure 2 March 1943, at 49, 1.1.9.9/ 11189489/ ITS Digital Archive, Bad Arolsen.
29. Alain Alexandra, Lecture at Mémorial de la Shoah, Paris 10 March 2019.
30. Phone conversation with B. Muntlak on 8 October 2018.

31. APMA-B, report A. Zaorski from 11 March 1971, collection statements, ed. 70, Bl. 212.
32. Cover letter Vanhems, file Hersz Strasfogel, EC 24.695, 21P 541 247, Service historique de la defense, DAVCC, Caen.
33. Email from J. Cohen, 22 August 2018. His father supposedly stayed in Paris from the spring of 1946 to January 1947 at the latest.
34. Interview with Leon Cohen, in Gideon Greif, *We Wept without Tears: Testimonies of the Jewish Sonderkommando from Auschwitz* (New Haven: Yale University Press, 2005), 304; Cohen, *From Greece to Birkenau*, 124, 131. A few months before his death in August 1989, Cohen states in an unpublished film interview with Gideon Greif (dir. Charles Tudor) that the letter was written by a French doctor from a transport gassed in the crematorium.
35. Bulletin 'Après Auschwitz', No. 19 (January/February 1948), 2.
36. The message was sent to his father-in-law Yehoshua Perahia in Saloniki, who died on 1 June 1955. Cohen, *From Greece to Birkenau*, 131. Cohen allegedly never saw the article in the bulletin.
37. Phone conversation with B. Muntlak on 8 October 2018. It was revealed that after the widow's death in 1997, her daughter sent copies of the letter and a photograph of the author to the Mémorial de la Shoah in 2002 with the intention of immortalizing her father's name on its memorial wall and confirming him as a victim of the Shoah. On 28 July 2003, the state secretary of veteran's affairs officially determined Strasfogel's date of death to be 'November 1944'. A colour copy of the letter disappeared in the archive of the Mémorial and was only registered as a 'letter from Birkenau' until found by the head of the archive Karen Taïeb in April 2018. After several weeks of absolute secrecy, she found the grandson of the author in Paris, who had not known anything about the distribution of the transcript and significance of the letter. It took several more months of secrecy until the family members decided on 7 October 2018 to make the original of the letter available for research and a planned exhibition. Phone conversation with Karen Taïeb on 8 October 2018.
38. A recording of the event is available at https://www.youtube.com/watch?v=vcomPqVg_rs (retrieved 20 May 2019).
39. E.g. Zaorski's assertion of the inclusion of an address to the Polish Red Cross as well as of bank orders left behind; in most editions, it states that it is the land of France that must be nourished, but in the original letter, it is written that it is the place to die (e.g. Ber Mark, *Des voix dans la nuit* (Paris: Plon, 1982), 326); Sonja Knopp suspects that the author had fled Poland with his family while fleeing from the Nazis ('*Wir lebten mitten im Tod*' (Frankfurt am Main: Peter Lang, 2009), 63); Pavel Polian assumes that the letter was not written until 26 November 1944 (mistranscribed date) (Pavel Polian, *Svitki iz pepla* (Moscow: Feniks, 2015) (in Russian), 478); Andrea Rudorff, writes of a brother-in-law of Lahana called Babani, but in the original, the brothers-in-law and brothers 'Babini' (two) are mentioned (Rudorff, *Auschwitz*, 508).

Bibliography

Cohen, Leon. *From Greece to Birkenau: The Crematoria Workers Uprising*. Athens: Kyanavgi, 2017.

Greif, Gideon. *We Wept without Tears: Testimonies of the Jewish Sonderkommando from Auschwitz*. New Haven: Yale University Press, 2005.

Herman, Chaim. [Herman Strasfogel]. 'Rękopis Chaima Hermana', *Wśród koszmarnej zbrodni: Rękopisy członków Sonderkommando. Zeszyty Oświęcimskie* 2 (1971), 175–84.

Kilian, Andreas. 'Abschiedsbrief aus dem Krematorium: das verschollene Original und sein anonymer Verfasser: Zur Autorenschaft des ersten überlieferten Sonderkommando-Manuskripts', *Mitteilungsblatt der Lagergemeinschaft Auschwitz, Freundeskreis der Auschwitzer* 38(1) (2018), 5–21.

Klarsfeld, Serge (ed.). *Le Mémorial de la déportation des Juifs de France*, Paris: Éditions Klarsfeld, 1978.

Knopp. Sonja. *'Wir lebten mitten im Tod': Das Sonderkommando in Auschwitz in schriftlichen und mündlichen Häftlingserinnerungen*. Frankfurt am Main: Peter Lang, 2009.

Mark, Ber. *Des voix dans la nuit: La résistance juive à Auschwitz*. Paris: Plon, 1982.

Nadjary, Marcel. *Manuscripts 1944–1947: From Thessaloniki to the Sonderkommando of Auschwitz*. Athens: Alexandria, 2018.

Polian, Pavel. *Svitki iz pepla: Evreĭskai͡a 'zonderkommando' v Aushvit͡se-Birkenau i ee letopist͡sy*. Moscow: Feniks, 2015.

Rudorff, Andrea (ed.). *Das KZ Auschwitz 1942–1945 und die Zeit der Todesmärsche 1944/45*. Berlin: de Gruyter, 2018.

Chapter 4

To Read the Illegible

Techniques of Multispectral Imaging and the Manuscripts of the Jewish Sonderkommando of Auschwitz-Birkenau

Pavel Polian and Aleksandr Nikityaev

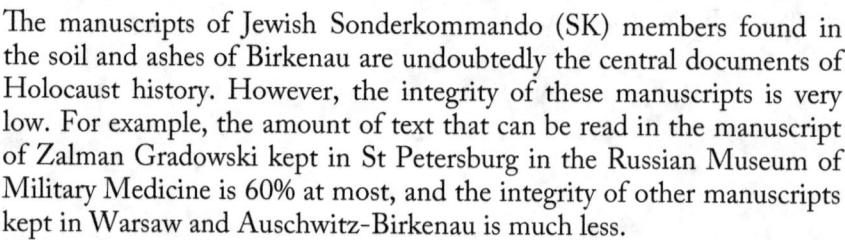

The manuscripts of Jewish Sonderkommando (SK) members found in the soil and ashes of Birkenau are undoubtedly the central documents of Holocaust history. However, the integrity of these manuscripts is very low. For example, the amount of text that can be read in the manuscript of Zalman Gradowski kept in St Petersburg in the Russian Museum of Military Medicine is 60% at most, and the integrity of other manuscripts kept in Warsaw and Auschwitz-Birkenau is much less.

At the same time, the application of state-of-the-art technologies and capabilities allows a noticeable gain in the readable content. Careful and skilled application of these technologies to the manuscripts of SK members would allow us to read for the first time the fragments that have not yet been deciphered, or at least significant part of these fragments. Unfortunately, the availability of specialized expensive hardware is not widespread in museums or archives. The corresponding skills are equally rare among archivists, historians and/or museum technicians.

However, using a regular desktop computer and image processing software, one can try to read scanned images of the damaged documents independently and at low cost. We received digital copies of the manuscript of Marcel Nadjary from the Auschwitz museum in early 2000. We used Adobe Photoshop CC software to handle the manuscript images. As a rule, any image processing begins with correcting its levels. The correction of levels is the most popular and primary processing not only of scanned documents, but of any images, as it allows you to bring up a representation of the image on the monitor and see the maximum number of details in terms of brightness. But in view of the successful reading of the illegible manuscripts, the most important point at this stage is to resist the temptation to make the image look visually good by overshooting the parameters of the levels filter, as it is very easy to cut off the boundary values of highlights and shadows that always convey necessary information that we still have to work with.

Computer monitors reproduce colour using the RGB (Red, Green and Blue) colour model, working as reproducing colours based on the combination of the three main colours listed above. Looking at Nadjary's manuscript in each individual colour channel, we noticed at once that in the red channel we could see the text, sometimes quite legibly. However, there is less text in the green channel and no text in the blue channel. This happens because various types of paper and ink have specific physiochemical properties that behave differently when illuminated by the light of different wavelengths. For light with a wavelength of 450 nm (which corresponds to the colour blue), the ink is quite indiscernible. For light with a wavelength of 750 nm (which corresponds to red light), the ink is at its maximum contrast to the paper. So the trend is that legibility grows from blue to red.

Working with the colour scanned images, we can try to see what happens to the text if we adjust the colour of each of seven main colours. Using Black&White filter, we can try to make the ink darker and the colour of the paper lighter. The parameters of this filter are adjusted "manually", i.e. visually. Legibility became better.

The nonuniformity of the manuscript brightness is the next problem. Dark spots prevented reading individual letters. To compensate for this, we used HighPass filter that could equalize these brightness gradients.

To compensate for leaked ink, we had to flip (mirror transform) the second folio and set its transparency at 50 per cent. Then we had to transform the layer to compensate for rotation angles. Next we had to invert its colours and apply the Gaussian Blur filter to get the effect of a natural spread of ink (a HighPass filter may also be applied here). As a result, the manuscript became much more legible in Black and white filter. For example, we found that the first page has a message in several languages concerning the importance of the text and to whom it should be given if found. This could not be read without the processing described above.

The following pretty simple algorithm of actions summarizes what we did:

Step 1: the correction (restoration of initial values) of levels in the digital file of the manuscript (Levels filter) as scanners tend to visually adjust balance to match the colours of scanned document.

Step 2: a channel-wise visual examination of the image to ascertain best contrast of signal and noise (as a rule in the red channel). The exposure and contrast of the initial image should be changed if the details are not highlighted by the Black&White filter (Photoshop CC).

Step 3: noise compensation. We compensated for defects of manuscript, e.g. ink leaked through from the other side.

As a result of this algorithm application, the whole text or its part, though being of low contrast, became more discernible.

The processing of the available low-quality trial scans of Marcel Nadjary's manuscript demonstrated obvious gains in legibility. In the case of Nadjary's manuscript, due to the application of MSI algorithm we had amazing success (see Table 4.1). From twelve pages of initial scans of which a third were completely illegible, they are all readable, so the gain of material was 100%. The total amount of text readable for the first time increased by a factor of four. The total amount of readable text increased by a factor of three, and the total share of readable text (rough visual estimate) was at least 80–85% of the total amount. New high-quality scanning of these pages and application of special hardware can confidently increase this share of read text to 95%.

Table 4.1 Gain of read text (in pages) of Marcel Nadjary's manuscript (characters and percentage).

# of page	Earlier read	Read for the first time	Total	Read for the first time, %
1	155	0	155	0
2	392	380	772	49
3	205	502	707	71
4	0	596	596	100
5	38	937	975	96
6	0	699	699	100
7	8	593	603	98
8	164	493	657	75
9	0	703	703	100
10	388	602	990	60
11	0	261	261	100
12	190	264	454	58
Total	1,540	6,030	7,570	75

Reading the fragments of Marcel Nadjary's manuscript not only allowed us to clarify the very vague content of one of central documents of the Holocaust, but also makes it possible to relate it to another manuscript by Nadjary and to gain a much more profound understanding of the author and Jews from Greece, their fate in the Holocaust, and their role in the life and death of the Jewish SK of Auschwitz-Birkenau.

Reading the unread in manuscripts of SK members is of tremendous interest in terms of history and culture research. Sooner or later, the barriers in this way will be overcome, but the more years wasted, the less will be the effect of the application of technologies. These manuscripts should be scanned again, ideally to multispectral imaging. The first phase of this project would involve processing the already-available scanned material. The second phase would rely on the application of more advanced techniques and state-of-the-art hardware for taking photos or scanning of original materials. It would be better to perform this after the completion of the first phase and analysis of its results.

Pavel Markovich Polian is a Russian geographer, historian and philologist (under the pen-name Nerler). He is Professor and Director of the Mandelstam-Center at the Higher School of Economics, Moscow, Senior Researcher at the Institute of Geography of the Russian Academy of Sciences and Professor of the North-Caucasus Federal University (former Stavropol State University), former Visiting Professor at the Universities of Freiburg, Cologne, Hanover and Konstanz, and fellow of the A. v. Humboldt Foundation, the Fullbright Foundation, the Kennan Institute, Princeton University, the United States Holocaust Memorial Museum, the Maison de Sciences de l'Homme, Paris and Manchester University. He is the author of more than 800 different publications, including forty books. Among them are *Between Auschwitz and Babyj Jar: Reflections and Investigations on the Shoah* (2010); *Zalman Gradovsky, in the Midst of Hell: Notes Found in the Ashes Near the Furnaces of Auschwitz* (2010; in English, 2015); *Scrolls from the Ash: Victims and Torture of Auschwitz* (2013); *Historycide, or Trepanation of Memory: Battles for the Truth about GULAG, Deportations, War and Holocaust* (2016); and *Geographical Arabesques: Spaces of Inspiration, Freedom and Non-freedom* (2017).

Aleksandr Nikityaev is a front-end web developer and user interface designer. He has experience working in web development, web design, image retouching, 3D graphics, magazine advertisement design, motion design, technical writing, system administration, automated retailing and point-of-sale hardware.

Chapter 5

'Like a True Greek'
The Last Will and Testament of Marcel Natzari

K.E. Fleming

The twelve-page letter penned in Birkenau by Emmanouil Natzaris/Marcel Natzari, one of the last survivors of the Sonderkommando (SK), in what he thought were his last days of life, is many things. First, it is just that – a letter, a letter to his best friend Dimitrios Athanasios Stephanides, nicknamed Misko. It is also a group letter to all of his closest friends – to Smaro Efraimidou of Athens, who had brought him packages of food as he languished in the Haidari concentration camp before being deported, the memory of whose kindness had sustained him during the months after deportation (Natzari's family had been deported from Thessaloniki; he himself had been deported from Athens some many months later). It is the letter of a young man in his mid twenties to his 'beloved' hometown 'paréa', the 'gang' or 'company' of which Natzari had been a part back in Thessaloniki: his cousin Ilias Cohen, his friend Giorgios Gounaris, Misko. At one level, it is a missive of the sort anyone might write to far-away, longed-for friends back home after isolating months away. As we read its opening sentences, we can imagine its author calling to mind the faces of his far-off, beloved pals, feverishly writing to tell them how much he misses them and how often he has thought of them over the course of the months in foreign lands.

But the feverishness derives of course from the fact that the document is far more than a letter written by a homesick lad abroad. It is also a last will and testament – as Natzari says in his closing line: 'This is my last wish'. It is the document of a dying man in his final days, who wishes to direct his reader as to the disposition of his personal effects: 'The property of my family I entrust to you, Misko'. And a few pages later: 'Misko, take my Nelli's piano from the Sionidou family and give it to [my cousin] Ilias . . . he loved her so much . . .' As Greek Jewish families were rounded up in Thessaloniki and forced into the Baron Hirsch Ghetto, the Nazi transit camp, many of them gave their possessions to Greek Christian families for safekeeping until their hoped-for 'return'. Evidently, the Sionidous had gotten the Natzari family piano – and now that Natzari realized there would be no one going home to claim it, he wanted to make sure it went to his cousin (in other instances, Greek Christian families swooped in to newly uninhabited Jewish homes, looting them. The disposition of Greek Jewish property after the war remains an open saga in Thessaloniki to this day).

At the same time, the letter is the deposition of an eyewitness to the greatest organized genocidal crime in history. It describes the camp, the Nazi gas chambers and the crematoria; it tells with haunting detail of the special, evil cans of Zyklon B gas brought to the chambers in a decoy Red Cross car, driven by two members of the SS. In stunningly straightforward language, it narrates to the reader an apparatus of death that by now has become familiar to us over the elapsed decades, over the course of so many tellings and retellings, after the filmic reconstructions and the videotaped testimonies. But at the time that Natzari was writing his letter, in the final days of the war, the things it recounted were unknown and unimaginable to the outside world. It limns the buildings of Auschwitz-Birkenau, the literal architecture of annihilation. Most jarringly, it is largely written in the *present* tense; unlike the Auschwitz interviews we all have seen, the descriptions with which we have become familiar, it doesn't bear witness to something that *happened*. It describes something that Natzari sees in real time, before his own very eyes:

> Under a garden there are two large underground chambers of enormous size. The one is used for undressing and the other as a chamber of death, where people go in naked and once it is filled with about 3000 people, it is closed up and they gas them, where after 6 to 7 minutes of agony, they give up the ghost.

Natzari's acute awareness of his own role as witness – as one of the few who could possibly give testimony to the crime of Auschwitz – is palpable. Natzari knew that his knowledge was dangerous: 'We have to vanish from the earth because we know so much about their abominable methods of abuse and reprisal'. Indeed, he was certain that imminently he would be murdered so as to guarantee his silence, so that he would never reveal the crimes that he had seen. His buried letter was his brilliant, desperate effort to make the truth known from beyond the grave. He knew that his knowledge was incredible – and dangerous. 'The dramas that my eyes have seen are indescribable', he writes, even as he attempts to describe them.

And beyond a testament to Nazi crimes, Natzari's letter is of course also a painful sort of confession, or more accurately an acknowledgement of the role that he himself had been forced to play in them: 'My beloveds you will say as you read what work I have done, how could I, Manolis, or anybody else do this work, burning my fellow believers'. The only consolation of being in the camp, the only gift given him by his proximity to death, was to have learned the intimate details of how others had met their end. So it is that he can reassure his cousin Ilias that Ilias' little sister Errika did not die alone: Natzari's own sister, Nelli, 'was with [her] ... until her very last dying moments'. We can feel in Natzari's words his hope that somehow some shred of good might come from his ghastly front-row status, from his horrible closeness to the deaths of so, so many – at least he can offer some small news, some scrap of comfort, some small detail of information that will be a balm on the mourning of others.

But in striking ways, Natzari's letter is above all and most potently an assertion of his own identity as a Greek – and of his devotion to and love for his Greek homeland. Indeed, the letter in its literary structure is designed as a declaration of Natzari's Greekness. This is the theme with which it opens and the assertion with which it closes. And it is the centrepiece of its discussion of death, which falls roughly at the letter's centre.

The letter's very opening line puts Greece and Natzari's status *as Greek* at the middle of his frame: 'to my beloved homeland "GREECE" where I have always served as a good citizen'. The remarkable document found beside the Birkenau crematoria thirty-five years after it was written is Natzari's *afieroma*, his tribute to Greece and to his own pride at being Greek. It is a letter written, above all, to GREECE, to the homeland to which he lays claim and from which he hails, and it is an assertion that he lived – and was determined to die – as a Greek.

The significance of this is difficult to overstate, for it was not at all a given that, in 1944, Jews living in Greece would think of themselves so definitively as Greek. Only since 1912 had the city of Thessaloniki – the famous 'Jerusalem of the Balkans' – been part of Greece, and its transition from being a multicultural, provincial and largely Jewish Ottoman city to being the second-largest city in a rapidly nationalizing, Christian Greece was not an easy one. The decades between 1912 (when the city 'became Greek') and 1943 (when Thessaloniki's Jewish community was deported) had been fraught ones. The First World War, the Great Thessaloniki Fire of 1917 (which left 70,000 people homeless and rendered over 50,000

Jews destitute), the 'population exchanges' of the early 1920s (which flooded the city with Asia Minor Greek Orthodox Christian refugees, further marginalizing the city's Jews), the Greco-Italian War (in which many Greek Jews, among them Natzari, fought in the Greek army) and then the Axis occupation that began in 1941 – these events were a succession of blows to Jews living in Greece. During this thirty-year period, the city of Natzari's parents ceased to be an Ottoman Jewish one and became instead a Greek one: street names were changed, Sunday (rather than Saturday) became the Sabbath, Jews were required to go to Greek schools and Ladino ceased to be allowed as a public language. Many Jews left, for Palestine or for the United States. Within a few short decades, the city that had long been the definitive stronghold of Sephardic Ottoman Judaism was rebuilt – physically and conceptually – as a Greek and Christian one.

But as Natzari's letter suggests, at the same time that these difficult transitions were taking place, a new first generation of truly 'Greek Jews' was coming into existence. Natzari, born in 1917, was a child of the new Greece and of the newly Greek Thessaloniki. He was educated in Greek schools, had Greek Christian friends and did not view the fact of being Jewish as something that was in conflict with the claim to 'Greekness'. And for Natzari, to be Greek was not simply cultural. He had not been 'made Greek' through historical circumstance; rather, Greek blood flowed in his very veins. He describes the few surviving members of the SK preparing for their own liquidation; of those members of the unit who were still alive, he recounts that twenty-six were Greek: 'At least we Greeks are determined to die as true Greeks, just as every Greek knows how to die by showing to the last moment, despite the superiority of the criminals, that Greek blood flows in our veins, as we showed in the war against Italy'.

To die like a 'true Greek' was to be Natzari's final act of defiance, and he wanted to be remembered for having done so: 'Whoever might ask about me, say that I no longer exist, and that I went like a true Greek'. We can only wonder who his imagined audience might have been, whom he imagined these people who might ask about him to be. His friends? To be sure. Greek Christians, who might have questioned his Greekness? Greek society at large – which in the 1940s was only slowly coming to accommodate the idea of Greek Jews? Possibly, but of course we cannot know for sure.

What we *can* know for sure is that for Natzari (who ultimately survived and who lived out his remaining decades in the United States, part of the sad and different saga of the difficulty Greek Jewish survivors had in settling in Greece after the War), what mattered most of all as he faced death in the cold Polish autumn of 1944 was Greece: 'I die happy because I know at this moment that our Greece is free, my last word will be : Long live Greece' (Πεθαίνω ευχαριστημένος αφού ξέρω ότι αυτή τη στιγμή η Ελλάς μας είναι Ελεύθερη η τελευταία μου λέξη θα είναι Ζήτω η Ελλάς). The letter of Marcel Natzari is a remarkable testament to its author's love of friends, of family and, ultimately, of homeland.

K.E. Fleming is the Alexander S. Onassis Professor of Hellenic Culture and Civilization in the Program in Hellenic Studies and the Department of History at New York University. She is a specialist on the religious history of early modern and modern Mediterranean and Greece, and author of *Greece: A Jewish History* (2008), which won numerous awards, among them the National Jewish Book Award and the Runciman Award. She has taught at New York University, the École normale supérieure and UCLA, and served for four years as Chair of the Board of the University of Piraeus in Greece. She holds degrees from Barnard College, the University of Chicago and the University of California at Berkeley, and has been awarded honorary doctorates from the University of Macedonia and Ionian University. In 2016, she was awarded honorary Greek citizenship by the Hellenic Republic.

Chapter 6

Disinterred Words

The Letters of Herman Strasfogel and Marcel Nadjary

Nicholas Chare, Ersy Contogouris and Dominic Williams

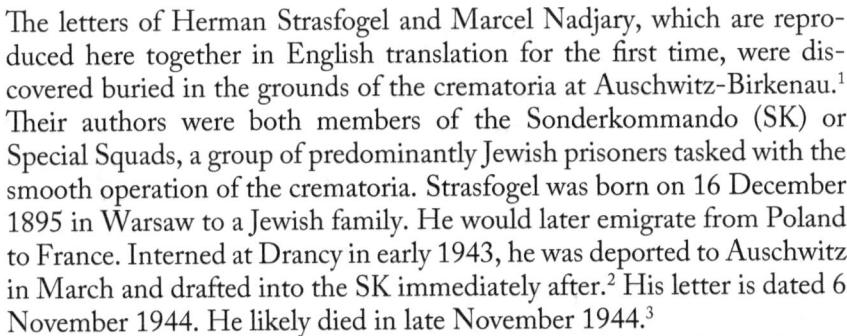

The letters of Herman Strasfogel and Marcel Nadjary, which are reproduced here together in English translation for the first time, were discovered buried in the grounds of the crematoria at Auschwitz-Birkenau.[1] Their authors were both members of the Sonderkommando (SK) or Special Squads, a group of predominantly Jewish prisoners tasked with the smooth operation of the crematoria. Strasfogel was born on 16 December 1895 in Warsaw to a Jewish family. He would later emigrate from Poland to France. Interned at Drancy in early 1943, he was deported to Auschwitz in March and drafted into the SK immediately after.[2] His letter is dated 6 November 1944. He likely died in late November 1944.[3]

Nadjary, a Greek Jew, was born on 20 November 1917 in Thessaloniki. In 1943, while in Athens receiving medical treatment for a foot injury, he was arrested because of his role in the Greek Resistance. On 30 December 1943, he was taken to Averoff prison. During his detention there he was tortured and subjected to brutal interrogation, in the course of which he revealed his name and that he was Jewish. In mid-February, he was then moved to the concentration camp at Haidari on the outskirts of Athens. On 2 April 1944, he was put on a transport from Athens to Auschwitz, where he arrived on 11 April. He began to work in the SK shortly after his arrival.[4] The letter he penned, which appears to be undated, was probably composed in late October 1944. It makes reference to the liberation of Greece (Athens was liberated on 14 October). It also refers to a transport from Theresienstadt having arrived on the day it was written. The last recorded transport from Theresienstadt reached Auschwitz on 28 October 1944. Nadjary survived Auschwitz and, after time in displaced persons (DP) camps, including Bari, returned to Greece. He would subsequently immigrate to the United States, where he died in New York in 1971.

The letters were written within days of each other, but found many years apart.[5] Strasfogel's letter was one of the first manuscripts (if not the very first) by a member of the SK to be discovered after Auschwitz-Birkenau was liberated in late January 1945. Sometime between 6 and 20 February 1945, Andrzej Zaorski came across a bottle in a mound of ashes in the environs of Crematorium 2 (III).[6] Inside was what Zaorski described as a document folded like a letter, with the outermost sheet serving as a 'makeshift envelope'.[7] This envelope, a page of grid paper from a notebook, included a message in French and Russian asking the finder to deliver it either to the French Consulate or the International Red Cross.[8] Zaorski was, by coincidence, a member of the Polish Red Cross. The envelope enclosed a letter in French by Strasfogel to his wife and daughter. Nadjary's letter was the last SK manuscript to be located. On 24 October 1980, a student who was clearing undergrowth near the ruins of Crematorium 2 (III) chanced upon a battered briefcase. It contained a broken thermos flask housing a largely illegible letter written in Greek. The letter was addressed to a number of Nadjary's friends from Thessaloniki.

The two letters form part of a remarkable archive of manuscripts handed down to us by members of the SK. In total, at least eight caches of documents by members of the squads have been discovered.[9] Strasfogel's and Nadjary's writings stand out both for their epistolary form and for being written in languages not local to the Generalgouvernement. The other manuscripts are almost entirely in Yiddish, although there is also an anonymous list of transports including a few words in Polish. The Yiddish writings are often treated as in a separate category to the letters. Ber Mark, for example, chose not to include Strasfogel's letter in his *Megiles Oyshvits* (translated as *The Scrolls of Auschwitz*) of 1977. In the 1982 French translation of Mark's book, *Des voix dans la nuit*, Strasfogel's letter is included, but as an annexe. The Auschwitz Museum Polish edition of the SK writings published in 1971 (translated into English in 1973) includes Strasfogel's letter as one of the manuscripts, but placed at the end.[10] The letter is mentioned only in passing in the preface by the editors and so might be said to have been given the status of an annexe once more.

Clearly no volume of the SK writings published prior to 1980 could include Nadjary's letter. Along with Strasfogel's letter, however, it is mentioned yet omitted from the 2005 French collection of SK writings *Des voix sous la cendre*. *Des voix* nevertheless includes the document dated 3 January 1945, 'Auschwitz', by Abraham Levite. This Yiddish preface, which was prepared as part of a broader project to bear witness to life in the camp, is of considerable historical interest. Yet in contrast to the letters, any direct relationship between this preface and the other SK writings is ambiguous. Nadjary's letter was added to the German translation of the Auschwitz Museum's edition of SK manuscripts and its translation into Italian.[11] The two letters have never before been published together in English. Versions of Nadjary's letter in English have previously been published as standalone texts in *Greeks in Auschwitz-Birkenau* and *Sephardi Lives*.[12] These versions of Nadjary's letter are based on the roughly 15% of text that is visible to the naked eye. This has rendered them, necessarily, fragmentary. The version we reproduce here features about 90% of the letter. Using multispectral analysis of pre-existing scans, Aleksandr Nikityaev, working in collaboration with Pavel Polian, has restored to view much of the writing that is invisible in the original. The hitherto fragmentary has been rendered almost whole. Through the revelation of formerly hidden characters, we are able to fill in many of the blanks that previously characterized the letter. The use of multispectral analysis has brought to light words previously buried as faded ink in the fibres of cellulose pulp that form the pages of Nadjary's letter. Viewing the enhanced version gives a sense of the letter as it appeared to its writer, the script in Greek reflecting his national heritage back to him. What he *saw* as he wrote held value for him as an articulation of his identity and his national pride. Since its discovery in 1980, much of this dimension to the letter, the visual power of the Greek script, has been veiled.

If a scholar consults Nadjary's letter in the original at the Auschwitz Museum today, they will not *see* the letter that we are now discussing, the version we are publishing here, which remains latent. No one now, however, would think about publishing the letter in the fragmentary form in which it is visible to the naked eye. The two renderings of the original letter that were published in English translation in 2009 and 2014 have been supplanted. Once comprehensive, they now lack. Thanks to technologies of image manipulation, it is today possible to look beyond what is there to be seen on the surface. There are therefore now two letters: a patchy paper version and a more substantial spectral version. This latter, disembodied letter is derived from the paper one, yet can be regarded as qualitatively different from it. It does not *look* the same.

Is this doubling cause for reflection? It bears thinking about if the materiality of the paper version begins to be overlooked, if we start to lose sight of what is not there to be seen and of its significance. The fading of the original ink and its becoming wraith-like, its slipping from being writing to being a trace of writing, holds a powerful testimonial significance. This disappearing, a disappearing figured in the blurring and smudging of the paper version, attests to the effects of the passage of time between 1944 and 1980. It is a product of the letter's need to be concealed and it signals that concealment. The restoration efforts of the Auschwitz Museum have already impacted this narrative, adding to its material history by rendering it more readily storable and legible, but muting some of the silences that spoke of its time in the earth. There is a danger that the new letter will work to amplify this muting, overwriting the old, rendering it redundant. There is a risk that the largely illegible letter held by the archive will be rendered obsolete, perceived as incomplete, undesirable. The hazy, smudgy, imprecise paper version may be replaced by the enhanced clarity of the spectral. Ideally, we would suggest, there is a need to find ways to look at both versions on equal terms, to see them as different, yet evenly weighted, moments in the life of Nadjary's writing. The letter can be regarded as palimpsestic, the writing overwritten by deterioration and the deterioration now overwritten in turn by the spectrally revived text. The hard-to-decipher letter in the Auschwitz Museum, however, retains a visual value in its distressed state that we should not overlook.[13]

Nadjary was himself attuned to the power of the visual, to its capacity to supplement the textual, to fill in where words were incapable. The testimony he wrote retrospectively in 1947 includes drawings as well as words.[14] One of these drawings provides a bird's-eye view of Birkenau as it was in 1944. The aerial perspective was clearly not one Nadjary ever attained. He has based his reconstruction of Birkenau from the air on his experiences on the ground. The overview he provides by way of the image is more effective at giving a sense of the layout of the camp than any passage of description. In Nadjary's letter, there is acknowledgment that words have their testimonial limits. He states after a summary of the process of extermination at Birkenau: 'The horrible things my eyes have seen are indescribable'. The word he uses here, which is translated as 'indescribable', is 'απερίγραπτα', which is etymologically linked to γράφω (gráphō), to writing.[15] What Nadjary has seen is, in a sense, unwritable. This reference to the limits of the description follows on from a lengthy narration in which, despite the multispectral analysis, there are still occasional gaps. There is thus a sense that as he is writing, Nadjary is reflecting back over his efforts to bear witness, his attempts to word what he has seen, and finding them wanting. His eyes have chronicled more than his pen is capable of recording.

In this context, there is something in Nadjary's letter about the insistence on eyewitnessing – he repeats the expression 'what my eyes have seen' three times – that is particularly striking. It is almost as if all that his body has done and suffered is incomparable to what he has witnessed through his eyes. He has seen, recorded, and is now transmitting this knowledge as best as he can, in contrast to Strasfogel, who wants to spare his readers – his wife and daughter – from this horror. It is a horror that Nadjary has registered primarily visually. There would have been other ways to communicate this same idea (for instance, with the expression 'what I have been through'; there is a very similar expression in Greek). But he uses 'what my eyes have seen'. Through keeping his eyes open, he has been able to record numbers and now have these be known. There is perhaps an agency here that belies the apparent passivity of the expression.

Although, in Nadjary's eyes, he cannot do justice to the horrors he has witnessed, his status as eyewitness has enabled him to record with remarkable precision the number of those murdered (he estimates 1,400,000 in total). His listing of how many people of different nationalities have been massacred renders his account comparable to (if less detailed than) the list of transports discovered with writings by Zalman Lewental and Leyb Langfus. The letter can therefore be viewed on a continuum with other manuscripts produced by members of the SK. Both letters are, however, often accorded peripheral status in comparison with the Yiddish writings.

This lesser status may, in part, be explained by qualitative differences between the documents. The major works of Zalman Gradowski and Langfus, for example, are carefully crafted, likely drafted in some form, and can legitimately be regarded as works of literature.[16] Their aim is clearly in significant part to bear witness to Nazi atrocities. Lewental's major manuscript, or what can be read of it, does not share such literariness. It is nevertheless a substantial undertaking in comparison to Strasfogel's and Nadjary's letters. Lewental seeks to detail his personal experiences and to provide a history of the SK and their preparations for revolt. He likely wrote the entirety of this document shortly after the SK uprising of 7 October 1944. He dates it 10 October.[17] If, as seems likely, Lewental started writing in the aftermath of the insurrection, he must have composed the work in great haste. In this, the rapidity of creation, the manuscript is similar to those of Strasfogel and Nadjary. Strasfogel and Nadjary also write after the revolt, although they do not greatly reflect back on it. It seems from Strasfogel's letter that despite the brutal suppression of the October revolt, further resistance was still viewed as a real possibility. Strasfogel states of his impending death: 'je m'en vais calmement et peut-être héroïquement (ça dépendra des circonstances)' (I'm going calmly and perhaps heroically (it will depend on the circumstances)).

Both Strasfogel and Lewental seem motivated to put pen to paper by the sense that their death is imminent. Nadjary writes of the likelihood that he will die but his immediate impetus to write a letter may straightforwardly have been that circumstances provided him with the materials and the opportunity to do so. The uneven script of his letter suggests that it was composed at speed and possibly on an uneven surface. Its novel mode of concealment may have been inspired by specific materials coming into his possession at that time. It is not inconceivable that the briefcase into which he stashed the flask holding the letter also contained the thermos and the writing materials when he first took ownership of it. The case may have served as his desk. Strasfogel's letter is composed on pages pulled from a notebook. It contains word formations that are inconsistent. The word 'Sonderkommando', for example, is written hyphenated (Sonder-Kommando) and unhyphenated (Sonder Kommando), and is misspelt at one point as Sonder-Komando. These variations, in particular, likely index the author's haste.

Despite possible differences in terms of the pace of writing between Nadjary and Strasfogel and such authors as Gradowski and Langfus, there is also crossover between them. Nadjary and Strasfogel, like Gradowski, start their documents with a short message in more than one language. Gradowski begins his account of the journey of a transport from Kiełbasin to Auschwitz with a plea to the manuscript's finder to take interest in it as it will be of value to historians. The message is in Polish, Russian, French and German. Nadjary's letter commences with a message in German, Polish and French directing the finder to take the letter to the Greek consulate. Strasfogel, as mentioned previously, asks the finder in French and Russian to take the letter to the French Consulate or to the Red Cross.[18] Nadjary also includes a relatively long account of the activities of the SK. He too is clearly thinking of the historical value of his account. Like Gradowski, Langfus and Lewental, he is openly setting out to bear witness. Strasfogel, by contrast, provides little direct insight into the experiences of the SK. His letter is more closed. He wishes to solely address his wife and his daughter, Simone. He does briefly acknowledge they may be dead, stating 'si vous vivrez' (if you live), but clearly this is not a reality he wants to countenance. Elsewhere, he views their survival as the ultimate victory: 'vous êtes en vie et . . . notre ennemi est perdu' (you are alive and . . . our enemy is lost). He is writing only to them, be they alive or dead. By contrast, there is a sense in Nadjary that although he wants to communicate with specific people, he also, at least at times, has a more general readership in mind.

In many ways, Nadjary's letter forms something of a hinge between Strasfogel's letter and the Yiddish writings. Like Strasfogel's letter, Nadjary's partly takes the form of a last will, albeit less directive. Also like Strasfogel, he finds comfort during what he thinks may be his last moments in the knowledge that his loved ones are safe. The liberation of Greece heartens him. Like Strasfogel, Nadjary asks his readers not to judge him harshly for his actions as a member of the SK and insists on the fact he has broken rules in carrying out his duties (for instance, on page 4, he writes that he told the truth to those on their way to the gas chamber) and that he dies with his head held high. The SK were acutely aware of how they were perceived by other camp inmates. Marco Nahon recounts that an Athenian member of the SK who encountered an old acquaintance, the newspaper reporter Bernardis, said to him: 'I knew what passed through your mind when you first saw me ... I could read in your eyes the shocking astonishment, the contempt, the utter disgust even, that my profession of today inspires in you, my profession of body burner'.[19] Here the SK member sees himself as viewed as abject, although, like Strasfogel and Nadjary, he goes on to contest this perception. In this context, Nadjary's insistence on 'what my eyes have seen' enacts a kind of detachment from events and may be interpreted as an unconscious means of reorienting responsibility towards the Nazis for the things he was forced to do as a member of the SK.[20]

Both Strasfogel's and Nadjary's letters manifest the haste of their composition through the styles of writing they adopt. Nadjary's letter uses a combination of different levels of written and spoken Greek, very little punctuation, a mix of tenses, and there are some digressions and quite a few spelling mistakes.[21] He also occasionally uses words in contexts that unnerve. For instance, on page 6, he writes that the SK have to be absent from the Earth (να λήψουμε) because of what they have witnessed. He also mentions the need for the Nazis to remove/subtract them (να αφαιρέσουν). These choices of phrase seem wrong in the context of a letter to dear friends and are very unsettling. The unfeeling language may be deliberate, designed to foreground the cold-bloodedness of the Germans.

In the context of Nazi brutality, for example, Nadjary describes the gas chamber after the SS have forced members of a transport into it as 'a real sardine tin of people after they sealed the door shut'. Referring to people as packed like sardines is commonplace, and likening those forced into the gas chamber to sardines is also unexceptional in Holocaust testimony.[22] Charles Bendel, for instance, writes of those about to be gassed that they are 'wedged in [*entassés*] like sardines'.[23] Here, however, we are presented with a slightly different image. The addition of the word 'real' (πραγματι) is crucial. The language is figurative but the reader is asked to take the metaphor literally. The gas chamber *is* an oversized tin rather than being like a tin. Sardines are, of course, also dead when they are packaged. The fate of the people in the chamber is prefigured in this choice of confining figure; it emphasizes the callous treatment meted out by the Nazis. Additionally, it is noteworthy that one of the major foodstuffs discovered by the SK in the possessions of those murdered, Dario Gabbai explains, was 'sardines in cans'.[24] The metaphor is therefore one 'found' in Nadjary's everyday existence. By chance or design, it acts to reinforce the industrial nature of mass death at Birkenau – that this is a death factory. Furthermore, sardines are a staple of the Mediterranean diet. The metaphor also connects with Nadjary's past in Thessaloniki.[25] It is striking how frequently Greek members of the SK resort to using sardines as an analogy or metaphor when recounting their experiences.

Some of this language, such as the reference to subtracting the SK, might alternatively attest to Nadjary's inability to find a more appropriate word because of his hurry. The letter was obviously written at considerable speed (there is a breathlessness to it), so the exactness with which he describes his experience at Birkenau underlines his desire to make known what he has witnessed and the sheer magnitude of it. The fact that he seems to pause and dedicate the time to spell out numbers in brackets after he writes them as figures is of particular note.[26] Despite his haste, he takes pains to make sure specifics are recorded as clearly as possible for his future readers, even if this takes extra effort and time. These specifics include the number of men in the SK when Nadjary joined it and also the names of two Greek compatriots who died in the revolt. He writes of the SK but also for them, foregrounding the heroism of the group and the fate of specific individuals.

The mixture of tenses also points to the ongoing nature of what Nadjary is describing. In one instance, however, he differentiates clearly between past and present – on page 8, he crosses out 'I wrote' and replaces it with the present tense 'I am writing' – in a manifest desire to assert that he is still alive. Yet, on the following page, he anticipates that by the time his friends read his letter, he will have been killed (a similar oscillation between hope and despair can also be identified in Strasfogel's letter). There is something about Nadjary's experience of time that is expressed through the ambiguities in the use of tenses. One instance is on page 8, when he writes: 'what always kept me was the revenge I wanted and want to live in order to avenge the deaths . . .', at first it reads as 'the revenge I wanted and want'. But then, we realize he has shifted to '[I] want to live in order to avenge the deaths of Dad of Mum and of my beloved darling sister'. The lack of punctuation coupled with the shifting tenses makes things hard to follow, but simultaneously also captures the complex experience of temporality members of the SK clearly had.

Like Lewental and Nadjary, Strasfogel's syntax is unwieldy and his sentences are not always punctuated, a sign of the hurry in which he describes himself to be writing. He observes, for example, of his chances of starting life afresh: 'that's out of the question no one gets out of here it's all over'. The asyndeton here, a running together of a triple negation of hope, indicates Strasfogel's haste and also lends a powerful sense of urgency, even desperation, to the writing. He calls his script 'étourdi', by which he likely meant not composed.[27] It is also clear that French is not his first language. There are numerous grammatical errors, particularly with prepositions, and he frequently omits accents. Additionally, some phrases seem to be marked by influences other than French. For example, he refers to himself as suffering at first from 'famine formelle' and being 'formellement squelettique', literally 'formal famine' and 'formally skeletal', expressions as odd in French as they are in English. The Polish equivalents are somewhat more acceptable – 'formalny' can mean 'sheer' or 'utter', especially in more colloquial usage. Some of his spelling also seems to have echoes of Polish.[28] Strasfogel is, however, occasionally capable of considerable eloquence. He writes of the physical changes to his body soon after his arrival at Auschwitz that 'mes mains n'ont même pas reconnu mon corps en le frottant' (when my hands rubbed my body they didn't even recognize it), which is oddly beautiful and could be called poetic. Overall, however, the letter is not characterized by literary flourishes. Here a comparison might be made with Zalman Lewental, whose written Yiddish is not of the standard of Gradowski and Langfus. In using a language in which they are not completely at home, Lewental and Strasfogel each show that they made a decision to use it, probably because it was the most appropriate for its anticipated readers, but perhaps for other reasons too. Yiddish was probably harder for the camp guards to get translated. French was, perhaps, a way to assert a particular identity. Strasfogel's choice of writing in French may simply be because it made it easier for his daughter to read his letter, but it also fits with his urging his wife and daughter to adopt French identities, never to return to Poland.

The fact that Strasfogel is writing to his wife and daughter, and that he wants his daughter to ensure some kind of continuation of the family line through her own children orients it much more towards the future. It is more a will than a testament of what he has seen, unlike Nadjary, for whom the 'will' part comes second. Strasfogel's primary reasons for writing are to comfort his wife and daughter, tell them he is dying in peace and give them instructions, whereas Nadary is motivated by the desire for revenge, which he sees as coming at least in part through his testimonial. Strasfogel leaves the testimonial to others. What does concern him is being judged harshly by his wife and child. He begs them explicitly not to do so: 'je vous prie de ne jamais mal me juger'. At multiple times he indicates that he broke rules and risked his life to help others, and that if he is still alive, it is not because he was a coward but by sheer luck.

When Strasfogel does indicate what he has experienced and witnessed, this is often expressed indirectly or even euphemistically: he talks about 'le vaste hall du Krematorium (vide)' (the 'immense chamber of the crematorium [empty]') where he shouts Simone's name. In all likelihood, this is the gas chamber, but he leaves its function unspecified.[29] The description of the SK as a kind of 'Chevra Kadischa' makes them sound as if they are carrying out the highest religious obligation in Judaism (although this euphemism is distanced from Strasfogel himself and put into the mouths of others) rather than violating its precepts to leave dead bodies intact.[30]

Strasfogel does straightforwardly tell of deportees who arrived in the camp with him and who were sent to the gas and the ovens, but he seems not to be able to connect these facts to himself. In justifying his own actions, he only hints apophatically at what is taking place: 'je faisais tout ce qui etait [*sic*] en mon moyen ne craignant ni risque ni péril pour soulager le sort de malheureux ou politiquement ce que je ne peux vous écrire du sort' (I did everything I was able to, never thinking about the danger or risk to ease the fate of the wretched [or] for reasons of discretion [what] I cannot write to you about their fate). Strasfogel both shows his need to justify himself, explaining that he did make efforts to help the victims, and makes a decision not to tell his family everything. The link between the two is syntactically odd. Why even hint at these facts? Perhaps he feels the need to acknowledge even if not to dwell on them because he knows that his family will hear something of them. Strasfogel's assumption seems to be that there will be a history of the SK available to read – perhaps one detailed enough even to allow the date of his death to be known. The simultaneous revelation and veiling of what has taken place also draws attention to the presence of complex emotions. Strasfogel needs to be seen to be compassionate in the eyes of his loved ones. This compassion also manifests in his desire not to 'show' them the horrors he has witnessed.

At times, Strasfogel seems to almost forget the circumstances in which he is writing, and to revert to the familiar and intimate back and forth of a conversation with his wife, when he writes of their relative Figlarz: 'à propos, qu'est-il devenu?' (on that subject, what happened to him?) as if they were chatting and he would be getting a response. Strasfogel also provides some detail about the community he has forged while interned: perhaps in 'ou Kolnidrés ce que nous avons improvisé chez nous' (or Kol Nidre which we improvised amongst ourselves) (to which 'chez nous' is he referring?), but definitely when he talks about David Lahana. It is striking that in the conditions in which he is writing, he devotes two paragraphs to Lahana as a fulfilment of a promise. His asking his wife to write to Lahana's family acts as a strengthening of the bonds that they had. He strives to reaffirm these bonds, but from the outside by inviting his wife to pass on the news of Lahana's fate.

At two different points, Strasfogel rehearses his intermittent belief that, by a miracle, he may survive:

> here I always thought if by some miracle I get out of here I will start over . . . but, alas! that's out of the question no one gets out of here it's all over.

> we are eyewitnesses must not survive, in spite of all, from time to time I retain a little spark of hope, perhaps by some kind of miracle, me who's already had so much luck one of the oldest here, who has overcome so many obstacles, one of two remaining from a hundred, perhaps this final miracle could happen? If so then let me be back before this buried letter is found.

The impression of these passages is very much of the writing following, or at least retracing, trains of thought, expressing or reliving them in the moment of writing, seesawing between hope and hopelessness. The act of writing and the closeness it brings to his family seem to reinvigorate his hope. Even with the passage that starts in the past tense, he switches to present and future forms, and in the second he dwells upon all the ways in which he has been lucky so far.[31] These painful moments of a man trying to face up to reality are difficult to read, and do not give the impression of attempts to spare his wife and daughter. The letter appears to give him space to express those feelings.

The newly legible text in Nadjary's letter affirms its emotional dimensions. There is also a great deal of love and humanity present (which speaks powerfully against the idea that members of the SK were dehumanized by their situation). This can be seen especially in his repeated use of the affectionate form 'μου' ('my Misko' or 'our Athens') and the diminutive forms '-ούλη' and '-ούλα' at the end of words and names. This aspect is deeply moving, signalling that Nadjary is hanging on to friendship, to connections, to the life he lived before, the life of a regular man in his twenties, with his παρέα (group of friends).[32] The emotional content has the effect of bringing the designated readers closer to him, re-creating the community he lost (a community the existence of which is expressed right at the beginning through the names of his friends and the word παρέα). There is a lightness in the repeated use of these terms, which then contrasts with the descriptions of his duties in the SK and of the numbers killed, and also with the sometimes business-like tone of the later pages in which he gives instructions for care of people and property (the letter is addressed to his loved ones, but it is really mostly to Misko (Dimitris) that he is writing and giving indications): at the top of page 9, 'I bequeath to you Misko' – there is no 'μου', but he then immediately reverts back to '-ούλη', '-ούλα', and 'μου'. On page 8, he writes about his desire to avenge the deaths of his parents and sister, and then, directly afterwards, triples the terms of endearment writing to his cousin Ilias when he asks him and his friends to know their duty, which simultaneously contradicts the solemnity of the word 'duty' but also reinforces the necessity that Misko know and carry out his duty. The abrupt transition between an expression of hatred (towards the Nazis) and a declaration of affection (to family and friends) registers that this is close to a stream of consciousness and also indexes the varied feelings that sustained Nadjary and, potentially, other members of the SK.

The discovery that the letter in French should be attributed to Herman Strasfogel also allows us to see even more how emotional ties bound the French and Greek members of the SK together. As Chare and Williams previously noted, Strasfogel made mention of Leon Cohen in his letter. We can now see the reciprocal nature of this naming: Cohen and Nadjary also referred to Strasfogel in their retrospective testimonies. Cohen's memories of Strasfogel appear to contain some errors about dates, but the affection for him is clear: he calls him a 'courageous' man from whom he was inseparable.[33] Nadjary too has warm words for Strasfogel, describing him as being among the best of his fellow prisoners and providing what appears to be a French nickname for him: 'Moineau' (sparrow).[34] Each of these two letters can be said to emerge from a community of feelings, as well as attempting to sustain and be sustained by a community of feelings with its recipients.

In Nadjary's letter, there is also the repetition of the word 'remember' that is striking: he uses the expression 'remembering' to say he often thinks of his friends and to ask them to think of him (there is an expression in Greek that is similar to 'thinking of' that he could have used), and also some references that only specific people would relate to (page 8), 'do you remember, the one who was at my house?' and pages 10–11, to Giorgo, '<Nea Evropi> do you remember . . .?', a sort of inside joke, maybe, regarding the Nazi newspaper Νέα Ευρώπη (*New Europe*) published in Thessaloniki during the occupation.[35] He wants his friends to know that 'Manolis has not forgotten them' (page 2), and he remembers Smaro's parcels and efforts to free him, which he describes as 'unforgettable' (page 2), bringing him comfort during the hardships he has endured. Nadjary referring to himself as Manolis (clearly a nickname) instead of Marcel in this context also works to affirm his closeness to those he is addressing. Although he anticipates death in the near future, Nadjary does not simply ask to be remembered, but asserts his place in a group bound together by shared memories. The space of the letter allows him to present himself as very much alive and still part of his group of friends, not simply determined by his present circumstances and marked for death.

Both the letters, in their distinct ways, embody agency and can be interpreted as vital testimonies of resistance. Their complex temporalities are part of this assertion of agency, moving between past, present and future.

This calls on us as readers to respond to the men who wrote them, but it might also offer us a way to reflect on the manuscripts they wrote. Instead of thinking purely of the moment at which the texts were written, we should also attend to the afterlife of the objects that these writings became. Strasfogel's letter was, for decades, known only in transcription and its authorship attributed to another man, Chaim Herman. What were taken to be one man's emotions and experiences have now been transferred to another, returned to him. Strasfogel posthumously reclaims this part of his life and is reunited with his letter. The letter itself has also been 'discovered' again. The urge to find it, which began in 2015, can be read as symptomatic of increasing recognition of the importance of the Scrolls of Auschwitz as a whole, as evidence of these writings coming to matter more.

The rediscovery of Strasfogel's letter enables us to fill in blanks in the transcription, most notably the section about wanting to express his gratitude to people for supporting his wife and daughter in his absence: 'I did not have the satisfaction of repaying them personally'. These words are absent from earlier published versions. The words show a desire to recompense, they register a sense of indebtedness, even if they cannot make good on that debt. Through these words, something of Strasfogel's personality, of his person, of the measure of the man, survives him. This dimension to his character was long obscured, a casualty of factors such as the failure to initially recognize the historical importance of the letter and the vagaries of copying. Now Strasfogel's honourableness, his sense of obligation, his wish to do right by the protectors of his family, is registered anew.

Chaim Herman, however, who it now appears probably did not work in the SK, seems fated to fade from view. Nothing of his emotional life or family ties, beyond the official records of illness and the postcard that the camp administration forced him to write, has survived.[36] The recognition of Strasfogel as the 'owner' of the emotions indexed by the letter necessarily, yet troublingly, comes at Herman's expense. Whatever feelings Herman had, in all their likely comparable complexity to Strasfogel's, are now only gestured towards by the fact that the ones expressed in the letter have been taken away from him. This accident of history reminds us of the hundreds of thousands of victims of Auschwitz-Birkenau whose last words were never recorded, a fate that Strasfogel himself suffered (at least in public life) for part of the afterlife of his letter. But at this point, Herman's loss might be said to take the form of a ghostly presence: we now accept we know nothing of his feelings in his final months at Auschwitz, yet that absence of knowledge is made painfully palpable at this moment of reattribution. In a similar way, the ghostly word-absences on Marcel Nadjary's manuscript might be said to be present in – are part of the meaning of – the text that he wrote, the period of their illegibility forming part of the manuscript's history as much as the periods of its original and restored readability. Even as we celebrate the fact that Nadjary's words have finally been brought back to us after seventy-five years, half of that time concealed in the earth, the other half obscured by the corrosion of ink and paper, we should remember that this history of their silence also tells us of the circumstances in which they were written and the future their author anticipated for himself.

Nicholas Chare is Associate Professor in the Department of History of Art and Film Studies at the Université de Montréal. In 2018, he was Diane and Howard Wohl Fellow at the Jack, Joseph and Morton Mandel Center for Advanced Holocaust Studies at the United States Holocaust Memorial Museum, Washington DC. He is the author of *Auschwitz and Afterimages: Abjection, Witnessing and Representation* (2011) and the co-author (with Dominic Williams) of *Matters of Testimony: Interpreting the Scrolls of Auschwitz* (2016) and *The Auschwitz Sonderkommando: Testimonies, Histories, Representations* (2019).

Ersy Contogouris is Assistant Professor of Art History at the Université de Montréal. Her research focuses on eighteenth and nineteenth-century art, as well as on the history of caricature and graphic satire. She is the author of *Emma Hamilton and Late Eighteenth-Century European Art: Agency, Performance, and Representation* (2018) and the assistant editor of *The Efflorescence of Caricature, 1759–1838* (2011).

Dominic Williams is Senior Lecturer in Holocaust and Genocide Studies at Northumbria University. He has published articles on modernist writing and antisemitism, contemporary Jewish poetry, and Holocaust memory and testimony. He and Nicholas Chare have coedited *Representing Auschwitz: At the Margins of Testimony* (2013), and co-authored *Matters of Testimony: Interpreting the Scrolls of Auschwitz* (Berghahn Books, 2016) and *The Auschwitz Sonderkommando: Testimonies, Histories, Representations* (2019).

Notes

1. See Andreas Kilian's chapter in this volume for the reasons for attributing the letter in French signed 'Herman' to Herman Strasfogel, and not Chaim Herman. Nadjary was the spelling adopted by Marcel for his surname when he immigrated to the United States. We have therefore used it here.
2. For a discussion of Drancy as a transit camp (July 1942 to July 1943), see Annette Wieviorka and Michel Lafitte, *À l'intérieur du camp de Drancy* (Paris: Éditions Perrin, 2012), 131–213.
3. See Erich Friedler, Barbara Siebert and Andreas Kilian, *Zeugen aus der Todeszone: Das Jüdische Sonderkommando in Auschwitz* (Munich: Deutsche Taschenbuch Verlag, 2005), 377. Although their suggestion refers to Chaim Herman, it still applies to Herman Strasfogel.
4. Nadjary was one of hundreds of Greeks drafted into the SK in preparation for the mass murder of Hungarian Jews. For a discussion of this period of enlargement of the SK, see Albert Menasche, Number 124454, *Birkenau (Auschwitz II). Memoirs of an Eye-Witness: How 72,000 Greek Jews Perished* (New York: Isaac Saltiel, 1947), 70. See also Steven Bowman, *The Agony of Greek Jews, 1940–1945* (Stanford: Stanford University Press, 2009), 96–99.
5. Leon Cohen gives the impression that at a specific moment there was a concerted effort among SK members to conceal letters. Cohen is directly referenced in Strasfogel's letter, and Strasfogel clearly provided his compatriot with the means to send a message to his loved ones. It is not inconceivable that Nadjary's letter also formed part of this particular endeavour. Nadjary may be referenced in Cohen's postliberation account (which was written in French) of his experiences at Birkenau. He describes an Albert Nadjari who went to America after the war. See Leon Cohen, *From Greece to Birkenau: The Crematoria Workers' Uprising*, trans. Jose-Maurice Gormezano (Tel Aviv: Salonika Jewry Research Center, 1996).
6. Jadwiga Bezwińska and Danuta Czech suggest this timespan for the finding of the letter. See *Amidst a Nightmare of Crime: Notes of Prisoners of Sonderkommando Found at Auschwitz*, trans. Krystyna Michalik (Oświęcim: Publications of State Museum at Oświęcim, 1973), 181n1.
7. Andrzej Zaorski, 'Relacja'. Unpublished manuscript in the archives of the Jewish Historical Institute, Warsaw. AZIH 301/7182, 11 March 1971.
8. We are grateful to Andreas Kilian for supplying us with information about the paper used to compose the letter and also regarding the layout of the composition itself. We have viewed some pages of the letter in photographic reproduction but have not been able to consult the original.
9. One manuscript by Leyb Langfus, which was discovered in 1945, was consigned to the finder's attic and forgotten about until it was donated to the Auschwitz Museum in 1970. It is possible that other manuscripts may also still be in private hands. It is also probable that the decaying remains of other manuscripts remain buried at Birkenau, yet the possibility of their still being legible is remote.
10. All of these publications attribute the letter to Chaim Herman. Chaim Herman, 'The Manuscript of Chaim Herman', in Jadwiga Bezwińska and Danuta Czech (eds), *Amidst a Nightmare of Crime: Manuscripts of Members of Sonderkommando*, trans. Krystyna Michalik (Oświęcim: Publications of State Museum at Oświęcim, 1996), 179–90. Chare and Williams also attribute the letter to Herman, which they analyse in *Matters of Testimony: Interpreting the Scrolls of Auschwitz* (New York: Berghahn

Books, 2016). Despite the reattribution of the letter, many of the observations made about it in *Matters* still stand.

11. Jadwiga Bezwińska and Danuta Czech (eds), *Inmitten des grauenvollen Verbrechens: Handschriften von Mitgliedern des Sonderkommandos*, trans. Herta Henschel and Jochen August (Oświęcim: Publications of State Museum at Oświęcim, 1996). Carlo Saletti (ed.), *La voce dei sommersi: Manoscritti ritrovati di membri del Sonderkommando di Auschwitz* (Venice: Marsilio, 1999).

12. See 'The Buried Manuscript of Marcel Nadjary', trans. Alexandra Apostolides, in Photini Tomai, *Greeks in Auschwitz-Birkenau* (Athens: Papasiziz Publishers, 2009), 160–67; 'Message in a Bottle: The Buried Manuscript of a Greek Jewish Inmate at Auschwitz [1944]', trans. Isaac Nehama, in Julia Philipps Cohen and Sarah Abrevaya Stein (eds), *Sephardi Lives: A Documentary History, 1700–1950* (Stanford: Stanford University Press, 2014), 285–86.

13. See, for example, the analysis of Nadjary's letter by Nicholas Chare and Dominic Williams in *Matters of Testimony*; the analysis by Chare in 'Material Witness: Conservation Ethics and the Scrolls of Auschwitz', *symplokē* 24(1–2) (2016), 81–97; and by Nicholas Chare and Marcel Swiboda in 'Introduction: Unforeseen Encounters', *Liminalities* 14(1) (2018), 1–25.

14. For further discussion of Marcel Nadjary's drawings, see Nicholas Chare and Dominic Williams, *The Auschwitz Sonderkommando: Testimonies, Histories, Representations* (Basingstoke: Palgrave Macmillan, 2019), Chapter 5.

15. We are grateful to K.E. Fleming for bringing this link to *gráphō* to our attention. The etymology of 'indescribable' also links it to 'writing' from the Latin *scribere*, to write, but this link is less obvious to an English reader than the clear connection available to a reader of Greek.

16. For an exploration of literary qualities in the works of these two authors, see the individual chapters devoted to them in Chare and Williams, *Matters of Testimony*.

17. The date is not placed at the end of the manuscript and it therefore appears that Lewental continued writing on or after this date. See ibid., 131.

18. The use of Russian by Gradowski and Strasfogel provides indications both of their interaction with Russian members of the SK and of their expectation that the camp would be liberated by the advancing Soviet army.

19. Marco Nahon, *Birkenau: The Camp of Death*, trans. Jacqueline Havaux Bowers (Tuscaloosa: University of Alabama Press, 1989), 100.

20. In video testimony, Dario Gabbai similarly distinguishes seeing from doing. He says that the nightmares he has about his time as a member of the SK do not relate to his own actions and observes of the terrors that haunt him: 'Whatever I did, I have nothing to do with it'. USC Shoah Foundation Interview Code 142. Dario Gabbai, interviewed by Stephen Smith on 1 May 2014 as a coda to testimony he initially provided to the USC Shoah Foundation in 1996.

21. Most of the letter is written in Demotic and informal Greek. There are some words, in particular plural, such as 'μήνας' and 'τας προσπαθείας' (at 2) that are in Katharevousa, and towards the end, there is a more formal level of Greek, but that is Demotic, such as when he begins the 'will' part of the letter, 'Την περιουσίαν της οικογενείας μου την παραχωρώ σε σένα Μήσκο <Δημήτριος Αθανασίου Στεφανίδην>' (at 9) and when he addresses the embassy (at 13). And there are some grammatical turns that are particular to Thessaloniki, for instance, 'με έμειναν' (it would be more common to say 'μου' instead of 'με').

22. Margo Selby (née Magda Roth), for instance, recounts of Birkenau: 'We slept on wide bunk beds ... squeezed together like human sardines'. Margo Selby, '37 Years after' (unpublished manuscript), 51. USHMM Accession Number 2007.469.1. The former SK member David Nencel says of the goods wagon in which he was transported to Auschwitz: 'We was packed in like, like sardines ... What I'm going to say sardines ... I don't want to use that word. [Sighs]'. For Nencel, the analogy is clearly problematic, dehumanizing. David Nencel, interviewed by Joe Russin in 1996. USHMM Accession Number 2003.76. RG 50.560.0001.
23. Charles Bendel, 'Le Sonderkommando', in *Témoignages sur Auschwitz* (Paris: Éditions de l'amicale des déportés d'Auschwitz, 1946), 162. Dario Gabbai also describes those in the gas chamber as 'like sardines' in his video testimony to Smith. Morris Venezia similarly observes 'they were like sardines inside'. USC Shoah Foundation Code 20405. Morris Venezia interviewed by Carol Stulberg on 27 October 1996. In an interview with Gideon Greif, the Greek SK member Shaul Chazan says of stacking corpses for burning at either Bunker 1 or Bunker II: 'We had to pile the bodies on top of each other like sardines'. Chazan, in Gideon Greif, *We Wept without Tears: Testimonies of the Jewish Sonderkommando from Auschwitz* (New Haven: Yale University Press, 2005), 264. For further discussion of sardines as analogy and metaphor, see Chare and Williams, *The Auschwitz Sonderkommando*, Chapter 5.
24. USC Shoah Foundation Interview Code 142. Dario Gabbai, interviewed by Carol Stulberg on 7 November 1996. Shlomo Venezia also speaks of finding tins of sardines (*scatole di sardine*) in possessions discarded by transports. He gave such a tin to his cousin Leone Venezia as a final meal before Leone's death. USC Shoah Foundation Interview Code 36179. Shlomo Venezia, interviewed by Manuela Consonni on 11 December 1997. In Kanada (the colloquial term used by inmates for the storage warehouses where possessions from the transports were housed and sorted), sardines were routinely found in luggage. Shirley Berger Gottesman recounts discovering a tin of sardines in the pocket of some clothing as she was sorting bundles and also attests that the men who worked in Kanada regularly brought the women who were working there sardines. See Shirley Berger Gottesman and Maryann McLoughlin, *A Red Polka-Dotted Dress: A Memoir of Kanada II* (Margate: ComteQ Publishing, 2011), 27. Henry Levy, who coincidentally befriended Nadjary at Birkenau, describes finding cans of sardines in a Red Cross parcel he was given just prior to his deportation from Thessaloniki to Auschwitz. See Henry Levy, 'The Jews of Salonica and the Holocaust: A Personal Memoir', in Solomon Gaon and M. Mitchell Serels (eds), *Del Fuego: Sephardim and the Holocaust* (New York: Sepher-Hermon Press, 1995), 229. Irene Weiss also refers to sardines in Red Cross packages found at the camp of Neustadt-Glewe. USC Shoah Foundation Interview Code 17212. Irene Weiss, interviewed by Ileane Kenney on 26 July 1996.
25. David (Dario) Pardo, for instance, tells of people queuing from 2 am in Thessaloniki to buy freshly caught sardines during the German occupation. USHMM Accession Number 1995.A.1261.201 RG Number: RG-50.431.0781. David Pardo, interviewed by Nancy Solomon on 12 May 1998.
26. Strasfogel does something similar at one point, writing that only '2 (*deux*)' of his transport are still alive.
27. Strasfogel does not write in his mother tongue, which, as we explore here, explains some of his odd choices of phrase. He also writes in a form of French that is distinct from contemporary French. His use of the word *étourdi* may seem unusual now but the 1919 Larousse defines the adjective *étourdi* as referring to acting without forethought and the verb *étourdir* as referring to being tired or distracted as in the Larousse's given example

of 'cet enfant m'étourdit'. These meanings would seem to fit with the circumstances of the writing of the letter. The word can also be used to describe a physical state akin to intoxication. In Julie Crémieux-Dunand's account of her time at Drancy, she describes an inmate as rendered 'étourdi, littéralement grisé' (punch-drunk, literally inebriated) by the barrage of information and questions he received upon his arrival at the camp. J. Crémieux-Dunand, *La vie à Drancy: 1941–1944* (Paris: Librairie Gedalge, 1945), 48.

28. For example, the spelling of 'Konsulat de France' on the 'envelope' instead of the standard French 'consulat'. He also appears to write of his physical sufferings as 'souffrances fosiques [i.e. physiques]' (cf. the Polish word *fizyczny*).

29. 'Hall' can mean an entrance hall or simply a large room. The reference then might just possibly be to the undressing room, the first to be entered by deportees. The need, however, to affirm its emptiness, the bracketed bareness, makes it more likely that Strasfogel is referring to the gas chamber.

30. The context suggests that the term is used ironically by some of the SK to refer to their labours. However, rabbis in the SK such as Langfus also seem to have issued *responsa*, interpreting religious precepts in new ways that responded to the unprecedented atrocities that the men were being forced to confront. David Nencel speculates that Langfus viewed the task of burning bodies in these terms. See David Nencel, interviewed by Joe Russin in 1996. Jeff and Toby Herr Oral History Archive, United States Holocaust Memorial Museum, Washington DC. Accession Number 2003.76. RG-50. 560. 0001. Yaakov Silberberg also gives one account along these lines in Greif, *We Wept without Tears*, 318–19. There are precedents in the Shoah that are linked to *chevrot kadischot*. Rabbi Ephraim Oshry, for instance, issued *responsa* (which he interred in cans in the ground) in the Kovno ghetto that related to burial practices. See Ephraim Oshry, *Responsa from the Holocaust* (New York: Judaica Press, 2001). We are grateful to David Deutsch for sharing his thoughts on Holocaust *responsa* literature. Drawing on remarks by Norman Lamn, Deutsch observes in 'Exhumations in Post-War Rabbinical Responsas' that *responsa* represent a kind of heroism as they manifest a 'commitment to tradition under harsh persecution'. David Deutsch, 'Exhumations in Post-war Rabbinical Responsas', in Jean-Marc Dreyfus and Elisabeth Anstett (eds), *Human Remains in Society: Curation and Exhibition in the Aftermath of Genocide and Mass-Violence* (Manchester: Manchester University Press, 2017), 90–112. Gideon Greif also provides a broad discussion of religious life in the SK in his chapter 'The Religious Life of Sonderkommando Members inside the Killing Installations in Auschwitz-Birkenau' in this volume.

31. In this context, it is noteworthy that he dates his letter, in contrast (as far as we can see) to Nadjary. This act of dating simultaneously makes the letter conventionally letter-like and forms a stamp of his presence at that moment. Against all the odds, he was still alive on 6 November 1944.

32. See also K.E. Fleming's chapter in this volume.

33. Cohen, *From Greece to Birkenau*, 60–61. See also at 52.

34. Marcel Nadjary, *Khroniko 1941–1945* (Thessaloniki: Etz Khaim, 1991), 48. As Nadjary tells it, Strasfogel seems much more part of the Poles when it came to the revolt itself (at 58 and 61).

35. Pepo Cohen observes that there were two major collaborationist newspapers in Greece publishing Nazi proclamations (and propaganda) during the occupation, Νέα Ευρώπη (New Europe) and Απογευματινή (Afternoon). See Pepo Cohen, 'Il n'y a pas de quartier juif à Salonique', in Miriam Novitch (ed.), *Le passage des barbares* (Paris: Presses du temps présent, n.d.), 13–15, at 13. Henry Levy remarks in video testimony that: 'The

Greek newspaper New Europe, *Νέα Ευρώπη*, started vitriolic articles writing every day ... The first day appeared "Death to the Jews"'. USC Shoah Foundation Interview Code 26580. Henry Levy, interviewed by Shelly Roberts, 10 February 1997.
36. See Andreas Kilian's chapter in this volume for a discussion of these documents.

Bibliography

Bendel, Charles. 'Le Sonderkommando', in *Témoignages sur Auschwitz*. Paris: Éditions de l'amicale des déportés d'Auschwitz, 1946.

Bensoussan, Georges, Philippe Mesnard and Carlo Saletti (eds), *Des voix sous la cendre: Manuscrits des Sonderkommandos d'Auschwitz-Birkenau*. Paris: Memorial de la Shoah/Calmann-Levy, 2005.

Bezwińska, Jadwiga, and Danuta Czech (eds). *Amidst a Nightmare of Crime: Notes of Prisoners of Sonderkommando Found at Auschwitz*, trans. Krystyna Michalik. Oświęcim: Publications of State Museum at Oświęcim, 1973.

———. *Inmitten des grauenvollen Verbrechens: Handschriften von Mitgliedern des Sonderkommandos*, trans. Herta Henschel and Jochen August. Oświęcim: Publications of State Museum at Oświęcim, 1996.

Bowman, Steven. *The Agony of Greek Jews, 1940–1945*. Stanford: Stanford University Press, 2009.

Chare, Nicholas. 'Material Witness: Conservation Ethics and the Scrolls of Auschwitz', *symplokē* 24(1–2) (2016), 81–97.

Chare, Nicholas, and Marcel Swiboda. 'Introduction: Unforeseen Encounters', *Liminalities* 14(1) (2018), 1–25.

Chare, Nicholas, and Dominic Williams. *Matters of Testimony: Interpreting the Scrolls of Auschwitz*. New York: Berghahn, 2016.

———. *The Auschwitz Sonderkommando: Testimonies, Histories, Representations*. Basingstoke: Palgrave Macmillan, 2019.

Cohen, Leon. *From Greece to Birkenau: The Crematoria Workers' Uprising*, trans. Jose-Maurice Gormezano. Tel Aviv: Salonika Jewry Research Center, 1996.

Crémieux-Dunand, Julie. *La vie à Drancy: 1941–1944*. Paris: Librairie Gedalge, 1945.

Deutsch, David. 'Exhumations in Post-War Rabbinical Responsas', in Jean-Marc Dreyfus and Elisabeth Anstett (eds), *Human Remains in Society: Curation and Exhibition in the Aftermath of Genocide and Mass-Violence*, Manchester: Manchester University Press, 2017, 90–112.

Friedler, Erich, Barbara Siebert and Andreas Kilian, *Zeugen aus der Todeszone: Das Jüdische Sonderkommando in Auschwitz*. Munich: Deutsche Taschenbuch Verlag, 2005.

Gottesman, Shirley Berger, and Maryann McLoughlin. *A Red Polka-Dotted Dress: A Memoir of Kanada II*. Margate: ComteQ Publishing, 2011.

Greif, Gideon. *We Wept without Tears*. New Haven: Yale University Press, 2005.

Herman, Chaim [Herman Strasfogel]. 'The Manuscript of Chaim Herman', in Jadwiga Bezwińska and Danuta Czech (eds), *Amidst a Nightmare of Crime: Manuscripts of Members of Sonderkommando*, trans. Krystyna Michalik. Oświęcim: Publications of State Museum at Oświęcim, 1996, 179–90.

Levy, Henry. 'The Jews of Salonica and the Holocaust: A Personal Memoir', in Solomon Gaon and M. Mitchell Serels (eds), *Del Fuego: Sephardim and the Holocaust*. New York: Sepher-Hermon Press, 1995, 213–46.

Mark, Ber. *Megiles Oyshvits*. Tel Aviv: Yisroel-Bukh, 1977.
——. *Des voix dans la nuit*, trans. Joseph Fridman and Liliane Princet. Paris: Plon, 1982.
Menasche, Albert, Number 124454. *Birkenau (Auschwitz II). Memoirs of an Eye-Witness: How 72,000 Greek Jews Perished*. New York: Isaac Saltiel, 1947.
Nadjary, Marcel. *Khroniko 1941–1945*. Thessaloniki: Etz Khaim, 1991.
——. 'The Buried Manuscript of Marcel Nadjary', trans. Alexandra Apostolides. In Photini Tomai, *Greeks in Auschwitz-Birkenau*. Athens: Papasiziz Publishers, 2009, 160–67.
——. 'Message in a Bottle: The Buried Manuscript of a Greek Jewish Inmate at Auschwitz [1944]', trans. Isaac Nehama. In Julia Philipps Cohen and Sarah Abrevaya Stein (eds), *Sephardi Lives: A Documentary History, 1700–1950*. Stanford: Stanford University Press, 2014, 285–86.
Nahon, Marco. *Birkenau: The Camp of Death*, trans. Jacqueline Havaux Bowers. Tuscaloosa: University of Alabama Press, 1989.
Novitch, Miriam (ed.). *Le passage des barbares*. Paris: Presses du temps present, n.d.
Oshry, Ephraim. *Responsa from the Holocaust*. New York: Judaica Press, 2001.
Saletti, Carlo (ed.). *La voce dei sommersi: Manoscritti ritrovati di membri del Sonderkommando di Auschwitz*. Venice: Marsilio, 1999.
Selby, Margo. '37 Years after'. Unpublished manuscript in the archives of the United States Holocaust Memorial Museum. USHMM Accession Number 2007.469.1.
Wieviorka, Annette, and Michel Lafitte. *À l'intérieur du camp de Drancy*. Paris: Éditions Perrin, 2012.
Zaorski, Andrzej. 'Relacja'. Unpublished manuscript in the archives of the Jewish Historical Institute, Warsaw. AZIH 301/7182.

Chapter 7

The Letter of Herman Strasfogel

Translated by Ersy Contogouris

Request from a dying man: please deliver this envelope[1] to the French consulate or to the International Red Cross for them to forward it to the address given. Thank you.[2]

Birkenau, 6th XI 1944.

To my very dear wife and daughter,
At the beginning of July of this year I was overjoyed to receive your letter (undated) which was like a balm for my sad days here, I reread it constantly and I will not let go of it until my last breath.

    I never had any opportunity to reply to you and if I write to you today at great risk and danger, it's to say that this is my last letter, that our days are limited and if one day you receive this message you must count me among the millions of our brothers and sisters who have vanished from this world. At this time I must reassure you that I'm going calmly and perhaps heroically (it will depend on the circumstances) only regretting that I cannot see you again for a moment. Nevertheless I want to convey to you here some instructions for you.[3] I know I haven't left you with much in the way of material goods to ensure your livelihood, but that after this war life will count, with a moderate determination and with their ten fingers everyone will be able to get by. Try to ally yourself with a knitter so you can work exclusively for them.

I hope that nothing of what you entrusted with your friends has been lost, if you do have some difficulties then approach the President of our fraternal benefit society who will take it upon himself to ascertain what is rightfully yours. I do not forget my great friend Mr Riss who I think of often who watches over you. I ask a major undertaking of my very dear, unforgettable Simone, that she leads her life socially and discreetly as she knew her father [to do], my wish is that she marries as soon as possible to a Jew on the condition that she has many children if destiny has deprived me of the continuation of my family name it's to her to Simone to secure my first name, the same as that of all the others of our family in Warsaw who are all gone.[4]

To you, my dear wife, I ask your forgiveness if at times in our life we had our little differences now I see that we didn't know how to cherish the time we spent together here I always thought if by some miracle I get out of here I will start over . . . but, alas! that's out of the question no one gets out of here it's all over. I know you are still young and you should remarry I give you carte blanche I order you even because I do not want to see you bereft but I also don't want to give Simone a stepfather try to marry her off as soon as possible, she should give up on further education after which you'll be free.

Never think of returning to Poland, that accursed land for us, it's the land of France that you must cherish and there die [*et là mourrir* (*sic*)] (unless circumstances take you elsewhere but never to Poland).[5]

I'm sure you're interested to know my situation here it is: abridged because if I had to write everything that's happened to me since I left you I'd have to write for my whole life so much has happened to me [*tant je suis passé*].

Our transport which was made up of 1132 people left Drancy on the 2nd March at the break of day and we arrived here in the evening on the 4th, in the cattle car without water, when we got off the train there were already many dead and gone mad.

One hundred people were selected to go to the camp (including myself) the rest went to the gas and then to the ovens. The next day after a cold bath and deprived of everything which we had with us (except for the belt which I still have with me) even the head shaved, don't even mention moustaches and beards, they put us as if by chance in the much talked about [*fameux*] 'Sonder-Kommando' there they told us that we came as reinforcements to work as 'undertakers' or as 'Chevra Kadischa'[6] twenty months have already gone by since then, it seems like a century, it's virtually impossible for me to write to you of all the pain[7] I've lived through, if you live you will certainly read quite a few works written about the 'Sonder- Komando' [*sic*] but I ask you to never judge me badly as if among us there were good and bad I was certainly not among the latter. During this period I did everything I was able to, never thinking about the danger or risk to ease the fate of the wretched for reasons of discretion I cannot write to you about their fate, that my conscience is clear and on the eve of my death I can be proud.

At the beginning I suffered a lot myself because of a distinct food shortage, I dreamed sometimes of a piece of bread even more of a little hot coffee, many of my comrades perished either through illness or simply from being killed each week, our numbers lessened at the present time only 2 (two) of us remain of our hundred, it's true that many found a more or less glorious mass death and if I was not amongst them it was not out of cowardice but simple happenstance in any case, my turn is coming probably in the course of this week.

My physical sufferings came to an end around September 43 starting when I taught my boss the rules of Belotte[8] through playing with him I was released from demanding and laborious work, at the time I had become really skeletal, when my hands rubbed my body they didn't even recognize it, but since, I've caught up, and at the present time with no lack of anything and especially since the month of May 44 we have everything in abundance (except beloved liberty) I am very well clothed, sheltered and fed, I'm in perfect health with no flab of course, very svelte and athletic except for my white hair people say I look like I'm 30 years old.[9]

During all these twenty months here, I've always thought of my favourite time [as being] on my bed where I've lain down thinking I'm with you both, that I'm talking to you and often I saw you in my dreams, sometimes I even cried with you, especially the first night of 'Kippur' or Kol Nidre which we improvised amongst ourselves, I wept a lot reflecting that you were doing the same somewhere in a corner of a hideaway thinking of me.[10]

I always saw Simone in the company of Madame [M-e] Vanhems on the day of the 17th February growing distant as I watched them from the window and more than once walking in the immense chamber of the crematorium (empty) I loudly spoke Simone's name as if I was calling to her and I heard my voice which echoed this precious name which I would unfortunately no longer get to use – that is the greatest punishment that our enemy could inflict on us.

Since I've been here I've never believed in the possibility of coming back, I knew like all of us that all connections with the other world are broken, it's another world here, if you will, it's Hell, but the Hell of Dante is completely laughable in the face of the real one here and we are eyewitnesses must not survive, in spite of all, from time to time I retain a little spark of hope – perhaps by some kind of miracle, me who's already had so much luck one of the oldest here, who has overcome so many obstacles, one of two remaining from a hundred, perhaps this final miracle could happen? If so then let me be back before this buried letter is found.

You should also know that all those who were transported from Drancy are dead, such as Michel, Henri, Adèle along with the children and all our friends and acquaintances whose names I do not record here.

I was happy in my suffering here believing you to be alive and since I've received a letter from you personally in both your handwritings that I kiss quite often, since then my happiness is complete, I'll die calmly knowing that you at least are saved, most of my friends here came with their whole families and the Poles especially are definitely the only survivors (for the moment) and we here are from different peoples or countries. Among the Poles there is a Figlarz who is a cousin of the father of our Figlarz (on that subject, what happened to him?) also people who knew Michel and Eva in the ghetto etc.

I'm asking you to do something for me; I shared life here with a mate from my transport, a French Jew, a certain manufacturer and tradesman from Toulouse called David Lahana it was mutually agreed between us to communicate news to the other's family in the case of the death of one of us and since by unfortunate bad luck he passed on before me, it's down to me to tell his family through you as intermediaries that his wife Mrs Lahana died three weeks after our arrival here (she went down to the camp alive with thirty other French women who are all already dead) and he himself was part of a transport to Lublin of 24th February 1944 comprising two hundred people all from the 'Sonder Kommando' where they were murdered a few days later.[11]

David was an angel, a friend without equal, tell his family that he was always thinking of his two sons with a father's deep love clearly believing them saved in Spain also of his mother and of his sisters and brothers in law. In misery, he was always saying 'Good God, Good God why cause me so much sorrow, have mercy, have mercy . . .' and it was I who consoled him, knowing no German, no Polish, no Yiddish he often found himself in bad spots which I got him out of but, as God is my witness, I could not save him from the transport. So write a letter to this family, they are certainly well known in Toulouse to tell them this news that concerns them, or by another means, his brothers in law Brothers Babani (if I'm not mistaken) have a shop selling silks and merchandises from China boulevard Malesherbes, try to get in touch that way.[12]

I ask you never to forget the good and the help our friends who have provided for you in my absence like the Martinellis, Vanhems and others if there have been, don't forget that if you're alive it's down to God and to them. Unfortunately, I will not have the satisfaction of repaying them personally, it's just left to me to send my sincerest thanks and my best wishes, the wishes expressed by a man before his death will be heard by Providence.

My letter is coming to an end, as are my hours and I bid you a last farewell forever it's the last goodbye, I hold you very very tightly for the last time and I ask once more *to believe me* that I'm going blithely knowing you are alive and our enemy has lost. It's even possible that through the history of the 'Sonder Kommando' you will learn the precise day of my death, I'm in the last squad of 204 people, we're currently shutting down Crematorium 2, where I am, with urgency and there's talk of our own liquidation this very week.

Forgive me for my confused [*étourdi*] letter and also for my French if you only knew the circumstances in which I am writing . . .

I ask that all my friends who I do not name for lack of space and who I bid a common goodbye to forgive me and say to them take revenge for your innocent sisters and brothers who fell at the scaffold.

Goodbye my dear wife and my treasured Simone, carry out my wishes and live in peace, may God watch over you.

A thousand kisses from your husband and father

Herman.

When you get this letter I ask you to tell Mrs Germaine Cohen of the Union Bank of Salonica S.A. – Greece that Leon shares my fate as he has shared my sufferings, he embraces everyone and particularly recommends Bill to his wife.[13] Daniel and Lili have been dead for a long time, the lawyer Yacoel died with his entire family a month ago

Herman.[14]

Notes

All notes are the translator's. A previous English translation of this letter that appears in the anthology of Sonderkommando (SK) writings *Amidst a Nightmare of Crime* attributes the letter to Chaim Herman based on it being signed Herman. Chaim Herman [Herman Strasfogel], 'Letter of Chaim Herman', in Jadwiga Bezwińska and Danuta Czech (eds), *Amidst a Nightmare of Crime: Notes of Prisoners of Sonderkommando Found at Auschwitz* (Oświęcim: State Museum of Oświęcim, 1973), 181–90. This attribution is now recognized to be incorrect. The letter was written by Herman Strasfogel (known to members of the SK by his non-naturalized name of Hersz Strasfogel). In this translation, the unconventional syntax and eccentric punctuation of the letter have been preserved as much as possible, although misspellings, of which there are many, are not indicated. Under immense pressure, Strasfogel has chosen to write in his second language. His situation manifests in the sometimes uneven prose of the composition. The script is, however, confident and clear. Strasfogel only very occasionally revisits and revises words he has penned.

1. The envelope was makeshift, simply a sheet of grid paper. This was the same paper used for the letter proper. A sheet of paper that has seemingly now been lost provided the Paris address of a family friend referenced in the letter, Mister Vanhems, for the letter to be delivered to. See Andreas Kilian's chapter in this volume.
2. This request was then repeated in Russian.
3. The multiple repetition of 'you' (*vous*) here occurs in the original.
4. Strasfogel identifies his daughter Simone by her first name, but conceals his wife's name (Chiona) throughout the letter, presumably because of its distinctiveness in a French context.
5. The word translated as 'unless' here is 'au moins'. It seems Strasfogel meant to write 'à moins'.
6. A *chevra kadisha* is a society of men and women tasked with following ritual and preparing the bodies of deceased Jews for burial in accordance with religious tenets.
7. This word is indistinct and could either be *peine* or *preuve* (épreuve), either 'pain/sorrow' or 'hardship'.
8. Belotte (more commonly belote in English) is a card game popular in France.
9. Strasfogel was forty-nine years old when he composed the letter.
10. *Kol Nidre* is a prayer in Aramaic that is said before the evening service on each Yom Kippur. The name derives from the opening words, which mean 'all vows'.
11. Becky Lahana (née Behar) died at Birkenau on 31 March 1943.
12. David Lahana's sister, Sarah Babani, was the wife of Israël Babani who lived in Toulouse. In the 1930s, the Maison Babani fabric shop Palais de la Soierie (Silk Palace) was located at 65 rue Alsace in the city. In 1937, the vice-president of the Association du Culte Israélite de Toulouse was Israël Babani and the treasurer was David Lahana. See Colette Zytnicki, *Les juifs à Toulouse entre 1945 et 1970: une communauté toujours recommencée* (Toulouse: Presses Universitaires du Mirail, 1998), 44.
13. Leon Cohen would ultimately survive and write a memoir of his experiences at Birkenau that makes mention of Strasfogel. See Leon Cohen, *From Greece to Birkenau: The Crematoria Workers' Uprising*, trans. Jose-Maurice Gormezano (Tel Aviv: Salonica Jewry Research Center, 1996), 60–61.
14. Strasfogel began writing this postscript lengthwise in the left margin of the page before continuing at the bottom of the page in smaller script. An arrow is used to guide the reader to this continuation of the postscript. Here the pitfalls of reading the letter in transcription manifest themselves as something of the visual complexity of the original manuscript is lost. The positioning of the postscript, initially at an angle to the text of the main body of the letter, serves to mark it as visibly different from the rest of the letter. Strasfogel is now writing on behalf of another rather than for himself. The message is discernibly an afterthought, forming a favour carried out once Strasfogel had finished the more important matter of writing to his loved ones. The translator is grateful to Andreas Kilian for information about the visual appearance of the letter.

Bibliography

Cohen, Leon. *From Greece to Birkenau: The Crematoria Workers' Uprising*, trans. Jose-Maurice Gormezano. Tel Aviv: Salonica Jewry Research Center, 1996.

Herman, Chaim [Hersz Strasfogel]. 'Letter of Chaim Herman', trans. Krystyna Michalik. In Jadwiga Bezwińska and Danuta Czech (eds), *Amidst a Nightmare of Crime: Notes of Prisoners of Sonderkommando Found at Auschwitz*. Oświęcim: State Museum of Oświęcim, 1973, 181–90.

Zytnicki, Colette. *Les juifs à Toulouse entre 1945 et 1970: une communauté toujours recommencée*. Toulouse: Presses Universitaires du Mirail, 1998.

Chapter 8

The Letter of Marcel Nadjary

Translated by Ersy Contogouris

Page 1
Bitte diesen Brief senden am dehm nerensten Griecheschen Konsulat[1]

Bardzo proszę niniejszy list doręczyć najbliższemu Konsulowi Greckiemu.[2]

... ces quelques mots par[s?] un condamné [?] à la mort ... le remettre en plus prochain Consulat de la Grèce[3]

Please this letter send to ……….. ………. the Greek Consulate

8 lines
Dimitrios A. Stefanides
Rue Kroussovo No 4
Thessaloniki
GRECE

Page 2
To my beloved ones, Dimitrios Athan. Stephanides, Ilias Cohen.– Georgios Gounaris My dear group of friends, Smaro Efraimidou < from Athens > and so many more whom I frequently think about and finally to my beloved homeland: "GREECE" of which I was always a good citizen.–

We set out from our Athens on 2 April 1944, after I had been tortured for months at the Chaidari camp where I always [crossed out] received the parcels that kind Smaro sent me and her efforts on my behalf have remained unforgettable to me during these awful days that I am living. [Future tense] .... always to .... her .... search .... my dear Misko, and some time [or from time to time?] .... to .... [my ....] but that you look after her addresses .... our Ilias and that you always help him .... and that Manolis has not forgotten them

Page 3
but even though it unfortunately seems that we will not be able to ever meet again.– After ten days of travel on 11 April, we arrived at Auschwitz, where they moved us to the Birkenau camp we stayed about a month in quarantine, and from there they separated us the healthy and strong, to where? where? my dear Misko? To a crematorium I will explain to you below the fine work that the Almighty wanted us to do It is a large building with a wide chimney with 15 <fifteen> ovens.
Under a garden there are two large underground chambers of enormous size. One is used for us to get undressed and the second chamber of death which the people enter naked and after it is full with about 3,000 individuals it shuts and they Gas them after about 6–7 minutes of agony, they give up the ghost.
Our work consisted first in welcoming them most of them

Page 4
did not know the reason .... They fell or were crying they were telling them that .... they were going to have a wash. . . . they were going unknowingly toward death.– To this day .... I said that every ... . [ro] to .... I would tell them that I do not understand the language they are speaking to me and to the people men and women who I saw were condemned I told the truth.– after ..... everyone was naked, they advanced toward the chamber of death in there the Germans had placed pipes on the ceiling .... so that they would think they were getting ready to bathe with whip in hand the Germans forced them to squeeze in so that they could fit as many as possible a real sardine tin of people after they sealed the door shut. The boxes of Gas arrived in the car of the Germ. Red Cross with two S.S. . . . They are Gassers who from some

Page 5
openings poured the Gas onto them. –
After half an hour we would open the doors and our work would begin we moved the bodies of those innocent women and children up to the

elevator that would take them to the oven chamber and from there they would place them into the ovens where they burned without the use of fuel because of the fat that they have. –

From one person there came out only about a few hundred grams of ashes of bones it [crossed out] that the Germans made us crush then pass through a coarse sieve and then a car took it and threw it into the river that runs near us Vistula and thus they eliminate every trace. –

The horrible things my eyes have seen are indescribable About 600,000 <six hundred thousand> Jews have passed before my eyes from Hungary – Frenchmen – about 80,000 Poles from Litzmannstadt and now lately

Page 6

have started to arrive about 10,000 ten thousand Jews from Theresienstadt in Czechoslovakia.– Today a transport arrived from Theresienstadt but thank God they did not bring them to us they kept them in the lager they say an order has come down not to kill Jews anymore and it seems to be true, now lately they have changed their minds but now there is not a single Jew left in Europe but for us things are different we have to be absent from the Earth because we know many of the unbelievable methods of abuse and reprisal of the. –

Our commando is called Sonder commando <special commando> made up of at the beginning 1,000 <one thousand> including 200 Greeks and the rest Poles and Hungarians and after a Heroic resistance because they wanted to get rid of only 800 <eight hundred> because (??? that is???) all of the one hundred outside the camp

Page 7

and the rest within. My good friends Viko Broudo and Minis Aaron from Thessaloniki fell. –

Now that this order has come down they will get rid of us as well, we are 26 Greeks in total and the rest are Poles. As for the Greeks at least, we are determined to die like true Greeks just as every Greek knows how to die by showing to the very last moments despite the superiority of the criminals that Greek blood courses through our veins just as we also showed it in the Italian war. –

My dear friends when you read this you will wonder about the work I did, how was I Manolis or anyone else able to do this work burning my fellow believers I was also thinking that at the beginning many times I thought of going in

Page 8
with them as well so as to finish but what always kept me was the revenge I wanted and want to live in order to avenge the deaths of Dad of Mum and of my beloved darling sister Nelli.– I am not afraid of death is it possible to fear it after all that my eyes have seen?
That is why my dear Ilias my beloved cousin if I myself do not exist that you must know – you and all my friends – your duty <I found out from my darling cousin Sarrika Chouli <do you remember the one who was at my house> she is alive today that Nellika was with your dear sister Errika during her last moments. –
My only wish is that your hands receive that which I wrote [crossed out] am writing you. –

Page 9
My family's property I bequeath to you Misko <Dimitrios Athanasiou Stephanidis> with the request that you take my cousin Ilias close to you Ilias is a Cohen and to consider him as if it were me in person that was with you, to always look out for him and if by chance Sarika [sic] Chouli my cousin returns to have [crossed out] treat her dear Misko the same way you treated my [crossed out] that beloved niece of yours Zmaragda, because all of us here are suffering to a degree that the human mind cannot imagine. –
Think of me now and then just as I think of you. –
It is not fated that I too see our Greece free just as you saw her on 12/10/43.
Whoever asks about me tell them that I no longer exist and that I went like a true Greek.– My dear Misko, help all those who return from the Birkenau

Pages 10–11
camp. –
I am not sad dear Misko that I am going to die, but that I will not be able to avenge myself in the way that I want and know. –
If you happen to receive a letter from our relatives living abroad answer appropriately that the family A. Nadjary was extinguished murdered by the civilized Germans <New Europe> do you remember my dear Giorgo? Nelli's piano dear Misko take it from the Sionidou family and give it to Ilias so that he always has it with him as a reminder of her he loved her so much and so did she. –
Almost every time they kill I ask myself if there is a God and in spite of it all I always believed in Him and still believe that God wants it so let His will be done

I die happy because I know that at this moment our Greece is Free my last word will be Long live Greece
Marcel Nadjary

Page 12
It has been about four years now that they have been killing the Jews .... they killed Poles, Czechs, Frenchmen, Hungarians, Slovakians, Dutchmen, Belgians, Russians and all of Thessaloniki except for about 300 who are still living in Athens, Arta, Corfu, Kos and Rhodes. –
In all about 1,400,000 in total

Page 13
The Honorable Greek Embassy which will receive this note is beseeched by a good Greek Citizen named Emmanouil or Marcel Nadjary formerly residing in Thessaloniki no. 9 Italias street
in Thessaloniki
To send it this note to the address below.
Dimitrios Athanasiou Stephanidis
no 4 Krousovou Street
Thessaloniki
Greece
This is my last wish sentenced to death, by the Germans because I am of the Jewish Faith
   Thank you
   Madjaris [Nadjary]

Notes

All notes are the translator's. The page numbering of this letter follows that of the Auschwitz Museum which failed to number all the pages correctly therefore giving the false impression that the letter has thirteen pages (it actually has twelve pages).

1. German: Please send this letter to the nearest Greek consulate.
2. Polish: Please send this letter to the nearest Greek consul.
3. French: . . . these few words from a man condemned to death . . . send it to the nearest Greek consulate.

Chapter 9

The Religious Life of Sonderkommando Members inside the Killing Installations in Auschwitz-Birkenau

Gideon Greif

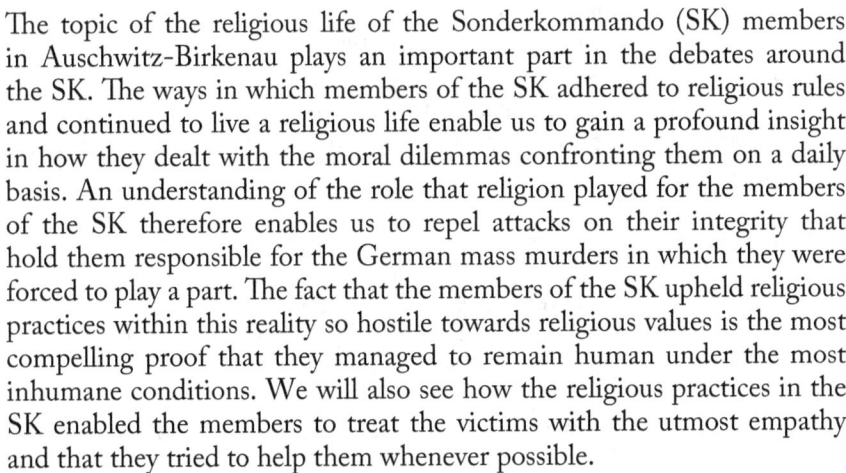

The topic of the religious life of the Sonderkommando (SK) members in Auschwitz-Birkenau plays an important part in the debates around the SK. The ways in which members of the SK adhered to religious rules and continued to live a religious life enable us to gain a profound insight in how they dealt with the moral dilemmas confronting them on a daily basis. An understanding of the role that religion played for the members of the SK therefore enables us to repel attacks on their integrity that hold them responsible for the German mass murders in which they were forced to play a part. The fact that the members of the SK upheld religious practices within this reality so hostile towards religious values is the most compelling proof that they managed to remain human under the most inhumane conditions. We will also see how the religious practices in the SK enabled the members to treat the victims with the utmost empathy and that they tried to help them whenever possible.

As we will see, religion played a very important part in the life of many SK members. We have to take into account the fact that the members of the SK were recruited among different Jewish movements. The inner structure of the SK was a copy of the diversity of the prewar Jewish communities. Orthodox traditionalists were recruited to the SK as well as reform Jews and nonreligious Jews of all kinds.

Some members of the SK tried to uphold the religious life they had led before their deportation to Auschwitz-Birkenau: they tried to adhere to the dietary laws, they prayed and they celebrated the Jewish holidays.

But the reality of Auschwitz-Birkenau in general and the reality of the gas chambers in particular made it impossible to continue with all religious practices in the same way they were used to when they were free. While the members of the SK had readier access to religious items such as prayer shawls because they could access the possessions of the victims, religious practices were forbidden for them as for all prisoners of the camp. The prisoner Gabriel Malinski reported that in 1942 more than 50 men were killed by the SS because they suspected religious authorities among them.[1] This explains the clandestine nature of the religious practices, as we can see in a report by Zalman Gradowski:

> I see the bunker [V] in front of my inner eye. A member would stand there and look if someone would come, in the meantime the religious Jews would deceive their oppressors. Very often they had to take off their tefillin quickly and run to work during their prayers as if nothing had happened. But in many cases, they were also caught in the act.[2]

How present religious life was within the SK, despite the cruel reality, is shown by the fact that, according to Mordechai Ciechanower, a group of about ten prisoners met daily for prayers.[3] To live according to the dietary laws, one prisoner in the SK only ate bread, margarine and onions, as Miklós Nyiszli reports.[4]

Especially in the later days of the commando, the Jewish religion was practised more confident and more in the open, as Shlomo Venezia remembers:

> Some prayed every day. I know that this was impossible and extremely dangerous in other parts of the camp. But in our commando, it was harmless because the Germans never entered the attic of the crematorium where we had our beds. We also could have organized prayer books easily, but these men did not need them. They knew all prayers by heart.[5]

In particular, prisoners with privileges used their status to enable religious practices. Abraham Dragon, for example, who had to do *Stubendienst* with his brother Shlomo, prepared matza for Sukkot:

> Yes. Only the people from the Sonderkommando. Because we could do whatever we wanted. We were locked in and no one saw that I baked matza. On Sukkot we prayed.[6]

The famous *Oberkapo* Kamiński also supported the religious Jews in the SK – he supplied them with prayer shawls and managed to relieve them of the harder work.[7]

Religious Authorities

One of the religious authorities supported by the other members of the SK was Zalman Gradowski, one of the so-called chroniclers of the SK. Yaakov Freimark, who noted that many members of the SK were indeed emotionally deaf, mentions Gradowski as a positive exception:

> Only Gradowski during the whole time said that he was going to pay with blood for the gruesome work he was forced to do. He was an intelligent man, religious. I cannot forget how he stood there and prayed . . . When I entered the block, I saw Salman in tallit and tefillin engrossed in prayer. After he had finished, I asked for whom he was saying the kaddish. He answered that he said it for the transport that arrived today and also for the holy books I had brought to burn the other day and for whose he had not said the kaddish yet. At that time everything was burned in the bunkers.[8]

Leyb Langfus, the former dayan from Maków Mazowiecki, was also assigned to relatively easy work and spent much of his time in the block.[9] The Kapos had assigned him the work of washing and cutting the victims' hair.[10] The specific situation of the SK made it possible for him to more or less adhere to religious rules until he was murdered in connection with the uprising of the SK. By Nyiszli and his comrades, Langfus was called 'the ascetic'.[11]

But what role did religious life play for the other members of the SK who were not religious authorities or especially pious Jews? There is no doubt that Jewish religious practices were extremely important for some of the SK members. It meant moral support and stability as well as strengthening a sense of community.

The importance religion held for many of the prisoners led to the fact that the religious authorities enjoyed a similar reputation in the commando as did the *Blockälteste*. But while the authority of the functionaries only derived from the role given to them by the German oppressors, the authority of the religious dignitaries was rooted in the prisoners' own tradition. This made the religious dignitaries extremely important to strengthen the moral stability of the prisoners in an environment governed by antisemitic terror. Pious prisoners were able to find answers to their questions and problems by asking the religious authorities in the commando, from whom they could get help in order to deal with their function within the commando and the reality of life in the camp. This also meant that the religious authorities were under pressure due to the expectations of other prisoners: they had to provide answers to their problems, they had to show how to deal with the inhumane situation of the camp and the gas chambers, and they had to resolve religious doubts. Nonreligious members of the SK and those who had lost their faith responded to the religious authorities with scepticism and rejection. For them, the religious practices seemed cynical due to the daily confrontation with mass murder and their own role in it. Shmuel Leibowicz remembers:

> Yes, there were Jewish prisoners in the Sonderkommando, they prayed. Outside the gas chambers. We laughed at them. At least I did. Because I was asking myself, where god was. On a daily basis, infants were murdered, mothers who had just given birth to a child. Where was god? But they prayed. They were no fanatics, but they were religious. One of them even had tefillin.[12]

On one occasion, Leibowicz had a discussion with an older man in the commando. He asked him to prove that there was a god. The man only answered that there was no answer to that question.[13]

The Polish-Jewish Kapo Lemke Pliszko asked the former dayan Langfus how he could still believe in the existence of god, given all that was happening. Langfus answered evasively and said that Pliszko should leave him to his work.[14] Filip Müller reports that due to different understandings of the Jewish faith, Langfus was isolated from the rest of the commando, together with a small group of extremely pious Jews surrounding him. He remembers that after a transport had been gassed, a conflict arose between the group around Langfus and another group within the SK:

> They insisted on their position that such a cruel reality as the one they were witnesses of could not exist if there indeed was a godly justness. 'Listen, dayan,' one of them said: 'not once I sensed only a hint of goodly justness here. After all, everything you put into my head in school is sheer nonsense. There is no god, and if there was one he would be an ox or the son of a whore!' It was a young boy from Makov, that threw these words into the face of his former teacher.

The dayan tried to argue against him:

> With a failing voice he tried to explain the meaning of the bible, that not only narrates the history of Judaism but also was the expression of an eternal law saying: What happened to the fathers, is the omen for their offspring. Another prisoner reacted enraged: 'Is that supposed to mean that the Nazis are allowed to murder because the pharaohs already murdered?' 'Of course not,' the dayan answered almost humble. 'I only wanted to say that the pious Jew does not read the bible like a legend but that he refers its content to the present... And if the haggadah orders that every man in every generation is supposed to see himself as if he himself would

emigrate from Egypt, then maybe those few who somehow will survive will read the haggadah, enlarged by their experiences in Auschwitz, Majdanek or Treblinka. In every generation, my brothers, there were pharaohs that wanted to annihilate us but – the holiest is praised – he always saved us from their hands'.[15]

According to Müller, most of the critics were appeased by the severity and the calm with which the dayan had spoken. Even if they did not believe in his words, they dispersed. After this incident, according to Müller, the dayan and his supporters were treated with respect.

Other members of the SK support the notion that the dayan was considered an authority among the SK and that prisoners asked him for counsel.[16] The functionaries within the commando also respected him and tried to protect him from hard labour by excusing him from work completely or assigning him easier tasks. They also supported him with food that suited the dietary laws. Langfus himself managed to avoid direct contact with the corpses, as did other religious prisoners. Mordechai Ciechanower and Yaakov Freimark noted on this matter:

> In the beginning, Langfuss worked like everyone else in the Sonderkommando. But after the commando got more organized, we made it possible – of course with the knowledge of the *Blockältester* – that he stayed in the block and write, while the other members of the Sonderkommando went to work in the crematorium.[17]

> Over and over he said how much it hurt him to see all this happening. Most of the time he worked in the undressing room. He was not among those who had to remove the corpses from the gas chamber. The dayan Langfuss had to clean the undressing room so he did not have to touch the corpses.[18]

In his diary, Langfus confirms that, 'on principle',[19] he never had direct contact with the corpses.

Holidays

During holidays, the religious authorities in the SK organized services and held speeches. On Passover, the other prisoners 'organized' (i.e. obtained illicitly) flour and baked unleavened matzo bread under the supervision of Langfus, as the Dragon brothers report.[20] Instead of wine, beet juice was served. On Sukkot, a sukkah was built outside the crematorium.[21]

Rosenblum reported that on Yom Kippur, he spoke to a rabbi within the commando:

> On Yom Kippur [1943] a rabbi spoke with the other prisoners in crematorium III. While he talked about the things happening in the camp and how thousands of Jewish women, men and children were murdered, I heard the screams, probably of 12- to 14-year-old children ... that were murdered in crematorium IV. The rabbi spoke about the general situation as well as our hope to be liberated – and he said that the annihilation of the Jewish people would come to an end very soon. Everyone thought of his loved ones and those he had to leave behind. We talked about the fear that the we would have the same fate as those brought to the gas chambers. As far as I remember, his name was Friedman, he was a foreman in the crematorium.[22]

Even if not all Jewish prisoners in the SK were religious, many of them showed some form of acknowledgement of the Jewish religion and the religious values by accepting the special nature of religious acts and the special meaning of the Jewish holidays. Many of them also shared the wish to uphold Jewish cultural traditions. In particular, because the daily work of the SK meant to take part in the actions of the murderers, the upkeep of religious practices could provide some form of solace.

A Moral Compass

Many SK members derived a special will to survive from the Jewish religion. The Jewish religion therefore has to be seen as a strong source of hope that helped many in the SK to survive. It strengthened the spirit because it enabled prisoners to set something against their German tormentors. Filip Müller, for example, reports how religion gave him the power to fight against the complete loss of emotions and prevented him from being broken by the misery surrounding him:

> I thought that all human feelings and emotions inside me had died. But when Schwarz said the kaddish ..., I felt this ineffable pain and deep sorrow in my soul, I am unable to describe these feelings. But the prayer helped me to overcome the pain and to ease my heart.[23]

The counsel of the religious authorities was especially important for upholding the morale of the other prisoners.[24] Müller remembers that one single believer, in this case the deeply religious foreman Goliath Fischl,[25] managed to provide stability to other religious Jews within the commando:

> When Fischl prayed, he gave us a signal with his hands to stand up, and every time he nodded with his head at a certain part of the prayer, we answered him: 'Omen!' [sic] To me it did not make any sense to pray in

Auschwitz and I considered it absurd to believe in god at such a place. In every other situation and in every other place I would not have taken Fischl, this wayward and abstruse person, seriously. But here, at the border between life and death, we willingly followed his example because we had nothing else and we felt how his faith gave us strength.[26]

It seems that the SS responsible for guarding the crematoria and the SK realized the importance of the Jewish religion to many members of the commando. Morris Venezia assumes that the SS collected information on the religious practices when he reports on an incident when the SS deliberately chose the holiday of Yom Kippur to collect the talitot (prayer shawls) from the men of the SK. The SS then had undershirts made from the talitot and forced the religious Jews in the commando to wear them.[27]

In connection with the daily work of the SK and the reality of the death camp, there was another dilemma for the strictly religious Jews due to the Jewish law 'Kiddush Hashem'. According to this principle, believers were obliged to sacrifice their own lives instead of committing a great sin. Of course, the daily life of the SK could be interpreted as such a great sin. We know that this question was indeed important to some members of the SK because when the uprising of the SK was planned, one of the prisoners asked the others to die according to the 'Kiddush Hashem' during the uprising. This discussion occurred after two Hungarian deportees raised their glasses to each other and were happy to die according to 'Kiddush Hashem'.[28] Bella Katz speaks about a SK prisoner who preferred to kill himself instead of touching corpses – he indeed preferred to die rather than commit a sin.

Confronted with the reality of the Holocaust, the Rabbi Yitzhak Nissenbaum who was in the Warsaw Ghetto developed the principle 'Kiddush Hachayyim', which in opposition to the 'Kiddush Hashem' emphasized the physical life as a holy thing and proclaimed the sustainment of life as the highest principle.[29] This principle made it possible for the Jewish faith to continue to be an important source of strength and morale for the members of the SK in their daily fight against the cruel reality of the gas chambers.

Doubts

But the longer the members of the SK had to carry out their cruel work in the gas chambers and crematoria, the more they began to doubt their faith. Many lost their faith in god during their time in Auschwitz – the same happened to many members of the SK, as we have already seen in the controversial debates among the prisoners. Morris Kesselmann reports how he himself began to doubt the existence of god: 'How can such awful things happen when there is a god?'[30] was the question he repeatedly asked himself, without being able to provide an answer. Other survivors also tell us about their religious doubts. Gabriel Malinski, for example, remembers how at a certain point he stopped to pray for his salvation. He did not feel up to it any longer and saw no meaning in the prayers after being confronted with the reality of Auschwitz for a certain time.[31] After Otto Moll brutally murdered an infant, Yaakov Silberberg also stopped believing in god.[32] The testimony of Zvi Schermer, who did not work in the SK but in the Kanada-Kommando, gives us an important insight in how conflicted the SK prisoners were concerning their religious beliefs. Schermer describes the impressions of the SK prisoners and their relationship to religion:

> The SK-guys always said: 'Look what became of us. Look, what kind of men we became'. They were depressed. They were anti-religious and had lost their faith in Judaism when they saw who they had to burn. That was the only thing we talked about. They were depressed.[33]

Suicide

When the SK prisoners had lost their faith as well as their individuality and emotionality, which were taken from them by the daily work and the reality of the camp, there was only one option left in order to escape the brutal life of the camp: many survivors of the death camp report that members of the SK committed suicide. In general, prisoners committing suicide was a very common phenomenon in Auschwitz. Many prisoners lost hope and wanted to make an end to their lives. It is important to note that the number of suicides in the SK was not higher than in other parts of the camp. However, for the SK prisoners, there was another reason to commit suicide: they did not want to continue the brutal work they were forced to do day after day. Lemke Pliszko reports that many prisoners killed themselves exactly for this reason: many prisoners 'hanged themselves or ran into the electric fences . . . They could not cope with the work anymore, so they committed suicide'.[34] Szaya Gertner also talks about cases of suicide among the SK connected to the work many prisoners simply could not do any longer:

> There only was one way out. During the 10 weeks I was a part of the Sonderkommando I saw many prisoners who threw themselves into the

electric fences. One corpse per minute. I thought they were doing the right thing . . . In the morning, I sometimes saw those who had walked into the fences during the night. They did not fall down, the electricity kept them up. They were standing upright with their hands stretched forward.[35]

Other prisoners, however, decided that according to their faith, suicide was not an option, thereby agreeing with the ideas of Rabbi Nissenbaum. Josef Sackar, for example, explains that 'it is written in the Torah that it is forbidden to take one's own life'.[36] Others used 'rational' arguments against a voluntary death, such as Morris Venezia, who said: 'What would have happened? Nothing. Someone else would have taken your position'.[37] Venezia might be correct that in the event that one worker was 'lost', the SS would have found a 'replacement' very quickly. However, one also has to take into consideration the fact that the system of mass murder would have been run less effectively for some time, since the new workers had to learn their jobs from scratch. The SK prisoners were considered 'valuable' workers from 1942 onwards. For this reason, the SS tried to prevent suicides in the SK. It was a central principle of the German camp system to react to every sign of resistance – and the suicide of a prisoner was considered as such – with the collective punishment of the whole group of prisoners. Yaakov Gabai describes the reaction of the SS after a suicide in detail. One or two months after the suicide of the SK prisoner Menachem Litschi, an SS man came to the remaining prisoners of the commando and asked to speak with prisoners who knew something about this case. Gabai responded and was taken for questioning:

> It was clear to me that I could not tell him that he simply committed suicide. When they asked me, how something like this could have happened, I said that he went to close to the fire while carrying the corpse, slipped and fell into the oven. Period. Woe is me if I had told them that he had killed himself . ! . They would have immediately killed me, too.[38]

After a suicide, the camp authorities always called the questioning and investigative unit of the Political Department – the so-called camp Gestapo – and the 'crime scenes' were photographed. The official reason for these measures was that it had to be determined whether a murder had occurred.[39] The SS also called physicians to examine the corpses. One of those physicians was Miklós Nyiszli, who worked as a pathologist in the crematoria for Josef Mengele. In his testimony, Nyiszli reports that one of the SK members once tried to kill himself with an overdose of luminal.[40] Nyiszli writes that this was a very common form of suicide among the SK prisoners because they could access medicine very easily due to their contact with the possessions of the victims. He continues:

The comrades standing beside the bed ask me to let the 'captain'[41] go his way. If he stayed alive this would only mean a prolongation of the sufferings he wanted to escape.[42]

Even though Nyiszli was aware that the SK was going to be 'liquidated' in a few weeks, he started to revive his patient as his professional ethics obliged him. But some time later, his assessment of the situation had changed – he no longer saw it through the eyes of a physician, but through those of a concentration camp inmate:

Now that I am no longer standing in front of him and his suffering face no longer calls forth my medical self, my human self agrees completely with his comrades. I should have let him go the way he chose, the one that was not leading toward the cold barrels of machine guns . . .[43]

Conclusion

Of course, the suicides of SK members were not investigated because the SS had no real interest in solving or preventing murders. And the physicians were not called in to save lives. Instead, the case illustrates that the total control in the camp and the SK was without limits; it also reached beyond the border between life and death. The prisoners should be stripped of every part of their autonomy, even the last bit of it: the decision to live or to die. This aspect of the reality of life in the camp shows the importance of religious practices in the SK. The orientation and strength provided by the religious laws and traditions helped the members of the SK to distance themselves from the brutal reality of daily life in the camp and enabled them to maintain some sort of autonomy against the brutal regime of the camp: they still were able to decide, they still had their own personal connection to god and to the Jewish religion. As we have seen, upholding a religious life in the vicinity of the gas chambers meant a daily struggle and presented the religious Jews in the SK with many dilemmas and problems. But it also gave them the strength to maintain some kind of autonomy, the feeling of upholding Jewish values in a place where European Judaism should be annihilated. The brutal clash between religion and the brutality of Auschwitz's death machinery can be seen in one incident reported by Yehoshuah Rosenblum, which occurred during the murder of the Hungarian Jews. At that time, the capacities of the crematoria and the undressing rooms were not sufficient and some of the deportees had to undress outside the crematoria buildings. Also, the Germans did not pay attention to the policy that men and women were divided as had once been the case.⁴⁴ Rosenblum, who became a member of the SK on 15 May 1944, remembers that in one case men and women had to undress in the same area. For the religious women in particular, this was a shock. Rosenblum reported on their reactions:

> There were cases in which the women did not want to undress in the presence of men. They were religious women. But after some shouts from the SS, threatening to hit the women, they finally undressed themselves.⁴⁵

The reality of the camp normally did not care about religious feelings; in a place created for mass murder, most of the time there was no space for religious feelings, religious traditions and the upkeep of religious life. However, many of the SK members managed to retain their religious values, even under the worst conditions imaginable. This is compelling proof that many of them stayed human and were not transformed by this inhumane place and the cruel work they were forced to carry out.

Gideon Greif is an Israeli historian, educator and pedagogue. He is the Chief Historian and Researcher at the 'Shem Olam' Institute for Education, Documentation and Research on Faith and the Holocaust, Israel, and the Chief Historian and Researcher at the Foundation for Holocaust Education Projects in Miami, Florida. He is considered a world-renowned historian-expert on the history of Auschwitz-Birkenau. His most famous contribution to the history of Auschwitz is his groundbreaking research *We Wept without Tears* on the history of the Sonderkommando. This research, first published at Yad Vashem, has become an international bestseller. The book *We Wept without Tears* inspired the Hungarian movie *Son of Saul*, which won an Oscar in 2016. Greif worked as a historical advisor for the film.

Notes

1. Gabriel Malinski, interview with GG on 1 December 1999 in Miami Beach, Private Archive GG.
2. Gideon Greif, *We Wept without Tears: Testimonies of the Jewish Sonderkommando from Auschwitz* (New Haven: Yale University Press, 2004), 35.
3. Mordechai Ciechanower, interview with GG on 30 July 1998 in Ramat Gan, Private Archive GG.
4. Miklós Nyiszli, *Im Jenseits der Menschlichkeit: Ein Gerichtsmediziner in Auschwitz* (Berlin: Karl Dietz, 2005), 138.

5. Shlomo Venezia, *Meine Arbeit im Sonderkommando Auschwitz* (Munich: Karl Blessing, 2008), 150.
6. Abraham Dragon, interview with GG in Ramat Gan, Private Archive GG.
7. Eliezer Welbel, interview with GG and Andreas Kilian on 17 October 1998 in Skokie, Private Archive GG.
8. Yaakov Freimark, interview with GG on 23 December 2005 in Herzliya, Private Archive GG.
9. Mordechai Ciechanower, interview with GG on 28 September 2000 in Ramat Gan, Private Archive GG.
10. Filip Müller, *Sonderbehandlung: Drei Jahre in den Krematorien und Gaskammern von Auschwitz* (Munich: Steinhausen, 1979), 104: 'Their work came down to the task to clean and dry the hair. As strictly religious men they dedicated all of their free time to pray for the dead and to study the Jewish texts. The books they owned came from fellow believers who had believed in a similar way before they were murdered in the gas chambers'.
11. Nyiszli, *Im Jenseits der Menschlichkeit*, 138.
12. Shmuel Leibowicz, interview with GG on 14 August 2000 in Hertzlyia, Private Archive GG.
13. Ibid.
14. Lemke Pliszko, interview with GG on 27 July 2001 in Givat Hashlosha, Private Archive GG.
15. Müller, *Sonderbehandlung*, 104ff.
16. Abraham Dragon and Shlomo Dragon, continuation of the interview with GG in Auschwitz, Private Archive GG, Video Nr. 15.
17. Mordechai Ciechanower, interview with GG on 1 October 1999 in Ramat Gan, Private Archive GG; Yaakov Silberberg, interview with GG on 22 January 1998 in Holon, Private Archive GG.
18. Yaakov Freimark, interview with GG on 23 December 2005, in Herzliya, Private Archive GG.
19. Leib Langfuss, *The Horrors of Murder*, 1944, printed in Ber Mark, *The Scrolls of Auschwitz* (Tel Aviv: Am Oved, 1985), 214.
20. Abraham Dragon and Shlomo Dragon, continuiation of the interview with GG in Auschwitz, Private Archive GG, Video Nr. 15.
21. Ibid.
22. Yehoshuah Rosenblum, Yad Vashem Archive Number P 25.
23. Müller, *Sonderbehandlung*, 76.
24. Yaakov Silberberg, interview with GG on 22 January 1998 in Holon, Private Archive GG. See also Teresa Świebocka, Franciszek Piper and Martin Mayr (eds), *Inmitten des grauenvollen Verbrechens: Handschriften von Mitgliedern des Sonderkommandos*, trans. Herta Henschel and Jochen August (Oświęcim: Verlag des Staatlichen Auschwitz-Birkenau Museums, 1996), 213f, and Mordechai Ciechanower, interview with GG on 1 October 1999 in Ramat Gan, Private Archive GG.
25. Fischl had been a foreman of the so-called Fischl-Kommando in the old crematorium (May/June 1942).
26. Müller, *Sonderbehandlung*, 47. The spelling 'Omen' is used to render the traditional Ashkenazi pronunciation of 'Amen'.
27. Morris Venezia, interview with GG on 14 September 1997 in Miami Beach, Private Archive GG.
28. Mendel Piekarz, *Hassidism in Poland: Between the Two World Wars and the Shoah* [in Hebrew] (Jerusalem: Bialik Institute, 1990), 414.

29. Nehemia Polen, 'Cultural and Religious Life in the Warsaw Ghetto', https://web.archive.org/web/20100106104231/http://motlc.wiesenthal.com/site/pp.asp?c=ivKVLcMVIsG&b=476145 (retrieved 16 May 2019).
30. Morris Kesselmann, interview with GG on 6 December 1999 in Aventura, Private Archive GG.
31. Gabriel Malinski, interview with GG and Andreas Kilian on 28 October 1998 in Montreal, Private Archive GG.
32. Yaakov Silberberg, interview with GG on 22 January 1998 in Holon, Private Archive GG
33. Zvi Schermer, Yad Vashem Archive Number 03/93 81, 21.
34. Lemke Pliszko, interview with GG on 22 October 2004 in Givat Hashlosha, Private Archive GG Lemke Pliszko, interview with GG on 16 December 2003 in Givat Hashlosha, Private Archive GG; Shmuel Leibowitz, interview with GG on 14 August 2000 in Herzliya, Private Archive GG.
35. Szaya Gertner, Yad Vashem Archive Number M 49E/348, 2.
36. Josef Sackar, interview with GG on 26 December 2003 in Holon, Private Archive GG.
37. Morris Venezia, interview with GG on 14 September 1997 in Miami Beach, Private Archive GG.
38. Gideon Greif, *Wir weinten tränenlos ...', Augenzeugenberichte des jüdischen Sonderkommandos in Auschwitz* (Cologne: Böhlau, 1995), 198. See also Yaakov Gabai, Yad Vashem Archive Number P 25, 6.
39. Nyiszli, *Im Jenseits der Menschlichkeit*, 175.
40. Luminal is a pharmaceutical introduced in 1912 normally used to treat epilepsy and for narcosis. Until the second half of the twentieth century, it was a widely used soporific.
41. 'Captain' was the nickname of the Greek Marine Officer Alberto Errera, who arrived in Auschwitz on 11 April 1944 and worked in the SK from May. After he had taken illegal photographs of the burning pits, he was killed during an escape attempt in September 1944. Nyiszli, *Im Jenseits der Menschlichkeit*, 78 and 175.
42. Ibid., 78.
43. Ibid., 79. Ellipses in original.
44. Morris Kesselmann, interview with GG on 13 December 1999 in Aventura, Private Archive GG.
45. Yehoshuah Rosenblum, interview with GG on 2 May 1995 in Haifa, Private Archive GG.

Bibliography

Ciechanower, Mordechai. Interview with GG on 30 July 1998 in Ramat Gan, Private Archive GG.
——. Interview with GG on 01 October 1999 in Ramat Gan, Private Archive GG.
——. Interview with GG on 19 February 2002 in Ramat Gan, Private Archive GG.
——. Interview with GG on 28 September 2000 in Ramat Gan, Private Archive GG.
Dragon, Abraham, and Shlomo Dragon. Continuation of the interview with GG in Auschwitz, Private Archive GG, Video Nr. 15.
——. Interview with GG in Ramat Gan, Private Archive GG.

Freimark, Yaakov. Interview with GG on 23 December 2005 in Herzliya, Private Archive GG.
Gabai, Yaakov. Yad Vashem Archive Number P 25, 6.
———. Yad Vashem Archive Number M 49E/348, 2.
Greif, Gideon. *We Wept without Tears: Testimonies of the Jewish Sonderkommando from Auschwitz*. New Haven: Yale University Press, 2004.
———. '*Wir weinten tränenlos . . .*', *Augenzeugenberichte des jüdischen Sonderkommandos in Auschwitz*. Cologne: Böhlau, 1995.
Kesselmann, Morris. Interview with GG on 6 December 1999 in Aventura, Private Archive GG.
———. Interview with GG on 13 December 1999 in Aventura, Private Archive GG.
Langfuss, Leib. 'The Horrors of Murder, 1944', in Ber Mark, *The Scrolls of Auschwitz*. Tel Aviv: Am Oved, 1985.
Leibowicz, Shmuel. Interview with GG on 14 August 2000 in Hertzlyia, Private Archive GG.
Malinski, Gabriel. Interview with GG and Andreas Kilian on 28 October 1998 in Montreal, Private Archive GG.
———. Interview with GG on 1 December 1999 in Miami Beach, Private Archive GG.
Müller, Filip. *Sonderbehandlung: Drei Jahre in den Krematorien und Gaskammern von Auschwitz*. Munich: Steinhausen, 1979.
Nyiszli, Miklós. *Im Jenseits der Menschlichkeit: Ein Gerichtsmediziner in Auschwitz*, trans. Angelika Bihari, ed. Andreas Kilian and Friedrich Herber. Berlin: Karl Dietz, 2005.
Piekarz, Mendel. *Hassidism in Poland: Between the Two World Wars and the Shoah*. Jerusalem: Bialik Institute, 1990 [in Hebrew].
Pliszko, Lemke, Interview with GG on 27 July 2001 in Givat Hashlosha, Private Archive GG.
———. Interview with GG on 16 December 2003 in Givat Hashlosha, Private Archive GG.
———. Interview with GG on 22 October 2004 in Givat Hashlosha, Private Archive GG.
Polen, Nehemia. 'Cultural and Religious Life in the Warsaw Ghetto'. Retrieved 22 October 2007 from http://motlc.wiesenthal.com/site/pp.asp?c=ivKVLcMVIsG&b=476145. Now available at: https://web.archive.org/web/20100106104231/http://motlc.wiesenthal.com/site/pp.asp?c=ivKVLcMVIsG&b=476145 (retrieved 16 May 2019).
Rosenblum, Yehoshuah. Interview with GG on 2 May 1995 in Haifa, Private Archive GG.
———. Yad Vashem Archive Number P 25.
Sackar, Josef. Interview with GG on 26 December 2003 in Holon, Private Archive GG.
Schermer, Zvi. Yad Vashem Archive Number 03/93 81, 21.
Silberberg, Yaakov. Interview with GG on 22 January 1998 in Holon, Private Archive GG.
Świebocka, Teresa, Franciszek Piper and Martin Mayr (eds). *Inmitten des grauenvollen Verbrechens: Handschriften von Mitgliedern des Sonderkommandos*, trans. Herta Henschel and Jochen August. Oświęcim: Verlag des Staatlichen Auschwitz-Birkenau Museums, 1996.
Venezia, Morris. Interview with GG on 14 September 1997 in Miami Beach, Private Archive GG.
Venezia, Shlomo. *Meine Arbeit im Sonderkommando Auschwitz*. Munich: Karl Blessing, 2008.
Welbel, Eliezer. Interview with GG and Andreas Kilian on 17.10.1998 in Skokie, Private Archive GG.

Part III

Retrospective Representations

Chapter 10

Doubly Cursed

The Sonderkommando in the Documents of the International Tracing Service

Dan Stone

Introduction: Sonderkommando Sources

In his account of his time at Birkenau, the Greek physician Marco Nahon describes a meeting between his friend, a journalist for *The Athenian* newspaper who was in the same barrack as Nahon and an old acquaintance of his from Athens, who was now a member of the Sonderkommando (SK):

> 'I knew what passed through your mind when you first saw me', says he, 'I could read in your eyes the shocking astonishment, the contempt, the utter disgust even, that my profession of today inspires in you, my profession of body burner. Ah! how far you all are from realizing how much I myself and my buddies from the Sonder are suffering from our situation. We at the Sonder are doubly cursed. But the Nazis are masters when it comes to educating their slaves to achieve the goal that they have fixed in their minds'.[1]

The SK, in this account, are doubly cursed, first by having to carry out the most dreadful tasks imaginable and second by being despised by their fellow Jews and the rest of humankind for undertaking those tasks. This negative judgement was prevalent even before the end of the war. In their famous report on the camp, the Auschwitz escapees Rudolf Vrba and Alfred Wetzler wrote of the SK that: 'On account of the dreadful smell spread by them, people had but little contact with them. Besides, they were always filthy, destitute, half wild and extraordinarily brutal and ruthless. It was not uncommon to see one of them kill another'.[2]

Today, scholars of the Holocaust no longer regard the SK men in this unforgiving light. There is far greater understanding that the men who were selected for the SK were given no choice in the matter and that, like Auschwitz inmates in other work details, they simply sought to stay alive for as long as possible. Indeed, given the appalling nature of their work and the documents (writings and photographs) that some of them produced at great risk to their lives, not to mention the fact that they rebelled against the camp administration, bringing about the destruction of one of the gas chambers, it is understandable that they are regarded today with a mixture of esteem and bewildered fascination. At the end of the war, however, and for several decades thereafter – in fact, until the 1990s – the SK men rarely spoke of what they had done for fear of being misunderstood as collaborators. Crucial in bringing about this change was Filip Müller's account *Eyewitness Auschwitz*, which was first published in 1979. But this book said nothing about what happened to him after his liberation, typifying the fact that there is very little documentation relating to the experiences of the surviving SK men – who were about eighty in number – after the end of the war.[3]

This situation is somewhat altered now that we have access to the International Tracing Service (ITS). Recently opened to researchers, with over 30 million documents, the ITS in Bad Arolsen (Hesse) is the world's largest single depository of material relating to Nazi persecution and its aftermath. It holds on the one hand vast quantities of material relating to the Nazi concentration camps, including the subcamps, documents relating to the huge number of German firms that used slave labour, and discrete collections relating to specific organizations, such as the Nazi *Lebensborn* programme, the Todt Organisation or the *Reichsvereinigung der Juden in Deutschland*. These are the so-called *Sachdokumente*, or factual documents, stemming from the wartime years. As well as documentation from many postwar trials, most copied from other bodies such as the Bundesarchiv, local German archives or the Zentralstelle in Ludwigsburg, the ITS also holds huge numbers of sources pertaining to the postwar experiences of survivors. This includes displaced persons (DP) registration forms, the CM/1 (Care and Maintenance) forms produced by the International Refugee Organization (IRO, the successor to the United Nations Relief and Rehabilitation Administration (UNRRA)), that same body's appeal proceedings, when people who had been initially refused IRO assistance received a second hearing, and correspondence relating to postwar compensation claims. The T/D (Tracing and Documentation) files of the ITS further add to this store of knowledge, in that researchers can follow the tracing process as it was carried out for over 3,000,000 requestors, including survivors themselves and victims' relatives.[4] And the centrepiece of the ITS is its Central Name Index (CNI), a vast collection of card files with details of over 17 million individuals; these are the starting point for research in ITS since they point the way to cross-referenced documents in which an individual's name occurs. Most of the documents at the ITS have now been digitized and a copy of the digital archive is deposited at a nominated repository in each of the countries that make up the International Commission that owns the ITS. In the United Kingdom, the Wiener Library in London is the access point for the ITS.

Documents relating to the men forced to work in the Auschwitz SK are sparse, so anything that can shed light on their experiences is worth consulting. This chapter is based on a simple research question: what documents exist in the ITS concerning the surviving members of the SK? It is more a scoping exercise than an analytical or argument-driven piece, and makes no claims to methodological originality. I hope only to show that when it comes to representing the SK, there exist postwar documents other than artistic, filmic and fictional, and that these can be used to understand the experiences and postwar lives of these men. In the ITS collections, one can find material relating to the operation of the Auschwitz-Birkenau death camp, in which the SK is mentioned (i.e. in the *Sachdokumente*), and one can also find documents pertaining to the postwar trajectories of the surviving SK members. For those, such as Zalman Gradowski, who did not survive but whose names are known to us through the so-called 'Scrolls of Auschwitz', we can find camp registration records that at least confirm that they were registered into the camp.

In this chapter, I will look at the second type of source: although the *Sachdokumente* contain some postwar reports and statements made by surviving inmates of Auschwitz I and II, references to the SK are fairly sparse and the documents are mostly copied from holdings elsewhere. Thus, I focus on the T/D files of the SK men, which are comparatively full and, in a few instances at least, offer an overview of the surviving SK men's postwar passage from survivors to displaced persons to stateless refugees to immigrants in new countries. For example, with respect to the Dragon brothers, we can see where they were living after the war (Salzburg, then Zeilsheim DP Camp, then Frankfurt am Main) and retrace their steps, showing how they applied for IRO assistance and finally left Europe for Israel. In the case of Shlomo Venezia, we can see how many years after the war (as late as 1982), he was engaged in correspondence with the ITS in respect of claims for compensation. Using these documents alongside interviews with surviving SK men, especially those conducted by Gideon Greif for his book *We Wept without Tears* and those conducted by the USC Visual History Archive, one can show in some detail how they managed to get by after 'liberation' and the end of the war, and bringing these sources together is a desideratum for future research.

The ITS documents are fascinating in their own right, but there is a particular reason for pursuing this research on the SK men: the documents offer an unspoken insight into why the SK men did not speak of their experiences for many years after the war. The writings of many Auschwitz survivors refer in a pejorative or at best disapproving tone to the SK, and the surviving SK men themselves never mention in their postwar documentation that this had been their lot (as the copies of the documents below confirm). Whilst it is always hard to discern an argument from silence, in this case, the silence appears to confirm what we suspect: that very soon after the war, in the confusion about what had taken place, having been a member of the SK was not something that one would openly admit. Only now, many years later when we have a clearer understanding of the history of the Nazi camps in general and the position of the SK in particular, can we see that these men were by no means collaborators or morally compromised, and that their experiences were in fact amongst the most brutal of all Holocaust victims. In the history of representations of the SK, these surviving early postwar statements, juxtaposed with the later self-representations of the SK survivors, offer us insights into how the SK were perceived – and perceived themselves – for much of the postwar period. The sources reveal that not only during the time of the camp's existence but also for decades afterwards, the SK men were indeed 'doubly cursed'.

The argument from silence also leads us to consider the role of the archive and the ways in which it shapes our ability to construct the past. The ITS, because of its huge scale, is perhaps the best example of what Jeffrey Wallen means when he talks about the tension between focusing on the human scale of the Holocaust on the one hand and the massive collective crime of the Holocaust on the other. Wallen writes: 'Paradoxically, in order to better understand the Holocaust, we need to move continually in opposing directions: from "paper" to "human beings" (as Wiesel urged historians to do), but also from "human beings" to "paper"'.[5] The example that he gives of the Gross-Rosen subcamp of Christianstadt shows how an awareness of these little-known subcamps can help us to make better sense of the complex history of the Holocaust, including how some inmates were taken from Birkenau to work in subcamps late in the war, and how that fact changes the dominant view of a single narrative of deportation and murder. When confronted with documents pertaining to SK men, these problems of scale and platitude (the 'flatness' of the documents) become especially acute. The documents are merely clues to personal trajectories, indicating where the men had been and where they ended up after the war; it is left to the historian to look elsewhere to discover the reasons for these trajectories and to try to comprehend what, in their cases, is hidden by the simple designation 'Auschwitz' on a card file. Here the clash between the bureaucratic administration and the simplicity of the files, and the horrific things the SK men lived through is glaring, but only if one already knows who these men are. The files themselves are of interest as supplements to our existing knowledge of the SK; they are in no ways replacements for it.

Postwar Trajectories

In order to get a sense of what is in the ITS, it is useful to start with a typical name card from the CNI, in this case Jakow (Yaakov) Gabai's.

The number on the top right of the card is Gabai's T/D reference; this allows the researcher to locate his tracing documents quickly and easily. The other information here includes Gabai's date and place of birth (Athens), the names of his parents and the fact that he was a stateless Jew ('isr./stls'.). Most importantly, it shows his wartime trajectory, from the time he was arrested in Athens and sent to a forced labour camp (ZAL) to Auschwitz (here his inmate number is given), and the fact that at

```
                                T/D    457 930
Name:           G A B A I    Jakow
                Elt.: Viktor u. Roza Beracha

BD: 26.9.1923  BP: Athen/Griechenld.  Nat: isr./stls.

     3. 1944    Athen verhaftet + ZAL Chaidari
     4. 1944    Auschwitz, Haeftl.Nr.: 182569
     1. 1945    Mauthausen
     3. 1945    Husen I ZAL.
     5.5.1945   Gusen befreit


     RBA f.Wg., Koblenz
     f. RA. Eckstein, Berlin
                                                  Mue.
```

Figure 10.1 CNI card for Jakow (Yaakov) Gabai. 0.1/21425601_0_1, International Tracing Service Digital Archive, Wiener Library, London (hereinafter ITS DAWL). The first part of the reference (0.1) refers to the subunit within the ITS (in this case, the CNI); the second is the individual page number. Courtesy of International Tracing Service Digital Archive, Wiener Library, London.

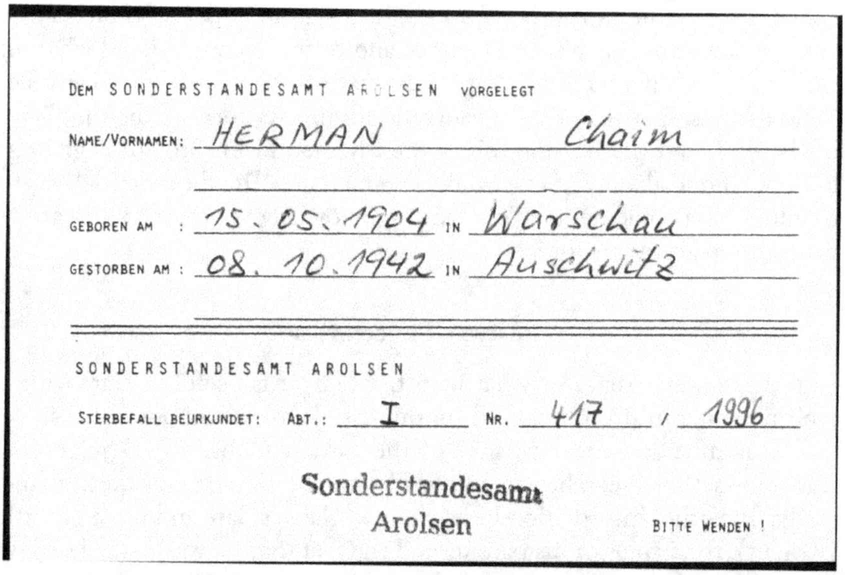

```
DEM SONDERSTANDESAMT AROLSEN VORGELEGT
NAME/VORNAMEN:  HERMAN          Chaim

GEBOREN AM :   15.05.1904  IN  Warschau
GESTORBEN AM : 08.10.1942  IN  Auschwitz


SONDERSTANDESAMT AROLSEN
STERBEFALL BEURKUNDET: ABT.:  I   NR.  417  /  1996

            Sonderstandesamt
                Arolsen              BITTE WENDEN !
```

Figure 10.2 Death certificate for Chaim Herman, 1996, 0.1/24537785_0_1, ITS DAWL. Courtesy of International Tracing Service Digital Archive, Wiener Library, London.

the end of the war he was transferred to Mauthausen, then that camp's subcamp of Gusen, where he was liberated (*befreit*) on 5 May 1945. The words at the bottom left refer to Gabai's compensation claim: 'RBA f. Wg., Koblenz' is short for the Rhineland-Palatinate Regional Restitution Office in Koblenz, and 'f. RA Eckstein, Berlin' means the case was being handled by the lawyer (*Rechtsanwalt*) Ludwig Eckstein, who dealt with thousands of Holocaust restitution claims in the 1950s and 1960s.

The ITS also recorded names of those who died and, in the early 1950s, the West German state opened a special register office (Sonderstandesamt) at Arolsen specifically for the purpose of issuing certificates of incarceration or death certificates in order to facilitate the restitution process. A typical card is like this one for Chaim Herman.

The reverse of the card shows that Herman, who was born in Warsaw, was captured in Paris and sent from Drancy to Majdanek on 2 March 1943, though this may be an error: it does not give any details of a subsequent transfer to Auschwitz. Such cards are useful in the case of the SK men for providing basic information, though it is what they do not tell us that is most intriguing.[6] Herman, it was recently discovered, was not the author of the only known SK text in French, a letter addressed to the writer's daughter. Indeed, it is questionable whether he was in the SK at

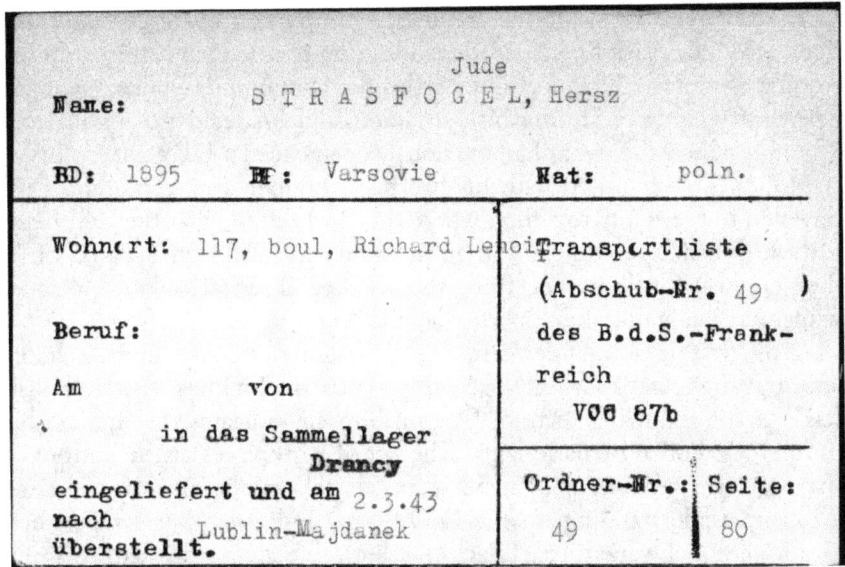

Figure 10.3   CNI card for Hersz Strasfogel, 0.1/42805817_0_1, ITS DAWL. Courtesy of International Tracing Service Digital Archive, Wiener Library, London.

all. But like Herman, Hersz Strasfogel – known in French as Herman – was deported on the 49th train from Drancy. Strasfogel, originally from Warsaw, had a daughter, Sima – Simone in French – and the original letter was in the family's possession for decades after the war.[7] Little is known about Strasfogel but his name does appear in ITS.

One of the aspects of these cards that is most interesting is knowledge of what happened to the survivors after the evacuation of Auschwitz. The SK men who managed to mingle with the general camp population were relatively fit by the standards of the camp in January 1945, and even with injuries, such as those Abraham Dragon sustained to his foot or Daniel Bennahmias to his legs, had a better than average chance of surviving the 'death march'.[8] Many of the surviving SK were on the same evacuation march out of Birkenau on 25 January 1945. Their destinations varied, but, along with the tens of thousands of camp inmates marched westwards in the face of the Soviet advance, they mostly ended up in subcamps of Mauthausen such as Gusen or Ebensee, or other camps in the Reich, such as Bergen-Belsen. An exception is Shlomo Dragon, who escaped from the death march whilst still in Poland. Following the 'liberation' of the camps, they then found themselves in DP camps, where they would wait for the chance to emigrate.

The DP registration forms are another important source of information. They take various shapes, depending on the date, and this form for Szloma (Shlomo) Dragon, noteworthy for containing a photograph, is an identity card confirming his DP status and his residence in an IRO assembly centre (i.e. what had previously been called a DP camp).

Shlomo was reunited with his brother Abraham in Austria and they travelled to Germany together, where they lived initially at the Zeilsheim DP camp near Frankfurt and then in Frankfurt itself. During that time, they applied for assistance from the IRO, and Abraham's CM/1 file, whilst typical, is full of fascinating detail.

In the first section, under nationality, Dragon designates himself 'stateless', but then next to it, the case worker (presumably) has written 'Polish Jew'. In the following section, Dragon himself indicates that he and his brother are Polish by nationality. The list of workplaces at the bottom of the page (the term 'employment' seems to be a euphemism or to betray a lack of understanding on the IRO's part) indicates that Dragon had performed 'Schwarzarbeit' (black market), which hardly explains the extent to which this was a necessity for survival in occupied Warsaw, and then shows his trajectory through Auschwitz and Mauthausen, which he describes as 'Zwangsarbeit' (forced labour), before ending up at Zeilsheim. Subsequent pages of the form indicate that Dragon had been receiving aid from the UNRRA and the Joint Distribution Committee (JDC, or 'the Joint', the world's largest Jewish charity), and explain his and his brother's desire to leave Germany. To the question 'do you wish to return to your country of former residence?', the answer is simply a firm 'Nein'; the reason, another one-word answer: 'Judenverfolgung' (persecution of Jews). A simple 'Nein' is also the answer to the question as to whether the applicant wishes to remain in Germany. On some of the CM/1 forms, one finds quite long narratives and details of relatives who supposedly live in the United States, Palestine or elsewhere; in this case, Dragon has simply written 'U.S.A.' across the whole of the final section dealing with hopes for emigration.

Shlomo, in an interview with Gideon Greif, notes with joy that he and his brother were never apart after their separation on the death march and that they left for Israel in 1949.[9] This is evidenced by Abraham Dragon's certificate of IRO eligibility from December 1948 (Figure 10.7), which approved his and Shlomo's receipt of IRO assistance in emigrating, a decision that was confirmed in a second IRO application of 28 July 1949, on which the case worker noted that in his opinion, Abraham was a racial persecutee and as such was eligible for IRO support in resettling.[10] Both brothers were therefore declared to be 'within the mandate'.[11]

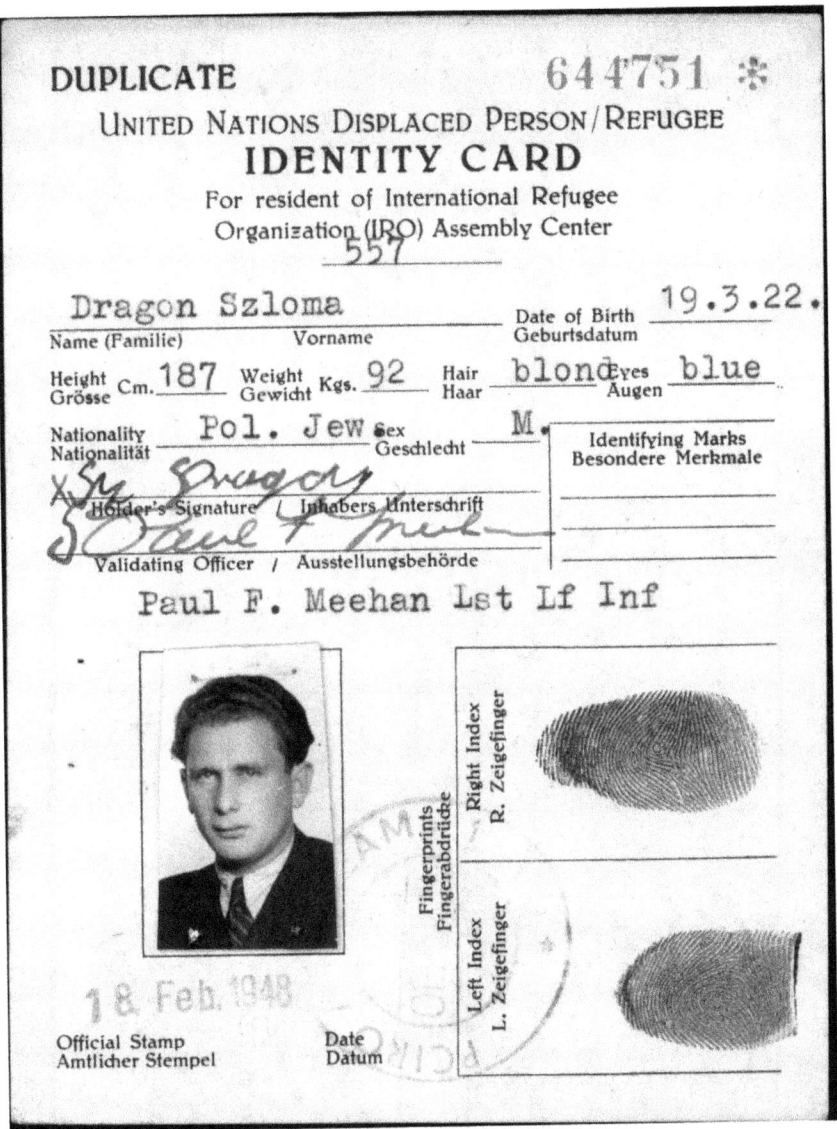

Figure 10.4 IRO DP identity card for Szloma Dragon, 1948. 3.1.1.1/66922794_0_1, ITS DAWL. Courtesy of International Tracing Service Digital Archive, Wiener Library, London.

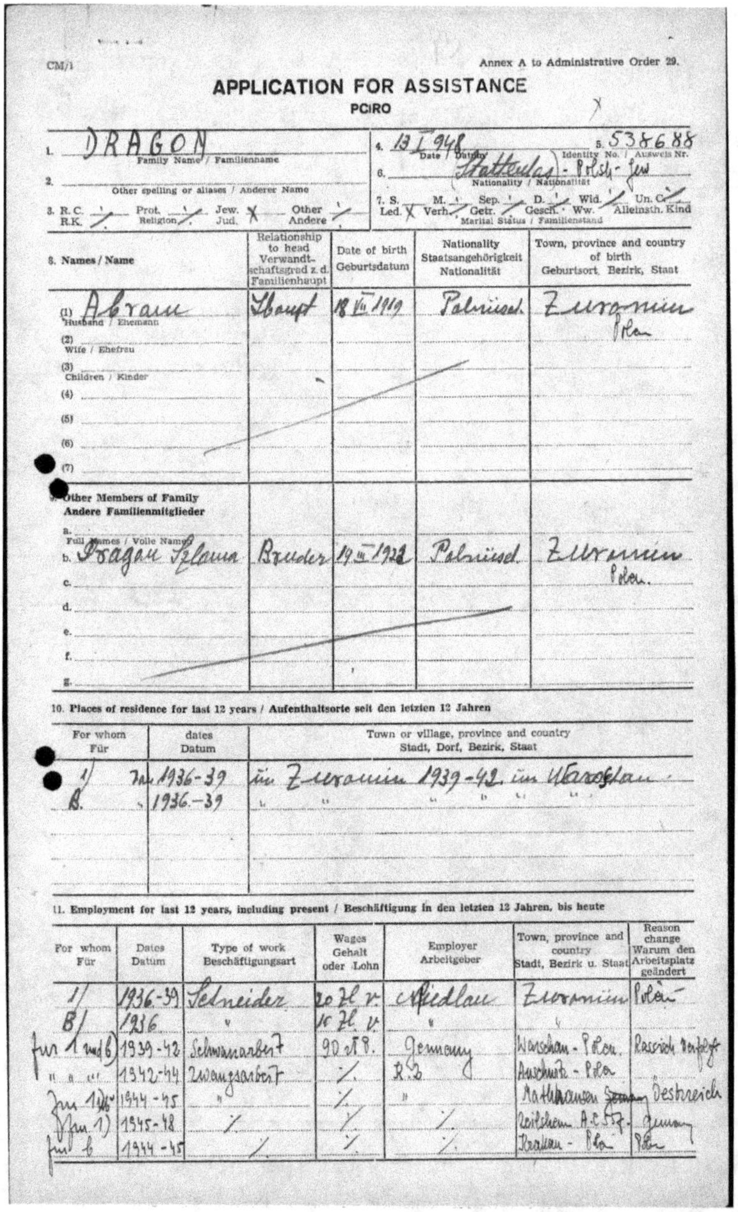

Figure 10.5 First page of Abraham Dragon's IRO application, 13 January 1948, 3.2.1.1/79042780_0_1, ITS DAWL. 'PCIRO' indicates that the document stems from the period of the Preparatory Commission of the International Refugee Organization, i.e. the interim period between UNRRA and full IRO administration. Courtesy of International Tracing Service Digital Archive, Wiener Library, London.

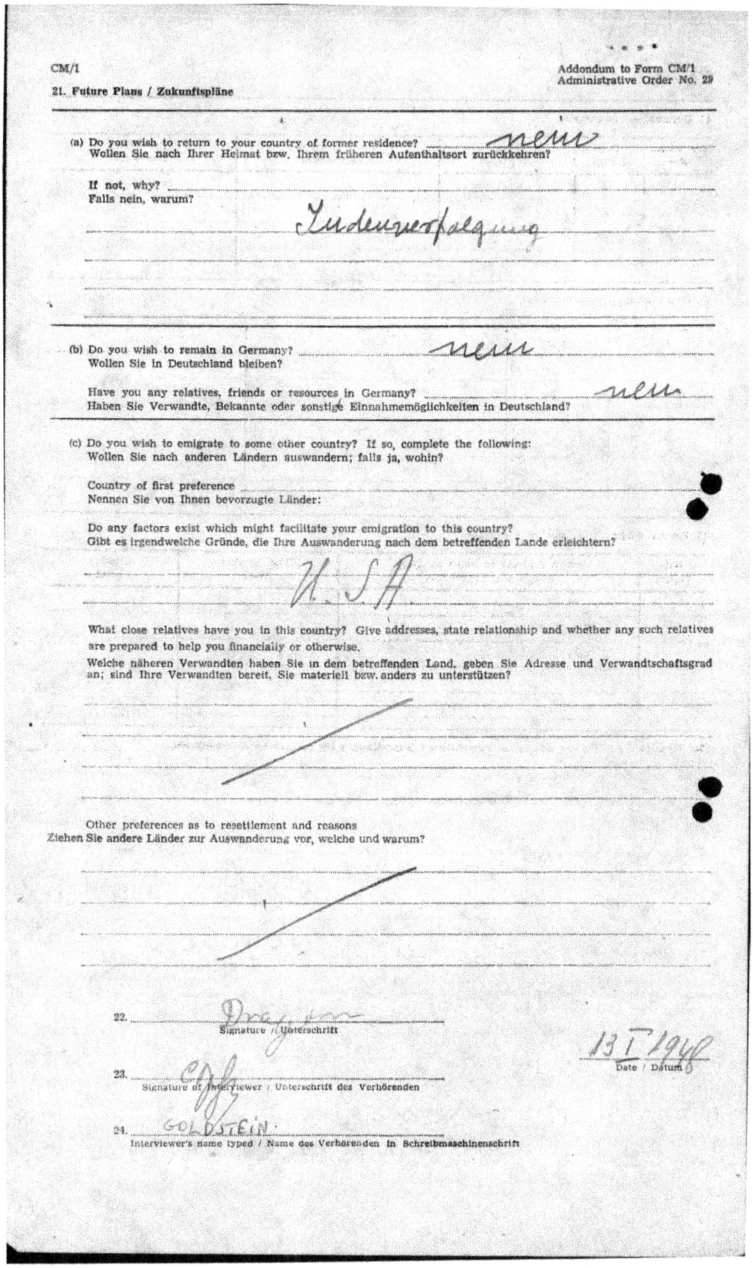

CM/1

Addondum to Form CM/1
Administrative Order No. 29

21. Future Plans / Zukunftspläne

(a) Do you wish to return to your country of former residence? nein
Wollen Sie nach Ihrer Heimat bzw. Ihrem früheren Aufenthaltsort zurückkehren?

If not, why?
Falls nein, warum?
Judenverfolgung

(b) Do you wish to remain in Germany? nein
Wollen Sie in Deutschland bleiben?

Have you any relatives, friends or resources in Germany? nein
Haben Sie Verwandte, Bekannte oder sonstige Einnahmemöglichkeiten in Deutschland?

(c) Do you wish to emigrate to some other country? If so, complete the following:
Wollen Sie nach anderen Ländern auswandern; falls ja, wohin?

Country of first preference
Nennen Sie von Ihnen bevorzugte Länder:

Do any factors exist which might facilitate your emigration to this country?
Gibt es irgendwelche Gründe, die Ihre Auswanderung nach dem betreffenden Lande erleichtern?
U.S.A

What close relatives have you in this country? Give addresses, state relationship and whether any such relatives are prepared to help you financially or otherwise.
Welche näheren Verwandten haben Sie in dem betreffenden Land, geben Sie Adresse und Verwandtschaftsgrad an; sind Ihre Verwandten bereit, Sie materiell bzw. anders zu unterstützen?

Other preferences as to resettlement and reasons
Ziehen Sie andere Länder zur Auswanderung vor, welche und warum?

22. Dragon
Signature / Unterschrift

13 I 1948
Date / Datum

23.
Signature of Interviewer / Unterschrift des Verhörenden

24. GOLDSTEIN
Interviewer's name typed / Name des Verhörenden in Schreibmaschinenschrift

Figure 10.6 Fourth page of Abraham Dragon's IRO application, 3.2.1.1/79042780_0_4, ITS DAWL. Courtesy of International Tracing Service Digital Archive, Wiener Library, London.

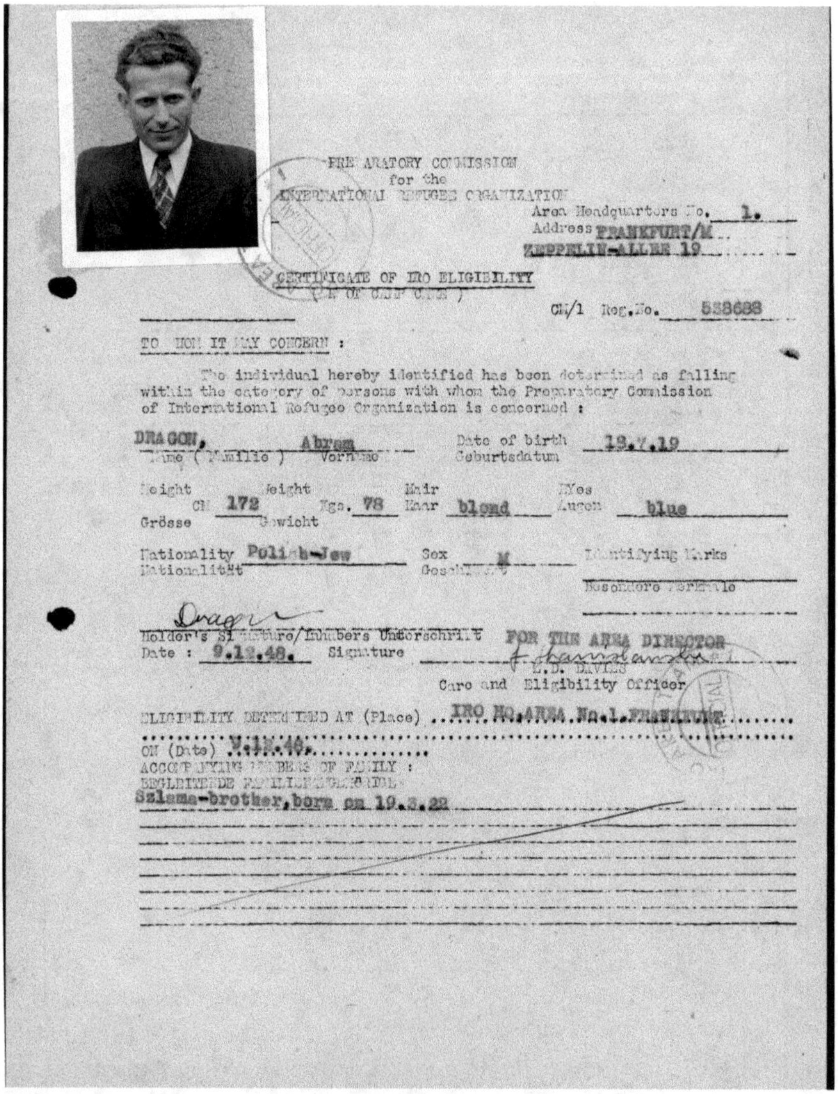
PREPARATORY COMMISSION
for the
INTERNATIONAL REFUGEE ORGANIZATION
Area Headquarters No. 1.
Address FRANKFURT/M
ZEPPELIN-ALLEE 19

CERTIFICATE OF IRO ELIGIBILITY

CM/1 Reg.No. 538688

TO WHOM IT MAY CONCERN :

The individual hereby identified has been determined as falling within the category of persons with whom the Preparatory Commission of International Refugee Organization is concerned :

DRAGON, Abram — Name (Familie) Vorname
Date of birth / Geburtsdatum 19.V.19

Height / Grösse CM 172
Weight / Gewicht Kgs. 78
Hair / Haar blond
Eyes / Augen blue

Nationality / Nationalität Polish-Jew
Sex / Geschlecht M
Identifying Marks / Besondere Merkmale

Dragon
Holder's Signature/Inhabers Unterschrift
Date : 9.12.48.
Signature
FOR THE AREA DIRECTOR
E.D. DAVIES
Care and Eligibility Officer

ELIGIBILITY DETERMINED AT (Place) IRO HQ.AREA No.1.FRANKFURT
ON (Date) 9.12.48.
ACCOMPANYING MEMBERS OF FAMILY :
BEGLEITENDE FAMILIENMITGLIEDER
Szlama-brother, born on 19.3.22

Figure 10.7 Abraham Dragon's IRO certificate of eligibility, December 1948. 3.2.1.1/79042781_0_1, ITS DAWL. Courtesy of International Tracing Service Digital Archive, Wiener Library, London.

One of the most important functions of the ITS as of the early 1950s was processing information for compensation claims, following the 1949 Bundesentschädigungsgesetz (Federal Indemnification Law). Indeed, the passing of this law was the occasion for the opening of the special register office at Arolsen. Many of the surviving SK men applied for compensation via German lawyers and some of the correspondence relating to the process – which often took many years – is held at the ITS. Daniel Bennahmias' correspondence, for example, covers over three decades, from the late 1960s until the early 1990s. His certificate of incarceration was issued in 1968, when the ITS was administered by the International Committee of the Red Cross (ICRC).

This shows, on the basis of ITS-held documentation, that he had been liberated at the Mauthausen subcamp of Ebensee, having previously been an inmate at Auschwitz. It gives his camp number, but does not mention his role in the camp.

Indeed, only more recently added documents are likely to provide such information. For Filip Müller, for example, who unsurprisingly has the fullest case file of any surviving SK man (he died in 2013), two T/D cards clearly illustrate the change in how the SK is spoken about. His first, from the 1960s, contains nothing other than his incarceration at Buna-Monowitz (Auschwitz III, the vast slave labour industrial plant).

This gives Müller's nationality as Czech (or, more specifically, 'Czechoslovak Socialist Republic') and only records his time at Monowitz, between March and August 1943, as part of the bricklaying commando (Mauererkommando). It is stamped with the details of Müller's lawyer, Henry Ormond, who had been a lawyer and judge since the Weimar Republic and was himself incarcerated in Dachau for five months before being released and spending the war years in the United Kingdom. One of the cofounders of *Der Spiegel* after the war, Ormond was one of the lawyers who helped former victims sue I.G. Farben in 1950. But it was during the Auschwitz Trial of 1963–65 that he came to prominence for his proposal that the court should visit Auschwitz on a so-called *Tatortsbesichtigung*, an official inspection of the crime scene, which produced 'one of the most dramatic and, in the context of the Cold War, politically significant moments in the trial'.[12] Indeed, Müller testified at the Auschwitz Trial, which explains his connection with Ormond.

The second is a card produced in 2003, following an inquiry from the Fritz Bauer Institute in Frankfurt.[13] According to the ITS's 25-year rule, the card cannot be published (although it can be viewed as part of the digital archive), but it notes that during the war, Müller was held at Auschwitz concentration camp and then explicitly adds that he was part of the Auschwitz SK.[14] In the decades before the twenty-first century, however, it was unusual for any such recognition to be present. Henryk Mandelbaum, for example, wrote from his home town of Gliwice to the ITS in 1973 asking for information about documents they might hold on him; he provided his Auschwitz number and gave the dates he was in the camp, but neither his letter nor the reply he

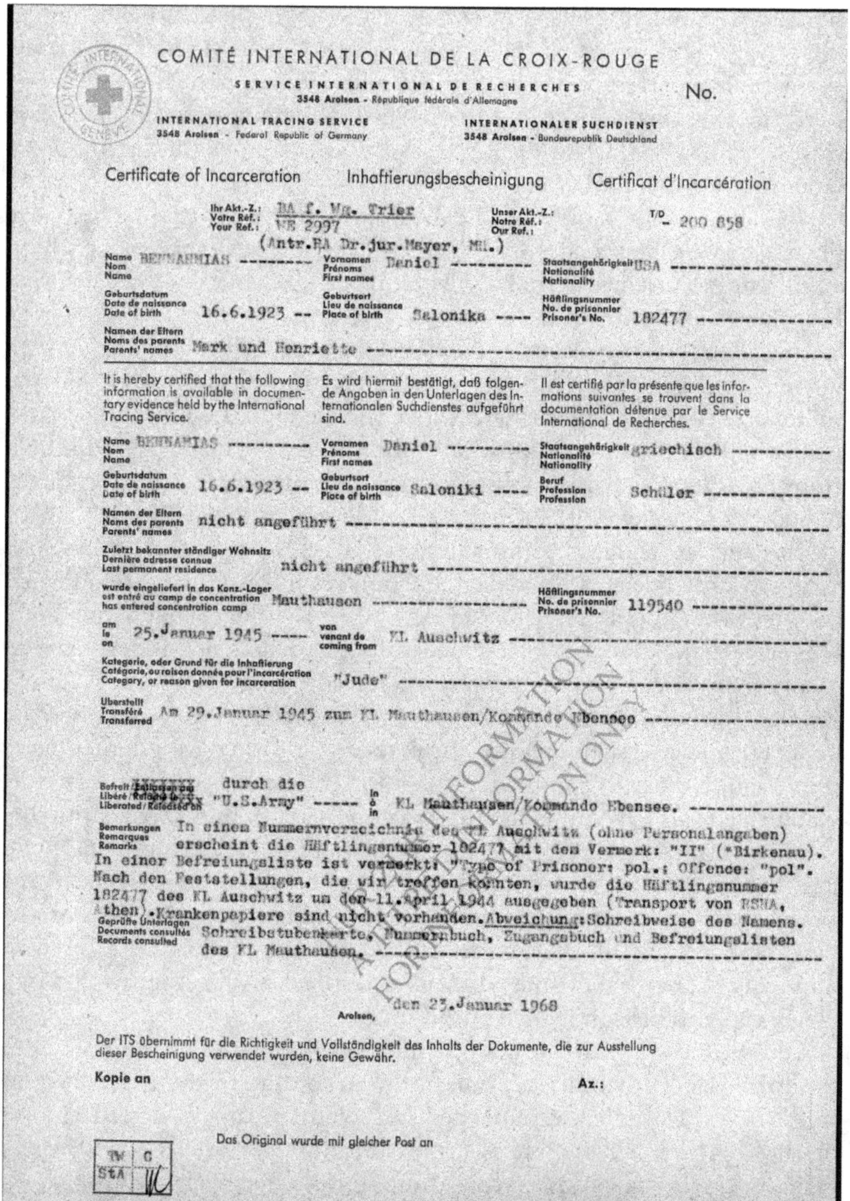

COMITÉ INTERNATIONAL DE LA CROIX-ROUGE

SERVICE INTERNATIONAL DE RECHERCHES
3548 Arolsen - République fédérale d'Allemagne

No.

INTERNATIONAL TRACING SERVICE
3548 Arolsen - Federal Republic of Germany

INTERNATIONALER SUCHDIENST
3548 Arolsen - Bundesrepublik Deutschland

Certificate of Incarceration   Inhaftierungsbescheinigung   Certificat d'Incarcération

Ihr Akt.-Z.: / Votre Réf.: / Your Ref.: BA f. Wg. Trier
WE 2997
(Antr.RA Dr.jur.Mayer, MR.)

Unser Akt.-Z.: / Notre Réf.: / Our Ref.: T/D - 200 858

Name / Nom / Name: BENNAHMIAS
Vornamen / Prénoms / First names: Daniel
Staatsangehörigkeit / Nationalité / Nationality: USA

Geburtsdatum / Date de naissance / Date of birth: 16.6.1923
Geburtsort / Lieu de naissance / Place of birth: Salonika
Häftlingsnummer / No. de prisonnier / Prisoner's No.: 182477

Namen der Eltern / Noms des parents / Parents' names: Mark und Henriette

It is hereby certified that the following information is available in documentary evidence held by the International Tracing Service.

Es wird hiermit bestätigt, daß folgende Angaben in den Unterlagen des Internationalen Suchdienstes aufgeführt sind.

Il est certifié par la présente que les informations suivantes se trouvent dans la documentation détenue par le Service International de Recherches.

Name / Nom / Name: BENNAMIAS
Vornamen / Prénoms / First names: Daniel
Staatsangehörigkeit / Nationalité / Nationality: griechisch

Geburtsdatum / Date de naissance / Date of birth: 16.6.1923
Geburtsort / Lieu de naissance / Place of birth: Saloniki
Beruf / Profession / Profession: Schüler

Namen der Eltern / Noms des parents / Parents' names: nicht angeführt

Zuletzt bekannter ständiger Wohnsitz / Dernière adresse connue / Last permanent residence: nicht angeführt

wurde eingeliefert in das Konz.-Lager / est entré au camp de concentration / has entered concentration camp: Mauthausen
Häftlingsnummer / No. de prisonnier / Prisoner's No.: 119540

am / le / on: 25.Januar 1945
von / venant de / coming from: KL Auschwitz

Kategorie, oder Grund für die Inhaftierung / Catégorie, ou raison donnée pour l'incarcération / Category, or reason given for incarceration: "Jude"

Überstellt / Transféré / Transferred: Am 29.Januar 1945 zum KL Mauthausen/Kommando Ebensee

Befreit/Entlassen am / Libéré/Relâché le / Liberated/Released on: XXXXXXX durch die "U.S.Army"
in / à / in: KL Mauthausen/Kommando Ebensee.

Bemerkungen / Remarques / Remarks: In einem Nummernverzeichnis des KL Auschwitz (ohne Personalangaben) erscheint die Häftlingsnummer 182477 mit dem Vermerk: "II" (=Birkenau). In einer Befreiungsliste ist vermerkt: "Type of Prisoner: pol.: Offence: "pol". Nach den Feststellungen, die wir treffen konnten, wurde die Häftlingsnummer 182477 des KL Auschwitz um den 11.April 1944 ausgegeben (Transport von RSHA, Athen). Krankenpapiere sind nicht vorhanden. Abweichung: Schreibweise des Namens.

Geprüfte Unterlagen / Documents consultés / Records consulted: Schreibstubenkarte, Nummernbuch, Zugangsbuch und Befreiungslisten des KL Mauthausen.

Arolsen, den 23.Januar 1968

Der ITS übernimmt für die Richtigkeit und Vollständigkeit des Inhalts der Dokumente, die zur Ausstellung dieser Bescheinigung verwendet wurden, keine Gewähr.

Kopie an

Az.:

Das Original wurde mit gleicher Post an

TW | C
StA |

Figure 10.8 Daniel Bennahmias' certificate of incarceration, 1968, 6.3.3.2/88197513_0_1, ITS DAWL. The ITS had been administered by the ICRC since 1955. Courtesy of International Tracing Service Digital Archive, Wiener Library, London.

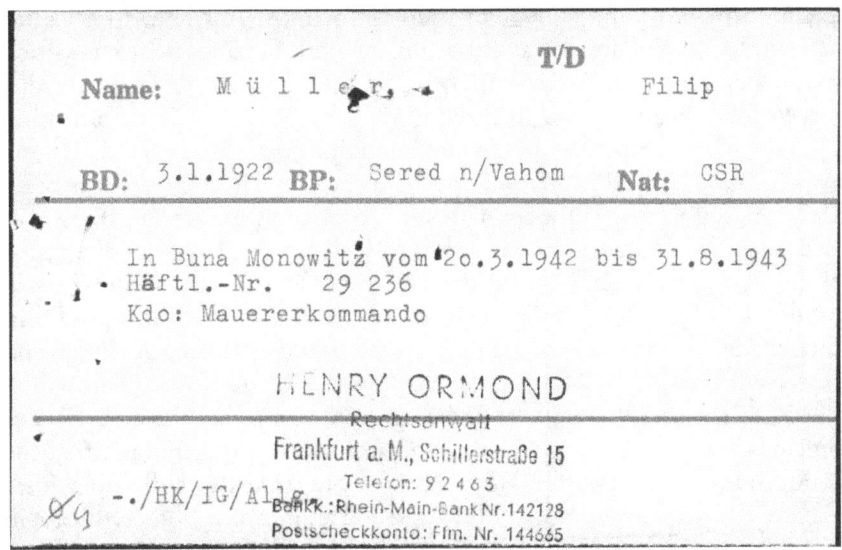

Figure 10.9 T/D inquiry card for Filip Müller, 6.3.3.2/104622108_0_1, ITS DAWL. Courtesy of International Tracing Service Digital Archive, Wiener Library, London.

received from the ITS mentioned the SK.[15] And even a year after the Fritz Bauer Institute inquired about Müller, a similar inquiry from the Italian Liaison Office (Italienische Verbindungsmission) in Bad Arolsen about Daniel Bennahmias gave rise to a card on which he is described simply as 'taken prisoner in Athens and interned in Mauthausen'.[16] Likewise, when Shaul Chazan wrote from Israel to the ITS in 1967 to ask for medical records in order to expedite his indemnification claim, he explained that he had been hospitalized in Wels and Linz for four months following his liberation at Gusen, but said nothing about the Auschwitz SK.[17] The ITS, in a rather curt fashion, furnished Chazan with a reply four months later, stating that its records on him end on 23 February 1945, with his incarceration in Gusen, and that the latter camp was liberated on 5 May 1945 by the American Army.[18] It is likely that Chazan knew that already. From the records we learn, however, that after leaving hospital in Austria, Chazan returned to Greece and that in December 1946 he was being held by the British at the Caraolas camp in Famagusta, Cyprus.

It is clear from the above that we can learn little new about the activities of the SK during the war years from the ITS records. Yet, what we can discover are snippets of information that show the survivors – like other Holocaust survivors – moving around after the war, seeking help and information, and trying, in the case of most of them, to settle in new lands. Correspondence regarding indemnification claims is a rich source here, for it shows that many of the surviving SK men were assiduous in filing claims – and in this too they were no different from other Holocaust survivors. The letters are sometimes unedifying in their tone and content, something that is revealing about the culture at the ITS and, especially, more broadly in West German officialdom in the 1960s and 1970s, as hinted at in the letter to Chazan cited above. When, for example, Josef Zakar wrote to the ITS regarding money and objects of value taken from him on his deportation to Auschwitz, and the ITS in turn made its own inquiries, other German bodies did what they could to see off the claim. Writing to the Restitution Office in Berlin, the Berlin Financial Office first stated that there was no record in its files of precious metal or jewellery relating to Zakar's claim and, second, that the claim as brought forward by the ITS possibly related to a different Josef Zakar. This was because the ITS had issued an incarceration certificate in 1963 pertaining to a Josef Zakar born on 4 March 1924 in Arta, Greece, whereas the applicant himself in his declaration under oath of November 1957 stated that he had been born on 15 July 1924 in Arta. He was therefore asked for further, more precise detail concerning the date of his deportation to Auschwitz, though how he was supposed to provide this evidence was not stated.[19] Whilst there are indeed many cases of individuals with the same name in the ITS, in this instance it might not have been too incautious to assume that these two pieces of information concerned the same person.

Indeed, the ITS did manage to resolve the case, at least as far as it was concerned. In a rather stiff letter to the restitution office, the ITS explained that many of the Auschwitz camp records had been destroyed, that the birthdates of Greek Jews were often unclear and, most importantly, that 'had we not been convinced that Josef Zakar born on 4 March 1924 in Arta was identical with Josef Zakar born on 15 July 1924 in Arta, then instead of a certificate we would have sent you a report, at the end of which would have read: "Because of the divergent personal files, we cannot be certain that this report is correct."' It concluded by stating that Zakar's tattooed number – to which it had already adverted in its first report – was the conclusive evidence and hoped that this matter was now dealt with to the satisfaction of the restitution office.[20]

On several occasions, the bodies handling reparations cases, whether that was the United Restitution Organization (URO, the forerunner of the Claims Conference), regional reparations offices in Germany or individual lawyers, felt obliged to write to the ITS to remind it to reply to their inquiries. One quickly gets a sense that, following the handover of the ITS to ICRC administration in 1955, the institution felt no special urgency in replying to survivors and their representatives, preferring to deal with the Bonn government and the special register office. Furthermore, the ICRC worried that the mandate of the ITS to certify compensation claims 'would jeopardize its humanitarian, neutral, and universal principles in the eyes of the public, which had begun to criticize the organization's policies during the Cold War'.[21] The URO, for example, wrote to the ITS in March 1956 to ask for a certificate of incarceration for Gabriel Malinski, and had to send a reminder in September of the same year.[22]

Nevertheless, despite the delays, the information the ITS did eventually send, though it might have been self-evident to the applicant, provided proof of a survivor's wartime and postwar path that was crucial for restitution claims. In David Nencel's case, for example, although the SK is, as we would by now expect, not mentioned in his correspondence, which dates from the 1950s and 1960s, his movements following his liberation at Ebensee provide a classic illustration of survivors' travails: from Ebensee, Nencel made his way to Rome, lived there for a year, then moved to Naples, then back to Cinecittà in Rome, where the famous film studios were being used as a DP camp, and in 1947 he emigrated for the United States.[23] The ITS sometimes took a long time to reply and was not always helpful, but, as in the case of Josef Zakar, it could also advance applicants' claims when it acted decisively.

Two Famous Cases

The ITS files provide information on the postwar fates of the surviving SK men, just as they do for most Holocaust survivors. For the majority of them, however, the files are limited to the ITS's name index cards, certificates of incarceration, some correspondence with lawyers and organizations handling restitution claims, and occasionally DP registration cards. Two cases provide exceptions to this: those of Filip Müller and Miklós Nyiszli.

Müller, as already noted, has the fullest file of any of the surviving SK in the ITS. This is because, having become well known following the publication of *Eyewitness Auschwitz*, numerous groups and individuals made inquiries with the ITS about him. Nyiszli, a more controversial figure who acted as an assistant to Josef Mengele whilst assigned to the SK, had also become famous thanks to his memoir *Auschwitz: A Doctor's Eyewitness Account*, written and published in Oradea (Nagyvarad) in 1946 and first published in English in 1952–53. In it, he documented his work as a pathologist, dissecting corpses in a special room set up for him by Mengele in the gas chamber complex.

In the case of Müller, the inquiries at the ITS (at least amongst the files thus far digitized) continue until less than ten years ago, when the ITS had to inform inquirers that, as his son told them, Müller's health no longer permitted him to deal with them. One such correspondent was Véronique Chevillon, whose website (www.sonderkommando.info) is dedicated to Müller and who hoped to interview Müller.[24] Similarly, the Fritz Bauer Institute asked for the ITS's help in locating Müller, so that it could obtain his permission to use a sound recording from the Auschwitz Trial in a future publication. Accompanying the request, it sent in copies of Müller's testimony from Claude Lanzmann's film *Shoah*. And the documents also show that Müller himself, via his new lawyer Werner Krechtler, was pursuing a compensation claim against the West German government, something he was able to do after moving from Prague to West Germany after the Prague Spring. Krechtler notes in his request for medical documents that Müller had written about his experiences, but neither his letter nor the details provided by Müller mention the very thing that occasioned the incoming inquiries in later decades: his membership of the SK.[25]

In his memoir, Nyiszli put it on record that the SK performed their tasks, especially that of hosing down the corpses in the gas chambers, 'by a voluntary act of impersonalization and in a state of profound distress'.[26] Yet the overall effect of his memoir was sensationalist and it should therefore be no surprise that outside agencies and individuals were interested in discovering more about him.[27] In 1980, an organization called Jewish Information, based in Sweden, included Nyiszli among a group of Holocaust victims they wanted to know more about, including Filip Müller, Anne Frank, Erich Kulka and Kazimierz Smoleń.[28] The latter was the Auschwitz-Birkenau State Museum director and an Auschwitz survivor, and he himself wrote to the ITS on behalf of the museum in July 1986, seeking more information on Nyiszli.[29] The letters from Jewish Information are also revealing about the secretive nature of the ITS during this period. Clearly having no concept of the vastness of the ITS's holdings, it noted that 'your International Tracing Service is generally little known and there may be important information which we have missed'.[30] The ITS's reply, sent on 23 July 1980, was worded in such a way as to discourage further communication: 'Please be advised that the task of the International Tracing Service consists in giving information about incarceration suffered or forced labour performed from the documentary material preserved in its archives to former victims of the National Socialist Persecution or their relatives'.[31] It crossed in the post with the Jewish Information request for information on specific individuals, however, and the ITS felt compelled to write again: 'According to the presently valid regulations pertaining to the laws for protecting of the rights of the individual, information can be given solely to third persons with the consent of the persons concerned or their assigns. The purpose of this measure is only the protection of the former persecutees' personal rights' – meaning that it could not provide Jewish Information with the information the latter was seeking.[32]

Not obtaining the information we are seeking is a fundamental characteristic of Holocaust historiography. The ITS acts as a kind of echo chamber of Holocaust research in general: we find millions of documents, yet they are not what we want. Endless rows of perpetrator documents, hundreds of thousands of pages of trial testimonies and postwar memoirs, yet the fundamental questions, at least in a more philosophical register, elude us. A positivist trawl through the ITS throws up exactly this problem. Our interest in the representation of the SK is stymied by the fact that there is no representation of the SK. There are documents pertaining to – and in many cases generated by – surviving SK men, but they do not mention the thing that engendered our interest in them in the first place. Here we have, in Wallen's terms, to move from documents to human beings. The documents help us to understand the lives the survivors led after the war, their leaving their homelands for DP camps in the lands of the perpetrators, their long wait to be resettled and their struggle for financial restitution. They are pieces in a larger puzzle. But to see the picture as a whole, the SK men's texts, their eyewitness statements given at trials and on film, the interviews they have conducted for books and documentaries are without question more significant. In this instance, the ITS gives us a sense of the struggles that the SK men endured after the war in terms of daily life and the attempt to return to 'normality'. But in order to understand what happened to them, to grapple with the lasting effects of their being members of the SK, we have to move to the human beings. As Shlomo Venezia says: 'Life. Since then I've never had a normal life . . . Everything takes me back to the camp . . . It's as if the "work" I was forced to do there had never really left my head . . . Nobody ever really gets out of the Crematorium'.[33]

Dan Stone is Professor of Modern History and Director of the Holocaust Research Institute at Royal Holloway, University of London. The author of some eighty scholarly articles, he has also written or edited sixteen books, including *Histories of the Holocaust* (2010); *Goodbye to All That? The Story of Europe since 1945* (2014); *The Liberation of the Camps* (2015); and *Concentration Camps: A Very Short Introduction* (2019). He is currently writing a book on the ITS for Oxford University Press and a book on the Holocaust for Penguin's revived Pelican series.

Notes

1. Marco Nahon, M.D., *Birkenau: The Camp of Death*, trans. Jacqueline Havaux Bowers (Tuscaloosa: University of Alabama Press, 1989), 100–1.
2. 'Report of Rudolf Vrba and Alfred Wetzler', in Henryk Świebocki (ed.), *London Has Been Informed...Reports by Auschwitz Escapees* (Oświęcim: Auschwitz-Birkenau State Museum, 2002), 214.
3. For a list of known members of the Auschwitz-Birkenau Sonderkommando, see 'Verzeichnis der Sonderkommando- und Krematoriumskommando-Häftlinge', in Eric Friedler, Barbara Siebert and Andreas Kilian, *Zeugen aus der Todeszone: Das jüdische Sonderkommando in Auschwitz* (Munich: Deutscher Taschenbuch Verlag, 2005), 371–91.
4. For a fuller history of the ITS, see Suzanne Brown-Fleming, *Nazi Persecution and Postwar Repercussions: The International Tracing Service Archive and Holocaust Research* (Lanham, MD: Rowman & Littlefield, 2016); Jennifer Rodgers, 'From the "Archive of Horrors" to the "Shop Window of Democracy": The International Tracing Service 1942–2013' (PhD thesis, Philadelphia: University of Pennsylvania, 2014). See also the yearbooks of the ITS, published under the title *Freilegungen: Jahrbuch des International Tracing Service* (2012–) and my articles 'The Memory of the Archive: The International Tracing Service and the Construction of the Past as History', *Dapim: Studies on the Holocaust* 31(2) (2017), 69–88 and '"The Greatest Detective Story in History": The BBC, the International Tracing Service, and the Memory of Nazi Crimes in Early Postwar Britain', *History & Memory* 29(2) (2017), 63–89.
5. Jeffrey Wallen, 'The Witness against the Archive: Toward a Microhistory of Christianstadt', in Claire Zalc and Tal Bruttmann (eds), *Microhistories of the Holocaust* (New York: Berghahn Books, 2017), 302. On Christianstadt, see also my essay 'Christianstadt: Slave Labour and the Holocaust', *Freilegungen: Jahrbuch des International Tracing Service* 4 (2015), 78–91.
6. On Herman, see Nicholas Chare and Dominic Williams, *Matters of Testimony: Interpreting the Scrolls of Auschwitz* (New York: Berghahn Books, 2016), Chapter 5.
7. See 'Archives: La letter retrouvée', on the Mémorial de la Shoah website: http://www.memorialdelashoah.org/archives-la-lettre-retrouvee (retrieved 5 April 2019). My thanks to Dominic Williams for this reference.
8. For Bennahmias, see Rebecca Camhi Fromer, *The Holocaust Odyssey of Daniel Bennahmias, Sonderkommando* (Tuscaloosa: University of Alabama Press, 1993), 92.
9. Gideon Greif, *We Wept without Tears: Testimonies of the Jewish Sonderkommando from Auschwitz* (New Haven: Yale University Press, 2005), 178.
10. Abraham Dragon, CM/1 form, 28 July 1949, 3.2.1.1/79042782_0_4, ITS DAWL. The case worker's original wording is: 'Meiner Meinung nach ist er ein Rassisch Verfolgte und kann die IRO Unterstützung bekommen. Er hat "screening" am 13. I. 1948 in Frankfurt a. M. gemacht mit seinem Bruder'.

11. For further discussion of the IRO terminology and procedures, see Dan Stone, *The Liberation of the Camps: The End of the Holocaust and its Aftermath* (New Haven: Yale University Press, 2015), Chapter 5.
12. Devin O. Pendas, *The Frankfurt Auschwitz Trial, 1963–1965: Genocide, History, and the Limits of the Law* (New York: Cambridge University Press, 2006), 92. The details about Ormond are also taken from Pendas' book.
13. 6.3.3.2/104622107_0_1, ITS DAWL.
14. 'Aufgeh'. is an abbreviation of *aufgehoben*, or 'held'.
15. Mandelbaum to ITS, 14 February 1973; 6.3.3.2/86759693_0_1, ITS DAWL. A. Opitz (head of Archives, ITS) to Mandelbaum, 17 April 1973; 6.3.3.2/86759697_0_1, ITS DAWL. On Mandelbaum, see *I was at the Auschwitz Crematorium: A Conversation with Henryk Mandelbaum, Former Prisoner and Member of the Sonderkommando at Auschwitz* (Oświęcim: Auschwitz-Birkenau State Museum, 2011).
16. 6.3.3.2/88197504_0_1, ITS DAWL. Bennahmias was liberated at Ebensee.
17. Chazan to ITS, 7 April 1967, 6.3.3.2/99941036_0_1, ITS DAWL. See also 6.3.3.2/99941037_0_2 for further details of Chazan's trajectory.
18. W. Jeck (Archives, ITS) to Chazan, 16 August 1945; 6.3.3.2/99941041_0_1, ITS DAWL. The ITS first wrote to Chazan on 15 June 1967, saying that it had no information on him and recommending that he contact the relevant hospitals in Wels and Linz.
19. Sondervermögens- und Bauverwaltung bei der Oberfinanzdirektion Berlin to Wiedergutmachungsämter von Berlin, 5 September 1966; 6.3.3.2/100272265_0_1, ITS DAWL.
20. ITS to Berlin Restitution Office, 21 February 1967, 6.3.3.2/100272271_0_1 and 100272272_0_1, ITS DAWL.
21. Jennifer L. Rodgers, 'Archive of Horrors, Archive of Hope: The ITS in the Postwar Era', *Freilegungen: Jahrbuch des International Tracing Service* 4 (2015), 30.
22. URO to ITS, 27 March 1956, 6.3.3.2/101429173#1, ITS DAWL; URO to ITS, 5 September 1956, 6.3.3.2/101429172#1, ITS DAWL. Malinski appears in Eric Friedler's film *Sklaven der Gaskammer*.
23. ITS Certificate of Incarceration for David Nencel, 15 April 1955, 6.3.3.2/98914336#1 and #2, ITS DAWL. On Cinecittà, see Noa Steimatsky, 'The Cinecittà Refugee Camp (1944–1950)', *October* 128 (2009), 23–50.
24. See http://sonderkommando.info/index.php/themes-lies/personnes/filip-muller for the page specifically on Müller (retrieved 5 April 2019). The text here is a slightly adapted version of the text sent to the ITS in 2009. Véronique Chevillon to Nathalie Letierce-Liebig, Mission française de Liaison, ITS, 31 October 2008, 6.3.3.2/104622122_0_1 and 104622123_0_1, ITS DAWL.
25. Dr W. Krechtler to ITS, 30 October 1969, 6.3.3.2/104622155_0_1, ITS DAWL.
26. Miklós Nyiszli, *Auschwitz: A Doctor's Eyewitness Account*, trans. Tibère Kremer and Richard Seaver (St Albans: Mayflower, 1973), 49. The German translation is more dramatic, being in the present tense: 'Eine furchtbare Arbeit, die das Sonderkommando nur in einem Zustand durchführen kann, der einer freiwilligen Aufgabe der eigenen Persönlichkeit gleichkommt und gleichzeitig von tiefster Verzweiflung begleitet ist'. See Miklós Nyiszli, 'Sonderkommando', in H.G. Adler, Hermann Langbein and Ella Lingens-Reiner (eds), *Auschwitz: Zeugnisse und Berichte* (Bonn: Bundeszentrale für politische Bildung, 2014 [1962]), 68.
27. On Nyiszli, see Marius Turda, 'The Ambiguous Victim: Miklós Nyiszli's Narrative of Medical Experimentation in Auschwitz-Birkenau', *Historein* 14(1) (2014), 43–58.

28. W. Clover, Jewish Information (Judisk Information) to ITS, 28 July 1980, 6.3.3.2/100393046_0_1, ITS DAWL.
29. Smoleń to ITS, 11 July 1986, 6.3.3.2/100393045_0_1, ITS DAWL.
30. W. Clover, Jewish Information (Judisk Information), to ITS, 15 April 1980, 6.3.3.2/100393047_0_1, ITS DAWL.
31. H. Siebel (ITS) to W. Clover (Judisk Information), 23 July 1980, 6.3.3.2/100393056_0_1, ITS DAWL.
32. H. Siebel (ITS) to W. Clover (Judisk Information), 6 October 1980, 6.3.3.2/104622189_0_1, ITS DAWL.
33. Shlomo Venezia, *Inside the Gas Chambers: Eight Months in the Sonderkommando of Auschwitz*, trans. Andrew Brown (Cambridge: Polity Press, 2009), 155.

Bibliography

Brown-Fleming, Suzanne. *Nazi Persecution and Postwar Repercussions: The International Tracing Service Archive and Holocaust Research*. Lanham, MD: Rowman & Littlefield, 2016.
Chare, Nicholas, and Dominic Williams. *Matters of Testimony: Interpreting the Scrolls of Auschwitz*. New York: Berghahn Books, 2016.
Friedler, Eric, Barbara Siebert and Andreas Kilian. *Zeugen aus der Todeszone: Das jüdische Sonderkommando in Auschwitz*. Munich: Deutscher Taschenbuch Verlag, 2005.
Fromer, Rebecca Camhi. *The Holocaust Odyssey of Daniel Bennahmias, Sonderkommando*. Tuscaloosa: University of Alabama Press, 1993.
Greif, Gideon. *We Wept without Tears: Testimonies of the Jewish Sonderkommando from Auschwitz*. New Haven: Yale University Press, 2005.
Mandelbaum, Henryk. *I was at the Auschwitz Crematorium: A Conversation with Henryk Mandelbaum, Former Prisoner and Member of the Sonderkommando at Auschwitz*. Oświęcim: Auschwitz-Birkenau State Museum, 2011.
Nahon, Marco. *Birkenau: The Camp of Death*, trans. Jacqueline Havaux Bowers. Tuscaloosa: University of Alabama Press, 1989.
Nyiszli, Miklós. *Auschwitz: A Doctor's Eyewitness Account*, trans. Tibère Kremer and Richard Seaver. St Albans: Mayflower, 1973.
——. 'Sonderkommando', in H G. Adler, Hermann Langbein and Ella Lingens-Reiner (eds), *Auschwitz: Zeugnisse und Berichte*. Bonn: Bundeszentrale für politische Bildung, 2014 [1962].
Pendas, Devin O. *The Frankfurt Auschwitz Trial, 1963–1965: Genocide, History, and the Limits of the Law*. New York: Cambridge University Press, 2006.
Rodgers, Jennifer. 'From the "Archive of Horrors" to the "Shop Window of Democracy": The International Tracing Service 1942–2013', PhD thesis. Philadelphia: University of Pennsylvania, 2014.
——. 'Archive of Horrors, Archive of Hope: The ITS in the Postwar Era', *Freilegungen: Jahrbuch des International Tracing Service* 4 (2015), 17–34.
Stone, Dan. '"The Greatest Detective Story in History": The BBC, the International Tracing Service, and the Memory of Nazi Crimes in Early Postwar Britain', *History & Memory*, 29(2) (2017), 63–89.
——. 'The Memory of the Archive: The International Tracing Service and the Construction of the Past as History', *Dapim: Studies on the Holocaust* 31(2) (2017), 69–88.

———. 'Christianstadt: Slave Labour and the Holocaust', *Freilegungen: Jahrbuch des International Tracing Service* 4 (2015), 78–91.

Vrba, Rudolf, and Alfred Wetzler. 'Report of Rudolf Vrba and Alfred Wetzler', in Henryk Świebocki (ed), *London Has Been Informed. … Reports by Auschwitz Escapees*. Oświęcim: Auschwitz-Birkenau State Museum, 2002.

Venezia, Shlomo. *Inside the Gas Chambers: Eight Months in the Sonderkommando of Auschwitz*, trans. Andrew Brown. Cambridge: Polity Press, 2009.

Wallen, Jeffrey. 'The Witness against the Archive: Toward a Microhistory of Christianstadt', in Claire Zalc and Tal Bruttmann (eds), *Microhistories of the Holocaust*. New York: Berghahn Books, 2017, 300–314.

Chapter 11

Enduring Witness

David Olère's Visual Testimony

Carol Zemel

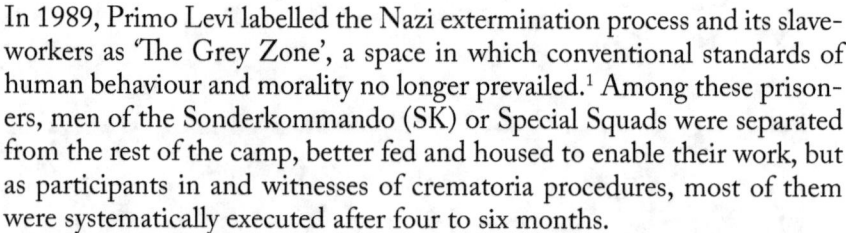

In 1989, Primo Levi labelled the Nazi extermination process and its slave-workers as 'The Grey Zone', a space in which conventional standards of human behaviour and morality no longer prevailed.[1] Among these prisoners, men of the Sonderkommando (SK) or Special Squads were separated from the rest of the camp, better fed and housed to enable their work, but as participants in and witnesses of crematoria procedures, most of them were systematically executed after four to six months.

Among the hundreds of drawings made by concentration camp prisoners, images of the killing process are rare. The Scrolls of Auschwitz, textual accounts of the extermination written and hidden by members of the SK, have been found, preserved, translated and published.[2] Four photographs taken in August 1944 by SK member Alberto (Alex) Errera in the dark and emptied Birkenau gas chamber have been exhibited and widely discussed.[3] But perhaps because visual art is often considered, narrowly, as self-expression rather than data or documentation or even cultural commentary, less attention has been paid to the postwar images of the killing process produced by the artist and SK member David Olère (1902–85).

Unlike the instantaneous and partly mechanical record of photographs, handmade images of events made after the fact are recollections: no matter how close in time they are to the depicted moment, they depend on the maker's visual memory and skilled reportage. David Olère's pictures of his SK experience are marked by their date, style, medium and testimonial purpose. Accessible as online biography and as teaching tools, Olère's images have not been widely used as official testimony and they scarcely appear in art historical studies.⁴

Olère kept his pictures during his lifetime, rarely exhibiting or selling them. After his death in 1985, Alexandre Oler deposited his father's work with the Klarsfeld Foundation in Paris;⁵ a lavishly illustrated catalogue was published in 1989, with a second edition in 1997. Some works were deposited in Israel at Lohamei Ha-Geta'ot (Ghetto Fighters' House) and Yad Vashem. Many pictures were restored and exhibited at the Museum of Jewish Heritage in New York; these works are now in the collection of the Auschwitz Museum in Poland. Despite their limited exhibition history, reproductions of Olère's pictures are readily accessible online.

The drawings' evidentiary status may be compared with the SK textual accounts, but the pictorial medium and, initially, a distinctive – almost impassive – visual style present their own form of testimony. At once compelling and troubling to see, Olère's drawings provoke both fascination and unease. This is trauma's hallmark. It signals, in Cathy Caruth's description, 'a crisis marked not by simple knowledge, but by the ways it simultaneously defies and demands our witness'.⁶

In this chapter, I consider the range of Olere's work – his initial postwar drawings, followed by the paintings he produced for the rest of his career and, finally, his totemic sculpture. Despite shifts in style and medium, they are lifelong testimony to the SK experience in the grey zone.

Born in Warsaw in 1902, David Olère attended the Warsaw Academy of Fine Arts. After the First World War, he worked briefly in Danzig and Berlin, where he built sets for Ernst Lubitsch's Europaische Film Allianz. Like many Jewish artists from Eastern Europe in those years, Olère moved to Paris in 1923, married Juliette Ventura in 1930 and became a French citizen. He continued his career designing film posters and theatre sets, genres that likely enhanced his skill in rendering dramatic space and expressive moment.

Olère was arrested by the Germans in February 1943, was deported in March from Drancy to Auschwitz, and two months later, was selected for the SK. Forced to participate in the procedures of mass murder, knowing its details and full extent, SK squads were systematically killed by the Nazis after a few months of work; Olère was one of the few to survive.⁷ Shortly before Auschwitz was liberated by the Soviet army in January 1945, he and approximately one hundred other SK members avoided execution and joined a prisoner death march that led first to Mauthausen (Austria), then to Melk and finally to Ebensee, where after months of hard labour he was liberated by the U.S. Army on 5 May 1945.⁸

Olère resumed drawing immediately on his return to Paris and with testimonial urgency: to convince his wife (and undoubtedly others) of the atrocities he had seen and experienced. He had no other subject. Caruth describes this state of being:

> The crisis at the core of many traumatic narratives ... often emerges as an urgent question – is the trauma the encounter with death or the ongoing experience of having survived it ... [It is] a sort of double telling, the oscillation between a crisis of death and a crisis of life: between the story of the unbearable nature of an event and the story of the unbearable nature of its survival.[9]

Trauma does not lessen the reliability or persistence of the artist's witness. Olère's pictorial report became a lifelong project, as realist drawing was followed by caricature, allegorical painting and finally sculpture. Despite their shifts in medium and style over the next forty years, the images all enact the urgency of pictorial testimony.

Unflinching in their content and directness, Olère's drawings are as unsettling to look at as SK testimony is to read.[10] Unlike those texts, however, the pictures have no narrative sequence; rather, their panoramic and close-up views render moments in the extermination process as a perpetual present, an emblematic timelessness, with no resolution or relief. With the impassive manner of an official report or traumatized witness, they are drawn in simple linear outlines, with little or no shading to inflect their design or to call out emphases. There is little sign of feeling or compassion in their presentation. There is nothing of the reverence found in Christian *Crucifixions* or images of martyrdom, none of the outrage stirred by the captioned etchings of Goya's *The Disasters of War* (1810–20)[11] or even by Olère's own elaborate later allegories. Direct but also impassive, like the moral limbo of the grey zone, the drawings are unflinching records of Nazi extermination practice.

Because Olère signed and dated his pictures by year, it is difficult to establish a precise sequence for the first postwar images.[12] To do so, however, might impose a visual narrative that belies both the fragmented and emblematic character of traumatic memory. Drawings dated 1945, for example, depict the artist's first weeks in Auschwitz as well as his final months in Ebensee. Their subjects include cold showers in the snow, the notorious standing cells of Auschwitz' Block 11 and a clandestine multifaith prayer service – an ecumenical motif that appears in Olère's later allegories. Only two drawings salute the liberators. One image, captioned in English 'It's all over now, is it a dream', pictures a burly American GI supporting a gaunt prisoner. But there is not much reference to this freedom or relief. For the rest of his career, both realist witness and lurid fantasy dominated Olère's pictures and history.

Prisoners in Auschwitz produced hundreds of secret drawings that testify to camp experience and atrocities.[13] Artists among them might also gain limited protection by making portraits of their captors or decorating officers' letters to family and friends. There are, however, almost no images of extermination procedures and, in this respect, Olère's pictures are unique.

Rather than working with execution squads and occasionally emptying bodies from the gas chamber, his 'only task', according to surviving SK member Dov Paisikovic, 'was to do paintings for the SS'.[14] This work involved decorating letters and drawing flattering portrait drawings for the notorious Oberscharführer Otto Moll, the commander of the crematoria, and other high-ranking Nazis in the camp.[15] These are conventional vignettes: a close-up of the officer's head and upper torso, carefully rendered with no trace of troubling character.[16]

A postwar drawing labelled 'For a Crust of Bread') conveys the context of this assignment. Gaunt, taciturn and in civilian dress, [17] Olère is framed within the fisted embrace of two Nazi officers. Despite the artist's place in the foreground, the dominant aspect of this triple portrait is the middle figure of the bald, uniformed officer – likely Moll – who leans forward to supervise the process and, with a rifle replacing the artist's pen, echoes his prisoner's pose.

This echoing enclosure appears in another self-image, dated 1947, in which Olère, in the striped prisoner uniform of the *Begrabungskommando* (gravediggers) and with tattooed number visible, shovels dead babies into a pit.[18] Seen through the framing contours of the artist's body, spade and arm, an SS officer in the background repeats the prisoner's pose. But such identifiable self-references are rare in Olère's early drawings, where everything – whether task or structure – illustrates Nazi efficiency and deceit.

Olère's architectural drawings, for example, testify to his eye for details, showing the elaborate and efficient structure of Crematorium III, which began operating in the summer of 1943.[19] A blueprint charts undressing, killing and postmortem areas, SS offices and SK quarters beneath the roof. In contrast, a view of a repurposed rustic farmhouse, its doorway labelled 'DESINFEKTION', illustrates Nazi euphemism and duplicity. As uniformed prisoners dig burial pits in the foreground, naked women and children proceed to the cottage entrance and death.

Unlike the irony in these drawings, Olère's pictures of extermination procedures are impassive renderings, a detached voice of traumatic testimony. *The Undressing Room* (1946) depicts a cavernous space, crowded with naked women and children. The setting might be a community bathhouse. There is little sign of distress, despite the SS guards who signal the inevitability of what will occur. Remarkably, Olère omits the SK, whose job it was to calm the victims and ease their compliance. Like a report, these drawings convey their data with realist detachment, allowing viewer witness to a secret spectacle.

The Cremation Room details the final steps of that process. Various stations include an elevator platform that lifted corpses to a sluice, from which they were set in piles, then placed through the open doors of flaming ovens, with crumbled bones and ash visible though the grates below. Corpses of women (all of them comely) and infants stacked in the foreground await disposal by bare-chested SK members. Undifferentiated 'pieces', as the Nazis called them, the dead are stripped of all but their gender identity. The scene, as Olère drew it, is a gendered theatre of death, with the viewer as both moral witness and titillated spectator.

Partnering the generic beauty of the women, the SK appear as faceless automatons. In one of the hidden Scrolls of Auschwitz, Zalman Gradowski described their impassivity and state of mind: 'The continual systematic death, the only life of everyone who lives here, deafens, confuses, and dulls your senses. You cannot feel, sense even the greatest suffering ... why am I sitting here quietly instead of lamenting, weeping over my tragedy, and why instead are we frozen, numb, drained of all emotion'.[20] And, in Zalman Lewental's account: 'We [the SK] were like dead men, like robots, when they [rushed?] us ... [No one] looked at anyone else ... none of us was alive at that time, none of us thought or contemplated'.[21]

No one in Olère's crematorium drawings – worker, guard or victim – is an individual; like a factory assembly line, their task and fate is their identity. The SS invariably appear as hypermasculine brutes, their coarse features twisted in a snarl, a rifle close at hand. Like all participants in the death process, they too are types, whose exaggerated machismo partners the women's conventional beauty and vulnerability. Beautiful women, robotic SK, grotesque SS: there is no identity beyond the rituals of death.

However impassive Olère's graphic report, the drawings' gender emphases bring a prurient voyeurism – an *eros-thanatos* coupling – to the crematorium views. Even pictures of postmortem procedures, such as removing teeth in a search for gold or cutting hair, split viewer attention between the gruesome action and the women's comeliness. Some drawings suggest a brothel: nude women pose and lounge about, while hulking SS men appear as both visitors and guards. There was, however, no brothel in the crematorium. One might consider this, however, a classic Oedipal vision: the beautiful Desired-Mother at the centre stands before us while threatened by the rapacious Rival-Father at the edge of the design. Such psychosexual positions pervade Olère's imagery and ultimately become vehicles of rage, with Nazi officers, always, as hulking brutes.

Olère's drawings also report postmortem medical procedures in the crematorium dissecting space, conveniently adjacent to the oven room. Miklós Nyiszli, [22] a Jewish forensic pathologist and a privileged SK who worked for Dr Josef Mengele, may be among the faceless white-coated surgeons gathered close around a female cadaver splayed on a dissecting table. With one leg cut to the bone and protruding into the foreground, the woman's naked body is the drawing's focus, as the viewer shares the position and attentive study of the medical team. The immediacy of this inclusive view is more unnerving than Olère's later painting of the scene in which the figure of a maddened Hitler is the dissector and the artist's head, as ghostly witness, floats overhead.

Two years after liberation, the sardonic force of caricature signals Olère's move from the crematorium drawings' impassive realism. One such taunt shows SS officer Ilse Koch stitching prisoner tattoos – flowers, fruit, hearts – onto a lampshade.[23] Infamously known as 'The Beast of Buchenwald', Koch had not worked at Auschwitz, but her likeness nonetheless hits the mark as a cliché of Nazi deviance. A rare example of female perversity in Olère's imagery, Koch also appears in an allegorical painting, where the inversion of masculine desire has her sadly pondering the genitals of a male corpse bearing Olère's prisoner number.

By 1947, and in line with the artist's film poster skills, the emotional displacements of allegory replaced the drawings' impassive realism. *Her Last Nursing* pictures a doomed family group: a beautiful mother nurses her baby, her naked daughter stands at her right, while an armed SS officer, his face contorted, grasps the woman's arm and shoulder, as if readying her for death. A smoking chimney in the background predicts the family's fate. The composition borrows Renaissance designs for a Christian Holy Family – Mother, Child and Joseph, who is recast here as an agent of death. The metaphor may be awkward, but the allusion intensifies the fusion of atrocity and sentiment.

With the move to allegory, cultural identities and sexual consorting replace the generic worker-prisoner population of the crematorium. SS officers remain grotesque giants, directing arrivals across the landscape towards the chimney flames. The prisoners have become a more ecumenical company. Men are led by an elderly rabbi in long black *kapote* and *Jude* badge, and a young priest in cassock and crucifix; each submissively bows his head. Women assemble as a distraught family of mothers, children and crone-like grandmother. Religious rituals – Jewish and Christian – are iconic in design. *Their Last Steps* mimes a Crucifixion, as three half-naked prisoners stand arm-in-arm, backed by crematorium flames; in *Kadish* (sic), a partial *minyan* of five men, their leader in a *tallit* (prayer shawl), stand together and recite the Jewish prayer for the dead.

Cultural identities also appear in Olère's few sculptural works, whose rough granite surface and emblematic figures invoke an ancient history. A naked mother crouches and cradles two babies, echoing a *Massacre of Innocents*. A father in a prayer shawl shelters his young son and a crouching man distils prisoner agony into totemic form.

Sexuality, however, is at the core of Olère's visual repertoire as the muffled eroticism of the crematorium drawings bursts into full-on bacchanal, and realism is replaced by overlapping sections of montage. The pictures are crammed with nudity: beautiful women and girls, fleshy copulating guards (the women wearing boots). The SS appear as deranged giants: one bestial officer, teeth gleaming, literally devours an adolescent girl. With chimney flames as a constant background, the paintings are frenzied displays of sex and death. The impassive realism and theatrical staging of the initial drawings gives way to erotic fantasy and the overlapping vignettes of poster montage.

What is the dimension of testimony in these lurid allegories? Are history and cultural memory well-served? As if in answer, Olère's self-image repeatedly enters the images in a separate register. No longer a robotic SK, he affirms a testimonial mission and floats above scenes of death and desecration as a ghostly apparition and witness.

Ultimately, Olère turned to the most prohibited sight: *Gassing* depicts the death chamber crammed with dying prisoners. SK texts describe such scenes, most vividly in Filip Müller's account of his despairing decision to join the prisoners in the chamber, only to be convinced by a group of young women of the importance of his testimony: 'perhaps you'll survive this terrible tragedy and then you must tell everybody what happened to you'.[24]

Müller's memoir *Eyewitness Auschwitz* (1979) fulfils this promise. Only Olère depicted the scene. There are, in fact, few pictures of the gas chamber – a sign of its secret status and ongoing mystification as forbidden sight.[25] But as a member of the SK, emptying the gas chamber was one of Olère's tasks; an early drawing shows him – barely identifiable – dragging the corpses of a young woman and baby outside the open chamber door.

There is no such setting in *Gassing*. The image is crammed edge-to-edge with tangled suffocating bodies of men, women and babies. Almost life-size (131×162 cm), the absence of foreground or any framing enclosure ambiguously places the viewer within and outside the space, as both victim and witness. Like a religious icon, the scene is timeless: there is only continuous agony for skeletal figures, blued by gas, open-mouthed and gasping to breathe. In a jumble of bony limbs, they are an iconic murdered company. Unusually for Olère, the picture has no signature. An open container labelled 'GIFT [poison] GAS ZYKLON B' is set at the lower right corner, where a name might be.

Olère's pictures are troubling visions, but they also raise a general juridical issue: to what extent can their content – especially the crematorium drawings – serve as data or evidence? Does their status as handmade imagery or art affect or diminish their testimonial status any more than a rescued diary or photo album? The answer seems ambiguous. Support for their testimonial position prevails in *The Evidence Room*, a recent installation at Toronto's Royal Ontario Museum,[26] in which a white chamber housing white sculpture replicas of gas chamber elements – an architectural column, door, ladder and pellet hatch – enable close scrutiny. The whitened objects and environment presumably enables close study and discourages the visitor from any experiential fantasy.

The exhibit also includes crematorium drawings by Olère and by Yehuda Bacon, a teenage prisoner in Auschwitz, to illustrate the phases and details of the extermination process.[27] In line with the architectural components, all the images have been recast from their original pen-and-ink format into white relief prints.[28] The viewer strains to see the images, which register as pattern, their content dimmed to near-erasure – although accessible to the visitor's touch.

One can, of course, cast – and quasi-replicate – almost anything. But the change from a two-dimensional image, with its illusionistic rendering of space and scale, to a barely palpable surface design scarcely translates, much less delivers pictorial information. Can one transform the culture-based language of pictorial illusion into comprehensible tactile form? And is this an enlightening synesthesia? What is the evidentiary status of these altered images, so distanced from their original format and impact? What prompts exhibition designers – intending accessibility – to narrow a visual record of atrocity to palpable pattern and design? [29]

One surely need not adjust the original formats of Holocaust history and testimony. All chronicles and accounts, whatever their medium, contain arguable assertions and inaccuracies. But nor should we alter or manipulate their evidentiary character. David Olère's pictures – whether impassive or sardonic, realist or allegorical – are first-hand declarations of experience. Difficult and disturbing as these pictures are, their testimony in its unaltered form enlarges our sense of moral compass and understanding of history.

Carol Zemel is Professor Emerita of Art History and Visual Culture at York University, Toronto. Her work focuses on Jewish and diasporic issues and on the ethics of visuality in modern and contemporary art.

Her book *Looking Jewish: Visual Culture and Modern Diaspora* was published in 2015. Her critical essays have appeared in *AJS Perspectives*, *C Magazine*, *Canadian Theatre Review*, *Images* and the Jewish daily *The Forward*. In the spring of 2017, she was Fellow at the Mandel Center, USHMM, Washington DC, completing archival research for her book *Art in Extremis*, a study of images made by prisoners in ghettos and camps during the Holocaust. Her current projects include a study of the modern 'Jewish nude', and Critical Israel, an exploration of contemporary art in Israel with a critical edge.

Notes

Portions of my study of David Olère's work appear in Carol Zemel, 'Right After: Aesthetics and Trauma in Survivor Visual Narratives', in Sophia Komor and Susanne Rohr (eds), *The Holocaust, Art, and Taboo: Transatlantic Exchanges on the Ethics and Aesthetics of Representation* (Heidelberg: Universitätsverlag Winter, 2010), 49–62.

1. Primo Levi, *The Drowned and the Saved* (London: Abacus, 1989), 53. For discussion of the term, see Sander H. Lee, 'Primo Levi's *Gray Zone:* Implications for Post-Holocaust Ethics', *Holocaust and Genocide Studies* 30(2) (2016), 276–97.
2. Nicholas Chare and Dominic Williams, *Matters of Testimony; Interpreting the Scrolls of Auschwitz* (New York: Berghahn Books, 2016).
3. For discussion of the photographs, see Nicholas Chare, 'Afterimages', in *Auschwitz and Afterimages: Abjection, Witnessing and Representation* (London: I.B.Tauris, 2011), 125–50; and Georges Didi-Huberman, *Images in Spite of All: Four Photographs from Auschwitz*, trans. Shane B. Lillis (Chicago: University of Chicago Press, 2008).
4. Thomas Geve, Alfred Kantor and Ella Lieberman-Shiber are among other artist-survivors who made pictorial narratives of their Holocaust experience. Olère was the only member of the SK to do so. See my essay 'Right after: Aesthetics and Trauma in Survivor Visual Narratives', in Sophia Komor and Susanne Rohr (eds), *The Holocaust, Art, and Taboo: Transatlantic Exchanges on the Ethics and Aesthetics of Representation* (Heidelberg: Universitätsverlag Winter, 2010), 49–61.
5. Serge Klarsfeld, 'Foreword', in *David Olère: A Painter in the Sonderkommando at Auschwitz* (New York: Beate Klarsfeld Foundation, 1989), 8–10. After conservation at the Museum of Jewish Heritage in New York, much of the work was sent to the Auschwitz Museum in Poland, where it remains. Several drawings were donated by the Olère family to Lohamei ha-Geta'ot (Ghetto Fighters' House) and to Yad Vashem in Israel.
6. Cathy Caruth, *Unclaimed Experience: Trauma, Narrative and History* (Baltimore: Johns Hopkins University Press, 1996), 5.
7. Approximately 80–100 of the 2,000 members of the SK survived. Chare and Williams, *Matters of Testimony*, 7; 'The Sonderkommando', www.jewishvirtuallibrary.org.
8. Klarsfeld, 'Foreword', 9.
9. Caruth, *Unclaimed Experience*, 7.

10. For the SK reports, see Gideon Greif, *We Wept without Tears: Testimonies of the Jewish Sonderkommando from Auschwitz* (New Haven: Yale University Press, 2005); and Léon Poliakov, *Harvest of Hate: The Nazi Program for the Destruction of the Jews of Europe* (New York: Holocaust Library, 1970). See also the accounts in Filip Müller, *Eyewitness Auschwitz; Three Years in the Gas Chambers* (Chicago: Ivan T. Dee, 1999); and Shlomo Venezia, *Inside the Gas Chambers: Eight Months in the Sonderkommando of Auschwitz* (Cambridge: Polity Press, 2009).
11. For viewer response to such images, see Susan Sontag, *Regarding the Pain of Others* (New York: Farrar, Straus & Giroux, 2003), 95–103.
12. I have followed dates accompanying the image signatures.
13. For comprehensive studies of Holocaust art, although with little discussion of Olère, see: Ziva Amishai-Maisels, *Depiction and Interpretation: The Influence of the Holocaust on the Visual Arts* (Oxford: Pergamon Press, 1993); Janet Blatter and Sybil Milton, *Art of the Holocaust* (New York: Routledge, 1981); Glenn Sujo, *Legacies of Silence: The Visual Arts and Holocaust Memory* (London: Philip Wilson Publishers, 2001).
14. "[Olère] était artiste peintre et, pendant tout le temps que je connus le kommando, il avait l'unique tâche to peindre des tableaux pour les SS, il était dispensé de tout autre travail pour le *Sonderkommando*'. Paisikovic, quoted by historian Leon Poliakov, *Auschwitz* (Paris: Éditions Gallimard, 2014), 208. Fluent in several languages, including English, Olère also translated British radio broadcasts of the war's progress for the SS.
15. Otto Moll was executed by the U.S. Allies in Landsberg-am-Lech prison on 28 May 1946. Retrieved 18 May 2019 from https://en.m.wikipedia.org/wiki/Otto_Moll.
16. Gideon Greif and Andreas Kilian, 'Significance, Responsibility, Challenge: Interviewing the Sonderkommando Survivors', *Sonderkommando Studien*. Retrieved 9 April 2019 from www.sonderkommando-studien.de/artikel.php?c=forschung/signifi cance.
17. Unlike most regular camp prisoners, SK members wore ordinary trousers and jackets, each with a red stripe or cross painted on the back.
18. Prisoners of the Begrabungskommando became the core of the SK.
19. The four crematoria at Auschwitz-Birkenau were designed by the architects Walter Dejaco and Fritz Ertel.
20. Zalman Gradowski, quoted in Greif, *We Wept without Tears*, 84.
21. Zalman Levental, quoted in ibid., 21.
22. Liberated, like Olère, at Ebensee, Nyiszli returned to medical practice in Romania in 1946. See his memoir, written first in Hungarian in 1947: *Auschwitz: A Doctor's Eye-Witness Account*, trans. Tibère Kremer and Richard Seaver (Geneva: Ferni, 1979). For discussion of his activities and testimony, see Marius Turda, 'The Ambiguous Victim: Miklós Nyiszli's Narrative of Medical Experimentation in Auschwitz-Birkenau', *Historien* 14 (2014), 43–58.
23. Olère caricatured himself doing the same, while seated beside fellow prisoner Kapo Julius Brück. See Klarsfeld, *David Olère*, 60.
24. Müller, *Eyewitness Auschwitz*, 113. See also Venezia's detailed account in *Inside the Gas Chambers*.
25. In 1945, Yehudah Bacon (1929–), a sixteen-year-old prisoner in Auschwitz, drew an image of his father's face rising from a fiery chimney in a cloud of smoke. Wiktor Siminski, a Polish political prisoner at Sachsenhausen, drew a gas chamber crowded with flailing, naked women, while a guard, eyes bulging, watches through a small window at the side.

26. Anne Bordeleau, Sascha Hastings, Donald McKay and Robert Jan van Pelt, *The Evidence Room* (Toronto: New Jewish Press, 2016), 2–16. The exhibition was first presented at the Venice Architectural Biennale, 2016.
27. For an account of his experience as an Auschwitz prisoner, see: www.yadvashem.org/articles/interviews/yehuda-bacon (retrieved 9 April 2019).
28. Anne Bordeleau, 'The Casts Court', in *The Evidence Room*, 113–18.

Bibliography

Amishai-Maisels, Ziva. *Depiction and Interpretation: The Influence of the Holocaust on the Visual Arts*. Oxford: Pergamon Press, 1993.
Bordeleau, Anne, Sascha Hastings, Donald McKay and Robert Jan van Pelt, *The Evidence Room*. Toronto: New Jewish Press, 2016.
Blatter, Janet, and Sybil Milton, *Art of the Holocaust*. New York: Routledge, 1981.
Caruth, Cathy. *Unclaimed Experience: Trauma, Narrative and History*. Baltimore: Johns Hopkins University Press, 1996.
Chare, Nicholas. *Auschwitz and Afterimages: Abjection, Witnessing and Representation*. London: I.B. Tauris, 2011.
Chare, Nicholas, and Dominic Williams. *Matters of Testimony: Interpreting the Scrolls of Auschwitz*. New York: Berghahn Books, 2016.
Didi-Huberman, Georges. *Images in Spite of All: Four Photographs from Auschwitz*, trans. Shane B. Lillis. Chicago: University of Chicago Press, 2008.
Greif, Gideon. *We Wept without Tears: Testimonies of the Jewish Sonderkommando from Auschwitz*, trans. Naftali Greenwood. New Haven: Yale University Press, 2005.
Klarsfeld, Serge. 'Foreword', in Serge Klarsfeld (ed.), *David Olère: A Painter in the Sonderkommando at Auschwitz*. New York: Beate Klarsfeld Foundation, 1989, 8–10.
Lee, Sander H. 'Primo Levi's *Gray Zone:* Implications for Post-Holocaust Ethics', *Holocaust and Genocide Studies* 30(2) (2016), 276–97.
Levi, Primo. *The Drowned and the Saved*, trans. Raymond Rosenthal. London: Abacus, 1989.
Müller, Filip. *Eyewitness Auschwitz; Three Years in the Gas Chambers*. Chicago: Ivan T. Dee, 1999.
Nyiszli, Miklós. *Auschwitz: A Doctor's Eye-witness Account*, trans. Tibère Kremer and Richard Seaver. Geneva: Ferni, 1979.
Poliakov, Léon. *Harvest of Hate: The Nazi Program for the Destruction of the Jews of Europe*. New York: Holocaust Library, 1970.
———. *Auschwitz*. Paris: Éditions Gallimard, 2014.
Sontag, Susan. *Regarding the Pain of Others*. New York: Farrar, Straus & Giroux, 2003.
Sujo, Glenn. *Legacies of Silence: The Visual Arts and Holocaust Memory*. London: Philip Wilson Publishers, 2001.
Turda, Marius. 'The Ambiguous Victim: Miklós Nyiszli's Narrative of Medical Experimentation in Auschwitz-Birkenau', *Historien* 14 (2014), 43–58.
Venezia, Shlomo. *Inside the Gas Chambers: Eight Months in the Sonderkommando of Auschwitz*. Cambridge: Polity Press, 2009.
Zemel, Carol. 'Right after: Aesthetics and Trauma in Survivor Visual Narratives', in Susanne Rohr and Sophia Komor (eds), *The Holocaust, Art and Taboo: Transatlantic Exchanges on the Ethics and Aesthetics of Representation*. Heidelberg, Universitatsverlag Winter, 2010, 49–61.

Chapter 12

The Sonderkommando and the Auschwitz-Birkenau Memorial Museum

Dominic Williams and Isabel Wollaston

In introducing the Auschwitz-Birkenau Memorial Museum's 2013 annual report, Piotr Cywiński, the Director, chose to reflect on the Sonderkommando (SK):

> *Geheimnisträger*, the bearers of secrets. This name was applied to a special group of prisoners in the camp. Above all, to those who had seen with their own eyes the heart of the Holocaust, the Sonderkommando prisoners who operated the Auschwitz-Birkenau crematoria. Prisoners in this category, separated from the others, were sentenced without exception to be murdered after finishing their work.
>
> In this way, no part of the grim secret would escape to the outside world. The *Geheimnisträger* were supposed to be the last link in the chain of memory. After them, nothing evermore. Silence.
>
> The plan failed. People survived and gave testimony.
>
> Today, thanks to their words and also to the original extant remains of the camp space, we remember and we try to understand. The knowledge we have obtained imposes a fearful obligation on us. Today, in a certain way, we are all *Geheimnisträger*, and what future generations will know, remember, and understand depends on us – exclusively on us.
>
> Let us bear witness to the truth.[1]

For Cywiński, the testimony of the SK is of importance precisely because they alone witnessed 'with their own eyes' the 'heart of hell'. His passing comment that the SK 'operated' the crematoria highlights the need for great care in how we use language in this context: the SK never 'operated the Auschwitz-Birkenau crematoria' in the sense of running the killing process and were (and are) acutely sensitive to any suggestion that they were collaborators and/or perpetrators.[2]

Cywiński's words are also telling in the way that the links in the chain of memory appear to turn all of humanity into SK, or at least to put them into a very direct relationship with them: 'we are all *Geheimnisträger*'. Here we see a number of problems that face anyone discussing the SK. On the one hand is the danger of accusing them of being little different from perpetrators. On the other is the temptation to blur the bounds between this group and the rest of the world, disregarding the extreme nature of their situation and the difficulty for those outside it to imagine it.[3] Cywiński's words indicate the central yet problematic place of the SK in the Museum's sense of what it wants the links in the chain of memory to pass on. As eyewitnesses, the SK seem to be key to the understanding of the site's history and its function as a centre of extermination. And yet their role as (relatively privileged) forced labourers within that exterminatory process raises questions that are difficult to address.

In this chapter, we will suggest that the Museum primarily deals with this problem by separating the former role from the latter.[4] While this approach is consonant with the Museum's desire to preserve the good name of the dead, it ends up leaving the human existence and suffering of the SK unexamined. This means that questions such as their place in the 'grey zone', their relationships and tensions with other prisoners, and even the ways that they might be said to have been anticipating the Museum's own mission are not addressed.

The Museum and the SK

The Museum itself is a complex and contradictory project. It spans multiple sites, which had different functions within the Nazi concentrationary and exterminatory universes. The museological spaces currently visible were also created at different times, in different contexts, from the mid 1950s onwards. In its present form, the site has multiple roles – primarily, as its name, and the 1947 law establishing it, indicate, as a memorial and a museum. Silke Arnold-de Simine notes that these two functions do not quite gel together: the memorial function (honouring the dead) and the museal function (critical interpretation and contextualization) can sometimes be at odds with each other.⁵ Added to that are the multiple groups who have a stake in the place: it is contested between survivors and their descendants, the Polish state and Israeli visitors, for example. Adding a further layer of complexity, none of these sometimes competing communities of memory or groups are themselves homogeneous, and are often riven by internal disagreements over the meaning and future of the site. This is not always a straightforward claiming of the space, however: the Polish state has attempted to legislate against calling it a 'Polish death camp', for example, and the Museum website does not use the domain suffix '.pl'.⁶ Much of the responsibility for documenting the prisoners of different nationalities, in the form of national exhibitions supplementing the permanent exhibition, was divided up amongst their home countries, which had very different agendas in approaching the history of the Holocaust and therefore different ideas of what the SK were and are.⁷ The survey that we provide of the representations of the SK in and by the Museum cannot, therefore, identify one coherent account of this group that emerges. But it is possible to trace some patterns, lacunae and commonalities among, and even emerging in the tensions between, the different approaches taken by the different sites and functions of the Museum.

Many of these commonalities stem from the problems that the SK would present to any museum. The SK often take a central role as forms of evidence because, as Jonathan Webber points out, they saw 'the apparatus of genocide close up'. But, as Webber also notes, the SK pose a problem for how to tell the story of what happened to the prisoners:

> The celebrated description of the Auschwitz survivor Primo Levi of what he called a moral and ethical 'grey zone' . . . with reference, for example, to the Sonderkommando prisoners at Auschwitz who were simultaneously victims as well as being collaborators with the perpetrators, and who therefore may in some sense be said to have shared some moral culpability for the mass murders there – is a constant reminder of the philosophical problems in finding a suitable way of telling the story of what happened in Auschwitz.⁸

If the museum is there to honour the dead, the SK might be difficult to honour. When people want to focus on victims and pay less attention to perpetrators, a group who some people find it difficult to fit straightforwardly into the former category might not be the easiest group to draw attention to.⁹

There are numerous other difficulties that the SK present to a museum. Simply dealing with what they witnessed is very difficult. All the questions about the ethics of representing violence are at work in the scenes that the SK depict.[10] As Ana Carden-Coyne puts it, for example: '[H]ow can the Holocaust be represented both accurately and ethically, without sensationalising, trading in "edutainment" or encouraging macabre fascination with atrocity imagery?'[11] Moreover, the testimony that they produced is hard to read as objects. The Museum provides numerous reproductions of forms and lists produced by the camp administration because they act as proof, but also because they are legible: they are typed, relatively well-preserved and in Roman script. The documents that the SK produced are none of these things: handwritten in unimaginably difficult circumstances (although not usually hastily scribbled), written for the most part in Hebrew script and damaged by being hidden in the ground. The photographs are more legible, but nothing like the clear delineation of the area of the ramp provided by the Auschwitz Album.

The decentralized and palimpsestic nature of the Auschwitz Museum means that these problems are not always dealt with in the same way, and the solution is often to ignore them. The information that the SK provide about the workings of the crematoria is cleaned up to make it as legible as possible, leaving the SK simply identified as sources of information. When they are acknowledged as people with their own experiences, they feature mostly as hero-witnesses to be honoured, whose actions should be 'lessons' or models of how to behave in such circumstances.

Birkenau: Crematoria IV and V

The site to which the SK are most linked is of course Birkenau.[12] This was the location of the crematoria in which they worked, the blocks in which they lived and the ground in which they buried their manuscripts. The latter two aspects are not drawn to visitors' attention. The focus is instead on two key moments of resistance: the uprising of 7 October 1944 in which Crematorium 3 (IV) was burnt, and the photographs taken in August 1944 around Crematorium 4 (V). Black information boards at a number of points on this site call attention to its histories, as well as, at times, serving a memorial function too.[13] The information board at Crematorium 3 (IV) certainly performs both functions for the SK, marking, and indeed celebrating, their uprising. It describes them as having 'organized the only armed revolt that ever took place at Auschwitz' and the 450 members who were 'murdered by the SS' as 'heroic prisoners'. The wording emphasizes the unique and extraordinary nature of the revolt. Its status as 'organized' and 'armed' is an important part of its meaning, although both are disputed terms.[14] Here all of these aspects set the SK

Figure 12.1 Birkenau. Memorial boards, near the site of Crematorium 4 (V). Photograph courtesy of Dominic Williams.

apart from the rest of the camp. Their forced labour is noted on the board, but might be said to be redeemed by their revolt.

Nearby, at Crematorium 4 (V), is the site at which the photographs were taken by a member of the SK (Figure 12.1). The notice boards here reproduce the three photographs that have identifiable content, rendering them as readable as possible. As both Isabel Wollaston and Georges Didi-Huberman point out, this means that the circumstances in which they were taken are elided: that they needed to be taken under cover, that some attempts to take them misfired and that they needed to be taken at a distance.[15] This is in the main a way of simply getting the information to the viewer as directly as possible, and could be said to fit with the likely intentions of the photographer to document the crimes and inform the world. But it can also be read as solving the problem of what to do with the SK by simply rendering them transparent. If visitors are not asked to contemplate what the taker of these photographs went through, they do not have to think of what made it possible for him to be there, of how they judge or refuse to judge him for being there. This fits too with the minimal account provided of the photographs' taking given by the information boards, which make no mention of the SK: 'Photos taken probably by Alex, a Greek Jew, in the summer of 1944'.[16] The link between this act of resistance and the October uprising, their situation in the ranks of the SK, is left unstated. Indeed, the idea that taking photographs might also be resistance is sidelined by the greater importance of using the photographs to provide information.[17] Moreover, no link is made between the photographer and the members of the SK who appear in the photograph, carrying out their task of disposing of bodies.

Permanent Exhibition: Auschwitz I. Block 4, *Zagłada/Extermination*

As Jonathan Huener notes, in its early days, the Museum decided to use the Auschwitz Stammlager as the site of its permanent exhibition, giving an overview of the workings of all parts of the camp. Visitors seeking an explanation of what happened in Birkenau had to go to Auschwitz.[18] This is still true today: Block 4 offers an account of 'Extermination', including elements that have been present from the 1950s. Unlike at Crematorium 4 (V), Room 4 ('Extermination Technique') now has all of the photographs on display (the fourth one – a mis-taken upwards one of treetops and the sky – did not use to be included), along with a range of other artefacts that make reference to the SK (Figure 12.2). Visitors, usually wearing headphones, which provide the guide's commentary as well as an accidental soundtrack of electronic whistlings and rustlings, are walked round the block in the best way possible to avoid overcrowding.[19] In the centre of the room in which the photographs are displayed is a cross-cut model of gas chamber and Crematorium 1 (II) by Miecysław Stobierski (1914–98). The back half of the room has now been cordoned off, due to the pressure of visitor numbers, one consequence of which is that visitors can no longer walk around the back of the model. Large blow-ups of all the four photographs are on the walls, around the entry door. Although all four are present, the only explanation of the fourth photograph is that it is one of those 'taken illegally by members of the Sonderkommando'. One photograph, taken at a slant with most of the image taken up by trees, is exhibited alongside a cropped blow-up of its bottom left-hand corner, with only the latter version given a caption: 'Jewish women being driven to a gas chamber'. The caption explaining the content of the final two is: 'Burning the dead bodies of the victims of the mass murder [Polish: *masowej zagłady*]'. Although the circumstances of the pictures' being taken are readable from the images, the captions still direct the visitors' attention almost exclusively to the content, except for the oddly chosen word 'illegally'.

Since 1951 Stobierski's large white plaster cut-away model of Gas Chamber and Crematorium 1 (II), including about 3,000 sculpted fig-

Figure 12.2 Auschwitz I, Block 4. Model of Crematorium 1 (II) and one of the Sonderkommando photographs. Photograph courtesy of Isabel Wollaston.

ures, has been central to the various iterations of its permanent exhibition.[20] The SK have therefore been represented in the Auschwitz Museum virtually from its inception. The model graphically portrays all the stages of the killing process from the line of people descending the steps, to the undressing room, the gas chamber and then the oven room. Reflecting on the impact the model in the United States Holocaust Memorial Museum had on him, Edward Linenthal confessed to finding 'the individual faces in Stobierski's model . . . among the hardest in the exhibit to look at, for he has sculpted, in exquisite detail, terror-stricken people in their desperate and feeble attempt to reach up toward the last air in the gas chamber'.[21] In contrast, the members of the SK are shown at work impassive and upright in the upper part of Crematorium 1 (II), unloading the lift of dead bodies, removing teeth, carrying bodies and working the ovens. They do not seem to be identifiable in other roles before that. There are figures of SS guards in the undressing room, but no one who seems to be a member of the SK. The space of the oven room is highly legible: large amounts of space are left between figures to render their actions clear. They become almost mechanical, part of the apparatus used to dispose of the bodies. Andrea Witcomb describes it as 'didactic', 'informative' about the 'process' of mass killing, but leaving her with a feeling of 'numbness'.[22]

Stobierski's model, and the SK photographs that surround it, arguably cross the threshold of what Michael Berenbaum terms the 'zone of privacy',[23] as do visitors jostling to see and /or take their own photographs. Linenthal acknowledges that not everyone responds to it in this way, observing that whilst visitors walked slowly by the model, they rarely paused to study the individual figures and faces. Our own recent experiences of visiting Auschwitz is that pausing to study the figures in the way that Linenthal suggests is practically impossible much of the time, given the pressure of visitor numbers, and because the model is clearly a designated spot where guides stop, using it as a backdrop to explaining how the killing process functioned, the significance of the SK photographs and related topics.

In a glass cabinet in the same room, documents produced both by perpetrators and resisters are also assembled to provide some sense of the extermination process. Typed memos offer information on the SK (one on their numbers from July 1944, one on the revolt and the deaths of three SS men). Incorrect information in Polish (and not English) is provided about the revolt. Documents are presented and summarized in a caption, but left untranslated. The logic of what unites the objects assembled here seems more to be about the SK than any other topic. But this is almost entirely unavailable to most visitors. The glass case is unlikely to be looked at by most of them. Here, laid out as evidence and explanation of the extermination process, are multiple items that feature the SK: as providers of evidence and as part of the machinery of death. It is hard to say that it amounts to a collective portrait of them, however. There seems to be some sense that the SK should be present here as more than simply part of the machinery of extermination, or providers of the photographs, but it is done in a way that makes it very unlikely that visitors will engage with it.

In Room 6 of the same block ('Plunder'), a reproduction of a double-page spread of Leyb Langfus's manuscript *The Deportation* in one cabinet serves to provide information about how the 'ghetto inhabitants of Maków Mazowiecki' were robbed, but only to visitors who can read the Polish translation or the Yiddish script of the original. The manuscript is attributed to 'the prisoner Lejb'. No mention is made of his membership of the SK, the position that probably gave him the time and resources to be able to record what had happened to his home town. The experiences of the SK are confined to their presence in the crematoria.

Block 27

The SK photos and images of their manuscripts also used to appear in Block 27, the block devoted to the history of the martyrdom of the Jews in the Auschwitz Museum's own exhibition from 1978, the second version of the exhibition, after one that opened in 1968.[24] This block has now been refurbished and a new exhibition curated by Yad Vashem was installed, opening in 2013. In this permanent exhibition, the decision was made to deal with the Shoah as a whole.

The entrance to the exhibition within the block is a black gateway marked 'Shoah' in Hebrew, Polish and English, with a definition of 'Shoah' given to the right, and to the left (in the same three languages), a paragraph from the manuscript written by Zalman Gradowski, one of the members of the SK, often identified as one of the leaders of the revolt, and the most famous of the 'scribes' of Auschwitz. Again, the circumstances in which this was written are not given, and Gradowski's status as a member of the SK is asserted mainly in order to confirm his participation in their revolt:

> 'Come here you free citizen of the world, whose life is safeguarded by human morality and whose existence is guaranteed through law. I want to tell you how modern criminals and despicable murderers have trampled the morality of life and nullified the postulates of existence'.
> Zalman Gradowski, who was murdered in the Sonderkommando revolt in Birkenau, 7 October 1944

This passage from Gradowski did not appear in the Auschwitz Museum's own editions of the SK manuscripts of the early 1970s, perhaps because it did not contain any facts.[25] But now, in the rather more experiential orientation taken by Yad Vashem to Block 27, Gradowski's incantatory words appear rather more appropriate. Whereas the approach at Crematorium 4 (V) and in Block 4 seems to be more fact-oriented, in Block 27 the approach is much more in line with appealing to emotions: it is an experiential, affective take on the whole of the Shoah, not a use of the objects and the site of the Auschwitz Museum as evidence or as a way to engage with its past.

Gradowski's soaring rhetoric, even in the somewhat bathetic form given it in its English translation, fits quite well with that approach. He is almost the 'voice' of the exhibition. But he also appears at the end of the exhibition, in the book of names collected by Yad Vashem. Here there is no Zalman Gradowski, however. He appears instead as Khaim Gradowski because his niece completed the Page of Testimony with the name Khaim Zalman. Zalman is how he signed himself, both with a number code when perhaps he thought he had a chance of surviving and did not want to risk identifying himself, and explicitly in a letter where the risk of being unremembered after his death seems to have been the greater one. As

Zalman he is a writer, murdered while resisting. He names himself. As Khaim he is simply murdered. Someone else names him.

Other Exhibitions

The SK feature in many other ways in Auschwitz I. There is a plaque – in Polish only – on the outside front wall of Block 27, unveiled on 7 October 1994, the fortieth anniversary of the SK uprising, in memory of Ala Gertner, Roza Robota, Regina Safirsztajn and Estera Wajcblum (the 'four women'), allegedly for smuggling gunpowder to the SK. National exhibitions also include references to them and their revolt. The Polish exhibition in Block 15 provides a photograph of Roza Robota. The French exhibition in Block 20 (lower floor) makes reference to the SK in a panel on resistance: Jankiel Handelsman and Józef Dorębus (known by the alias of Josel Warszawski in the camp), with photos and names on deportation lists, as well as a reproduction of David Olère's *The Revolt of the Sonderkommando*. All were deported to Auschwitz from Drancy. In 'The Citizen Betrayed', the national exhibition of Hungary (Block 28, upper floor), three of the SK photos appear in installations projected on to the walls. The SK also appear in the permanent exhibition *The Resistance at KL Auschwitz* (Block 11, rooms 8–9, opened 14 June 2018). The two panels devoted to them discuss them as testifiers and resisters, and the David Olère painting included in the exhibition is of obtaining food, suggesting subversion of the camp regime and even altruism. Here they are made part of a general movement of resistance in the camp, part of a collective enterprise to inform the world about the crimes taking place there.[26]

The Auschwitz Museum's Presence beyond Oświęcim

References to the SK are placed at key sites in the physical space of the Museum, but it also has a location on the Web, or in fact multiple locations. In addition to its own website, which provides what it calls 'online lessons', the Museum has a number of exhibitions on Google Arts and Culture (created by the Google Cultural Institute (GCI)).[27] Currently, nine exhibitions are included. One of them is on the SK.[28] This would suggest they anticipate that this topic would be of public interest, as does the fact that they are included as one of the four graphic novels in the series *Episodes from Auschwitz* (see Table 12.1).

Unlike the other GCI exhibitions, the SK are presented without much sense of them as individual people. 'Before They Perished' – family photo

Table 12.1 Online lessons, Google exhibitions and *Episodes from Auschwitz* graphic novels.

Online lesson	Google Arts and Culture	*Episodes from Auschwitz*
Auschwitz – Concentration and Extermination Camp		
Art at Auschwitz*		
Auschwitz Museum in the First Years of its Operation*		
Christian Clergy and Religious Life at Auschwitz*		Sacrifice [on Maksymilian Kolbe]
Deportations of Hungarian Jews to Auschwitz		
Escapes from KL Auschwitz		
Evacuation and Liberation of KL Auschwitz*	The Evacuation and Liberation of Auschwitz	
Extermination of Jews at KL Auschwitz*		
Fate of Soviet Prisoners in Auschwitz*		
First Deportations of Poles to Auschwitz		
From the Uprising Warsaw to Auschwitz	The deportations of Warsaw residents to Auschwitz after the outbreak of the Warsaw Uprising	
Holocaust – the Destruction of European Jews – course*		
Preparation to the Visit at the Auschwitz Memorial for Students 13-15 years old		
Resistance Movement in KL Auschwitz	Polish military resistance movement at Auschwitz	Witold's Report
Roma in Auschwitz	Roma in Auschwitz*	
Sonderkommando	Sonderkommando	Bearers of Secrets
	14 June 1940†	
	From Ghetto in Theresienstadt to Auschwitz II-Birkenau	
	Traces of Them Remain . . .	
	Before They Perished	
	Tragic Love at Auschwitz‡	Love in the Shadow of Death [on Mala and Edek]

*Added since 2016
†Added since 2017
‡Available on Google Arts and Culture until March 2017

albums that now appear in the exhibition in the Sauna block in Birkenau – offers images of individuals and usually some identifying details. The other exhibitions include individuals' testimony. In the 'Resistance in Auschwitz' exhibition, Witold Pilecki's letters are translated as well as shown; 'Liberation of the Camp' includes the words of survivors. The SK exhibition names people and shows the photographs and a picture of some of what they buried, but no translation or explanation of their documents is provided. Instead, there is just an objective, neutral account. Does that suggest a judgement being made about the SK, that perhaps it is less possible to engage with them at a human level? Or perhaps that the facts need to be set straight and certain legends dealt with (for example, the legend that the SK were liquidated in their entirety every three or four months is shown to be wrong) because people are *too* eager to think they know what the SK are?

However, a different version of this exhibition also appears (in what the Museum calls an 'online lesson') on the Museum's website, which does include testimony.[29] There are also numerous small differences between them. The two sites describe the texts written by members of the SK in different ways, for example:

> Realising that the SS would in the future try to erase evidence of their crimes committed in Auschwitz, *Sonderkommando* prisoners secretly wrote notes of their experiences, emotions and the events that occurred at the crematoria. (Auschwitz website)

> Realising that the SS would endeavour to obliterate the traces of the crime, SK prisoners made clandestine notes describing their experience and the events taking place in the crematoria. (GCI)

According to the Auschwitz Museum, the SK's writings discuss experiences, emotions and events, while the GCI lists only experiences and events (although other aspects of the wording in the English translations vary, the original Polish sentences are different only in the inclusion or omission of this word). Given the frequent claims that members of the SK were unable to feel emotions, it is disquieting to see that references to them can be included or excluded so casually.

In displaying the photograph of Zalman Gradowski, one site includes his wife Sonya, while one crops her out of the image. Quite different effects (and affects) arise from these two versions. One is Gradowski with family ties. These are the family ties that he stressed repeatedly in one of his manuscripts, each of whose three sections begins with a memorial to the murdered members of his family and also actually in the way that he asked to be memorialized: he requested that his manuscript be published with a photograph of him and his wife together. The other is Gradowski as one heroic individual, dressed in such a way to indicate his earlier life, but singled out as the leader, the voice of his people. This too is an image he provides of himself in his writings.[30] Contingent decisions in putting together these websites lead to one image being favoured over another.

Episodes from Auschwitz

Episodes from Auschwitz is a series of short graphic novels that are supposed to present the events 'as seen by the victims'. There are four so far, produced by comic artists and writers with the oversight of Auschwitz's historians and published by the Auschwitz Museum.[31] Two of the topics, Witold Pilecki and the SK, also appear in the GCI and the museum's online lessons. The story of 'Mala and Edek' overlaps with a (now defunct) GCI exhibition, and that of Maximilian Kolbe with the recent online lesson on the Auschwitz website about clergy. For the former, the desire to cover Polish resistance and tell the story of a Polish hero seems clear. The prominence of the SK seems better explained by a sense that their story allows the camp's exterminatory function to be made understandable.

In every other graphic novel, there is a focus on one central figure or couple (Witold Pilecki, Mala and Edek, Maximilian Kolbe), and all of them die a more or less heroic death. *Bearers of Secrets* has much less of an identifiable figure than Mala and Edek, Witold or Saint Maximilian Kolbe. Nominally, the story follows Joshua, who 'combines biographies of a few prisoners', but the narrative 'voice' is one of a Sonder who survived and gave testimony at Otto Moll's trial. It is just about possible that this voice occurs all the way through the graphic novel, but the actual voice varies wildly, from the impersonal introduction (which feels more like an omniscient third-person or a historian) to the last page, where the narrator absolutely has an individual existence as someone who has a brother and went to Israel.[32] At times this voice is retrospective, while at times it is contemporaneous. Strangely – at least for anglophone conventions – the narrative is given in a word bubble (a tail-less speech bubble) rather than a box. It blends with other uses of word bubbles, which are used whenever words are not spoken from an identifiable place in the picture, such as thoughts, or even words from someone 'off-camera'. This particular use of a word bubble may simply be the choice of Michał Pyteraf, who was not the artist for any of the other *Episodes from Auschwitz*. But it indicates the difficulty that the graphic novel has of giving the SK a voice, as indeed the introductory remarks express: 'it has not been possible to fully understand the magnitude of their tragedy and reflect what inmates of this "special detail" went through and experienced'. The graphic novel does try to take an interest in the psychological state of the SK, but finds it hard to do so convincingly. They are not crystallized into a particular person's story or a set of readily identifiable emotions, as the slack postures and rather bland range of expressions indicate.

Indeed, the fact that it has been judged suitable for readers aged 14 and over (rather than 16 and over, as for the stories of Mala and Edek and Kolbe) seems quite appropriate, as the level of emotional involvement it promotes is much less.[33] Even in media where there is a much greater expectation that the viewer/reader will become emotionally involved, empathy with or understanding of the SK appears harder to articulate.

Social Media: Twitter

The Museum also has a presence on social media, both on Facebook and Twitter. On both sites, representatives of the Museum respond to new events, commemorate anniversaries, offer links to resources produced by the museum and battle against denial, trivialization and misunderstanding. It fulfils all of these functions with respect to the SK too. They are certainly not central to the Twitter account's concerns: they do not feature in even 1% of its tweets and only appear as a hashtag twenty-six times (eighteen of these from 2018). A search of its Twitter timeline for the term 'SK' between 2012 and 2018 (see Table 12.2) reveals 222 tweets, with 128 of these from 2016 and 2017. This increase in interest in them may well stem from the release of *Son of Saul* (2015), as ten out of fifty tweets in 2016 referred to the film (by 2018, however, the account ceased referring to it).

The tweets often link to the online lessons provided by the museum's website. There are fairly frequent corrections of other Twitter users' misconceptions: people who tweet about twelve (rather than two) SK squads or the blowing up (rather than burning) of a crematorium during the October revolt often find the Auschwitz Museum Twitter account telling them that they have got their facts wrong.[34] This need to establish hard facts is also evident in the way in which films are discussed: *The Grey Zone* is often denounced as bad history; *Son of Saul*, followers are warned, is not a documentary, although at some point the feed begins to negotiate this problem with the idea that the film is part symbol, part history. The feed also serves a memorial function, commemorating the revolt on 7 October each year, as well as the public hanging of the four women on 6 January. The Twitter feed does act as a form of interaction between the Museum

Table 12.2 Breakdown of tweets mentioning 'sonderkommando' from @AuschwitzMuseum.

	Total Tweets	On 7 October (percentage of tweets for that year)	Other anniversaries (percentage of tweets for that year)
2012	3	2 (67%)	
2013	4	3 (75%)	
2014	10	7 (70%)	
2015	7	5 (71%)	
2016	50	13 (26%)	1 (11 April) 1 (29 Aug) 2 (3 Dec) (8%)
2017	78	12 (15%)	12 (29 Aug) 3 (9 Oct) 3 (10 Oct) 6 (3 Dec) (31%)
2018	70	4 (6%)	2 (6 Jan) 2 (27 Jan) 4 (4 Mar) 2 (5 Mar) 2 (16 Mar) 2 (9 May) 2 (29 Aug) 6 (10 Dec) (31%)

and those interested in its work, but in the main it uses its position of authority to assert the institution's prevailing understanding of the SK: making sure that the facts are correct (even to the point of pedantry) and honouring their memory.

Conclusion

The Museum very much presents itself as the Site (with a capital 's'), as the ultimate trace of what happened there. It claims, for example, that: 'Exhibitions about Auschwitz and the Holocaust can be presented in various places all over the world. Only at the site, however, can the message of the exhibition be accompanied by the experience of the authentic grounds and the original vestiges of the camp – things that themselves are eyewitnesses to their tragic history'.[35] This approach parallels much of what visitors expect to experience. Avital Biran, Yaniv Poria and Gila Oren identify 'a sense of "see it to believe it," and interest in having an emotional heritage experience' as among visitors' motives.[36] Visiting a site of the Holocaust is a way of getting close to it, for whatever reason that might be: walking in the footsteps of the victims, 'seeing' (visually or proprioceptively) how the machinery of death worked, paying homage at their resting place, observing (with sight or with other senses), and reacting to the traces that remain. For the Museum and for its visitors, the encounter with the materiality of the site (seeing) is transformative. The SK and their testimony and photographs are part of what the Museum uses to assert this relationship with the past. They provide traces, even physical connections to what happened there. The act of putting archival photographs at the place at which they happened (or are thought to have happened) is making that connection very concrete: reading texts and seeing images at the places where they happened. As this chapter has shown, one primary concern in doing so is to make the information as easily available as possible. In this, the Museum could certainly said to be in line with one of the desires of the SK. Indeed, the SK can be counted among those who started to carry out some of the key functions the Museum identifies for itself before it started to exist: 'documentation of extermination', 'collection ... and [attempted] preservation of the history of KL Auschwitz' by burying artefacts as well as documents in the ground, and even 'disseminating the history of KL Auschwitz', with writings targeted at an outside audience and photographs smuggled outside the camp.[37]

The information boards and displays, as well as the organization of routes, are also ways to manage the 'raw' experiences, sites and artefacts using some kind of a framework, providing means for memorialization, understanding and even celebration to take place. Texts and images are provided to inform, but also to channel and provoke people's emotions. The SK too did all of those things themselves in their writings, as Nicholas Chare and Dominic Williams have demonstrated.[38] However, the idea that there might be a continuity between what the Museum is doing and what the SK did is not really present.

This lack of acknowledgement may simply be the result of the process that the Museum takes to all its historical material, separating its role as a memorial from its function of establishing facts. But it is consistent with the lack of any sense that the SK might have mediated and synthesized their experiences. The Museum performs the absolute opposite of synthesis, disaggregating the different aspects of the SK, sometimes even separating their testimony from the idea of resistance, and giving little attention to their lives. This disaggregation is not only the result of contradictions within the multiplicity of the Museum and its sites, but also seems to be used as a solution to the difficulties that the Museum has with this particular group. Moreover, it leaves out entirely the more fraught questions about the SK, or indeed about prisoner life in general: the painful moral dilemmas and 'choiceless choices' they faced or the realm of privilege and collaboration that makes up the grey zone. Insofar as any portrait of the SK emerges, it is in the form that Piotr Cywiński gave: *Geheimnisträger*, the most significant links in the chain of memory. As far as possible, they are made part of the Museum's emphasis on witness as a form of resistance.

Dominic Williams is Senior Lecturer in Holocaust and Genocide Studies at Northumbria University. He has published articles on modernist writing and antisemitism, contemporary Jewish poetry, and Holocaust memory and testimony. He and Nicholas Chare have coedited *Representing Auschwitz: At the Margins of Testimony* (2013) and have coauthored *Matters of Testimony: Interpreting the Scrolls of Auschwitz* (Berghahn Books, 2016) and *The Auschwitz Sonderkommando: Testimonies, Histories, Representations* (2019).

Isabel Wollaston is Senior Lecturer in Jewish and Holocaust Studies at the Department of Theology and Religion, University of Birmingham. Her recent publications include 'The Absent, the Partial and the Iconic in Archival Photographs of the Holocaust', in Hannah Ewence and Helen Spurling (eds), *Visualizing Jews through the Ages: Literal and Material Representations of Jewishness and Judaism* (2015), 265–93; and 'Emerging from the Shadows? The Auschwitz Sonderkommando and the "Four Women" in History and Memory', *Holocaust Studies: A Journal of Culture and History* 20(3) (2014), 145–70.

Notes

1. Auschwitz-Birkenau State Museum (hereinafter 'the Museum'), *Annual Report 2012*, 5
2. This is a recurring theme in testimonies of Auschwitz survivors and many studies of the SK. See Gideon Greif, *We Wept without Tears: Testimonies of the Jewish Sonderkommando from Auschwitz* (New Haven: Yale University Press, 2005); and Nicholas Chare and Dominic Williams, *Matters of Testimony: Interpreting the Scrolls of Auschwitz* (New York: Berghahn Books, 2016).

3. See, for example, the claims of Henryk Mandelbaum in Jan Południak, *Sonder: An Interview with Sonderkommando Member Henryk Mandelbaum*, trans. Witold Zbirohowski-Kościa (Oświęcim: Frap-Books, 2008).
4. Our observations are based on numerous visits by the authors to the Museum, observing how its representation of the SK has evolved since the Museum began to re-structure and re-present itself after 1989, up to early November 2018.
5. Silke Arnold-de Simine, *Mediating Memory in the Museum: Trauma, Empathy, Nostalgia* (Basingstoke: Palgrave Macmillan, 2013).
6. Poland and Israel jointly sponsored a request to UNESCO to formally change its name in UNESCO documentation. On 27 June 2007, UNESCO agreed to rename it 'Auschwitz-Birkenau: German Nazi Concentration and Extermination Camp (1940–1945)'. See https://whc.unesco.org/en/list/31 (retrieved 9 April 2019). This is the name favoured by the current Polish government, e.g. its renaming of 14 June as the National Remembrance Day for Victims of the German Nazi Concentration and Extermination Camps. See also http://auschwitz.org/en/museum/news/there-were-no-polish-death-camps-there-is-a-simple-tool-to-prevent-this-mistake-from-recurring,1192.html (retrieved 9 April 2019).
7. On the complex history of Auschwitz as a museum and as a site, see Andrew Charlesworth, 'Contesting Places of Memory: The Case of Auschwitz', *Environment and Planning D: Society and Space*, 12(5) (1994), 579–93; Jonathan Huener, *Auschwitz, Poland, and the Politics of Commemoration, 1945–1979* (Athens, OH: Ohio University Press, 2003); Jonathan Webber, 'The Kingdom of Death as a Heritage Site: Making Sense of Auschwitz', in William Logan, Máiréad Nic Craith and Ullrich Kockel (eds), *A Companion to Heritage Studies* (Chichester: John Wiley & Sons, 2015), 115–32; Zofia Wóycicka, *Arrested Mourning: Memory of the Nazi Camps in Poland, 1944–1950* (Bern: Peter Lang, 2013); and Marek Kucia, Marta Duch-Dyngosz and Mateusz Magierowski, 'The Collective Memory of Auschwitz and the Second World War among Catholics in Poland: A Qualitative Study of Three Communities', *History and Memory*, 25(2) (2013), 132–73. On the Museum's current position regarding national exhibitions, see http://auschwitz.org/en/museum/news/new-permanent-exhibition-concept-approved,37.html (retrieved 9 April 2019).
8. Webber, 'The Kingdom of Death', 127.
9. In this they are not unique, of course; Kapos and other privileged prisoners could also be cited. But only the SK perform the other functions so important to the Museum, of witnesses and resisters.
10. SK testimony has taken many forms: the buried texts, interviews (in many genres), affidavits/testimony at war crimes trials, photographs, sketches and art. There is a tendency to overlook visual forms of 'testimony' other than the SK photographs. On this, see Nicholas Chare and Dominic Williams, *The Auschwitz Sonderkommando: Testimonies, Histories, Representations* (London: Palgrave Macmillan, 2019).
11. Ana Carden-Coyne 'The Ethics of Representation in Holocaust Museums', in Jean-Marc Dreyfus and Daniel Langton (eds), *Writing the Holocaust* (London: Bloomsbury, 2011), 167. See also Susan A. Crane, 'Choosing Not to Look: Representation, Repatriation, and Holocaust Atrocity Photography', *History and Theory* 47(3) (2008), 309–30.
12. The presence of the Fischl-Kommando and other precursors of the SK who worked at the crematorium in Auschwitz I is not referenced.
13. Visually, the black information boards are quite similar in colour (if not in shape) to the markers/mtzeva marking the locations where human ashes were scattered.

14. Zalman Lewental recorded the plans for an uprising, but the relationship between them and what actually took place on 7 October is uncertain; the explosives that the women of the Unionwerke smuggled out are often linked to the SK's revolt, but what use was made of them is also unclear. See Chare and Williams, *Matters of Testimony*, esp. 136–43; Isabel Wollaston, 'Emerging from the Shadows? The Auschwitz Sonderkommando and the "Four Women" in History and Memory', *Holocaust Studies*, 20(3) (2014), 137–70.
15. Isabel Wollaston, 'The Absent, the Partial and the Iconic in Archival Photographs of the Holocaust', *Jewish Culture and History* 12(3) (2010), 443–45; Georges Didi-Huberman, *Écorces* (Paris: Éditions de Minuit, 2011), 48–49.
16. Claire Griffiths notes, however, that Alex is identified as Alberto Errera and as a member of the SK by some of the guides on the tour. Claire Griffiths, 'Encountering Auschwitz: Touring the Auschwitz-Birkenau State Museum', *Holocaust Studies* 25(1–2) (2019), 192.
17. Henryk Mandelbaum acted as guide to and/or interpreter of the site of Crematorium 4 (V), the burning pits, the woods where the photographs taken. This is recorded in the documentary *Sonderkommando: The Living Dead of Auschwitz* (Yesterday, 2012).
18. Huener, *Auschwitz*, 123–27.
19. The use of headsets, although not the noise, is discussed in Susan Henderson and Lindsay Dombrowski, 'What Can Onto-epistemology Reveal about Holocaust Education? The Case of Audio-Headsets at Auschwitz-Birkenau State Museum', *Holocaust Studies* 24(3) (2018), 305–28.
20. The model is used by Claude Lanzmann in *Shoah* to illustrate Filip Müller's testimony about the liquidation of the Terezín Family Camp. Versions of it are included in the permanent exhibitions of Yad Vashem, the United States Holocaust Memorial Museum and the German Historical Museum, Berlin.
21. Edward Linenthal, *Preserving Memory: The Struggle to Create the American Holocaust Museum* (New York: Viking, 1995), 210. Linenthal discusses the version of this model in the United States Holocaust Memorial Museum, which contains some small differences from the model at Auschwitz.
22. Andrea Witcomb, 'Remembering the Dead by Affecting the Living: The Case of a Miniature Model of Treblinka', in Sandra H. Dudley (ed.), *Museum Materialities: Objects, Engagements, Interpretations* (New York: Routledge, 2010), 39.
23. This is what he terms the 'domain that forever eludes us', the experience of the gas chambers that we will never know. Michael Berenbaum interviewed in *Nazi Scrapbooks* (National Geographic Channel, 22 April 2013).
24. The 1978 exhibition was produced in conjunction with the Jewish Historical Institute, Warsaw, with consultation from international partners including Yad Vashem. See Huener, *Auschwitz*, 196.
25. Jadwiga Bezwińska and Danuta Czech (eds), *Wśród koszmarnej zbrodni: Notatki więźnów z Sonderkommando w Oświęcimiu* (Oświęcim: Wydawnictwo Państwowego Muzeum w Oświęcimiu, 1971), 75. It is also not included in the Polish second edition (1973, at 133). The recent translations of the Gradowski's writings published by the Museum do finally include it: Zalmen Gradowski, *From the Heart of Hell: Manuscripts of a Sonderkommando Prisoner, Found in Auschwitz*, trans. Barry Smerin and Janina Wurbs (Oświęcim: Auschwitz-Birkenau State Museum, 2017). The manuscript itself is held in St Petersburg, but a photographed reproduction is held in the Auschwitz archive.
26. The SK also featured in some temporary exhibitions. There was a panel on the SK uprising and four members of the SK were listed, as part of a panel on 'international'

(i.e. non-Polish) resistance movements, amongst the leaders of Jewish resistance in the camp (Zalman Gradowski, Leyb Langfus, Józef Deresiński and Jankiel Handelsman) in the exhibition *Resistance Movement at the Auschwitz Camp* (dating from the 1970s). There was a panel on the four women, their role in supplying the SK with gunpowder and their execution in the exhibition *Punishments and Executions at the Auschwitz Camp*. Both exhibitions were located on the first floor, Block 11 (the 'death block'), but are currently closed. The SK were the focus of a temporary exhibition to mark the seventieth anniversary of the SK uprising (autumn 2014). They also formed a constant thread in the more recent temporary exhibition *Auschwitz: Death Factory*, produced by Gideon Greif and the National Socialism Documentation Centre, Cologne, in conjunction with the Museum, in the autumn of 2016. The content of these exhibitions in Block 11, floor 1 seems to have partly been absorbed – and updated, into the new 2018 exhibition on resistance on the ground floor. The exhibition *David Olère: The One Who Survived Crematorium III* ran from the end of October 2018 to March 2019.

27. Holocaust Education has been key to the GCI all the way through. Yad Vashem was the very first partner of what was to become the GCI in January 2011. See the GCI's major exhibitions launched in October 2012 covering the Holocaust, the Berlin Wall, and Apartheid: https://www.google.com/culturalinstitute/about/partners (retrieved 9 April 2019).

28. https://artsandculture.google.com/exhibit/gQgsxfhh (retrieved 9 April 2019). There are also references to the SK in the exhibitions on Resistance Movements in the camp and in the one on Escapes. The full range of exhibitions is available at: https://artsandculture.google.com/partner/auschwitz-birkenau-state-museum (retrieved 9 April 2019).

29. English version: http://lekcja.auschwitz.org/en_10_sonder; Polish version: http://lekcja.auschwitz.org/ 10_sonder (retrieved 9 April 2019).

30. Chare and Williams, *Matters of Testimony*, 60–92.

31. Michał Gałek and Marcin Nowakowski, *Love in the Shadow of Death*, trans. David R. Kennedy (Oświęcim-Babice: K&L Press, 2009); Michał Gałek, *Witold's Report*, trans. David R. Kennedy (Oświęcim-Babice: K&L Press, 2009); Michał Gałek and Łukasz Poller, *Sacrifice*, trans. David R. Kennedy (Oświęcim-Babice: K&L Press, 2013); Michał Gałek and Michał Pyteraf, *Bearers of Secrets*, trans. Piotr Beluch (Oświęcim-Babice: K&L Press, 2013). Graphic novels on the Holocaust are quite common and there are also a few graphic novels/comics on the SK, including a comic based on the childhood/adolescence of the X-Men's supervillain Magneto. Greg Pak and Carmine di Giandomenico, *X-Men Magneto: Testament* (New York: Marvel, 2009).

32. Gałek and Pyteraf, *Bearers of Secrets*, 7, 38.

33. Some editions of *Sacrifice* are labelled as suitable for readers aged '14+'.

34. E.g. nine tweets from the @AuschwitzMuseum account posted on 9 December 2018 corrected claims that Crematorium 3 (IV) was blown up rather than set on fire. This constitutes nearly 13% of the account's tweets from 2018 mentioning the SK.

35. Auschwitz Birkenau State Museum, *Annual Report* 2009, 43. Piotr Cywiński, the Museum's current director, insists that: 'A visit to this Memorial Site is not like a visit to an ordinary museum, heritage park or palace garden. The purpose is not to be taught, but to personally experience. Therefore other exhibition methods should be applied. Strongly believing in the evocativeness of the Place itself, I am convinced that minimalism is the most sensible option'. See Piotr Cywiński, *Epitaph* (Oświęcim: Auschwitz-Birkenau State Museum, 2012), 91.

36. Avital Biran, Yani Poria and Gila Oren, 'Sought Experiences at (Dark) Heritage Sites', *Annals of Tourism Research* 38(3) (2011), 836.

37. These match items 1, 2 and 5 of its objectives, outlined at: http://auschwitz.org/en/public-information/organisational-rules-of-the-auschwitz-birkenau-state-museum/ (retrieved 9 April 2019).
38. These moments would include (as discussed by Chare and Williams): Leyb Langfus's emotion-provoking stories, Zalman Gradowski's stirring invocation of the reader, Zalman Lewental's writing providing a gravestone for his dead comrades, Marcel Nadjary expressing patriotism or Chaim Herman (now known to be Herman Strasfogel) expressing paternal love and controlling concern; Chare and Williams, *Matters of Testimony*, 104–15, 64–8, 142–3, 166, 164–5.

Bibliography

Arnold-de Simine, Silke. *Mediating Memory in the Museum: Trauma, Empathy, Nostalgia*. Basingstoke: Palgrave Macmillan, 2013.
Auschwitz Birkenau State Museum. *Annual Report* (2009). Retrieved 9 April 2019 from http://auschwitz.org/en/museum/museum-reports.
——. *Annual Report* (2012). Retrieved 9 April 2019 from http://auschwitz.org/en/museum/museum-reports.
Bezwińska, Jadwiga, and Danuta Czech (eds). *Wśród koszmarnej zbrodni: Notatki więźnów z Sonderkommando w Oświęcimiu*. Oświęcim: Wydawnictwo Państwowego Muzeum w Oświęcimiu, 1971.
Biran, Avital, Yaniv Poria and Gila Oren. 'Sought Experiences at (Dark) Heritage Sites', *Annals of Tourism Research* 38(3) (2011) 820–41.
Carden-Coyne, Ana. 'The Ethics of Representation in Holocaust Museums', in Jean-Marc Dreyfus and Daniel Langton (eds), *Writing the Holocaust*. London: Bloomsbury, 2011, 167–83.
Chare, Nicholas, and Dominic Williams. *Matters of Testimony: Interpreting the Scrolls of Auschwitz*. New York: Berghahn Books, 2016.
——. *The Auschwitz Sonderkommando: Testimonies, Histories, Representations*. London: Palgrave Macmillan, 2019.
Charlesworth, Andrew. 'Contesting Places of Memory: The Case of Auschwitz', *Environment and Planning D: Society and Space* 12(5) (1994), 579–93.
Crane, Susan A. 'Choosing Not to Look: Representation, Repatriation, and Holocaust Atrocity Photography', *History and Theory* 47(3) (2008), 309–30.
Cywiński, Piotr. *Epitaph*. Oświęcim: Auschwitz-Birkenau State Museum, 2012.
Didi-Huberman, Georges. *Écorces*. Paris: Éditions de Minuit, 2011.
Gałek, Michał, and Arkadiusz Klimek. *Witold's Report*, trans. David R. Kennedy. Oświęcim-Babice: K&L Press, 2009.
Gałek, Michał, and Marcin Nowakowski. *Love in the Shadow of Death*, trans. David R. Kennedy. Oświęcim-Babice: K&L Press, 2009.
Gałek, Michał, and Łukasz Poller. *Sacrifice*, trans. David R. Kennedy. Oświęcim-Babice: K&L Press, 2013
Gałek, Michał, and Michał Pyteraf. *Bearers of Secrets*, trans. Piotr Beluch. Oświęcim-Babice: K&L Press, 2013.
Gradowski, Zalmen. *From the Heart of Hell: Manuscripts of a Sonderkommando Prisoner, Found in Auschwitz*, trans. Barry Smerin and Janina Wurbs. Oświęcim: Auschwitz-Birkenau State Museum, 2017.

Greif, Gideon. *We Wept without Tears: Testimonies of the Jewish Sonderkommando from Auschwitz*, trans. Naftali Greenwood. New Haven: Yale University Press, 2005.

Griffiths, Claire. 'Encountering Auschwitz: Touring the Auschwitz-Birkenau State Museum', *Holocaust Studies* 25(1–2) (2019), 182–200.

Henderson, Susan, and Lindsay Dombrowski. 'What Can Onto-epistemology Reveal about Holocaust Education? The Case of Audio-Headsets at Auschwitz-Birkenau State Museum', *Holocaust Studies* 24(3) (2018), 305–28.

Huener, Jonathan, *Auschwitz, Poland, and the Politics of Commemoration, 1945–1979*. Athens, OH: Ohio University Press, 2003.

Kucia, Marek, Marta Duch-Dyngosz and Mateusz Magierowski, 'The Collective Memory of Auschwitz and the Second World War among Catholics in Poland: A Qualitative Study of Three Communities', *History and Memory* 25(2) (2013), 132–73.

Linenthal, Edward. *Preserving Memory: The Struggle to Create the American Holocaust Museum.* New York: Viking, 1995.

Pak, Greg, and Carmine di Giandomenico. *X-Men Magneto: Testament*. New York: Marvel, 2009.

Południak, Jan, *Sonder: An Interview with Sonderkommando Member Henryk Mandelbaum*, trans. Witold Zbirohowski-Kościa. Oświęcim: Frap-Books, 2008.

Sonderkommando: The Living Dead of Auschwitz (documentary, Yesterday, 2012)

Webber, Jonathan, 'The Kingdom of Death as a Heritage Site: Making Sense of Auschwitz', in William Logan, Máiréad Nic Craith and Ullrich Kockel (eds), *A Companion to Heritage Studies*. Chichester: John Wiley & Sons, 2015), 115–32.

Witcomb, Andrea. 'Remembering the Dead by Affecting the Living: The Case of a Miniature Model of Treblinka', in Sandra H. Dudley (ed.), *Museum Materialities: Objects, Engagements, Interpretations*. New York: Routledge, 2010, 39–52.

Wollaston, Isabel. 'The Absent, the Partial and the Iconic in Archival Photographs of the Holocaust', *Jewish Culture and History* 12(3) (2010), 443–45.

———. 'Emerging from the Shadows? The Auschwitz Sonderkommando and the "Four Women" in History and Memory', *Holocaust Studies* 20(3) (2014), 137–70.

Wóycicka, Zofia, *Arrested Mourning: Memory of the Nazi Camps in Poland, 1944–1950*. Bern: Peter Lang, 2013.

Chapter 13

Early and Late Testimonies of the Sonderkommando Survivors

Gideon Greif

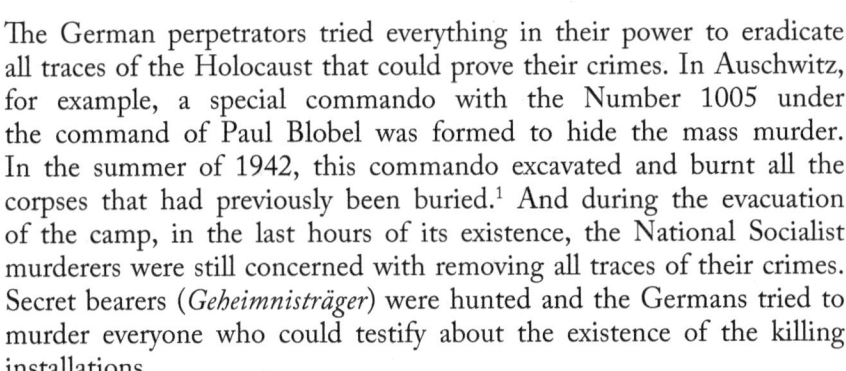

The German perpetrators tried everything in their power to eradicate all traces of the Holocaust that could prove their crimes. In Auschwitz, for example, a special commando with the Number 1005 under the command of Paul Blobel was formed to hide the mass murder. In the summer of 1942, this commando excavated and burnt all the corpses that had previously been buried.[1] And during the evacuation of the camp, in the last hours of its existence, the National Socialist murderers were still concerned with removing all traces of their crimes. Secret bearers (*Geheimnisträger*) were hunted and the Germans tried to murder everyone who could testify about the existence of the killing installations.

Despite all these efforts, several members of the Sonderkommando (SK) were able to deliver reports, testimonies, letters or photos to the public and to posterity. Even though the SS had planned to murder all members of the SK, some survived and were able to testify about the reality of the mass murder in Auschwitz after their liberation. In some cases, members of the SK managed to smuggle information and documents out of the camp or buried them in the vicinity of the gas chambers for future researchers and investigators to retrieve them. The testimonies as well as the documents delivered to us by members of the SK are crucial for our understanding of the reality of the gas chambers and the mass murder during the Holocaust, and for reconstructing the reality of the biggest concentration and extermination camp.

The reports and testimonies not only document the crimes of the Germans but also convey the thoughts and feelings of those who had direct contact with the killing installations and the victims. They enable us to get closer to an understanding of something that can never fully be understood. The reconstructive work of today's historical research on the reality of the camp predominantly depends on the testimonies of the former SK prisoners. The German attempts to destroy all proof of their crimes led to a documentary vacuum that can only be filled by the memories of the survivors. Even the story of one single witness can help to reconstruct history.[2]

The testimonies of the SK members are especially important for Holocaust Studies, not only because we need the testimonies to realize that something as unthinkable as the crimes perpetrated in the German death factories in fact happened, but also because the members of the SK were among the few who saw the gas chambers from the inside and came out alive. Only they can report on the reality of the mass murder, on the cruel details of the killing process, as well as on the last moments in the life of the victims. Of course, very few members of the SK managed to survive the camp; 95% were murdered before Auschwitz was liberated by the Red Army.[3] This means that the existing testimonies only represent a small part of the reality of the gas chambers. However, the testimonies of the SK members are not only the sole source that can substitute the missing documentation, but also deliver the other layer of the camp's reality, one that is not delivered by the simple facts: the feelings of those who had to work in the killing installations, their doubts, fears and moral dilemmas. Only the testimony of the witnesses who experienced all this themselves can shed light on those subjective aspects of history. In combination with other sources, this enables the historian to draw a broader picture of the past.

As we can see, we are extremely lucky to have these testimonies. And we are especially lucky that the testimonies we can use for our research have been recorded over a long period of time. This means that many of the survivors were interviewed several times – some of them at intervals of several decades. Comparing these interviews, we can even reach a more detailed picture and become more certain on the adequacy of crucial reports given to us by the survivors. In some cases, survivors used the exact same words to describe certain situations, which speaks for the consistency of their memories.

Also, the comparison of interviews given at different times enable us to write another history: the one of the SK testimonies themselves. This history is closely connected to the way in which the survivors dealt with their experiences after their liberation in 1945. The type of testimonies that have been used in SK research in the last few decades became possible because of developments that are part of this history and that can be understood by looking at the different type of testimonies given by the survivors of the SK.

Collecting testimonies delivered by contemporary witnesses already played an important role in prewar Easter European Judaism. As a result of their social position as pariahs and due to the experiences of the pogroms, the Jewish population had already established a tradition of Jewish historiography in the nineteenth century that was based on the experiences of eyewitnesses. The Jewish everyday world as well as painful experiences of antisemitic exclusion and deathly violence were recorded in collections of testimonies. These collections were then made accessible for historical research. The impetus behind these collections was to establish a different picture from that of official historiography by focusing on the experiences of those who had no place in that historiography. In this respect, these early collections of testimony can be seen as predecessors of the collection of testimonies after 1945, with both aiming to record the experiences of Jewish victims in order to inform the public and posterity about the crimes perpetrated against them. They wanted to make experiences heard that otherwise would have been silenced. During the Holocaust, the famous Jewish historian Shimon Dubnow asked the Jews in the Riga ghetto to record everything they experienced: 'Yidn shraybt un farshraybt!' (Jews, write down and document!). [4] This central idea has been deeply rooted in Jewish tradition since the time of the First and Second Temple and the expulsion of the Jewish people as well as the pogroms during the Crusades.

Having this in mind, it is not surprising that immediately after the liberation, 'Jewish historical commissions' were formed to collect as many testimonies of survivors as possible. The commissions worked in displaced persons (DP) camps all over Europe, where they tried to record every testimony they could. The members of these commissions were survivors themselves and they recruited their personnel among many different trades. Only a few of those working for the commissions were schooled historians. These commissions created the first collections similar to today's oral history collections. But, of course, there were several important differences, the most important being that these interviews were ignored in most cases by official historical research due to the fact that they had normally been recorded by amateurs.[5] Today, most of these testimonies can be found in two big archives: in the Żydowski Instytut Historyczny (ŻIH) in Warsaw and in the Yad Vashem Archive in Jerusalem. It is no exaggeration to call these testimonies a treasure. These early testimonies recorded very fresh memories of Holocaust survivors. Even if the way in which these interviews were conducted differs widely from today's methods, which makes it difficult to compare them, due to the relative short time between the interviews and the actual events, they deliver a huge amount of information that is missing in later interviews.

In this context, one also has to mention the secret scrolls written by members of the SK. These records written by the members of the SK *during* their time in Auschwitz provide even more immediate access to the experience of the SK prisoners because there is almost no time difference between the events and the recording. It was the clear wish of those members of the SK who wrote the scrolls to give testimony and to prevent the cruelty of the gas chambers from being forgotten. In the words of Zalman Gradowski:

> We, the Sonderkommando, wanted to make an end to this cruel work that has been forced on us by agony for a long time ... Posterity will judge us based on these scriptures. The world will learn from them even if it is only a small part of the tragic world we live in.[6]

He also writes:

> I wrote these things while I was a member of the Sonderkommando ... These records and many others want to keep an eternal and living testimony for future, peaceful days so the world will know what happened here.[7]

Other testimonies given by members of the SK directly after their liberation were those for Soviet or Polish investigative commissions. Shlomo Dragon, for example, supplied the Soviet commission with a written statement. He and Henryk Tauber also returned to Auschwitz only a few weeks after their liberation in order to serve as witnesses for a Soviet investigative commission.[8] Their testimonies are accessible for researchers in the Archive of the Auschwitz-Birkenau State Museum.[9] Yehoshuah Rosenblum was brought to Auschwitz by Soviet officers only months after the liberation to explain the functional principles of the death installations: 'The Russians only wanted to see the crematoria and the pits. Maybe they also made recordings'.[10] During the trials against commanders and guards of the Auschwitz camp, SK survivors gave testimony as well: Henryk Mandelbaum was a witness in the Auschwitz Trial that took place in Krakow in 1947.[11] Miklós Nyiszli, a Romanian doctor who had worked for Josef Mengele as a pathologist, was a witness for the International Military Tribunal in Nuremberg, where he reported on the SK in Auschwitz-Birkenau. Later, the SK members Milton Buki, Filip Müller, Dov Paisikovic and Simon Gotland were witnesses in the Auschwitz Trial in Frankfurt in 1963.[12] And in 1974, Yehoshuah Rosenblum gave testimony in a trial against two Ukrainian SS men in Frankfurt.[13]

The testimony given by Alter Feinsilber (under the name of Stanisław Jankowski) on 13 April 1945 was published by the Auschwitz-Birkenau State Museum.[14] By looking closely at the form of a given testimony, we can elaborate upon differences between the testimonies given for investigative purposes immediately after the liberation and those testimonies conducted for historical research in recent decades.

Feinsilber's testimony provided the investigative commission at the court of Krakow with detailed information about the killing process and the killing installations in Auschwitz-Birkenau. Since only a few months had passed since liberation, Feinsilber remembered many facts and was able to give relatively exact descriptions of the crematoria buildings and the gas chambers, even though the measurements included in his testimony were not exact.[15] Feinsilber was also able to give detailed information on the number of victims who were murdered and burnt in the gas chambers and crematoria,[16] and on the capacities of the crematoria.[17] However, while his estimate of the total number of victims is incorrect,[18] and he obviously did not have a complete overview, he emphasizes that he is quite sure about the numbers he mentions for certain transports because he was able to count how many corpses he had to burn on that particular day.[19] It becomes evident that the testimony was a part of an official investigation because of the repeated assurance that the information stated in his testimony is based on his own eyesight or hearing.[20] In addition, the testimony is extremely precise in relation to the names of the perpetrators. Feinsilber lists all the perpetrators he is able to name in order to enable the authorities to prosecute them:

> The commandant of all crematoria in Birkenau was Oberscharführer Foss. Additionally, also the SS-men: Kurschuss, Steiberg, Keller, the Volksdeutsche from Lodz, Kell, Scharführer Buch, an Oberscharführer from Lublin, Unterscharführer Zajc ... and Oberscharführer Moll were working there.[21]

While the precise information provided by these early, official testimonies is extremely helpful for the reconstruction of the reality of the gas chambers and the work of the SK, one central aspect is missing: the witnesses in these official testimonies almost never talk about their personal experiences, their emotions and their individual problems. They try to give an objective report; their own personality only counts when it is necessary to give reassurance that they really saw or heard what they are reporting. This is also true for the testimony of Feinsilber. Only once does his personal perspective shine through. In order to explain that he cannot give additional information on the Capo Mietek, he talks about his personal point of view: 'It was difficult to hear something about details of his life because he was very unapproachable, also we were afraid to talk to him'.[22]

Even if, as we have seen, a variety of early testimonies by the SK exist, there was no systematic research or collection of testimonies on the SK in the immediate period after 1945. The testimonies just mentioned were the only source on the SK and the reality of the gas chambers for decades. In the 1960s and 1970s, however, employees of the Israeli Holocaust Memorial Yad Vashem in Jerusalem conducted several interviews with survivors. These interviews have not been published, but are accessible for research and were used for different historical publications, as they provide detailed insight into the reality of the daily work of the SK as well as into the living conditions of the SK prisoners and the procedure of mass murder in Auschwitz-Birkenau. Yet, these interviews had almost no influence on general public opinion about the SK. Conducted by professionals of Yad Vashem and only used for historical research, they could not influence the general picture of the SK and its role in the camp.

The reason for this gap in historical research is the general perspective historians and the general public held regarding the Holocaust for several decades. The way one used to look at the Holocaust period led to the reality of the gas chambers as well as the SK being taboo. This taboo was mainly based on the fact that many were unsure how to deal with the reality of the gas chambers. Was it possible to understand the process of mass murder? How should one talk about it? Could one even talk about it? Was it possible to aesthetically represent the reality of the gas chambers?[23] Could we understand what happened there?

Instead of trying to find answers to these questions, many preferred to leave this aspect of the Holocaust and the history auf Auschwitz untouched. To some, researching the reality of the gas chambers and those prisoners who were forced to work there seemed to be a defilement of something holy, an intrusion into a place reserved for the victims. Some even considered it a desecration of graves. Also, it was a very common position that the details of mass murder were less important than the spirit and the heroism of the victims and their spiritual fight. Dealing with the technical details of mass murder and the daily life of those forced to help with it was considered either morally wrong or unnecessary. In relation to the 'Scrolls of Auschwitz', Nicholas Chare and Dominic Williams have pointed out how disturbing and confronting the testimonies of SK members can be:

> These remarkable witness accounts, furtively written by men trapped at the core of a 'death factory', while distinctive in many ways are also like all Holocaust testimony in that they require responsibility and sensitivity

of their readers. The Scrolls were therefore sometimes daunting to engage with. They provide eyewitness accounts of the most horrendous events and pose complex, at times very troubling, questions about the nature and limits of testimony. The physical documents, distressed and fragmentary, seem haunted by their authors and the circumstances in which they wrote. They are unnerving to touch.[24]

This is why the history of the SK continued to be a black hole for so long. Additionally, many of the SK survivors did not want to talk about their personal history and their time in Auschwitz. Their memories were too difficult for them and they preferred to be silent about their past. For many survivors, the most important task was to cope with the new reality that came after their liberation. They did not know how to deal with their past openly because their social contacts normally did not know much about the Holocaust or the SK. Consequently, most of the survivors were left alone with their memories. Also, many of them feared that no one would believe them because the cruelty of the things they had seen made them difficult for most people to imagine. Shaul Chazan explains how difficult it was to talk about his time in the SK: 'I cannot explain to others what I have seen. I do not know how to explain it. How can I explain it?'[25] Even family members did not believe the things he remembered.[26] Joseph Sackar, another SK survivor, says that fear of not being heard was the reason why he did not talk about his time in the SK for so long: 'I thought one would not believe me. Even today, many do not believe that I was a part of the Sonderkommando and got out alive. Maybe even you don't believe it'.[27]

This silence forced onto the survivors by their social environment made life extremely difficult for them as they could not forget what they had seen.[28] Even if many survivors felt a moral obligation to give testimony, they tried not to talk about their memories publicly. In some cases, they even kept their memories from their families.[29] And, indeed, breaking their silence could make them relive their Holocaust experiences and lead to a retraumatization.[30] The public debates on the role of Kapos and functionaries did not make it easier to publicly talk about the experience as a member of the SK. As well as Kapos and functionaries, members of the SK had been publicly attacked for their alleged crimes in Auschwitz.[31]

This shows that it should not be taken for granted that the SK survivors finally decided to give testimony and take part in interviews. Due to their personal situation and the public picture of the Holocaust and the role of the SK, an open discussion about the reality of their life and work in Auschwitz-Birkenau was extremely complicated.[32] It seemed almost impossible to talk about their experiences because what they had to say did not appear to be socially adequate. This also influenced the recordings of testimonies and the information made accessible for historical research. The general atmosphere made it difficult to collect information on the reality of the SK and the gas chambers, and led to a situation where interviews with many SK survivors were only conducted in the 1980s or even later.

Only once the public picture of the Holocaust and the nature of public debate had changed did the interviews conducted in recent decades become possible. After the general atmosphere had changed, some SK survivors also started to visit schools and talk about their experiences with students, while others visited the Auschwitz-Birkenau Memorial in Poland with youth groups and told the participants about their experiences.[33] Shlomo Venezia and Henryk Mandelbaum took part in these trips almost until their deaths.

An important step was the publication of the English translation of *The Scrolls of Auschwitz*,[34] which put the SK on the agenda as far as historical research was concerned. Not only are the published Scrolls extremely valuable for historical research, but they also provide the individual story of every author. This made it possible to bring broader attention to the reality of the SK and was an important milestone in changing the way in which the work of the SK was perceived. A very important aspect was that the simple existence of these scrolls proved that SK members were not the cruel helpers of the Nazis they were seen to be by many, but, instead, were individuals who tried to cope with the cruel reality they were confronted with. The *Scrolls* also proved the SK men did everything they could to document or even stop the crimes that took place in the gas chambers and crematoria of Auschwitz-Birkenau. According to the former Polish Foreign Minister Władysław Bartoszewski, the *Scrolls* were:

> a rejection from the other side of the graves against the criminal system that the authors of the documents experienced in an especially drastic way. They also are an important contribution for the understanding of the influence this criminal system had on the mental condition and the behaviour of the prisoners of the Sonderkommando who were exposed to its relentless influence. At the same time, they are a comment which enables a glimpse into a situation and on events in front of which the imagination and the capacity to morally judge his own actions of every normal man had to fall short.[35]

Another important step for historical research on the Holocaust in general and the SK in particular was made in the mid 1980s. The perspective with which both historical research and general public were looking at certain aspects of the Holocaust changed radically. Controversial and delicate topics like the role of the Judenräte and the assumption that the Jews had only passively endured what happened to them were analysed from a new perspective and no longer only interpreted based on a simple black-and-white pattern. Historical research and public debate became open to the 'grey zones' of the Holocaust and almost all aspects were dealt with in a deeper, multifaceted way. The same was the case for the SK. In this context, the author began to try to convince those former prisoners of the SK who were still alive to talk about their memories and to collect and record their testimonies. Over a period of nineteen years, he talked to former prisoners of the SK as well as to other prisoners of Auschwitz-Birkenau who had been in contact with the members of the SK. The first interview was conducted with a Greek survivor of the SK. After the interview was finished and this first testimony was recorded, it became clear that it was extremely important to record the testimonies of all those members of the SK who were still alive.

The interviews conducted in the following years were the result of the author's solitary and independent decision to try to find all the remaining survivors and to document their legacy in order to stop the neglect of the oral documentation of the memories of the SK prisoners. Before the author started with the collection of the testimonies, sixty former SK members who had survived Auschwitz had already died and there was a clear danger that the memories of the other survivors would be lost as well. When the author realized that no systematic research and no systematic collection of testimonies had been initialized until 1986, he was shocked. It became clear to him that it was necessary to start immediately and to prevent even more memories from being lost forever. The effort to document the memories of the SK survivors came at the last minute!

Since there was no time left, he simply began to collect the testimonies, without being assigned to an official organization or to an official research institution. The interviews were conducted in Israel, the United States, Canada, Poland, Italy, Greece and the Netherlands, in Hebrew, Polish (with an interpreter), German, English and Yiddish.[36] In most cases, the author visited the survivors in their homes, where the conversations took place. Only some interviews – for example, those with Henryk Mandelbaum – were conducted at Birkenau, next to the ruins of the crematoria. Some survivors were only interviewed once or twice, while with others, the author met them several times. In some cases, up to twenty interviews were recorded. Audio records were made during all the interviews and in some cases the testimonies were recorded on video as well. The transcription of the interviews was done by Beatrice Greif, the author's mother. The interviews conducted in Hebrew and English were then translated into German by Beatrice Greif, who is an experienced translator. Those interviews that had been conducted in Yiddish were first translated into Hebrew. Beatrice Greif then made the translations into German. For the interviews conducted in Polish, Jan Kaplon, a research professional at the Auschwitz-Birkenau State Museum, was responsible for the translations. During the translation process, all the translators tried to preserve the survivors' spirit and personality. Corrections in relation to style and language were not introduced. In most cases, due to their level of education, the survivors used rather simple formulations. These formulations were not changed during the translation in order not to alter the special spirit in which the survivors reported their experiences. Particular care was also given to the transcription and translation of names. Confusion over names had to be prevented since SS men with similar names had been stationed at Auschwitz. All the transcriptions and translations are now a part of the author's private archive in Israel.

In order to conduct the interviews, the author had to overcome one central obstacle. Many of the survivors had gotten used to staying silent about their experiences. They were not used to talking about their memories, their feelings and their thoughts. The decades-long taboo atmosphere made it very difficult to get them to talk. With every question, the interviewee risked hurting the survivor. Therefore, it was extremely important to start very carefully. Only step by step was it possible to gain the trust of the survivors; with every meeting, every conversation and every interview, they shared a bit more. Some of them told their suppressed memories to the author over periods of many years. In some cases, he was the first person they had spoken with about what they had experienced. In many cases, the author slowly became friends with the survivor and stayed in contact with them for the rest of their life.

Normally, the questions for the survivors were not prepared in advance. The author adhered to this method as a means to follow the stream of memories together with the survivor and in order to adapt the questions according to the aspects that he remembered during the conversation. In most cases, the author only asked questions and did not correct the survivors if they were stating something that the author knew was incorrect; he only intervened in the case of clear mistakes relating to places or dates. These methods produced a very flexible and free atmosphere, and enabled conversations without great restrictions. After the interview, all facts were compared with the existing research in order to check the accuracy of the mentioned facts.

The results of the interviews were the basis for the author's dissertation at the University of Vienna under the title 'Das jüdische Sonderkommando in Auschwitz Birkenau 1940–1945' and were then published in the book *We Wept without Tears*.[37] Originally published in German, the book was later translated into English and many other languages. Currently, a Chinese edition is being prepared. Several articles based on the interviews were also published in academic journals. These interviews, and the ones conducted after the publication of this first book, were also the basis for the authors' *Habilitation* under the title *Im Zentrum der 'Endlösung' – Alltag in der Todesfabrik Auschwitz*, as well as a more recent publication on the uprising of the SK, written with Itamar Levin.[38] Besides this, the published interviews have been the basis of ongoing historical research by other historians and have thus provided an important basis for the understanding of the SK's reality.

While the early SK testimonies could not change the general view of the SK and only a few historians – among them the Auschwitz survivor Erich Kulka and Ber Mark – took an interest in the history of the SK prisoners, this fundamentally changed after the publication of the late interviews. Especially in Germany, where the first edition of *We Wept without Tears* was published, to huge attention, the quantity of research published on the SK rose significantly afterwards. Due to the fact that the interviews were the first effort to systematically collect testimonies from the survivors of the SK, it is now considered a pioneer publication that changed perspectives on Auschwitz and the 'Final Solution'.[39]

The interviews not only deliver broad facts and information that provide a central basis for historical research, but – in contrast to official testimonies – also convey the emotional situation of the SK members, their moral dilemmas as well as their emotional and spiritual responses to the reality of the camp. Like the 'Scrolls of Auschwitz' they are 'not simply sources of information (although they are this), but are also archives of feelings'.[40] And because they are both sources of information and archives of feelings, they are an important source for the reconstruction of the reality of the camp and of the gas chambers.

Unlike those interviews that are only accessible to researchers, the publication of the late SK testimonies also had a strong influence on public perceptions of the SK and its role in the 'Final Solution'. As a result of the publication of the interviews, filmmakers started to develop an interest in the history of the SK. In recent years, three important films were made about the SK and its work in the gas chambers and crematoria. In 2001, the film *The Grey Zone*, directed by Tim Blake Nelson, was released. In 2008, it was followed by a documentary, directed by Emil Weiss, entitled *Sonderkommando Auschwitz-Birkenau*. Another milestone was the film *Son of Saul*, directed by László Nemes, which was released in 2015. The film shows the reality of the SK from the perspective of one of its members and won an Oscar in 2016. Even though the film does not use the testimonies of the survivors directly and is a fictitious story,[41] it is closely based on the information the survivors provided during the interviews. As we can see, today's perspective on the reality of the SK has fundamentally changed. This change is closely connected to the differences between the early testimonies of the SK members and the late interviews. While the changing perspective of historical research made these interviews possible in the first place, the interviews, in their turn, also helped to amplify this change in perspective.

Gideon Greif is an Israeli historian, educator and pedagogue. He is the Chief Historian and Researcher at the 'Shem Olam' Institute for Education, Documentation and Research on Faith and the Holocaust, Israel, and the Chief Historian and Researcher at the Foundation for Holocaust Education Projects in Miami, Florida. He is considered a world-renowned historian-expert on the history of Auschwitz-Birkenau. His most famous contribution to the history of Auschwitz is his groundbreaking research *We Wept without Tears* on the history of the Sonderkommando. This research, first published at Yad Vashem, has become an international bestseller. The book *We Wept without Tears* inspired the Hungarian movie *Son of Saul*, which won an Oscar in 2016. Greif worked as a historical advisor for the film.

Notes

1. On the history of this commando, see Jens Hoffmann, *Diese außerordentliche deutsche Bestialität: Wie die Nazis die Spuren ihrer Massenmorde in Osteuropa beseitigten. Augenzeugenberichte und Gespräche* (Hamburg: KVV Konkret, 2013).
2. Carlo Ginzburg, 'Just One Witness', in Saul Friedländer (ed.), *Probing the Limits of Representation*. Cambridge, MA: Harvard University Press, 1992, 82–96.
3. Sonja Knopp, *'Wir lebten mitten im Tod': Das 'Sonderkommando' in Auschwitz in schriftlichen und mündlichen Häftlingserinnerungen* (Frankfurt am Main: Peter Lang, 2009), 22.
4. Michael Brenner, *Propheten des Vergangenen. Jüdische Geschichtsschreibung im 19. und 20. Jahrhundert* (Munich: C.H. Beck, 2006), 145.
5. On the Jewish postwar commissions and their roots in prewar Jewish historiography, see Laura Jockusch, 'Jede Überlebende ist ein Stück Geschichte', in Martin Sabrow and Norbert Frei (eds), *Die Geburt des Zeitzeugen nach 1945* (Göttingen: Wallstein, 2012); and Laura Jockusch, *Collect and Record!* (Oxford: Oxford University Press, 2012).
6. Salman Gradowski, 'Der Brief', in Świebocka et al. (eds), *Inmitten des grauenvollen Verbrechens* (Oświęcim: Verlag des Staatlichen Auschwitz-Birkenau Museums, 1996), 139.

7. Ibid., 137.
8. Ibid., 309.
9. Henryk Mandelbaum, Auschwitz-Birkenau Museum Archive, DPR-HD/26, No. 48347/4, Volume 26b.
10. Yehoshuah Rosenblum, interview with GG on 2 May 1995 in Haifa, Private Archive GG.
11. Henryk Mandelbaum, Auschwitz-Birkenau Museum Archive: DPR-Hol/26, No. 48347/4, Volume 26b.
12. Hermann Langbein, *Der Auschwitz-Prozess: Eine Dokumentation* (Frankfurt am Main: Neue Kritik, 1995); and Eric Friedler, Barbara Siebert and Andreas Kilian. *Zeugen aus der Todeszone* (Lüneburg: zuKlampen, 2002), 310.
13. Yehoshuah Rosenblum, interview with GG on 2 May 1995 in Haifa, Private Archive GG.
14. Stanisław Jankowski (Alter Feinsilber)'s testimony, in Świebocka et al. (eds), *Inmitten des grauenvollen Verbrechens* (Oświęcim: Verlag des Staatlichen Auschwitz-Birkenau Museums, 1996), 25–60.
15. Ibid., 36.
16. E.g. ibid., 46, 50.
17. Ibid., 43.
18. Ibid., 47, 53.
19. Ibid., 53.
20. Ibid., 34, 38, 41.
21. Ibid., 45.
22. Ibid., 43. However, the suffering the witnesses often had to endure during their testimonies becomes clear when we look at the documentation of the Auschwitz trial in Frankfurt. A protocol of the hearing of Dov Paisikovic mentions that he collapsed after an identification parade (Friedler et al., *Zeugen aus der Todeszone*, 311f).
23. A question that was intensively discussed in connection to the work of Georges Didi-Hubermann (Georges Didi-Hubermann, *Images malgré tout* (Paris: Minuit, 2004)).
24. Nicholas Chare and Dominic Williams, *Matters of Testimony* (New York: Berghahn Books, 2016), vii.
25. Shaul Chasan, interview with GG in August 1984 in Holon, Private Archive GG.
26. Shaul Chasan, interview with GG on 21 September 2000 in Holon, Private Archive GG.
27. Josef Sackar, interview with GG on 22 September 2000 in Holon, Private Archive GG.
28. The survivors were forced to cope with their memories alone. According to psychological research, the place that the memories would take in daily life differs widely. While in some cases the survivors had to deal with their memories on a daily basis immediately after the liberation, in other cases the memories only returned decades after liberation. Cathy Caruth, 'Trauma als historische Erfahrung', in Ulrich Baer (ed.), *Niemand zeugt für den Zeugen* (Frankfurt am Main: Suhrkamp, 2000), 84ff.
29. Friedler et al., *Zeugen aus der Todeszone*, 313.
30. Dori Laub, 'Zeugnis ablegen oder die Schwierigkeiten des Zuhörens', in Ulrich Baer (ed.), *Niemand zeugt für den Zeugen* (Frankfurt am Main: Suhrkamp, 2000), 68ff. In the case of Eliezer Eisenschmidt, a visit to Auschwitz made the memories return and led to massive sleep disorders. In his dreams, he returned to the SK: 'And everything is just as it was. And everything happened as it had happened in the past'.

Eliezer Eisenschmidt, interview with GG on 12 February 2004 in Givatayim, Private Archive GG.
31. Gerhard Botz, 'Widerstand, Überleben und Identität', in: Alexander Friedmann et al. (eds), *Überleben der Shoa – und danach. Spätfolgen der Verfolgung aus wissenschaftlicher Sicht* (Vienna: Picus-Verlag, 1999), 51.
32. The difficult personal situation of the SK survivors is vividly illustrated by the testimonies two of their wives gave to the authors of *Zeugen aus der Todeszone*, Friedler et al., *Zeugen aus der Todeszone*, 315ff.
33. 'Why [should I go to Birkenau]? For the sad memories to return? I see no reason for that. But I can go there just to tell to the young people, the young Jews, what happened there. For that, I would do it! To tell the stories. But I would not go there just to have a look, no' (Morris Venezia, interview with GG on 15 September 1997 in Kalamares, Private Archive GG).
34. Ber Mark, *The Scrolls of Auschwitz* (Tel Aviv: Am Oved, 1985).
35. Władysław Bartoszewski, 'Nachwort', in in Świebocka et al. (eds), *Inmitten des grauenvollen Verbrechens* (Oświęcim: Verlag des Staatlichen Auschwitz-Birkenau Museums, 1996), 275.
36. The interviews conducted in Israel were conducted in Hebrew or Yiddish.
37. Gideon Greif, 'Das Kommando im Inferno: Geschichte, Image und Problematik des jüdischen "Sonderkommandos" in Auschwitz-Birkenau 1940–1945', Ph.D. dissertation (Vienna: University of Vienna, 2000).
38. Gideon Greif and Itamar Levin, *Aufstand in Auschwitz: Die Revolte des jüdischen 'Sonderkommando' am 7 Oktober 1944* (Cologne: Böhlau, 2015).
39. Among the work continuing the research on the SK is Friedler et al., *Zeugen aus der Todeszone* and the relatively new research by Sonja Knopp ('*Wir lebten mitten im Tod*').
40. Chare and Williams, *Matters of Testimony*, 220.
41. Dominic Williams criticized this and asked to use 'the increasing interest in the Sonderkommando ... as an opportunity to attend to the stories they themselves told, rather than simply placing them within easier, wider narratives'. See Dominic Williams, 'Stories from Holocaust Prisoners Forced to Work in the Gas Chambers Should Be Heard, Not Silenced', https://theconversation.com/stories-from-holocaust-prisoners-forced-to-work-in-the-gas-chambers-should-be-heard-not-silenced-65862 (retrieved 17 April 2019).

Bibliography

Bartoszewski, Wladyslaw. 'Nachwort', in Świebocka et al. (eds), *Inmitten des grauenvollen Verbrechens*. Oświęcim: Verlag des Staatlichen Auschwitz-Birkenau Museums, 1996, 275–77.
Botz, Gerhard. 'Widerstand, Überleben und Identität', in Alexander Friedmann, Elvira Glück and David Vyssoki (eds), *Überleben der Shoa – und danach. Spätfolgen der Verfolgung aus wissenschaftlicher Sicht*. Vienna: Picus-Verlag, 1999.
Brenner, Michael. *Propheten des Vergangenen. Jüdische Geschichtsschreibung im 19. und 20. Jahrhundert*. Munich: C.H. Beck, 2006.
Caruth, Cathy. 'Trauma als historische Erfahrung', in Ulrich Baer (ed.), *Niemand zeugt für den Zeugen*. Frankfurt am Main: Suhrkamp, 2000, 84–100.
Chare, Nicholas, and Dominic Williams. *Matters of Testimony: Interpreting the Scrolls of Auschwitz*. New York: Berghahn Books, 2016.

Chasan, Shaul. Interview with GG in August 1984 in Holon, Private Archive GG.
——. Interview with GG on 21 September 2000 in Holon, Private Archive GG.
Didi-Hubermann, George. *Images malgré tout*. Paris: Minuit, 2004.
Eisenschmidt, Eliezer. Interview with GG on 12 February 2004 in Givatayim, Private Archive GG.
Friedler, Eric, Barbara Siebert and Andreas Kilian. *Zeugen aus der Todeszone*. Lüneburg: zuKlampen, 2002.
Ginzburg, Carlo. 'Just One Witness', in Saul Friedländer (ed.), *Probing the Limits of Representation: Nazism and the 'Final Solution'*. Cambridge, MA: Harvard University Press, 1992, 82–96.
Gradowski, Salman. 'Der Brief', in Świebocka et al. (eds), *Inmitten des grauenvollen Verbrechens*. Oświęcim: Verlag des Staatlichen Auschwitz-Birkenau Museums, 1996, 137–38.
Greif, Gideon, and Itamar Levin. *Aufstand in Auschwitz: Die Revolte des jüdischen 'Sonderkommando' am 7 Oktober 1944*. Cologne: Böhlau, 2015.
Hoffmann, Jens. *Diese außerordentliche deutsche Bestialität: Wie die Nazis die Spuren ihrer Massenmorde in Osteuropa beseitigten. Augenzeugenberichte und Gespräche*. Hamburg: KVV Konkret, 2013.
Jankowski, Stanisław. Aussage von Stanislaw Jankowski (Alter Feinsilber), in *Inmitten des grauenvollen Verbrechens*. Oświęcim: Verlag des Staatlichen Auschwitz-Birkenau Museums, 1996, 25–60.
Jockusch, Laura. *Collect and Record! Jewish Holocaust Documentation in Early Postwar Europe*. Oxford: Oxford University Press, 2012.
——. 'Jede Überlebende ist ein Stück Geschichte', in Martin Sabrow and Norbert Frei (eds), *Die Geburt des Zeitzeugen nach 1945*. Göttingen: Wallstein, 2012, 113–44.
Knopp, Sonja. *'Wir lebten mitten im Tod': Das 'Sonderkommando' in Auschwitz in schriftlichen und mündlichen Häftlingserinnerungen*. Frankfurt am Main: Peter Lang, 2009.
Langbein, Hermann. *Der Auschwitz-Prozess: Eine Dokumentation*. Frankfurt am Main: Neue Kritik, 1995.
Laub, Dori. 'Zeugnis ablegen oder die Schwierigkeiten des Zuhörens', in Ulrich Baer (ed), *Niemand zeugt für den Zeugen*. Frankfurt am Main: Suhrkamp, 2000, 68–83.
Mandelbaum, Henryk. Auschwitz-Birkenau Museum Archive, DPR-HD/26, No. 48347/4, Volume 26b.
Mark, Ber. *The Scrolls of Auschwitz*. Tel Aviv: Am Oved, 1985.
Rosenblum, Yehoshuah. Interview with GG on 2 May 1995 in Haifa, Private Archive GG.
Sackar, Josef. Interview with GG on 22 September 2000 in Holon, Private Archive GG.
Świebocka, Teresa, Franciszek Piper and Martin Mayr (eds). *Inmitten des grauenvollen Verbrechens: Handschriften von Mitgliedern des Sonderkommandos*, trans. Herta Henschel and Jochen August. Oświęcim: Verlag des Staatlichen Auschwitz-Birkenau Museums, 1996.
Venezia, Morris. Interview with GG on 15 September 1997 in Kalamares, Private Archive GG.
Williams, Dominic. 'Stories from Holocaust Prisoners Forced to Work in the Gas Chambers Should Be Heard, Not Silenced'. Retrieved 17 April 2019 from https://theconversation.com/stories-from-holocaust-prisoners-forced-to-work-in-the-gas-chambers-should-be-heard-not-silenced-65862.

Chapter 14

From Special Operations Executive to Sonderkommando

Sebastian Faulks and the Anxiety of Invention

Sue Vice

The British author Sebastian Faulks is best known for his novels about the two world wars. Such works include what is referred to as his 'French trilogy', of which the first volume, *The Girl at the Lion d'Or* (1989), focuses on interwar France, while *Birdsong* (1993) is set during the First World War and *Charlotte Gray* (1999) centres on a young woman working alongside the French Resistance in the Second World War. Faulks' interest in the extreme events, undercover operations and psychology of war, particularly as it affects British individuals and national culture, is equally evident in his novel *Where My Heart Used to Beat* (2015), in which the protagonist looks back from the vantage point of London in 1980 to his wartime experience in Italy. In the writer's 2012 novel, *A Possible Life*, which is my concern in the present chapter, the plot addresses in overt terms, for the first time in Faulks' oeuvre, the world of the wartime extermination camps. While the collaborations of Vichy are anatomized in *Charlotte Gray* and we learn of the arrest of two young orphan brothers prior to their deportation to Auschwitz, the camp universe remains outside that novel's conceptual frame. In the case of *A Possible Life*, by contrast, the greatest possible confrontation between a British backdrop and the machinery of genocide is presented in the form of a British soldier's experience of forced labour as part of the Sonderkommando (SK) unit in Auschwitz.

A Possible Life is unconventional in consisting of five apparently unrelated novellas. Yet, as the title suggests, each story is highly individual, while at the same time presenting the radically contingent implication that its central character could, at a different historical moment, have had an entirely different existence. Such an idea is reinforced by the appearance of the same buildings and landscapes in two stories, each of which is set at a different historical moment. Thus, it is implied, the apparent specificity of these biographical stories is fortuitous, even as we read such distinctive narratives as that of a British soldier interned in Auschwitz, a Victorian child of the workhouses making good as a landlord, an Italian scientist in the near future identifying the location of human self-consciousness in the brain, the ambiguous religious revelation of an uneducated French peasant, and a Californian folk-singer achieving stardom.

'A Different Man'

In the opening section of *A Possible Life*, 'A Different Man', on which I will focus here, the life of the protagonist, Geoffrey Talbot, a Latin master at a minor English preparatory school, is interrupted by the outbreak of the Second World War. Geoffrey's wartime work in the British Special Operations Executive (SOE) in France ends when he is betrayed to the Gestapo by a fellow agent, resulting in his being sent to Auschwitz along with his friend 'Tiny' Trembath. Geoffrey's deportation to Auschwitz constitutes an abrupt geographical dislocation, as well as an ironic linguistic transfer between these very different 'special' units. In the camp, Geoffrey's volunteering his linguistic services as a translator leads to his being co-opted into the Special Force, that is, the SK, although that term is never used in the novel, and made to work as a stoker of the crematorium furnace.

In narrative and compositional terms, this transition from the SOE to the SK has the metatextual effect of marking a clash between the different kinds of source material drawn on by Faulks in constructing this narrative world. These texts include Roderick Bailey's *Forgotten Voices of the Secret War* (2008), an oral history of the SOE, and Andrey Pogozhev's *Escape from Auschwitz* (2007), a memoir by a Russian former prisoner-of-war (POW) of a break-out from the camp. These two documentary works are blended with a third, a purported eyewitness account, Donald Watt's *Stoker* (1995), by a captured Anzac soldier who claims he was made to work alongside the SK members in the role of keeping the crematorium furnace alight. In the present chapter, I will trace the effects of these various intertextual elements on the construction and significance of the fictional Geoffrey's experiences in the SK in Faulks' novel, and their relevance for British memories of the war.

In Faulks' much more expansive story of Charlotte Gray in the eponymous novel, the narrative of Charlotte's assumed identity and acts of subversion in Vichy France has the space to be told with local and personal detail. By contrast, Geoffrey is constructed in the present case in minimalist fashion as a man of his time – or, in more metafictional terms, it is clear that the demands of the time have constructed him. Thus, we read that after his graduation: 'In September 1938, after a series of rebuffs, Geoffrey found himself at a boys' preparatory school in Nottinghamshire, where he was to teach French, Latin and elementary maths'.[1] The date is significant not in terms of Geoffrey's personal biography, but to alert us to where he will be a year hence, on the declaration of war. Likewise, the sense of Geoffrey's lack of agency, as conveyed in the passive constructions of the description of his job – he 'found himself', 'he was to teach' – is not so much a realist character trait as an element crucial to his being swept up in a horrifying war. Such phrasing makes plain Geoffrey's novelistic role as a cipher in those events and within *A Possible Life* as a whole. While the characters in the other sections of Faulks' novel might have historical or literary forebears – Flaubert's servant-girl Félicité from his *Un Cœur simple* is perhaps the forebear for the French servant Jeanne in 'A Door into Heaven', and Helen Dunmore sees Joan Baez as the inspiration for the folk-singer Anya King in 'You Next Time'[2] – Geoffrey is constituted out of a discordant variety of earlier sources.

The effect on *A Possible Life* of the competing discourses represented by each of these sources is compounded by the invented status of those sections of Watt's *Stoker* that represent the Holocaust. In the memoir, Watt recounts his experience of escape from a POW camp in 1944. This was followed by imprisonment in Auschwitz, via a week in Bergen-Belsen, as punishment for his failing to talk under brutal interrogation. While Watt's history of arrest in Greece in 1941 and his transfer to two different POW camps in Germany, where he was held captive until the liberation in 1945, appears in his official records, the period he claims was spent in Auschwitz does not.[3] Nor, as Paul O'Shea points out, is the presence of an 'English-speaking, non-Jewish prisoner, sent to work as a stoker' mentioned in any other account.[4] The only exception to this is the corroboration that appears to be given to Watt's story by Denis Avey. Avey, the author of the bestselling memoir *The Man Who Broke into Auschwitz* (2011), gives an account of his war experience that includes not just his imprisonment as a POW in the Auschwitz complex close to the Monowitz camp, but also his apparently having changed places on two occasions with a Jewish prisoner in order to gain access to Auschwitz-Birkenau. In the summary given of his oral interview deposited at the Imperial War Museum in London, we read that while he was a prisoner, Avey heard of an Australian POW who worked as a stoker in the crematorium.[5] In the interview, Avey claims that the reason for breaking into Auschwitz was in part to get in touch with the Australian stoker, but that he failed to do so. As Russell Wallis argues, such a claim on Avey's part appears to offer independent corroboration of Watt's story, but, given the falsity of the latter, 'can only have been based on a reading of Watt's book *Stoker*' and not on Avey's own experience. It appears that Avey thus 'project[ed] Watt's latter-day claims backwards in time', at the very least making himself appear unreliable as an eyewitness.[6] Far from Avey corroborating Watt's account, the unreliability of each memoir compounds the other.

Like Avey's memoir, *Stoker* was a bestseller, but plans to make a film about Watt's experience, the screenplay to be composed by the Australian writer and director Barrie Kosky, foundered after definitive doubt was cast on the veracity of the account. These published rebuttals include an article by Konrad Kwiet, concluding that the 'stoker story' is 'unbelievable', as well as the verdict by Gideon Greif, the historian of the SK experience, that due to its 'various falsehoods and major errors', Watt's story is 'definitely an invention'.[7] Kwiet's exposé was published as early as 1997, yet *Stoker*'s central premise – that an Allied POW could have been enlisted into the body of Jewish prisoners who made up the SK – underlies Faulks' novel of over a decade later. It seems likely that the novelist was unaware of the memoir's contested status. Partly for that reason, it is the very episodes with which Kwiet takes issue that feature most centrally in Faulks' novel. Although Watt claims that he and his fellow stokers worked alongside, rather than as members of, the SK team, this simply compounds the inaccuracy of his account, as Paul O'Shea argues, since the stokers did not work separately in this way.[8] However, Watt's claims of this kind have the effect of implying that the SK members are not considered by him in terms of the moral dubiety of the 'grey zone'. Rather, the use made of *Stoker* in turn for fictional purposes in *A Possible Life* also suggests that the SK experience is one taken to be the quintessentially horrifying aspect of Auschwitz in terms of setting the prisoners to work in disposing of their fellow-inmates' bodies, a labour they carried out under fear of death themselves. Although both memoir and novel show the terrible suffering and psychological breakdown undergone by the SK members, it is implied that such an experience demanded the highest standards of personal and ethical resource on the part of the 'stoker' in each case to survive it.

The Special Operations Executive

Sebastian Faulks' interest in the historical experience and significance of the SOE preceded *A Possible Life*, as is clear in his introduction to Roderick Bailey's oral history of the organization, *Forgotten Voices of the Secret War*. Despite the nonfiction status of this introduction, Faulks emphasizes the appeal of using Churchill's 'secret army' for novelistic purposes, by reason of such factors as its offering the potential for unconventional and extreme individual action, many examples of which feature in Bailey's anthology. As Faulks concludes, this 'extraordinary organisation' is one that, 'however much you know about it, never loses its power to make you gasp – in admiration, humour, amazement and disbelief'.[9] Indeed, the profusion of remarkable detail in Bailey's collection of testimonies about life as an SOE operative in occupied Europe, including its agents' hair's-breadth escapes, ingenious ruses and acts of inventive sabotage, reveals how hard it must have been to decide which to retain in such a condensed narrative as the eighty-page 'A Different Man'.

Faulks' claim in the introduction to Bailey's *Forgotten Voices* that the SOE 'epitomised all the most memorable aspects of the British war effort', in a 'mixture of cussedness, heroism and amateurishness', underlies his decision to make such events part of the present novel. Yet the narrative of Geoffrey's life is not in the main concerned with this topic. Faulks was clearly struck by the moral incongruity of a British military prisoner incarcerated in the Nazi 'concentrationary universe'. He makes this clear when describing in his introduction the 'terrible dangers' agents faced if they were arrested, since they were not seen as 'regular prisoners of war' but 'faced torture and death in a concentration camp'.[10] Some of the most striking accounts in *Forgotten Voices* are by captured British SOE agents who were incarcerated in just this way, not in POW camps but in concentration camps. The starkness of the ontological contrast between the SOE ethos and that of the Nazis, when placed in such close proximity to one another, is one that must have attracted Faulks' novelistic instinct. It is put in such terms by Robert Sheppard in *Forgotten Voices*, when he describes his arrival in the first of the four concentration camps, which included Mauthausen and Dachau, where he was held prisoner: 'We were entering the world of the German concentration camp, which we didn't know. It was really entering a new life. We were absolutely shocked by the way [the Germans] behaved'.[11] It is this traumatic confrontation of worldviews, onto which Faulks' reading of Watt has been grafted, that underlies the premise of his novel's placing a British SOE agent not in a concentration camp, but in Auschwitz-Birkenau itself.

In *A Possible Life*, the SOE context serves primarily as a backdrop and as the means for getting Geoffrey plausibly to be in Nazi-occupied Europe. Faulks draws on the historical experiences of SOE members in representing the detail of Geoffrey's joining the organization and his wartime life in France before being sent to Auschwitz. Thus, Faulks describes his high regard for Benjamin Cowburn's memoir *No Cloak and No Dagger* (1960), a work of 'gritty understatement' judged by the novelist to be 'for my money the best of the SOE memoirs', in which the former operative regularly travelled between free and Vichy France 'in a hollow compartment beneath the engine of a locomotive'.[12] Geoffrey arrives in France by just such means, in a fashion that is meticulously imagined and described. However, the novel's moral centre lies with a different kind of train, the 'cattle truck' into which Geoffrey and his friend 'Tiny' Trembath are put after they are betrayed to the Gestapo, along with 'thirty others . . . most of them Russians' (36). This very change of trains signals to the reader the new track the narrative is about to take.

A similar divergence from the SOE narrative to one more appropriate to imprisonment in an extermination camp is clear in relation to Faulks' fictive use of the frequent assertions in *Forgotten Voices* on the part of the captured SOE agents in prisons and camps about the importance of behaving with what they refer to as a sense of British 'dignity'. Thus, Robert Sheppard describes how in Dachau: '[The Germans] wanted us to be beasts and they nearly, nearly reached it . . . [But] all the way through I wanted to keep my dignity as a British officer'.[13] Despite, or indeed because of, Faulks' clearly high regard for such maintenance of honourable behaviour in thoroughly dishonourable circumstances, since he quotes these comments by Sheppard in his introduction,[14] in *A Possible Life* the notion of dignity is shown to be a liability in the world of an extermination camp. Geoffrey's friend Trembath invokes the term in a way that is used to demonstrate its irrelevance, at a moment when he is 'impatient' to take action: '"Listen, Talbot . . . it's important that we don't let ourselves descend to the level of some of these people. They've lost their dignity."' (43).

Just as Geoffrey earlier prevented Trembath from remonstrating with a guard over the summary execution of an old man in the barracks, he reasons otherwise with his friend here, to caution against rash action that is sure to bring terrible reprisals. Sheppard's experience in Dachau informs the debate between Geoffrey and Trembath in such a way that the two fictional characters take shape from the division in the former SOE agent's comments between his idealism and a pragmatic sympathy for the other inmates. Sheppard describes the camp in the last months of its existence as a 'living cemetery', where starving prisoners were reduced to fighting over bowls of soup. While Geoffrey voices a version of the former agent's words – as Sheppard puts it, 'you cannot reproach these people for behaving like that' – Trembath embodies instead Sheppard's concluding remark: 'It needed tremendous force of character to live through that, to try and keep your dignity'.[15] However, we learn that Trembath's prewar morality has no place in Auschwitz, as is conveyed by his death in an attempted escape from the camp, related in retrospect by Geoffrey (64). By means of the battle for meaning over the term 'dignity', the novel acknowledges the difference between Trembath's determination to be a figure like that of the real-life Robert Sheppard and the impossibility of any such wish in Geoffrey's situation as an SK member in Auschwitz.

Donald Watt, *Stoker*

A Possible Life thematizes in this way its own intertextual history, moving away from the SOE accounts of daring subversion and resolve to reliance on Donald Watt's memoir *Stoker* in its representation of a world without even Trembath's moral compass. Watt's account is subtitled *The Story of an Australian Soldier Who Survived Auschwitz-Birkenau* and relates the atrocities he witnessed. It also recounts his own experience in being forced to take part in work as a stoker feeding the crematorium furnace, along with a group of Polish political prisoners. As Watt puts it in describing this labour:

> My job, stoking the fires, was despicable work, and I knew it ... We worked at the side of the crematorium, where there were five three-door furnaces ... We fed the wood through [the doors] and onto a grate that looked as though it was made from cast-iron bars. The wood came in from the forest of fir trees to the northwest of the camp ... The bodies were thrown in through an opening just above the stoking hole ... One person had a long pole with a steel plate on the end, which he used to push the bodies through the opening and into the furnace as they built up.[16]

The everyday and apparently down-to-earth view that Watt offers on genocidal atrocity, from the perspective of an Australian POW incarcerated in the camp, must have attracted Faulks' attention for the sake of his own fiction. In the description quoted above, Watt is keen to emphasize the factual detail of his forced labour, which appears in turn in Faulks' novel. We learn that when Geoffrey is put to work as a stoker, in a way that echoes Watt's account:

> [The] furnaces at knee-height had to be kept roaring day and night with logs cut from the pine forests ... The corpses came in on trucks with chutes

at the back ... Some stokers were given metal poles and detailed to prod the corpses down into the fire in groups of six or eight at a time, urged on by the screaming SS officers. (53)

Yet even the designation of a 'stoker' in the burning process is not used accurately in Watt's account, since the term was reserved for those who cremated corpses, not those who stoked the fires, as is described in his memoir.[17] Naturally, this error is repeated in *A Possible Life*. Watt's other inaccuracies, as identified by Kwiet and others, include his description of the non-Jewish stoking crew who work separately from the SK. Of the latter, Watt says in order to distinguish them that 'the other prisoners with the really rotten jobs were the people conscripted into the special squads, or *Sonderkommando*'.[18] Equally, his error about the kind of fuel used to incinerate corpses, which was coke rather than wood, disrupts the very basis of Watt's memoir. But because of its presence in *Stoker*, the historical solecism is adopted for a significant thread of meaning in Faulks' novel. This thread arises once more from a stark ontological contrast: this time between the natural world, including the English countryside, embodied by the pine trees, and their co-option into the process of mass murder. Geoffrey's prewar awareness of the 'sandy pine' landscape of Norfolk (8), as he travels to his job as a schoolmaster for the first time, possesses an innocence that is thoroughly lost to the post-traumatic 'flash-memories of pine-logs' that assail him after his return to Britain at the war's end (65).

In a complex instance of foreshadowing, 'A Different Man' lays the seeds for what will become the triggers for Geoffrey's post-traumatic state in the war's aftermath. As his SOE interviewer puts it, with more aptness than could then have been envisaged: "'You may see things that none of us has ever seen.'" (21). In an ambivalent set of correspondences, the militaristic discourse of public school life, with its 'barrage' at cricket against a school that Geoffrey's has failed to 'beat' at anything, and the recommendation he receives not to seek promotion, but to remain a 'foot soldier' (3, 5), strikes a disturbing note in the run-up to war. In the postwar era, such language sounds even more jarring. Yet it appears that the ironic correspondence is meant to establish difference rather than similitude between the militaristic discourse of British educational practice and its extreme expression in the Nazi camps. The world of the public school is not put forward for analysis in terms of its systemic 'soft violence', as Pierre Bourdieu would phrase it. The irony of Geoffrey's postwar 'flash-memories' is not that they reveal a likeness between past and present, but that they emphasize their absolute difference.

As a counterpart to these elements of British life, in the early wartime period of 'A Different Man', we encounter a different kind of self-conscious temporality in the form of the failure of individuals to predict accurately what the reader knows to have been the war's outcome. In the light of Geoffrey's eventual fate, such forecasts as that of his employer, the headmaster Mr Little, possess extra irony, as he invokes his own experience during the First World War: '"You'll be all right, Talbot. No trenches this time. It'll be all tanks and movement and high-level bombing."' (7). The 'trenches' that Geoffrey does eventually encounter are those characteristic of a quite different kind of war, designed for the mass burial of the victims of genocide. Geoffrey's thoughts on the war could be viewed as an example of what Michael André Bernstein calls sideshadowing, in imagining a genuinely open play of historical contingency at any given moment rather than an insistence on the inevitability of what actually took place. His view early in the war is that: 'The Scandinavians would offer little resistance, yet the French could be relied on to hold out until British reinforcements came to help' (6). However, so crucial are the events that he gets wrong in relation to his own story that such a miscalculation merely makes him appear out of touch. Later, he notes that: 'Europe was entirely under occupation; France had not put up the resistance that Geoffrey, raised on stories of heroic resistance on the Marne, had expected' (16). Even more significant here is the blurring of third-person narrative with free indirect discourse, making it hard to distinguish what is being reliably established from what is more impressionistic and subjective. Indeed, at times it is precisely subjective impressions that are reported upon. Such a blurring is crucial to the period of his war experience that Geoffrey spends in Auschwitz.

In *A Possible Life*, Geoffrey's role has a defamiliarizing effect similar to Watt's, as a British onlooker at extermination in the moment of its occurrence, and without the explanatory narrative of genocidal mass murder offered by historical hindsight. The reader is enlisted to supply the missing historical framework. Thus, we know before Geoffrey does that the unnamed camp where he arrives and that had 'obviously been built for some other purpose before the war', set in 'marshy land with pine forests all around' (38), is Auschwitz, although its name is never given.

This reimagining of how the camp might appear to a contemporary onlooker even includes Geoffrey's awareness of a scene modelled on that shown in one of the four 'Sonderkommando photographs', taken secretly in August 1944. The photograph in question depicts the cremation of corpses in the open air at Birkenau: 'Geoffrey could see what looked like bonfires in clearings among the trees, attended by further prisoners in striped uniforms ... Columns of smoke with an unfamiliar smell emanated from the pyres' (40). Geoffrey's perspective replicates in geographical terms that of the SK member, a Greek Jew known as

Alex, who is believed to have taken the photographs. However, while Alex's look through the camera viewfinder was motivated by the urgent wish of the SK to capture the reality of genocide, at this moment in Faulks' novel, Geoffrey's view lacks precisely that awareness. His gaze at this scene registers a radically cognitive version of the 'understatement' admired by Faulks, since Geoffrey cannot judge what he sees in any other way. Such understatement operates here as both technique and epistemology. Antisemitism itself, in particular its eugenic, eliminationist variety, is also misrecognized by Geoffrey, his puzzlement revealed through the free indirect discourse of a rhetorical question: 'What on earth was the point of taking a French seamstress from a back-street in Lyons and transporting her across Europe to be murdered, on the grounds that some distant ancestor might have once plied his trade from Dan to Beersheba?' (49). Both Geoffrey's conception of Jews in the mythical terms of the Bible and his failure to understand 'the point' of the practical and ideological effort of genocide constitute a stark reimagining of the racialized basis of Nazi mass murder, one whose apparent logic might have started to seem dangerously self-evident in the present, over seventy years later.

Stoker supplies another significant feature of Faulks' novel in the form of Watt's apparent ability to transcend the extreme circumstances of his SK duties by mental effort. In Faulks' version, this becomes a further expression of the gulf between German and British sensibility, as well as fitting his novel's overall theme of the migration of selfhood between individual consciousnesses. It is prepared for as early as the psychological examination Geoffrey has to undertake as part of his SOE recruitment, during the course of which the examiner, Dr Samuels, asks him: '"Are you good at being on your own? Do you have resources? In your head?"' (22). The origin in *Stoker* of the importance for *A Possible Life* of 'inner resources' is readily apparent. For Watt, 'switching off mentally', as he puts it, 'by shutting out the grisly nature of what was happening around me', takes the form of supporting what he frequently terms his 'larrikin' sensibility,[19] that of a specifically Australian kind of authority-flouting maverick. The appearance of this term is a clue to the ideological motivation of Watt's memoir, characterized by Kwiet as an attempt to forge a connection between 'the Anzac legend', one of antipodean courage and comradeship in the face of adversity, 'and the reality of the Holocaust'.[20] In Brian Woodley's description of Watt's memoir, as 'the story of an intrepid Aussie Digger locked up in the engine room of the Holocaust', the significance of the Auschwitz setting, forming the ultimate challenge to the Anzac spirit, is made clear.[21] Looking back at his time as a stoker, Watt describes his habit of '[letting] my mind wander back to the sun and the wheatfields, to the beaches of Melbourne, to the wineries around

Mildura, to my motorbikes, to Mum and Dad and my mates'.[22] His ability to summon up such memories is presented as a virtue that is as typically Australian as the landscape itself.

As we have seen, an analogous contrast is established in Faulks' novel between British values, or what Geoffrey thinks of as 'democracy and the RAF' (39), and Nazi brutality, which on many occasions shocks him by reason of its unmotivated cruelty. In Geoffrey's case, the imagery he calls upon to escape the camp's reality takes the form of a construct of British masculinity, as a counterpart to the Australian version invoked by Watt:

> He pushed his mind as far as he could from his surroundings. There was a particular cricket ground that had meant a great deal to him when he was growing up. It had a cedar tree in one corner, near the pavilion, a hedge that ran along the road ... It was, for a club ground, remarkably flat and true. (41)

The distance from his circumstances invoked here by Geoffrey is not just spatial and temporal but also moral. We are shown that there is a profound distinction between the status of cricket, the 'true' nature of its ground a virtue in several senses, and the Nazi guards' 'sport' with the camp inmates. Such behaviour includes the episode that Geoffrey describes with laconic irony as the 'game' of the guards taking turns to let fly a leather whip at the prisoners' bodies (41), based on Watt's description of such an incident. It is the toll of the first day of duty as a 'stoker' at the crematorium that makes Geoffrey's internal escape strategy fail: 'That night nothing of England would come to him: no river, almshouse or cricket-ground'. Like Primo Levi and other survivor-witnesses, Geoffrey finds himself ontologically confused and unable any longer to say which is the real world: that of the camp or of his prewar ordinary life. As he concludes of the images of England: 'It was these places that had taken on the vague outlines of something he had dreamed' (55).

Faulks' reliance on the details of Watt's account extends to the latter's postwar inability to talk about his time in the camp, as he describes the day of his arrival at a POW camp towards the war's end: 'From that day on, for 44 years, I didn't mention a word about Auschwitz to anybody'.[23] In the case of the fictional Geoffrey, apart from an effort to describe his experiences to a fellow-teacher after the war, his post-traumatic disorder means that cannot share the details of the reasons for his eventual mental breakdown. It is hard not to read Watt's accounting for his silence in this way as an alibi for his suddenly starting to describe the memory of his time in Auschwitz at a time when the Australian government was offering compensation to those affected. While even Kwiet endorses Watt's right to compensation of this kind for what he did undergo, and which he was duly awarded, this was not for his Auschwitz experiences as recounted in *Stoker*.

Andrey Pogozhev, *Escape from Auschwitz*

Faulks' third intertext, Andrey Pogozhev's *Escape from Auschwitz*, exerts a particular pressure on the plot of *A Possible Life*. No fictional character equivalent to Pogozhev himself appears in the novel. However, Geoffrey encounters Sergei, a POW – in Pogozhev's account, he is the Russian who 'stirred up' the plan to escape – for the first time immediately after his visions of England have failed to sustain him, suggesting that only direct action will now do. Pogozhev was not a member of the SK and describes their different activities during the confusion that took place just before the Russian prisoners' escape. The historical intertexts Faulks chose determine the direction of his plot, and for this reason it is the Russian POWs' escape of November 1942, rather than the SK uprising of October 1944, that provides Geoffrey's exit from the camp. Nonetheless, the two events are conflated in Geoffrey's postwar account of his experience to his fellow-schoolteacher Gerald Baxter: "'When we escaped, there was a riot. They managed to blow up a crematorium'" (64). Such poetic licence taken with historical fact suits the detail of the novel's plot, with its focus on Geoffrey's forced labour at just such a crematorium in the camp.

Geoffrey and Trembath discuss the possibility of escape soon after arriving in Auschwitz, but, following Pogozhev's memoir, it is the Russian POWs who put such a plan into practice. Sergei's appearance in the novel marks the conclusion of *Stoker*'s influence and establishes that the resolution of Geoffrey's plight will take place by different means from those of Watt. A detail from Pogozhev's memoir even amplifies the notion of inner escape that is so significantly borrowed from Watt for Geoffrey's story. For Pogozhev, the 'world of fantasy' allows him to be 'far, far away' in the realm of 'the beloved past'.[24] This is a generalised return to 'events and episodes' from his earlier life. However, Pogozhev's description of the Russian prisoners' 'verbal retelling of novels, humorous stories, anecdotes and fables', as a way to 'transport you to a different world',[25] underlies the depiction of Geoffrey's 'night-time discipline', that is, his efforts to recall entire novels. He considers contributing to the equivalent of the scene described by Pogozhev, that of the Polish prisoners' recitation of 'folk stories, legends or the entire plots of books', including what are in the circumstances such ironically named works as Dickens' *Great Expectations* (52).

As well as these details, Pogozhev's memoir most notably provides the resolution of Geoffrey's plight in the camp. While Watt is simply – if, according to O'Shea, implausibly[26] – returned to a POW camp in Germany in 1944 after seven months in Birkenau, Pogozhev was one of seventy Russian POWs who undertook a mass escape from Birkenau in 1942, a year after his arrival in the camp. Of this number, Pogozhev was one of only four to survive. In *A Possible Life*, Geoffrey flees Birkenau under cover of the break-out by, in the fictive version, the fifty Russians who made up a search party for the body of a recently executed prisoner outside the camp's fence. Faulks' narrative follows Pogozhev's account closely, yet shapes the memoir's detail to suit his fictive requirements and exigencies. Thus, in the moments before his shelter is toppled, the SS guard in the watchtower looks down at the Russians, 'calmly' in Pogozhev's original[27] and, with even greater dramatic irony, 'complacently' in Faulks' version (59). The sudden eruption of violence, which Pogozhev explicitly likens to a 'volcano',[28] is conveyed by Faulks as 'there comes a roar of Russian, fifty men hurling iron and rocks and rushing the wooden tower'. Although Faulks prefers a wordless 'roar', in Pogozhev's account we hear the Russian words which are not quoted here:

> Suddenly a voice cut through the silence: 'For the Motherland! Forward!' A discordant 'Hurrah!' exploded, unleashing a hail of rocks, lumps of iron and assorted missiles at the SS watchman.[29]

Faulks' decision to omit the utterances quoted by Pogozhev acts both to retain the consistency of Geoffrey's uncomprehending anglophone perspective and also to sidestep the question of Pogozhev's having felt obliged to assert his patriotic credentials in the memoir. However, the phrase does appear, perhaps more fittingly, in the form of Geoffrey's earlier conversation with the novel's Sergei, described as an individual who 'could speak a little English', and rendered in free indirect discourse so that his words are filtered through Geoffrey's consciousness. Sergei 'assured Geoffrey that all the Russians were determined to escape in order to get back to Moscow and help the Motherland repel the Fascist invader' (55). Finally, Pogozhev notes with mournful irony the final words uttered by the historical Sergei, whose surname the memoirist can no longer recall: 'I heard Sergei's voice for the last time, some distance behind: "Don't rush! Don't waste your strength! Run sensibly!"'[30] All alone as Geoffrey must be, as both a fictional character and a British escapee, the words of selfless advice issue instead from his own inner voice: 'steady, Talbot, pace yourself; leave something for the later stages' (59).

After an ellipsis in the novel following the narrative of the break-out, we jump forward to 1946 and Geoffrey's return to life at his Nottinghamshire school as a Latin master. The apparent unfurling of events in Geoffrey's narrative of the camp without the benefit of hindsight turns out to be an illusion, since we learn that the apparently present-time relation of events has been a version of a postwar recapitulation of his experiences in a pub conversation with his fellow schoolmaster Gerald Baxter. This notion is made plain when Baxter abruptly asks Geoffrey, without any such story having been told: "'So . . . after you'd escaped from this wretched POW place, what happened then?'" (63). It seems that the narrative we have just read must have been the tale Geoffrey told Baxter, and it ends at what is clearly the same point, that of the escape. Yet Baxter's understated description of the experience he has just been told about, as 'this wretched POW place', suggests that there has been a miscommunication of some kind: either Geoffrey's inability to tell his story has already taken hold or Baxter cannot comprehend what he has heard. Nonetheless, we learn how Geoffrey got away from the vicinity of the camp in his answer to Baxter's question. He 'got his bearings' in order to travel west, away from Auschwitz, by following "'the stars'" (63). This detail registers a final debt to Pogozhev, who describes 'the Great Bear' as 'our only guide'.[31] It is hard not read this reference to the 'Great Bear' in patriotic as well as astrological terms, and as revelatory of the particular structures that inform any such documentary account.

Conclusion

The section 'A Different Man' from Sebastian Faulks' novel *A Possible Life*, on which my discussion here has centred, is titled thus to convey the great toll taken on its protagonist by his experience in the SK. Not only does Geoffrey Talbot return to Britain in an entirely different psychic state; as well as this, the postwar plea, 'Let somebody else live my life for me, Geoffrey thought' (82), reveals that he wishes in a more literal sense to be a 'different man'. The severe psychological effects of what Geoffrey underwent turn at the story's conclusion into narrative ones. It is no longer post-traumatic stress disorder, but, rather, preparation for the novel's conceit of migrating subjectivity that underlies Geoffrey's final realization that 'some subtle rearrangement of particles had taken place within him; he felt with joy and resignation that he was not the same man' (83).

It is to this profoundly literary conclusion that the extremity of the novel's setting in the SK at Auschwitz-Birkenau has tended. Faulks' reliance on historical intertexts, particularly those of a popular kind, to construct this historical world is a method shared by most Holocaust novels, ranging from William Styron's *Sophie's Choice* (1979) to John Donahue's *The*

Death's Head Chess Club (2015). Such fiction uses documentary material as context or inspiration with varying degrees of fidelity, and equally as a way to demonstrate its historical credentials. In relation to the contextual impulse, Faulks' reliance on *Stoker*, as a memoir that has been shown to be unreliable, does not in itself make a detrimental ethical or literary difference to his novel, given that the imagined nature of Watt's account of his time in Birkenau feeds fittingly into another fiction. Indeed, Faulks' judgement that *Stoker* was suitable for his novelistic purposes might redouble our sense of the memoir's imaginary status.

However, even if we do not agree with Helen Dunmore's verdict that Faulks' representation of the mechanism of genocide goes 'beyond his capacity',[32] it is clear that none of Faulks' intertextual sources focuses on the SK members themselves. The topic is all-encompassing in the novel, yet also approached indirectly, by means of accounts of the experience of SOE agents in concentration camps, Russian POWs in Auschwitz and an invented Australian 'stoker'. The Jewish prisoners of the SK are only ever in the background of Faulks' novel, because that is their position in his documentary sources. He did not choose to draw upon any of the SK's own contemporary writings or any of their number's postwar testimonies. What is finally conveyed by the reliance of *A Possible Life* on *Stoker* is that it was chosen because it offers an anglophone readership a perspective on the world of the camp that matches their own. The reason that it is the only text to do so, and therefore the only one that Faulks could have chosen for the task, is because it is an impossible viewpoint.

Sue Vice is Professor of English Literature at the University of Sheffield. Her most recent publications include the coedited volume *Representing Perpetrators in Holocaust Literature and Film* (2013) with Jenni Adams, the monograph *Textual Deceptions: False Memoirs and Literary Hoaxes in the Contemporary Era* (2014) and the coauthored study *Barry Hines: 'Kes', 'Threads' and Beyond*, with David Forrest (2017). She is currently working on a study of the outtake footage for Claude Lanzmann's 1985 film *Shoah*.

Notes

1. Sebastian Faulks, *A Possible Life* (London: Vintage, 2013 [2012]), 2. All further references are by page number in the text.
2. Helen Dunmore, review, *The Guardian*, 20 September 2012.
3. Konrad Kwiet, 'Anzac and Auschwitz: The Unbelievable Story of Donald Watt', *Patterns of Prejudice* 31(4) (1997), 53–60.
4. Paul O'Shea, 'From the Manning to Majdanek: The War History of Private Ernest Maxwell Sawyer, NX1488', unpublished MA dissertation, Macquarie University 1997, 258.
5. Imperial War Museums oral history record for Denis George Avey, interview, July 2001. Retrieved 12 April 2019 from http://www.iwm.org.uk/collections/item/object/80020527. On the details of the discrepancies between the five-hour interview and the published account, see Nicholas Hellen, 'Hero of Holocaust Changed Key Elements of His Story', *Sunday Times*, 13 November 2011.
6. Russell Wallis, *British POWs and the Holocaust: Witnessing Auschwitz* (London: I.B. Tauris, 2017), 278–79. See also Tony Kushner, 'Loose Connections? Britain and the "Final Solution"', in Caroline Sharples and Olaf Jensen (eds), *Britain and the Holocaust: Remembering and Representing War and Genocide* (London: Palgrave Macmillan, 2013).
7. Kwiet, 'Anzac and Auschwitz', 52; Gideon Greif, *We Wept without Tears: Testimonies of the Jewish Sonderkommando from Auschwitz* (New Haven: Yale University Press, 2005), 82.
8. O'Shea, 'From the Manning to Majdanek', 255.
9. Roderick Bailey, *Forgotten Voices of the Secret War: An Inside History of Special Operations in the Second World War* (London: Ebury 2008), ix.
10. Ibid., ix–x.
11. Ibid., 196.
12. Ibid., x.
13. Ibid., 197.
14. Ibid., x.
15. Ibid., 299.
16. Donald Watt, *Stoker: The Story of an Australian Soldier Who Survived Auschwitz-Birkenau* (London: Simon & Schuster, 1995), 96, 103.
17. O'Shea, 'From the Manning to Majdanek', quoting Darren O'Brien.
18. Watt, *Stoker*, 96.
19. Ibid., 114–15.
20. Kwiet, 'Anzac and Auschwitz', 53.
21. Brian Woodley, 'Shadow of Doubt', *The Australian*, 29–30 March 1997.
22. Watt, *Stoker*, 109.
23. Ibid., 121.
24. Andrey Pogozhev, *Escape from Auschwitz*, trans. Vladimir Krupnik et al. (Barnsley: Pen and Sword, 2007), 126.
25. Ibid., 128.
26. O'Shea, 'From the Manning to Majdanek', 265.
27. Pogozhev, *Escape from Auschwitz*, 146.
28. Ibid., 147.
29. Ibid.
30. Ibid.

31. Ibid., 148.
32. Dunmore, review.

Bibliography

Bailey, Roderick. *Forgotten Voices of the Secret War: An Inside History of Special Operations in the Second World War*, London: Ebury, 2008.

Faulks, Sebastian. *A Possible Life*. London: Vintage, 2013 [2012].

Greif, Gideon. *We Wept without Tears: Testimonies of the Jewish Sonderkommando from Auschwitz*, New Haven: Yale University Press, 2005.

Kushner, Tony. 'Loose Connections? Britain and the "Final Solution"', in Caroline Sharples and Olaf Jensen (eds), *Britain and the Holocaust: Remembering and Representing War and Genocide*. London: Palgrave Macmillan, 2013, 51–70.

Kwiet, Konrad. 'Anzac and Auschwitz: The Unbelievable Story of Donald Watt', *Patterns of Prejudice* 31(4) (1997), 53–60.

O'Shea, Paul. 'From the Manning to Majdanek: The War History of Private Ernest Maxwell Sawyer, NX1488', unpublished MA dissertation. Macquarie University, 1997.

Pogozhev, Andrey. *Escape from Auschwitz*, trans. Vladimir Krupnik et al. Barnsley: Pen and Sword, 2007.

Wallis, Russell. *British POWs and the Holocaust: Witnessing Auschwitz*. London: I.B. Tauris, 2017.

Watt, Donald. *Stoker: The Story of an Australian Soldier Who Survived Auschwitz-Birkenau*. London: Simon & Schuster, 1995.

Chapter 15

Out of the Plan, Out of the Plane 2
Stripping, Fourth Letter to Gerhard Richter

Georges Didi-Huberman

Paris, 8th July 2016

Dear Gerhard Richter,
After paying you another visit two weeks ago, I've returned to writing these letters. I was happy to see you again – and to see you so calm – alone in your studio where new works hung on the walls, some part-finished, some still untouched. We did not speak much. You seemed almost surprised that I had so few questions to ask you. I just wanted to sound out your feelings. I did not want to burden you with questions about the meaning of a process already undertaken by your painting. In my heart, deep down, there was only one question: I just wanted to know if the figurative images of the four Sonderkommando photographs you had painted already were dry or not when you decided to switch to 'abstraction'. Did you scrape [*raclé*] the paint while it was still workable – knowing that it was a work in oil and not acrylic – or did you rather 'recoat' a painting that was already dry? You replied to me: 'Yes, dry . . .' Then, after a moment's thought, you added: 'But not fully . . .' I will try to briefly explain why, in my eyes, that detail is so important.

   Whichever it was, you understood that the issue of process was very important to me. So you went off in search of something in your library, and after looking here and there for a while, you handed me a publication that you said was not commercially available (having no publisher or logo in fact, nor a publication date): it was a book of colour photographs by

Joe Hage which documented, over a very specific period – that of his visits to your studio – the evolution of your work on the Birkenau series.[1] It was quickly apparent that this collection of photographs contributed significantly to the debate I'm exploring here: your debate with the much discussed 'subject' that some art critics have wanted to pronounce dormant but which seems to remain as necessary as it is aporetic for you. I come back then to the subject, what you commonly refer to as *Gegenstand*, the 'object' of a painting, and what an art historian would name, on the other hand, as the 'subject' as well as the 'topic' or *subject matter* of that same painting.

You have emphasized this feature for a long time: '... the essential: what is to be painted [*was zu malen ist*], the subject [*das "Thema"*]'.[2] Or alternatively: 'Appearance [*Schein*] is my life's work [*mein Lebensthema*] ... The painter sees the appearance of things and reproduces it'.[3] We would no doubt be mistaken if we deduced from such *phrases* that painting for you is reducible to 'giving the appearance' of visible things: what you say on the contrary, is that such an appearance, in its obviousness, renders the object unintelligible or incomprehensible. After what I said about *September*, I can deduce that this dual aspect makes a full-blown pictorial *trauma* of any painted *subject*, something like an obviousness which only reveals itself by way of its *dramatic* and unintelligible aspects that are characteristic of traumatic situations: '[When] the painting is finished, I then have an outcome that I perceive as if the unintelligible [*Unverständliches*] and the autonomous [*Selbständiges*] themselves are facing me'.[4]

Painting would thus to be to provide access, visually, to this 'imperceptible' obviousness which is, fundamentally, to do with *the unintelligibility of time*: 'Painting is to create an analogy for the imperceptible and the unintelligible which thereby take form and become accessible'.[5] In 1982 you said that 'the more a painting depicts an inexpressible reality, the more beautiful, clever, mad it is, the more intense, expressive and unintelligible [*irrsinniger und extremer, je anschaulicher und unverständlicher*] it is, the better it is ...' And you add that it is because of this that 'art is the ultimate form of hope' [*die Kunst ist die höchste Form von Hoffnung*].[6] This is a way for you to profess the practice of painting as the 'production of truth' [*machen eine Wahrheit*] and, at the same time, to express a radical scepticism regarding the possibility of rendering that truth clear and intelligible.[7] There is truth but it is inaccessible or it is only approachable through the form of this primary movement [*mouvement fondamental*] contained in the word 'hope'.

From such a perspective, *Birkenau* appears to be the limit case of your general recognition of images in terms of historicity, of suffering and of trauma. Suffering is not sentimentality, or not of the kind you have castigated for a long time, for example, in 1981, when you write: 'I want to obtain a content [*densité*] [*Inhaltlichkeit*] without sentimentalism [*ohne Sentimentalität*], one as humane as possible'.[8] It needs restating here that the 'dissolution of the subject' as a singular response to 'spectacular fetishism' [*fétichisme spectaculaire*] arises not just from a simplistic view of things but also from a superficial reading of Adorno, whose wonderful Hegelian phrase: 'As long as there is an awareness of suffering among human beings there must also be art as the objective form of that awareness', I reminded you of earlier.[9] But that is what you say yourself, my dear Gerhard Richter, when you state that 'art has always had a link with distress, despair, disarray'.[10] Or when you speak of 'capturing the sadness, the sympathy, the pain [and] also the fear' in your paintings.[11]

What then is the 'subject' of a painting for you? If the four Sonderkommando photographs from Birkenau are truly the subject of your *Birkenau* series, how is that the case? How do you reach that point? How, essentially, do you put this subject together and set it out for others? How does this subject *exist* because it's not *shown*, not openly in your four abstract paintings, even if it is ultimately – and very gently – laid out [*disposé*] in the way the paintings are hung, as I saw at Baden-Baden? It's simultaneously a very concrete question, a very material one, which is linked to your creative processes and to your exhibition preferences . . . and a very profound, philosophical question.

Permit me to say a few words on the philosophical dimension of this issue: although it will fittingly lead me to the soundest schema [*au plan le plus concret*] of your pictorial practice. One which nonetheless seems quite complicated. Firstly, the four photographs from 1944 were your 'object': it was as if they stood in front of you, of your horrified eyes, 'thrown before you', what, in Latin, is called *ob-jecta*. When, in German, you say *Gegenstand*, it automatically adds a conflictual quality which renders 'objects' dangerous or traumatizing things, things created from an almost hostile standpoint (*Stand*), a standpoint 'against' (*gegen*) you. There would then be, if I simply listen to your choice of words, something like a pre-existing struggle between particular objects and your decision to make them the subject of some of your paintings.

As with Hegel, perhaps, in the best cases, this *struggle* – in which desire is bound up with doubt, or rather with risk, sometimes, with revulsion – ends up being *recognized*. That which was for *oneself* is worth something only through becoming *for others*. And that's when the hostile or threatening object, that which 'issued from your eyes', became the overarching *subject* of your pictorial practice. What kind of 'subject'? A *logical* subject if we consider that your four paintings appear in public space under their 'proper name' of *Birkenau*. A *material* subject if we consider that the four images from 1944 are always 'inherent' to the grey, green or red paint that has covered them. It's not by chance that the two meanings of the word 'subject' co-exist in Aristotle, the philosopher who led us so well on the path of thinking through difficulties [*la méthode diaporématique*]. In *The Categories* and *Metaphysics*, Aristotle never ceases questioning and commenting upon the 'logical subject' and the 'inherent subject', in their interrelation.[12]

For our purposes, what we can take from these discussions would perhaps be the movement by which the 'subject' becomes identified little by little with the substance itself (what the Greeks called *ousia* that described true being and that Hegel would take up again on his own account subsequent to his impassioned reading of Aristotle).[13] But this movement is double: the more it narrows to *substance*, the more it becomes – as Pierre Aubenque says in a key work on *The Problem of Being in Aristotle* – '*ecstatic*'.[14] It's a movement of dispersal. In reality, essence or substance only becomes incarnated – in our everyday life – in contingent beings who can always become *other* than who they are. Birkenau may well have been your 'subject' but there was nothing stable or 'substantial' about it in your practice, it only came to take on a body in your paintings by way of a long series of changes, of doubts, of trials and errors, of processual branching offs [*bifurcations processuelles*].

That explains why the 'subject', albeit fundamental, is never univocal nor stable nor possessed once and for all. It endures what Aubenque named an 'essential splitting' ['scission essentielle'] (that *Spaltung* that Freud would much later observe at the heart of psychic life).[15] But Aristotle expressed this 'split in the subject' in terms that a painter such as you would understand immediately: it's nothing other than the perpetual drama between subject and form. That's why we can say that even for a 'Master of Truth' such as Aristotle, *the subject is imperfect*, even 'in the imperfect' ['à l'imparfait'], which precisely expresses the canonical expression that philosophy has retained through the term 'quiddity': being . . . is that which was (or [being is] the 'what it was to be'). In this crucial Aristotelian – and Anti-Platonic – expression, which is '*to ti ēn einai*', the infinitive time of being (*einai*) cannot be without the imperfect time (*ēn*) which divides it in two as its unconscious memory, between substance and chance, form and matter, etc.

But that's not all. If the subject is imperfect or 'in the imperfect' that does not prevent – and it is the same situation – its other fundamental 'ecstasy': *the subject is sub-jacent*. That's precisely what the Latin word we are all familiar with, the *sub-jectum*, says. Like the Greek word it is a translation of, *hypokeimenon*: thrown underneath [a thing underlying]. Always, in fact, the subject continues beneath: either in the sense of being subjugated (like when we speak of a sovereign's 'subject') or in the opposite, more interesting, sense of exercising its own independence [*souveraineté*] but from beneath the visible world. Aristotle uses the word 'subject' to indicate the most concrete meaning of being or of matter: it is that which lies (*keitai*) beneath our feet, under our noses or at the heart of our spoken words. An ambiguity, however, remains, as if, for Aristotle, the subject was the locus of an irresolvable conflict between form and matter. Something the philosopher clearly recognizes – after having proposed the conflictual or dialectical nature of the principals of all things – in the *Physics*: 'We first said that only oppositions were principles, then that it was necessary for something else to be subjacent . . . But the question of knowing whether it is the form or the substratum which is matter is not yet clear'.[16]

My dear Gerhard Richter, let's leave the philosophers to their debates on general principles, endless and moving as they are. Regarding our specific context, we both know that the four Sonderkommando photographs form the 'subject' of your *Birkenau* series. Subject-conflict? Subject-form? Subject-matter? All those things at once. And in every case, according to Aristotle's profound lesson: *imperfect subject* or 'in the imperfect' but equally *subjacent subject*. This is our new step forward, from which, inevitably, new questions will arise.

First question, why would the 'subject' of *Birkenau* be *imperfect*? Because it is anchored in a historical past that is simultaneously vanished and not foreclosed. This subject is not a 'simple past' [*passé simple*], a tense [*temps*] that one could simply use to relate the history.[17] It is 'in the imperfect': because it does not allow itself to be simply told, and because it never ceases to haunt us. It dwells in our present and continues to shape many aspects of it. It is our memory and yet one lacking clear remembrances. Because this memory is itself 'imperfect' in the same way that the four photographs – urgent, necessary, lacking, partial – which you decided to work upon are imperfect. That means your art practice itself is marked by this imperfection: you wanted and then doubted, did then undid, painted then 'unpainted' (in accordance with the act of *Vermalung* which you often claim is an integral aspect of your work). Then you remade, reshaped your desire, and shouldered your paintings.

It's in that sense that your images, your *Bilder*, are, like all images, perhaps, *Nachbilder*, or 'afterimages'. They render their 'subject' an example of deferred action, of *Nachträglichkeit* as Freud referred to it: they take on the act of 'bringing' or of 'bringing back' (*tragen*) their subject from an antecedence which, at the same time, makes them operate as acts of memory (towards a past) and stirs of desire (towards a future). All of a sudden, active, they ratify the 'blow' [*coup*] of the present, a 'blow' that had struck you in a far more muted way a long time ago.[18] Similarly to how Freud observed symptoms in psychic life, they are like tears in the present for a loss that happened a long time ago without the precise nature of the loss being established. In the present, these works form the traumatic character – obvious and unintelligible – of a memory of that past that you did not know what to do with up until then. They are then both anterior and ulterior, somewhere between the *too early* of your discovery of the images from 1944 and the *too late* of your decision, seventy years later, to paint something again afresh.

The Freudian model of deferred action enables us to define what Benjamin meant by the work of 'excavation' and memory: it's a time which, at the very moment it makes something appear, clarifies it but makes it sink back into the strata of memory.[19] It only reveals the character of the 'blow,' suddenly, by way of the unintelligible, re-covered intricacy of its structure of *afterward*. It is revelatory – like your paintings – only by showing the temporal complexity of an archaeological site. This is what Freud wrote to Wilhelm Fliess on the 6th December 1896: 'As you know, I am working on the assumption that our psychic mechanism has come into being by a process of stratification: the material present in the form of memory traces being subjected from time to time to a *rearrangement* in accordance with fresh circumstances – to a *retranscription*. Thus what is essentially new about my theory is the thesis that memory is present not once but several times over, that it is laid down in various kinds of indications'.[20] Could we not say that your paintings implement this kind of enduring work of stratifying, of revising and of rewriting signs?

Could we not, at once, understand the 'subject' in work of this kind as only thinkable by way of a dialectical process of latencies and emergences, of visible lacunae and of reversions underneath? Isn't that precisely what your lengthy work regarding the four photographs from 1944 has been? And isn't that what will open a pathway to responding to the other great question of the 'subject', that of knowing why it only essentially acts from its *subjacent* position? The object was thrown before us (*ob-jectum*): strange and hostile. It only becomes a subject by way of immersion within, beneath (*sub-jectum*): always strange but henceforth intimate. Inherent to you as a psychic being, inherent to paint as a material being. There, where Eric Santner saw a big theatre of 'stranded objects' – something we could also note of Joesph Beuys or Tacita Dean – it is something different again in your work: not landscapes of collapsed ruins but strata of buried ossuaries, to again take up the allegorical image running through Lukács, Benjamin or Adorno.[21]

The subject is not 'in the painting' – which is to say in a particularly significant iconographic detail of a painted representation – as Daniel Arasse believed.[22] It is *in the paint*, which is to say layered [*couché*], coiled in a material, underlying all the representational composition – or even abstract, as in the present case – of the picture. And, once again, it's there, all the meaning of the Balzacian story of the *unknown masterpiece*, by way of what, precisely, is in play in the 'underneath of the painting' as Hubert Damisch was able to say.[23] Namely somewhere between 'subject' and 'subjectile'.[24] This status of inherence or of subjacency is essential: it allies both the phenomenological materiality of the painting and its capacity to 'signify according to the other', from baroque allegories analysed by Benjamin to the devices of classical painting studied by Louis Marin in terms of 'deposition', a word which evokes the *hypokeimenon* of the Greek philosophers as much as the reality of burial, the entombment of a human body.[25]

How then, my dear Gerhard Richter, did you pictorially – materially and semiotically – get out of the plan [*sorti du plan*]?[26] Firstly, by taking on the *imperfect*, past, lacunary character of your 'subject': a way by which to position yourself in time and before history. Then by taking on the *underlying* [*sous-jacente*] role of this same 'subject'. Starting with an object (*Gegenstand*) which was before you, beneath your eyes, like an aporia, you thus got 'out of the outline' – but *out of the outline through the underneath*: through the inside, through the within of painting. You did not 'dissolve' your subject. Rather you formed it by 'ossifying' it, if I can put it like that, by burying it, encrypting it in the eventful material of four patches [*pans*] of non-figurative painting. Louis Marin said that 'representation buries or tries to bury time in the tomb of the artwork'.[27] You too, my dear Gerhard Richter, you too have created a tomb but of an altogether different kind: simultaneously a homage to some dead, in accordance with the poetic sense of the literary genre of the 'tomb'[28]; and as a procedure of material burying or encrypting of your subject.

This is precisely what we see in the photographs of your studio collected together by Joe Hage over a period stretching from February 2014 to January 2015. In pictures dated 1st February 2014, we first see you plunged in gloom.[29] An epidiascope projects an enlargement of one of the Sonderkommando photographs. You seem to be calmly carrying out your artistic work, going over the outlines of the image projected on white canvas with graphite. Your shadow is also clearly outlined on the canvas. This makes us think, of course, of the classical myths of the origins of painting – the daughter of the potter Dibutades tracing the contours of the shadow of her lover who was leaving for war – except that here it's an issue of death without hope and no longer of love, one of fundamental mourning and not of desire. With this gesture, are you not returning to your earliest practices of pictorial preparation? Like in 1964–1965 when you observed the following: 'Perhaps it's because the photograph leaves me inconsolable, because it vegetates, leads a pitiful existence despite being a complete image, that I want to highlight it, valorise it, make it (even if what I make is worse). Make without understanding or thinking or reasoning. I never stop painting photos because I never uncover their secret and because the only way to copy them is to paint them and that excites me, to give myself over to something which I have so little hold over'.[30]

This photograph of your work – graphic – on a projected photograph is quite fascinating. It mixes your shadow from 2014 with the shadows of a document from 1944, as if your paintings of *Birkenau* had night – but also a simple ray of light in the midst of obscurity – as their initial matrix. That said, the results of this first work completely invert the values of the initial setting: once finished and illuminated, the drawings, in contrast with the large masses of shadow in the initial document, only provide a vision of a few fragile lines on still completely white canvases.[31] Neither paintbrushes nor colours have yet intervened. Yet the energy of your lines already has something eminently pictorial about it. The two drawings of the forest, photographed on the 25th July 2014, foreground an intensity and a particular dynamism, even if only by way of your graphic elimination of contrasts between masses of shadow and luminous overexposures, which the documents which were your starting point manifested in an entirely different way. As for the strategic zone of the women running in the forest – and it was that, above all, that the member of the Sonderkommando wanted to bring to the attention of the outside world – you have treated it differently to all the rest, as if it had to be isolated in an unsettled aura of greyness and of terror.

It's at the end of July 2014 that the first use of colours – blacks, greys – really came to transform the Sonderkommando photographs into paintings worthy of the name.[32] Yet it required a period of roughly six months for the graphic treatment of the images, such as we see in the photograph from February 2014, to be taken up in a more specifically pictorial way. On 25th July, we see, for instance, how – using brushstrokes of black and grey – you have tried to visually render the smoke which surrounds the human bodies and will disappear in the foliage of the trees in the background. At this moment, we can discern an entire inventory of formal solutions – or, rather, hypotheses – in the picture, which go from simple line to blur and from white reserve to an almost formless conglomeration of coloured brushstrokes.

It's then that a striking gap arises in Joe Hage's collection of photographs.³³ Between the 25th July and the 14th August, suddenly everything has changed. In reality, it is during this time lapse – with nobody watching you – that you *recovered the images* you had painted, at the calculated risk of losing everything, of destroying it all, foregrounding a symphony of red and green paint where, little by little, grey intervened, initially discreetly then more and more forcefully.³⁴ Between 14th August and 15th September, a new pictorial calamity seems to arise: it is as if you once again *contradict everything by obscuring* your paintings where, from now on, black and grey along with some irregular passages of white become dominant, leaving perceptible, nevertheless, vestiges of the earlier work with red and green.³⁵ On the 5th September 2014, a photograph captured the brief instant of literal chance when a black butterfly spotted with yellow landed on the surface of one of your four paintings.³⁶

From this moment, the *Birkenau* series seems finished (but I know you put your hand to it again, here and there, later), exhibited silently in your impeccably clean studio.³⁷ Anyhow, already, on the 19th September, the photographic work on the abstract oeuvres took over: the 'details' which would soon come to comprise *Birkenau* are arranged on a big table in front of the paintings themselves, as if to replay the dialectic table-painting [*table-tableau*] which has long linked your photographic *Atlas* with your painted works.³⁸ A series of photographic 'details' sampled from the four paintings will follow, integral to what you have named their *Fotoversion*.³⁹ A few images at the end of the collection show your large scale photographic proofs – exactly the same as that of the paintings – taped to the frames and, because of this, giving the 'organised' impression that the painting has moulted by itself, like a skin in profile born as an outgrowth from the canvas itself.⁴⁰

Over a year ago you wrote to me that if your *Birkenau* paintings were really 'finished', you remained nevertheless profoundly 'involved in the subject'. But were you not also saying, more fundamentally, that the *subject remains involved in your painting*, whatever the procedures of 'abstraction'? There are undoubtedly many ways to make abstract painting with a view to 'desubjectivising' it: it's a powerful motivation of formalist criticism and it's the lesson that Benjamin Buchloh wanted to trace back to you from the beginning. It's nonetheless not what you do. The 'power of the negative' central to your painting is not a formalist *tabula rasa* of the subject. So, how does this subject happen, how does it involve itself in your great morphologies of destruction? On the plane of meaning, it involves itself or implies itself as *allegory* (in the sense that I have tried to restore to this word, following Benjamin: exegesis and expression, 'deserted image', allegorical documentary).

And on the plane of the pictorial materials? Well, it is encysting [*enkystement*], encryption, putting to the bottom. You redrew and then painted the photographic images from Birkenau, which had been enlarged by projection, on the surface of your white paintings. Then you encysted or encrypted them in conflictual movements of red, green and grey paint (I think there are even other colours in play in this whole process). You did not 'dissolve' anything in doing this: to the contrary, you put your *subject* in a position of *sub-jection*, of *sub-jacency*, of *hypokeimenon*. You therefore preserved, *deposited* your subject in the bed of your painting, in the same way as we speak of a riverbed or of a funerary bed upon which some recumbent figure lies in their sarcophagus.[41]

What then, consequently, is the work of the negative in your four paintings? In the sense that the 'abstract' painting is made to become a *mould* in relation to the initial painted images of Birkenau. That's why you waited, as much as possible, for the paint to dry before coating it (and if the paint was not completely dry, this implies that the painted images of Birkenau had to show through [*transparaître*], even if imperceptibly, by way of a porosity in the thickness of your abstract painting. And from that time on we are before these paintings as if before an operation of *imprinting* of which the internal process, by definition, escapes us – and also escaped you – thus, as Gilbert Simondon noted in his beautiful description of what happens, and what exceeds us [*ce qui se passe, et nous dépasse*] in a moulding: 'The perspective of the man who works is still far too removed from the taking on of form, which is technique in and of itself. You would have to enter the mould with the clay, be both mould and clay, live and feel their shared process to be able to comprehend the taking on of form in itself. . . . [The artisan] puts the clay in the mould and the press; but it's the *setup* constituted by the mould and the pressed clay which is conditional for the taking on of form; it's the clay that takes form by virtue of the mould, not the worker who gives it form. The man who works prepares the intermediation [*la médiation*] but he does not accomplish it: the going between accomplishes itself by itself after the conditions have been produced; even though the man is very close to this process, he does not know it; his body pushes it to happen, permits it to happen, but the representation of the technical operation does not appear in the work. The essence is missing, the active centre of the technical operation remains veiled'.[42]

So it's plainly as *underlay* [*sous-jacent*] that you laid down – affirmed in one sense, deposited in another – as your *subject*. By doing this, you maintained it in its fundamental inaccessibility: an inaccessibility which is not a beyond, not transcendental (as the metaphysicians of the Shoah would like it to be) but, very precisely, below, immanent, *just beneath our ability to see it clearly*. You yourself, you can no longer see your subject: by covering it, you only show the rhythmic screed [*la chappe rythmique*] of coloured material which forms the mould. That is how you make your subject what it most essentially should be: imperfect and underlying. Now, by this procedure – which is material – you give the idea of *form* its most radical consistency, which is that of *negative form*: which is to say the mould, as we still hear it in the Italian word *formaggio*, for instance, namely the cheese as hardened milk, dried into a gouged 'form', this receptacle capable of the broadest processual and aesthetic virtues.[43]

Finally, you successfully left the plane behind [*vous êtes bien sorti du plan*]. But by way of the interior, the within: by the subjacency of the subject. The movement of *ana*, from which the word *anamnesis* derives, now takes on all its dimensions, all the richness of the Greek language: *in climbing back* towards the past (here by way of the images of Birkenau), then by proceeding *through* the pictorial matter (here within the pictorial process), as would an archaeologist through his field of excavation.[44] The psychoanalysts Nicolas Abraham and Maria Torok have, perhaps, best discussed this movement when rethinking the notion of anamnesis by way of the correlative ideas of anti-semantics [*l'antisémantisme*] – in summary, they say that thinking about the subject is nothing other than foregrounding its inaccessibility, a way to put in doubt all unilateral judgements regarding it: it's the very ethic of psychoanalysis – and, above all, of *anasemia* [*l'anasémie*].[45] What is anasemia? It's the dual unity, in all psychic subjects, of the 'shell' and the 'kernel'. The kernel is 'introjected', encysted, placed in a crypt: this relates particularly to obvious processes of mourning and melancholia.[46] Nicolas Abraham stated that it is to create a psychic spectre and to guarantee the 'communication of the unconscious from one generation to another' at one and the same time.[47] Isn't that precisely what you are doing by exhibiting your pictorial and photographic series of *Birkenau*?

But the strangest thing about this process of 'anasemia' is expressed by way of what Nicolas Abraham perceives to be the *dialectic of the shell and the kernel*. To think through this dialectic would be to 'highlight the existence of discontinuities and confusions in the shell of vocables [but it should also be said, of images]'.[48] A way to redefine what folk psychology calls *what you feel in your heart of hearts* [*for intérieur*] from the standpoint – well glossed by Jacques Derrida – of an 'excluded outside on the inside'.[49] I would say then that if the exhibition of your paintings in Dresden was dedicated to your artistic 'heart of hearts' in the unstudied sense of the term (you, faced with yourself), then that of Baden-Baden opened this 'heart of hearts' towards a far more fruitful meaning: that of your response to – or your responsibility towards – certain ghosts of European history.

Could the word *rind* [*écorce*] ultimately name this strange relation that your paintings (*Birkenau*, 2014) have to their subject-matter (Birkenau, 1944)? Could this be the relation of the four big pieces of rind to their common core? Strange return of things, or alternatively the effect, after the fact, of a sort of originary scene which would undoubtedly have conditioned the very direction of my questioning: the first day that I came to see you in Cologne, in December 2013, I wanted to give you, in its German translation, a little book about Birkenau entitled *Écorces* [*Barks*].[50] You thanked me, saying at the same time that you already had the book and had already read it. Why did I speak of barks in relation to Birkenau? Because the bark of the birches of *Birkenwald* are omnipresent, of course, but, more importantly, to try to construct a 'thought picture' relating to an *anamnesis* of place and of time which would also be *anasemia*: its subject residing inherently in the still visible surfaces even if it is henceforth unobjectifiable, indecipherable as such because fallen into the beneath. The life of the surface having encysted its kernel without, for all that, revoking it, repressing it, dissolving it, or forgetting it.

Confronted by your paintings of the *Birkenau* series, I find something of the insight of *Écorces*: an encrypted subject, nonetheless attached, inherent, subjacent to the very matter of the visible. Like the flesh underlies the skin, not clearly exposed but inseparable from it. Like the flesh that appears through symptoms – the pains, the wounds – on the surface. Here then, *painting becomes a shell of the subject*. The burying and 'scraping' of the figurative images certainly generates the 'discontinuities' and 'entanglements' that Nicolas Abraham spoke of in relation to the psychic shell: morphologies of destruction, scars of never forgotten wounds. This shell is afterlife (*Nachleben*) as well as survival (*Überleben*): paradoxical life, yet obstinate life, life in spite of all. The distance between it and the kernel is ultrathin, and yet already a field of tensions and possibilities opens up. It produces an eerie feeling, one of non-recognition: where have the four photographs of the Sonderkommando from Birkenau gone in the *Birkenau* paintings? And yet the kernel – the subject – dwells just beneath, right next to us. *Implied*, as you put it so well.

It's as if the act of scraping that you hold dear, by way of its violence, had made both the wound and its scar. Which, ultimately, is to say: its crust, with its memory of the blows, the accidents, its bas-relief rough edges which have become stratified like so much scar tissue. Living surfaces upon which the labour of death is written. It's as if, reciprocally, from inside, the encysted kernel never ceased to push the shell into the foreground. From this perspective, the *Birkenau* series seems like a novel experiment – for you, who has never stopped making variants – regarding the paradoxical power of painting. Paradoxical because of the crossover of the intrinsic and the extrinsic, of pictorial matter and of historical matters, of visible forms and psychic shifts: in short, of shells and kernels. Cannot the whole exploration of relations between painting and photography, so crucial in your work, be brought out by this dialectic between the shell and the kernel?

If the recovery of figurative images through a lengthy process of abstract morphogenesis was able to turn your paintings into images (*Bilder*) thought of as 'afterimages' (*Nachbilder*), what do we make, to conclude, of the *photographic excrescences* which made of *Birkenau* something more than a group of four paintings? I'm struck by the fact that hardly had the paintings been finished than the photographic montage began. Joe Hage's book is there to show how the two undertakings are contemporaneous and solidary: the *worktable* [*table*] of photographic details positioned against the *artwork* [*tableau*] is then perceivable as a collection of biological sloughs.[51] It's as if new dermises were dropping from the *skin-picture* [*l'écorce-tableau*], new pellicles, new skin-photos [*écorces-photos*]. A phenomena rendered even more spectacularly in the final illustrations in the collection: the photographic paper laid against the canvas itself forms nothing less than a big outgrowth in relief, like a rind [*écorce*].[52]

I'm not surprised that Friedel wanted to use your excellent series from 1978, the *128 Fotos von einem Bild*, in the Baden-Baden exhibition.[53] In this series, haven't you looked at your singular pictorial 'image' from the angle of its innumerable scraps of rind? And these bits of rind were they not simultaneously ruins (a process of destruction) and scars (a life process arising from destruction)? Cannot the same be said – putting the artistic process to one side – of a simple scrap of bark photographed at Birkenau? At the level of planning [*le plan pictural*], don't your *Birkenau* paintings have something to do with this process: stripping [*écorcement*].[54]

Here then, my dear Gerhard Richter, the question with which I began has shifted slightly, even if our shared *Skepsis* towards what answer to give, in order to finish up, remains. The aporia of the subject that motivated your desire to paint these four pictures, does it persist still in the *Birkenau* series? Don't we need, however, to rephrase the question in these terms: how has the kernel of the subject 'survived' in the shell of your paintings?
Translated by Nicholas Chare and Dominic Williams

Georges Didi-Huberman is a philosopher and art historian based in Paris, where he teaches at the École des Hautes Études en Sciences Sociales. Recipient of the 2015 Adorno Prize, he is the author of more than fifty books on the history and theory of images, including *Images in Spite of All:*

Four Photographs from Auschwitz (2003); *The Surviving Image: Phantoms of Time and Time of Phantoms: Aby Warburg's History of Art* (2016); and *Bark* (2017).

Notes

1. Joe Hage, *Making the Birkenau Paintings*, n.p., undated, c. 2016.
2. Gerhard Richter, 'Notizen 1985', in Dietmar Elger and Hans-Ulrich Obrist (eds), *Text 1961 bis 2007: Schriften, Interviews, Briefe* (Cologne: Verlag der Buchhandlung Walther König, 2008), 142. Translator's note: this collection of essays has been translated into English as *Gerhard Richter – Text: Writings, Interviews and Letters, 1961–2007* (London: Thames & Hudson, 2009). The translation of this note by Richter can be found on 141.
3. Gerhard Richter, 'Notizen 1989', in *Text 1961 bis 2007*, 223 (215 in the English translation).
4. Gerhard Richter, 'Interview mit Wolfgang Pehnt' (1984), in *Text 1961 bis 2007*, 136 (also 136 in the English translation).
5. Gerhard Richter, 'Notizen 1981', in *Text 1961 bis 2007*, 120 (also 120 in the English translation).
6. Gerhard Richter, 'Text für Katalog Documenta 7' (1982), in *Text 1961 bis 2007*, 121 (also 121 in the English translation).
7. Gerhard Richter, 'Notizen 1962', in *Text 1961 bis 2007*, 15 (also 15 in the English translation).
8. Richter, 'Notizen 1981', in *Text 1961 bis 2007*, 119 (also 119 in the English translation).
9. Theodor W. Adorno, *Métaphysique: Concept et problèmes*, trans. Christophe David (Paris: Payot & Rivages, 2006 [1965]), 165. Translator's note: this work was translated into English as Theodor W. Adorno, *Metaphysics: Concepts and Problems*, trans. Edmund Jephcott (Stanford: Stanford University Press, 2000).
10. Gerhard Richter, 'Notizen 1983', in *Text 1961 bis 2007*, 129 (also 129 in the English translation).
11. Gerhard Richter, 'Gespräch mit Jan Thorn-Prikker über den Zyklus 18. *Oktober 1977*' (1989), in *Text 1961 bis 2007*, 245 (236 in the English translation).
12. Aristotle, *Catégories*, 1b, *Œuvres complètes*, ed. and trans. Pierre Pellegrin (Paris: Flammarion, 2014), 32; Aristotle, *Métaphysique*, 1024b, *Œuvres complètes*, ed. and trans. Pierre Pellegrin (Paris: Flammarion, 2014), 1825. See Jean-Marie Le Blond, *Logique et méthode chez Aristote: Étude sur la recherche des principes de la physique aristotélicienne* (Paris: Vrin, 1973 [1939]), 374–83; Paul Ricœur, *Être, essence et substance chez Platon et Aristote: Cours professé à l'université de Strasbourg (1953–1954)*, ed. Jean-Luis Schlegel (Paris: Éditions du Seuil, 2011), 271–92.
13. See Gilbert Gérard, 'Hegel, lecteur de la métaphysique d'Aristote : La substance en tant que sujet', *Revue de métaphysique et de morale* 74 (2012), 195–223.
14. Pierre Aubenque, *Le problème de l'être chez Aristote : Essai sur la problématique aristotélicienne* (Paris: PUF, 1972 [1962]), 456.
15. Ibid., 456–84.
16. Aristotle, *Physique*, 191a, *Œuvres complètes*, 530. See also Aristotle, *De la génération à la corruption*, 320a, *Œuvres complètes*, 816.

17. Translator's note: Didi-Huberman is playing with the dual sense of the word *temps* here, which means both 'time' and 'tense' in French.
18. Translator's note: Didi-Huberman is punning on the French translation of Nachträglichkeit as *après-coup*.
19. Translator's note: see Walter Benjamin's 1932 essay, 'Excavation and Memory', in Benjamin *Selected Writings, Volume 2*, Marcus Paul Bullock, Michael William Jennings, Howard Eiland and Gary Smith (eds) (Cambridge, MA: Belknap Press, 2005), 576.
20. Sigmund Freud, *The Complete Letters of Sigmund Freud and Wilhelm Fliess, 1887–1904*, ed. and trans. Jeffrey Moussaieff Masson (Cambridge, MA: Belknap Press, 1985), 207. See also Jean Laplanche, *Problématiques, VI: L'après-coup* (Paris: PUF, 2006), 56–87. Translator's note: the letter is dated 6th December 1896.
21. Eric L. Santner, *Stranded Objects: Mourning, Memory, and Film in Postwar Germany* (Ithaca: Cornell University Press, 1990).
22. Daniel Arasse, *Le sujet dans le tableau : Essai d'iconographie analytique* (Paris: Flammarion, 1997).
23. Hubert Damisch, *Fenêtre jaune cadmium, ou les dessous de la peinture* (Paris: Éditions du Seuil, 1984), 9–45.
24. Georges Didi-Huberman, *La peinture incarnée* (Paris: Les Éditions de Minuit, 1985), 38–40. Jacques Derrida, 'Forcener le subjectile', in *Antonin Artaud: Dessins et portraits* (Paris: Gallimard, 1986), 55–59. Translator's note: the word *subjectile* is used in French art criticism and theory to refer to the surface upon which a layer of paint is applied. It forms a support. Derrida writes of the subjectile as '[b]etween the beneath and the above, it is at once a support and a surface'. Jacques Derrida, *The Secret Art of Antonin Artaud*, trans. Mary Ann Caws (Cambridge, MA: MIT Press, 1998), 64.
25. Louis Marin, 'Le tombeau du sujet en peinture', in *De la représentation* (Paris: Gallimard/Éditions du Seuil, 1994), 267–81. Translator's note: this collection of Marin's essays was published in English translation as *On Representation*, trans. Catherine Porter (Stanford: Stanford University Press, 2002).
26. Translator's note: the word *plan* has multiple meanings in French, including 'plan' or 'outline' and also 'plane', as in picture plane.
27. Louis Marin, 'Déposition du temps dans la représentation peinte', in *De la représentation* (Paris: Gallimard/Éditions du Seuil, 1994), 282.
28. Translator's note: Didi-Huberman is making reference to 'Le tombeau poétique', a literary genre that can be traced back to Classical Greek epitaphs and is bound up with honouring the dead. This genre is not to be confused with the literary output of the Graveyard Poets, which might be more familiar to an anglophone reader.
29. Hage, *Making the Birkenau Paintings*, 15–28.
30. Gerhard Richter, 'Notizen, 1964–1965', in *Text 1961 bis 2007*, 31 (also 31 in the English translation).
31. Hage, *Making the Birkenau Paintings*, 29–40.
32. Ibid., 41–70.
33. Ibid., 70–71.
34. Ibid., 71–124. Translator's note: Didi-Huberman writes that Richter 'avez *recouvert les images* peintes'. Recouvrir means to coat, cover or re-cover. It is proximate to the word 'recouvrer', which means 'recover'.
35. Ibid., 125–36.
36. Ibid., 137.
37. Ibid., 138.
38. Ibid., 140–63.

39. Ibid., 164–209.
40. Ibid., 210–13.
41. Translator's note: Sarcophagi in Western Europe in the Middle Ages and Renaissance frequently featured recumbent sculpted figures also known as recumbent effigies.
42. Georges Simondon, *Du mode d'existence des objets techniques* (Paris: Aubier-Montaigne, 1969), 243.
43. See Georges Didi-Huberman (ed.), *L'Empreinte* (Paris: Éditions du Centre Georges Pompidou, 1997), 15–192. Reprinted in Georges Didi-Huberman, *La Ressemblence par contact : Archéologie, anachronisme et modernité de l'empreinte* (Paris: Les Éditions de Minuit, 2008).
44. Translator's note: the Ancient Greek prefix *ana* (ἄνἄ) translates as 'up' and as a prefix can mean upwards and also backwards. Didi-Huberman is exploiting its rich semantics here.
45. Nicolas Abraham, 'L'écorce et le noyau' (1968), in *L'écorce et le noyau* (Paris: Flammarion, 1987), 209-211. Translator's note: anti-semantics forms one of the linguistic mechanisms identified by Abraham and Torok as capable of disrupting language's powers of expression or representation. See Nicholas Rand's 'Editor's Note', in Abraham and Torok, *The Shell and the Kernel*, 105.
46. Nicolas Abraham and Maria Torok, 'Deuil *ou* mélancolie: Introjecter – incorporer' (1972), in *L'écorce et le noyau*, 259–75.
47. Nicolas Abraham, 'Note du séminaire sur l'unité duelle et le fantôme' (1974–75), in *L'écorce et le noyau*, 411.
48. Nicolas Abraham, 'L'écorce et le noyau' (1968), in *L'écorce et le noyau*, 226.
49. Jacques Derrida, 'Fors: Les mots anglés de Nicolas Abraham et Maria Torok', in Nicolas Abraham and Maria Torok, *Cryptonomie : Le verbier de l'Homme aux loups* (Paris: Aubier-Flammarion, 1999 [1976]), 13. Translator's note: the term 'for intérieur' in French refers to a judgement of conscience in contrast to a 'for extérieur' or a judgement linked to apparatuses of human justice; in ecclesiastical law, *for* refers to 'legal authority'.
50. Georges Didi-Huberman, *Écorces* (Paris: Les Éditions de Minuit, 2011). Translator's note: the word *écorce* has multiple connotations which Didi-Huberman exploits in his book of that name and in this letter to Richter. *Écorce* can describe the bark of a tree, the peel or rind of a fruit and, figuratively, the outward appearance or semblance of something. Etymologically, the word also refers to skin.
51. Hage, *Making the Birkenau Paintings*, 140–63.
52. Ibid., 210–13.
53. Gerhard Richter, *Gerhard Richter: 128 Fotos von einem Bild (WVZ 432-5)* (Cologne: Verlag der Buchhandlung Walther König, 1998 [1978]). See Helmut Friedel (ed.), *Gerhard Richter, Birkenau* (Cologne: Verlag der Buchhandlung Walther König, 2016), 16.
54. Translator's note: the word *écorcement* refers to the action of stripping bark from a tree, but can also describe the flaying of skin from a body.

Bibliography

Abraham, Nicolas. 'L'écorce et le noyau' (1968), in Nicolas Abraham and Maria Torok, *L'écorce et le noyau*. Paris: Flammarion, 1987, 203–26.
Abraham, Nicolas, and Maria Torok. 'Deuil *ou* mélancolie: Introjecter – incorporer' (1972), in *L'écorce et le noyau*. Paris: Flammarion, 1987, 259–75.
Adorno, Theodor W. *Métaphysique: Concept et problèmes* (1965), trans. Christophe David. Paris: Payot & Rivages, 2006.
——. *Metaphysics: Concepts and Problems*, trans. Edmund Jephcott. Stanford: Stanford University Press, 2000.
Arasse, Daniel. *Le sujet dans le tableau: Essai d'iconographie analytique*. Paris: Flammarion, 1997.
Aristotle. *Catégories*, 1b, *Œuvres completes*, ed. and trans. Pierre Pellegrin. Paris: Flammarion, 2014.
Aubenque, Pierre. *Le problème de l'être chez Aristote : Essai sur la problématique aristotélicienne*. Paris: PUF, 1972 [1962].
Benjamin, Walter. 'Excavation and Memory', in Walter Benjamin, *Selected Writings, Volume 2*, ed. Marcus Paul Bullock, Michael William Jennings, Howard Eiland and Gary Smith. Cambridge, MA: Belknap Press, 2005, 576.
Hubert Damisch. *Fenêtre jaune cadmium, ou les dessous de la peinture*. Paris: Éditions du Seuil, 1984.
Derrida, Jacques. 'Forcener le subjectile', in *Antonin Artaud: Dessins et portraits*. Paris: Gallimard, 1986, 55–59.
——. *The Secret Art of Antonin Artaud*, trans. Mary Ann Caws. Cambridge, MA: MIT Press, 1998.
——. 'Fors: Les mots anglés de Nicolas Abraham et Maria Torok', in Nicolas Abraham and Maria Torok, *Cryptonomie: Le verbier de l'Homme aux loup*s. Paris: Aubier-Flammarion, 1999 [1976], 7–73.
Didi-Huberman, Georges. *La peinture incarnée*. Paris: Les Éditions de Minuit, 1985.
——. (ed.). *L'Empreinte*. Paris: Éditions du Centre Georges Pompidou, 1997.
——. *La Ressemblence par contact: Archéologie, anachronisme et modernité de l'empreinte*. Paris: Les Éditions de Minuit, 2008.
——. *Écorces*. Paris: Les Éditions de Minuit, 2011.
Freud, Sigmund. *The Complete Letters of Sigmund Freud and Wilhelm Fliess, 1887–1904*, ed. and trans. Jeffrey Moussaieff Masson. Cambridge, MA: Belknap Press, 1985.
Friedel, Helmut. (ed.). *Gerhard Richter, Birkenau*. Cologne: Verlag der Buchhandlung Walther König, 2016.
Gérard, Gilbert. 'Hegel, lecteur de la métaphysique d'Aristote: La substance en tant que sujet', *Revue de métaphysique et de morale* 74 (2012), 195–223.
Hage, Joe. *Making the Birkenau Paintings*, n.p., undated, c. 2016.
Laplanche, Jean. *Problématiques, VI: L'après-coup*. Paris: PUF, 2006.
Le Blond, Jean-Marie. *Logique et méthode chez Aristote : Étude sur la recherche des principes de la physique aristotélicienne*. Paris: Vrin, 1973 [1939].
Marin, Louis. 'Déposition du temps dans la représentation peinte', in *De la représentation*. Paris: Gallimard/Éditions du Seuil, 1994, 282–300.
——. 'Le tombeau du sujet en peinture', in *De la représentation*. Paris: Gallimard/Éditions du Seuil, 1994, 267–81.
——. *On Representation*, trans. Catherine Porter. Stanford: Stanford University Press, 2002.

Rand, Nicholas. T. 'Introduction', in Nicolas Abraham and Maria Torok, *The Shell and the Kernel Volume 1*, trans. Nicholas T. Rand. Chicago: University of Chicago Press, 1994, 1–22.

Richter, Gerhard. *Gerhard Richter: 128 Fotos von einem Bild (WVZ 432-5)*. Cologne: Verlag der Buchhandlung Walther König, 1998 [1978].

———. *Text 1961 bis 2007: Schriften, Interviews, Briefe*, ed. Dietmar Elger and Hans-Ulrich Obrist. Cologne: Verlag der Buchhandlung Walther König, 2008.

———. *Text: Writings, Interviews and Letters, 1961–2007*. London: Thames & Hudson, 2009.

Ricœur, Paul. *Être, essence et substance chez Platon et Aristote : Cours professé à l'université de Strasbourg (1953–1954)*, ed. Jean-Luis Schlegel. Paris: Éditions du Seuil, 2011.

Santner, Eric L. *Stranded Objects: Mourning, Memory, and Film in Postwar Germany*. Ithaca: Cornell University Press, 1990.

Simondon, Georges. *Du mode d'existence des objets techniques*. Paris: Aubier-Montaigne, 1969.

Chapter 16

Greeks in the Birkenau Sonderkommando

Representation and Reality

Steven Bowman

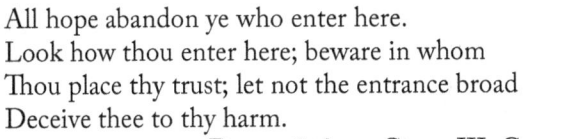

All hope abandon ye who enter here.
Look how thou enter here; beware in whom
Thou place thy trust; let not the entrance broad
Deceive thee to thy harm.
—Dante, *Inferno*, Canto III, Canto V

FIRE. Satan's soothing bathwater. Emblem of Hell. Instrument of Mass destruction. Fire devoured everything in its path without concern
For value or worth.
—Harlan Corbin, *Play Dead*

It was hell on earth. If there is a hell after death, I think it must look like that. It was hell, real hell ... Cremations took place every day. Day and night they burned the bodies of Jews there. The furnaces burned day and night, and we always had to clean up the crematorium and the cremation facilities.
—Eliezer Eisenschmidt in Gideon Greif, *We Wept without Tears*

The story of Greek Jews in the Birkenau Sonderkommando (SK) and their role in the uprising of October 1944 has been shrouded in mystery among survivors and historians for nearly seventy years. It is time to examine both the confusion and the sources that might enable us to shed some light and restore accuracy to the memory of this heroic episode of the Shoah, in the face of this two-generation-old neglect and confusion.

The following examination will compare the early sources on the SK with Greek sources in various interview and written accounts. It will show the various ways in which Greeks carried out acts of resistance. And finally it will discuss the various accounts of the SK uprising, showing how the Greek sources add new insights into this epic event that, despite its failure and disastrous conclusion, was unique during the period of the Shoah.

The earliest scholarly mention of the SK uprising was by Philip Friedman in several articles in 1946 and 1947.[1] He dates the revolt to September 1944, a not egregious error since that is the date that most Greek survivors and others cite (see below). Otherwise, his brief summary of the event and its aftermath, although lacking in details, is fairly accurate and a reflection of the interviews and reports at his disposal.[2] Another contemporary brief account is by Pery Broad, a 20–21-year-old guard who first served at Auschwitz and later at the Politische Abteilung. In 1959 he was arrested and in 1965 he was sentenced to four years in prison, which included his time under investigated detention.[3]

A more important description of the SK was written as part of the autobiography of Rudolf Höss, which he wrote during his imprisonment in January and February 1947; he was executed by the Polish authorities in April 1947 following his trial in March.[4] These observations can be supplemented by the surviving documents and interviews with SK slaves, which will be discussed below. I will mainly discuss the Greek materials since the other documents are treated in specific chapters in this volume. Though Höss was commandant of Auschwitz from May 1940 to December 1943 and again briefly in May and June 1944, his authenticated autobiography represents the report of an experienced administrator and, for our purposes, a detailed description of the men drafted into the SK during that period.[5] Despite its shortcomings (see below), it clarifies the process that contributed to the efficiency of the mass murder process:

> The eager help given by the Special Detachment in encouraging them to undress and in conducting them into the gas chambers was most remarkable.[6]
>
> ... They carried out all these tasks with a callous indifference as though it were all part of an ordinary day's work. While they dragged the corpses

about, they ate or they smoked. They did not stop eating even when engaged in the grisly job of burning corpses which had been lying for some time in mass graves[7] . . . Were [they] really able to hide . . . emotions so completely, or had [they] become too *brutalized* to care . . .

Notwithstanding Höss' emphasis on *eager help* and *callous indifference*, the actual attitude of the SK men was based on two complementary principles: one was the absolute discipline imposed by SS weapons that killed any dissent immediately; the other was the attempt by the slaves *to spare the victims any undue terror at their imminent fate*. Both of these modes of coping were totally incomprehensible to the Nazi operators, as attested by Höss' observations.

There also substantial commentary on the historiography of the SK by victims and researchers. We noted Philip Friedman among the latter, to whom we should add Ber (and Esther) Mark, who summarized written and oral reports, primarily those of non-Greek sources.[8] Yisrael Gutman, a survivor of several concentration camps, including Auschwitz, left several studies on his experiences and research, but emphasized the role of the Yiddish sources with which he was more familiar. Once I asked Gutman about the Greek role in the SK revolt and he dismissed its importance. Ben too reports that in his Hebrew *Anashim va'efer: Sefer Auschwitz-Birkenau*, Gutman recorded that the claim that the revolt was prepared and executed by Greek Jews, former officers in the Greek army, was 'an unreasonable opinion'.[9] Most of the studies on the SK rely on memoirs and interviews by Ashkenazi Jews. Reuben Ainsztein's *Jewish Resistance in Nazi-Occupied Eastern Europe* has a long and detailed account of the revolt with no mention of Greeks.[10] Fictional and film representations of the topic also pay scant attention to the Greek experience. The Greeks are totally absent from the film *The Grey Zone* (2001) and they are represented by only a cringing rabbi in *Son of Saul* (2015).[11] *Triumph of the Spirit* (1989) is the only film to date that captures a slice of the Greek experience in Auschwitz-Birkenau and stresses their role in the uprising of 7 October 1944.

The Greek experience lasted for about two years, from the spring of 1943 to the spring of 1945 (plus the Greeks of France deported in November 1942). Several Hebrew volumes on the Greek experience have been most informative, including the Hebrew version of Ber Mark's book, which was the basis for several chapters in Joseph Ben's *Greek Jewry in the Holocaust and the Resistance 1941–1944*, and David Recanati's two edited volumes comprising *Zichron Saloniki* and the edited volume *Salonik, 'Ir ve-em beyisrael*.[12] The classic study is the Hebrew version of Molho-Nehama, *In Memoriam* of 1948, which was revised and expanded in 1965 as *Shoat Yehudei Yavan 1941–1944*.[13] And from Greece, there is a photographic essay, including memoirs of the Auschwitz experience, *Greeks in Auschwitz-Birkenau* by Photini Tomai.[14] See also my *Jewish Resistance in Wartime Greece* and *The Agony of Greek Jews, 1940–1945*.[15] Greek participation has been treated more recently in English by Yitzhak Kerem in 'The Role of Greek Jews in the Sonderkommando Revolt in Birkenau' in the edited volume *Remembering for the Future: Armenia, Auschwitz and Beyond*.[16] Kerem's account is based on a wide variety of interviews with Greek SK survivors. In Hebrew, Gideon Greif and Itamar Levin's *Revolt in Auschwitz* provides a comprehensive summary based mainly on Greif's earlier interviews with SK survivors, including Greeks.[17]

A growing number of memoirs of the Greek experience during the Holocaust have appeared and especially of the eleven Greek SK survivors whom Recanati interviewed for his Hebrew *Memorbuch*. Eight Greek survivors are listed here: Daniel Bennahmias, Marcel Nadjary, Leon Cohen, Shlomo Venezia, Josef Sackar, Yaakov Gabai, Shaul Chazan and Mois Mizrahi, and several other non-Greek survivors (Abraham and Shlomo Dragon, Eliezer Eisenschmidt and Yaakov Silberberg) (interviewed by Greif).[18] The following is a partial reconstruction of the SK experience drawn from the memoirs listed above.

Jacob Maestro opined that the Greek men of the SK had two choices: suicide or rebellion. Only two chose the first option. Others, such as Joseph Baruch, already a hero of the Greek resistance (who found the gassed bodies of his parents and that of his good friend Yomtov Yakoel), vowed vengeance and planned a revolt with the Polish Oberkapo Jakub Kamiński, a former army officer.[19] Some were obsessed with the necessity to survive in order to bear witness to the slaughter of the masses of Jews who passed through the gas chambers and crematoria. Some of the feelings of these men were recorded in the memoirs of the handful of survivors listed above. How could decent young men survive the shock of the first experiences of the SK, witnessing the sight of thousands (averaging 2,000–3,000) of gassed corpses that tumbled out of the crematoria and the shock of the various tasks they were condemned to perform: aiding at first their own families and friends to undress and to enter the gas chamber, bundling the clothes and glasses and other remnants of the victim, cleaning the gas chambers of the fluids and waste left behind by the victims, separating with special tools (canes and rakes) the tangled corpses and pulling them out by belts, dragging the lifeless bodies across the floor to the elevator, stripping the corpses of hair and gold teeth, throwing the bodies into the ovens, shoveling the ashes into pits or into the river? They became accustomed to the pressure of the SS guards to hurry, hurry. After the first few days, they ceased to think or care. 'We wept without tears'; 'We became robots' or even 'living corpses'.

After their own transports, the Greeks could not understand the languages of the newly arrived people assembled in the undressing area and, in any case, were forbidden to speak other than to calm them and guide them into the chamber. 'First take a shower and from there go to work ... I didn't have the guts to tell them [their fate]. Why should I scare and upset them right before their death ... Could they defend themselves?'[20]

'What helped you to survive?' asks Greif. 'The will to live, so that I could tell it to future generations, so that the truth would come out ... Otherwise they'll think the Holocaust never happened', responds Joseph Sackar.[21] Yaakov Gabai adds: 'With my own eyes I saw millions of Jews murdered ... I survived because I'd hoped to emerge from Auschwitz alive from the moment I'd entered. I survived because I was optimistic'.[22] Shaul Chazan was deported to Auschwitz in April 1944 and was drafted from the quarantine block to the SK along with 200 other Greeks to work in a 'factory'. They arrived

> at a little rustic house, a cottage ... The whole interior of the house was filled with bodies from a transport, more than a thousand corpses ... Shrieking, beatings, they didn't give us a chance to think about what we'd just seen ... We had to pile the bodies on top of each other like sardines ... [in] a deep pit, called "a bunker". Other workers split logs and we did everything in sequence – wood, corpses, wood, corpses, corpses, corpses, until the whole pit was filled ... A barrel of gasoline ... The SS man poured the gasoline ... and set the gasoline on fire ... The fire took hold, and corpses, corpses, corpses, corpses, throw 'em in, throw 'em in' burn 'em, burn 'em, burn 'em. On and on endlessly ... "Move it! Move it!" Beatings all the time. "Burn all these corpses and wipe out the transport!" ... Twelve hours [a shift], but ... never twelve hours ... we didn't leave until ... twenty-four hours straight.... As time passed, we got particularly depressed. We didn't feel like thinking people anymore. We just worked, ate, and slept, like automatons ... Whenever we lagged even a little, they beat us right away'.

After being assigned to Crematorium III, Chazan confesses: 'I'd stopped being human by then. If I'd been human, I couldn't have endured it for even one minute. We kept going because we'd lost our humanity'.[23]

Leon Cohen, due to his facility with German and French, was the spokesman for the 150 Greeks in the quarantine taken to work in the SK. These were divided among the four crematoria in Birkenau. 'When we reached our workplace ... someone in my group saw what the work consisted of – cremating dead Jews – he threw himself into the flames'. These Greeks worked first at the burning pits. 'It was terrifying. I can't describe it in words. It was terrible'.

Later Cohen worked in Crematorium III. 'We were never left alone, even for a moment. The Germans ... ordered us to mislead the victims. Anyone who'd dared to tell the Jews the truth would have been murdered straight away ... the Germans were afraid ... that chaos would erupt, a riot would break out, and the quiet process would be disrupted'. '[P]eople asked various questions ... simple questions from people who have no idea what's going to happen to them a few minutes later ... we had no choice but to answer [simply] ... because the idea was to dispel their fear of the unknown ... Few of them imagined that they were about to die in such a cruel and imminent way'. His final assessment was: 'We were dehumanized ... We'd become robots'.[24]

Yet were they indeed just mechanized inhuman robots? After the slow-down following the end of the Hungarian transports and the SK's slow reduction in number, the 'mechanized inhuman robots' realized that their end was nigh, especially the experienced veterans who continued to plan a revolt. With the help of the Polish partisans, they obtained a camera and film and succeeded in taking some clandestine photographs that were smuggled out of the camp.

The Four Photographs

The four photographs taken by Alek (alias Alekos Alexandris?), one of the Greeks in the SK, are 'unquestionably the most important documents that we have'.[25] They provide 'a representation of what they saw, unfettered by the fragilities of memory'.[26] The growing bibliography on them is discussed from a variety of postmodern perspectives, especially the critical reading of the Lacanian analysis of Didi-Huberman provided by Chare and Williams in *Matters of Testimony*.[27] My reading of them, by contrast, places them in toto in a dialogue with the actual experiences recorded in interviews and memoirs of the SK survivors themselves, acting as an 'unvoiced witness'. To my mind and others, these photographs present a narrative. The four pictures are assumed to portray the hurried snapping of the views captured by Alek (not securely identified, although occasionally taken to be Alberto Errera) with the aid and support of the small photographic crew that planned and carried out the complicated and dangerous assignment.[28]

The first two photographs show the SK crew at the burning pits into which they tossed the bodies of the gassed victims. These are framed in a way that indicates that they were snapped from inside a building assumed to be the crematorium. The third captures a group of naked women running towards the gas chamber. The fourth is a picture of the sky above the trees that gave the name Birkenau to the location of the camp officially known as Auschwitz II. The first two pictures show the men (possibly Greeks) at their terrible task. In most reproductions, the third picture is shown deliberately cropped. The fourth has been explained as a hurried, even off-balance shot. Rather, I would suggest that the fourth picture could be a deliberate choice, more an epilogue, a final slice of life in the reality of the crematorium, which is Alek's intentional commentary on the horrific scene that he was photographing as a witness for posterity, a visual memory of the SK refrain: 'They're going to heaven'.

What we should remember in any discussion of these unique photographs is that a *pshat* (surface reading) statement is a first step in their analysis. They were consciously created in an attempt to provide visual proof of the atrocities and the method of their implementation to a world that could not even conceive of the massacres that occurred daily in the concentration camps. Even as they buried written testimony and especially teeth as exhibits, the SK, whatever they believed about their possible survival, knew that the Nazis planned to kill them as they had all previous SKs. The undeveloped film was sent to a resistance committee in Cracow on 4 September 1944.[29] Fully authenticated, these four photographs remain the most positive and compelling emotional proof of the Holocaust of European Jewry, over and above the myriads of documents and testimonies of perpetrators and survivors.

Greek resistance took a number of other forms, which have received less consideration. One major medium was their love of music, which was appreciated and exploited by the guards. Greeks often sang when they worked in the crematorium and later during their rest periods. Greeks changed the words of their popular songs to pass on information, the women news of those surviving and the men news of their experiences. One song sung nightly by an SK worker is recorded by Berry Nahmia, who heard it after her transfer to Brzezinka to a camp opposite the crematorium:

> Greek girls
> who hear me
> tra-la-la-la-la-la
>
> I'm singing this as song
> so you won't get me wrong.
> The chimneys up far,
> Do you know what they are?
> They're factories of Death.
> That's what they are.
> Thousands of Jews
> all without blame

> old, young, and children
> in the arms of the flame.
> Soon non-existent
> burnt I will be
> unable to tell
> what my tired eyes see.
> Girls, can you hear me?
> the horror is true
> please now believe me
> I live it as a Jew.
> Greek girls, please
> if one day you get out
> explain to the world
> what I'm singing about.[30]

I learned this song by heart, she writes. I bring these words to these pages of mine to be read by my readers, just as he urged me to do: 'explain to the world what I'm singing about'. This SK communication is as informative as it is touching. It was the first indication to the women prisoners of what went on in the 'general grimness of the environment' of the closed-off crematorium areas. Other prisoners recall in their memoirs how they sang in code as they marched to work and thus passed information about other Greeks through the ranks of prisoners.

The SK slaves had many means to communicate with other prisoners, especially those in the Kanada-Kommando. Toward the end of September, Errikos Sevillias' brother-in-law David Persiades warned him that a general revolt was being planned and on 5 October informed him that everything was ready for 4 p.m. on the following day.[31] Berry Nahmia reports a letter from Marcel Nadjary that was smuggled to the Greek girls in the Sauna and is worth quoting here:

> Dear cousin Sarika,
> I saw you from a distance and recognized you. I imagine there are many Greek girls there, as I have many Greek men here with me. I want to inform all of you about something you must keep secret for a while. Know that in two or three days, here in the crematorium, we are preparing a revolt against the Germans. Ready yourselves and be careful, girls. Maybe we'll be fortunate enough to succeed, come and save you, and all get out of this hell.
> Marcel Nadjari

Another letter written by Nadjary as his final statement after the revolt, was discovered in 1980. It is extremely fragmentary due to the vicissitudes of its burial, but what survives is a testament to the nationalist spirit and pride of the former resistance fighter who survived the war. His later testimony recalled his slavery in the SK. Berry includes a portion of his later memoir in her own (*A Cry for Tomorrow 76859*), which also includes a miscellany of material gleaned from survivors with whom she remained in contact.

There were apparently several Greek small rebellions reported in the literature that anteceded the major revolt planning and uprising from late July to 7 October 1944. Molho-Nehama reports without any supporting source that a Salonican Jew stabbed an SS man to death who had been torturing him.[32] From an April transport from Greece, 320 men were selected in early May 1944 to work near the crematoria; one hundred of them, nearly all from Athens, refused to participate when they reached the crematoria: 'this was a real rebellion'. The hundred were immediately surrounded and shot; some were killed and others wounded. All were tossed quickly into the oven. Molho-Nehama's preliminary report ends with the attempted escape of Alberto Errera and his killing of one guard in the process.[33]

More important is the report of the 400 (or 435) Greek Jews who were drafted out of Quarantine Camp B-IIb on 21 July 1944 for work in the SK. According to Tuvia Friedman of the Haifa Documentation Center, they refused to work and were gassed the following day.[34] However, a near-contemporary account has survived in Olga Lengyel's memoir of Birkenau:

> An extra shift of the Sonderkommando was added ... Still it was not enough. At least four hundred Greeks from the Corfu and Athens transport were ordered in the Sonderkommando. Now, something truly unusual happened. These four hundred demonstrated that in spite of the barbed wire and the lash they were not slaves but human beings. With rare dignity, the Greeks refused to kill the Hungarians! They declared that they preferred to die themselves first. Sadly enough, they did. The Germans saw to that. But what a demonstration of courage and character these Greek peasants had given. A pity the world does not know more about them.

Lengyel was a nurse in the women's camp which bordered on the SK (Camp B1) and thus was close enough to be privy to the events inside that area.[35]

The Revolt or, More Accurately, the Uprising

The discussion of the leaders of the rebellion dominates the literature of the revolt and usually ignores the Greeks. A contemporary account of the uprising by Zalman Lewental was discovered on 17 October 1962 buried alongside Crematorium III.³⁶ It is dated 10 October 1944, when the confused events were still fresh, and constitutes the best summary by an Ashkenazi Jew of the events, including his impressions of the character of the men involved. He emphasizes the betrayal of the Polish partisan allies who were more interested in buying weapons with SK gold than in joining the actual revolt, which they continually delayed. Lewental's contemporary report illuminates details of the uprising that are undeveloped in most accounts, including that by Leon Cohen, who is the major source for the Greek role. There is no mention of Greeks however since they had no common language with him and the different ethnolinguistic groups kept their own counsel, save for general planning through their own leaders.

However, as it happened, in addition to a few named Greeks among the leadership of the revolt, most of the Greek SKs participated too, especially as it became more apparent that the crews of Crematoria IV and V were about to be murdered.

Recently, a new source has emerged that sheds light on these other Greeks and also illuminates one of the mysteries of the story: how did all the dynamite get into the SK area? We are all familiar with the story of the Union munitions factory and the role of the women there in smuggling powder to the men in the crematoria, and the heroic fate of the four women captured and tortured and hung for their connection with the affair.³⁷ But the story is more complicated and the new source illuminates it with a new hero. Jacob Maestro, known as 'Jackito', was a street wise young teenager from the Baron Hirsch quarter in Salonika, skilled in black market operations. When he arrived in Auschwitz and made himself known as a clever youngster who knew German, he was assigned to the Politische Abteilung and the office of work assignments, which allowed him free access to the whole camp. His position allowed him to save a number of Greeks by getting them into salubrious commandos rather than the more deadly ones, and to get sick and weak men to hospital when necessary. One day he was visiting the Schuhkommando where a number of Greek girls were working. One of the girls (non-Greek) took him aside and drafted him to assist with the SK request to obtain dynamite and weapons for them. He agreed only to the former. But from what source, since all the dynamite was under guard? So he went to the few Greeks who were in the Strassenbau Brzeszeze, who used dynamite to build roads. He obtained explosive powder, smuggling it to the Greek girls – Matilda Hagoel, Allegra Uziel and Arlette Yeruziel – who passed it on to girls in the Union factory with connections to the SK (e.g. Yisrael Gutman and Jehuda Lehrer) and eventually to Joseph Baruch, who had ordered it.³⁸

As noted earlier, most Greek memoirs and later studies date an uprising to 6 or 9(?) September 1944, while only a few recognize the official dating of 7 October 1944.[39] The earlier date is somewhat strange, given the relationship to the upcoming Jewish New Year and attendant holidays, which fell towards the end of September that year. Be that as it may, and contemporary dates are widely variant in the memoirs,[40] the preparatory stages of planning and delays in the execution of the revolt, the distribution of specific roles, the accumulation of explosive materials, etc. have been fully discussed on the basis of Ashkenazi Jews' memoirs.[41] Many of these were prepared as final wills and testimonies by those who prepared for the anticipated 15 August revolt, which was postponed. Insofar as the Greek role is concerned, Hermann Langbein, citing the Dutch doctor (and psychiatrist) Eduard de Wind, who remained with the sick after the camp was abandoned, lists the following Greek leaders: 'Eduard de Wind recalls a conversation that he had shortly after the evacuation of Auschwitz with [Isaac] Kabeli, a professor of literature at the University of Athens, who, like de Wind, had remained in the camp. Kabeli, who had served on the Sonderkommando for a year, named some Greek Jews whom he knew to have participated in the organization of the uprising: Baruch, Burdo, Carasso, Ardite, and Jachon'.[42] An earlier account notes that after 200 SK workers were lured to the main camp in September 1944, the chief kapo Jakub Kamiński suggested organizing a general uprising, but the main camp resistance leaders were against it.[43] Kamiński, however, met with two Greeks – one named Alberto Errera from Larissa[44] and the other 'a very intelligent Greek ... known for his beautiful singing' according to Dov Paisikovic, a youth of twenty recently drafted into the SK[45] – to plan an uprising of the SK that was supported by the leaders of the camp resistance. One important name is missing from this partial recall of Greek leaders: Pep(p)o-Yoseph Varouh (also Joseph Baruch),[46] who, according to Leon Cohen, was 'the man chosen to lead our [Greek] revolt'. He survived the uprising and reportedly died at Ebensee on the eve of its liberation. In actuality, however, the mastermind of the revolt is cited as a Russian officer (possibly a colonel and suspected to be Jewish) who planned the strategies. Additionally, the highly praised Jakub Kamiński, the Polish chief kapo of the SK camp, worked closely with Joseph Baruch in organizing the slaves.

While most of the Greek Jews in the SK appear to have been informed of the intended revolt and given individual assignments,[47] a number of them have been named by survivors as being among the resistance planning leadership. These include, for example, David Persiades, husband of Errikos Sevillias' sister who informed Errikos of the planned revolt.[48] Leon Cohen indicates that 'everyone in Birkenau became involved' and assignments were distributed among different groups for the planned 15 August[49] 'insurrection': a group of prisoners were to disarm the watchtower guards during the change of shift and tie up the SS in the crematorium. The next stage would be a signal from the steam engineers of the disinfection unit who would set the gauges to the limit to explode, whereupon the guards would be disarmed and their weapons seized. The Kanada-Kommando would set the warehouses on fire; the 'Sonder' men's job was to disconnect telephone and electric lines. Another group was to cut the barbed wire to the women's camp to allow the 40,000 women to join the men. One commando was to shoot any wounded: 'Our orders were: "No mercy for anyone!"' Each group was to run to the partisans who were expecting them. Leon Cohen and four others were to set the mattresses on fire and burn the crematorium:

> We all agreed that even if only one man managed to escape, it was worth undertaking. If you are to die may it be with dignity, holding a gun in your hand rather than shamefully being dragged to the gas chamber like an animal to the slaughter-house.[50]

But this plan was delayed since it counted on the Russian army interfering, which it did not. Kaminski, according to Cohen, volunteered to make the rounds to postpone the rebellion, but when he reached Crematorium II, the SS (perhaps just the sadist Moll) beat him nearly to death before throwing him into the oven. Shortly thereafter, the new commandant of the camp arrived, who turned out be the former head of the Haidari prison in Athens and therefore knew the Greeks and their watchword 'Sirma' ('wire' in Greek) by which they called him. He recognized the term and was apparently pleased that they remembered him, and left the crematorium ordering the punishment of the men (which, however, was not implemented, to their delight). The story spread through the camp according to Cohen. The failure of Errera's heroic escape attempt (see above), which resulted in the death of an SS guard and Errera's own 'honorable death', encouraged the Russian officers to sympathize with the Greeks' plans to rebel. Joseph Varouh (Baruch) of Crematorium III was chosen as leader and the final plan in coordination with Crematoria IV and V was to attack the SS guards, set the crematorium on fire and escape via Crematorium II, a slight update to the August plan. However, the signal of a burning rag did not arrive and the SS quickly gained control of the situation outside the barricaded Crematoria IV and V. The crew of Crematorium II cut the fence and fled, while the men of Crematoria III and the burning pit stayed put, locked in by the Germans. Crematorium IV was burned down:

The few surviving Greeks became legendary figures. The Schupo staff was so impressed that they called us 'the Greek bandits'. Every time we went to the kitchen the Russians who worked there praised us for what they saw as revenge for the earlier murder of their comrades.[51]

The report of the rebellion spread throughout the other camps, even to Mauthausen and its satellites in Melk and Ebensee, and encouraged the prisoners there. Cohen's encomium reflects the Greek survivors' memory in all their memoirs:

> this handful of Greek Jews, who, like David, had risen against a modern and bloodthirsty Goliath. As Jews and as Greeks, they had fought for their nation and for their country. To sum up, we, the Birkenau survivors, must always remember the extraordinary bravery of a handful of our fellow citizens. In the annals of extermination camps, heroism of that order was exceptional. As a rule, all deportees allowed themselves to be slaughtered like cattle. May the memory of our friends stay with us, forever.

Further details in other occasional sources do not add much to our understanding of the uprising and its after-effects.[52] Many of the SK were killed during or after capture and others were killed later on (452 in total). Less than a hundred, including twenty-five Greeks,[53] succeeded in escaping massacre by mixing with the other prisoners when the camp was evacuated. It was years before a few SK memoirs became available and a generation before the Greeks began to tell their stories, following Isaac Kabeli (as noted above) and, later on, Leon Cohen's detailed memoir.

While the revolt was a failure, as were other revolts of doomed Jews, even as they were castigated by ill-informed later commentators (viz. Hannah Arendt), they were nonetheless honoured by other prisoners to whom they gave courage and pride in their attempt, and showed that rebellion was possible.[54] Indeed, they showed that they were not all 'sheep led to the slaughter', that some of the men had character, that they were considerate of the doomed victims, that some maintained their dignity as human beings, that many prized life and were enslaved to the SS rather than collaborators, participating against their will in the murder of European Jews to which only they were trustworthy eyewitnesses. Among these SKs now should and can be counted the testimonies of Greek Jews who lived and died as proud Greeks.

Steven Bowman is Professor Emeritus of Judaic Studies at the University of Cincinnati. He is the author of *Jewish Resistance in Wartime Greece* (2006) and *The Agony of Greek Jews, 1940–1945* (2011). He is editor of the

Sephardi and Greek Holocaust Library, which has published five wartime memoirs and other studies. Well published in Byzantine and Jewish studies and a popular lecturer, he is Visiting Professor at College Year in Athens (CYA) (May–June 2019), where he is offering a course on the Greek-Jewish Encounter through the Ages, a survey of what he defines as the double helix of Western civilization whose creativity continues to unfold in all its complexity.

Notes

1. The latter published in English in Philip Friedman, *Roads to Extinction: Essays on the Holocaust*, Ada June Friedman (ed.) (New York: JPSA, 1980), 211–43. An independent account was published by J. (Isaiah) Eiger in Yiddish: 'Resistance Movement in the Concentration Camp Auschwitz-Birkenau', *From the Last Extermination: Journal for the History of the Jewish People during the Nazi Regime* 10 (1948), 70–75.
2. Friedman, *Roads to Extinction*, 233.
3. His brief 'Reminiscences' was published by the Auschwitz-Birkenau State Museum in *KL Auschwitz Seen by the SS* (Oświęcim: State Museum of Auschwitz-Birkenau, 1997). The discussion of the SK revolt can be found at 138f.
4. *KL Auschwitz Seen by the SS* (ibid.) includes only the Auschwitz part of his autobiography. The full text is in Rudolf Hoess, *Commandant of Auschwitz: The Autobiography of Rudolf Hoess*, trans. Constantine Fitzgibbon (New York: World Publishing Company, 1959).
5. Hoess returned to Auschwitz in May–June 1944 to direct the extermination of some 400,000 Hungarian Jews, and these comments on the SK may reflect that later period, which was more intense than the earlier one. The Greeks were very visible in this last SK, as we shall see below.
6. Hoess, *Commandant*, 165.
7. Ibid., 168.
8. Ber Mark, *The Scrolls of Auschwitz* (Tel Aviv: Am Oved, 1985) – supplemented by his wife Esther Mark and originally in Yiddish, translated into Hebrew and then into English by Sharon Neemani.
9. Joseph Ben, *Greek Jewry in the Holocaust and the Resistance 1941–1944* (Tel Aviv: Institute of the Saloniki Research Center, 1985), 149. See my *The Agony of Greek Jews, 1940–1945* (Stanford: Stanford University Press, 2009), 271 fn 6 for a correction of Gutman's erroneous view. Gutman's summary of the revolt in his *Anashim va'efer* can be found at 151–57.
10. Reuben Ainsztein, *Jewish Resistance in Nazi-Occupied Eastern Europe* (New York: Barnes & Noble, 1974), 769ff.
11. The latter is a somewhat strange lacuna in view of the fact that Gideon Greif was a major consultant for the film (see below).
12. Ben, *Greek Jewry in the Holocaust*; David Recanati (ed.), *Zichron Saloniki*, 2 volumes (Tel Aviv: El Commitato por la Edition del Livro Sovre la Communita de Salonique,

1972–85); Baruch Uziel et al. (eds), *Saloniki, 'Ir ve-em beyisrael* (Tel Aviv: Centre de recherches sur le judaisme de Salonique, 1967).
13. Michael Molho, *In Memoriam: Hommage aux victims juives des Nazis en Grèce* (Thessaloniki: Éditions N. Nicolaidès, 1948), revised and expanded as *Shoat Yehudei Yavan 1941–1944* (Jerusalem: Yad Vashem, 1965), especially 194–201.
14. Photini Tomai, *Greeks in Auschwitz-Birkenau*, 2nd edn (Athens: Papazisis, 2009).
15. Steven Bowman, *Jewish Resistance in Wartime Greece* (London: Valentine Mitchell, 2006) and *The Agony of Greek Jews*. See below n. 39 for Isaac Kabeli and his influence.
16. Yitzhak Kerem, 'The Role of Greek Jews in the Sonderkommando Revolt in Birkenau', in Michael Birenbaum, Richard Libowitz and Marcia Sachs Little (eds), *Remembering for the Future: Armenia, Auschwitz and Beyond* (St Paul, MN: Paragon Books, 2016), 121–37.
17. Gideon Greif and Itamar Levin, *Revolt in Auschwitz: The Uprising of the Sonderkommando in the Gas Chambers, 7.10.1944* [Hebrew] (Rishon LeZion: Miskal – Yedioth Ahronoth Books & Chemed Books, 2017). Greif also produced a documentary in which he led several SK survivors, including Greeks, to Birkenau to give their testimony in situ; this documentary illustrates the interviews he published in his collection *We Wept without Tears*. Other interviews are recorded on the disc included with Tomai, *Greeks in Auschwitz-Birkenau*.
18. Rebecca Camhi Fromer, *The Holocaust Odyssey of Daniel Bennahmias, Sonderkommando* (Tuscaloosa: University of Alabama Press, 1993); Leon Cohen, *From Greece to Birkenau: The Crematorium Workers' Uprising* (Tel Aviv: Salonika Jewry Research Center, 1996) (Hebrew version: *Pe'amim* (1986)); Shlomo Venezia, *Inside the Gas Chambers: Eight Months in the Sonderkommando of Auschwitz* (Cambridge: Polity Press, 2009); Gideon Greif, *We Wept without Tears: Testimonies of the Jewish Sonderkommando from Auschwitz* (New Haven: Yale University Press, 2005), interviews with Josef Sackar, Yaakov Gabai, Shaul Chazan, Leon Cohen and several other non-Greek survivors (Abraham and Shlomo Dragon, Eliezer Eisenschmidt, and Yaakov Silberberg); Marcel Nadjary, *Chroniko 1941–1948* (Thessaloniki: Hidryma ETS ACHAIM, 1991). Part of Nadjary's postwar memoir can be found in Berry Nahmia, *A Cry for Tomorrow 76859 . . .*, trans. David R. Weinberg (Jacksonville, FL: Sephardic House, 2011), 79–88; Mois Mizrahi of Chios, oral testimony deposited in Gratz College; Albert Menasche, *Birkenau (Auschwitz II). How 72,000 Greek Jews Perished* (New York: I. Saltiel, 1947; Hebrew version, 1967; Greek version, 1974); and a report on the uprising in Uziel et al., *Salonik, 'Ir ve-em beyisrael*, 309; Errikos Sevillias, *Athens-Auschwitz*, trans. and ed. Nikos Stavroulakis (Athens: Lycabettus, 1983); René Molho with Rebecca Camhi Fromer, *They Say Diamonds Don't Burn* (Berkeley, CA: Judah L. Magnes Museum, 1994); Yad Vashem file #03/2484, report of Isaac Cohen, eyewitness report of SK revolt from the Kanada-Kommando; Marco Nahon, *Birkenau: The Camp of Death*, trans. Jacqueline Havaux Bowers (Tuscaloosa: University of Alabama Press, 1989); Greif and Levin, *Revolt in Auschwitz;* and Gideon Greif, *The Merciful Angel from Auschwitz: The Story of Jacob 'Jaquito' Maestro from Thessaloniki Greece* [in Hebrew] (Jerusalem: Memorial for the Thessaloniki and Greece Jewry Publishing House, 2014), which relates Jackito's interaction with the SK (at 190f). Molho, Nahmia, Nahon and Maestro spoke with SK men during 1943 and 1944 in Birkenau and report their experiences.
19. The role of trained officers in the camp revolts has not been sufficiently emphasized. They were able to organize the youth drafted to the SKs in Treblinka and Birkenau. Among these officers were Greek veterans and officers, Poles and later Russians who

were active in the organization of the revolt, while few of the majority SK men (Poles and Hungarians) participated in the actual uprising.
20. Greif, *We Wept without Tears*, 102 and 103.
21. Ibid., 121.
22. Ibid., 213 and 214. Dr Anton Dick-Boldes wrote and produced a play based on Gabai's interview which was performed in Berlin in 1997, according to Greif (ibid., 182).
23. Ibid., 264, 273
24. Ibid., 294, 296, 298, 305
25. Dan Stone, 'The Sonderkommando Photographs', *Jewish Social Studies* 7(3) (2001), 132–48.
26. https://www.academia.edu/2552802/THE_SONDERKOMMANDO_PHOTOGRAPHS and commentary by Gary Spicer.
27. Nicholas Chare and Dominic Williams, *Matters of Testimony* (New York: Berghahn Books, 2016), 183–213.
28. Jonathan Webber and Connie Wilsack, *Auschwitz: A History in Photographs* (Bloomington, IN: Indiana University Press; Warsaw: Książka i Wiedza, 1993), 42f, 172ff; Bowman, *Jewish Resistance*, Chapter 7; Bowman, *The Agony of Greek Jews*, 271. Since Alek(o) is a nickname for Alekos, the pseudonym for Alberto Errera, a naval officer and potential hero of the SK for his attempted violent escape, it is understandable that he was chosen as the man behind the name Alek, and maybe he was … but there is no absolute identification even though there were perhaps too few other Alekos in the SK. Errera's attempted escape is not listed in the usually comprehensive Danuta Czech, *Auschwitz Chronicle 1939–1945* (New York: I.B. Tauris, 1990). A summary of his attempted escape by Moshe Shmuel is in Recanati, *Zichron Saloniki*, vol. 2, 610. Nikos Stavroulakis in his notes to Sevillias' *Athens-Auschwitz*, 103n suggests his attempt was between 21 and 29 September 1944, while Chare and Williams, *Matters of Testimony* suggests late in August.
29. Czech, *Auschwitz Chronicle*, 701. If Errera was the photographer, this would to date his attempted escape and its impact on the Greeks and Russians. Czech's *Auschwitz Chronicle* notes a transport from the Łódź ghetto on 2 September, which might help identify the women in the photographs.
30. Citations from Nahmia, *A Cry for Tomorrow 76859*, with kind permission of her translator David R. Weinberg.
31. Sevillias, *Athens-Auschwitz*, 51f. The date of 6 October is one day short of the official date of the revolt accepted by scholars; however, the time is correct. See also the testimony of Isaac Ieremias, a crematorium worker, in the Jewish Museum of Greece archives.
32. Molho, *Shoat Yehudei Yavan 1941–1944*, 194. Moshe Shmuel notes this event in his comments on the revolt in Crematorium IV in Recanati, *Zichron Saloniki*, vol. 2, 610.
33. Molho, *Shoat Yehudei Yavan 1941–1944*, 194f.
34. Czech, *Auschwitz Chronicle*, entry for 21 July 1944. No mention of this further data is included for 22 July 1944.
35. Olga Lengyel, *Five Chimneys: The Story of Auschwitz* (Chicago: Ziff-Davis, 1947), cited in Fromer, *Holocaust Odyssey*, xviiif. An independent account by Moshe Shmuel designates this act by 100(!) Greeks in May 1944 as the beginning of the revolutionary actions against the Germans. Shmuel, in Recanati, *Zichron Saloniki*, vol. 2, 610.
36. Described by Mark, *The Scrolls of Auschwitz*, 160f and translated at 216–35. The manuscript was heavily damaged and 50 per cent illegible, yet the revolt is clearly described. See the discussion in Chare and Williams, *Matters of Testimony*, 125–53.

37. See Lore Shelley, *The Union Kommando in Auschwitz: v. XIII: The Auschwitz Munition Factory through the Eyes of its Former Slave Laborers* (Lanham, MD: University Press of America, 1996). Apparently their arrest and tortured interrogation was for sabotage rather than smuggling gunpowder. The latest contribution to the subject is by Ronnen Harran, 'The Jewish Women of the Union Factory, Auschwitz 1944: Resistance, Courage and Tragedy', *Dapim* 31 (2017), 45–67. See below for the names of three Greek women who participated.
38. See Greif, *The Merciful Angel from Auschwitz*. Many of his Salonikan contacts had come on the first transport to Auschwitz in late March 1943. See above for an earlier interview summary. See also Yitzhak Kerem, 'New Finds in Greek Jewish Heroism in the Holocaust', *Sephardi Horizons* 2(4) (2012).
39. Ben and the Hebrew version of Molho-Nehama rely on an early Hebrew article of Isaac Kabeli cited as 'Revolt of the Greek Jews in Auschwitz', dated May 1946 (not seen). Actually Kabeli cites this article published earlier in P.A.M.E.M. in May 1946 (which I have not found) and other sources in his longer Hebrew article 'The Jews in the Greek Underground', *Sefer ha-partizanim ha-Yehudim* (1958), 417–27 (see note to 423), especially 426–27, where he lists a number of Greek Jewish leaders in the revolt. These included Joseph Baruch, Yoseph Levi, Morris Aharon, Yitzhak Baruch, Sam Karasso and Yom Tov Yacoel. In addition, Kabeli is responsible, among other things, for the September date of the uprising and for the erroneous data on casualties. See Ben, *Greek Jewry in the Holocaust*, 150f for a summary (his revised MA Thesis); and Greif, *The Merciful Angel from Auschwitz*. Ben writes a more detailed version of which the following is a partial summary: on 9 September, a French Kapo came to Crematorium III, called out the numbers of 100 Hungarian workers and left. He returned and called out the numbers of 100(!) Greek workers. The Greeks rebelled, the Hungarians joined them. The SS surrounded the crematorium, 300 were killed and others later. Only Isaac Venezia escaped to the Kanada-Kommando, where he hid. This 'revolt' supposedly occurred the day before the Theresienstadt transport arrived in Birkenau (see Czech, *Auschwitz Chronicle*, sub 29 September 1944 and 6 October 1944). Obviously this version is partly a confused collation with the 7 October uprising, which follows directly in Ben's reconstructions based on Kabeli. See Greif's introductory chapter for a chronology and description of the October uprising. (*We Wept without Tears*, 40–46). It is very strange that Greif does not mention the Greeks in his summary of the revolt, even though some of the Greek leaders are mentioned in the subsequent interviews in his book and elsewhere by SK survivors, and also in the memoir of Jacob Maestro that Greif edited! The problem with Ben's version and the date stems from Kabeli, whose essays on the Greeks during the Shoah have not been critically examined. See remarks of the Ber Mark (*The Scrolls of Auschwitz*, Chapter 13): 'This information provokes certain reservations'. We noted above that Philip Friedman already dated the revolt to September 1944. Did he read Kabeli's article of May 1946? We cannot account for Kabeli's erroneous date and other data that he collected from survivors of the SK other than the confusion of the survivors with whom he talked at the time. In any case, many of the Greek memoirs, especially Greif's recent interview with Jackito, and subsequent scholarship rely heavily on Kabeli, and all these reports must be held suspect with regard to a too-often-cited September revolt. There is no mention of a revolt in September 1944 in Czech's data-packed *Auschwitz Chronicle*, nor do any Greeks appear in her summary of the revolt on 7 October! The Greeks are sadly unmentioned in most online accounts of the revolt. For the latest sequence of events, see Kerem, 'The Role of Greek Jews'.

40. Recall Thucydides warning about eyewitnesses: 'different eye-witnesses gave different accounts of the same events, speaking out of partiality for one side or the other from imperfect memories (I,22)'. None of the memoirs mention any Jewish holidays connected with the revolt.
41. See the classic Ber Mark, *The Scrolls of Auschwitz*.
42. Hermann Langbein, *People in Auschwitz*, trans. Harry Zohn (Chapel Hill: University of North Carolina Press, 2004), 202. These names refer to Joseph Varouh, Brudo, Sam Carasso and Arditi, perhaps Raoul or his brother Alberto (see Fromer, *Holocaust Odyssey*, 60) – two of the four Yachon brothers were earlier sadistically tortured and shot by Moll. The Jachons were related to Dr Albert Menasche (see above). A different Isaac Kabeli from Salonika was interviewed for the Spiegel Collection at USC with no reference to the revolt.
43. The SK veterans, namely Poles and other Ashkenazim who had a common language, had their own committee to plan their role in the general camp planning. When the SK capo asked for a list of men to be sent to another camp the day before the uprising, the leadership decided to supply the names of Greeks and Hungarians with whom they had no common language, i.e. the latest to be drafted for the SK. This necessitated independent action by the Greeks, who had their own planning committee, which was in contact with the main SK committee, when they learned of this intended sacrifice on the eve of their transport to destruction. Noah Zabludowicz, an electrician given free run of the camp, gave two accounts of his role as messenger in YVA 03/1187 in 1959 and TR3/8 in 1961, on which this account is based.
44. Alberto Errera was a Greek naval officer (also identified as an army officer) who joined the Greek resistance before he was caught and sent to Auschwitz.
45. Langbein, *People in Auschwitz*, 196 and 200. This latter may be Isaacquino (a diminutive of Isaac) Venezia, known for his beautiful singing voice and for his courage Fromer, *Holocaust Odyssey*, 70n.
46. While all the sources identify him as Joseph Baruch, his registration form from Birkenau carries the signature Varouh [YIVO Archives S-2 87 #182722] and his military experience in the Greek army as a regular army officer (1937–41) in the Third Artillery Regiment of Corinth; he later fought in the Greek resistance. The B (beta) in Greek is pronounced V. To pronounce it as B, it is written MP as in MProudo (Broudo) or MPen (Ben). Hence, Pep(p)o-Yoseph wrote his name as it was pronounced in Greek (Varouh), and therein lies the confusion of this hero's name in the non-Greek sources. See further details on him in Fromer, *Holocaust Odyssey*, 63.
47. Daniel Bennahmias mentions that he was part of the conspiracy to revolt. He and Dario Gabbai were assigned to kill an SS guard.
48. Sevillias, *Athens-Auschwitz*, 50–54. He may have been just one of the active participants rather than a leader.
49. A major Christian holiday celebrating Mary's dormition.
50. Cohen, *From Greece to Birkenau*, 58ff. He was in Crematorium III along with Daniel Bennahmias and many other Greeks. Cohen, according to Bennahmias, tended to exaggerate (interview with author).
51. Ibid., 89. These were recent Russian victims. Much earlier, some 50,000 Russian POWs were marched to Auschwitz and settled in a field with barbed wire strung around them and starved. Only about 100 survived and were treated as special by the SS.
52. See *The Architecture of Crime: The 'Central Camp Sauna' in Auschwitz II – Birkenau*, trans. William Brand (Oświęcim: Auschwitz-Birkenau State Museum, 2001), 99

from the memoir of Irena Strzelecka: 'I heard the *International* being sung in Greek, and then some sort of explosions, screams, and gunshots'.
53. Figure cited by Marcello Pezzetti in Venezia, *Inside the Gas Chambers*, 187, based on his research in the Museum Archive at Auschwitz.
54. See the passage from Yisrael Gutman's *Anashim ve-efer*, (153f), quoted in Greif, *We Wept without Tears*, 45.

Bibliography

Ainsztein, Reuben. *Jewish Resistance in Nazi-Occupied Eastern Europe*. New York: Barnes & Noble, 1974.
Ben, Joseph. *Greek Jewry in the Holocaust and the Resistance 1941–1944*. Tel Aviv: Institute of the Saloniki Research Center, 1985.
Bowman, Steven. *Jewish Resistance in Wartime Greece*. London: Valentine Mitchell, 2006.
———. *The Agony of Greek Jews, 1940–1945*. Stanford: Stanford University Press, 2009.
Chare, Nicholas, and Dominic Williams, *Matters of Testimony: Interpreting the Scrolls of Auschwitz*. New York: Berghahn Books, 2016.
Cohen, Leon. *From Greece to Birkenau. The Crematorium Workers' Uprising*. Tel Aviv: Salonika Jewry Research Center, 1996.
Corbin, Harlan. *Play Dead*. New York: British American Publishing, 1990.
Czech, Danuta. *Auschwitz Chronicle 1939–1945*. New York: I.B. Tauris, 1990.
Eiger, J. [Isaiah] 'Resistance Movement in the Concentration Camp Auschwitz-Birkenau', *From the Last Extermination: Journal for the History of the Jewish People during the Nazi Regime* 10 (1948), 70–75 [in Yiddish].
Fromer, Rebecca Camhi. *The Holocaust Odyssey of Daniel Bennahmias, Sonderkommando*. Tuscaloosa: University of Alabama Press, 1993.
Greif, Gideon. *We Wept without Tears: Testimonies of the Jewish Sonderkommando from Auschwitz*. New Haven: Yale University Press, 2005.
———. *The Merciful Angel from Auschwitz: The Story of Jacob 'Jaquito' Maestro from Thessaloniki Greece*. Jerusalem: Memorial for the Thessaloniki and Greece Jewry Publishing House, 2014.
Greif, Gideon, and Itamar Levin. *Revolt in Auschwitz: The Uprising of the Sonderkommando in the Gas Chambers, 7.10.1944*. Rishon LeZion: Miskal – Yedioth Ahronoth Books & Chemed Books, 2017 [in Hebrew].
Harran, Ronnen. 'The Jewish Women of the Union Factory, Auschwitz 1944: Resistance, Courage and Tragedy', *Dapim* 31 (2017), 45–67.
Hoess, Rudolf. *Commandant of Auschwitz: The Autobiography of Rudolf Hoess*, trans. Constantine Fitzgibbon. New York: World Publishing Company, 1959.
Hoess, Rudolf, Pery Broad, and Johann Kremer. *KL Auschwitz Seen by the SS*. Oświęcim: State Museum of Auschwitz-Birkenau, 1997.
Kabeli, Isaac. 'The Jews in the Greek Underground', *Sefer ha-partizanim ha-Yehudim*. Merhavia: Sifriyat Po'alim, 1958, 417–27.
Kerem, Yitzhak. 'The Role of Greek Jews in the Sonderkommando Revolt in Birkenau', in Michael Birenbaum, Richard Libowitz and Marcia Sachs Little (eds), *Remembering for the Future: Armenia, Auschwitz and Beyond*. St Paul, MN: Paragon, Books, 2016, 121–37.

Langbein, Hermann. *People in Auschwitz*, trans, Harry Zohn. Chapel Hill: University of North Carolina Press, 2004.

Lengyel, Olga. *Five Chimneys: The Story of Auschwitz*. Chicago: Ziff-Davis, 1947.

Mark, Ber. *The Scrolls of Auschwitz*, trans. Sharon Neemani. Tel Aviv: Am Oved, 1985.

Menasche, Albert. *Birkenau (Auschwitz II). How 72,000 Greek Jews Perished*. New York, I. Saltiel, 1947.

Molho, Michael. *In Memoriam: Hommage aux victims juives des Nazis en Grèce*. Thessaloniki: Éditions N. Nicolaidès, 1948.

Molho, René, with Rebecca Camhi Fromer. *They Say Diamonds Don't Burn*. Berkeley, CA: Judah L. Magnes Museum, 1994.

Nadjary, Marcel. *Chroniko 1941–1948*. Thessaloniki: Hidryma ETS CHAIM, 1991.

Nahon, Marco. *Birkenau: The Camp of Death*, trans. Jacqueline Havaux Bowers. Tuscaloosa: University of Alabama Press, 1989.

Nahmia, Berry. *A Cry for Tomorrow 76859 . . .*, trans. David R. Weinberg. Jacksonville, FL: Sephardic House, 2011.

Recanati, David. *Zichron Saloniki*, 2 vols. Tel Aviv: El Commitato por la Edition del Livro Sovre la Communita de Salonique, 1972–85.

Sevillias, Errikos. *Athens-Auschwitz*, trans. Nikos Stavroulakis. Athens: Lycabettus, 1983.

Shelley, Lore. *The Union Kommando in Auschwitz: v. XIII: The Auschwitz Munition Factory Through the Eyes of its Former Slave Laborers*. Lanham, MD: University Press of America, 1996.

Stone, Dan. 'The Sonderkommando Photographs', *Jewish Social Studies* 7(3) (2001), 132–48.

Tomai, Photini. *Greeks in Auschwitz-Birkenau*, 2nd edn. Athens: Papazisis, 2009.

Uziel, Baruch, et al. (eds), *Salonik, 'Ir ve-em beyisrael*. Tel Aviv: Centre de recherches sur le judaïsme de Salonique, 1967.

Venezia, Shlomo. *Inside the Gas Chambers: Eight Months in the Sonderkommando of Auschwitz*. Cambridge: Polity Press, 2009.

Webber, Jonathan, and Connie Wilsack. *Auschwitz: A History in Photographs*. Bloomington, IN: Indiana University Press/Warsaw: Książka i Wiedza, 1993.

Part IV

Cinema and the Sonderkommando

Chapter 17

'We Did Something'

Framing Resistance in Cinematic Depictions of the Sonderkommando

Barry Langford

Some forty minutes into Tim Blake Nelson's *The Grey Zone* (United States, 2001),[1] the Sonderkommando Hoffman (played by David Arquette) is helping 'process' a newly arrived selection of his fellow Hungarians in one of the Auschwitz-Birkenau crematoria.[2] As Hoffman moves through the undressing room, one deportee – a middle-aged man – rejects his reassuring bromides about the fate that awaits them. Resisting Hoffman's efforts to subdue him, he decries the Sonderkommando (SK) as accessories to mass murder. Challenged to admit that the 'showers' are a lie – 'Look me in the eye and tell me I'm not going to be killed', the man demands (*TGZ* 40/46) – Hoffman all but abandons pretence, repeatedly urging him simply to stay quiet, but without success. As the confrontation mounts, Hoffman notices the man's wristwatch and demands he hand it over. When the man refuses – spitting in his face and calling him a 'fucking Nazi liar' (*TGZ* 40/47) – Hoffman breaks and assaults him in full view of the other Jews assembled in the undressing room, the SS guards and his fellow SK member Cohen as well as the man's increasingly hysterical wife. 'Berserk', Hoffman ends up beating the older man to death with his bare hands. Insane with horror at what she has witnessed, the wife continues to scream uncontrollably until an SS guard puts a bullet in her brain. Processing resumes under Cohen's supervision. Finally, as the naked deportees file into the gas chamber, a second SS man unstraps the watch from the murdered man's wrist and with a sardonic half-smile offers it to Hoffman, who has slumped to the floor, physically drained and stupefied by his own actions. Numbly, Hoffman accepts it.

Strategically placed early in the film's second act,[3] this lengthy scene is disturbing on several levels. Though, given its setting, murder is obviously ubiquitous in *The Grey Zone*, this is nonetheless by some measure its most graphically as well as *intimately* violent scene. Other individual killings punctuate the film, but those murders (all by gunshot) are markedly less gruesome, less protracted and more matter of fact than the blows Hoffman rains down on his defenceless fellow Jew's head and face. The chaotic violence of the uprising at the film's climax – even the burning alive of an SS guard – has a far less traumatic impact, being experienced by the spectator as not only justified but cathartic, and involving mostly anonymous SK squad members and SS. In fact, the only death that readily compares to this act by Hoffman in terms of either screen time or dramatic emphasis is another Jew-upon-Jew killing, Rosenthal's (David Chandler) asphyxiation of the nameless[4] older SK with which the film opens.

Yet the two acts are not equivalent and are also readily distinguished by the spectator. Although, beyond the opening title card outlining the history of the SK, no narrative context is supplied to explain Rosenthal's actions, and notionally at least the audience's point of identification in the scene is either Dr Nyiszli (movie doctors being generically coded as sympathetic, pro-social characters)[5] or Hoffman, who has called Nyiszli to the scene and from whose point of view we enter the film, nonetheless body language and dialogue cues – 'Easy now, old friend. Easy', Rosenthal murmurs as he smothers the old man (*TGZ* 4/4) – strongly imply this is a mercy killing, not a cold-blooded murder (audiences might recall the end of *One Flew over the Cuckoo's Nest*) and that Nyiszli's anger and horror are misplaced or mistaken (as he himself later acknowledges). Rosenthal's willingness to take decisive action helps establish him (as well as Schlermer (Daniel Benzali), who aids him) as a tough, hard-bitten and at the same time compassionate realist (qualities that play out strongly in his subsequent attitude to the girl who survives the gassing). The younger Hoffman, by contrast, here appears as a more unformed character whose learning curve, we might surmise, will unfold over the ensuing action. His only appearance between the opening scene and the murderous encounter in the undressing room reiterates this contrast and underlines the character's naivety: a dialogue with Abramowics (Steve Buscemi, described in the screenplay as 'slightly older . . . and more than slightly harder' than Hoffman) in which the latter brutally slaps down what he regards as Hoffman's delusions that the SK might survive to be liberated by the advancing Red Army (*TGZ* 7/8).

This sense that Hoffman is a 'softer' character than his nihilistic comrades (Abramowics instructs him to 'Believe it. You're dead already . . . It's just a matter of deciding how') (*TGZ* 7/10) encourages the audience, as they search for a subject of identification amidst the hellish netherworld of the crematoria, to believe they have located him in Hoffman: a conviction promoted by the very first shot of the film, a painterly close-up of Hoffman's mournful, reflective face in half-shadow (characterized by Axel Bangert as an 'Ecce Homo').[6] This identification is then shockingly disrupted by his actions in the undressing room, for which nothing in his demeanour or behaviour hitherto has prepared us. Indeed – given that Hoffman very clearly instantly repents his actions – this episode occurs in something of a dramatic vacuum. Although Hoffman accepts the key motivating prop of the watch, almost it seems as a token of his own damnation, it is never referred to again thereafter (it is presumably intended to bribe the SS, as seen elsewhere in the film with other looted items, to permit SK squad members to move between their assigned crematoria, but we never see it used for this purpose). His homicidal frenzy goes unseen by any of the film's other principals, German or Jewish (the SK Cohen is a minor character) and indeed prompts no response from anyone stronger than the 'curious bemusement' of the SS guards. Absent the focalizing presence of other main characters, we lack any sense of whether his actions should be understood as profoundly transgressive (as they obviously strike us) or simply an occupational hazard and logical extension of the deadening work the SK habitually perform. The only dramatically meaningful witness, in fact, is the nameless (and mute) young girl who will miraculously survive the gas chamber and whose preservation Hoffman subsequently pursues as a means of symbolic restitution or absolution. Since she is present here (as in all the scenes prior to her resuscitation) only via an (unremarked) optical point-of-view shot at the head of the scene and again at its close as she and her family enter the gas chamber, her blank perspective – uncomprehending of the meaning of the terrible events around her – is essentially also that of the audience. All of this means that unlike the killing of the old man, Hoffman's crime occurs in isolation from narrative context and unknown to any of the other main characters whose response might help mediate or explain them for the spectator.

It is of course possible that Nelson incorporates Hoffman's unexplained and apparently uncharacteristic moral collapse as a quasi-Brechtian gesture intended to suggest, precisely, that the kinds of broadly consistent behaviour we expect from characters in realist cinema, grounded in related conventionalized assumptions concerning dramatic verisimilitude and psychological coherence, are irrelevant and/or unachievable given the unique condition and experiences of the SK. (As we shall see, there is some suggestion of this in László Nemes' portrayal of his title character's 'addled consciousness' in *Son of Saul* (Hungary, 2015).)[7] But this interpretation is belied by the portrayal of the other principal SK characters Rosenthal, Schlermer and Abramowics, whose consistent characterization and rationality, however hard-pressed, never ruptures at any stage of the film.[8] Hoffman himself, for that matter, not only behaves consistently either side of the undressing room scene, but betrays no evident emotional or psychological consequences of his murderous outburst: although his quixotic mission to save the girl follows immediately (she has arrived in the same transport as the man Hoffman murders), there is no suggestion that this is directly prompted by guilt or remorse; indeed, his actions seem consistent with his response to the old man's death in the opening scene. Significantly, it is the latter episode, and *not* the killing in the undressing room (which Hoffman must realize the girl had witnessed) to which he returns when, guarding the girl following her resuscitation, he offers her a halting quasi-confessional monologue.

Standing out in relief from their dramatic context, Hoffman's actions underscore the scene's glaringly didactic purpose. The murder – like Rosenthal's earlier killing of the old man, but far more emphatically and, indeed, stridently – is very obviously intended to foreground the titular 'grey zone' into which their enforced complicity with the Nazi murder programme drove the SK, a domain of ethical and moral uncertainty also repeatedly invoked in Nelson's dialogue. Our sense that the undressing room scene has been conceived as an exemplary, almost parable-like, self-contained morality play is intensified by the realization that it is wholly invented: no such episode is recorded anywhere either in the 'Scrolls of Auschwitz' (the testimonies secreted by members of the Auschwitz SK) or in postwar testimony by SK survivors. Indeed, given the alacrity with which self-proclaimed guardians of Holocaust memory react to perceived or actual transgressions of 'Holocaust propriety', it is somewhat surprising that this scene – admittedly, in a film that largely failed to find much of an audience – seems not to have attracted condemnation or even much comment. That it has not perhaps reflects the continuing ambivalence with which the SK are viewed compared to other, 'purer' Holocaust victims.[9] Perhaps it was the absence, given the original play's claustrophobic concentration on the 'work' in the crematoria (only partly opened up in the film by the scenes featuring the female conspirators), of any external dramatic perspective from which the SK could be 'framed' in moral or even eschatological terms – that is, the standpoint of a Primo Levi – that made Nelson feel the need for such an extreme and, arguably, schematic enactment of the predicament of the SK.

In dwelling at length on this sequence, I wish to draw out the significance of Nelson's decision not only to invent such a lurid scene through which to render the extremity and ethical impossibility of the SK's experience, but to do so through by presenting an act of violence: a dramatic choice, I would suggest, he makes almost by default. Dominic Williams notes the predominance in popular narrative representations of the SK of generic paradigms focusing on narrative arcs of character development, and on violence as the primary index of (male) self-determination. This tendency works to promote depictions of the SK as inhabiting a permanent existential crisis ('living in a crisis situation', as indeed Auschwitz SK survivor Filip Müller memorably puts it in his testimony in Lanzmann's *Shoah*) and, concomitantly, a dramatic focus on armed resistance as the principle, or even sole, authentic response to this crisis.[10] Thus, for example, both in films focusing on the Birkenau SK, including *The Grey Zone* and *Son of Saul*, as well as the partly different experience of the slave workers at Sobibór (in the so-called 'living camp') such as *Holocaust* (Marvin Chomsky, NBC TV, 1978) and *Escape from Sobibor* (Jack Gold, United Kingdom/United States, 1989), preparation and execution of the insurrections at these camps are to varying degrees dramatically central. This structure not only conforms to mainstream dramatic conventions but also restores the often-controversial figure of the SK to the ranks of Holocaust martyrology, expiating the suspicion of collaboration in fiery self-sacrifice (allying these films with other recent screen portrayals of armed Jewish resistance such as *Uprising* (Jon Avnet, United States, 2001) and *Defiance* (Edward Zwick, United States, 2007)).

However, accommodating them to generic templates of sacrificial heroism arguably perpetuates the tendency to instrumentalize the SK – that is, to subordinate their uniquely terrible experiences to *a priori* models of historical and/or moral interpretation that ignore or simplify the complex subjecthood of the historical SK themselves. The most persistent of these interpretations is to conceive of the SK as embodiments of, in Erin McGlothlin's words, 'utter abjection in a realm of pure death',[11] a condition in which not only must conventional ethical judgments be suspended (as Levi famously suggests), but also normative assumptions about subjecthood, identity and agency. Arguably even Claude Lanzmann's approach to the SK reflects these approaches (albeit in a very different vein) in his insistence that his SK survivor interviewees[12] are (solely) 'spokesmen of the dead' and thus labour under the ethical obligation to reincarnate – at whatever personal cost – their dreadful histories. Williams has wisely observed that such attitudes tend to foreclose upon the idea that the SK might wish to be more than simply 'witnesses to themselves'. Conscription into the ranks of the damned in the innermost circles of hell at Auschwitz-Birkenau did not necessarily, in and of itself, extinguish altogether the possibility of formulating reflective, self-conscious and even historically, philosophically and ethically aware articulations of self that included, but were not altogether limited to, a wide variety of responses to the catastrophe that had befallen the SK themselves and European Jewry as a whole.[13]

Hoffman's invented descent into Judeocide – presented, as I have been arguing, in stylized fashion as almost a fable of self-slaughter – figures on the one hand as an inversion of the heroic reinstantiation of the SK (i.e. through legitimate violence directed against the SS), perhaps reflecting Nelson's stated reluctance to make an 'uprising film' populated by 'refugees from a Hollywood action picture'.[14] However, it can also be seen as the logical corollary of the (perhaps quintessentially American) idea of 'regeneration through violence',[15] for insofar as the life-world of the SK is understood as always-already delimited by violence as its starting and end-point, it is only in and through violence that their subjecthood can be figured. But the identification of resistance with violent rebellion alone is always likely to marginalize the other forms of social practice – individual and collective – through which, under conditions of unimaginable privation, the SK at once preserved their own humanity and undertook to record and comprehend their and the Jewish people's experience. These too demand to be conceived as acts of resistance: for example, the literary and evidential content alike of the 'Scrolls of Auschwitz' and the variety of continuing social practices to which, as Nicholas Chare and Dominic Williams meticulously document, the Scrolls themselves bear material witness through the very conditions of their fabrication and preservation.[16] The following section of this chapter aims to explore the (very limited) extent to which screen representations of the SK explore their subjecthood beyond violence to self and/or others, and the consequences of those self-imposed limits of thinking and seeing the SK in their full (historical) humanity.

Social Practice and/as Resistance

The persistence of social and even cultural life even in the abyss of the gas chambers and crematoria poses significant and disturbing challenges of conceptualization, comprehension and representation – challenges to which cinematic representations of the SK have generally failed to rise. The received image of the SK – if indeed we can speak of such – is of men brutalized and traumatized to the point of psychic, emotional and spiritual death, reduced to shambling zombies or near-automata who undertook their atrocious assignments in a numbed stupor of repetitive, grinding physical labour. Indeed, the image of the crematorium slaves as 'robots' – in so many words – is a trope repeatedly invoked by the SK themselves. The testimonies (both those discovered posthumously and the interviews assembled by Gideon Greif) include, as Michael Berenbaum notes, numerous variations on this theme: 'I could not cry. I could not think. Like a robot' and many other similar statements.[17] Representations of the SK on film have frequently followed this lead. Thus, in *Escape from Sobibor*, our only, very brief glimpse of the workers within the 'Upper Camp' (the enclosed extermination compound, roughly analogous to the Birkenau crematoria as the 'living camp' was analogous to 'Canada') reveals silent, immobile figures slumped in catatonic dejection against the walls of the gas chamber itself or across the carts they will shortly use to transport the corpses to the pyres. Filmed in long shot in an optical point-of-view shot through the horrified eyes of a Jewish child labourer sent on an errand from the 'living camp' (where the remainder of the action takes place), the corpse handlers are presented as the walking dead themselves, variants of the abject 'Müsselmann' figure. There is zero possibility of a human encounter, let alone dramatic identification, with such figures, and bar a brief dialogue exchange where the impossibility of including the 'Upper Camp' workers in the uprising and proposed mass breakout is cursorily agreed, they are never seen or referred to again. In the seminal 1978 miniseries *Holocaust*, following his deportation to Auschwitz Karl (James Woods), eldest brother of the central Weiss family, ends up as a SK member, seen (with a sledgehammer irony characteristic of the show) unwittingly clearing away his own mother's clothes after she has entered the gas chamber. As a major character throughout the show, Karl cannot be distanced from the viewer like the anonymous mute zombies of *Escape from Sobibor*; however, Woods plays the scene with a hollow-eyed, blank-faced stare and robotic gait that fully corresponds to the cliché of the SK as living dead. That Karl is a gifted artist makes his degradation all the more apparent and poignant.

The Grey Zone also incorporates this robot motif. Several of the wide shots of the exterior of the crematoria grounds discover squad members (not the handful of individuated central characters, but anonymous extras) sitting or standing, statue-like, between shifts. Perhaps more striking is the long slow push in towards Schlermer, silent and expressionless, drinking mechanically, almost metronomically from a bottle of spirits as he waits in deep shadow alone and silent outside the offscreen gas chamber (*TGZ* 20/24–25).[18] At the tail of the scene, Rosenthal enters, unrecognizably insectoid in a gas mask, rubber gauntlets and apron, and hands another gas mask and pair of gauntlets to Schlermer, who, wordlessly and without acknowledging Rosenthal, dons them and renders himself equally dehumanized.[19] The starkly industrial *mise-en-scène* and the ominous mechanical grinding on the soundtrack – the extractor fans powering up to ventilate the death chamber – combines with the sinister cyborg-like visage of the fully-garbed SK in their protective gear to lend this scene, like some others in the film, a flavour almost of dystopic science fiction.

Nelson's deployment of science-fiction tropes is tactical rather than a consistent dimension of the film; nevertheless, it both offers the audience a generic 'map' through the disorienting netherworld of the crematoria[20] and is bound up with his general conception of the Holocaust as industrialized murder (indeed, the generic discourses of dystopic SF themselves relate importantly to philosophical claims for the Holocaust as a perversion – or alternatively the logical culmination – of rational scientific modernity).[21] This idea is repeatedly emphasized in the Director's Notes Nelson circulated to cast and crew ahead of principal photography. In contrast to the Nazis' 'crude' pre-Auschwitz methods of murder – 'ranging from the improvised to the quasi-systematic' – he stresses the idea of Auschwitz as 'an enormous factory, plain and simple':

> This is why, throughout the script, I go again and again to the image of a factory, and why you will hear me throughout our process, in often callous ways, pushing us past the immediate and unimpeachable horror of the images and situations we'll depict to a place that's colder, more ruthless, more *true*.[22]

There is no need to litigate the historical 'truth', as Nelson claims, of Auschwitz-as-factory, except to note that this governing concept leads him to depict the slaughter as a far calmer, more streamlined, smoothly running and altogether 'cleaner' process than by most accounts it typically was (including an unhistorical depiction of the camp orchestra playing serenely at the very entrance to the Crematorium II[23] undressing room).[24] So the portrayal of the SK as dehumanized robots is allied to, and supports, a generalized understanding, first of the Birkenau gas chambers and crematoria as the ultimate iteration of or perhaps in some sense the 'authentic' Holocaust in ways that the 'Holocaust by bullets', the Chełmno gas vans or even the Operation Reinhard camps were not, and, second, of its industrial aspect as the defining quality of this 'authentic' Holocaust, characterized (as Nelson says in relation to the Birkenau contracting and construction process) by its 'absolute bloodlessness'.[25] (*Son of Saul*, by contrast, portrays a chaotic environment – 'filled with cries and shouts, haste and violence'[26] – where structure, authority and even language constantly teeter on the verge of collapse, very far removed from the image of Auschwitz as in any sense a sterile death factory. The two films' contrasting depictions of the open-air pyres to which the SS resorted when the crematoria were overwhelmed by the sheer volume of deportations during the liquidation of Hungarian Jewry – atrocious yet quotidian in *The Grey Zone*, frenzied, phantasmagoric and all-but-anarchic in *Son of Saul* – exemplifies Nelson's and Nemes' different approaches.) The question then is whether this somewhat abstract and oversimplified thesis concerning the Holocaust generally also promotes the abstraction of the SK themselves from the multidimensional complexity of their lived reality, as terrifying and terrible as that was.

Posing the question of whether the SK 'lost their sense of humanity' as the SS unquestionably had, Gideon Greif argues that a close reading of SK testimonies reveals 'a different aspect' of their daily life – one in which 'emotional and human sentiment' did not, despite everything, vanish.[27] Greif points out the intense anguish at the slaughter – far from numbed acceptance – ubiquitously present in the surviving testimonies. In their pioneering analysis of the material textuality of the 'Scrolls of Auschwitz', paying attention not only to their narrative and informational content but also to the histories densely encoded in the artefacts themselves, Chare and Williams point out that the very existence and preservation of the Scrolls testifies to collaborative action amongst squad members, conscious of the vital importance of the act of testifying: the need to 'organize' writing materials and the opportunity to safely write with them could not have been come by easily or, in all likelihood, in a purely solitary way.[28] They note too the varied self-conceptions of the different writers whose testimonies have been recovered – as historian, in the case of Zalman Lewental, or poet and polemicist, in the case of Zalman Gradowski: identities that simply by existing and by commanding our recognition, *as* consciously held (and, indeed, fashioned) identities, challenge 'many of the conventional understandings of Holocaust writing (that the Shoah went unwitnessed, that its victims lost all sense of self)'.[29] No more than the SK writers themselves, who note the diverse responses and coping strategies amongst their comrades – including, certainly, the retreat of some into a neutered, robotic shell – do these commentators suggest that the capacity for sustained observation of self and environment, let alone for translating those observations into literary forms, was universal amongst the SK, any more than it would be in any random group thrown together. But this is surely precisely the point: as unique and inconceivably terrible – and of course wholly unbidden by the victims themselves – as their circumstances were, the men of the SK were not utterly consumed by them, or not, at least, to the point where their subjecthood and self-understandings, or even the possibility thereof, were entirely annihilated even as they confronted their own inevitable and impending deaths. And in such circumstances, neither self-definition nor resistance itself was confined exclusively to the forms or discourses of violent action.

The idea of cultural practice and the persistence of 'ordinary' (in this context, of course, not ordinary at all) life as forms of resistance in the 'concentrationary universe' is a familiar one and has been especially well documented in Holocaust historiography: for instance, the persistence in the ghettoes of (often clandestine) communal religious observance, political activism and publication, children's religious and secular education, and musical and theatrical performances. In the extreme environment of the death camps, the specific *forms* of resistance through culture were enormously reduced and attenuated, but the *mode* of such resistance, as recent analysts of SK testimonies have shown, was consistent with Jewish practice elsewhere under Nazi rule. This cultural continuity itself reflects the larger sense in which the members of the SK did not simply cease to be themselves – as individuals, as Jews and as members of their particular communities – at the moment of their induction into the 'special squads'; rather, as Gideon Greif observes, their experiences 'strengthened existing character lines and sharpened others'.[30] Indeed, given the systematic German practice of dehumanizing and denaturalizing Jewish experience – for example, by insisting on referring to deportees as 'cargo' or bodies as 'pieces' – this stubborn refusal to accept the preferred Nazi avatar of Jewish slaves as inhuman/ahuman/subhuman drone, in favour of an attachment to character and through it to selfhood, might itself be considered a form of resistance.

Little of this complex and multifaceted subjectivity is to be found in screen depictions of the SK. Psychic and – whatever form these might take – cultural forms of resistance are generally subordinated to more obvious and externalized gestures, typically the preparation and execution of armed insurrection.[31] In the process, the struggle to preserve subjecthood as itself a kind of resistance tends to be treated either as a nonissue (because the integrity of the self is not seen to be seriously imperilled by the environment of the extermination camps) or unachievable (because the self is obviously annihilated by this environment). An example of the former is *Escape from Sobibor*. Admittedly, by confining its principal action and characters, as previously noted, to the 'living camp' (relegating the SK-like corpse handlers in the 'Upper Camp' to the narrative margins and placing them effectively beyond representation), the film allows them and itself a degree of distance, in terms of their daily duties and conditions, from the ultimate horrors of the murder apparatus. Nonetheless, the viewer is struck by the lack of evident trauma amongst the camp's worker Jews – almost of all of whom have lost their entire families upon arrival at Sobibór – and their relatively calm adaptation to their situation. Though the film tracks some new arrivals through the shock of realization (of their families' true fates), the blandly mimetic mode of Gold's direction and

Reginald Rose's script convey at best a superficial sense of their internal process. Rather, the narrative moves swiftly on to its principal business: the planning of the uprising and mass escape.

Escape from Sobibor is nonetheless unusual in films set in the death camps for the particular attention it pays to personal (including sexual) relationships amongst the prisoners.[32] Though these relationships are in themselves little more than indifferent sketches, they mandate a number of scenes in the Jewish barracks depicting the persistence of social life including cooking, music-making, gambling and general kvetching as well as sex and romance. The lengthiest of these scenes features an SS-sponsored dance accompanied by a prisoner ensemble. As portrayed in the film, the dance creates an affective space in which the routines of movement to music allow couples to make their attraction known and pair off, thus appropriating the voyeuristic spectacle intended by the SS for some degree of authentic emotional exploration and exchange. The testimony of Sobibór survivor Thomas Toivi Blatt characterizes such vignettes as atrophied, emotionally depleted rote enactments of the contentless forms of social intercourse, using the by-now familiar metaphor: as a fellow prisoner tells him, 'it's because we've become robots; our survival instincts have taken over'.[33] In the film, however, and notwithstanding the central character Leon Feldhandler's (Alan Arkin) assertion that every day of continued life in the camp is 'an agony of conscience', in general the Jews of Sobibór neither succumb to nor even evidently grapple with the impact of their trauma. Rose's script uses Toivi's (Jason Palmer) enraged response to scenes of social life in the barracks and accusations of passivity or even complicity as the pretext for a rather formulaic but authoritative declaration by the film: 'What is there to do but survive? Yes, we sing, we dance, sometimes we make jokes . . . we make love. If not, we deny life. We work for them [i.e. the Germans] so we may survive. And we survive for a reason. Revenge. And someday we'll have it'. Thus, social practice in itself is presented as, at best, marking time prior to the opportunity for decisive, meaningful action in the form of armed revolt.

The all-male environment of the Birkenau crematoria, unlike the Reinhard camps, rules out the exploration of (heterosexual) romantic or sexual encounters in SK films (though *Son of Saul* suggests that Saul, perhaps prior to joining the SK but perhaps not, maintained a relationship with a woman working in the 'Canada' compound – his SK comrade Abraham also notes that Saul 'used to talk about women'). Jewish religious observance, by contrast, was in some fashion a universal presence in every camp, yet almost no films pay meaningful attention to its persistence (or abandonment) amongst the SK, let alone its role either in fostering (armed) resistance or as a form of resistance itself. Survivor testimony, however – especially the Scrolls of Auschwitz – makes it clear that Orthodox Jews (like the Scrolls writers Leyb Langfus and Zalman Gradowski) were well represented amongst the Birkenau SK, and that their faith and religious practice both persisted throughout their captivity. Gideon Greif notes the role of Orthodox Jews in offering spiritual guidance, consolation and sustenance to their tormented colleagues, and that although not necessarily in any straightforwardly causal way, religious convictions drove several of the resistance leaders and perhaps empowered them in taking on leadership roles. None of this is explored in any of the films that depict SK experience.[34] Indeed, although, as the foregoing indicates, religious practice was no barrier to active participation or leadership in armed resistance – if anything it was the reverse – the tendency in screen depictions has been at worst to associate faith and observance, explicitly or by implication, with passivity and acquiescence, and at best to treat it as irrelevant to more obviously meaningful (and cinematic) acts of violent resistance.

The unproduced 2008 screenplay *Seven Blades of Grass*, a more stylized though still broadly realist account of a Reinhard camp compared to *Escape from Sobibor* – in this case Treblinka – is very much the exception not only in portraying a mix of observant, secular and assimilated Jews, but also in making at least one central character's reconnection to Jewish tradition, and the Kabbalistic mysticism of another, feed directly into the preparation for the uprising around which this script too is dramatically centred.[35] By including dream sequences and fashioning individualistically idiomatic dialogue – hard-boiled, scholarly, devout, cynical, pedantic, etc. – for its characters, the script also departs from the tendency in SK dramas (especially apparent in *The Grey Zone*, where although the characters represent different stances on, for example, the timing of the revolt, the fate of the girl, etc., they all speak in very much the same way) towards a pervasive flattening of affect and deindividualization belied by the evidence of the Scrolls. Religion in *Seven Blades of Grass* is not (as in Frank Cottrell Boyce's 2008 BBC television drama *God on Trial*) the pretext for formal theological debate about God's existence or accountability for the Holocaust as such, but a bulwark and redoubt of Jewish collective and individual identity as well as an important device through (or against) which the persistent interiority and imaginative worlds of the Treblinka prisoners can be accessed dramatically.

Religious observance of any kind is notably absent from both *Escape from Sobibor* and *The Grey Zone*: none of the principals or indeed a single speaking character is characterized as devout,[36] and none of the numerous (i.e. individual) deaths in either film receives any commemoration or mourning, even in the form of a muttered Kaddish. By contrast, religious ritual is very obviously central to *Son of Saul* and is indeed explicitly identified as an act of resistance in its own right, as important if not more so than the armed uprising that here too helps structure the drama. However, Saul's is a ritual of a very particular and highly individualistic, indeed, arguably solipsistic kind that places it at a remove from the communal traditions that, according to SK testimonies, the religious amongst the SK sought to preserve and maintain, to say nothing of the forms of solidarity that religious observance may have helped uphold and that in their turn ultimately contributed to the Birkenau uprising. A small group of Orthodox Jews are briefly glimpsed observing Shabbat in the margins of Saul's constantly moving point of view, but their prayers are immediately counterpointed by offscreen heckling and mockery from other SK members. It is made clear elsewhere in the film that the SK have established their own commemorative practices: when Saul first identifies a dead youth as his son, he is directed to a rabbi working as a Kapo at the ovens, who says Kaddish for SK family members (indicating that 'processing' one's own family is a predictable occurrence); later, in the face of Saul's insistence on a full Jewish burial, the rabbi upbraids him for not conforming to established SK practice. As Saul's quixotic quest proceeds, searching for (another, better) rabbi, first amongst the other SK units – leading directly to the death of the squad member he approaches – and subsequently amongst the newly arrived deportees, we see repeatedly that his mission is undertaken not only in isolation from the collective project of the resistance in the crematoria, but also in effect against it. By bringing the youth's purloined body into the SK living quarters, Saul imperils his comrades by potentially drawing the attention of the SS, in turn threatening to expose the plans for the uprising; by deviating to the fire pits in search of a rabbi upon his return from the women's camp, he misplaces the vital gunpowder entrusted (improbably) to him; once the revolt (presented in the film, notwithstanding scenes of conspiratorial planning, as not so much premature as spontaneous and virtually anarchic) breaks out, Saul makes very clear his disinclination to contribute, instead exploiting the chaos amidst the fighting to make his escape, still shouldering the body of his 'son' and accompanied by the 'rabbi' he rescued from the fire pits, into the surrounding woods. Saul's indifference, even hostility, to any acts of resistance beyond his own is not confined to the rebellion: when a squad member obstructs him as he brings the body into the SK living quarters, Saul threatens to reveal to the SS where the objector has buried his secret writings.

Saul's behaviour is consistent with Nemes' overall portrayal of the Hobbesian condition of SK life as atomized, conflictual and culturally antagonistic (whereas in *The Grey Zone* the SK are all Hungarian – meaning they speak unaccented American English – the squads in *Son of Saul* are multinational and polyglot, leading to frequent episodes of mutual incomprehension and frustration). If *Escape from Sobibor* depicts an implausibly homogeneous prisoner community and *The Grey Zone* a beleaguered and resentful yet still functional platoon-like unity of purpose,[37] Nemes' vision seems to owe more to the Sartrean concept of 'seriality', whose infection of European Jewry – with paralysing consequence for effective resistance – Simone de Beauvoir attributes to Nazi 'divide and rule' strategies in her preface to Jean-François Steiner's controversial 1966 nonfiction novel *Treblinka*.[38] In de Beauvoir's account, it was the acknowledgement of the universal nature of the Nazi extermination project – an acknowledgement that for the slave workers in the death camps (and equally the Auschwitz SK) was uniquely unavoidable – that ultimately countermanded this seriality and enabled the collective resistance whose most dramatic expression was the armed uprisings undertaken in the full and, crucially, *shared* acceptance of certain death. Not only the pervasive atmosphere of mutual hostility but even the internal organization of the SK living quarters – which in *Son of Saul* replace the bunks, bed linens and well-supplied dining table shown in *The Grey Zone* (and recorded by Nyiszli) with a shanty town-like milieu of sheets serving as partitions, mattresses or heaps of rags on floors, etc. – give an impression of an almost completely socially de-evolved environment. Against such a backdrop, the *acte gratuit* to which Saul commits himself – his private, inscrutable and ephemeral act of restitution – and its precedence over the work of testimony and bearing witness become comprehensible and even justifiable.

Conclusion

Visualizing the lived historical reality of the SK – and, albeit perhaps to a lesser extent, that of the slave workers in the Reinhard death camps – in ways that a mainstream audience will find comprehensible and/or tolerable is a huge challenge; in his very positive review of *Son of Saul*, historian Nikolaus Wachsmann nonetheless admits to finding the film 'almost impossible to watch'.[39] It is entirely understandable that filmmakers seeking to lend narrative and interpretative form – which is also to say communicative effectivity – to these experiences, so horrific and so profoundly disturbing at a number of levels, should limn that form via the extraordinary heroism and moral courage of the uprisings mounted in the death camps against all conceivable odds. Nor should filmmakers embarking on such deeply unpromising terrain (in purely commercial terms) be unduly criticized for trying to give their work a minimal marketplace foothold by organizing narratives around recognizable motifs of armed resistance to absolute evil. Tim Blake Nelson admits candidly that 'without the rebellion the movie is but a bleak portrait of the twelfth *Sonderkommando*, and I dare say it would have no audience'.[40] Indeed, one might imagine that the film's coda – 'this is how the work continues' – gives a flavour of what this nonexistent alternate version of *The Grey Zone* might look like, and its stylized affectlessness feels further removed from lived history than anything else in the film.

However, this chapter has sought to identify other elements of the SK experience, as identified by historians and analysts of SK testimony, and to consider the implications of eliding those elements – such as friendship, religious observance, the interior worlds of imagination and fantasy – in favour of more obviously photogenic acts of armed struggle. We can see that the films discussed here understand the life-world of the SK as wholly circumscribed by violence and death and do not seriously attempt to think dialectically the relationship of individuals and groups to such extreme situations in terms of the defence and preservation of coherent forms of subjecthood. This critique extends to *Son of Saul*, notwithstanding its departure from many of the operative conventions of other SK films, insofar as Nemes depicts a disintegration of the self that is in some ways the most complete and disabling of all.

The protagonists of *The Grey Zone* and *Son of Saul* both end their stories – and their lives – in passages of quiet intimacy that starkly contrast to the ubiquitous violence and conflict of their existence in the crematoria. For Hoffman and Rosenthal, it is the moments before their execution along with the rest of the squad after the insurrection has been crushed by the SS, during which they exchange details of their pre-Holocaust lives in Hungary that, apparently, they have never shared before, and discover that in another world they might have been 'neighbours'. Saul, in keeping with the solitariness of his whole narrative, seems to experience a private epiphany upon glimpsing a young Polish boy peering into the barn where he and the other SK escapees have taken refuge; perhaps the smile that, only now, creeps across his face indicates that he sees in the boy the spirit of the 'son' whose mortal remains he has tried to honour, or perhaps it is the sight of a free boy – any boy – that rekindles a warmth lost in the crematoria. In both these cases, it is the certainty and inescapability of imminent death that enables these stolen moments: death perversely releases the SK back into a humanity functionally extinguished by life in the crematoria. Again, in fact, we see that *life* in the crematoria is regarded as an impossibility.

'We did something', Rosenthal and Hoffman tell each other in *The Grey Zone* instants before the SS executioner reaches them, a line that with presumably deliberate ambiguity Nelson allows a double reference to the uprising and the attempt to save the girl. What perhaps none of the films discussed here has fully been able to demonstrate is that in every moment and in all the ways they succeeded in preserving, however precariously, their own identities amidst the unimaginable nightmare of the gas chambers and crematoria, the SK 'did' as much as they did in the more overt and melodramatic ways depicted in their onscreen portrayals.

Barry Langford is Professor of Film Studies at Royal Holloway, University of London. His publications include *Film Genre: Hollywood and Beyond* (2005), *Teaching Holocaust Literature and Film* (2008, with Robert Eaglestone) and *Post-classical Hollywood* (2010). He is a member of the Holocaust Research Institute at Royal Holloway and has published widely on Holocaust film and television. He is currently completing a monograph on Holocaust film, *Darkness Visible: The Holocaust in Cinema*. He is also a professional screenwriter whose credits include the award-winning 2005 Holocaust-themed short film *Torte Bluma*.

Notes

1. Scene 40/page 46 of *The Grey Zone* published shooting script (New York: Newmarket, 2003): all scene references hereafter in the format '*TGZ* [scene nbr]/[page nbr]'.
2. Nelson's screenplay follows Miklós Nyiszli's memoir, his principal source, in his numbering of the Auschwitz crematoria – identifying the principal location of the action as 'The Number One Crematorium' (*TGZ* 1/1) when it is evidently Crematorium II at Auschwitz-Birkenau that is being depicted, not Crematorium I (the original gas chamber and crematorium located just outside the perimeter fence of the Auschwitz I camp and no longer used for killings by October 1944, when the action of *The Grey Zone* takes place). A high-angle shot establishing shot of the crematoria complex as a whole (not included in the final release cut) depicting a factory-like serial array of identical buildings and smokestacks also indicates erroneously that all four Birkenau crematoria were located in the same zone of the camp and built to a uniform architectural pattern (in fact, as Nelson's 'Director's Notes' acknowledge, Crematoria II and III, the largest installations, with subterranean gas chambers, were mirrored designs at the camp's western extremity while Crematoria IV and V were more cheaply fabricated wholly above-ground buildings on its northern margins). Here too, the historical inaccuracy is evidently intended to simplify for the audience the geographical, hence logistical, relations between the SK teams planning the uprising.
3. The scene begins on page 44 of the 121-page screenplay and ends on page 49.
4. Identified in the script only as 'Old Man' and referred to as such by Hoffman in his later account of the episode to the girl.

5. Erin McGlothlin discusses the ways in which Nyiszli's characterization works with and against 'the trope of the doctor-hero': '"The Doctor is Different": Ambivalent Ethics, Cinematic Heroics and the Figure of the Jewish Doctor in Tim Blake Nelson's *The Grey Zone*', in Oleksandr Kobrynskyy and Gerd Bayer (eds), *Holocaust Cinema in the 21st Century: Memory, Images, and the Ethics of Representation* (New York: Wallflower, 2015), 188–93.
6. Alex Bangert, 'Changing Narratives and Images of the Holocaust: Tim Blake Nelson's Film *The Grey Zone* (2001)', *New Cinemas: Journal of Contemporary Film* 6(1) (2008), 22.
7. Megan Ratner, 'Imagining the Unimaginable: Interview with László Nemes on *Son of Saul*', *Film Quarterly* 69(3) (2016), 58.
8. Abramowics, who as noted earlier in the film derides Hoffman's hopes of liberation and aggressively insists that the SK are all 'dead already', later rejects Rosenthal's assumption of the uprising as a suicide mission, revealing he plans to escape: 'Fuck you, Max . . . I hope I live 'til I'm ninety' (*TGZ* 66/84).
9. At the Cannes press conference for *Son of Saul*, lead actor Géza Röhrig responded angrily to suggestions that the SK were 'half victims, half hangmen': no one should have 'the slightest doubt that the *Sonderkommando* were not just equally victimised but more victimised'. Retrieved 12 April 2019 from https://www.theguardian.com/film/2015/may/19/geza-rohrig-son-of-saul-interview-auschwitz-jewish-prisoner-sonderkommando. On *The Grey Zone* as an example of 'Holocaust impiety', see Matthew Boswell's analysis of the film in *Holocaust Impiety in Literature, Popular Music and Film* (Basingstoke: Palgrave Macmillan, 2012), 159–78.
10. Dominic Williams, 'Figuring the Grey Zone: The Auschwitz *Sonderkommando* in Contemporary Culture', *Holocaust Studies* 25(1–2) (2019), 141–57.
11. McGlothlin, '"The Doctor is Different"', 188.
12. Lanzmann asserts that 'the survivors in *Shoah*, they are all members of the *Sonderkommando*, who testify for the dead' ('Seminar with Claude Lanzmann, 11 April 1990', *Yale French Studies* 79 (1991), 99). This is obviously factually incorrect. Even if one ahistorically extends the category of the SK (as a designation for Jewish slave workers in extermination sites, apparently applied by the SS only to the Birkenau crematoria squads, though the word 'Sonderkommando' – meaning simply 'special squad' – can be found elsewhere in the history of the Holocaust) to include not only the Chełmno survivor Simon Srebnik, who as a body handler performed directly comparable duties, but also survivors of the 'living camps' at Treblinka and Sobibór such as Richard Glazar and Abraham Bomba, who were not directly engaged in the killing process (no survivors of the extermination compounds at the Operation Reinhard camps are featured in the film), there remain a number of other Jewish witnesses in the film including the Warsaw Ghetto fighter Itzhak Zukermann and Auschwitz survivor Rudolf Vrba, none of whom were at any stage SK members. Assuming this is not simply carelessness on Lanzmann's part, it may reflect his tendency both to collapse the Holocaust as a whole into the 'industrialized' death factories in Poland, and within that further to collapse Jewish experiences of martyrdom into their most extreme, mortified and – in the testimonial sense, because of their unparalleled proximity to the 'invisible' scene of death in the gas chamber – privileged form, the SK.
13. Williams, 'Figuring the Grey Zone', 151.
14. Tim Blake Nelson, 'Director's Notes', in *The Grey Zone* shooting script, 158–59.
15. The reference here is to Richard Slotkin's celebrated discussion in *Gunfighter Nation: The Myth of the Frontier in Twentieth-Century America* (Norman: University of

Oklahoma Press, 1998) of the Western as a paradigmatic expression of the ontological centrality of violence to American culture.
16. See Nicholas Chare and Dominic Williams, *Matters of Testimony: Interpreting the Scrolls of Auschwitz* (Oxford: Berghahn Books, 2016).
17. Gideon Greif, *We Wept without Tears: Testimonies of the Jewish Sonderkommando from Auschwitz* (New Haven: Yale University Press, 2005), 339, quoted in Michael Berenbaum, '*Sonderkommando:* Testimony from *Evidence*', in Jonathan Petropoulos and John K. Roth (eds), *Gray Zones: Ambiguity and Compromise in the Holocaust and its Aftermath* (New York: Berghahn Books, 2005), 65.
18. In a subtle touch, Schlermer's repetitive drinking here associates him (and by extension the SK generally) with SS Muhsfeldt (Harvey Keitel), who in a later scene also knocks back shots of spirits several times in succession – albeit from a cut-glass decanter (*TGZ* 42/49).
19. Adam Brown describes Schlermer's demeanour in this scene, which he takes to illustrate the 'air of normality' the SK adopt to their assigned tasks, as 'calm', whereas I take it rather to be emotionally null and dehumanized. See Adam Brown, *Judging 'Privileged' Jews: Holocaust Ethics, Representation, and the 'Grey Zone'* (New York: Berghahn Books, 2013), 175.
20. On the 'genericization' of the Holocaust as representational strategy, see Barry Langford, *Film Genre: Hollywood and Beyond* (Edinburgh: Edinburgh University Press, 2005).
21. On the Holocaust in/as science fiction in contemporary cinema, see Barry Langford, 'Globalizing the Holocaust: Fantasies of Annihilation on Contemporary Media Culture', in Axel Bangert, Robert Gordon and Libby Saxton (eds), *Holocaust Intersections: Genocide and Visual Culture at the New Millennium* (London: Routledge, 2013), 123–24.
22. Nelson, 'Director's Notes', 143, 145, emphasis in original.
23. As noted above, Crematorium I in the film.
24. Ironically enough, given Nelson's stated determination to distinguish his film from the 'sentimentalize[d]' versions of Auschwitz in 'other films' (he feels no need to name them), the implausible placidity of this scene echoes Steven Spielberg's highly stylized depiction of the crematoria in *Schindler's List* immediately following the infamous 'shower scene'.
25. Nelson, 'Director's Notes', 144.
26. Nikolaus Wachsmann, 'Nightmare of Crime', *Sight and Sound* 26(5) (2016), 19.
27. Gideon Greif, 'Everyday Life in the *Sonderkommando*', in Petropoulos and Roth (eds), *Gray Zones*, 44.
28. Chare and Williams, *Matters of Testimony*, 32–49.
29. Ibid., 85.
30. Greif, 'Everyday Life in the *Sonderkommando*', 44.
31. *The Grey Zone* poster featured the strapline: 'While the world was fighting . . . a secret battle was about to erupt'.
32. The Operation Reinhard camps included female seamstresses and laundresses amongst their slave workers, at Sobibór from the outset and at Treblinka apparently only following an outbreak of typhus. (Little detail is known of Bełżec, from which there were only two known survivors.) On living conditions and social life in the Reinhard camps, see Yitzhak Arad, *Belzec, Sobibor, Treblinka: The Operation Reinhard Death Camps* (Bloomington: Indiana University Press, 1987), 199–208, 226–37.

33. Thomas Toivi Blatt, *From the Ashes of Sobibor* (Evanston, IL: Northwestern University Press, 1997), 96.
34. Frank Cottrell Boyce's Auschwitz-set BBC television play *God on Trial* (2008) explicitly debates Jewish theological interpretations of the Holocaust, but excludes the SK – never seen and referred to only briefly in dialogue, where they are characterized as collaborators – from participation or consideration.
35. Full disclosure: the present writer coauthored *Seven Blades of Grass* (with Benjamin Ross).
36. Nelson's *Grey Zone* script identifies the SK workers in the 'hair room' (which did not exist in the actual crematoria) as 'mostly Orthodox Jews', but this (unhistorical) identification is not obvious onscreen. It is not clear what Nelson's purpose here was, unless it was to suggest (also unhistorically) that religious Jews comprised a discrete, self-sufficient or even quarantined subgroup within the SK (*TGZ* 48/47).
37. A recurrent motif in *The Grey Zone* is the lack of solidarity between the different national Jewish communities – in the film, Polish and Hungarian – in the SK: 'What's another week to these guys [i.e. Polish Jews]? Another ten thousand Hungarians? They don't care about us. They never have' (*TGZ* 30/32–33).
38. De Beauvoir, 'Preface'; Jean-François Steiner, *Treblinka*, trans. Helen Weaver (New York: Meridian, 1994), xxi–xxiii.
39. Wachsmann, 'Nightmare of Crime', 20.
40. Nelson, 'Director's Notes', 158–59.

Bibliography

Arad, Yitzhak. *Belzec, Sobibor, Treblinka: The Operation Reinhard Death Camps*. Bloomington: Indiana University Press, 1987.
Bangert, Alex. 'Changing Narratives and Images of the Holocaust: Tim Blake Nelson's Film *The Grey Zone* (2001)', *New Cinemas: Journal of Contemporary Film* 6(1) (2008), 17–32.
Berenbaum, Michael. '*Sonderkommando*: Testimony from *Evidence*', in Jonathan Petropoulos and John K. Roth (eds), *Gray Zones: Ambiguity and Compromise in the Holocaust and its Aftermath*. New York: Berghahn Books, 2005, 61–69.
Blatt, Thomas Toivi. *From the Ashes of Sobibor*. Evanston, IL: Northwestern University Press, 1997.
Boswell, Matthew. *Holocaust Impiety in Literature, Popular Music and Film*. Basingstoke: Palgrave Macmillan, 2012.
Brown, Adam. *Judging 'Privileged' Jews: Holocaust Ethics, Representation, and the 'Grey Zone'*. New York: Berghahn Books, 2013.
Chare, Nicholas, and Dominic Williams, *Matters of Testimony: Interpreting the Scrolls of Auschwitz*. New York: Berghahn Books, 2016.
De Beauvoir, Simone. 'Preface', in Jean-François Steiner, *Treblinka*, trans. Helen Weaver. New York: Meridian, 1994.
Greif, Gideon. 'Between Sanity and Insanity: Spheres of Everyday Life in the *Sonderkommando*', in Jonathan Petropoulos and John K. Roth (eds), *Gray Zones: Ambiguity and Compromise in the Holocaust and its Aftermath*. New York: Berghahn Books, 2005, 37–60.
———. *We Wept without Tears: Testimonies of the Jewish Sonderkommando from Auschwitz*. New Haven: Yale University Press, 2005.

Langford, Barry. *Film Genre: Hollywood and Beyond*. Edinburgh: Edinburgh University Press, 2005.
——. 'Globalizing the Holocaust: Fantasies of Annihilation on Contemporary Media Culture', in Axel Bangert, Robert Gordon and Libby Saxton (eds), *Holocaust Intersections: Genocide and Visual Culture at the New Millennium*. London: Routledge, 2013, 113–29.
Lanzmann, Claude. 'Seminar with Claude Lanzmann, 11 April 1990', *Yale French Studies* 79 (1991), 82–99.
McGlothlin, Erin. '"The Doctor is Different": Ambivalent Ethics, Cinematic Heroics and the Figure of the Jewish Doctor in Tim Blake Nelson's *The Grey Zone*', in Oleksandr Kobrynskyy and Gerd Bayer (eds), *Holocaust Cinema in the 21st Century: Memory, Images, and the Ethics of Representation*. New York: Wallflower, 2015, 188–93.
Nelson, Tim Blake. *The Grey Zone*. New York: Newmarket, 2003.
Ratner, Megan. 'Imagining the Unimaginable: Interview with László Nemes on *Son of Saul*', *Film Quarterly* 69(3) (2016), 58–66.
Slotkin, Richard. *Gunfighter Nation: The Myth of the Frontier in Twentieth-Century America*. Norman: University of Oklahoma Press, 1998.
Wachsmann, Nikolaus. 'Nightmare of Crime', *Sight and Sound* 26(5) (2016), 18–20.
Williams, Dominic. 'Figuring the Grey Zone: The Auschwitz *Sonderkommando* in Contemporary Culture', *Holocaust Studies* 25(1–2) (2019), 141–57.

Chapter 18

'We Can't Know What We're Capable Of'

Approaching the 'Grey Zone' in Holocaust Film

Adam Brown

> I would like you to judge my actions so as to tell me how one should have behaved and you would have behaved in my place.
>
> —Ryszard Kordek, 'Epilogue',
> in Jan Południak, *Sonder*

In his epilogue to a transcribed interview with Holocaust survivor Henryk Mandelbaum, Ryszard Kordek recounts the above request being made by Mandelbaum of a group of American-Jewish youths some fifty years after the war's end. Mandelbaum was speaking at the ruins of Crematorium V in Auschwitz-Birkenau, the camp where much of his family had been murdered in 1943 and where he himself – then in his early twenties – would suffer several horrific months working in its gas chambers and crematoria. As one of the few surviving members of the Auschwitz Sonderkommando (SK), Mandelbaum would go on to be actively involved in educating new generations about the Nazi past, appearing in two documentaries and telling his story in person throughout Poland and Germany.

Speaking to a group of young people far removed from the unprecedented events he witnessed, Mandelbaum's suggestion that day was followed by marked silence among his audience. Simultaneously inviting judgement and implying that his listeners have no right to judge, in one brief sentence Mandelbaum elucidates the fundamental dilemma encountered when attempting to understand the extreme situations of the death camp crematorium workers. Responses to this problem often form around what is essentially a rhetorical question: 'What would you have done?' The intersecting problems of judgement and representation that stem from this, articulated so powerfully in Primo Levi's paradigmatic essay on the 'grey zone', are no more evident than in artistic explorations of the liminal figures of the SK.

This chapter examines how Holocaust fiction films have engaged with the traumatic circumstances Mandelbaum could only inadequately describe as 'hell'.[1] The increased interest in the Auschwitz SK in particular raises important questions about the ongoing role of this group of victims in the formation of historical understandings and collective memories. Contextualized within the genre of Holocaust film and the growing fascination with the antiheroic generally, recent filmic depictions of Jewish victims forced into morally ambiguous positions reveal them to be at the forefront of broader shifts in Holocaust popular culture that eschew a redemptory aesthetic and seek to unearth ethical complexities that have long been taboo.

'Here One Hesitates to Speak of Privilege': Judging the Sonderkommando

When I began my research for what would become *Judging 'Privileged' Jews: Holocaust Ethics, Representation, and the 'Grey Zone'*,[2] it was evident from an early stage that the ethical dilemmas that confronted members of the SK would be central to my work. In fact, Tim Blake Nelson's response to Levi's writings in his film *The Grey Zone* (2001) had been a major catalyst for the project. The resulting book began with a passage from Zalman Lewental's unearthed SK manuscript and ended with Günther Anders' evocative poem 'What Would You Have Done?', although the study's overall focus is situated more broadly on representations of so-called 'privileged' Jews. This category also includes the leaders and other administrative officials of the Judenräte (Jewish councils); the members of the Jewish ghetto police (or Ordnungsdienst); the Kapos (chiefs) of forced labour squads in the camps; the prisoner-doctors who worked in *Lager* infirmaries, and various prisoner-functionaries. According to Levi's multilayered and often contradictory essay, these inhabitants of the 'grey zone' cannot be praised, but should also not be condemned for their controversial behaviour in extremis.[3] At the same time, Susan Pentlin emphasizes in her essay 'Holocaust Victims of Privilege' that in order to develop a deeper understanding of the Holocaust and its ethical implications, one must listen to the 'voices from the grey zone' and explore the often marginalized issues of 'position and privilege'.[4]

While I have encountered occasional wariness over my use of the term 'privileged' when delivering presentations at conferences and other forums,[5] I also witnessed on several occasions scepticism over my grouping of the SK alongside the other prisoner categories mentioned above. As Levi himself wrote of the crematorium workers in 'The Grey Zone': 'Here one hesitates to speak of privilege: whoever belonged to this group was privileged only to the extent that – but at what cost – he had enough to eat for a few months, certainly not because he could be envied'.[6] Yet, like Levi, my interest in the 'privileged' figures of the 'grey zone' is not concentrated on their better rations, limited exposure to the elements, or greater access to extra items for trade, but on the dynamics that have given rise to widespread (and generally negative) moral judgements on their behaviour by those attempting to come to terms with an inherently complicated past. Levi's writings on the 'grey zone' raise crucial questions: if Holocaust victims are not to be judged for their behaviour in a situation so utterly beyond their control, can judgement be suspended in representations of their experiences? And if judgement is indeed inevitable as soon as language is brought to bear on the issue, how should they be portrayed?

That the 'special squads' were – and I would argue increasingly are – being conceptualized as 'exceptional' is a curious development. This development partly arises from – and results in – moral distinctions being drawn between the minimal agency afforded to the crematorium workers and the seemingly greater ethical freedom (and therefore burden) of those with 'privileged' positions in the ghettos and camps who played very different roles. Compelled to undertake their ghastly duties or face immediate execution, the workers in the Birkenau SK would usually only be granted a reprieve of four months at most. The specific nature of their experiences, encased within an incomprehensible environment of constant, systematic mass killing, makes their common differentiation from other 'compromised' groups somewhat understandable. Any criticism of their 'cooperation' or 'participation' (the words themselves provide unwanted connotations) would implicitly suggest that those men who undertook the work should have 'chosen' to die instead. The correlation between refusal and death appears to be more decipherable for the SK when compared with the diverse situations of other 'privileged' prisoners; however, as soon as such distinctions between victims are made, a spectrum of blameworthiness imminently follows. This is not to suggest, of course, that the SK have completely avoided moral condemnation.

Gideon Grief's substantial study of the crematorium workers devotes many pages to 'the moral problematics' of his subject, stressing that 'while non-Jewish survivors expressed harsh criticism of the Sonderkommando, Jewish survivors have been the most pungent critics of all'.[7] Even Levi, who argued that any judgement on the SK should be suspended, cannot abstain from passing judgement through his rhetorical choices, literary allusions and implicit construction of moral binaries.[8] Nonetheless, as Bryan Cheyette points out, 'the ethical uncertainty at the heart of Levi's writings is the necessary critical yardstick by which one ought to understand present-day films and novels, many of which glibly assimilate the Holocaust in a breathtakingly untroubled manner'.[9] The way in which the paucity of language plays itself out varies widely across genres, and previous research has revealed that clear-cut judgements have for many decades been a central facet of representations of 'privileged' Jews in Holocaust memoir, video testimony, historical writing, documentary and fiction film.[10]

The substantial and ever-expanding scholarship on Holocaust cinema has long taken the discussion beyond that of representational limits alone, opening up avenues of thought on the medium's ethical potentialities, where dramatization inhabits an important place in the (re)negotiation of this traumatic past. Yet Levi's ambivalence is hardly something that is likely to be perceived as easily translatable or attractive to filmmakers. The representation of the SK in this arena has seen both an overshadowing of their experiences in films that appropriate their circumstances for various ends, and more recent and serious attempts to engage with their ethical dilemmas amidst a growing interest in themes of trauma, guilt and compromise.

Avoiding the 'Grey Zone': Appropriating the Crematorium Workers

The provocative figures of the 'special squads' have served as convenient plot devices at frequent intervals throughout Holocaust film history. In a reflection on the use of screen texts in Holocaust education, Barry Langford notes that the SK appear in cinema 'out of all proportion to their actual numbers or (arguably) historical significance'.[11] In one sense this has been the case, yet images of their presence and activities nearby or inside the gas chambers and crematoria (generally in Auschwitz) have often been loaded with meanings that repurpose their extreme situations for various political ends. In a more important sense than the merely quantitative, an engagement by filmmakers with the ethical dilemmas of those victims forced into the SK has usually been found wanting. On the whole, appearances of crematorium workers in fiction films have been governed by disparate ideological agendas and seldom dwell on the crucial questions with which Levi and others have been concerned. Instead, the experiences of the SK have been appropriated to communicate messages of Zionist legitimacy, Christian martyrdom and the triumph of Jewish resistance.

In the heavily politicized film *Exodus* (1960), which is based on Leon Uris' 1958 novel about the founding of Israel, experiences in an Auschwitz SK form the traumatic background of Dov Landau, a central character. Desperate to join the Irgun fighters in Palestine, Landau reluctantly admits in a particularly dramatic scene to his involvement in the crematoria. The filmmaker's creative licence is highlighted when Landau's expertise with dynamite (evidently valuable for the Irgun's activities) is revealed to have been obtained from the making of mass graves in Auschwitz. Additionally, a stark and simplistic judgement goes unquestioned in this scene when an Irgun leader forces Landau to admit 'you saved your own life by working in that camp as a *Sonderkommando*'. The imminent death that awaited the vast majority of crematorium workers is not addressed, hence the viewer is left to assume that Landau had other options before compromising himself.

The horrific experiences of the 'special squads' are appropriated in a very different way in Costa-Gavras' *Amen* (2002), which focuses on the issue of the Vatican's complicity with Nazi Germany through the story of historical figure Kurt Gerstein, an SS officer who attempted to expose the genocide. Based on Rolf Hochhuth's controversial 1963 play *The Deputy*, this film incorporates the heroic priest Riccardo Fontana (an invented character) to stand as the epitome of virtue and contrast with the marked indifference of the Catholic hierarchy. When his appeals to Pope Pius XII to intercede in the mass deportation of Rome's Jews fall on deaf ears, Fontana pins a yellow badge to his chest in order to be transported to Auschwitz as well. There he becomes a member of a SK and is at one point visited by Gerstein. Despite Gerstein's protestations, Father Riccardo refuses to leave his persecution in the crematoria, thereby sacrificing his life in protest. While *Amen*, like Hochhuth's stage play, generated controversy around 'Hitler's Pope',[12] the film does little to elucidate the complexities of 'privileged' positions in Auschwitz.

Looking beyond the above examples of appropriations of the 'special squads', the subject of Jewish resistance has collided even more strongly and frequently with depictions of SK in Holocaust films. Narratives that pivot on the actions of Gentile rescuers, armed Jewish resisters or those victims who undertake more spiritual forms of opposition, as in Roberto Benigni's *La vita è bella* (*Life is Beautiful*, 1997) or Peter Kassovitz's *Jacob the Liar* (1999), rarely visit the setting of the gas chambers in a detailed manner. Even where crematorium workers do appear on screen, they often do so as extras in the background whose circumstances are at best alluded to and at worst overlooked entirely. The prioritization of heroic deeds and happy endings is perhaps predictable in the context of what Ilan Avisar describes as the 'trivialising melodramatic action' and 'traditional clichés of conventional heroics' common to Hollywood Holocaust films dealing with rescue and resistance.[13]

Marvin J. Chomsky's immensely popular television miniseries *Holocaust: The Story of the Family Weiss* (1978) remains one of the most influential Holocaust screen texts and holds a particularly important place in filmic portrayals of the SK. Temporally situated in the middle of two other landmarks of Holocaust film history, George Stevens' *The Diary of Anne Frank* (1959) and Steven Spielberg's *Schindler's List* (1993), *Holocaust* has been credited with pushing the historical event into mainstream memory culture, helping to establish the Jewish particularity of the event and reaching hundreds of millions of viewers worldwide. On the other hand, its melodramatic tendencies and profuse sentimentality which signal the production's reliance on soap opera tropes to render the unprecedented past palatable have attracted considerable criticism for 'trivializing' the Holocaust.[14] Levi himself wrote several articles on the NBC miniseries, finding it to be fundamentally flawed in terms of its historical substance and generic conventions.[15] In a letter to a friend, Levi acknowledged the benefits of the mass dissemination of the miniseries, but wrote that 'it is, however, sad to think that in order to reach the man [*sic*] on the street, history has to be simplified and digested to such an extent'.[16] The eight-hour *Holocaust* miniseries follows the story(s) of various members of the wealthy, assimilated Weiss family as they experience the incremental antisemitic assault and euthanasia programme in Germany, hiding in Czechoslovakia and Ukraine, the Babi Yar massacre, and incarceration in Buchenwald, the Warsaw Ghetto, Theresienstadt, Sobibór and Auschwitz. Questions of moral compromise and complicity with the Nazi overseers are raised prominently throughout the narrative, particularly in relation to the role(s) played by the Kapos in the camps and the Jewish Council and ghetto police in Warsaw. Nonetheless, similar issues are avoided in regards to the SK. Instead, *Holocaust* marginalizes the ethical dilemmas of the 'special squads' and to a large extent conceals the nature of their existence inside the death camp crematoria.

Significantly, the very first reference to the SK in *Holocaust* is made at a high-level meeting of Nazi perpetrators. The ambitious SS officer Erik Dorf, who is the focal point of one of the miniseries' major plot threads, is shown explaining Birkenau's extermination process to senior colleagues with the assistance of a slide projector. The scene alternates between actual historical photographs being screened for Dorf's audience and the mostly expressionless faces of the SS officers as they are stepped through the sequence of dehumanization and death. Long pauses in Dorf's narration seem to allow the images to 'speak for themselves' in telling the story, though the exchange of dialogue is crucial to the meanings conveyed in the scene:

> Dorf: Sorting of clothing. All the labourers are Jews, special teams.
> SS officer: What happens to them?
> Dorf: They go eventually.[17]

The deployment of the 'Nazi gaze' onto these images – not all of which were taken from the perpetrators' perspective – is an ethically fraught strategy, one exacerbated by the unquestioned adoption of the oppressor's euphemistic language. Dorf's statement that the crematorium workers 'go eventually' is not dwelt upon; he simply moves on. Furthermore, the use of archival images to construct a narrative is dubious not only due to the employment of the perpetrator's perspective, but also due to the fact these images are taken out of context on multiple levels – some photographs (such as those of the crematoria ovens) were taken after the war.

Of more significance to the portrayal of the SK in this scene, the slide that Dorf uses to highlight what happens after a gassing is an image of crematorium workers surrounded by a pile of bodies next to an outdoor pyre. This image is a cropped portion of one of several photographs taken secretly and at immense personal risk by a member of a 'special squad' in August 1944; the film was then smuggled out of Auschwitz by the Polish resistance. With the Nazis unaware of their existence, the photographs have long stood as a formidable example of opposition to the Holocaust's perpetrators within the direst of circumstances. In his detailed reflection on what he argues to be 'unquestionably the most important [visual] documents that we have' in relation to the Nazi genocide, Dan Stone writes that 'the *Sonderkommando* photographs are especially harrowing, not only because of their content but also because of the extreme difficulties involved in taking them, smuggling the film out of the camp, and having them developed in Kraków'.[18] However, the use of one of these photographs in *Holocaust* undermines the image's power by altering the context of production. Indeed, as much time is spent in the scene on Dorf's unsuccessful attempts to obtain a transfer back to Berlin as on the details of the mass killing process. The multifaceted adoption of the Nazis' perspective on the crematorium workers – a perspective that has been shown to be deeply problematic, not least of all in the recollections of SS-Obersturmbannführer Rudolf Höss[19] – sets up a disturbing framework through which the later experiences of the narrative's Jewish victims are portrayed.

In the second half of the miniseries, the two brothers of the Weiss family – Rudy and Karl – find themselves recruited into work squads attached to the mass-murder machinery of Sobibór and Auschwitz-Birkenau respectively. Both characters had previously been engaged in different forms of resistance activities. Rudy joins the Sobibór SK just as it is in the midst of finalizing its plan for the revolt that would see approximately 300 prisoners escape the camp. Upon proving he has a partisan background, Rudy is recruited to the effort; his conversation with the other prisoners never broaches the subject of their work in the death camp. He is instrumental to the triumphant uprising, instigating the event by killing the first two German guards with a hammer and an axe, which allows the resisters to break into the armoury. Rudy then shoots three more soldiers, somersaults over a group of dead prisoners to throw a grenade into a car, and blows up a guard tower with a final grenade. Taking on the role of the solitary hero familiar to audiences of Hollywood Westerns, after the uprising Rudy refuses to travel east towards safety and instead leaves his companions, determined to find his family. A lingering camera shot watches a courageous Rudy walk along train tracks into the unknown with only the miniseries' sentimental soundtrack to accompany him.

Rudy's brother endures his SK experience somewhat differently. At one point, an emotionally shattered Karl is shown collecting the clothing of Jewish women who have just been led into a Birkenau gas chamber – which, unbeknownst to him, includes his mother. Curiously, unlike the men around him, Karl does not appear to benefit from the 'privileges' commonly associated from work in the 'special squad'; his body emaciated, he hobbles slowly through the barracks, dragging his feet wrapped in rags and clutching a tattered blanket around his worn camp uniform. When Weinberg, an old acquaintance from Buchenwald, tries to boost his spirits with rumours of Allied military victories, Karl responds for the most part with an empty expression until the man provides him with drawing instruments. A desolate Karl begins to sketch a picture of a 'Muselmann', paying particular attention to the figure's hollowed-out eyes.[20] A subsequent scene shows that Karl has collapsed and died atop his drawing during the Nazis' evacuation of the camp. In *Holocaust*'s final minutes, Karl's wife Inga and her newborn son joyfully reunite with Rudy. Inga, who has learnt of Karl's fate and come into possession of the final image he had sketched, frames her husband's death through a discourse of spiritual resistance: 'He begged for something to draw with right up to the end'.[21] Rudy, on the other hand, joins the effort to smuggle Greek Jewish orphans into Palestine, allowing the film to conclude on a cathartic note as he plays football with the children. Thus, instead of being confronted with the ethical dilemmas at the core of the SK experience, the two Weiss brothers are 'liberated', one through armed rebellion and the other through artistic creation, replacing the turmoil of their incarceration with a final appeal to the power of the human spirit.

A similar dynamic to that of the *Holocaust* miniseries is evident in later screen narratives that depict the 'special squads'. Jack Gold's *Escape from Sobibor* (1987), for instance, focuses on the 'privileged' death camp inmates charged with greeting deportees upon arrival and sorting their belongings. The ethical dilemmas inherent in their situation are raised in the film's early scenes; however, the majority of its plot is preoccupied with the preparations for, and implementation of, the uprising. The film ends with the surviving prisoners streaming out of the camp and into the forest amidst a jubilant musical score. Significantly, Sobibór's death machinery was serviced by a separate group of Jewish prisoners isolated from those who took part in the uprising. As a result, *Escape from Sobibor* contains only a momentary image of these workers standing exhausted outside the gas chambers, along with a brief acknowledgement of the regret felt by the resisters that they could not coordinate their plans with them.

A few years later, Robert M. Young's *Triumph of the Spirit* (1989) would engage more frequently and intensely with the distrust, theft and conflict between camp prisoners. The film dramatizes the story of Salomo Arouch, a Greek Jewish boxer from Salonika deported with his family to Auschwitz. The protagonist becomes 'privileged' insofar as he is enlisted to fight for the entertainment of the SS, thereby gaining access to extra food, cigarettes, alcohol and easier, indoor work. While several anguished expressions convey Arouch's increasingly disturbed conscience over his activities – his victories, while keeping him alive, condemn his defeated opponents to death – the film goes to some lengths to avoid taking its exploration of moral ambiguity and compromise into the crematoria. When Arouch's brother glimpses the ovens after being drafted into the camp's SK, he states determinedly: 'I won't do it'. In the following scene, news reaches Arouch that the Greek Jews refused to cooperate and were executed; the protagonist is saluted with a 'Bravo' for his sibling's act of resistance. As the film draws to a close, Arouch ultimately refuses to continue fighting for the Nazis' pleasure and is himself taken to work in the SK. However, the squad begins its armed revolt at the exact moment he arrives, preventing (or *saving*) him from being able to perform any duties – or refuse to. Nonetheless, like other filmic depictions of the SK revolt that would follow in the decades to come, *Triumph of the Spirit* portrays the event briefly and without exaggerated SS casualties or a mass exodus of prisoners. Moving towards the end of the twentieth century, there were increasing signs that screening the horrific reality that faced the 'special squads' would not remain taboo much longer.

Asking the Question: Screening the Ethical Dilemmas of the Sonderkommando

In an essay on Holocaust representation and its perceived 'limits', Frank Stern mentions Tim Blake Nelson's *The Grey Zone* (2001), which was at the time he was writing yet to be released, and predicts that more 'films that are preoccupied with problematic or marginal aspects of the Shoah will doubtlessly follow in the coming years. Beyond all questionable and purely market-oriented film productions, this development indicates a shift in cinematic culture'.[22] This has certainly been the case. Since the first direct engagement with the extreme circumstances of Birkenau's crematorium workers in *The Grey Zone*, the provocative figures of 'privileged' Jews and their 'choiceless choices' have attracted the increased interest of filmmakers. Joseph Sargent's *Out of the Ashes* (2003) dramatizes the experiences of Gisella Perl, a prisoner-doctor in Auschwitz who used her position to save the lives of pregnant women by performing abortions while navigating a precarious closeness to Mengele's pseudo-scientific endeavours.[23] Audrius Juzenas' German film *Ghetto* (2006), on the other hand, adapts Joshua Sobol's play to explore the moral ambiguities of victim behaviour in the Vilna Ghetto. Particular attention is given to the controversial behaviour of Jacob Gens, who struggles to balance his forced implementation of Nazi edicts with his desire to render the ghetto sustainable and save a remnant of the Jewish population.[24] Stefan Ruzowitzky's 2007 drama *Die Fälscher* (*The Counterfeiters*) also focuses on the ethical dilemmas of 'privileged' Jews through its portrayal of a group of prisoners assigned to a Nazi counterfeiting operation in the Sachsenhausen concentration camp. In other words, the figures of Levi's 'grey zone' have finally been exposed in very different ways from previous trends in Holocaust film.

The overriding thematic emphasis on resistance and rescue in Holocaust cinema since the mid 1980s[25] has been significantly altered by an increased interest in moral ambiguities and the antiheroic. Acts of resistance play an intrinsic part of recent films that depict victims with 'privileged' positions – the SK included – yet how that 'resistance' is conceptualized is often more nuanced in these films than in those earlier productions that glorify 'fighting back' at the expense of other Jewish responses to persecution. In addition to armed rebellion, historiographical debates over what constitutes 'resistance' have seen many include the 'passive', psychological resistance that comprised the daily struggle for survival through maintaining hope, human dignity and a will to live.[26] Philip Friedman views anything that constitutes 'noncollaboration' as Jewish 'resistance',[27] although in the context of victims with 'privileged' positions, even this is not clear-cut.

In representing the Auschwitz SK, both Nelson's *The Grey Zone* and László Nemes' *Saul fia* (*Son of Saul*, 2015) eschew an uncritical embrace of spiritual triumph, unproblematic survival and cathartic heroism – reassuring messages that have for the most part permeated mainstream Holocaust cinema. In doing so, these productions move towards the indecipherable realm of moral ambiguity that Levi points to in his writing. Substantial analyses of each film have been published in recent years.[28] Unlike existing studies, Nelson's and Nemes' films (and their reception) will be examined alongside one another here to draw out some of the key distinctions in the ways in which each addresses issues of 'privilege' and 'complicity'.

While *The Grey Zone* and *Son of Saul* veer sharply away from each other in their modes of delivery, the films share thematic similarities. Each narrative provides a fictional representation of experiences within the twelfth special squad (of a supposed thirteen) in Birkenau. Importantly, this particular squad instigated the armed revolt of October 1944 in a partially successful attempt to sabotage the camp's extermination machinery. Both productions conflate actual historical incidents to construct their storylines: the focalizer of Nemes' film, Saul Ausländer, witnesses the shooting of the clandestine SK photographs on the same day the uprising takes place; whereas in Nelson's film, a group of crematorium workers preparing for the revolt try to save a young girl who they discover has survived the gas chamber (each incident happened long before the uprising).[29] *The Grey Zone*'s muted portrayal of the attempt to save – or at least prolong – the life of the Jewish girl, ostensibly to rekindle a semblance of the dignity or 'humanity' the traumatized prisoners feel they have lost (or at least to find a way to deal with their self-loathing), mirrors another key feature of *Son of Saul*. Nemes' main character spends much of the film desperately trying to find a willing rabbi to give a young boy he claims to be his son a traditional Jewish burial. The boy in *Son of Saul* has also survived the gas, but is immediately asphyxiated by the SS. These acts on behalf of children are a source of conflict in both films: on the one hand, several members of the SK in *The Grey Zone* bicker about whether they should kill the girl to avoid the potential undermining of their resistance plans; on the other hand, Ausländer's engagement in what the director Nemes himself has called 'a seemingly vain and useless deed'[30] to have the boy prayed for and buried is questioned by all those around him – the rest of the squad doubt he has a son at all and are let down when he fails to procure valuable gunpowder from women working in a munitions factory.

The unsentimental detachment of both Nelson's and Nemes' representations of the Auschwitz SK reveal that their strategies share more than plot similarities. Neither filmmaker positions his audience to identify with certain characters through sympathetic portrayals; the crematorium workers exhibit many unappealing traits and their interactions are defined more by animosity than solidarity. In this way, both directors reject the simplistic binary opposition between 'good Jews' and 'bad Jews' that has often characterized representations of those with 'privileged' positions, and avoid what Avisar describes as the problematic 'inducement of emotional involvement with the fate of the characters' in sentimental Holocaust films.[31] Instead, Nemes and Nelson construct a claustrophobic environment defined by selfishness and cruelty, where affection has no place, theft is a common occurrence, and internecine suspicions and hatreds between Polish and Hungarian Jews are frequently given voice. For the crematorium workers in these films, reliance on the Nazis' euphemistic language is a necessity and, entirely at the whim of the perpetrators, survival from moment to moment is uncertain. As in *Triumph of the Spirit*, the ultimate futility (in a 'military' sense) of the SK revolt is made clear through the refusal to resort to heroic action sequences or mass Nazi casualties. Further, the unorthodox characterization within the *The Grey Zone* and *Son of Saul* makes clear the desensitization of the 'special squads' to the daily mass killing they were forced to work in close proximity to, reflecting the admission in Zalman Lewental's SK manuscript that the workers 'of necessity [got] used to everything'.[32] In these ways, the films provide intricate depictions of the inherently complex nature of 'resistance' and 'cooperation' in a world of industrialized death, blurring Levi's own aforementioned moral distinction between the crematorium workers who planned and took part in the uprising, and those 'miserable manual labourers of the slaughter'.[33] At the same time, while the SK characters in both films are shown to be deeply mired in the extermination process, the anti-redemptory discourse adopted by Nelson and Nemes involves major differences that result in distinct approaches to addressing the issue of moral complicity.

The Grey Zone spends considerable time visually representing aspects of the SK's daily routine and the 'privileges' they are afforded due to this work. Rough, hand-held camerawork takes the audience through the various 'stages' of the killing process in several short vignettes, graphically depicting the squad's deception of Jews about to be gassed, cleaning of the chambers, and transporting, pillaging and burning of the corpses. The soundtrack is immersed in ambient noise, most notably the roar of the crematorium furnaces, which serves as a constant reminder of the industrial genocide taking place and offers no calming respite for either characters or viewers. In one scene, well-clothed prisoners are shown eating and bartering jewellery at a table laden with various kinds of food, alcohol and cigarettes, presenting a considerably different picture from the brief scenes that portray emaciated, silent and expressionless munitions factory workers residing in the camp proper. Yet these benefits are shown to be entirely transient: the 'special squad' is fully aware that its days are numbered and all depicted crematorium workers perish in the uprising or the reprisals that follow. Nelson's film also resists conventional narrative closure, showing the next 'special squad' burning the bodies of their murdered predecessors while the disembodied voice of the girl the squad unsuccessfully attempted to rescue tells the viewers that 'this is how the work continues'.[34]

Another defining characteristic of Nelson's representation of SK workers is his film's greater use of dialogue (in contrast to Nemes' minimalist script) to signal the ethical complexities of their experience. This is undoubtedly due in part to *The Grey Zone* having been adapted from Nelson's stage play of the same name, which has led some critics to describe the film as 'stagy' and slow-moving.[35] Aggressive debates consisting of staccato dialogue between prisoners articulate the ethical dilemmas they face, invariably without any resolution being found. During a heated argument over what is to be done with the girl, Abramowics chastises Rosenthal for any hope he may have of moral redemption for his involvement in the extermination process. When Rosenthal declares he has no pretensions of being a hero, Abramowics spitefully responds: 'Not a hero, not a killer. What are you, Max?'[36] When Abramowics is suddenly executed by an SS officer, the question is left open. In the clearest example of the film's encouragement of viewers to contemplate the dilemma of what they would do if confronted with the same extreme situation, Hoffman (another SK member) makes an emotional appeal to the girl who has survived the gas:

> I used to think so much of myself ... What I'd make of my life ... We can't know what we're capable of, any of us ... How can you know what you'd do to stay alive until you're really asked? I know this now ... For most of us, the answer is anything.[37]

Here the film's hitherto realist mode of representation breaks down in a sequence comprising one of the narrative's few restrained appeals to audience emotion. Hoffman's pivotal monologue is punctuated by pauses that seem ill-fitting alongside the *The Grey Zone*'s otherwise fast-paced exchanges, while a slow-motion image of workers pulling gold teeth from the mouths of naked corpses is followed by a close-up shot of an anonymous crematorium worker crying hysterically as he rocks back and forth. Tormented by the daily activities of the SK, Hoffman asks the girl (who never speaks and is arguably the closest thing to an audience surrogate to be found in *The Grey Zone*): 'You can hear me, can't you?' When the girl motions with a subtle nod of her head, Hoffman breathes a sigh of relief and almost manages a smile. He repeats the words: 'I thought so'. Just as Levi's closing reflection in 'The Grey Zone' that 'we are all in the ghetto' evokes the contemporary relevance of the Holocaust's ethical dilemmas for his readers,[38] Nelson's film attempts, in the director's own words, 'to put its audience squarely in the position of having to face what these men faced: As an audience member you ask yourself, how would I have responded? What would I do to save my own life?'[39] In this way, *The Grey Zone* implicates its audience in the fraught question of complicity that so disturbed Mandelbaum, but also effectively articulates the nature of the 'choiceless choices' that governed Jewish responses to Nazi genocide.

Nemes' film differs markedly from *The Grey Zone* in various ways, taking Nelson's unorthodox characterization to a new level and omitting clear images of the killing process, while at the same time leaving questions of moral complicity far more implicit. The constricted narrative of *Son of Saul* takes place over a 24-hour period and entirely within the realm of consciousness and experience of its main character, limiting the viewer to Ausländer's perceptions by frequently lingering on his face in close-up or hovering just behind his shoulder. In contrast to the graphic portrayal of violence in *The Grey Zone*, the shallow depth of field frequently obscures all that surrounds Ausländer. This literal blurring of atrocity can be read as signalling the character's own instinctive desire to desensitize himself as much as possible to the chaos and misery around him – something he can never fully accomplish given the occasional emergence of clear images of murder and death, and the intrusions of the soundscape's regular screams, gunshots and other loud noises. Genocide is obscured, not hidden; the omnipresence of the dead is evident despite the unfocused lens, and clearer images appear when Ausländer closely inspects bodies piled on a crematorium lift or when he narrowly escapes being shot into a pit. In *Son of Saul*'s opening sequence, several long takes follow Ausländer as he accompanies Jews from a newly arrived transport on their walk to the undressing room, helps them hang their coats and other items on hooks, and then guides them into the gas chamber. Nudging or on a few occasions pushing those soon to be killed along their way, Ausländer maintains a coldly inexpressive composure. His jaw clenches momentarily as he stands listening to the dying scream and bang on the door. He looks downwards slightly before the screen cuts to the film's title, then back to Ausländer scrubbing blood from the gas chamber floor. This introductory sequence sets up what might be called the 'intimate distance' that at once permits viewers to imagine, but prevents them from grasping, Ausländer's inner thoughts – a distance that seldom diminishes throughout the rest of the film.

The staccato dialogue that proliferates Nelson's script is replaced by sparse and often interrupted conversations between the characters in *Son of Saul*, who seem constantly aware that a misplaced word or a look in the wrong direction could result in their demise. When Ausländer's preoccupation with the boy is criticized as risking his entire squad, he curtly replies: 'We're already dead'.[40] Even when Ausländer is quietly declared to have 'saved the day' when he hides a camera in a pipe to prevent the SS from finding the SK photographs, participation in anything that might be labelled 'resistance' is never glorified. With the squad's liquidation drawing near, an argument between two prisoners over whether attacking the SS or photographing the extermination should be given priority points to the practical limitations of each. One asks: 'You think you can blow up this whole thing?', while the other replies: 'Your pictures will bring an army here to free us?'[41] Just as no neat separation between 'heroism' and 'betrayal', 'innocence' and 'complicity' can be found in *The Grey Zone*, the seemingly antithetical concepts of 'resistance' and 'cooperation' are presented as intrinsically connected by Nemes. While Ausländer cleans up a feast enjoyed by the SS, the SK's Oberkapo Biederman is briefly shown anguishing in the background over a blank piece of paper, on which he has been ordered to make a list of seventy names to be killed the following morning. The men to be murdered must come from the squad he supervises, who are preparing the uprising with him. Shortly after this scene, Biederman is shown reporting the news to his colleagues – even though he will still need to complete the task or be killed himself. Yet despite rare and subtle gestures to the ethical dilemmas of 'privileged' prisoners (of which Biederman's anxiety is perhaps the most obvious), *Son of Saul* borders on eluding the crux of Levi's 'grey zone' – albeit in a different way from films that simplistically condemn or absolve them, or otherwise hide their more controversial behaviour under a shield of their own or others' heroism.

Nemes' strategy of 'aesthetic withdrawal' has been praised by his film's proponents, who frame this as an ethical and appropriate response to the Holocaust and the 'limits' the event has placed on representation.[42] Richard Alleva argues that this 'pictorial shallowness' has the effect of imprisoning 'us so convincingly within Ausländer's horrible reality that we are kept from making facile judgments about a person whose enslavement has forced him to make choices no one should ever have to make'.[43] Stuart Liebman likewise notes that Nemes' 'spare, imagistic script does not criticize his iconoclastic antihero'.[44] To be sure, although an acquaintance named Abraham accuses Ausländer of having 'failed the living for the dead' when he loses the gunpowder, the positioning of the audience in relation to the latter's behaviour is far more complex.[45] To the extent that human motivation and action can be 'understood' in the shadow of Birkenau, Abraham's judgement might be 'understandable' when taking into account his involvement with the resistance, but so is Ausländer's frantic attempt to grant his 'son' a (somewhat) decent burial. Indeed, in a film that seeks to generate little emotion towards the liminal figures on screen, the viewer's sympathies are perhaps appealed to most strongly when Ausländer is beaten and cursed as a 'stupid Jew' for the same mistake by another inmate. As in Nelson's film, all attempts to salvage something positive from the SK's circumstances lead to death; from that finality there is no escape. Thus, Ausländer's efforts to accomplish his objective see Nemes' and Nelson's films both converge and diverge, with the evocation of paternal instinct and human dignity enabling some form of diluted affirmation to be attached to the crematorium workers' existence.

The narratives of *Son of Saul* and *The Grey Zone* fall short of anything that could be described as 'redemptive', yet the different kinds of care afforded to the films' child figures is highly significant to the muted affect they generate. The characters of Hoffman and Rosenthal briefly connect while awaiting execution at the end of Nelson's story, agreeing that 'We did something' just before being shot.[46] Even though the girl is not saved – she is shot at the end of the same scene – they have maintained or rekindled some part of their 'humanity'. Appeals to audience emotion are even more subtle in *Son of Saul*. When the first rabbi Ausländer talks to tells him to be satisfied with the saying of a prayer, he quietly but with some intensity tells the rabbi that it is 'Not enough'.[47] Liebman identifies 'a moral epiphany of sorts' in Ausländer's first sighting of the boy, for which Nemes employs a rare standard point-of-view shot 'to provide possible insight into what Ausländer is thinking, although precisely what that is remains hard to grasp'.[48] Nonetheless, the character subsequently throws himself into his quest, coming perilously close to being killed (or indirectly causing the deaths of others) on several occasions as he negotiates with the prisoner-doctor assigned to dissect the boy's corpse and prevents another rabbi (or a man who claims to be) from being shot by giving him his own clothing. Ausländer even slows himself down by carrying the body out of the camp during the brief escape of a small group of SK members. When he loses the body in the current of the Vistula River, Ausländer hides in a cabin with several other exhausted prisoners. He smiles broadly when he sees a young Polish boy of approximately the same age as his 'son' appear in the doorway, just before the escapees are discovered and killed by the

SS. The film's final shot watches the boy running to safety amid the forest greenery as machine guns sound in the near distance.

In their own ways, both *Son of Saul* and *The Grey Zone* reflect a theme that arises in Lewental's buried manuscript that: 'so long as man is able to do anything, has the energy, can undertake risks, so long does he believe that by his conduct he may achieve something'.[49] Significantly, not only does Nemes include the doomed uprising in his film, but also a tense depiction of the photographs being taken, a brief reference to the burying of SK testimonies, and the aforementioned escape (which Nelson filmed a few brief scenes of for *The Grey Zone*, but decided to leave out of the final cut).[50] The glimmer of hope in finding some form of positive meaning within the SK's nightmarish circumstances is as transient as it is faint in both films – and particularly so in *Son of Saul* – but it is still there; audiences need to be engaged and left 'satisfied', relatively speaking, in one form or another. Even Lawrence Langer, who has long expressed scepticism over many fictionalized representations, concedes that the Holocaust 'so threatens our sense of spiritual continuity that it is agonizing to imagine or consent to its features without introducing some affirmative values to mitigate the gloom'.[51] Setting aside their unrelenting reliance on setting-specific noises, both films introduce soft music to accompany their end credits, mourning the tragic loss of millions and offering some respite from the ethical quagmire of the death camp crematoria.

The Grey Zone and *Son of Saul* reveal the potential of works in the genre to capture something of the 'essence' of the Holocaust without losing track of the event's historical specificity; yet, both have attracted some controversy in turn, and the reception of these films is instructive. Kristin Hohenadel's characterization of Nelson's *The Grey Zone* as 'a Holocaust horror story without a Schindler' is representative of the considerable praise for the film following its release.[52] Commentary on *Son of Saul* seemed to similarly identify a new landmark in the cinematic representation of the Holocaust. Even Claude Lanzmann, who has for decades rejected fictionalized representation without exception, praised Nemes' film as the 'anti-*Schindler's List*'.[53] Indeed, Steven Carr's reflection on the alleged 'crisis of Holocaust film' dismisses the 'neatly manicured visual spaces' constructed by Spielberg and Nelson in favour of Nemes' 'radical negotiation of familiar Holocaust film tropes'.[54] The restrained narrative of *The Grey Zone* may appear to some contemporary viewers to be almost 'epic' in contrast to *Son of Saul*'s stark minimalism; however, bearing in mind that Nelson's film was made less than a decade after Spielberg transformed the genre with his 1993 blockbuster, *The Grey Zone* – and various other films exploring trauma, guilt and compromise that followed – also signalled a deep shift in Holocaust cinematic culture. Financed at the turn of the century under the assumption that it would not return a profit,[55] Nelson's film was in large part a repudiation of *Schindler's List* – and I would argue an effective one. While at the time Nelson himself noted that without including the uprising, his 'movie's but a bleak portrait of the twelfth *Sonderkommando*, and I dare say it would have no audience',[56] some fifteen years later another viable step could be taken into the miasma of the crematoria that focused even less on active opposition to the Nazis. Nemes still relies on several slightly more oblique examples of resistance. Nelson's and Nemes' films deviate in significant ways, but each must be considered in context, and lumping *The Grey Zone* together with more sentimental films such as *Schindler's List* (problematic in its reliance on moral binaries, but also highly valuable in its own ways, given its own context) is simplistic.

Rather than shock viewers with brutally visualized SK duties, Nemes seeks a visceral impact by invoking the theme of the 'unpresentable' in a way that declares a refusal to represent. In turn, *Son of Saul* has been condemned by Stefan Grisseman as an 'innovative art-house thriller', 'an exploitation film not despite but *because* of its technical skill and resolute cunning'.[57] Again I have to disagree with this assessment, as Nemes' film is far from unenlightening or exploitative, and characterizing it as such only takes us backwards to redundant theoretical prohibitions on representation generally. Yet now, just as Nelson's *The Grey Zone* has become somewhat 'normalized' and its own innovativeness has faded over the years, I do share some of Richard Alleva's uneasiness about *Son of Saul*'s 'tunnel vision', not so much for its potential reinforcement of the Nazis' dehumanization of their victims (which is one of Alleva's concerns), but for its broader open-endedness – and how this intersects with the overwhelming adulation the film has been greeted with.[58] For Alleva: 'By shunning flashbacks, exposition, depth of focus, crosscutting and by refusing to clarify supporting characters, [Nemes] casts a present-tense, you-are-there, hypnotic spell on the viewer, but also turns everything in the visual and narrative background into a blur'.[59] The lack of multiplicity in perspective and array of unanswered questions and unexplored issues is not something that detracts from the film *per se* (they are in fact key facets of its power), but the exaltation of its *techniques* risks situating the film above others in a way that implies a comprehensiveness that its makers had never aspired to. In relation to depictions of the SK and the ethical dilemmas they confronted, Nemes does not seek to implicate his audience in the question 'What would you have done?' to the extent that some other portrayals of 'privileged' Jews have. For this reason, I am sceptical that *Son of Saul* actually does ask 'what it might mean to be enlisted as one of [the] laborers', as one reviewer suggests.[60] And my uneasiness only grows when I read commentators who praise the film by describing it as 'bear[ing] witness to the Holocaust through the eyes of a morally complicit prisoner' or who write of 'the work of the *Sonderkommando* [as] a form of complicity far beyond the merely untenable'.[61] Levi's reflection in the 'The Grey Zone' on the need to continue to develop a nuanced understanding of moral ambiguity and compromise, and how this plays out through the twin problems of judgement and representation, could not be more relevant than it is today.

Between Redemption and the Radical Negation of Hope

In a Levi-inspired reflection on Holocaust representation, Dominick LaCapra identifies two main approaches to the Nazi genocide: the affirmation of redemption involving 'absolute recovery with no essential loss' and 'the denial and absolute negation of redemption'. The latter comprises a conceptualization of redemption that views it 'as unavailable, absent, or repeatedly and aporetically in question', where 'any hope of recovery' lies only in the 'radical negation of hope in redeeming the past or making sense of it in the present'.[62] LaCapra calls these competing discourses 'working through' and 'acting out' respectively, and goes on to disagree with both perspectives, positing a compromise that promotes:

> a view of working through not as full redemption, total recovery, or unmitigated caesura but as a recurrent process that, with respect to extreme trauma or limit events, may never totally transcend acting out or compulsive repetition but that does provide a measure of critical distance on problems and the possibility of significant transformation . . .[63]

An engagement with the experiences and behaviour of the SK would seem to require us to navigate this tenuous space. This chapter has highlighted the important role that fiction films have in this endeavour by emphasizing their potential to eschew simplistic moral binaries, explore themes of trauma, guilt and compromise, and look for meaning where nothing might readily or ever present itself with clarity.

The intersecting problems of judgement and representation identified in Levi's 'grey zone' will continue to influence and confound efforts to understand this realm of moral ambiguity and compromise; some form of simplification is inevitable. As Levi wrote in his essay, 'without profound simplification the world around us would be an infinite, undefined tangle that would defy our ability to orient ourselves and decide upon our actions'.[64] Even within the anti-redemptory framework of *The Grey Zone* and *Son of Saul*, Nelson's traumatized prisoners find some brief succour in that they 'did something', while Ausländer's quiet commitment to a fellow prisoner that 'I have to take care of my son' and his crazed pursuit of this goal gives his final day in the camp purpose. Some gesture to hope without resorting to outright redemption and catharsis would seem to be at the very least a productive step forward.

Anton Kaes has noted in an early work on Holocaust-related cinema that a violation of the 'mainstream' conventions of representation established by innumerable feature films serves to 'enable, if not to force, the viewer to maintain [a] critical distance'.[65] Both Nelson and Nemes establish this distancing effect, pushing the viewer back from empathizing with their characters in a burgeoning glare of affect. At the same time, the implication of *The Grey Zone*'s audience in the dilemma 'What would I have done?' is rhetorical; Hoffman explains to the young girl and temporary audience surrogate: 'We can't know what we're capable of'. In an important sense, the multilayered distancing effect of *Son of Saul* does not result in the same questions being asked of the viewer as in *The Grey Zone*, but both films do offer a direct and serious engagement with the experiences of the Auschwitz SK in ways that earlier films have not. Produced fifteen years apart, Nemes' and Nelson's films portray Birkenau's systematic killing as an industrial, factory-like process, attempting to construct an immersive experience for their audience that is immediate and 'of the present'.[66] In a further fifteen years from now, it is more than likely that the practice of, and key discussions around, engagement and immersion will have for the most part moved far away from Holocaust films as they are conventionally conceived and onto textual experiences that are 'participated in' rather than merely 'consumed'. The historical, aesthetic and ethical issues that arise for that time are yet to be made front and centre, but past, present and future developments in Holocaust film will undoubtedly play a significant role in shaping them.

Adam Brown is Senior Lecturer in Digital Media at Deakin University, creator of the *Social Media Stories* podcast and co-host of the *Our Gamified World* web series. He is the author of *Judging 'Privileged' Jews: Holocaust Ethics, Representation and the 'Grey Zone'* (Berghahn Books, 2013) and coauthor of *Communication, Digital Media and Everyday Life* (2015). His interdisciplinary research has spanned Holocaust representation across various genres, women in film, surveillance cinema, mediations of rape, digital children's television, nonhuman animal ethics, transmedia storytelling, and gaming cultures. Further details and social media links can be found at adamgbrown.wordpress.com.

Notes

1. Jan Południak, *Sonder: An Interview with Sonderkommando Member Henryk Mandelbaum*, trans. Witold Zbirohowski-Kościa (Oświęcim: Frap-Books, 2008), 30.
2. Adam Brown, *Judging 'Privileged' Jews: Holocaust Ethics, Representation, and the 'Grey Zone'* (New York: Berghahn Books, 2013).
3. See Primo Levi, *The Drowned and the Saved*, trans. Raymond Rosenthal (London: Michael Joseph, [1986] 1988), 41, 43, 49.
4. Susan L. Pentlin, 'Holocaust Victims of Privilege', in Harry James Cargas (ed.), *Problems Unique to the Holocaust* (Lexington: University Press of Kentucky, 1999), 39, 26.
5. For a discussion of the use of this term, see Brown, *Judging 'Privileged' Jews*, 5.
6. Levi, *The Drowned and the Saved*, 34.
7. Gideon Greif, *We Wept without Tears: Testimonies of the Jewish Sonderkommando from Auschwitz* (New Haven: Yale University Press, 2005), 51.
8. See Brown, *Judging 'Privileged' Jews*, 59–61.
9. Bryan Cheyette, 'The Uncertain Certainty of *Schindler's List*', in Yosefa Loshitzky (ed.), *Spielberg's Holocaust: Critical Perspectives on* Schindler's List (Bloomington: Indiana University Press, 1997), 227.
10. See, for example, Brown, *Judging 'Privileged' Jews*; Adam Brown, 'Witnessing Moral Compromise: "Privilege", Judgement and Holocaust Testimony', *Life Writing* 14(3) (2017), 327–39; Adam Brown, 'Confronting "Choiceless Choices" in Holocaust Videotestimonies: Judgement, "Privileged" Jews, and the Role of the Interviewer', *Continuum: Journal of Media and Communication Studies* 24(1) (2010), 79–90; Adam Brown, 'Narratives of Judgement: Representations of "Privileged" Jews in Holocaust Documentaries', *LISA e-journal* 12(1) (2014), http://lisa.revues.org/5652, retrieved 12 April 2019.
11. Barry Langford, 'Mass Culture/Mass Media/Mass Death: Teaching Film, Television, and the Holocaust', in Robert Eaglestone and Barry Langford (eds), *Teaching Holocaust Film and Literature* (Basingstoke: Palgrave Macmillan, 2008), 73.
12. Frank J. Coppa, *The Papacy, the Jews, and the Holocaust* (Washington DC: Catholic University of America Press, 2006), ix.
13. Ilan Avisar, *Screening the Holocaust: Cinema's Images of the Unimaginable* (Indianapolis: Indiana University Press, 1988), 38.
14. For detailed reflections on the *Holocaust* miniseries and its reception, see Judith E. Doneson, *The Holocaust in American Film*, 2nd edn (New York: Syracuse University Press, 2002), 141–96; Jeffrey Shandler, *While America Watches: Televising the Holocaust* (New York: Oxford University Press, 1999), 155–78.
15. Primo Levi, *The Black Hole of Auschwitz*, trans. Sharon Wood (Cambridge: Polity Press, 2005), 56–66.
16. Ian Thomson, *Primo Levi: A Life* (New York: Henry Holt and Company, 2002), 376–77.
17. Marvin J. Chomsky, *Holocaust: The Story of the Family Weiss* (United States: Titus Productions, 1978, DVD).
18. Dan Stone, 'The Sonderkommando Photographs', *Jewish Social Studies*, 7(3) (2001), 132.
19. See Greif, *We Wept without Tears*, 60.
20. *Muselmänner*, or 'Muslims', was the name given by camp inmates to the barely conscious 'skeletons' of the camps; those nameless, voiceless prisoners who merely *existed*

on the threshold of death and invariably perished in a short period of time. See Levi, *If This is a Man; and, The Truce*, 96.
21. Chomsky, *Holocaust*.
22. Frank Stern, 'The Holocaust: Representing Lasting Images in Literature and Film', in Konrad Kwiet and Jürgen Matthäus (eds), *Contemporary Responses to the Holocaust* (Westport: Praeger, 2004), 213.
23. For a detailed discussion of Perl and the representation of her experiences in *Out of the Ashes*, see Adam Brown, '"No One Will Ever Know ...": The Holocaust, "Privileged" Jews, and the "Grey Zone"', *History Australia* 8(3) (2011), 95–116.
24. An in-depth analysis of *Ghetto* and other filmic depictions of Jewish leaders can be found in Adam Brown, 'The "Grey Zone" in Holocaust Film: Screening the Ethical Dilemmas of Jewish Leaders', *Holocaust Studies: A Journal of Culture and History*, in press.
25. See Annette Insdorf's conceptualization of the 'second wave' of Holocaust film in *Indelible Shadows: Film and the Holocaust*, 3rd edn (Cambridge: Cambridge University Press, 2003 [1983]), 247.
26. Robert Rozett, 'Resistance, Jewish', in Israel Gutman (ed.), *Encyclopedia of the Holocaust* (New York: Macmillan, 1990), 1267.
27. Philip Friedman, 'Problems of Research on the European Jewish Catastophe', in Yisrael Gutman and Livia Rothkirchen (eds), *The Catastrophe of European Jewry: Antecedents, History, Reflections* (Jerusalem: Yad Vashem, 1976).
28. On *The Grey Zone*, see Brown, 'Judging "Privileged" Jews', 170–86; Axel Bangert, 'Changing Narratives and Images of the Holocaust: Tim Blake Nelson's Film *The Grey Zone* (2001)', *New Cinemas: Journal of Contemporary Film* 6(1) (2008), 17–32. On *Son of Saul*, see Chari Larsson, 'Making Monsters in László Nemes' *Son of Saul*', *Senses of Cinema* 81 (2016), 1–22.
29. See Miklós Nyiszli, *Auschwitz: A Doctor's Eyewitness Account*, trans. Tibère Kremer and Richard Seaver (New York: Arcade, 1993 [1960]), 114–20.
30. Cited in Stuart Liebman, 'Son of Saul', *Cineaste* 41(1) (2015), 47.
31. Avisar, *Screening the Holocaust*, 35.
32. Salmen Lewenthal, quoted in Jadwiga Bezwińska and Danuta Czech (eds), *Amidst a Nightmare of Crime: Manuscripts of Prisoners in Crematorium Squads Found at Auschwitz* (New York: Howard Fertig, 1992 [1973]), 139.
33. Levi, *The Drowned and the Saved*, 42.
34. Tim Blake Nelson, *The Grey Zone* (United States: Lions Gate Home Entertainment, 2001, DVD).
35. See, for example, Elbert Ventura, 'The Grey Zone', *PopMatters*, 31 October 2002. The film's use of staccato dialogue has also been criticized in Ed Gonzalez, 'The Grey Zone', *Slant*, 14 October 2002.
36. Nelson, *The Grey Zone*, DVD.
37. Ibid.
38. Levi, *The Drowned and the Saved*, 51.
39. Nelson, The Grey Zone*: Director's Notes and Screenplay* (New York: Newmarket, 2003), ix.
40. Nemes, *Son of Saul*, DVD.
41. Ibid.
42. See, for instance, Chari Larsson, 'Making Monsters in László Nemes' *Son of Saul*', *Senses of Cinema* 81 (2016), 20.
43. Richard Alleva, 'Fixed Focus: *Son of Saul*', *Commonweal* 143(7) (2016), 26.

44. Liebman, 'Son of Saul', 48.
45. László Nemes, *Son of Saul*. Hungary: Sony Pictures, 2005, DVD.
46. Nelson, *The Grey Zone*, DVD.
47. Nemes, *Son of Saul*, DVD.
48. Liebman, 'Son of Saul', 48.
49. Quoted in Bezwińska and Czech, *Amidst a Nightmare of Crime*, 136.
50. See 'Deleted Scenes' on Nelson, *The Grey Zone*, DVD.
51. Lawrence L. Langer, 'The Dilemma of Choice in the Deathcamps', in Alan Rosenberg and Gerald E. Myers (eds), *Echoes from the Holocaust: Philosophical Reflections on a Dark Time* (Philadelphia: Temple University Press, 1988), 118.
52. Kristin Hohenadel, '*The Grey Zone*: A Holocaust Horror Story without a Schindler', *New York Times*, 7 January 2001, http://www.nytimes.com/2001/01/07/movies/film-a-holocaust-horror-story-without-a-schindler.html, retrieved 12 April 2019.
53. Jonathan Romney, 'Dead Man Walking: László Nemes' Troubling *Son of Saul* Conveys the Holocaust's Full Horror by Keeping it out of Focus', *Film Comment* 51(6) (2015), 24.
54. Steven Alan Carr, '*Son of Saul* and the Crisis of Holocaust Film', *Film Criticism* 40(3) (2016), 25.
55. Hohenadel, 'The Grey Zone'.
56. Nelson, The Grey Zone: *Director's Notes*, 158–59.
57. Stefan Grisseman, 'Atrocity Exhibitionism: Why *Son of Saul* is an Opportunistic and Highly Problematic Work of Meta-exploitation', *Film Comment* 51(6) (2015), 28–29.
58. Alleva, 'Fixed Focus', 27.
59. Ibid., 27.
60. Romney, 'Dead Man Walking', 25.
61. Debruge, 'An Unblinking Horror', 65; Romney, 'Dead Man Walking', 24.
62. Dominick, LaCapra, 'Approaching Limit Events: Siting Agamben', in Michael Bernard-Donals and Richard Glejzer (eds), *Witnessing the Disaster: Essays on Representation and the Holocaust* (Madison: University of Wisconsin Press, 2003), 262.
63. Ibid., 263.
64. Levi, *The Drowned and the Saved*, 22.
65. Anton Kaes, *From Hitler to Heimat: The Return of History as Film* (Cambridge, MA: Harvard University Press, 1989), 114.
66. See comments by the directors and crew members in Hohenadel, 'The Grey Zone'; Peter Debruge, 'An Unblinking Horror: Laszlo Nemes' *Son of Saul* Bears Witness to the Holocaust through the Eyes of a Morally Complicit Prisoner', *Variety* 330(10) (2015), 65.

Bibliography

Alleva, Richard. 'Fixed Focus: *Son of Saul*'. *Commonweal* 143(7) (2016), 26–27.
Avisar, Ilan. *Screening the Holocaust: Cinema's Images of the Unimaginable*. Bloomington: Indiana University Press, 1988.
Bangert, Axel. 'Changing Narratives and Images of the Holocaust: Tim Blake Nelson's Film *The Grey Zone* (2001)', *New Cinemas: Journal of Contemporary Film* 6(1) (2008), 17–32.

Bernard-Donals, Michael and Richard Glejzer (eds). *Witnessing the Disaster: Essays on Representation and the Holocaust*. Madison: University of Wisconsin Press, 2003.

Bezwińska, Jadwiga, and Danuta Czech (eds). *Amidst a Nightmare of Crime: Manuscripts of Prisoners in Crematorium Squads Found at Auschwitz*. New York: Howard Fertig, 1992 [1973].

Broder, Jonathan. 'Treblinka Survivor Called "Liar" at Trial', *Chicago Tribune*, 3 March 1987. Retrieved 12 April 2019 from http://articles.chicagotribune.com/1987-03-03/news/8701170312_1_defense-attorney-mark-o-connor-judge-dov-levin-eliyahu-rosenberg.

Brown, Adam. 'Confronting "Choiceless Choices" in Holocaust Videotestimonies: Judgement, "Privileged" Jews, and the Role of the Interviewer', *Continuum: Journal of Media and Communication Studies* 24(1) (2010), 79–90.

———. '"No One Will Ever Know . . .": The Holocaust, "Privileged" Jews, and the "Grey Zone"', *History Australia* 8(3) (2011), 95–116.

———. *Judging 'Privileged' Jews: Holocaust Ethics, Representation, and the 'Grey Zone'*. New York: Berghahn Books, 2013.

———. 'Narratives of Judgement: Representations of "Privileged" Jews in Holocaust Documentaries'. *LISA e-journal* 12(1) (2014). Retrieved 12 April 2019 from http://lisa.revues.org/5652.

———. 'Witnessing Moral Compromise: "Privilege", Judgement and Holocaust Testimony'. *Life Writing* 14(3) (2017), 327–39.

———. 'The "Grey Zone" in Holocaust Film: Screening the Ethical Dilemmas of Jewish Leaders', *Holocaust Studies: A Journal of Culture and History*, in press.

Cargas, Harry James (ed.). *Problems Unique to the Holocaust*. Lexington: University Press of Kentucky, 1999.

Carr, Steven Alan. '*Son of Saul* and the Crisis of Holocaust Film', *Film Criticism* 40(3) (2016), 24–26.

Chomsky, Marvin J. *Holocaust: The Story of the Family Weiss*. United States: Titus Productions, 1978. DVD.

Coppa, Frank J. *The Papacy, the Jews, and the Holocaust*. Washington DC: Catholic University of America Press, 2006.

Costa-Gavras. *Amen*. United States: King Video, 2002. DVD.

Debruge, Peter. 'An Unblinking Horror: Laszlo Nemes' *Son of Saul* Bears Witness to the Holocaust through the Eyes of a Morally Complicit Prisoner'. *Variety* 330(10) (2015), 64–65.

Doneson, Judith E. *The Holocaust in American Film*, 2nd edn. New York: Syracuse University Press, 2002.

Eaglestone, Robert, and Barry Langford (eds). *Teaching Holocaust Film and Literature*. Basingstoke: Palgrave Macmillan, 2008.

Gold, Jack. *Escape from Sobibor*. United States: Digital Works, 1987. DVD.

Gonzalez, Ed. 'The Grey Zone', *Slant*, 14 October 2002.

Greif, Gideon. *We Wept without Tears: Testimonies of the Jewish Sonderkommando from Auschwitz*. New Haven: Yale University Press, 2005.

Grisseman, Stefan. 'Atrocity Exhibitionism: Why *Son of Saul* is an Opportunistic and Highly Problematic Work of Meta-exploitation', *Film Comment* 51(6) (2015), 26–29.

Gutman, Israel (ed.). *Encyclopedia of the Holocaust*. New York: Macmillan, 1990.

Gutman, Yisrael, and Livia Rothkirchen (eds). *The Catastrophe of European Jewry: Antecedents, History, Reflections*. Jerusalem: Yad Vashem, 1976.

Hohenadel, Kristin. '*The Grey Zone*: A Holocaust Horror Story without a Schindler', *New York Times*, 7 January 2001. Retrieved 12 April 2019 from http://www.nytimes.com/2001/01/07/movies/film-a-holocaust-horror-story-without-a-schindler.html.
Insdorf, Annette. *Indelible Shadows: Film and the Holocaust*, 3rd edn. Cambridge: Cambridge University Press, 2003 [1983].
Kaes, Anton. *From Hitler to Heimat: The Return of History as Film*. Cambridge, MA: Harvard University Press, 1989.
Kwiet, Konrad, and Jürgen Matthäus (eds). *Contemporary Responses to the Holocaust*. Westport: Praeger, 2004.
Larsson, Chari. 'Making Monsters in László Nemes' *Son of Saul*'. *Senses of Cinema* 81 (2016), 1–22.
Liebman, Stuart. 'Son of Saul'. *Cineaste* 41(1) (2015), 46–48.
Levi, Primo. *The Drowned and the Saved*, trans. Raymond Rosenthal. London: Michael Joseph, 1988 [1986].
———. *If This is a Man; and, The Truce*, trans. Stuart Woolf. London: Abacus, 1995 [1979].
———. *The Black Hole of Auschwitz*, trans. Sharon Wood. Cambridge: Polity Press, 2005.
Loshitzky, Yosefa (ed.). *Spielberg's Holocaust: Critical Perspectives on* Schindler's List. Bloomington: Indiana University Press, 1997.
Nelson, Tim Blake. *The Grey Zone*. United States: Lions Gate Home Entertainment, 2001. DVD.
———. The Grey Zone: *Director's Notes and Screenplay*. New York: Newmarket, 2003.
Nemes, László. *Son of Saul*. Hungary: Sony Pictures, 2005. DVD.
Nyiszli, Miklós. *Auschwitz: A Doctor's Eyewitness Account*, trans. Tibère Kremer and Richard Seaver. New York: Arcade, 1993 [1960].
Południak, Jan. *Sonder: An Interview with Sonderkommando Member Henryk Mandelbaum*, trans. Witold Zbirohowski-Kościa. Oświęcim: Frap-Books, 2008.
Preminger, Otto. *Exodus*. United States: MGM Home Entertainment, 1960. DVD.
Romney, Jonathan. 'Dead Man Walking: László Nemes' Troubling *Son of Saul* Conveys the Holocaust's Full Horror by Keeping it out of Focus'. *Film Comment* 51(6) (2015), 22–25.
Rosenberg, Alan, and Gerald E. Myers (eds). *Echoes from the Holocaust: Philosophical Reflections on a Dark Time*. Philadelphia: Temple University Press, 1988.
Shandler, Jeffrey. *While America Watches: Televising the Holocaust*. New York: Oxford University Press, 1999.
Sharpe, Matthew, Murray Noonan and Jason Freddi (eds). *Trauma, Historicity, Philosophy*. Newcastle upon Tyne: Cambridge Scholars Press, 2007.
Stone, Dan. 'The Sonderkommando Photographs', *Jewish Studies* 7(3) (2001), 132–48.
Ventura, Elbert. 'The Grey Zone'. *PopMatters*, 31 October 2002.
Young, Robert M. *Triumph of the Spirit*. United States: MGM Home Entertainment, 1989. DVD.

Chapter 19

The Sonderkommando on Screen

Philippe Mesnard

Cinema is one of the major cultural modes for raising awareness of extreme violence, whether through documentaries, narrative film, docudramas, blockbusters or television series. To put it provocatively, perhaps: how would the consciousness of the Shoah have developed in Western culture without Marvin Chomsky's *Holocaust* (1978), Claude Lanzmann's *Shoah* (1985), Steven Spielberg's *Schindler's List* (1993) and the many films that have been produced since then, to which we might add the many video testimonies that now appear on YouTube?

As such, we could ask how the highly distinctive and ambivalent figures of the Sonderkommando (SK) can appear on screen, since they are at one and the same time the closest witnesses to the final phase of the Nazi exterminatory process and bear most upon the always vexed question of enforced collaboration with the SS. Are they not therefore the best placed to allow us to face the challenges and dilemmas of representation? What analogies, what images has the great reservoir of the historical imagination accorded in film to these men, so easy to take for brutes or cowards, in order to give them a presence, to make them active in a history, indeed in a fate that was precisely what they were stripped of as soon as they were drafted into the 'special squads' whose name they bear?

From Shame to Martyrdom, the Paths of Fiction

While the SKs and the *Arbeitsjuden* (Jews for work) were the only ones from the Nazi concentrationary and exterminatory system to revolt at Treblinka (2 August 1943), Sobibór (14 October 1943) and Auschwitz (7 October 1944), the first time they were portrayed in cinema, in Otto Preminger's *Exodus* (1960), was through the ambiguous character of Dov Landau. To become a member of the Zionist army Irgun, Landau boasts of his skills as a munitions expert who learnt how to handle dynamite digging trenches to bury victims, while, he says, a member of the SK at Auschwitz. Not only is this explanation entirely fanciful, but, in addition, he claims the SS used him like a woman. The myth-making film links clichés about feminine 'weakness' and homosexuality with the shame of those who helped murder their own people.

Discrediting the SK in this way fits perfectly with the cultural framework of the time which was dominated by resistance fighters. In truth, the scope of representation, which is to say the possibilities for rendering the SK visible (*c'est-à-dire les possibilités de faire émerger les Sonderkommandos dans le champ du visible*), has always been restricted. The alternatives are either to reproduce a stigma that is already present in popular consciousness, one immediately expressed by the inmates themselves, or alternatively to reduce them to a singular heroic act which stifles issues raised by the lived experience of these men. It is more or less this latter tendency that characterizes the development of their representation from the 1990s onwards.

By way of the revolt of 7 October 1944, the SK reappeared differently, tentatively at first in Robert Milton Young's *Triumph of the Spirit* (1989) and then at the heart of Tim Blake Nelson's *The Grey Zone* (2001), in portrayals significantly informed by their role as fighters. It is this exemplary act of sacrifice, moreover, which comes to redeem them in the eyes of an audience and to render them worthy of a place in the Shoah. These films are characterized by a wish to show everything through a mass of omniscient shots without any ethical restraint. They reproduce plot devices and patterns of conduct already used in Wanda Jakubowska's *The Last Stage* (*Ostatni etap*) (1947), Gillo Pontecorvo's *Kapo* (1960) and Armand Gatti's *Enclosure* (*L'Enclos*) (1961).

Triumph of the Spirit is inspired by the story of the boxer Salomo Arouch (played by Willem Dafoe) who was deported from Greece to Auschwitz with his family in 1943. In line with realist conventions, the film links documentary elements with a dramatic storyline that is sustained by plot twists and by boxing matches to entertain the SS. On the basis of the ring, it would have been possible to develop the question of the grey zone because in order to survive and to enable his family to survive, the boxing champion had to knock out his opponents in the knowledge that every loser would be killed by the SS. But this dimension is not developed, undoubtedly because of the requirements of mainstream cinema. Many scenes show the ditches where they burned bodies and, since one of the parents of the protagonist is drafted into the SK, it is possible to learn through his eyes of the workings of the Crematorium.

The main issue with this film relates to the number of inconsistencies that build towards the end. Suddenly the main character is drafted into a squad of the SK and is simultaneously thrown into the heart of the revolt that has broken out. This is described in a semi-dream-like way. After the revolt has been ruthlessly suppressed, he emerges from the ruins of a bunker in the area of the gas chambers that has been blown up. The heap of blocks of concrete leads the viewer to believe the blast has pulverised the building, a flagrant inaccuracy if we are referring to the sabotage which only damaged Crematorium IV during the revolt of 7 October 1944. This depiction instead corresponds with the results of the dynamiting of the facilities by the SS in January 1945 just before they fled. After this, the hero is captured and tortured. Feigning innocence, he miraculously escapes death. He is not evacuated during the death marches which we see being organized and finds himself, again miraculously, outside the block where he had been tortured. The camp is then abandoned by the SS. There is a final addition to this series of improbable events: the grass is green, vernal and weather is mild, in contrast to the prevailing conditions on 27 January 1945 in the heart of Poland.

By contrast, *The Grey Zone*, the project of Tim Blake Nelson, the grandson of survivors, is driven as much by a concern for exactitude as by a special attachment to testimony. Nelson surrounded himself with advisors, including, notably, Andreas Kilian who co-authored a reference book on the subject.[1] Before that, he had also carried out his own research reading the (often imprecise) testimony of the Hungarian doctor Miklós Nyiszli and Primo Levi's essay on 'The Grey Zone' in *The Drowned and the Saved*.[2] Before devising the film, Nelson wrote a play of the same name that he staged in many theatres in the United States in 1996. The project therefore passed through a preliminary phase of dramatic development in order to arrive at the film six years later. *The Grey Zone* was released in 2001.

If the main story concerns the revolt, embedded in it can be found the event, inspired by Nyiszli's testimony and taken up by Primo Levi, of the young woman who survived a gassing only to be murdered by a member of the SS. Except for this occurrence, the unfolding of the action up to the revolt and the ensuing blood bath is unsurprising. The predictable aesthetic inclination to show everything involves an unwholesome artifice: a scene depicts the interior of a gas chamber during a gassing, medium shots portray the last moments of the main characters who, lying on the ground, are executed one by one. It is not so much a case of making visible as of producing a totalizing visibility that imposes its own codes on the real taken as subject, described at once by way of stereotypes and generic characterization.

The revolt plunges us briefly into the genre of the 'war film': explosions, bodies flying through the air, attack, counterattack, assaults, loud detonations. Neither 'Auschwitz' nor the Shoah, however, is war. All we have of the SK is a causal chain constructing plausibility carried along by the temporality of a realist narrative. Everything is there so that it contributes to the plot.

These three films preserve only the dimension of resistance of the SK and limit the lives of these men to stock situations. The last two films are also led them to tackle the thorny question of the grey zone. In each case, the exceptional circumstances of the SK are used to render them foils to the action plot and what is unique about their experience is neglected. Is there then a form of fiction and a kind of narrative which would enable this destiny to be conjured up? It is to the witnesses themselves that we should now turn our attention and, in doing this, to those films that have given them a place as such.

Witness Testimony and Plot Devices

Two films accord a key role to one or more of these survivors: Claude Lanzmann's *Shoah* (1985) and Karl Fruchtmann's *Ein einfacher Mensch* (*A Simple Man*, 1986). Despite their very different forms, these two contemporaneous films have a number of points in common: they combine plot devices with their documentary aims. This gives them an experimental dimension that should be seen as entirely suitable for the cinematic treatment of the SK.

It was in Israel that Karl Fruchtmann came to film Yacov (Yaakov) Silberberg, upon whom *Ein einfacher Mensch* is centred. The documentary framework rests on a scenario of psychodrama in which Silberberg succeeds in testifying in the company of his wife Luba and his two children. On camera, no communication occurs between Yacov and Luba until, with the pressure on their relationship building, she forcefully calls upon him to snap out of the deadening lethargy that paralyses him (a state clearly hammed up by Yacov, who assumes the role of himself, to show the psychic damage he suffered). In order to enable this maieutic method, Fruchtmann opts for a rather strange docudrama. Contrary to the genre, he includes no archival material and gives no screen time to experts alongside his characters. The story unfolds through the depictions of each member of the family, filmed as themselves in their normal living and working environments. Yacov is a baker, so the film opens and closes with shots showing dozens of bread rolls being inserted into a bakery's oven – a visual metaphor of cremation that could be judged excessive, but which nonetheless illustrates the alienation the former SK member still endures. If Yacov was able to physically survive this disaster, his mind is still imprisoned in the environs of the gas chambers at Birkenau, as the blank gaze of his inexpressive face shows.

Fictionalization characterizes the overall approach of Yacov. For this to happen, the family accept not only to be directed by Fruchtmann but also to perform some highly fictionalized scenes. That the couple are filmed repeatedly in their marital bed, each beside the other, separated by their own stories is nothing compared to the race which will surprise the spectator two-thirds of the way through the film. This long sequence, which lasts nearly six minutes, unfolds through alternating scenes of a sunlit cemetery and of a station yard in which goods wagons – a clear reminder of deportation – are parked in sidings. A real chase begins in the cemetery when Yacov is pursued by his children and his wife who never stops calling out: 'Yacov, bleib stehen Yacov bleib stehen' (Yacov, stand still . . .).

Really, this film is a rewriting of an earlier film by Fruchtmann, *Zeugen: Aussagen zum Mord an einem Volk* (*Witnesses: Testimonies of the Murder of a People*) (1980–1), which gathered together the accounts of sixty survivors of the genocide against the Jews who were living in Israel or Poland, with a tightening of focus on Silberberg. The yardstick against which this project, which focuses on the personality of a single witness, is to be measured is an entirely conventional documentary. The issue of support and of restoring confidence in another (the interlocutor, the interviewer) lends the conception its humanity and its spirit. This issue is even more forcefully present in *Shoah* (1985).

Abraham Bomba, a barber in Częstochowa in Poland, was deported to Treblinka in September 1942, where he was tasked with cutting the hair of Jews just before they were gassed. His testimony resonates with the preceding example, its *mise-en-scène* exemplary as a plot device, meaning that it can be more easily taken as a template than *Ein einfacher Mensch* with its psycho-dramatic excesses. Abraham Bomba is not the only person in *Shoah* to attest to this kind of experience; the first scenes of the film introduce us to Simon Srebnik, followed by Michael Podchlebnik, the sole survivors of Chełmno on the Ner, the first extermination site to use gas vans. We also hear from a survivor from Treblinka, Richard Glazar, and from Auschwitz, Filip Müller.

Bomba appears six times in *Shoah* to give accounts of his deportation and his imprisonment at Treblinka. The filming was done in September

1979 in Israel, where he had moved after his retirement, having previously worked as a barber in New York. His appearances in the film do not exceed one minute and 40 seconds. Until the longest sequence, which is thirteen minutes in length. Bomba is positioned by the director in a barber's shop, which he himself had chosen, where – in contrast to previous scenes – in replicating the task he carried out on Jewish victims at Treblinka, he becomes an actor of his own testimony not only in the way Yacov Silberberg did at around the same time, but also by way of *interpretation* in the musical sense of the term. In fact, in front of the camera and the mirrors of the shop, he mimics the gestures of his twin pasts: that of *Arbeitsjude* and that of hairdresser who worked at Grand Central Station for most of his career. In the barber's shop in Tel Aviv, with a friend from Częstochowa playing a customer, he reproduces the ghastly gestures he practised thousands of times at Treblinka. This link with his job is clearly reminiscent of Silberberg spending a significant period of his life working in front of the ovens as a baker.

After having recounted his story in a very controlled way, under pressure from Lanzmann something emerges from Bomba. First, he can no longer speak; only his silence accompanies the methodical gestures he makes in front of the mirror. Then he says he can no longer express himself. Finally another voice comes as if from the depths of this man, a different mode of expression (*parole*) that the descriptive account had enabled him to escape up until then. It is only after muttering a few words in Yiddish, his mother tongue, itself impacted by the history of genocide, that his emotion becomes bound once again to their lingua franca (*langage véhiculaire*). Bomba then tells an additional story in English. One day a transport arrived from Częstochowa in which he knew most of the Jews, some of very closely. He then uses the third person to attribute the story to one of his co-workers from the same town assigned to the same detail:

> They knew the minute they said a word, not only the wife and sister (who were to die already) but also they would share the same path with them. In a way they tried to do the best for them, to stay with them a second, a minute longer, just to hug them and kiss them because they knew they would never see them again.[3]

This literal staging and the implicit presence of Claude Lanzmann suspends the remit of what comes under the category of the survivor-witness' voluntary memory, in order to bring out the involuntary memory of he who, at another time, was *witness*. We cannot know if the person of whom he speaks was himself, if he could only describe himself in the third person, or someone else.

These two films go beyond the genre of the documentary in which many wish to place them; the part which precisely renders them not of that genre is the invasion of fiction as a device, but not as narrative content. In *Ein einfacher Mensch*, as is the case with *Shoah*, real people can only express their stories, stories that distance them (*qui les aliène*) from themselves, only by becoming actors playing themselves and no longer simply witnesses – as if they had to be freed from their testimonial capacity. Indeed, the value of fiction cannot be reduced to a narrative framework: it provides the filmmaker with a means to call upon fictional devices – without the film becoming 'fiction' – that enable a truth to be brought to the screen and communicated. What then about other forms of film in which members of the SK also appear? What role do they have?

Testimony as Expertise

There exist a number of recordings of testimony which speak only to the demands of the documentary format, a format showing no evidence of artistry either in its conception or in its making and the accounts that accompany that. How do the men whose stories were marginalized for so long appear in these?

Dario Gabbai, a Greek who was assigned to the Auschwitz-Birkenau SK in April 1944, testifies for three minutes in *The Last Days* (1998), a documentary by the made-for-television director James Moll for which Steven Spielberg was an executive producer. This film is characteristic of the vast project of recording video testimonies which were amassed by the director of *Schindler's List*. Gabbai, having been recruited before the summer, takes part as a major witness to the methodical killing of the Hungarian Jews. The second, more recent example is provided by the filming of the survivors in the grounds of Auschwitz-Birkenau itself. *Mémoire demain* (*Tomorrow's Memory*), a DVD-ROM produced in 2009 under the guidance of Raphaël Israel and Isabelle Ernot, gives voice to twenty deportees, including the former SK member Henryk Mandelbaum. With its branching structure designed for interactive use, it becomes more than a film; it is a pedagogical tool for teachers and cultural educators. During the scene dedicated to Mandelbaum, he shows the precise location and layout of the gas chambers that were destroyed by the SS just before they fled, how the gassings unfolded and what the SK did. Mandelbaum is working as a specialist and a field man, and it is there, precisely, that we are surprised to see the SK in the garb of expert. The more the other survivors, called upon as individuals, recount their own personal experiences of the Shoah, the more the SK, required as a specialist, sticks to the script which the directors have unwittingly assigned to him – a script which he has also undoubtedly taken refuge in and cannot escape from. We find once again a kind of technical hyper-positivism of which Jean-Claude Pressac was one of the most active advocates. Genocide is thus reduced to a clearly complex set of technical processes and the SK reappears as bereft of feeling, it having been engulfed by his skills. Twelve years before, the Italian filmmaker Ruggero Gabbai, with the historians Marcello Pezzetti and Liliana Picciotti working as writers on the project, made *Memoria* (1997), where you can already see, as with Mandelbaum, Shlomo Venezia not only precisely describing the process by which victims met their deaths, but also pacing the ruins of Crematorium V in the company of Pezzetti. Faced with such stage-managing, we might ask ourselves: is this where the lost soul of the SKs roams? It certainly isn't revealed through this strictly informational account.

Among the survivors of the SK, Mandelbaum was certainly the most sought-out. He is also to be found in two documentaries about the special squads: *Sklaven der Gaskammer: Das Jüdische Sonderkommando in Auschwitz: Aus der Todeszone* of 2001 and in the British documentary *Sonderkommando: The Living Dead of Auschwitz* of 2009. In this last film, Mandelbaum, who died shortly after filming, is questioned from start to finish; he repeats – and this is probably why he participated – the same gestures accompanying the same words as the previous times, as if on demand. Paying the docudrama's usual obeisance to the authenticity of images, the British film brings extraneous material to the topic as if it is necessary at all costs to show corpses in order to bestow greater credibility on the person invited to speak as an expert. *Sklaven der Gaskammer*, a more reliable effort, was made in 2001 for the Westdeutscher Rundfunk (WDR) by Eric Friedler, with Barbara Siebert and Andreas Kilian acting as consultants. Friedler would edit the volume *Zeugen aus der Todeszone* with them a year later, the most comprehensive treatment of the SK at Auschwitz to date. Following each other on camera were Shaul Chazan, Morris Kesselman, Gabriel Malinski, Henryk Mandelbaum, Chaim Lemke Pliszko, Yehoshuah Rosenblum, Yacov Silberberg and Shlomo Venezia. The film provides a means for these former SK members to tell the story of their role and of the murder of the Jews by gassing: some are filmed in a personal setting, such as a room in their house or their business, others, such as Mandelbaum, in an airport, on the bed of a hotel, or at Birkenau near to the crematoria. If this short film of 45 minutes is clearly a documentary, we can nevertheless keep in mind that the ways in which these witnesses have been filmed involves a minimal *mise-en-scène*. Friedler is thus able to juxtapose these men returned from death and the everyday setting in which they let themselves be filmed today. Nonetheless, he also uses archival photographs as if he needed to sometimes guarantee, sometimes illustrate the words of the witnesses. This is what Karl Fruchtmann, with *Ein einfacher Mensch*, and Claude Lanzmann, with *Shoah*, managed to avoid doing twenty years earlier.

Writings in Spoken Words

Claude Lanzmann never accorded significance to the written testimonies of the SKs, although admittedly they did not fit with his requirements. After their publication, which only happened in France between 2001 and 2005, it took a long time for a director to become interested in them. In *Sonderkommando* (2007), we listen for 52 minutes to readings in French and Yiddish of the manuscripts that were buried by the SK members Zalman Gradowski, Leyb Langfus and Zalman Lewental, to extracts from witness statements given by Shlomo (also Szlama) Dragon, Henryk Tauber and Alter Feinsilber, who were able to escape the liquidation of the SKs, and to pages from Miklós Nyiszli's book. Without pathos, voices recite these texts – which have been chosen as some of the most revealing of the Shoah – without creating a spectacle of horror. The camera shots derive from actual sites in Birkenau and from within the ruins of the crematoria, where Emil Weiss animates his camera through zooming out, through shifts in depth of focus and by working with the speed of the camera's movements such that it follows the very rhythm of the diction of the testimonies. If there is a strategy at work here, it is one directed at the viewer which aims to promote the act of listening: there are no characters, no people to be seen, the places are empty – unreal, in some way, because usually they are full of tourists and visitors. A turning point has probably been achieved because, twenty years after *Shoah*, the words of the SK become audible, despite not a single French historian showing any interest in them.

A sign of this change is that, inspired by the release of Weiss' film, Alain Timar, the director of Théâtre des Halles in Avignon, staged extracts from the first manuscript of Zalman Gradowski under the title *Une voix sous la cendre* (*A Voice beneath the Ashes*) at Festival Off from 7–30 July 2009. The 80-minute performance featured the actor François Clavier reciting the texts alone on stage with a white curtain – which moved forward during the reading – as a backdrop. The actor here gave a 'one man show': joining a number of similar events such as the adaptation of Charles Reznikoff's *Holocaust* (1975) by Claude Régy in 1998 or, more recently, of Imre Kertész's *Kaddis a meg nem született gyermekért* (*Kaddish for an Unborn Child*) (1990) organized by different stage directors in Paris and in Brussels.

In fact, on the subjects of both documentary and dramaturgy, a work that is now almost forgotten accorded an important place to the 'special squads' at the same time as the Frankfurt Auschwitz trials of a number of SS who worked at the camp, and notably at Birkenau, were taking place. Thus, in 1965, *Die Ermittlung* (*The Investigation*), an oratorio in eleven songs devoted its last song to the SKs: 'Gesang von den Feueröfen' ('Song from the Crematorium Ovens'). This provided accounts of fictitious events from those designated as witnesses No. 2 and 7 and then 1 and 3, to confront the German public of the time with the systematic killing process at Birkenau. Applying his idea of documentary theatre, Peter Weiss repeats quotations taken from the testimonies of survivors and spares no detail regarding the method or the lies with which the victims were swamped (Reznikoff, then Régy, are inspired by the same principle in their versions of *Holocaust*). The SKs appear simultaneously incredibly cynical ('The men of the commando shouted quick, quick, the water's getting cold') and heroic, because the revolt is described at length.

Back to the Fable

A new stage in the history of films of the SK was reached in 2016, with the release of the film *Son of Saul*, directed by László Nemes. In October 1944, in the area of the gas chambers at Auschwitz-Birkenau, Saul Ausländer, an SK, witnesses a young boy who has survived a gassing being revived and then murdered by the SS. The body is taken to the medical block to be autopsied. Auslander, however, wants the body to be left untouched at all costs and insists that it is his son. He must not be burnt like the others. Convinced that he needs a rabbi to say kaddish, the Jewish prayer for the dead, he spends much of the film looking for one.

In following Saul's wanderings around the camp, the camera sees what cinema has so far never really shown. Not watchtowers, electric fences, wooden barracks, inmates in striped uniforms and dying prisoners, but, instead, the harrowing tempo of the work of the SKs in the undressing room at the moment of the arrival of those about to die, and then after their murder, of the funnelling of the corpses to the ovens. We are witness to the dumping of human ashes into the Vistula (or the Soła), the shooting of Jews and their burning in pits when the gas chambers were insufficient to cope with the quantity of arrivals, the everyday life of the SK in their quarters, and the revolt of 7 October 1944. Nemes shows the functioning of the extermination site at Birkenau in a way it has never been shown before, without pandering to voyeurism in the slightest.

To write and produce this film, Nemes and Clara Royer, his co-scriptwriter, grasped the few possibilities that the history of cinema relating to the Nazi camps and the Shoah had not yet used. Thus, *Son of Saul* is a fable that takes its place among the films which we have examined all too briefly above, the documentaries (because the director also takes note of them for his film) as well as the fictional ones. *Son of Saul* takes advantage of all the possibilities that the films which preceded it either could not or did not know how to capitalize on. In some ways, the film is driven by the issues that the earlier films knew to broach, examine and reflect upon, but on which they foundered. Nemes found a way to present these issues which had not been tried before, either aesthetically or thematically.

We are concerned here with the central character (upon whom the entire work rests) in the sense that he resists all the categories that, up until now, have been assigned to the SK. Additionally, Saul Ausländer does not match any of the SK members whose existence we know of, something which is not the case for a number of other characters. The film does makes reference to individuals who did really exist, such as Zalman Gradowski, one of the resistance leaders and the author of some of the buried manuscripts, or one of the handymen of the squad who took a photograph looking out from the gas chamber of Crematorium V. Similarly, we can easily identify Miklós Nyiszli, the Hungarian doctor who became an assistant to Josef Mengele, and some SS (the Oberscharführers Voss and Busch). 'Ausländer', however, remains forever a stranger, as his surname derived from the German clearly indicates.

Without ever tipping into excessively subjective camerawork, *Son of Saul* shows us the essential character of this reality at the head height of Ausländer or through his eyes. One of the specific aesthetic aspects of the film is the way in which the camera focuses on the head or neck of the protagonist. Most of the time, we are supposed to see with him or see what he sees. Nemes and Royer make Ausländer play the role of the innocent, a literary formula popularized by Candide and Fabrice de Dongo. He moves around all the different extermination sites, as no member of the SK would have been able to, and through this, he becomes our guide. Let us note two characteristics of this antihero to better grasp what makes him stand out: fatherhood and resistance.

First, the paternal. Nemes and Royer had read the buried manuscripts, most notably Gradowski's second manuscript, and learnt there that some of the SK members secretly performed funeral rites. As such, Ausländer's wish to give his 'son' a Jewish burial is an act that – in its symbolic and, at the same transcendent, dimension – becomes a means to resist the crushing atmosphere of the extermination site. As to the fact that Ausländer insists on the need for a rabbi when Judaism authorizes the saying of kaddish without one, it is necessary to see this, according to the director, as the symptom of a character who has lost all connection with a religion which he now seeks to find once more.

If we retain the idea that the film follows on from the other films that have featured the SK in their plot, then the relation of the son to the father refers to another fable about Auschwitz in which the question of filiation was central, Roberto Benigni's *Life is Beautiful* (1997). Although controversial, this film advances very normative and conservative arguments, as is usually the case in our times. At the film's conclusion, the father Guido protects his son Giosuè to the point of going to his death having hidden the child beforehand, playing *il fanfarone* (the braggart) to distract him. It is very much the case of a 'new father', to borrow the insightful idea of Sophie Ernst. In a very controversial way, Benigni perpetuates the well-established model of the family unit as sacrosanct. By contrast, the child who Ausländer designates as his son brings into question a genetic filiation that is of concern to both the Jewish community and to the maintenance of the heterosexual family unit. In a world in which everything has been taken away, including the freedom of death, the resistors are trying to reappropriate the latter. Ausländer stubbornly acknowledges a son, a dead son, to recover what seemed irrecoverable, simultaneously opting for an act of freedom, the opposite, clearly, of the choiceless choice of Sophie in the eponymous novel of Styron (1979) and Pakula's film (1983).

Regarding resistance, the deconstruction accomplished by *Son of Saul* is equally effective. In fact, the plot of *Son of Saul* does not conform to the canons of a genre in which courage and resistance would 'naturally' be the cornerstone, nor, such is its subtlety, does it give in to an alternative (or additional) generic expression of victimhood. This was in fact one of the major concerns of Nemes from the project's outset: no voyeurist aesthetics, no Hollywood realism, a film that was neither lament nor Western (the end of *The Grey Zone* very much resembles one). It is for this reason that *Son of Saul* hardly ever shows the body: heroic martyrdom and its diametrical opposite, the depiction of helpless victimhood, both need the body to be visible, either in its glory or by way of its injuries and its abasement. Here the body is generally blurred.

Wandering in parallel with preparations for the revolt, Ausländer is not a fighter. He saves the photographer and the photographs through hiding the camera shortly before being roughly searched by the SS, thus playing the role of a *deus ex machina*. He lets himself be carried along by the revolt, not out of conviction but because he is preoccupied with his own quest. Such is the case in the scene with the gunpowder that he recovers from Kanada, but which he loses during the shambles of the killings of the transport. Ausländer's quest enables another kind of resistance to be articulated, a transcendental one this time, which makes him stand up to the resistance fighters. It is for this reason that he threatens the one presumed to be Gradowski with revealing the whereabouts of his hidden writings. In the face of rough treatment from a Red Army officer, he affects an indifference that is reminiscent of Bartleby, another 'naïve' of literature. The climax occurs as the revolt breaks out when – travelling behind a wagon that protects members of the SKs from the fusillades of the SS – he carries the body of the dead boy on his back. Ausländer's mission provides an alternative to the binary fate of hero or victim.

Son of Saul is, perhaps, the last film about 'Auschwitz', not only because it is the last addition to a list which is already pretty long, but also because its deductive cleverness has enabled it to take into account the possibilities that these films, and perhaps the history of cinema, bequeathed it. Could we not say that *Son of Saul* marks a new stage in our relationship to Auschwitz, indeed an end to our relationship with this place which, in our culture, is as much symbolic as real, an end which it does not dictate but which it bears witness to?

Philippe Mesnard is Professor of Comparative Literature at the Université Clermont Auvergne (UCA) and a member of CELIS. He is a member of the Institut Universitaire de France. His research interests include issues of memory and testimony in the twentieth and twenty-first centuries.

Notes

Translated by Nicholas Chare and Dominic Williams.
1. Eric Friedler, Barbara Siebert and Andreas Killian, *Zeugen aus der Todeszone: Das Jüdische Sonderkommando in Auschwitz* (Munich: Deutscher Taschenbuch Verlag, 2005).
2. See Miklós Nyiszli, *Auschwitz: A Doctor's Eyewitness Account*, trans. Tibère Kremer and Richard Seaver (London: Penguin, 2013); Primo Levi, *The Drowned and the Saved*, trans. Raymond Rosenthal (London: Michael Joseph, 1988).
3. Abraham Bomba – Treblinka, Claude Lanzmann Shoah Collection, Transcript of Interview with Abraham Bomba, 59, United States Holocaust Memorial Museum, Accession Number 1996.166; RG-60.5011.

Bibliography

Friedler, Eric, Barbara Siebert and Andreas Killian, *Zeugen aus der Todeszone: Das Jüdische Sonderkommando in Auschwitz*. Munich: Deutscher Taschenbuch Verlag, 2005.

Levi, Primo. *The Drowned and the Saved*, trans. Raymond Rosenthal. London: Michael Joseph, 1988.

Nyiszli, Miklós. *Auschwitz: A Doctor's Eyewitness Account*, trans. Tibère Kremer and Richard Seaver. London: Penguin, 2013.

Afterword

Tracing Topographies of Memory and Mourning

Victor Jeleniewski Seidler

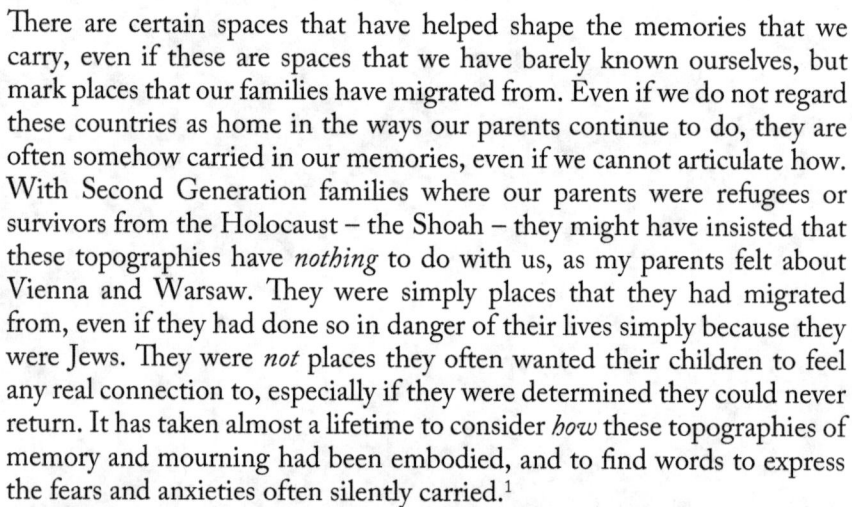

There are certain spaces that have helped shape the memories that we carry, even if these are spaces that we have barely known ourselves, but mark places that our families have migrated from. Even if we do not regard these countries as home in the ways our parents continue to do, they are often somehow carried in our memories, even if we cannot articulate how. With Second Generation families where our parents were refugees or survivors from the Holocaust – the Shoah – they might have insisted that these topographies have *nothing* to do with us, as my parents felt about Vienna and Warsaw. They were simply places that they had migrated from, even if they had done so in danger of their lives simply because they were Jews. They were *not* places they often wanted their children to feel any real connection to, especially if they were determined they could never return. It has taken almost a lifetime to consider *how* these topographies of memory and mourning had been embodied, and to find words to express the fears and anxieties often silently carried.[1]

My parents, talking more personally, wanted to cut their connections rather than feel the pain of rejection, as my mother felt about Vienna, when Hitler's German army marched in to be celebrated by the overwhelming mass of the population. The Jewish population felt terribly isolated and, their fate sealed, recognized that they had to use whatever means were available to escape. They often insisted that these places had nothing to do with their children. On some level, it was a gesture of revenge. Even though my mother carried a love of Vienna with her, especially its food and music, she was often silent in the face of questions, saying 'I have suffered more than enough'. As children, we soon learnt *not* to ask, for we did not want to add to her suffering. It shows *how* spaces and memories can be connected in topographies of loss and mourning.

On some level, it was because our parents had been 'lucky enough', as they framed it, to have escaped inevitable death in concentration camps that they often *refused* to talk about what happened and did their best to protect their children from these histories. They did *not* want to remember themselves because the memories they carried were too painful and it was important for them to insist that topological mappings that might connect London to Vienna and Berlin could have *no* reality for their children. They insisted that because we were born in London, as a matter of logic that could not be disputed, this meant that we belonged exclusively to London and had to make British national history and imperial geographies our own as we sought to *become English*. The places where they had lived, sometimes for many generations, they insisted had *no* connection to us.

They did not want to think of themselves as refugees because they feared that this could make it harder for their children to belong. Even if we knew that our parents were 'foreign' – that they were 'continentals' – this was a way of making the topographies imprecise and the affective connections to Vienna and Warsaw difficult to engage with. This was especially so in relation to Warsaw, which existed in a kind of virtual space as we were growing up, locked away behind the Iron Curtain. Europe existed as a divided topography and there were spaces that barely existed on the same affective map, but that nevertheless could make themselves *felt* unconsciously through our dreams. As the same time, there was ambivalence because the Warsaw Ghetto uprising had an intense personal resonance, for at some level we knew relatives had lived in the ghetto. But it was to take many years to trace topographies and thus connections to Vienna and Warsaw, and to begin to recognize *how* these places continued to resonate as part of an affective geography. I was helped in this process, as I will explore through the literary and artistic explorations of others, including those who carried unresolved legacies of the perpetrator generation.

Growing up within a liberal moral culture, you often learn as part of a liberal 'common-sense' to forget the past – to put the past behind you – as you learnt to focus upon the present and opportunities for the future. We learnt in the 1950s and 1960s to accept a topography of progress that meant that you could turn your back on the past as *if* it was over and had *no* bearing on the present. Some people might have an interest in history, but within liberal schooling there was a progressive discourse that insisted that the past could not be changed, so you should forget about it. This was particularly true in relation to the mass deaths of European Jewry in the extermination camps – it would be morbid to remember, and what would be the point? This liberal common-sense supported our parents, who were anxious to insist that these painful histories they had lived through had nothing to do with their children.

On another level, we also embodied an awareness that it was because they were Jews that our families had been in danger and so many had been murdered. There were also stories circulating in schools, as Paul Morrison, director of the BBC film *From Bitter Earth* about art that was created in the camps and ghettoes of the Second World War, explains: 'It was my contribution to nailing the lie that was pervasive when I was growing up, that it was the Jews' own fault they perished, because they didn't fight back. The film describes this extraordinary cultural resistance'. Those of us who had been more directly affected were haunted by a sense that *if* others got to know that we were Jews, we could be murdered – 'if it happened to them, it could happen to us'. This unspeakable fear existed in an ambivalent relationship with postwar liberal notions that held that religion was a private and personal matter of individual belief, so could *not* really stand in the way of you becoming *like everyone else*.

But this involves thinking beyond the terms of postmemory because it was not that we could *not* remember what our parents had lived through, but that we had not lived through these experiences ourselves. Thinking in terms of postmemory is often to frame memory in cognitive terms and to represent it within a visual grammar that says that the Second Generation can only inherit photographic images of what happened, not the real thing. But often this is not helpful because, growing up in a different world, children *embody* different affective memories, even if they are positioned differently, as they seek to come to terms with their own historical experiences.

As we learnt in the late 1980s to begin to identify a particular 'Second Generation' experience, this was sometimes achieved through the language of postmemory, but that can make it harder to grasp *how* children were affected in quite different ways, depending also on what parents were ready to share, as survivors or refugees and the strategies and silences they insisted upon to protect their children from this 'difficult knowledge', as Eva Hoffman has called it. I was struck by Primo Levi's admission that living through the horror, one could not conceive it in its full magnitude and his awareness, expressed in *The Drowned and the Saved*, that the victim 'felt overwhelmed by an enormous edifice of violence and menace but could not form for himself a representation of it because his eyes were fastened on the ground by every single minute's needs'.[2]

I want to argue that Levi's concern at the time that the *Lagers* did not provide a good 'observation post'[3] from which to fully comprehend the true scope of the catastrophe that was unfolding is not met within a positivist historiography that insists that perspective is gained from spatial distance or through temporal lapse. We might have learnt to bring new questions to these horrors and we might question the tendency at the time to think of the concentration camps as a 'living hell'. It is partly because of the continued silences of the perpetrator generation that we can still feel overwhelmed by these catastrophic events. On some level, within a liberal moral culture we might find it harder, not easier, to gain a perspective on these histories, even if we have listened carefully to the stories of survivors and refugees.

We might still feel speechless as we reflect upon these sites of mass destruction and seek to trace our own connections, as I am still seeking to do in relation to Treblinka, where many of my father's large Warsaw family were murdered. As I was growing up, I do not recall hearing much about Treblinka and only decades later did I realize that this was also because the records, so carefully kept at Auschwitz, had been destroyed. It took me time to acknowledge *how* I was impacted by the murder of family members in the Holocaust – the Shoah – since for years I wanted to accept the narrative that these histories could *not* shape my felt experience because I had not lived through these times myself and, at the most, they were 'postmemories'. But in time I was to learn otherwise, as I realized I was carrying fears, anxieties – even memories that were not my own alone – but had been *embodied* through the silences and tensions that shaped my life in the family as I was growing up.

Holocaust Hauntings

Keeping these wider concerns in mind, I want to trace hauntings of the Holocaust – the Shoah taking an indirect path that also learns from the artistic practice of Anselm Kiefer. A topological methodology that also allows us to trace disconnections is helpful because within a liberal moral culture that was determined in large part to turn its back on the recent events of the Shoah it was easy to feel as a child of refugees that *if* you do not think about something and put it into words, then it is *not* real and at some level you can remain disconnected from embodied histories and fears you learn to carry silently. Hauntings can be ignored too, if not your dreams and everyday fears and anxieties as you learn to identify with the school histories of Britain that you learn as your own

It is not a matter, as postmemory theory suggests, that you did not live through these experiences yourself so that you cannot remember as a matter of logic, but that you *also* know how hard it is for the victims themselves to understand what they lived through. Freud understands the significance of transgenerational and ancestral legacies, and how they seep through, even if parents have sought to exclude and banish them. He also knew that it made a difference *if* there was a conversation that happened across generations and that there was a language in which adults were willing to speak to their children. But he also recognized the power of silence and the difficulties of different generations finding the words in which they could voice their embodied memories.

There could also be the pressure of normalization and so to become *like everyone else*, as I explored in *Shadows of the Shoah: Jewish Identity and Belonging*, that can enforce its own forms of splitting as disavowal and unknowing. You can feel the hollowness of your own words, as if you are not really daring to occupy them when you, for example, share your family history, somehow assuming that there is nothing unusual about saying that 'nobody in my father's large family in Warsaw survived – they were all murdered'.

You just assume that other children have had similar histories and there is nothing strange – but then watching the shock on their faces, you quickly withdraw into yourself, feeling uneasy and disturbed at what has just happened. But on another level, it can also make it hard for you to *trust* the world and feel a sense of ontological security – to feel that others *can* really *be there for you*. On some level, you can be caught in an unspeakable isolation and loneliness as you learn to be silent about what you carry as family history, while at the same time able to be friendly and accommodating to others.

It is not a matter of sharing a personal narrative that others might learn from, but of developing a form of narrative analysis that allows you to *think through the personal*, even if this is not immediately evident in the literary and artistic work I will also be thinking through. I also want to show how a certain topography of memory and mourning that allows you to visit different spaces and draw upon different affective memories and sense experiences can also help you to *shape* a language that can speak to people on different levels. This is to go beyond the cognitive terms of much work in cultural memory and suggest different ways of thinking relationships between bodies, memories and emotions. This is also to trace topographies between different forms of artistic expression as they are placed in relation to each other.

In this way, I bring different artistic productions into relation and so trace a topography between them that draws upon the *very different ways* they have had to draw upon their own personal histories and experiences in order to come to terms with these *spaces of terror*. These are spaces that they have not lived through themselves, but have in some way been implicated in and have somehow embodied as *traumatic memories*. At some level, for example, some children of Nazis both seek to engage their father's histories and experiences while at other times attempting to identify with the victims of Nazi violence and destruction. This speaks beyond an easy categorical distinction between perpetrators, bystanders and survivors that can become too rigid and help to avoid difficult and unsettling questions.

As people find the courage to voice their embodied memories and shape a language, however haltering, that seems helpful, so we open up possibilities of dialogue between younger generations that are positioned as 'German' and 'Jewish' who are dealing as Second and now Third Generations with these complex emotional legacies of shame, guilt, anger and rage. As people engage with the emotional work in different ways, and also through artistic practices, they can learn something important for themselves as well as for others. We also know that *if* we turn our backs on these histories, insisting that they belong to a history long past that is not allowed to echo in the present, there will be a price to pay.

Sometimes this shows itself as we become more rigid in our bodies and attitudes, as we refuse to consider concerns that we have closed down, often shutting off access to ourselves in some way. As we remain haunted in some unspeakable ways, there will also be *gaps* in the ways we think and feel as we find certain emotional paths blocked to us. In our rigidity and silence, we will often unknowingly pass on to the next generations traumatic memories we have not been able to engage with ourselves.

Forgetting Horrors

I was born in December 1945 and so I was born in the 'shadows of the Shoah', but into a Jewish world that could only feel safe *if* it learnt how to forget a traumatic history that was still surfacing. As children, we were to see the images of what was called the 'liberation of Belsen' – but we were to see and at the same time not see, not witness, what 'Hitler had done to the Jews' – this was the lesson, whatever it meant, that we were to absorb into our bodies as we saw these terrible images of dead bodies that were being moved by enormous tractors into large pits. But what were we seeing – and as children part of us knew that we could have been seeing our relatives – uncles, aunts, cousins. We did not know, but we feared that this could be the case. We were to watch in silence.

The adults who were also watching while the sombre words of Richard Dimbleby were being spoken also sat in tense silence. This is not what our parents wanted their children to see. They were shocked at the images and they wanted to pretend that *nothing was happening* – that we were *not seeing* what we were seeing. This was everything that adults wanted to protect us from, but here they were defeated by the television schedules.

They had not known what was going to be shown and if they had known, they would have done their best to turn the TV off – but now it was too late and as children we had been *captured by these terrible images*. They were never to go away – we were never to be able to escape their hauntings. But the adults pretended that we had *not* seen them at all – it had all been some terrible accident. They took refuge in the notion that as children we were too young to understand what we had seen – to absorb the images and to be hurt by them – and that we would soon forget what we had seen. These were things the adults as refuges from Nazi-controlled continental Europe needed to believe, but it had no connection with the Second Generation, who were often *marked by what they had seen*. But as with so many big philosophical and ethical questions emerging from the horrors of the Holocaust, we learnt *not* to ask about them and felt that we somehow owed it to our parents to forget – or at least to pretend that we could forget.

Images of Absence

Anselm Kiefer was born in Germany in 1945. As Jonathan Jones writes of the recent major exhibition of his work at the Royal Academy: 'To enter the world as the Third Reich fell was to be a baby surrounded by human ash'. If this seems a tasteless way of putting it, he assures us that Kiefer is not tasteful and that: 'Ever since he posed for a photograph in 1969 giving the sea a Nazi salute, he has resurrected the terrors of the 20th century in a shocking, pungent and explicit way that defies both the politeness of forgetting and the evasiveness of appropriate speech. He would rather you were angry than amnesiac. He will not let the ashes of history's victims blow away, but thrusts them in our face as a handful of truth'.[4]

I could *not* have written these words – I am too close to the victims – but I was pleased that Jones could be so direct. He notes that Kiefer's gigantic painting *Ash Flower*:

> has ash scattered over its surface to create a vast, obscuring veil. Through this splattering of death dust, the lines create the enormous ghost of a building. The structure is a chilling neoclassical hall, some grandiose relic of Hitler's insane empire. Over the ash on the lower part of the painting, Kiefer has added cracked clay – a layer of brown earth crumbling as it dries. Dangled down the entire height of the painting is a single, dried colossal sunflower.

As Jones recognizes: 'To find straightforward affirmations of life here would signal a complete misunderstanding of Kiefer's art . . . At some level Kiefer . . . wonders if he even has the right to make art'. Kiefer's *Ash Flower* is a painting that seems to span epochs. As Jones recognizes: 'It is ancient'. He notes that: 'Kiefer includes time in his art (as a matter of fact it took from 1983 to 1987 to build up *Ash Flower*, and every minute shows). His tangled archaeological surfaces, layered with paper, woodcuts and charred photographs, are mirrors of time itself'.

The traumatic history of the Holocaust – the Shoah – cannot be placed securely in the past, as a matter of history. Rather, it is a continuous present that each generation has to come to terms with in its own way. It is constantly rising to the surface as the dead demand to be heard for justice to be done to their memory. As Kiefer recognizes, this is an uncomfortable realization and people would prefer to bow their heads in reverential silence on the days that the state has assigned for remembering and then get on with their everyday lives as if due respect has been given to history. But Kiefer also insists that if this is a terrible history that Germany has to carry, it is *also* part of a wider European history, as Simone Weil also insisted, in which Hitler was carrying out ideals of power and greatness that are already there in the way we still teach our children to admire Caesar and the Roman Empire as well as the British Empire that sought to emulate it (as Hitler also wanted to do).

This was why Hitler felt that the British would understand and not go to war against Germany – a Britain that is still to come to terms with its own legacies of colonial violence and mass killings. This was why Kiefer could appropriately give his Nazi salute at the Colosseum in Rome. It is also telling that he felt a need to dress in his father's Nazi uniform to do the salute; as he said on the occasion of the Venice Biennale in 1980, he had to 're-enact what they did just a little bit in order to understand the madness'. He needed to experience these feelings through his own body – to embody them in order to make what happened more real to him. He used his own body to violate the ban on artistic representations of Nazism, through the genre of the self-portrait.

As Daniel Arasse recalls, it was Joseph Beuys, a teacher and supporter of Kiefer when he was being severely criticized, who was the first in the visual arts with his Auschwitz memorial window in 1955 'to attack this "ground zero of visual amnesia", to break the silence and to affirm the need for artists to confront German society's collective past in their work'.[5] Kiefer took an active part in the efforts of his generation of the 1960s to overcome the wholesale obliteration of the past, but as Arasse notes, 'unlike Beuys, whose Auschwitz window was allegorical, Kiefer was violently provocative and broke a collective taboo. *Heroic Symbols* and *To*

Genet, along with the large self-portraits painted from photos, made him the first to tackle the representations of Nazism head on, using his own body'. Kiefer would later acknowledge ambivalence as 'the central theme of all my work'.[6]

Acts of Memory as Acts of Mourning

Daniel Arasse helpfully points out that 'Anselm Kiefer's "acts of remembering" have the associations of an "act of mourning" – as is made perfectly clear by the German subtitle of *Occupations: Besetzungen*'.[7] It also means the assumption of a role in a play – Kiefer appears to rehearse in his studio the performance he is preparing to play in public. But there is also the meaning associated with Freud's *cathexis*, meaning retention or holding fast to the lost one, often found related to an act of mourning and accompanied by a lack of interest in the outside world. Arasse argues that by taking relatively little interest in contemporary debates in the arts in German society and 'by concerning himself exclusively with subject matter and imagery connected with German's past (recent or remote), and by "holding fast" to Nazi imagery even to the point of having his own body re-enact its abject rallying gesture, Kiefer was through the act of remembering performing an act of mourning'.[8]

Lisa Saltzman argues that the apparently endless nature of the mourning seems to relate it to melancholia – the 'mourning which never ends'. She believed in 1999 that Kiefer's work was 'fundamentally melancholic in its thematics, mood, and allegorical operations', and when she considered the question of whether painting is capable of accomplishing an act of mourning or is itself 'melancholic', a petrified object, an allegorical fragment, a ruin, she suggested that his artistic programme is 'necessarily melancholic'.[9]

But Saltzman suggests that this melancholia should not be reduced to the classical definition that is Freudian in origin. She believes it extends beyond Freud and touches the melancholia of a Renaissance humanism often associated with Durer's engravings. I think it marks something particularly modern in the ways that the Holocaust is tied up with European modernities and the industrialization of death. It breaks with a dream of modernity – the possibility that the dead will not return to haunt us, but can somehow be erased completely, as if they had never really existed at all. It also breaks with the individualization of loss and the processes of mourning that we find in Freud.

But the picture that stopped me and brought me to tears – I just wanted to sit in front of it forever – was a large picture, *Black Flakes*

(2006), which incorporates a lead book along with materials such as branches and plaster within a landscape of earth covered by snow. There is a sense of terrible coldness and you *fear* what has taken place in this place and whether it has somehow been held, witnessed or recorded in the book. I had already been struck by a programme note that had said something about the importance of books for Kiefer and it somehow reflected a remark made by the architect David Chipperfield that there 'is a quality that Kiefer's works seems to share and aspire to, a deep emotional record, a search not for truth but for memory'. Is this book showing us that whatever terrors happened in this place will not be forgotten, but will somehow be recorded in the book – a book made of lead and therefore of a material that lasts forever?

Books of Memory and Mourning

What inspires Kiefer to make his books out of lead and thus place a book made of lead in the middle of the field covered with snow and an abiding sense of loss – as if beneath the earth, or close by, there lie the remains of dead bodies? As Kathleen Soriano says in her programme notes: 'Kiefer regards lead as an important material, one that affects him more than all the other metals . . . He believes that lead is the only material heavy enough to carry the weight of human history, and that it's properties most closely resemble ours. "It is in flux. It's changeable and has potential to achieve a higher state of gold."'[10]

Kiefer's interest in alchemy resonates with his interest in Kabbalah – the Jewish mystical tradition. Soriano suggests that this fascination 'is perhaps a metaphor for the way his art attempts to transform and redeem the past. The snowy, barren landscapes that we see here feature often in Kiefer's painting. In Celan's poems, snow and ice often refer to the landscape of the Holocaust and symbolise the oblivion and silence that descended over Europe at that time'.

But we need to be careful about *how we think* about the nature of this 'oblivion and silence', for there were also screams that were endless, but were not heard. There were concentration camps across Europe where people were being held, worked to death and murdered on an industrial scale, as is often said. This was a world that Kiefer was born into, but his history lessons at school only touched lightly on the Third Reich. He was drawn to address this collective absence of memory and, as Soriano also notes: 'Books have been central to Kiefer's practice since 1968. He considers them works in their own right – but also as intimate visual diaries in which he seeks to "re-create a memory"'. She also reminds us that: 'For many years, Kiefer has moved between the worlds of poetry and painting. He has spoken of poems as being "like buoys in the sea. I swim to them, from one to the next: without them I am lost".

These terrible histories leave us in a different relationship to them – for example, as Jews or as Germans, we are positioned differently. But there are moments when these histories cease to be framed as history lessons at school and somehow become 'our' histories – however we understand this – that we have to *come to terms with as individuals and as collectivities*. At the same time as we have a relationship to histories, we also have a relationship with nature and so we exist between heaven and earth.

Re-Membering Treblinka

It has taken me far too long to remember Treblinka – and even when I remember it, I often slip away, finding it hard to *keep* my attention on it. So often the important things remain unspeakable and we realize – but can seem to do so little about it – that while we are talking what is *not* being talked about is what really matters, but somehow we cannot find the words. We move on and feel an edge of frustration as we wonder what that was about. As a teenager, people would ask me about my father's family and I might say 'none of them survived in Warsaw'. Often it was difficult for me to engage their shocked responses because I had also learnt to think that, born in London, I was *like everyone else*. I thought that other friends must carry similar histories, but they did not. I knew that some of my uncles, aunts and cousins had died in Treblinka but, as I have said, it was only decades later while visiting the museum at the Holocaust memorial in Berlin that I discovered that so little was known about Treblinka, as opposed to Auschwitz and some other camps, because all the records had been destroyed. There were no lists of names that had been carefully preserved; there was just oblivion.

Samuel Moyn in his preface to *The Last Jew of Treblinka* points out that 'Chil Rajchman's memoir of that place lay in Yiddish manuscript for decades, and the very name "Treblinka" became widely known only decades after the war's end . . . Nazis had long since tried to wipe [it] from the map'. He also notes a different typography: 'Unlike in the West, the victims in the east were dealt immediate extinction on arrival, and died as Jews targeted as Jews by the regime. Next to no one survived'. He also knows that: 'Only those few who, like Rajchman, were selected to operate the machinery of extinction in the *Sonderkommando* of the killing centre, and not put to death themselves along the way or at the end, could tell what happened'.[11]

Possibilities for survival are also gendered, since, as Moyn records: 'Arrival there meant the immediate loss of his sister, along with all other women and children: the only work for which selection is possibly at a death camp is for the handful of men needed to run the camp itself... the logistics of destruction call for only a few dozen SS, some more Ukranian assistants, and the Jews themselves'. He notes that: 'Rajchman tells of the internal division of labour, through which the steps in the process of extermination are carefully apportioned, and whose shifting roles allow him to survive'.[12]

As Moyn writes:

> If the 'work' evolves as Polish Jewry meets its end, it is because the Nazis sought a way to eliminate the evidence of their deeds. They order thousands of corpses dug for burning, after a policy change alters the methods of disposal from burial to cremation. In the early days Jews are told to layer sand over the tombs carefully, but – as if in a sickening act of posthumous resistance – the blood of the Jews is 'unable to rest' and 'thrusts itself upwards to the surface'... Women, Floss (the cremation specialist); placed at the base, they are torches that will consume the rest. But there are still fragments of bones that the Nazis make the Jews painstakingly collect...[13]

Rajchman recalls:

> I am given the same work as the day before, sorting clothes. While sorting I find the dress that my sister was wearing. I stop, grasp the dress, hold it for a moment, and examine it from every angle. I show it to my neighbour. He forgets himself for a moment and pities me. Then immediately he shouts – You are forgetting yourself. Naturally, who can help himself? Our fate is so wretched. But remember, you can get the whip for that.
>
> I tear off a piece of the dress and I hide it in my pocket. (I had that piece of the dress with me for ten months, the whole time I was in Treblinka.)[14]

He writes earlier: 'I lie there and remind myself that I wronged my poor sister. A few minutes before her death I dissuaded her from eating a piece of bread and she was driven hungry to her death. Did she forgive me? The murderers robbed us all of our understanding'.[15]

> I look at my friend Leybl and he at me, and our tears pour like rain. Each of us asks the other why he is crying. I cannot answer. I have lost the power of speech. We try to comfort and calm one another as much as possible. Leybl, I say to him, yesterday at this time my young sister was still alive. He answers – And my whole family, my brothers and twelve thousand poor Jews from my town.

And yet we are still alive and witness this great misfortune and are so hardened that we can eat and endure the heartbreak. How can one be so strong, have such unnatural strength to endure?[16]

Before me sits a young woman. I cut her hair and she grabs my hand and begs me to remember that I too am a Jew. She knows that she is lost. But remember, she says, you see what is being done to us. That's why my wish to you is that you will survive and take revenge for our innocent blood, which will never rest . . .[17]

Telling Terrible Truths

As Samuel Moyn reports:

Even for Vasily Grossman, in 1944, the Jewish identity of Treblinka's victims is clearly registered, but not emphasized. And by a year later, when in collaboration with Ilya Ehrenberg he finished a *Black Book* detailing Nazi crimes against Jews, and sought to reincorporate his Treblinka essay, the Soviets could not accept the realities of predominantly Jewish victimhood. Though Grossman's essay had circulated on its own (and had been translated into French), the plates of the *Black Book* were destroyed. Whether in the west, where Belsen and Buchenwald were so prominent, or the east, where it was 'humanity' not Jewry who above all suffered, not one else could allow themselves to see what Rajchman and his fellow survivors of the Treblinka revolt did. What the Nazis did to Jews as Jews at these killing centres – exterminate them in millions on arrival – did not easily serve existing agendas at the time.[18]

Things were slow to change, at least in the West, in the 1980s, when it became possible to speak of the Holocaust as the Shoah – but if there was a public discourse that also allowed a Second Generation to find words to voice their own experience growing up in families that has been scarred by these traumatic histories, it was not an easy task. There are difficulties in somehow connecting to these fearful events and finding words that go beyond the individualized notions of mourning and melancholia.

Having grown up to *be normal* within the culture of assimilation that was dominant in Britain in the 1950s and 1960s – when belonging meant *becoming like everyone else* – it can be difficult to voice differences without still fearing rejection. It can be difficult to insist that these memories of the Shoah do *not* belong to a past that is history, but very much echo in the present as formative experiences that not only shape the individual lives of Jews but also have come to speak more widely about experiences of racial violence and the ease with which human beings can abuse and mistreat each other through identifying them as 'other'.

Traditions of European Enlightenment have rendered it too easy to treat others as if they are *less than human*. This has been integral to the decentring of Europe that has been part of a postcolonial critique. We have shaped new forms of social and cultural theory as we learnt to speak from the margins in ways that can insist on the integrity and dignity of difference, as people are encouraged to engage critically with their own cultural and historical traditions and memories. As we shape new typographies of mourning, so we learn with Benjamin to honour *each* death and name *each* victim, not as part of a history that has been ordered through historical notions of progress. With Benjamin, we need to question ideas of progress as we learn to name sources of oppression and inhumanity that have long been implicitly legitimated in theories of historical and cultural relativism.

Rather than visioning with Marx and traditions of liberal humanism that *the human* is to be grasped through a transcendence of differences that are thereby shamed, we can learn with Jewish traditions – an insight also shared by many other traditions – that it is only though recognition of the personal and the emotional and ways they can be undermined and harmed that we can create new democratic visions of *the human*. This also involves shaping formative social and cultural theories willing to trace new typographies of memory and mourning. As Vasily Grossman writes: 'It is the writer's duty to tell the truth, and it is the reader's civic duty to learn this truth. To turn away, to close one's eyes and walk past is to insult the memory of those who have perished'.[19]

The Scrolls of Auschwitz

As Eva Hoffman notes in the Preface she wrote to *Representing Auschwitz: At the Margins of Testimony*, 'we can see that catastrophes of these dimensions and complexity demand, and generate, not one but many kinds of investigation and genres of testimony'.[20] Referring to the fragments of text that have become known as 'The Scrolls of Auschwitz' produced by the Sonderkommando (SK), who worked in the gas chambers, she observes these:

> seem to represent, especially in their half-destroyed form, not so much acts of written recollection, as enactments of direct, almost physical witnessing; emanations from the underworld, driven by a compelling need to reach the world above, to record and tell. Primo Levi has famously said that the true witnesses of the annihilation did not speak. The Scrolls of Auschwitz are as close as we can come to hearing voices from the site of death.[21]

Hoffman faces the ethical difficulties in asking: 'What kind of response is called for – or possible – to the evidence inscribed or implicit, in the Auschwitz Scrolls? It is hard, when confronted with these shards of darkness, to avoid moral ambivalence or confusion ... those ambiguities are part of the difficult knowledge brought to us by the Shoah's extremity'. As she writes: 'But perhaps the most powerful aspect of the Scrolls' significance is the very fact of their existence. In the closest proximity to the horrifying processes of annihilation, and facing their own almost certain death, the scribes of Auschwitz were determined that what happened there should not be deleted from human memory or knowledge'.[22]

For Hoffman, the documents testify to 'the need to register the evidence of suffering and terrible injustice – to give expression to one's own existence, so that it is not entirely lost – is a fundamental and profound part of being human. In turn, the desire to respond to those voices – to preserve that evidence and to restore justice even in memory – is what makes history a reparative as well as an analytical exercise'.[23]

My father was the only member of his large Warsaw family to be outside the country, in the relative safety of London where he had moved from Leipzig recognizing the threats to Jewish existence when Hitler came to power. I still have a black notebook where he did his English comprehension lessons in preparation for his move to London. But he was not to anticipate the mass deaths of his family who had moved from Suwałki in northeast Poland to Warsaw in the late 1920s or early 1930s – the details are unclear. It was not possible for him to live with this 'difficult knowledge' and he died in 1950, in New York, leaving four sons under the age of seven for my mother and grandmother to bring up.

I have looked endlessly for references to the Jeleniewski family, so it was striking to see a reference to Suwałki as the place where one of the scribes, Zalman Gradowski, was born. He came from a fairly prominent family, which is mentioned in the town's *yizker-bukh*, and he was in Auschwitz to become one of the leaders of the uprising of 7 October 1944. As a young man in Suwałki, he had received some religious education at the Łomża yeshiva and he became active in both religion and politics as he worked in father's tailoring business. My father was in the fur business, but also seemed identified with Betar, the Zionist youth movement of Vladimir Jabotinsky's revisionist party. He moved with his family to Warsaw.

This explains why some in my father's family were murdered in Treblinka rather than Auschwitz. But it seems they both came from religiously orthodox families carrying the Lithuanian traditions. As reported in *Matters of Testimony*: 'According to Yaakov Freimark, Gradowski worked in Crematorium 4 and each day would put on tallis and tefilin and say kaddish for the dead, crying out that he was a sinful man'.²⁴ After the uprising he helped to lead, he was captured and tortured to death.

As Nicholas Chare and Dominic Williams put it: 'members of the Sonderkommando had a modicum of agency, some sense of themselves, even an ability to interpret the environment in which they were living and dying. This inevitably calls into question both the prevalent images of the SK and more general assertions that the Shoah was an "event without a witness"'.²⁵ They argue that 'the literary forms had to be what he could find on the inside: drawn from the history that he brought with him, reliant upon whatever bodily condition that he could maintain . . . It testifies to the kind of man who was in Birkenau, and what being there did to him; and also the conditions in which he found it possible to write, and to which he had to adapt how he wrote'.²⁶

In relation to Gradowski's style of writing, they suggest: 'In its repetitions it comes across as a kind of ritual, a spell . . . to summon [a reader] up before himself, so that he has a witness to whom he can speak. And even the converse: expecting to be dead by the time his text is found, Gradowski has to summon himself up before the reader, as a kind of ghost. Each figure, reader and writer, is a ghost to the other, never coinciding'.²⁷ Gradowski presents himself 'as an individual who has undergone specific experiences, as well as the narrator tasked with the responsibility of speaking for all the dead'. As he writes about Auschwitz: 'And there I was appointed by these demons watchman at the gates of hell, through whose doors there passed and still pass millions of Jews from all over Europe . . . They <entrusted> me with their last life-secrets . . . They told me about everything, how they were torn from their homes and underwent a chain of agonising suffering until they reached their final destination as victim of the devil'.²⁸

Echoes, Traces and Resonances

When Gradowski begins to tell the story of the transport from Auschwitz, he does more than explain what happened to him and his family. As Chare and Williams note: 'He uses his journey as a literary device, permitting him to survey the condition of Jews in Poland' – including my father's family in some way, starting as it does from Suwałki. On the journey, the train comes close to Treblinka, a site whose function the passengers know all too well. As he writes: 'We are approaching a station well known to the Jews, Treblinka, which, according to various reports we have received, has swallowed up and destroyed the majority of Jews in Poland, as well as from abroad'. As they reach the station at Warsaw, the grim reality is evident: 'You see no trace now of a Jew at Warsaw, a station once filled with Jews'.[29]

There is a second document, written in the spring of 1944, which contains a part that is framed as a lengthy address to the moon. As Chare and Williams explain:

> if the moon is any kind of escape, the text acknowledges its impossibility by placing this view of her in the past . . . He denounces her for shifting on indifferently while his people are being slaughtered, and even for failing to give them darkness in which to hide. He asks why she is still shedding her light on the perpetrators, and finally says that the world is not worthy of her light, but she should serve as a memorial candle for his people: 'May your eternal ray, may your mournful light always shine at the grave of my people. May this be their yahrzeit-candle, which you can still alone provide for them'.[30]

Gradowski writes of himself as imagining some of the women as dead, even as they are alive: 'I stand now by a group of women, ten to fifteen in number, and a wheelbarrow will contain all their bodies, all their lives in a wheelbarrow of ashes'.[31] He is clearly determined to describe every part of the process, from the opening of the doors of the gas chambers to the burning of the bodies in the ovens:

> Our eyes are riveted, hypnotised [*tsugeshmidt, farhipnotizirt*] by the sea of naked dead bodies, which has now appeared before us. We have now caught sight of a world of nakedness, They lie fallen, intertwined, twisted together like a tangled skein, as if the devil before their deaths had played a special devilish game with them, and laid them out in such poses . . . You see only parts of human bodies on the surface of this naked world.
> In this great sea of nakedness heads float about . . . These heads – dark, fair, brown – are the only individual parts that break out of the universal nakedness.[32]

The SK cannot stand there for long before they need to begin to process of disposing of the bodies:

> We must deaden out feeling hearts, dull every feeling of grief in ourselves. We must forswear [*farshrayen*] the horrific sufferings in us, which like a storm sweeps through every part of our bodies. We must turn into robots [*oytomatn*], which see nothing, feel nothing and understand nothing.[33]

Chare and Williams acknowledge: 'Here we see what that knowledge has done to him. But it is clear that this affectless state is what is writing is fighting against. He wants to see and feel, just as he wants his readers to do as well. Becoming robots like this simply makes the process of getting rid of the bodies more efficient'. They also recognize that: 'The lengthy, lavish even, description of the destruction of a body forms material for the kind of envisioning that Gradowski desires of his readers . . . he is not simply telling us what he has seen; he is . . . *showing* it to us'.[34] Gradowski writes:

> The first to catch fire is the hair. The skin swells us into blisters and splits in a few seconds. Now the arms and legs begin to move – this is the blood vessels tightening and this moves the limbs. The body in its entirety is now blazing strongly; the skin has split, the fat flows and you hear the sizzling of the fire burning. You know long see a corpse – only a chamber of hellish fire, in the middle of which lies . . . something. The stomach splits. The guts and entrails quickly spill out of it, and in minutes there is no trace of them left. The last to burn is the head; from its two eyes two little blue flames now flicker – these are the eyes burning with the brain inside, while from the mouth the tongue also still burns now. Twenty minutes for the entire procedure, And a body, a world, has been turned to ashes.[35]

I still recall the shock I first felt upon reading this description. It was part of a process that had become routine, but could never really be. It was a human world that had been turned to ashes, but it was also a vision of European modernity that had gone up in flames, even though many philosophers and social theorists wanted to carry on after the war as if nothing had really happened and they could return to their traditional forms of reason and rationalism. As Chare and Williams read it, possibly in too literary and distancing a form: 'In the striking imagery of the burning bodies, a sight that transfixes the viewer, it is the tongue, a means of speech, which burns to ashes last of all. In this context, the writings he composed and concealed can be read as resisting oblivion like the enduring tongue. A trace of Gradowski's world will survive in and through his literary endeavours'. Also, the readers are implored to take action against these horrors and thus to see to it 'that its flames devour those who kindled it'.[36]

Dan Stone in his essay 'The Harmony of Barbarism: Locating the Scrolls of Auschwitz in Holocaust Historiography' reminds us that Gradowski also wrote more generally about 'the dialectic of civilisation and barbarism': 'The more highly developed a culture, the more cruel its murderers, the more civilised a society, the greater its barbarians'. He also emphasized the willing submission of individuals to Nazi ideology, noting that: 'This violent pirate and his gang have begun their torture by crushing their egos, sacrificing their souls to their Aryan God'.[37]

Stone also reminds us helpfully that 'at the same time that Gradowski was writing those words in Birkenau, Horkheimer and Adorno were writing their not dissimilar *Dialectic of Enlightenment* in exile in California'. He also notes that 'Gradowski's text provides a rare insight into the way in which the Sonderkommando men were inducted into their role and how they were forced to come to terms with the murder of their families and then with what the Nazi authorities were expecting them to do for the short time they were supposed to remain alive'.[38]

Difficult Legacies

There is a hope that if the Second Generation do some of the emotional work that their parents unwittingly passed on to them while at the same time insisting that these terrible histories had nothing to do with them, the Third Generation would somehow be spared. Different generations will still have to come to terms with these histories in their *own* way, even if the task is made easier if some of the emotional memory work has already been done. If there is a conversation that has been opened up between generations, a younger generation will he hopefully helped in the ways in which they carry these unspeakable pasts and family legacies of violence and humiliation that leave their own scars.

But it is also not surprising if the Second Generation insist, in ways that still echo their parents, that the work they have done and the conversations they have had somehow mean that their children have little work of their own to do. Different generations hear in their own way and have issues of their own in establishing relationships with these topographies of destruction that have often been turned into tourist attractions. Different generations grow up in different technological worlds, and with social media and the Internet they can feel surrounded by images of horror that disturb their nights. They need to deal with ways these images have become normalized and even banal so that they face their own issues in making these historical experiences, as family histories, real to them. They might also have to trace their own relationships of memory and mourning as they discover *how they are related emotionally* to those who have been murdered.

They will often have their own questions and they might wonder why there are still silences in their own families when issues around the Holocaust – the Shoah – have been raised as part of the school curriculum. In Jewish survivor and refugee families, there is often a topography of memory that means grandparents feel easier telling their stories to their grandchildren while *still* wanting to protect their children. In perpetrator families in Germany, it has often been the state that has taken responsibility for collective memory and there has often been an enduring silence from the perpetrator generation within families. Sometimes it is their grandchildren who insist that their grandparents could not have been Nazis and that in any case they carried their own sufferings from the war, the Allied bombing and the population displacements.

But it can also be difficult for those who grew up in the aftermath of the Second World War knowing that their parents had identified with the Nazis and even possibly carrying the name of 'Adolph' as a hidden identification their parents had assigned to them and that they might carry as a hidden second name. They lived through their own topographies of memory as parents refused to answer their questions and they felt that their words somehow fell into the gap between them as parents insisted that the past was *not* a respectable topic of conversation. They could feel that no one was there that they could talk to and feel recognized, but rather that their questions were to be dismissed. Often, as they grew up, they felt that they needed to leave Germany and Austria to be able to engage with questions that they felt they could not shape in the country that insisted on its own amnesia in the postwar period.

They had to leave the spaces they had grown up in and find a different topography that allowed their questions to be framed. Or in a later generation, Kiefer had to raise difficult questions as he traced his own topography of memory and mourning as he moved across Europe. He had to make connections between histories too easily separated as if the Nazis had not been welcomed into different countries and their antisemitic project perpetrated in a topography that countries across Europe are still coming to terms with. It has been too easy for Eastern European and Baltic states to talk about European values of the Enlightenment that were so radically challenged in the relationship between the European modernities and the Holocaust – the Shoah.

Though Europe remembers and memorializes the Holocaust at particular events like the liberation of Auschwitz, there are still ways it tends to treat it as a historical aberration that was at odds with European values rather than acknowledging ways that it also continued a European colonizing tradition of empire, power and greatness that was prepared to engage in mass murder, even genocidal murder, to sustain its position. The concentration camps serve as a constant reminder of genocidal murder, but also as a constant question of values we so often take for granted, knowing that these events happened at the heart of Europe.

Victor Jeleniewski Seidler is Emeritus Professor of Social Theory in Sociology at Goldsmiths, University of London. He also teaches Jewish philosophy and Jewish thought at the Leo Baeck College, London. His research on social theory, philosophy and ethics has been combined with a focus upon gender, particularly critical work around men and masculinities, and his recent publications include: *Transforming Masculinities: Men, Cultures, Bodies, Power, Sex and Love* (2006); *Urban Fears and Global Terrors: Citizenship, Multicultures and Belongings after 7/7* (2007); *Jewish Philosophy and Western Culture* (2007); *Remembering Diana: Cultural Memory and the Reinvention of Authority* (2013); and *Remembering 9/11: Terror, Trauma and Social Theory* (2013). His most recent book is *Making Sense of Brexit: Democracy, Europe and Uncertain Futures* (2018).

Notes

1. My thinking for this chapter began to take form in a keynote lecture presented to the conference 'Tracing Topographies: Revisiting the Concentration Camps Seventy Years after the Liberation of Auschwitz', held at the Jewish Museum in London, 6–8 January 2015, which was organized by Vered Weiss and Joanne Pettitt. It was a chance to think across the boundaries of the personal and the academic, and hopefully *show* limits to a language of 'postmemory' through drawing upon a variety of literary and artistic hauntings. It was at this event that Dominic Williams spoke about Zalman Gradowski and 'The Scrolls of Auschwitz', and I realized that Gradowski had come from Suwałki, where my father had also lived as a young man, sharing a similar orthodox Jewish life and politics. It helped to open up new lines of memory and mourning.
2. Primo Levi, *The Drowned and the Saved* (London: Abacus, 1989), 6.
3. Ibid.
4. *The Guardian*, 22 September 2014.
5. Daniel Arasse, *Anselm Kiefer* (London: Thames & Hudson, 2001) 30.
6. Ibid., 35.
7. Ibid., 36.
8. Ibid., 38.
9. Ibid., 41.
10. *Anselm Kiefer*, exhibition catalogue, Royal Academy, 2014.
11. Samuel Moyn, 'Preface', in Chil Rajchman, *The Last Jew of Treblinka: A Memoir* (New York: Pegasus, 2012), xi–xii.
12. Ibid., xv.
13. Ibid., xvi.
14. Chil Rajchman, *The Last Jew of Treblinka: A Memoir* (New York: Pegasus, 2012), 31–32.
15. Ibid., 27
16. Ibid., 26
17. Ibid., 40
18. Moyn, 'Preface', xviii.
19. Epigraph to Chil Rajchman, *The Last Jew of Treblinka* (New York: Pegasus, 2012), vii.
20. Eva Hoffman, 'Preface', in Nicholas Chare and Dominic Williams (eds), *Representing Auschwitz: At the Margins of Testimony* (Basingstoke: Palgrave Macmillan, 2013), viii.

21. Ibid.
22. Hoffman, 'Preface', ix.
23. Ibid., x.
24. Nicholas Chare and Dominic Williams, *Matters of Testimony: Interpreting the Scrolls of Auschwitz* (Oxford: Berghahn Books, 2016), 63.
25. Ibid., 61.
26. Ibid.
27. Ibid., 66.
28. Ibid. The angled brackets indicate an editorial reconstruction of a word rendered illegible by damage to the manuscript.
29. Ibid., 69.
30. Ibid., 71.
31. Ibid., 80.
32. Ibid., 81–82.
33. Ibid., 82.
34. Ibid., 82–83.
35. Ibid., 83.
36. Ibid., 84.
37. Dan Stone, 'The Harmony of Barbarism', in Chare and Williams (eds), *Representing Auschwitz*.
38. Stone, 'Harmony of Barbarism', 23–24.

Bibliography

Adorno, Theodor, and Horkheimer Max. *Dialectic of Enlightenment*. London, Allen Lane 1973.
Agamben Giorgio. *Home Sacer: Sovereign Power and Bare Life*, trans. Daniel Heller Roazen. Stanford: Stanford University Press, 1998.
———. *Remnants of Auschwitz: The Witness and the Archive*, trans. Daniel Heller Roazen. New York: Zone Books, 2008.
Arendt, Hannah. *The Origins of Totalitarianism*. New York: Meridian Books, 1958.
Bartov, Omer. *Mirrors of Destruction: War, Genocide and Modern Identity*. Oxford: Oxford University Press, 2000.
Bataille, Georges. *Literature and Evil*, trans. Alistair Hamilton. London: Marion Boyars, 1985.
Bauman, Zygmunt. *Modernity and Ambivalence*. Cambridge, Polity Press, 1991.
———. *Postmodernity and its Discontents*. Cambridge, Polity Press, 1997.
———. *Modernity and the Holocaust*. Cambridge, Polity Press, 2000.
Blum, Lawrence, and Victor J.J. Seidler. *A Truer Liberty: Simone Weil and Marxism*. New York: Routledge, 1991.
Arasse, Daniel. *Anselm Kiefer*. London: Thames & Hudson, 2001.
Chare, Nicholas, and Dominic Williams (eds). *Representing Auschwitz: At the Margins of Testimony*. Basingstoke: Palgrave Macmillan, 2013.
———. *Matters of Testimony: Interpreting the Scrolls of Auschwitz*. Oxford: Berghahn Books, 2016.
Felman, Shoshana, and Dori Laub. *Testimony: Crises of Witnessing in Literature, Psychonanalysis and History*. New York: Routledge, 1992.

Hartman Geoffrey (ed.). *Holocaust Remembrance*. Oxford: Blackwell 1994.
Hirsch, Marianne. *Family Frames: Photography, Narrative and Postmemory*. Cambridge, MA: Harvard University Press, 1997.
Hoffman, Eva. *After Such Knowledge: Memory, History and the Legacy of the Holocaust*. New York: Public Affairs 2003.
———. *Lost in Translation: Life in a New Language*. London: Vintage 2008.
LaCapra, Dominick. *History and Memory after Auschwitz*. Ithaca: Cornell University Press, 1998.
———. *Writing History, Writing Trauma*. Baltimore, MD: Johns Hopkins University Press, 2001.
Lang, Berel. *Holocaust Representation: Art within the Limits of History and Ethics*. Baltimore, MD: Johns Hopkins University Press, 2000.
Langer, Lawrence. *Holocaust Testimonies: The Ruins of Memory*. New Haven CT: Yale University Press, 1991.
Levi, Primo. *The Drowned and the Saved*, trans. Raymond Rosenthal. London: Abacus, 1989.
Rajchman, Chil. *The Last Jew of Treblinka: A Memoir*, trans. Solon Beinfeld. New York: Pegasus, 2012.
Rothberg, Michael. *Traumatic Realism: The Demands of Holocaust Representation*. Minneapolis: University of Minnesota Press, 2000.
Seidler, Victor Jeleniewski. *Shadows of the Shoah: Jewish Identity and Belonging*. Oxford: Berg, 2000.
———. *Jewish Philosophy and Western Culture* London: I.B. Tauris, 2007.
Young, James. *Writing and Rewriting the Holocaust*. Bloomington: Indiana University Press, 1988.
———. *The Texture of Memory*. New Haven: Yale University Press, 1993.
Weil, Simone. *The Need for Roots*. 2nd edn. London: Routledge, 2001.

Index

A

Abraham, Nicolas 19–20, 257–258, 262 n45
abstraction 19–20, 247, 249, 253, 255–256, 259
Adorno, Theodor 19, 34, 40–42, 43, 249, 252, 363
aesthetics xi, 37, 40, 42, 43, 46–47, 49, 50, 59–60, 220, 257, 308, 321, 326, 334, 342–343
affect 37, 43, 50, 51, 60, 189, 201, 204, 297, 298, 301, 322, 326, 347–348, 350, 362
afterimages 251, 259
Agamben, Giorgio 14–15
agency xii, 4, 10–11, 115, 122, 232, 291, 309, 361
allegory 36, 37, 187, 255
Alleva, Richard 321, 324
Amariglio, Erika Myriam Kounio 7–8
Amen (film) 311
amidah 6, 9, 11
analogy 118, 126n22, 248
anamnesis 257–258
Anders, Günther 12, 308
antiheroism 308, 316, 322, 342
Anzac 231, 239
Arasse, Daniel 253, 353, 354
archaeology x, 19, 252, 257, 353
architecture 107, 185, 189, 302n2
archives 3, 17, 42, 112, 162–163, 217, 225
Arendt, Hannah 12–13, 34–35, 37–38, 53, 54–57, 81, 86n45, 277
Aristotle 43, 250–251
armed struggle 4, 5–6, 7, 8, 196, 291, 296, 297–298, 300, 301, 315, 316, 317
Arnold-de Simine, Silke 194
Arolsen/Bad Arolsen 160, 164, 170, 173

Arouch, Salomo 315–316, 333–334
Arquette, David 287
assimilation 298, 312, 358
Ashkenazi 154n26, 267, 274, 275, 282n43
asyndeton 118
Athenian, The (newspaper) 159
Athens 106, 111, 121, 138, 139, 142, 159, 163, 173, 273, 276
Aubenque, Pierre 250
Auschwitz Album 196
Auschwitz-Birkenau State Museum 18, 22n6, 84n13, 91–92, 93, 95, 98n4, 102, 112, 113, 114, 125n9, 142, 176, 183, 190n5, 193–213, 218, 219, 224, 283n53
Auschwitz-Birkenau (overall camp complex) 18, 234, 236
Auschwitz I (Stammlager) 24n35, 64n33, 92, 161, 198–202, 210n12, 302n2
Auschwitz II (Birkenau)
  evacuation of 165
  liberation of 112
  mass killings at 1, 4–5, 8, 23n17, 24n35, 36, 39, 45, 48, 53–54, 62n9, 91, 94, 107, 114, 118, 123, 136n11, 161, 191n19, 194, 196–19, 198, 220, 250, 287, 294, 302n2, 312, 314, 326, 336, 341
  other prisoners in 7, 98n7, 126n22, 127n24, 159, 162, 223, 273, 275
  photos taken in and smuggled out of 11, 182, 196–197, 238, 249, 256–258
  Scrolls of Auschwitz discovered at 9, 16, 102, 108, 111–112, 125n9, 273–274
  as a site visited after liberation 196–198, 204, 223, 228n33, 258, 259, 307, 338, 340

Auschwitz II (Birkenau) *(cont.)*
  SK working at ix, 3, 4–5, 11, 16, 17, 19,
    20, 24n35, 38, 51, 53, 57, 92, 95, 97,
    98n1, 98n8, 100n37, 105, 106, 118,
    125n5, 136n13, 143–144, 196–197,
    201, 218, 219, 221, 222, 242, 243, 244,
    256, 267, 269, 277, 291, 297, 298, 299,
    303, 309, 314, 316, 317, 322, 338, 341,
    361, 363
  as a unit of Auschwitz-Birkenau 41, 114,
    139, 141, 232, 271
Auschwitz III (Monowitz) 41, 171, 232
Ausländer, Rose 34
Australia 232, 233, 236, 239–240, 244
automatons. *See* robots
authenticity 26n60, 97, 207, 271, 294, 297,
    339
Avey, Denis 232–233, 245n5

B
Babi Yar 312
Bacon, Yehuda 85n26, 189, 191n25
Baden-Baden 249, 258, 259
Bailey, Roderick 231, 234
Balzac, Honoré de 253
banality xi, 13, 50, 51, 364
Bartoszewski, Wladyslaw 222
Baruch, Joseph 268, 274, 275, 276, 281n39,
    282n46
Bauer, Yehuda 6
Bauman, Zygmunt 52
Beckett, Samuel 42, 61
Bełżec 41, 53, 304n32
Ben, Joseph 267, 281n39
Bendel, Charles 117
Benjamin, Walter 252, 253, 255, 359
Bennahmias, Daniel 165, 171–173, 268,
    282n47, 282n50
Bergen Belsen 41, 63n18, 165, 232, 351
Berlin 183, 313, 347, 356
Bernstein, Michael André 238
Besson, Rémy 26n60
Betar 360
Bettelheim, Bruno 12–13
Beuys, Joseph 252, 353
Bezwińska, Jadwiga 91, 125n6
Białystok, 5

Birkenau. *See* Auschwitz II
Blatt, Thomas Toivi 297
Blobel, Paul 215
block 145, 196, 334
  Block 4 (Auschwitz) 198–200, 201
  Block 11 (Auschwitz) 184, 202,
    211–212n26
  Block 15 (Auschwitz) 202
  Block 20 (Auschwitz) 202
  Block 27 (Auschwitz) 200–202
  Block 28 (Auschwitz) 202
Boder, David 12
Bomba, Abraham x, 20, 51–52, 303n12,
    336–337
Bourdieu, Pierre 237
Bowman, Steven 17, 20, 26n76
boxing 315, 333–334
Bresson, Robert 46
Brown, Adam 2, 20, 25n53, 71, 83n5,
    304n19
Browning, Christopher 71
Brussels 340
Buchenwald 41, 48, 62n9, 187, 312, 314,
    358
Buchloh, Benjamin 19, 27n80, 255
Buki, Milton 218
burial x, 34, 36–37, 38, 52, 57–59, 66n59,
    128n30, 253, 299, 317, 322, 357
burning pits 2, 19, 34, 59, 238, 269, 270,
    276, 299, 341
Butler, Judith 13–14

C
Caraolas camp 173
Card, Claudia 14, 71, 79
Carden-Coyne, Ana 196
Caruth, Cathy 9, 183, 184
catharsis 288, 314–315, 317, 326
Cayrol, Jean 57, 62n8
Celan, Paul 33–34, 60, 355
Chazan, Shaul (also Chasan, Hazan)
    127n23, 173–174, 179n17, 179n18,
    221, 268, 269, 279n18, 339
Chełmno 1, 9, 10, 41, 53, 294, 303n12,
    336
Chevra Kadischa ix–x, 119–120, 128n30,
    132, 136n6

Cheyette, Bryan 310
childhood 6, 296, 346, 347–348, 349, 351–352
choiceless choice 14, 209, 316, 320, 343
Chomsky, Marvin 291, 312, 332
Chouli, Sarrika 141
Christianstadt 162, 178n5
chronology 2, 281n31
chronotope 41
Churchill, Winston 63n13, 234
Ciechanower, Mordechai 144, 147
cinematography xi, 46, 49–50, 289, 293, 303n2, 314, 320, 333, 334–335, 336, 340
Clavier, François 340
claustrophobia 45, 290, 318
Clendinnen, Inga 79
Cohen, Boaz 21
Cohen, Ilias 106, 107, 108, 121, 138, 139, 141
Cohen, Leon 94, 96, 100n34, 100n36, 122, 125n5, 135, 136n13, 268, 269–270, 274, 275–277, 282n50
colonialism 353
collaboration 2, 15, 51, 56, 65n45, 70, 72, 81, 128n35, 160, 162, 194, 195, 209, 230, 277, 291, 305n34, 317, 332
colour 103–104, 254, 256, 257
complicity 12–13, 15, 35, 50, 56, 297, 311, 312, 317, 318, 320, 321, 325
concentrationary universe. *See* univers concentrationnaire
Counterfeiters, The (film) 316
Cowburn, Benjamin 235
crematorium ix, xii, 1, 2, 8, 11, 16, 24n35, 45, 64n26, 93, 94, 96, 107, 108, 111, 119, 133, 139, 144, 147, 149, 151, 152, 182, 185, 186–187, 188, 189, 191n19, 194, 218, 219, 222, 223, 231, 233, 236, 240, 268, 271, 273, 287, 289, 290, 292–293, 297, 301, 302n2, 309, 310, 311, 313, 318, 324, 334, 339, 340
  Auschwitz I Crematorium 210n12
  Crematorium 1 (II) 8, 24n35, 198–199, 276, 294, 302n2

Crematorium 2 (III) 24n35, 91, 98n1, 112, 135, 148, 185, 269, 270, 274, 276, 281n39, 282n50, 302n2
Crematorium 3 (IV) 24n35, 148, 196, 276, 280n32, 302n2, 334
Crematorium 4 (V) 19, 24n35, 196, 197, 198, 211n17, 276, 302n2, 307, 339, 342, 360
Crémieux-Durand, Julie 127n27
crime 3, 7, 8, 13, 14, 21, 34, 48, 55, 91, 107–108, 162, 171, 197, 202, 204, 215–216, 217, 221, 222, 289
cruelty 34, 35–36, 37, 51, 54, 61, 218, 221, 240, 318
cultural memory x, 4, 38, 39, 40, 41, 43, 63n18, 188, 350
Cywiński, Piotr 193–194, 209, 212n35
Czech, Danuta 91, 125n6, 135, 280nn28–29, 281n39

D

Dachau 41, 171, 234, 235
Damisch, Hubert 253
data 92, 182, 186, 189
Dawidowicz, Lucy 6
De Beauvoir, Simone 300
death factory 4, 36, 41, 54, 79, 118, 294
deceit. *See* duplicity
deferred action 251–252
Defiance (film) 291
dehumanization xi, 6–7, 36, 38, 55, 60, 121, 126n22, 270, 293, 294, 296, 304n19, 313, 324
Dejaco, Walter 191n19
desire 53, 59–60, 118, 121, 123, 186, 187, 249, 251, 254, 320, 360
dialectic 19, 35, 251, 252, 255, 257, 259, 301, 363
dialogue (in film) 288, 290, 298, 313, 319, 321
diaries 5, 20, 25n45, 74, 77, 147, 189, 355
Diary of Anne Frank, The (film) 312
Dickens, Charles 241
didacticism 199, 290
Didi-Huberman, Georges 18–20, 47, 64n33, 197, 227n23, 270
Dimbleby, Richard 351

displaced persons (DP) 112, 160, 161, 165–166, 175, 177, 217
documentary film 20–21, 225, 279n17, 335–338, 339, 341
Donahue, John 243–244
Dorembus, Josef (also Józef Dorębus) 94, 202
Dragon, Abraham 144, 147, 161, 165–170, 268, 279n18
Dragon, Shlomo (also Szlama, Szloma) 144, 147, 161, 165–170, 218, 268, 279n18, 340
Drancy 92, 93, 94, 95, 111, 124n2, 127n27, 132, 134, 164, 165, 183, 202
drawings x, 17–18, 114, 182, 183–189, 254, 314
Dubnow, Shimon 217
Dunmore, Helen 232, 244
Dworzecki, Meir (Mark) 6–7, 8–9, 11, 21

E
Ebensee 17, 165, 171, 175, 179n16, 183, 184, 191n22, 275, 277
Eichmann, Adolf 48, 51
Einfacher Mensch, Ein/A Simple Man (film) 335–336, 338, 340
emasculation 8
emotions. *See* feelings
encrypting 253, 256, 258
encysting 256, 257, 258
epidiascope 253
erasure 48, 63n18, 189, 204, 354
Errera, Alberto 155n41, 182, 211n16, 270, 273, 275, 276, 280n28, 280n29, 282n44
eroticism 188
Ertel, Fritz 191n19
Escape from Sobibor (film) 291, 293, 296–297, 298, 300, 315
ethics ix, 4, 5, 11, 13, 14–15, 16, 46, 52, 57, 71, 75–76, 80, 195–196, 244, 257, 290, 291–292, 308, 309–310, 312, 313, 315, 316, 319, 320, 321, 324, 326, 333, 352, 360
evidence x, xi, 59, 75, 76, 80, 91, 93, 174, 189, 195, 200, 201, 204, 357, 360
Evidence Room, The (art installation) 189

evil 14, 45, 53, 79, 86n45, 301
Exodus (film) 25n54, 311, 333
exterminatory universe 4, 194
eyewitness 2, 6, 107, 114–115, 121, 133, 177, 194, 207, 217, 221, 231, 233, 277, 282n40

F
facts xi, 16, 50, 71, 72, 74–76, 82, 120, 160, 162, 201, 204, 206–207, 208, 216, 219, 224, 225, 236, 303n12
Faulks, Sebastian 18, 230–246
family 52, 81, 93–94, 96–97, 107, 119, 120–121, 132, 134, 141, 187, 204–205, 221, 299, 336, 343, 349, 350, 360, 364
fear 56, 79, 148, 160, 216, 221, 233, 249, 270, 348, 349, 351, 355, 358
feelings ix, 5, 9, 23n19, 77, 79, 120, 121–122, 123, 145, 148, 184, 186, 201, 204, 206, 208, 216, 224, 225, 258, 268, 271, 292, 295, 297, 304n19, 318, 319, 322, 337, 339, 351, 353, 355, 362, 364
Feinsilber, Alter (Stanisław Jankowski) 219, 340
Felman, Shoshana 9, 49
female perversion 187
femininity 8, 333
Festival Off (theatre festival) 340
fiction 13, 18, 20–21, 42, 43–44, 45, 47, 231, 232, 233, 236, 244, 267, 317, 323, 335, 336, 338, 342
figuration 9, 19, 38, 58, 117–118, 247, 253, 259
fire pits. *See* burning pits
First World War 63n13, 108, 183, 230, 238
Fischl, Goliath 148–149
Fischl-Kommando 154n25, 210n12
Flaubert, Gustave 232
Fleming, K.E. 17, 126n15
football match 15, 73, 79, 84n14, 86n38
form (in art) 248, 250, 251, 256, 257
formalism 19, 42, 255
'Foss'. *See* Voss, Peter
Franco, Lucia 7

Frank, Anne 176
Frankfurt Auschwitz trial (1963–65) 171, 218, 227, 341
Freimark, Yaakov 145, 147, 360
French resistance 230
Freud, Sigmund xii, 250, 251–252, 350, 354
Friedel, Helmut 259
Friedländer, Saul 39
Friedman, Philip 266, 267, 281n39, 317
Friedman, Tuvia 273
Fritz Bauer Institute (Frankfurt) 171, 173, 176
From Bitter Earth (film) 348
Fruchtmann, Karl 335–336, 340

G

Gabai, Yaakov (also Jakow) 151, 163–164, 268, 269
Gabbai, Dario 86n36, 117, 126n20, 126–127n23, 282n47, 338
Garbarini, Alexandra 77
Gartner, Szaya 150
gas chamber ix, 1–2, 8, 52, 57, 59, 60, 73, 107, 117, 119, 139, 146, 160, 176, 182, 188–189, 191n25, 198–199, 211n23, 216, 219, 220, 268, 293–294, 311–312, 334, 338, 362
gaze 40, 45, 313
Geheimnisträger 193, 194, 209, 215
Gell, Alfred 10
gender 17, 59, 186, 357
Germany 3, 34, 41, 48, 53, 62n9, 62n18, 77, 166, 174, 225, 232, 242, 307, 311, 312, 352, 353, 364, 365
Germany, West 176
Gerstein, Kurt 311
Gestapo 151, 231, 235
gesture 6, 337, 339
ghetto 4, 6, 43, 48, 63n13, 134, 296, 308, 309, 320, 348
    Łódź 5, 70, 280n29
    Lwów 20
    Maków Mazowiecki 200
    Riga 217
    Vilna 6, 316
    Warsaw 5, 149, 303n12, 312, 347

Ghetto (film) 316
Ghetto Fighters' House 183
Gilbert, Martin 2, 22n6
Glazar, Richard 303n12, 336
Gliwice 171
God on Trial (television play) 298, 305n34
Godard, Jean-Luc 40, 42, 63n18
Gold, Jack 291, 296, 315
Goldberg, Amos 9, 10, 25n43, 25n45
gorgon 74
Gotland, Simon 218
Gottesman, Shirley Berger 127n24
Gottlieb, Roger 8
Gounaris, Giorgios 106, 138
Goya, Francisco 184
Gradowski, Zalman (also Salman, Salmen, Zalmen) 10, 13, 21, 22n6, 23n11, 25n49, 59, 85n26, 102, 115, 116, 119, 126n18, 144, 145, 161, 186, 201, 204, 211n25, 212n26, 213n38, 218, 295, 298, 340, 342, 344, 360–364, 366n1
graphic novel 202, 205–206, 212n31
Greenberg, Clement 19
Greif, Beatrice 223–224
Greif, Gideon 17, 18, 25n53, 100n34, 127n23, 161–162, 166, 212n26, 223–225, 233, 268, 269, 278n11, 279n17, 281n39, 293, 295, 296, 298
grey zone 4, 14–15, 69–86, 183, 184, 194, 209, 223, 233, 290, 309, 333
'Grey Zone, The' (essay) ix, 13–14, 16, 35, 69–86, 182, 195, 308, 309, 321, 325, 335
Grey Zone, The (film) 20, 206, 225, 267, 288, 291, 293, 295, 298, 299–300, 301–302, 305n36, 305n37, 308, 316–320, 321, 322, 323–324, 325, 326, 333, 334–335, 343
Greek Jews xi, 16–17, 20, 94, 98n7, 106–110, 111, 118, 125n4, 138–142, 174, 197, 223, 238, 265–283, 314, 315, 338
Grisseman, Stefan 324
Grossman, Vasily (also Vassily) 54, 358–359
Gross-Rosen 162
Gusen 164, 165, 173

Gutman, Yisrael (also Israel) 5, 267, 274, 278n9, 283n54

H
Hage, Joe 248, 253, 255, 259
Haidari 106, 111, 139
Handelsman, Jankiel 94, 202, 212n26
happiness xi, 61, 109–110, 134, 142, 149, 247, 312
Hegel, G.W.F. 57, 249, 250
Herman, Chaim 16, 86n44, 91–94, 98n3, 99n13, 123, 125n3, 164
heroism 5, 9, 128n30, 220, 234, 291, 300, 317, 321
Herskowicz, Josef 10
Hilberg, Raul 2, 12–13, 22n5
Hirsch, Marianne 37
historical reconstruction 42, 216
historiography x, 6, 177, 217, 267, 296, 316, 349
Hitler, Adolf 187, 311, 346, 351, 352, 353, 360
Hochhuth, Rolf 311
Hoffman, Eva 348, 359–360
Holocaust (television series) 63n13, 291, 293, 312–315, 327n14, 332
Horkheimer, Max 363
Höss (Hoess), Rudolf 8, 266–267
Huener, Jonathan 198
humanism 354, 359
humanity 6, 11, 13, 56, 121, 269, 292, 295, 317, 322, 336, 358
Hungary 48–49, 64n26, 140, 203, 301

I
identity 5, 7, 166, 186, 291
  assumed 232
  civic 38
  collective 186, 298
  gender 186
  individual 17, 108, 113, 119, 186, 298
  Jewish 52, 358
ideology 35, 363
immersion 36, 38, 44–45, 53, 252, 326
imperceptibility 248, 256
Imperial War Museum 232
improvisation 4, 6, 120, 133, 294

incarnation 2, 250
instrumentalization 59, 70, 291
International Refugee Organization (IRO) 160, 161, 166, 179n11
International Tracing Service (ITS) 17, 159–180
interpretation x, 4, 39, 194, 291, 305n34, 337
interviews 11–12, 50, 107, 161, 166, 177, 216–217, 218, 220, 221–222, 223–226, 232–233, 266, 267, 268, 293, 307, 336
Investigation, The (play) 341
Irgun 311, 333
irony 185, 237, 238, 240, 242, 293
Israel 43, 161, 166, 173, 183, 205, 210n6, 223, 224, 228n36, 311, 335, 336, 337

J
Jacob the Liar (film) 311
Jones, Jonathan 352–353
Judenräte 223, 308
judgement 14, 70, 71, 79, 82, 159, 204, 257, 262n49, 307–308, 310, 311, 322, 325
  moral xi, 69, 71, 75, 80–81, 309, 325
  value 75

K
Kabbalah 298, 355
Kaddish 37, 47, 58, 64n37, 65n44, 145, 148, 187, 298, 299, 341, 343, 361
Kamiński, Jakub 144, 268, 275–276
Kanada-Kommando 7, 127n24, 150, 281n39, 343
Kaplon, Jan 224
Kapos 4, 70, 144, 145, 146, 191n23, 210n9, 221, 268, 275, 281n39, 299, 308, 312, 321
Kenig, Murray 23n19
kernel (psychoanalysis) 19–20, 257–259
Kertész, Imre 36, 48–49, 340
K., Morris 7
Kesselman, Morris 150, 339
Kiefer, Anselm 349, 352–356
Kiełbasin 10, 116
Kilian, Andreas 84nn13–14, 125n8, 136n14, 334, 339
Klarsfeld Foundation 183

Kłodziński, Stanisław 98n5
Koch, Ilse 187
Kol Nidre 120, 133, 136n10
Kolbe, Maximilian 203, 205, 206
Koltai, Lajos 48–49
Kordek, Ryszard 307
Kosky, Barrie 233
Kraków Auschwitz trial (1947) 218, 219
Kulka, Erich 176, 225
Kwiet, Konrad 233, 237, 239, 240

L
LaCapra, Dominick 325
Ladino 109
Lahana, Becky 134, 136n11
Lahana, David 94, 100, 120, 134, 136n12
Lang, Berel 71
Langbein, Hermann 8, 70, 72, 76–77, 80, 82–83n3, 83–84n13, 275
Langer, Lawrence 13, 14, 26n60, 323
Langford, Barry 20, 310
Langfus, Leyb (also Leib Langfuss) 2, 24n35, 59, 85n35, 115, 116, 119, 125n9, 128n30, 212n26, 298, 340
Lanzmann, Claude x, 1–2, 3, 26n60, 37, 46–47, 48, 49–52, 66n51, 211n20, 303n12, 323, 337, 340
Last Days, The (film) 338
Last of the Unjust, The (film) 50–51
Laub, Dori 9
Lazarus 36, 38, 43, 47, 57, 62n8, 65n39
Lebović, Đorđe 2
Lee, Sander H. 71
Leibowicz, Shmuel 146
Lengyel, Olga 273
letters 16–17, 18–19, 81, 82, 185, 204
Levi, Primo ix, 2, 13–15, 16, 33, 35, 69–87, 182, 195, 240, 290, 291, 309, 310, 311, 312, 317, 325, 334, 359
Levin, Itamar 225
Levite, Abraham 112–113
Lewental, Zalman (also Leventhal, Lewenthal, Loewenthal) 5, 8, 9, 11, 22n6, 23n17, 24n35, 59, 83–84n13, 86n36, 115–116, 118, 119, 126n17, 186, 211n14, 273–274, 295, 308, 318, 323, 340

Liebman, Stuart 321–322
Life is Beautiful (film) 3, 311, 343
Linenthal, Edward 199–200, 211n21
lists 10, 24n35, 92, 94, 95, 112, 115, 196, 202, 282n43, 321, 356
Litschi, Menachem 151
Łódź (also Litzmannstadt) 5, 8, 70, 140, 219, 280n29
London 161, 230, 232, 347, 356, 360
Low, Erna 7
Lubitsch, Ernst 183
Lublin 134, 219
Lukács, Georg 252

M
Maestro, Jacob 268, 274, 279n18, 281n39
Majdanek 147, 164
Maków Mazowiecki 145, 200
Mala and Edek 203, 205, 206
Malinski, Gabriel 144, 150, 175, 179n22, 339
Mandelbaum, Henryk 7, 171, 210n3, 211n17, 218, 222, 223, 307–308, 320, 338, 339
Mann, Franceska 8
Mann, Louis 253
Mark, Ber 5, 100n39, 112, 225, 267, 278n8, 281n39
Mark, Esther 267, 278n8
Marne 238
Marx, Karl 359
masculinity 8, 186, 240, 297
mass killing. *See* mass murder
mass murder 1, 12, 19, 34, 35, 36, 37, 53, 54, 63n13, 79, 91, 125n4, 143, 146, 151, 153, 183, 195, 198, 199, 215–216, 220, 237, 238, 239, 266, 287, 309, 313, 314, 318, 353, 365
materiality 114, 208, 249–250, 252, 253, 256, 295
Matters of Testimony (Chare and Williams) 21, 59, 85n26, 125n10, 270, 280n28, 360–361
Mauthausen 57, 164, 165, 166, 171, 173, 183, 191n25, 234, 277
McCabe, Colin 46
McGlothlin, Erin 303n5

melancholia 257, 354, 358
Melk 183, 277
memory 34, 39, 51, 63n16, 182, 184, 193, 194, 195, 209, 250, 251–252, 258, 270, 271. 290, 312, 337, 346, 350, 353, 355–356, 359, 360, 364–365
Mengele, Josef 151, 175, 187, 218, 342
Merleau-Ponty, Maurice 78–79
Mesnard, Philippe 15, 20–21
metaphor 117–118, 187, 297, 336, 355
mise-en-scène 293–294, 336, 339
'Misko' (friend of Nadjary). *See* Stephanidis, Dimitrios.
Mizrahi, Mois 268, 279n18
Model of Crematorium 1 (II) 198–199
Moll, James 338
Moll, Otto 150, 185, 191n15, 205, 219, 276, 282n42
Mooney, Catherine 73, 78, 79
Moore, Michael F. 72, 83n12
Morawa, Mieczyslaw ('Capo Mietek') 219–220
mourning xii, 34, 36, 38, 47–48, 56, 60, 61, 108, 254, 257, 298, 323, 346–347, 354, 358, 359, 364, 365
morality 11, 12–14, 16, 34, 35, 36, 38, 55, 56, 57, 59–60, 69, 70–71, 72, 75–76, 77, 78, 79–80, 81–82, 84n20, 143, 145, 162, 182, 184, 186, 189, 195, 201, 209, 216, 222, 225, 236, 240, 289, 290, 291, 308, 309–310, 312, 316, 317, 322, 324, 325, 347, 349, 360
Moyn, Samuel 356–357, 358
Müller, Filip 2, 11, 13, 26n60, 51, 52, 72, 92, 93, 146–147, 148, 171–173, 175–176, 218, 291, 336
Muhsfeldt, Erich 71, 73, 79, 304n18
multispectral analysis 16–17, 105, 113–114
Murmelstein, Benjamin 50–51, 65n44, 65n45
Muselmann 14, 26n65, 314, 327–328n20
Museum of Jewish Heritage 183, 190n5
music 40, 42, 271–272, 296, 297, 315, 323, 347

N

Nadjary, Marcel (also Natzari) 10, 11, 17, 80–82, 94, 102–105, 106–110, 111–128, 138–142, 213n38, 268, 272–273
Nahmia, Berry 271–272, 279n18
Nahon, Marco 117, 159, 279n18
nakedness 37, 59, 60, 107, 139, 185, 187, 188, 287, 362
narrative cinema 20–21, 38, 40, 43, 44, 52, 300–301, 315, 317, 319, 320, 322, 332
nationalism 17, 108, 272
Nea Evropi/New Europe (newspaper) 122, 128n35, 141
Nelson, Tim Blake 20, 22n10, 225, 287, 289–292, 294, 301, 302, 304n24, 305n36, 308, 316–324, 326, 333, 334
Nemes, László x, 20, 36, 44–49, 51–52, 59–60, 225, 289, 295, 299–301, 317–324, 326, 341–343
Nencel, David 126n22, 128n30, 175
Neustadt, Melech 5–6, 23n20
Nikityaev, Aleksandr 16–17, 113
Nissenbaum, Yitzhak 149, 151
number of victims 10, 115, 118, 121, 140, 142, 219
numbering of crematoria 24n35, 302n2
numbness (emotional) 186, 199, 295
Nussbaum, Martha 78
Nyiszli, Miklós 12, 15, 72–73, 75, 78, 79, 83n13, 84n14, 86n39, 144, 151–152, 175–176, 187, 191n22, 218, 288, 300, 302n2, 303n5, 334, 340, 342

O

O'Shea, Paul 232, 233, 242
Oler, Alexandre 94, 183
Olère, David 17, 92–93, 94, 98n9, 182–192, 202, 212n26
ontology 234, 237, 240, 350
Operation Reinhard 34, 41, 53, 294, 297, 298, 300, 303n12, 304n32
Ormond, Henry 171
Oshry, Ephraim 128n30
Out of the Ashes (film) 316

P

painting 3, 17–18, 19–20, 184, 187–188, 202, 352–353, 355–356
Paisikovic, Dov 185, 218, 227n22, 275
Palestine 109, 166, 311, 314
Pardo, David (Dario) 127n25
palimpsest 114, 196
Paris 16, 17, 36–37, 49, 91, 92, 93, 94, 95, 96, 97, 98n8, 100n33, 100n37, 164, 183, 340
partisans 43, 270, 274, 276, 314
passive heroism. *See* heroism
passivity 12, 115, 186, 297, 298
Passover 147
Pentlin, Susan 308
Perl, Gisella 316, 328n23
Persiades, David 272, 275
photographs 60, 63n18, 151, 166, 182, 200, 202, 204–205, 247–248, 253, 254–255, 257, 259, 268, 312–313, 339–340, 352, 353
Pilecki, Witold 205
Plato 43, 250
Pliszko, Lemke 146, 150, 339
Podchlebnik, Michael (also Michał, Mordechai) 336
poetic licence 241
poetry 12, 34, 43, 308, 356
Pogozhev, Andrey 231, 241–243
pogroms 217
Poland 5–6, 9, 34, 41, 54, 62n9, 91, 111, 119, 132, 165, 183, 190n5, 210, 222, 223, 303, 307, 334, 336, 360, 361
Polian, Pavel 16, 100n39, 113
Polish (language) 24n35, 85n28, 112, 116, 119, 128n28, 134, 200, 201, 202, 204, 223, 224
Pollock, Griselda 13, 16, 65n39, 66n62
Pope Pius XII 311
positivism 177, 339, 349
postcolonialism 359
Postec, Ziva 1, 22n1
postmemory 21, 37, 348–349, 366n1
postmodernism 270
prayer 96, 144, 145, 148–150, 184, 187, 299, 322, 341
Pressac, Jean-Claude 339
Presser, Jacob (Jacques) 70, 82n2
privileged prisoners 4, 15–16, 74, 76, 144, 194, 209, 210n9, 309–310, 314, 315, 316, 318, 321
psychic life 9, 78, 243, 250, 252, 257, 258, 292, 335
psychoanalysis xii, 19–20, 186, 250, 251–252, 257–258, 270, 350, 354
psychological breakdown 34, 79, 233, 243
psychosexuality 186
Putnam, Hilary 75
Pyteraf, Michał 205

Q

quarantine 139, 269, 273
quietude 19

R

Radlitzky, Zvi 20
Rajchman, Chil 356–358
Rancière, Jacques 43, 47, 50
realism 44, 184, 186, 187, 188, 189, 232, 289, 298, 319, 333, 335, 343
rebellion. *See* revolt
Recanati, David 267, 268
Red Army 34, 41, 54, 216, 288, 344
Red Cross 91, 96, 100n39, 107, 112, 116, 127n24, 139, 171
re-enactment 2, 60, 353, 354
Régy, Claude 340
Reznikoff, Charles 340, 341
religion 17, 58, 141, 143, 144, 145, 148–149, 150, 152–153, 298, 343, 348, 360
 religious beliefs 150, 298
 religious practices 60, 119–120, 128n30, 143, 144, 145, 146, 149, 152, 298
 religious ritual 38, 136n6, 187, 298–299
representability 37, 39, 42, 47, 54, 296, 321, 324, 332, 333, 353
resistance xi, 2, 9, 17, 20, 21, 115, 197–198, 202, 205, 238, 266, 275, 318, 321, 335, 343, 357
 aesthetic 40, 59
 armed 4–5, 8, 140, 196, 267, 291, 298, 301
 collective 58, 202, 292, 299, 300

resistance (*cont.*)
  cultural 9–10, 11, 271–272, 292, 296, 348
  passive 5–6, 316
  political 58
  psychic 296
  spiritual 6, 8–9, 297, 298–299, 314
  symbolic 7–8, 24n34
  unarmed 6
  witnessing and 10, 209
  women and 7–8, 202, 206, 211n14, 274
responsa literature 128n30
restoration (of SK manuscripts) 114
revenge 10, 77, 80–81, 118, 119, 135, 141, 277, 297, 346, 358
revolt 5, 6, 7, 23n20, 43, 54, 58, 73, 268, 270, 273, 277, 292, 297, 316
  Auschwitz-Birkenau xi, 2, 4–5, 9, 12, 23n19, 57, 64n26, 94, 115, 118, 145, 149, 196–197, 200, 201, 202, 206, 211n14, 211–212n26, 225, 241, 266, 267–268, 272, 273–277, 279–280n19, 280n31, 280n36, 281n39, 282n40, 288, 292, 298, 299, 301, 315, 317, 318, 319, 323, 324, 333, 334–335, 341, 343–344, 360–361
  Sobibór 53, 66n51, 293, 297, 314, 315, 333
  Treblinka 12, 53, 54, 279–280n19, 298, 333, 358
rhetoric 15, 201, 310
Richter, Gerhard 3, 18–20, 247–262
Röhrig, Géza 45–46, 60, 61, 303n9
robots 9, 186, 188, 268, 270, 293, 294, 295, 297, 362–363
Roma 36, 41, 54, 56, 62n9, 63n13
Rose, Reginald 297
Rosenblum, Yehoshuah 148, 152–153, 218, 339
Rosenthal, Raymond 72, 83n4
Rothberg, Michael 41, 79–80
Royal Ontario Museum 189
Royer, Clara 85n29, 342
Rumkowski, Chaim 70, 72, 83n5
Russian prisoners 126n18, 231, 235, 241–242, 244, 275, 276, 277, 279–280n19, 280n29, 282n51

S

Sachsenhausen 316
Sackar, Josef (also Zakar) 151, 174–175, 221, 268, 269
sacralising xi
Salonika. *See* Thessaloniki
Saltzman, Lisa 354
Santner, Eric 252
Sanyal, Debarati 15
sardines 117–118, 126n22, 126–127n23, 127n24, 139, 269
Schermer, Zwi 150
Schillinger, Josef 8
Schindler's List (film) 3, 22n10, 42, 304n24, 312, 323, 324, 332, 338
Schoenberg, Arnold 42
science-fiction 294
Scrolls of Auschwitz 2, 10–11, 24n35, 52, 59, 112, 123, 161, 182, 186, 218, 220–221, 222, 225, 290, 292, 295, 298, 359–364, 366n1. *See also* Sonderkommando manuscripts
Second Generation 37, 60, 346, 348, 352, 358, 364
Second World War x, 18, 230, 231, 348, 365
Seidler, Victor 21
Selby, Margo (Magda Roth) 126n22
semiotics x, 253
Sephardi 109
seriality 300, 302n2
Seven Blades of Grass (screenplay) 298
Sevillias, Errikos 272, 275
sexuality 76, 188, 297, 333
sexual relationships 297
Shabbat 109, 299
shame 71, 79, 333, 351
shell (psychoanalysis) 19–20, 257–259
Sheppard, Robert 234, 235–236
Shoah (film) x, 1, 2, 20–21, 22n1, 26n60, 43, 46–48, 49–50, 51–52, 86n38, 176, 211n20, 291, 303n12, 332, 335, 336–338, 340
Silberberg, Yaakov (also Yacov) 128n30, 150, 268, 335–337, 339

silence 21, 40, 49, 114, 124, 162, 221, 307, 348, 349, 350, 351–352, 353, 355, 364–365
Siminski, Wiktor 191n25
Simmel, Georg 52
Simondon, Gilbert 256
Sklaven der Gaskammer (film) 179n22, 339
Slotkin, Richard 303n15
Smoleń, Kazimierz 176
Sobibór 3, 41, 53, 66n51, 291, 293, 296–297, 298, 300, 303n12, 304n32, 312, 314, 315, 333
Son of Saul (film) x–xi, 3, 5, 20–21, 36–38, 44–53, 57–61, 84n18, 85n29, 206, 225–226, 267, 289, 295, 298–301, 317–318, 319, 320–326, 341–344
Sonderkommando ix, 1, 12, 17, 22n1, 34, 69, 82, 91, 102, 106, 111, 116, 143, 159, 178n3, 182, 190n7, 193, 209n2, 210n10, 215, 230, 251, 254, 266, 287, 303n9, 307, 332, 359
  manuscripts 10–11, 21, 22n6, 24n35, 25n49, 52, 59, 102, 113, 116, 119, 123, 145, 161, 182, 186, 201–202, 204–205, 213n38, 218, 220–221, 222, 225, 280n36, 290, 292, 295, 298, 359–361, 361–364
  photographs 2, 3, 11, 19–20, 59, 155n41, 160, 182, 196–198, 200, 208, 238–239, 247, 249, 251–252, 253, 254, 258, 270–271, 313, 317, 321, 323, 343
  uprising (*see* revolt Auschwitz Birkenau)
Sonderkommando Auschwitz-Birkenau (film) 225, 340
Sonderkommando: The Living Dead of Auschwitz (film) 211n17, 339
songs 271–272, 341
Sophocles 58
Soriano, Kathleen 355–356
soundtrack (film) x, 51, 61, 198, 293–294, 318–319
Special Operations Executive (SOE) 231, 234–235, 236, 237, 239, 244
spectrality 113–114
Spielberg, Steven 42, 43, 304n24, 312, 323, 332, 338

SS (Schutzstaffel)
  acts of resistance against 8, 200, 273, 276, 282n47, 292, 315
  as camp administration 11, 34–36, 37, 57–58, 92, 151–152, 204, 267, 268, 277, 281n39, 282n51, 294, 299, 301, 303n12, 332, 334, 338, 357
  as guards at Auschwitz 79, 83, 185, 199, 268, 289, 315, 321, 333
  ideology and ethos of 34–36, 37, 54–56, 58, 295
  individual SS officers 8, 15, 73, 151, 219, 224, 311, 313 (*see also* entries for Kurt Gerstein, Rudolf Höss, Erich Muhsfeldt, Otto Moll, Josef Schillinger, Peter Voss)
  participation in football matches at Birkenau 15, 73, 79, 84n14
  post-war trials of 205, 218, 341
  representations of in art, film and fiction 52, 57, 185–188, 237, 242, 287, 288, 297, 304n18, 312–313, 317, 319, 321, 323–324, 333, 341, 342, 343, 344
  violent and criminal acts of 37, 50, 54, 59, 61, 63n18, 107, 117, 144, 149, 153, 196, 215, 269, 276, 334
Stalingrad 34
starvation 35, 38, 63n18, 235–236, 282n51
Steiner, Jean-François 300
Stephanidis, Dimitrios Athanasiou 105, 107, 121, 139, 141, 142
Stevens, George 312
stigmatisation xi, 333
Stobierski, Mieczyslaw 198–200
Stone, Dan 17, 65n41, 179n11, 313, 363–364
Strasfogel, Chiona 95, 136n34
Strasfogel, Herman ix–x, 16, 80–82, 91–100, 111–128, 131–136, 165, 213n38
Strasfogel, Simone 93, 94–95, 96, 99n24, 116, 120, 132, 133, 135, 136n4, 165
Styron, William 243, 343
subject matter 38, 45, 248, 354
suicide 55, 94, 150–152, 268
Sukkot 144, 147

Suwałki 360, 361, 366n1
symbolism 5, 7–8, 56, 77, 206, 342, 355
Szmaglewska, Seweryna 11

T
Tarr, Béla 46, 49, 51, 60
tattooing 7, 174, 185, 187
Tauber, Henryk 8, 218, 340
television 20, 97, 305n34, 312, 332, 338, 352
temporality 15, 58, 118, 122, 237–238, 240, 252, 335, 349
tense (grammar) 107, 117, 118, 121, 179n26, 251, 261n17, 324
Terezín/Theresienstadt 50, 51, 111–112, 140, 203, 281n39, 312
theatre 42, 183, 334, 340, 341
Theresienstadt. *See* Terezín
Thessaloniki (also Salonika) 106, 107, 108, 109, 111, 112, 118, 122, 126n21, 127n24, 127n25, 140, 142, 274, 281n38, 282n42, 315
Third Generation 37, 60, 351, 364
Timar, Alain 340
Todorov, Tzvetan 13, 71
tomb 36, 56–57, 253, 261n28, 357
Tomai, Photini 268
topographies (of memory) 346–348, 350–351, 364–365
Torok, Maria 19, 257, 262n45
Toulouse 94, 136n12
trauma x, 9–10, 17, 25n45, 35, 37, 39, 51, 60, 183, 184, 185–186, 221, 234, 237, 240, 243, 248, 249, 252, 288, 292, 296, 297, 308, 310, 311, 317, 323, 325–326, 350–351, 353, 358
Treblinka x, 1, 3, 12, 20, 41, 52, 53, 54, 147, 279n19, 298, 303n12, 304n32, 333, 336–337, 349, 356–358, 360, 361
Treblinka (novel) 300
Twitter 206–207

U
Ukraine 41, 48, 312
undressing room 8, 107, 127–128n29, 139, 147, 152, 185–186, 199, 269, 287, 288, 289, 290, 294, 320, 341

unintelligibility 248, 252
Union Munitions Factory 211n14, 274, 281n37
United Nations Relief and Rehabilitation Administration 160, 166
United Restitution Organization 174, 175
univers concentrationnaire x, 37, 53, 62n9, 65n46, 194, 230, 234, 296
uprising. *See* revolt
USC Visual History Archive 161

V
Vanhems, Mr 95, 96, 133, 134, 136n1
Venezia, Shlomo 7, 127n24, 144, 161, 177, 222, 268, 339
Venezia, Morris 127n23, 149, 151, 228n33
Venezia, Isaac 281n39, 282n45
vengeance. *See* revenge
Ventura, Juliette 183
Vice, Sue 18
Vichy France 230, 232, 235
victimisation 12, 290, 303n9
video testimony 5, 7, 85n26, 223, 310, 332, 338
Vienna 51, 346, 347
Vilna/Vilnius 95
violence xii, 2, 5, 6, 15, 20, 34, 35, 58–59, 196, 217, 237, 242, 258, 288, 291, 292, 295, 298, 301, 303–304n15, 320, 332, 348, 351, 353, 358, 364
Vistula 140, 322, 341
visual memory 182, 271
Voss, Peter (also recalled as Foss, Forst) 219, 342
voyeurism ix, 17, 186, 297, 341, 343
Vrba, Rudolf 159, 303n12

W
Wachsmann, Nikolaus 300
Wallen, Jeffrey 162, 177
Warsaw 164, 165, 166, 183, 217, 346, 347, 349, 350, 356, 360, 361–362
Warsaw ghetto. *See* ghettos
Warsaw Ghetto uprising 5, 95, 102, 111, 132, 203, 303n12, 347

Watt, Donald 18, 231, 232–233, 234, 236–241, 242, 244
We Wept Without Tears (Gideon Greif) 161, 224, 225, 281n39
Webber, Jonathan 195
Weil, Simone 353
Weiss, Irene 7, 127n24
Weiss, Peter 341
Weiss, Emil 225, 340
Weissglas, Immanuel 34
Wetzler, Alfred 159
White, Hayden 75
Wiesel, Elie 36, 49, 65n39, 162
Williams, Dominic 13, 16, 17, 18, 20, 59, 122, 125n10, 126n13, 208, 213n38, 220–221, 228n41, 270, 280n28, 291, 292, 295, 361–363, 366n1
Wollaston, Isabel 18, 197
women's camp 11, 273, 276, 299
writing 9–10, 14, 51, 59, 106, 113–114, 116, 117, 118–119, 121, 127n27, 134, 135, 136n14, 141, 213n38, 247, 361, 362–363
Wyschogrod, Edith 76

Y
Yad Vashem 6, 9, 183, 190n5, 201, 211n20, 211n24, 212n27, 217, 220
Yiddish 11, 16, 112–113, 115, 116, 119, 134, 200, 223–224, 267, 337, 340, 356
Yom Kippur 136n10, 147–148, 149

Z
Zakar, Josef. *See* Sackar, Josef
Zaorski, Andrzej 91, 96, 100n39, 112
Zeilsheim DP camp 161, 166
Zemel, Carol 17–18
Zeugen: Aussagen zum Mord an einem Volk (film) 336
ŻIH (Żydowski Instytut Historyczny) 211n24, 217
Żywulska, Krystyna 11, 85nn27–28